Lecture Notes in Computer Science 7373

Commenced Publication in 1973
Founding and Former Series Editors:
Gerhard Goos, Juris Hartmanis, and Jan van Leeuwen

T0241200

Hafizur Rahaman   Sanatan Chattopadhyay
Santanu Chattopadhyay (Eds.)

Progress in VLSI Design and Test

16th International Symposium, VDAT 2012
Shibpur, India, July 1-4, 2012
Proceedings

 Springer

Volume Editors

Hafizur Rahaman
Bengal Engineering and Science University Shibpur
Department of Information Technology
P.O. Botanic Garden, Howrah-711103, India
E-mail: rahaman_h@it.becs.ac.in

Sanatan Chattopadhyay
University of Calcutta
Department of Electronic Science
92, A.P.C. Road, Kolkata 700009, India
E-mail: scelc@caluniv.ac.in

Santanu Chattopadhyay
Indian Institute of Technology Kharagpur
Department of Electronics and Electrical Comm. Engg.
West Bengal 721302, India
E-mail: santanu@ece.iitkgp.ernet.in

ISSN 0302-9743   e-ISSN 1611-3349
ISBN 978-3-642-31493-3   e-ISBN 978-3-642-31494-0
DOI 10.1007/978-3-642-31494-0
Springer Heidelberg Dordrecht London New York

Library of Congress Control Number: 2012940576

CR Subject Classification (1998): B.7-8, C.0, C.2.1, C.2-4, F.3, D.2.4

LNCS Sublibrary: SL 1 – Theoretical Computer Science and General Issues

Typesetting: Camera-ready by author, data conversion by Scientific Publishing Services, Chennai, India

Printed on acid-free paper

Springer is part of Springer Science+Business Media (www.springer.com)

Message from the Steering Committee Chair, VLSI Design Conference

It is a pleasure to welcome you to the proceedings of the 16th International Symposium on VLSI Design and Test (VDAT) held in Shibpur, India. From a modest beginning in January 1998 at Chennai, this meeting has become a recognized forum for technical exchange in India.

Let me begin by expressing thanks to the entire VDAT Organizing Committee, headed by Indranil Sengupta and Biplab Sikdar, for their tireless effort in putting the symposium together. Beside the technical papers and tutorials, this year we had a PhD forum that invited doctoral students to present their research. This was sponsored by the VLSI Society of India (VSI) and the Women in Engineering (WiE) group of the IEEE Kolkata Section. Expansion of education in India still has a long way to go and the PhD effort in engineering is just starting. This forum is a step in the right direction and we hope that other conferences will follow the lead.

The Program Chairs, Hafizur Rahaman and Sanatan Chattopadhyay, and their Program Committee selected the papers that appear in this book. Their peer reviewing process accepted less than 30% of the submitted papers. The topics are indicative of the wide variety of research in India and abroad. Some of the unconventional or emerging topics are quantum logic, reversible circuits, 3D stacked integrated circuits, carbon nanotube devices, finFETs, quantum dot cellular automata, and Vedic arithmetic. You are least likely to see the last item anywhere else.

Continuing the VDAT tradition, we had tutorials, an education day and invited talks. I am pleased that VDAT is publishing the papers in Springer's *Lecture Notes in Computer Science* (LNCS) Series, so that they get the worldwide attention they deserve.

The *VDAT Symposium Series* http://vlsi-india.org/ is sponsored by the VLSI Society of India http://vlsi-india.org/vsi/. A ten-member VLSI Design Conference Steering Committee looks after the continuity of this symposium and the International Conference on VLSI Design, presently scheduled for January 5–10, 2013, in Pune, India http://vlsidesignconference.org/.

July 2012   Vishwani D. Agrawal

Message from Advisory Committee Patron

I am extremely happy that Bengal Engineering and Science University, Shibpur, in collaboration with IIT Khragpur, IIM Calcutta, ISI Calcutta, Calcutta University and Jadavpur University, India, organized the 16th International Symposium on VLSI Design and Test (VDAT 2012) during July $1–4^{th}$, 2012, with the objective of strengthening VLSI education and research in India.

To mark this important event, eminent keynote speakers and authors of research papers from industry, research institutions, and universities presented their work. I am sure that these presentations have inspired the creative minds of young researchers to take up advanced innovative research in diverse areas of VLSI technology.

The role of VLSI technology in shaping our lives can never be over emphasized. From computing to healthcare, energy, the environment, transportation, natural resource harnessing or industrial product development, mankind finds VLSI technology in all aspects of everyday life.

I would like to thank the officials of the VLSI Society of India for consenting to host this symposium at our university. I would also like to express my thanks to the keynote speakers and the tutorial speakers for kindly agreeing to deliver their lectures. We would like to thank the authors of all the papers for submitting their quality research work. Finally, on behalf of the Organizing Committee of VDAT 2012, I heartily welcome all the delegates, presenters and speakers for helping to make this event a grand success.

Let all our efforts in education and research be directed toward the welfare of mankind.

Ajoy K. Ray

Message from the Technical Program Chairs

It is great pleasure to welcome you to the proceedings of the 16th International Symposium on VLSI Design and Test (VDAT 2012) held at Bengal Engineering and Science University, Shibpur (Kolkata), India. VDAT 2012, sponsored by the VLSI Society of India (VSI), was organized by the Bengal Engineering and Science University, Shibpur, in collaboration with IIT Kharagpur, IIM Calcutta, ISI Calcutta, Calcutta University, and Jadavpur University. This annual event was initiated 16 years ago in 1997 by the VSI and has gradually matured into one of the topmost international VLSI conferences.

The technical program included (a) four keynote talks and a banquet talk from eminent people in the field of VLSI, (b) four invited talks from well-known researchers in their respective areas of expertise, (c) 54 peer-reviewed papers and (d) six half-day tutorials on some of the hottest topics in VLSI, (e) Half Day Education Day, and (f) Half Day PhD Forum.

This year we received 135 papers from all over the world. After a rigorous review process, the Program Committee (PC) selected 30 regular papers, 10 short papers and 13 poster papers. In all, 146 expert reviewers were involved in rating the papers and each paper received at least three independent reviews made by the 64 PC members and also by additional external experts. The papers along with the reviews were scrutinized by the PC members during final selection phase. We would like to thank the authors of all the papers for submitting their quality research work. Special thanks go to the PC members and the external reviewers who gave their precious time in reviewing and selecting the best set of papers.

We would like to thank Vishwani D. Agrawal, V. Ramgopal Rao, Krishnendu Chakrabarty, M. Balakrishnan, and Rolf Drechsler for readily accepting our invitation to deliver keynote and invited talks at the symposium. The main conference program was preceded by a day of tutorial presentations. We would also like to thank the tutorial speakers for kindly agreeing to deliver their lectures. We would like to express our thanks to the Keynote Chairs, Prasun Ghosal and S. Ramesh, and the Tutorial Chair, Partha Sarathi Dasgupta and Partha Bhattacharyya, for their active initiation and enthusiasm to make the sessions a success.

This year we introduced a new half-day session of a PhD forum hosted by the VSI and Women in Engineering (WiE) Affinity Group of the IEEE Kolkata Section. The efforts made by Susmita Sur-Kolay and B.B. Bhattacharyya in this regard deserve special mention. We would like to express our thanks to the staff of EasyChair for providing assistance with the online submission. We must thank the staff of Springer for agreeing to publish the proceedings of VDAT 2012 as part of Springer's *Lecture Notes in Computer Science Series.* Our Publication Chair, Santanu Chattopadhyay, did a great job of composing the technical contents of the proceedings in the LNCS format.

We hope that you will find the VDAT 2012 proceedings technically rewarding.

July 2012   Hafizur Rahaman
                                                      Sanatan Chattopadhyay

Message from the General Chairs

The International Symposium on VLSI Design and Test (VDAT), which was first held in 1998 as a small workshop in Chennai, has been successfully organized every year in different parts of the country. The 16th symposium in this series, VDAT 2012, was held during July 1–4, 2012, at the Bengal Engineering and Science University (BESU), Shibpur, West Bengal. Over the last one and a half decades, the symposium has left its mark in the field of VLSI design and test.

This year, VDAT attracted a large number of submissions (135) from India and abroad. With painstaking effort, the Program Committee selected 30 regular papers, 10 short papers, and 13 poster presentations. Also, this is the first time the proceedings of the symposium are published as a Springer LNCS volume.

The program of the symposium spanned over four days and included, in addition to a high-quality technical program during the last two days, six half-day tutorials on the first day delivered by eminent researchers and practitioners in the field, giving young researchers and students an excellent opportunity to learn about the latest trends in VLSI design and test.

In addition, an Education Day and a PhD Forum were organized during the second day to encourage the budding researchers and academicians in this field.

The Program Chairs, Hafizur Rahaman and Sanatan Chattopadhaya, along with the PC members did an excellent job in completing a rigorous review process. We take this opportunity to record our appreciation to the Program Committee members. We would also like to thank V. Ramgopal Rao, Krishnendu Chakrabarty, M. Balakrishnan, Rolf Drechsler, and Vishwani D. Agrawal for readily accepting our invitation to deliver keynote and invited talks at the symposium.

We would also like to thank the Tutorial Speakers for kindly agreeing to deliver their lectures. The efforts made by the Keynote Chairs, Prasun Ghosal and S. Ramesh, and the Tutorial Chair, Partha Sarathi Dasgupta and Partha Bhattacharyya, in this regard deserve special mention.

The Organizing Committee, headed by Arindam Biswas and Chandan Kumar Sarkar, should be commended for taking the necessary steps to ensure that the symposium could be successfully conducted at BESU. We are indebted to the sponsors of the event who contributed significantly even in a period of financial crunch. We would also like to thank Sumit Goswami and Mrinal Das, Industry Liason Chairs, for their active initiatives in getting sponsorship.

Our Publication Chair, Santanu Chattopadhyay, did a great job of composing the technical contents of the proceedings in the LNCS format. Finally, we would like to thank Aloke Maity and Chandan Giri, the Finance Chairs, for doing all the hard work in the background, thereby making the event a grand success.

July 2012

Indranil Sengupta
Biplab Kumar Sikdar

Organization

Advisory Board

Vishwani D. Agrawal	Chairman, VLSI Conference Steering Committee
Ajay K. Ray (Patron)	Vice Chancellor, BESUS, India
Susmita Sur-Koley	ISI Calcutta, India
B.B. Bhattacharyya (Chair)	ISI Calcutta, India
P.P.Chakrabarti	IIT Kharagpur, India
Amit K. Das (Dean)	FET, BESUS, India
Susanta Sen	Calcutta University, India
C.P. Ravikumar	Texas Instruments, Bangalore, India
Debesh K. Das	Jadavpur University, Kolkata, India
Susmita Sur-Koley	ISI Calcutta, India
Jayanta Lahiri	ARM, India
Pradip Dutta	Synopsys India Limited, India

General Chairs

Indranil Sengupta	Indian Institute of Technology, Kharagpur
Biplab K. Sikdar	Bengal Engineering and Science University, Shibpur, India

Program Chairs

Hafizur Rahaman	Bengal Engineering and Science University, Shibpur, India
Sanatan Chattopadhyay	Calcutta University, India

Publication Chair

Santanu Chattopadhyay	Indian Institute of Technology, Kharagpur, India

Tutorial Chairs

Partha Sarathi Dasgupta	Indian Institute of Management, Calcutta, India
Partha Bhattacharyya	Bengal Engineering and Science University, Shibpur, India

Program Keynote Chairs

Prasun Ghosal	Bengal Engineering and Science University, Shibpur, India
S. Ramesh	General Motors, Bangalore, India

Organizing Chairs

Arindam Biswas	Bengal Engineering and Science University, India
Chandan Kumar Sarkar	Jadavpur University, India

Finance Chairs

Aloke Maity	Bengal Engineering and Science University, Shibpur, India
Chandan Giri	Bengal Engineering and Science University, Shibpur, India

Fellowship Chairs

Partha Pratim Das	Indian Institute of Technology, Kharagpur, India
Partha Ray	Intel Corporation, Bangalore, India

Publicity Chairs

Pranab Roy	Bengal Engineering and Science University, Shibpur, India
Susanta Chakraborty	Bengal Engineering and Science University, Shibpur, India

Industrial Liaison Chairs

Mrinal Das	Sankalp Semiconductor, India
Sumit Goswami	Intel Corporation, India

Local Arrangements Chairs

Surajit Roy	Bengal Engineering and Science University, Shibpur, India
Tamaghna Acharya	
Indrajit Banerjee	

Registration Chairs

Tuhina Samanta   Bengal Engineering and Science University,
                               Shibpur, India

Sukanta Das

Program Committee

Abhijit Sanyal   Saha Institute of Nuclear Physics, India
Adit Singh   Auburn University, USA
Ajit Pal   IIT-Kharagpur, India
Am Jabir   Oxford Brookes University, UK
Anindya Dhar   IIT-Kharagpur, India
Anshul Kumar   Indian Institute of Technology Delhi, India
Bharadwaj Amrutur   Indian Institute of Science, India
Bhargab Bhattacharya   Indian Statistical Institute, Calcutta, India
Biplab Sikdar   BESU
Chitta Mandal   IIT KGP, India
C.P. Ravikumar   TI India
D. Nagchoudhuri   DAIICT, Gandhinagar, India
Debdeep Mukhopadhyay   IIT Kharagpur, India
Debesh Das   Jadavpur University, India
Dhiraj Pradhan   University of Bristol, UK
Dipanwita Roychowdhury   IIT Kharagpur , India
Dong Xiang   Tsinghua University, China
Hafizur Rahaman   BESU, Shibpur, India
Huawei Li   Chinese Academy of Sciences, China
Indranil Sengupta   IIT KGP, India
Jacob Abraham   University of Texas at Austin, USA
Jayanta Lahiri   ARM
Koushik Maharatna   University of Southampton, UK
Krishnendu Chakrabarty   Duke University, USA
M. Balakrishnan   Indian Institute of Technology Delhi, India
Mathew Jimson   University of Bristol, UK
Michael Goessel   University of Potsdam, Germany
Nagarajan Charudhattan   IBM India
Nagi Naganathan   LSI, USA
Navakant Bhat   Indian Institute of Science, India
Pallab Dasgupta   IIT KGP, India
Parthapratim Das   IIT Kharagpur, India
Partha Sarathi Dasgupta   Indian Institute of Management, Calcutta,
                               India
Pradip Mandal   IIT Kharagpur, India
Pramod Meher   NTU, Singapore
Preetiranjan Panda   Indian Institute of Technology Delhi, India

Rajatsubhra Chakraborty	IIT Kharagpur, India
R.M. Patrikar	NIT Nagar
Rohit Kapur	Synopsys Inc.
Rolf Drechsler	University of Bremen, Germany
Roy P. Paily	IIT G, India
Samir Ray	NITTTR, Kolkata, India
Sanatan Chottopadhyaya	University of Calcutta, India
Sandip Kundu	U Mass, Amherst, USA
Santanu Chattopadhyay	IIT KGP, India
Santosh Biswas	IIT Guwahat, India
Saraju Mohanty	University of North Texas, USA
Shawn Blanton	Carnegie Mellon, USA
Simon Hollis	University of Bristol, UK
Srimat Chakradhar	NEC Labs America, USA
Srinivasan Anuradha	Intel, India
Srivaths Ravi	Texas Instruments
Subhasish Mitra	Stanford University, USA
Sudeb Dasgupta	IIT R, India
Sukumar Nandi	IIT Guwahati, India
Susmita Sur-Kolay	ISI, Kolkata, India
Swapna Banerjee	IIT KGP, India
Tarun Bhattacharya	IIT Kharagpur, India
V. Kamakoti	IIT Madras, India
V. Sahula	National Institute of Technology, Jaipur, India
Vinod Prasad	Nanyang Technological University, Singapore
Virendra Singh	Indian Institute of Science, India
VishwaniAgrawal	Auburn University, USA

Additional Reviewers

Abhijit Mallik	Biswajit Patra	Karthik Ramkumar
Abhirup Das Barman	Bratati Mukherjee	Kunal Sinha
Amlan Chakrabarti	Chandan Giri	Laxmi Karthikeyan
Andrew Madison	Chandra Narla	Mahesh Gautam
Anindita Das	Chester Rebeiro	Mamata Dalui
Anirban Bhattacharyya	Chirasree Roychaudhuri	Manikandan R.R.
Arpita Das	Debaprasad Das	Manodipan Sahoo
Avik Chatterjee	Debotosh Guha	Mathias Soeken
Baohu Li	Eleonora Schoenborn	Mousumi Saha
Basavaraj Talwar	Elias Kougianos	Mridul Sengupta
Basudev Nag	Farhana Rashid	Mukesh Agrawal
Chaowdhury	Geng Zheng	Nachiketa Das
Bei Zhang	Goutam Dalapati	Narender Ponna
Bibhash Sen	Jins Alexander	Nicole Drechsler
Bidesh Chakraborty.	Jyoti Kaushik	Nitin Yogi

Oghenekarho Okobiah
Oleg Garitselov
Partha Bhattacharyya
ParthaPratim Roy
ParthaSarathi Gupta
Pranab Roy
Prasun Ghosal
Praveen Venkataramani
Preetham
   Lakshmikanthan
Priyadharshini
   Shanmugasundaram
Prof. P.K. Basu

Rahul Shrestha
Rajeswari D.
Rob Aitken
Robert Wille
Shailendra Jain
Sivaram Subramanian
Smitha Kavallur
Pisharath Gopi
SomsubhraTalapatra
Soumyajit Poddar
Soumya Pandit
Srinivasan Srinath
Stefan Frehse

Stephan Eggersglüß
Sudip Ghosh
Sudipta Bhawmik
Suman Sao
Sumit Darak
Swaroop Ganguly
Tuhina Samanta
Udayan Ganguly
Vijay Sheshadri
Vikram Chaturvedi
Vinay Rao
Yang Zhao

Table of Contents

Design Techniques I

Algorithms and Applications I

Lower Power II

Analog VLSI Design II

Test and Verification II

Design Techniques II

Algorithms and Applications II

Emerging Technologies

Algorithms and Applications III

NoC and Physical Design

Poster Presentation

Invited Talk

An Efficient High Frequency and Low Power Analog Multiplier in Current Domain

Anu Gupta and Subhrojyoti Sarkar

Dept. of Electrical and Electronics Engineering
Birla Institute of Technology and Science, Pilani, Rajasthan
anug@bits-pilani.ac.in, sarkar.subhrojyoti@gmail.com

Abstract. A new CMOS Analog Multiplier in Current Domain using very negligible amount of static power is presented. This circuit uses the concept of harmonics along with the square law of current in a saturated MOS and is simulated using 90nm Technology Node of UMC. The supply voltage Vdd is kept at +1V. The circuit, when drawn using the Cadence Virtuoso Schematic Editor and simulated using the Spectre Simulator, gave a -3dB bandwidth of 2.07GHz with a load capacitance of 10fF.

Keywords: Analog, multiplier, low power, current mode, static power consumption, bandwidth.

1 Introduction

An analog multiplier is a circuit which takes two inputs and produces an output which is a product of the two. So, if two sinusoids of the same frequency are taken as inputs, the output sinusoid has double the frequency. And if the two input sinusoids are different, the resulting wave will be an Amplitude Modulated one which will have beats having a beat frequency equal to the difference between the frequencies of the two input sinusoids.

Frequency translation is an important concept in radio transmission. The base frequency is generated using a crystal oscillator which is a very stable reference for low frequencies but is not practical to manufacture for a higher frequency. As such, the low frequency signal is translated to a higher one.

A four quadrant analogue multiplier is a basic building block of many signal processing circuits. They have several applications in modulation, detection, frequency translation, automatic gain controlling, Fuzzy systems and neural networks. Several four quadrant CMOS current multiplier circuits have been published, with the transistor operating in the saturation region, which have been discussed at length in the subsequent sections. The major drawback faced by them was that they had limited bandwidth.

In this report, a new design of an analog multiplier is proposed. The circuit is symmetric and thus is able to reduce distortions. Also, the proposed circuit is a four quadrant multiplier. It works with a supply voltage of +1V and uses just 59.5μW power. It also has a very high bandwidth (f-3dB = 2.07GHz) mainly due to the reason that the main signal path does not have high parasitic capacitances. This circuit uses 10 MOS and thus does not occupy much area thereby resulting in cost reduction on silicon chip.

H. Rahaman et al. (Eds.): VDAT 2012, LNCS 7373, pp. 1–9, 2012.

2   Basic Operation and Design

Shown in the figure 1 is the design of proposed analog multiplier. The underlying principle is the square law of bias current through a saturated MOS transistor.

Here, $Ia = I1 + I2$ and $Ib = I3 + I4$.

$Vx\_Pos = V + vx$, $Vx\_Neg = V - vx$, $Vy\_Pos = V + vy$ and $Vy\_Neg = V - vy$.

$$I1 = 0.5\mu_n Cox(W/L)(Vx\_Pos - Va - kvy - Vtn)^2 \qquad \{ \text{Ignoring } \lambda \} \text{------------------ (i)}$$

$$I2 = 0.5\mu_n Cox(W/L)(Vx\_Neg - Va + kvy - Vtn)^2 \qquad \{ \text{Ignoring } \lambda \} \text{---------------- (ii)}$$

$$I3 = 0.5\mu_n Cox(W/L)(Vx\_Pos - Vb + kvy - Vtn)^2 \qquad \{ \text{Ignoring } \lambda \} \text{------------------(iii)}$$

$$I4 = 0.5\mu_n Cox(W/L)(Vx\_Neg - Va - kvy - Vtn)^2 \qquad \{ \text{Ignoring } \lambda \} \text{----------------(iv)}$$

Clubbing the DC terms together into a term Vdc, we get,

$$Ia = 0.5\mu_n Cox(W/L)((vx - kvy)^2 + Vdc^2)$$

$$Ib = 0.5\mu_n Cox(W/L)((vx + kvy)^2 + Vdc^2)$$

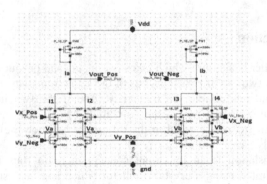

Fig. 1. Proposed Multiplier Topology

These two currents are then sensed by the diode connected PMOS and the outputs are Vout_Pos and Vout_Neg. The difference between these two output voltages gives us the product of the two input voltages vx and vy.

$$I_{diff} = Ia - Ib = \mu_n Cox(W/L)k(vx)(vy)$$

In this case, we have used N_10_SP and P_10_SP as NMOS and PMOS respectively wherein SP denotes "Standard Performance" and N_10 denotes an NMOS with 1V Vdd with corresponding values for P_10. Here we must note that in umc90nm library the minimum channel length can go to 80nm.

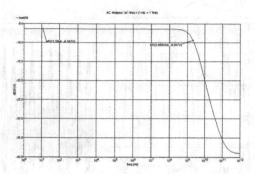

Fig. 2. AC Response showing -3dB Frequency of proposed multiplier

We have used a channel length of 100nm for both NMOS and PMOS and the W/L values have been set up by purely considering the case where all the MOS's, except those NMOS's whose sources are connected to the ground, are in saturation.

Here, it is important to mention that we have not used any current mirror in order to reduce power that would have been consumed by adding a separate branch for current reference, when we can do without it using a diode connected PMOS, which keeps the DC level of Vout more or less constant across corners. In this way, this circuit is different from Gilbert's Cell. Also, since we are concerned with a high bandwidth, so we have used very small devices. Since there are only ten MOS, the area of the chip will be much less. The circuit was tested for an Input signal of 1GHz for :

1)　Typical NMOS and Typical PMOS at a temperature of 27^0C,
2)　Fast NMOS and Fast PMOS at a temperature of 100^0C, and
3)　Slow NMOS and Slow PMOS at a temperature of 0^0C.

It was also tested for two signals, one at 1GHz and the other at 50MHz and the output was checked on all three corners.

3　Performance at Corners

Here in the figure2, we can see that the -3dB frequency of proposed analog multiplier ,for typical case, is at around 2.069GHz. This high bandwidth comes from the fact that we are using extremely small devices. The load capacitance used was 10fF, which is the standard for 90nm devices. We can use devices having a larger channel length in order to suppress the DIBL effects and other short channel effects such as velocity saturation and hot carrier effects but that would compromise on the bandwidth. Suppose we increase the both channel width and length by a fixed ratio 'x'. The bias current won't increase but the parasitic capacitances will increase by 'x^2' leading to smaller bandwidth. If after that, we try to increase just the channel width by a particular ratio 'y', so as to increase the bias current, the bandwidth will not be affected much because the parasitic capacitances too will increase by 'y'.

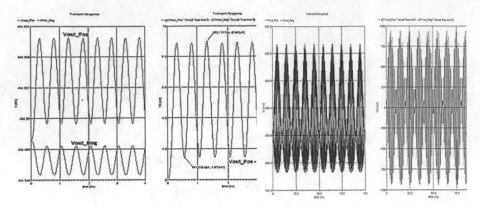

Fig. 3. Frequency Doubling   **Fig. 4.** Amplitude Modulation

The performances are shown for Typical NMOS and Typical PMOS at a temperature of 27^0C.

To show that the circuit works at very high frequencies, we take a double ended input signal of frequency 1GHz and apply it to the two input terminals of the circuit, Vin_Pos and Vin_Neg. The transient response is plotted for 4 nanoseconds.

As we can see clearly from the figure 3, the input signals have 4 peaks whereas the output signal "Vout" has 8 peaks for the same time slot of 4 nanoseconds. This shows that the above circuit doubles the input frequency even at very high frequencies.

The figure 4 shows the Amplitude Modulation of a carrier signal of 1GHz by a message signal of 50MHz.

Table 1 summarizes the characteristics of proposed multiplier at extreme corners and typical case--

Case1: Fast NMOS and Fast PMOS (FF) working at a temperature of 100^0C.
Case2: Slow NMOS and Slow PMOS (SS) working at a temperature of 0^0C.

The table 1 shows % variation in -3dB frequency of multiplier at corner cases . the important point observed is the frequency doubling and amplitude modulation characteristics were retained even at extreme corner cases which shows the correctness of design.

Table 1. Characteristics of proposed multiplier at extreme corners and typical case

Case	-3dB frequency	% Variation
FF	2.451GHz.	0.18
SS	1.44GHz.	0.30
TYPICAL	2.069GHz	

For the case of amplitude modulation, as well as frequency doubling, we checked the Power Spectral Density (PSD).

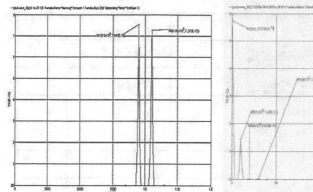 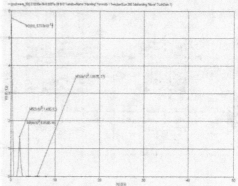

Fig. 5. Power Spectral Density for Amplitude Modulation

Fig. 6. Power Spectral Density for Frequency Doubling

The figure 5 shows the PSD for the case of amplitude modulation of a 1GHz wave by a 50MHz wave. Here we observe that the PSD plot shows that two sinusoids are summed, one having a frequency of 1.05GHz and the other having 0.95GHz, which perfectly tallies with our claim.

The figure 6 shows the PSD for the case when a 1GHz signal is given as input and the output is a signal having 2GHz frequency. The figure 6 shows that the higher order harmonics are more than 1000 times weaker than the main output signal which has a frequency of 2GHz. The total harmonic distortion was found out to be 0.0346%.

4   Comparison with Existing Multipliers

For comparison, the circuit for Analog Multiplier given in reference [3] and proposed circuit shown in Figure 1 has been designed and compared in 90 nm technology node. The design of reference [3] is given in figure 7. All the channel lengths and widths of the devices present in this circuit have been chosen keeping in mind the W/L's mentioned in [3]. The devices chosen are again N_10_SP and P_10_SP from UMC's 90nm library.

Transient simulation were done for typical NMOS and typical PMOS, with a Vdd of 1V and at a temperature of 27^0C. A differential signal of 1GHz frequency was applied to both the ports of the circuit, namely, Vin_Pos and Vin_Neg. Figure 8 shows that for reference [3[circuit, there was an initial delay of roughly 1ns for the output to get stabilized. This was particularly because of the reduced bandwidth due to large number of devices which produce more parasitics in the path of the main signal.

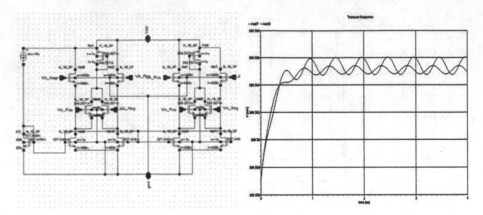

Fig. 7. Circuit given in in reference [3]   **Fig. 8.** Transient response for Circuit in reference [3] for 1GHz Signal

For comparison, we have also designed the circuit proposed in reference [4] , as shown in figure 15 and 16, using UMC's 90nm technology libraries

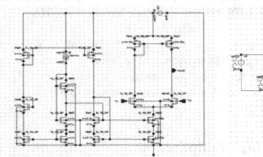

Fig. 9. Differential Amplifier for Summation   **Fig. 10.** complete circuit of reference [4]
in reference [4]

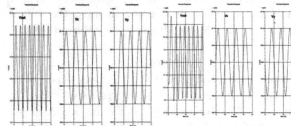

Fig. 11. Transient Response   **Fig. 12.** Transient Response   **Fig. 13.** Transient Response
of reference [4] for 1MHz   of reference [4] for 200 MHz   of reference [4] for 500MHz
Signal input   Signal input   Signal input

In figure 9, we have shown the differential amplifier used for summation of two input signals (in reference [4]) to be applied at Vx and Vy and complete circuit of reference [4] is in figure 10. The circuit performance is again checked against the performance of proposed multiplier. We have obtained transient response of this circuit using a signal of 1MHz, 200MHz, 500 MHz as given in figures 11, 12, 13. Here, the response deteriorates starting from 200MHz itself. For higher frequencies, we observed that the circuit is not able to stabilize at and beyond 500 MHz input. Therefore we can say that circuit of reference [4] does not work at SHF (-3dB frequency of 3.96GHz) in 90 nm technology.

Table 2 gives a comparison of performance of proposed multiplier with the circuits in the references [10] and [4]. The data for the performances of the circuits presented in [10] and [4] have been taken from the respective papers themselves.

Here it is important to mention that in some cases the exact channel lengths and widths as given in the papers are difficult to maintain for simulation using 90nm technology. This is because the short channel effects become pretty profound and the V_{th} fluctuates with V_{DS} as well as channel length, making design of bigger circuits like amplifiers more prone to process variations. That's where a small and simple circuit has more uses.

5   Advantages of Proposed Multiplier

Proposed multiplier is a current mode circuit as it is the difference between the output currents which is finally the product of the input voltages. And these currents are sensed by diode connected PMOS's in order to ensure that there is no resistor which is highly sensitive to PVT variations. No bandgap circuit has been used to bias the circuit as it is self - biasing due to the presence of the diode connected PMOS thereby reducing the power consumption further. If this circuit is used for simple frequency doubling, then this circuit can be used as a standalone device to feed its output to the next stage to get a frequency that is 4 times the original frequency because the output produced is differential. Also, the differential output contributes to the reduction in noise

The greatest advantage of the circuit presented in this work is its simplicity and extremely small size. There are only 10 devices which can be perfectly used for multiplication and the PSD plots also support our claim. This multiplier can also be used for frequency translation. A crystal oscillator cannot produce a stable signal at a very high frequency. This circuit is highly specialized and can be inserted in such a system to produce a signal that can have a very high frequency. Also, given the fact that DSP technology is yet to evolve properly to be used for high frequency applications at a bearable cost, an analog solution such as this is much more feasible. The very high bandwidth of 2.069GHz and an extremely low power consumption of 59.5µW will make it a valuable addition to modern communication systems to generate a very high frequency carrier signal to be modulated by the main signal and can also be used in modulation.

6   Conclusion

A new circuit for Four Quadrant Analog Multiplication using 90nm technology node has been proposed. This circuit has a bandwidth of 2.069GHz and consumes only 59.5μW power to achieve this. This circuit has been designed using the Standard Performance MOSFETs of UMC's 90nm Technology Library. The schematic has been drawn using Cadence Schematic Editor and is simulated using the Spectre Simulator at all the three extreme corners. Further, this circuit does not have any body effect.

The circuits of references cited are also four quadrant analog multipliers. These circuits multiply analog signals by using harmonics. But proposed multiplier achieves better performance over these circuits with less complex schematic. As silicon cost is very high, so we need to minimize the area occupied so as to reduce the cost per chip. Here, proposed multiplier has only 8 NMOS and 2 PMOS. We have further used small devices in our design. The width of the PMOS's is 500nm and that of the NMOS's is 300nm. The length of all the MOS's is only 100nm.

Table 2. Comparison of performance of proposed multiplier with circuits of reference [4], reference [10]

Characteristics	Reference [10]	Reference [4]	Proposed multiplier
Technology	350nm	180nm	UMC's 90nm
Supply	±1V	±1V	1V
No. of MOS	12	36	10
Bandwidth	1.74GHz	3.96GHz	2.069GHz
Power	0.85mW	0.588mW	0.059mW
Simulator Used	HSPICE	PSPICE	Spectre
Input Range	±20μA	±100mV	±250mV
THD	-	-	0.0346%

References

1. Li, S.C., Cha, J.C.: 0.5V- +.I5 V VHF CMOS LV/LP Four-Quadrant Analog Multiplier in Modified Bridged-Triode Scheme. In: Proceedings of the 2002 International Symposium on Low Power Electronics and Design, ISLPED 2002, pp. 227–232 (2002)
2. Sawigun, C., Mahattanakul, J.: A 1.5V, Wide-Input Range, High-Bandwidth, CMOS Four-Quadrant Analog Multiplier. In: IEEE International Symposium on Circuits and Systems, ISCAS 2008, pp. 2318–2321 (2008), doi:10.1109/ISCAS.2008.4541918
3. Al-Nsour, M., Abdel-Aty-Zohdy, H.S.: A Wide Input Range Analog Multiplier For Neuro-computing. In: Proceedings of the 40th Midwest Symposium on Circuits and Systems, vol. 1, pp. 13–16 (1997), doi:10.1109/MWSCAS.1997.666022

4. Hidayat, R., Dejhan, K., Moungnoul, P., Miyanaga, Y.: OTA-Based High Frequency CMOS Multiplier and Squaring Circuit. In: International Symposium on Intelligent Signal Processing and Communications Systems, ISPACS 2008, pp. 1–4 (2009), doi:10.1109/ISPACS.2009.4806748

5. Prommee, P., Somdunyakanok, M., Kumngern, M., Dejhan, K.: Single Low-Supply Current-mode CMOS Analog Multiplier Circuit. In: International Symposium on Communications and Information Technologies, ISCIT 2006, pp. 1101–1104 (2006), doi:10.1109/ISCIT.2006.339949

6. Mahmoud, S.A.: CMOS Fully Differential CMOS Four-Quadrant Analog Multiplier. In: International Conference on Microelectronics, ICM 2008, pp. 27–30 (2008), doi:10.1109/ICM.2008.5393543

7. Li, S.C.: A Very-High-Frequency CMOS Four-Quadrant Analogue Multiplier. In: Proceedings of 1997 IEEE International Symposium on Circuits and Systems, ISCAS 1997, vol. 1, pp. 233–236 (1997), doi:10.1109/ISCAS.1997.608681

8. Ramirez-Angulo, J., Carvajal, R.G., Martinez-Heredia, J.: 1.4V Supply, Wide Swing, High Frequency CMOS Analogue Multiplier with High Current Efficiency. In: Proceedings of the 2000 IEEE International Symposium on Circuits and Systems, ISCAS 2000 Geneva, vol. 5, pp. 533–536 (2000), doi:10.1109/ISCAS.2000.857489

9. Diwakar, K., Senthilpari, C., Singh, A.K., Soong, L.W.: Analog Multiplier with High Accuracy. In: First International Conference on Computational Intelligence, Communication Systems and Networks, CICSYN 2009, pp. 62–66 (2009), doi:10.1109/CICSYN.2009.10

10. Ghanavati, B., Nowbakht, A.: + 1V high frequency four quadrant current Multiplier. Electronics Letters 46(14), 974–976 (2010), doi:10.1049/el.2010.1020

11. Chen, C., Li, Z.: A low-power CMOS analog multiplier. IEEE Transactions on Circuits and Systems II: Express Briefs 53(2), 100–104 (2006), doi:10.1109/TCSII.2005.857089

Design of Push-Pull Dynamic Leaker Circuit for a Low Power Embedded Voltage Regulator

Biswajit Maity and Pradip Mandal

Dept. of E & ECE, IIT Kharagpur, 721302, India
biswajitmaity.iitkgp@gmail.com, pradip@ece.iitkgp.ernet.in

Abstract. A novel technique of fast transient response for a low power voltage regulator for embedded applications has been presented in this paper. Push-pull dynamic leaker circuit has been used to get fast transient response. Push-pull dynamic leaker paths help to reduce both peaks and dips at the output due to momentary load transients or line transients. Leaker paths work either as a source or sink path for the load current depending upon the requirement of load current and supply voltage. Introduction of push pull dynamic leaker paths in parallel to a linear regulator also helps to drastically reduce settling time with marginal increment of static power loss. Proposed dynamic leaker circuit is implemented with current control voltage regulator in 0.18µm CMOS process for 3.3V to 1.35V conversion and tested in silicon. Measurement result shows, 10% settling time of the regulator is less than 200ns, whereas peak at the output is 1.49V and dips at the output is 1.04V due to 15mA load transient in 1nS.

Keywords: Push-pull, dead band, dynamic leakage path, settling time, peaks and dips.

1 Introduction

With the advancement of the technology, internal supply voltage for subcomponents of battery-operated hand held portable device is decreasing. Whereas, voltage of battery does not scale down with the same proportion. It leads to a mismatch of the required supply voltage of an IC and the available battery voltage. To mitigate this problem an external and/or an embedded (within IC) DC-DC converter is used. Switched capacitor DC-DC converter gives limited conversion ratio and has high noise in on-chip converters but recent research shows any voltage level at the output can be achievable from switched capacitor converter [1]. Due to the portable nature, low cost and low noise, low dropout linear regulators (LDO) were mainly used in embedded DC-DC converter [2]. Transient performance of linear regulator is good as compared to switching converter or inductor based embed converter. In high speed digital applications, load might change momentarily from maximum to minimum or vice-versa. Even in linear regulator, peaks at the output voltage are higher than nominal value due to variation of load current from high to low whereas dips are less than nominal value when load current changes from low to high value. In addition, the settling time due to the load transient in the converter is very high and hence reliability of the hand held devices is a major concern. In [3], dual loop feedback LDO

H. Rahaman et al. (Eds.): VDAT 2012, LNCS 7373, pp. 10–18, 2012.

has been used for fast transient response. But circuit uses off-chip component not suitable for embedded application. In [4], dual loop feedback is used in push-pull configuration to improve the transient performance of the embedded voltage regulator. For digital applications, peaks and dips are still high due to its limited close loop bandwidth. In [5], settling time of the regulator is improved with the help of 1μF off-chip capacitor. In [6] capacitive-coupled feedback (CCFB) is used to improve the transient performance of fully integrated voltage regulator. Based on post layout results of [5], it can be noted that transient performance is improved significant with the help of large static power loss. CCFB based circuit can't be used in low power application as it will affect directly on the power efficient of the regulator. In [7], peaks, dips and settling time of the regulator are significantly large to maintain power efficiency of switched capacitor based regulator in current control loop. On the other hand dynamic leaker path in [8] is used in current control regulation loop to reduce peaks and settling time due to variation of load current from high to low value. In addition, in [8] off-chip capacitor has been used to reduce peak and settling time.

We are proposing similar dynamic leaker paths for embedded application but in push pull configuration to reduce peaks and dips at the output during transient time. This proposed dynamic leaker helps to improve transient response of the converter while power efficiency of the voltage regulator remains almost unchanged over the load current (i.e. contrast to [7]). At the same time settling time to reach pre-specified voltage level, is reduced drastically. Performance of embedded regulation is tested in silicon and results are presented. It can be noted that this dynamic leaker circuit is also suitable for switching converters. Section 2 of this paper deals with the working principle and implementation of push-pull dynamic leaker. In section 3, simulation and measurement result of proposed voltage regulator have been discussed and in section 4 conclusion is given based on the measurement results of the regulator.

2   Working Principle and Implementation of Push-Pull Dynamic Leaker Circuit

With In figure 1, simple schematic diagram of has been shown (similar to [2]). It mainly consists of error amplifier and a pass transistor. Error amplifier is implemented cascode differential amplifier [9] to improve operating current range. Due to unavailability of large load capacitor for low power embedded applications and to make the converter stable irrespective of load current, internal pole is made dominant as compared to the output pole. It can be mentioned that the quiescent current of the LDO is 90μA. This simple voltage regulator is stable throughout the load current (0.25mA to 30mA). Unity-gain bandwidth of the regulator is 10Mz. Due to its limited bandwidth, transient response of the low power regulator is poor, specifically in case of digital applications where load changes momentarily form low to high and vice-versa. Due to fast changes of load current from high to low, output of error amplifier becomes momentarily high and as a result of this output voltage reaches toward supply voltage. If chip switches again to high current during the time when output voltage is not stabilized, the output voltage falls much below than its specified lower limit as it is shown in figure 2. In this figure 2, transient performance of the voltage regulator is illustrated where load current changes from 0.25mA to 15.25mA and vice-versa. From this figure, it can be observed that peak voltage at the output is 1.63V while dip in the output is 0.64V. In addition settling time required to precisely adjust the output voltage is more than 1μs. All these parameters restrict the use of simple voltage regulator in embedded digital applications where load changes frequently.

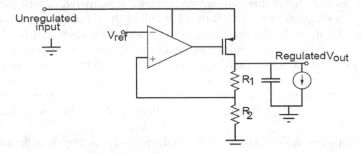

Fig. 1. Schematic diagram of a Linear rugulator

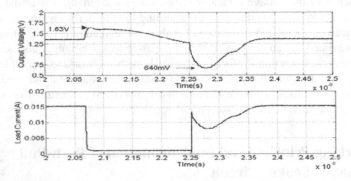

Fig. 2. Transient performance of the voltage regulator without dynamic leaker

To improve the transient performance of voltage regulator without affecting other performance parameters (power efficiency and output ripple), we are proposing push pull dynamic leaker path in parallel to the existing current control loop of LDO. Schematic diagram of embedded voltage regulator based on proposed push pull dynamic leaker is illustrated in figure 3. In figure 3, upper leaker path and lower leaker path are added in parallel with the existing current control loop in figure 1. Parallel path works during transient time and provides a leakage current path during that transient time. Proposed configuration is called push-pull dynamic leaker as one of the leaker path works either as a source or sink of load current during load or line transient. Each of the leaker paths is driven by hysteresis op-amp (intentionally made offset in operational amplifier). Detailed circuit diagram of lower leaker path and upper leaker path has been illustrated in figure 4 and figure 5 respectively. Let's assume, load current changes from maximum to minimum value within 1ns. During this transient time, transistor M2 of figure 4 becomes stronger than M1 and output of the differential amp becomes high and this lead to switch on the lower leaker path. This leaker path remains switched on until output voltage reaches within dead band (below 1.4V) as it is shown in figure 6. Due to faster response of leaker path, settling time to enter into the dead band is drastically reduced. At the same time peaks at output, during this load transient is decreased. Positive offset of differential amp may make the dynamic path permanently on. To avoid the flaw, we intentionally make negative offset in the differential amplifier by making size of the transistor M1 more than M2 in figure 4.

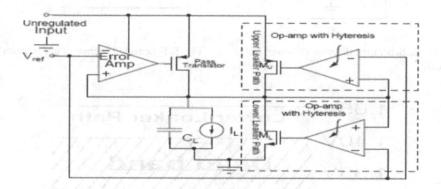

Fig. 3. Block diagram of voltage regulation with dynamic leaker

Similar structure in figure 5 has been adopted for the upper dynamic leaker path to minimize output dips. A hysteresis differential amplifier is also used in the upper dynamic leaker path. This leaker path works when load current changes from low to high. Upper dynamic leaker path helps to supply the load current and hence brings back output voltage into the dead band (more than 1.3V) as shown in figure 5. Similar to lower hysteresis op-amp, negative offset is made in upper hysteresis op-amp by making size of transistor M1 more than transistor M2. From the above discussion it can be mentioned that during transient time, leaker paths acts either as a source or sink of load current to stabilize the output voltage quickly. It can be mentioned that size of M_U and M_L is made large to reduce the drop during transient time. But sizes of these leaker path output transistors are ~10% of pass transistor size. We did rigorous stability analysis for the regulator. It can be noted that dynamic leaker path are much faster than LDO path and dominant pole of LDO sits at the output of error amplifier. For LDO, for max current (30mA) phase Margin (PM) is 78^0 whereas for low load current (10µA) regulator PM is 25^0. Due to addition of upper and lower leaker path, there is slight degradation of stability due to non-dominant poles at the gate of MU/ML (gates of upper/lower leakage path output transistor). Still proposed regulator is stable from 50uA to 26mA load current.

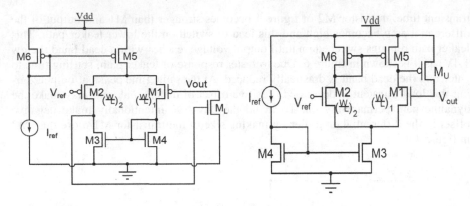

Fig. 4. Schematic diagram of lower leaker path

Fig. 5. Schematic Diagram of upper leaker path

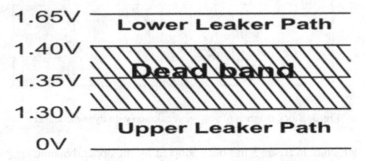

Fig. 6. Operating voltage range of push pull dynamic leaker

It can be noted that once the output reaches into the dead band, leaker path becomes switched off and current control loop takes over to bring back the output to its steady state output voltage as it is shown in figure 7.

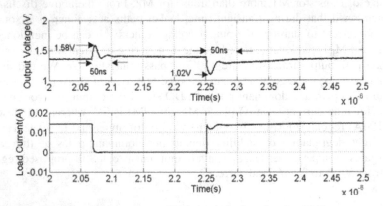

Fig. 7. Transient performance regulator with dynamic leaker circuit with the same condition of fig 2

It can be noted that figure 2 and figure 7 are used to illustrate transient performance of voltage regulator without and with dynamic leaker circuit respectively. Performances are shown for the same load transient (15mA) and same load transient time
(i.e. 1ns). Huge transient performance improvement is achieved due to use of the
proposed push pull dynamic leaker circuit path. Settling time is reduced to 50ns from
1us, peak in the output is reduced to 1.58V from 1.63V whereas dip in the output is
reduced to 1.02V. In digital applications, normally, the chip runs at high frequency.
Consequently, the chip transits from minimum load current to maximum load current
point in few ns time. Dynamic leaker consumes almost zero static power in steady
condition. At the same time it improves the transient behavior of the voltage regulator
when the load current varies momentarily from minimum to maximum or vice versa.

3   Results

Performance of proposed push pull dynamic leaker circuit for the embedded voltage
regulator is implemented in 0.18um CMOS technology to get 1.35V output from 3.3V
supply voltage. In the regulator, only 50pF load capacitor has been used. This capacitor is implemented using PMOS transistor in n-well process.

Performance of low power embedded regulator is first characterized in simulation
and then verified in silicon. Here we are illustrating load regulation of voltage regulator (variation of load current from 0.25mA to 15.25 mA and vice-versa in 1ns time).
Figure 8 is used to illustrate simulated performance of the voltage regulator with proposed dynamic leaker circuit. It can be noted that in figure 2 figure 7, load transient
has occurred in 1μs interval whereas in figure 8, load transient is occurred in 2.2μs
interval (i.e. load transient is occurred once output reaches to steady state value). In
figure 8 peak output voltage is 1.58V and settling time is 100ns.Whereas dips output
voltage is 1.04V and settling time is 100ns. In this figure 8, dynamic leakage current
due to load transient has also been illustrated. It can be noted that leakage current
flows only during transient time.

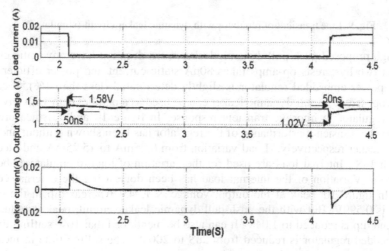

Fig. 8. Load transient of voltage regulator with dynamic leaker circuit (simulated)

Hence dynamic leaker paths work as a sink or source of load current during transient time and quickly bring the output within the dead band of the dynamic leaker. It can be noted from the figure that once output voltage is reached within the dead band (output is within 1.30V to 1.40V) of dynamic leaker, current control loop takes the control to get precise output voltage. Figure 9 is used to illustrate simulated line regulation of proposed voltage regulator (variation of line voltage or supply from 3.6V to 3.0V and vice-versa in 1ns) while load current remains at 10mA. From this figure, it can be observed that as supply voltage is decreased from 3.6V to 3.0V, output is quickly settled to pre-specified voltage level with the help of upper dynamic leaker paths. Similarly lower leaker path works while line voltage changes from 3.0V to 3.6V. From the leaker current waveform in figure 9 it can also be mentioned that push pull dynamic leaker circuit gives one extra current path during transient time and brings the output voltage level within the dead band.

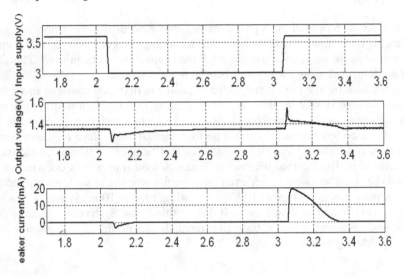

Fig. 9. Line transient of regulator with dynamic leaker circuit (simulated)

Though proposed push pull dynamic leaker paths does not have any static current path, but two hysteresis op-amps takes 80uA static current and power efficiency of the low power embedded regulator is slightly deteriorated (less than 1%). It can be noted proposed push-pull dynamic leaker can be used as a parallel path with any other voltage regulator to improve transient response. In figure 10 and 11, measurement result for the transient performance of the regulator has been shown without and with dynamic leaker respectively. (Load variation from 0.25mA to 15.25mA and vice versa within 1nS). Internal load are used for the variation of load to emulate embedded application. Variation of the internal load has been done using the external control signal. In figure 10, peak at the output voltage is 1.94V whereas dip in the output voltage is 0.599V. But with the push-pull dynamic leaker circuit, peak is reduced to 1.54V and dip is reduced to 1.04V. It can also be mentioned that 10% settling time of the embedded regulator is reduced from 2uS to 200nS. The selling time in measurement is more compared to simulation due to measurement parasitic.

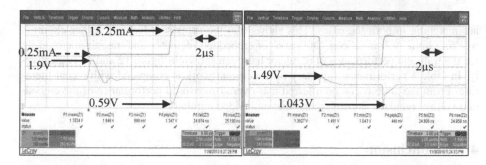

Fig. 10. Load regulation of the regulator without Dynamic Leaker

Fig. 11. Load regulation of the regulator with Dynamic Leaker

Fig. 12. Die photo proposed dynamic leaker

Fig. 13. Measurement setup the regulator for transient performance

Table 1. Performance comparison of the proposed converter

	Ref[3] Simulated and off-chip cap	Ref [4] Simulated	Ref[6] Measured	Ref[7] Measured	Ref[8] Simulated and Off-chip cap	Proposed Regulator Measured
Imax	100mA	26mA	50mA	10mA	200mA	26mA
Input Supply	5V	3.3V	3.5V	1.8V	3.3V	3.3V
Vout	3V	1.35V	2.8V	0.8V	1.9V	1.35V
Cout	10 uF	50pF	100pF	574 pF	10nF	50 pF
Settling Time	10us	<500ns	15us	120ns	-	<200ns
Peak or Dip	1mV	230mV	90mV	250mV	242mV	300mV
Technology	0.5μm CMOS	0.18μm CMOS	0.35μm CMOS	45nm CMOS	0.18μm CMOS	0.18μm CMOS

Similarly peaks and dips is slightly degraded in measurement But, performance trends are matching in both the cases. This shows that the proposed dynamic leaker circuit is working quite well in silicon. Die photo of embedded regulator and measurement set-up for the transient performance of regulator has been shown in figure 12 and 13 respectively. In table 1 performance summary of the current work is compared with recent literature. From the table it can be inferred that overall measured performance of the embedded voltage regulator is better than other embedded regulator.

4   Conclusion

Proposed regulator is tailored to fast transient loads and established in silicon. Performance characterization in simulation and verification in silicon for proposed voltage regulator based on push pull dynamic leaker circuit gives us enough confidence to use the circuit in high-speed digital applications (specifically in SRAM) where load current changes frequently. Due to the use of dynamic leaker circuit, power efficiency of the embedded voltage regulator remains almost unchanged while transient performance (settling time, peaks and dip at the output) is improved to a large extent. Push pull dynamic leaker circuit helps to bring the output voltage level within the dead band of dynamic leaker in few ns time. Introduction of dead band helps to mitigate output noise, process variation and temperature variation in the circuit.

Acknowledgment. The authors would like to acknowledge NSC for the support to use their process.

References

1. Hanh-Phuc, L., Seeman, M., Sanders, S.R., Sathe, V., Naffziger, S., Alon, E.: A 32 nm fully integrated reconfigurable switched-capacitor DC-DC converter delivering 0.55W/mm at 81% efficiency. In: Proc. ISSCC, pp. 210–211 (2010)
2. Rincon-Mora, G.A., Allen, P.E.: A Low Voltage, Low Quiescent Current, Low Drop-Out regulator. IEEE Journal of Solid-State Circuits 33(1), 36–44 (1998)
3. Chen, W., Ki, W.-H., Mok, P.K.T.: Dual-Loop Feedback for Fast Low Dropout Regulators. In: IEEE Power Electronics Specialist Conference, Vancouver, British Columbia, Canada (June 2001)
4. Maity, B., Bhagat, G., Mandal, P.: Dual Loop Push-Pull Feedback Linear Regulator for Embedded DC-DC Converter. In: IEEE PEDES 2010 (2010)
5. Lu, S.-H., Huang, W.-J., Liu, S.-I.: A Fast Settling Low Dropout Linear Regulator with single Miller compensation. In: Asian Solid-State Circuits Conference, pp. 153–156 (November 2005)
6. Miliken, R.J., Silva-Martínez, J., Sánchez-Sinencio, E.: A Full On-Chip CMOS Low-Dropout Voltage Regulator. IEEE Trans. Circuit and System I 54, 1879 (2007)
7. Ramadass, Y., Fayed, A., Haroun, B., Chandrakasan, A.: A 0.16mm^2 Completely On-Chip Switched-Capacitor DC-DC Converter Using Digital Capacitance Modulation for LDO Replacement in 45nm CMOS. In: ISSCC 2010, February 7-11 (2010)
8. Maity, A., Raghavendra, R.G., Mandal, P.: On chip voltage regulator with Improved Transient Response. In: Proceeding of VLSID 2005 (2005)
9. Allen, P.E., Holberg, D.R.: CMOS Analog Circuit Design. Ox. University Press (2004)

Power Modeling of Power Gated FSM and Its Low Power Realization by Simultaneous Partitioning and State Encoding Using Genetic Algorithm

Priyanka Choudhury and Sambhu Nath Pradhan

Dept. of ECE, NIT Agartala, 799055, India
{priyanka.choudhury22,sambhu.pradhan}@gmail.com

Abstract. Partitioning is an effective method for synthesis of low power finite state machines (FSM). To make the partitioning more effective power gating can be applied to turn OFF the inactive sub-machine. During transition from the states of one sub-machine to the states of other sub-machine, the supply voltage is required to be turned OFF for one sub-machine and turned ON for other sub-machine. This adjustment of supply voltage needs some amount of time. Hence, it effects the partitioning of FSMs for its power gated implementation as both the sub-machines are ON during this time. In this paper we have considered this issue by developing a new probabilistic power model of the power-gated design of FSM. As effective partitioning and encoding of FSM decides the power consumption of final power gating implementation, in this paper Genetic Algorithm (GA) has been used to solve this integrated problem of both bi-partitioning and encoding. Experimental results obtained show the effectiveness of the approach in terms of total dynamic power consumption, compared to the technique reported in the literature.

1   Introduction

Nowadays most of the emerging computing devices and wireless communication systems require high speed computation and complex functionality with a low power consumption and they are also control dominated. The controllers continue to run even when parts of data path are shut down. So, good amount of system power is consumed by the controller. Since most of the controllers are implemented as FSMs, power efficient synthesis of FSM has come up as a very important problem domain.

An FSM can be partitioned into two or more coupled sub-machines such that most of the time only one of the sub-machines is active. The other sub-machine which is inactive does not consume any power. A good encoding can help the logic minimizer to achieve a better realization in terms of area and power. So, power consumption can be reduced by applying state encoding to a partitioned FSM. The power can further be reduced by applying power gating technique. Power gating is a technique for saving both leakage and switching power by shutting off the idle blocks of the circuit.

In this paper, after suitably modeling the power metric of power gated FSM we have considered partitioning and state encoding together for low power realization of FSM. The contributions of this paper are as follows:

H. Rahaman et al. (Eds.): VDAT 2012, LNCS 7373, pp. 19–29, 2012.
© Springer-Verlag Berlin Heidelberg 2012

- GA based approach for simultaneous partitioning and state encoding of FSMs with power reduction as the objective using power gating.
- Effectiveness of our encoding technique has been established by comparing the results with that of NOVA encoding [14].
- The power model presented in [12] has been modified to accommodate power consumption during cross transition.
- It compares the dynamic power consumed by the combinational part of the circuit by SIS [13] with the power consumed by the circuit using NOVA [14].
- Power calculation is done considering the boundary depths 1 and 2 separately.
- CPU computation time, which was not recorded in [12] has been reported in this work.

The rest of the paper is organized as follows: the accumulative detail of the previous works is portrayed as literature review in section 2. Section 3 presents partitioning of FSM and architecture for power gating implementation. In section 4 the process of steady state probability calculation is explained. Proposed power model of power gated FSM is described in section 5. Section 6 describes the genetic algorithm for partitioning and state encoding. Experimental results are presented in Section 7. Finally, Section 8 concludes the whole work along with the future scope.

2   Literature Review

A physical partitioning of FSM has been proposed in [1] with considerable increase in area of the circuit. To sort out this problem some encoding strategies [2, 3] are used which result in significant power savings in the synthesized circuit.

The technique in [11] uses the probabilistic model of an FSM to obtain state encoding that minimizes the average number of signal transitions on the state lines for a general State Transition Graph (STG).

The clock gating technique for low power FSM decomposition has been reported in [4, 5]. An analysis of the efficiency of power-gating for Clocked Storage Elements has been presented in [6]. The works in [7, 8, 9] address the design of a power gating structure with high performance in the active mode, low leakage and short wakeup time during standby mode. The authors in [10] presented a simulated annealing based power-gating technique for FSM decomposition targeting low power, but it did not considered state encoding. The authors in [3, 12] considered the problems of FSM decomposition and state encoding together, targeting low power dissipation in power-gating technique. In [12] it was mentioned that during the cross transition power is consumed by both the sub-machines but while calculating the total power they did not considered this issue. In [12] it is considered that during cross transition power is consumed only by the sub-machine which is going to be active after the transition. In our paper we have modified the power model in [12]. Here the power modeling is based on state probability, considering partitioning and state encoding together. After verifying the results authors in [12] claimed that power will be less for the FSM whose boundary state probability is less. Instead of taking boundary depth 2 (as in [12]), if we take boundary depth 1, the boundary state probability may reduce as number of boundary states will reduce. So, we have carried out experiments taking boundary depth 1 and 2. It has been observed that better results are obtained when boundary depth is taken as 1.

3   Partitioning of FSM and Power Gating Implementation

Authors in [3] have briefly described the structure of a low power partitioned FSM. The low power architecture developed in [3] is such that if the inputs to an idle machine are held to a fixed value then the outputs will also be at a fixed value and power will not be consumed but since the sub-machine is not completely OFF it will consume some power. This problem was overcome in [12]. Power gating technique was used in [12] by adding a PMOS sleep transistor between Vdd and the combinational circuit or by adding NMOS sleep transistor between combinational circuit and ground as shown in Fig.1 which is the proposed circuit architecture for power-gating in [12]. In our work we have considered the same architecture as in Fig.1. The description and partitioning strategy of the circuit was described in [12].

Next, we state some of the definitions of [12] to enable us to formulate our partitioning and state encoding problem.

Boundary Depth (BD): It is defined as the number of clock cycles needed to turn ON the sub-machine to be activated.

Boundary States (BS): A boundary state between two sub-machines is a state in one sub-machine which is within the boundary depth of another machine. We use $D(F_1, F_2)$ to denote the set of boundary states in F_1 leading to F_2. The sum of the boundary state probability (BSP) of $D(F_1, F_2)$ is denoted as $P_D(F_1,F_2)$. Similarly, the sum of the boundary state probability of $D(F_2, F_1)$ is denoted as $P_D(F_2, F_1)$.

Next section onwards we will use BD, BS and BSP in place of *Boundary depth*, *Boundary states* and *boundary state probability* respectively.

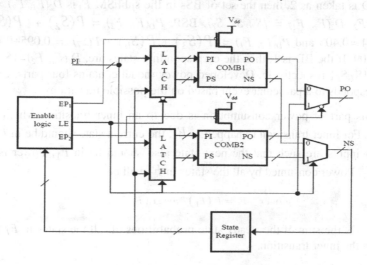

Fig. 1. Power-gating architecture

4   Steady State Probability Calculation

It is possible to compute the steady state probabilities of the states and the transition probabilities from the specific input line probabilities. The steady state probability $P(S_i)$ is the probability of the finite state machine being in the state S_i at a time instant. The state transition probability for the transition from S_i to S_j is defined as $P(S_{ij})$ and it is computed as $P(S_{ij}) = P(S_i) * P(k)$

where $P(k)$ represents the probability of the primary input combination holding true for which the transition S_i to S_j takes place. The steady state probabilities of the FSM states are calculated using the following equations.

$$\Sigma i\, P(S_i) = 1, \qquad P(S_i) = \Sigma j P(S_{ij})$$

By solving this set of linear equations using the Gauss-Jordon Elimination method, the steady state probabilities have been determined.

5   Power Modeling

Here we present our power model to estimate the total power consumed by the bipartitioned FSM. We need this model only during the execution of the GA based partitioning and state assignment procedure we have used. We assume that the combinational logic has been implemented in a two-level PLA. It may be noted that our fitness calculation targets two-level realization.

Fig.2 is an example of dk27 benchmark circuit showing the bipartitioning of a state transition graph (STG) into F_1 and F_2. For this example, the transitions between the states of $F_1 = \{S_1, S_2, S_4, S_6\}$ and the transitions between the states of the sub-machine $F_2 = \{ S_3, S_5, S_7\}$ are the inner transitions. The transitions from state S_2 to S_3, S_2 to S_5, S_5 to S_2, S_5 to S_1, S_7 to S_6 are the cross transitions.

If the BD is taken as 2, then the set of BSs in the subFSM F_1 is $D_2(F_1, F_2) = \{S_2, S_6\}$ and for F_2, $D_2(F_2, F_1) = \{S_3, S_5, S_7\}$. BSP, $P_D(F_1, F_2) = P(S_2) + P(S_6) = 0.191+0.214 =0.405$ and $P_D(F_2, F_1) = P(S_3) + P(S_5) + P(S_7) = 0.095+0.167 + 0.047 = 0.209$. If the BD is 1, then the corresponding states are, $D_1(F_1, F_2)=\{S_2\}$ and $D_1(F_2,F_1)=\{S_7,S_5\}$ respectively. Developed power model contains four parts, each of which corresponds to a particular event based on the possible transitions.

Part_1: This part of power consumption is due to an inner transition which takes place in F_1. For inner transition to happen in F_1, the current state should be in F_1 and the primary inputs are such that the next state also should be in F_1. Power is consumed in F_1. Power consumed by all the states in F_1 will be,

$$power\_F_1 = P(F_1) Power(F_1) \tag{1}$$

where $P(F_1)$ is the sum of the steady state probabilities of all the states in F_1 which takes part in the inner transition.

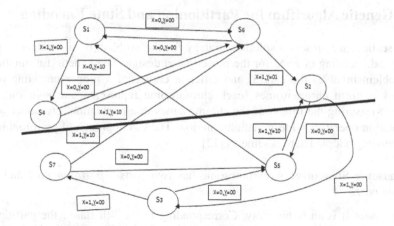

Fig. 2. Bipartitioning of STG of dk27 benchmark circuit

Part_2: Similar to part_1, this part of power consumption is due to an inner transition which takes place in F_2. For inner transition to happen in F_2, the current state should be in F_2 and the primary inputs are such that the next state also should be in F_2. Power is consumed in F_2. Power consumed by all the states in F_2 will be,

$$power\_F_2 = P(F_2)Power(F_2) \tag{2}$$

where, $P(F_2)$ is the sum of the steady state probabilities of the states in F_2 which takes part in the inner transition.

Part_3: This is due to the cross transitions which takes place from F_1 to F_2, both the sub-machines are ON and power is dissipated in both the machines but while taking the sum of the steady state probabilities only those states from which the transitions will take place are considered. So, power consumed for the transition from F_1 to F_2 is given by, $power\_F_{12} = P_D(F_1,F_2)[Power(F_1)+Power(F_2)] \tag{3}$

where, $P_D(F_1,F_2)$ is the sum of steady state probabilities of the states of F_1 from which the transition takes place to F_2.

Part_4: Similarly, when cross transition takes place from F_2 to F_1, both the sub-machines are ON and power is dissipated in both the machines but while taking the sum of the steady state probabilities only those states from which the transitions will take place are considered. So, the power consumed for this event is given by,

$$power\_F_{21} = P_D(F_2,F_1)[Power(F_1)+Power(F_2)] \tag{4}$$

where $P_D(F_2,F_1)$ is the sum of steady state probabilities of the states of F_2 from which the transition takes place to F_1.

So, from equations 1,2,3 and 4 we can say that the total power consumed will be,

$$Total\ power = P(F_1)Power(F_1)+P(F_2)Power(F_2)+P_D(F_1,F_2)$$
$$[Power(F_1)+Power(F_2)]+P_D(F_2,F_1)[Power(F_1)+Power(F_2)] \tag{5}$$

6   Genetic Algorithm for Partitioning and State Encoding

In this section, we present a solution strategy for the problem of simultaneous partitioning and encoding of FSM for the power gated design. The genetic formulation of any problem involves the careful and efficient choice of a proper encoding of the solutions to form chromosomes (each chromosome represents one solution), cost function measuring the fitness of the chromosomes in a population, crossover operator, mutation operator and termination criterion. The GA approach of partitioning and state encoding adopted here is same as [12].

Chromosome Structure: A chromosome has two parts- *partition part* and *state encoding part*.

Partition part: It is an N bit array. Corresponding to the i-th state , the partition bit determines the partition to which the state belongs i.e partition 1,if the bit is '0' and partition 2 if the bit is '1'.

State encoding part: It determines the codes assigned to the states. The most significant bit (MSB) of the state code is set to '0' for states in partition 1, whereas , the bit is set to '1' for state in partition 2. The number of bits required for encoding is given by $n = 1 + max (\lceil log k \rceil, \lceil log l \rceil)$, where, k is the number of states in partition 1 and l is the number of states in partition 2.

Step 1: Generation of the Initial Population: In the partition array the number of genes was equal to the number of states of the FSM. To determine whether the particular state is in partition 1 or partition 2, a number between 0 and 1 is generated randomly and if the number is less than or equal to 0.5 , the state is considered to be in partition 1 and if the number is greater than 0.5 ,the state is in partition 2. To avoid the migration of all the states to a particular partition, the criterion $(k\ or\ l) \geq N/5$ is maintained i.e., the minimum number of states in each partition should not be less than 20% of the total number of states. The code array is generated randomly with each element taking any value between 0 and $2^{n-1}-1$ such that state codes are non-repetitive in a particular sub-FSM.

Step 2: Fitness Measure: The combinational logic parts corresponding to the two partitions are extracted, then minimized using ESPRESSO and finally corresponding dynamic power values are computed using the *power_estimate* command of SIS[13]. The values are then combined in Eqn. 6 to compute the total power which is the fitness function of our GA based partitioning and state encoding.

Step 3: Use of Genetic Operators: In this step three genetic operators are used to evolve the new generations. The description of the operators is as follows:

Direct Copy: First the initial population is sorted according to fitness value. The selection process must ensure that the individuals with better fitness are more likely to get selected. So, 20% best chromosomes are directly copied to the next generation.

Crossover: To select a chromosome participating in crossover we have followed the same process used in [12]. 70% of the total population has been generated via the crossover operation.

Mutation: To perform mutation also we have used the process in [12]. The mutation rate is 10%of the total population.

Step 4: Termination: The GA terminates when there is no improvement in result over the previous 20 generations.

7   Experimental Results

The proposed power-gating decomposition technique has been implemented in C language on a Pentium 4 machine with 3GHz clock frequency and 3 GB main memory. For the power calculation we have used the 'power_estimate' command of SIS [13]. SIS assumes a supply voltage of 5V and operating frequency of 20 MHz. It may be noted that SIS is a quite old power estimator. So, it is a representative case study for validation of our power gaiting approach. However, the developed method can also be validated using recent power estimator. It may also be noted that SIS gives only the dynamic power estimation (it does not provide the leakage power).

7.1   Result for GA Encoding

To see the impact of state-encoding, we have formulated another GA in which only state-encoding has been performed for the whole FSM—it does not do any partitioning. The dynamic power consumed by the combinational part of the resulting circuit has been estimated using SIS and noted in the column marked GA of Table 1. Column NP gives NOVA power and column %SAV gives %saving. As it can be computed from the table, the GA that performs state encoding only requires 52% lesser dynamic power than NOVA encoding. This clearly establishes the impact of our GA-based encoding.

Table 1 (a, b). Comparison of power result for NOVA encoding and GA based encoding

(a)

CIRCUIT	NP (μW)	GA (μW)	% SAV
bbara	977.0	743.9	21.48
cse	3247.2	2599.6	62.45
dk16	3559.0	2170.2	25.79
dk512	759.9	306.5	49.53
keyb	6353.3	2507.9	80.63
modulo12	348.9	174.8	48.55
s1	7894.3	3245.1	43.19
s208	556.2	669.2	57.89
s386	2115.6	1385.0	71.61

(b)

CIRCUIT	NP (μW)	GA (μW)	% SAV
s510	7068.0	4111.8	67.42
s820	3312.4	3244.3	79.68
sand	11967.6	8361.0	49.81
dk27	277.7	134.2	55.90
planet	17462.8	9391.3	57.25
s832	3109.0	3220.9	78.83
bbtas	295.8	167.8	43.27
ex4	659.5	641.5	2.73
donfile	1559.1	959.5	38.46

7.2   Result for BD 2

Table 2 presents the combinational power results obtained by our approach considering BD 2. The details of the columns of Table 2 are as follows: Column *I/O/S* notes the number of primary inputs, outputs and states. Column $P_D(F_1,F_2)$ is the sum of steady state probabilities of all the BSs in F_1. Similarly, $P_D(F_2,F_1)$ represents the sum of steady state probabilities of all the BSs in F_2. Column $P(F_1)$ represents the sum of steady state probability of the states in F_1. The power-gating results are obtained by estimating the power consumed by the combinational logic of F_1 and F_2 respectively and summing them using Eq.(5) as described in Section 5.

Column GP in Table 2 notes the dynamic power only for 2-level realization of the resulting combinational circuits. Column NP notes the power required by the combinational logic generated by the state assignment tool NOVA [14] with "–e ioh" option. The % power saving of each individual circuit compared to NOVA is noted in column %SAV. The result shows on an average 36.5% saving in dynamic power. Saving is higher for the cases with lower BSP. For FSMs with higher BSP, both the machines are always ON, thus requiring higher power. Circuits, such as *s820, s832* and *s510* have lower BSP, so lower power dissipation. Last column gives CPU time required to get solution.

Table 2. State probabilities and combinational power of our power-gating technique (BD is 2)

CIRCUIT	I/O/S	$P_D(F_1,F_2)$	$P_D(F_2,F_1)$	$P(F_1)$	NP (μW)	GP (μW)	% SAV	TM (μS)
bbara	4/2/10	0.33224	0.04912	0.95087	977	939.7	3.82	56.1
cse	7/7/16	0.05024	0.00014	0.99985	3247.2	1643.6	49.38	87.7
dk16	2/3/27	0.64792	0.35207	0.64792	3559	3306.6	7.09	229.0
dk512	1/3/15	0.40773	0.37797	0.62202	759.9	521.0	31.44	75.3
keyb	7/2/19	0.000002	0.05365	0.000002	6353.3	1767.3	72.18	324.5
modulo12	1/1/12	0.16666	0.16666	0.66666	348.9	210.9	39.56	694.3
s1	8/6/20	0.48942	0.14184	0.85815	7894.3	6617.9	16.17	265.6
s208	11/2/18	0.01464	0.00098	0.99903	556.2	301.0	45.88	75.3
s386	7/7/13	0.01813	0.0003	0.99969	2115.6	779.8	63.14	66.8
s510	19/7/47	0.0283	0.28302	0.62264	7068	2479.9	64.91	406.9
s820	18/19/25	0.03	0.01	0.99	3312.4	705.7	78.69	628.1
sand	11/9/32	0.33364	0.20225	0.7359	11967.6	9479.9	20.79	524.2
bbtas	2/2/6	0.41739	0.34782	0.41739	295.8	247.5	16.32	17.5
dk27	1/2/7	0.66666	0.33333	0.66666	277.7	161.9	41.69	21.9
planet	7/9/48	0.15955	0.20901	0.57814	17462.8	8749.1	49.89	457.7
s832	18/19/25	0.03	0.01	0.99	3109	763.5	75.44	234.5
ex4	6/9/14	0.17391	0.08695	0.69565	659.5	713.7	-8.22	623.8
donfile	2/1/24	0.66666	0.33333	0.66666	1559.1	1733.0	-11.16	366.5

7.3   Result for BD 1

One way of reducing BSP is to reduce the BD. It is expected that if BD is reduced from 2 to 1, BSP will be reduced because the states, which are on the boundary are considered and consequently power saving will be high. This has motivated us to carry out experiment taking BD 1.The experiments described in Section 7.2 have been carried out for BD 1. In this case, $P_D(F_1,F_2)$ and $P_D(F_2,F_1)$ values are lower than the corresponding values when BD is taken as 2. This is because the states, which are on the boundary, only they are considered. The result shows on an average 51.23% saving in dynamic power w.r.t NOVA. As expected in this case, the average power saving is higher to that of the saving when BD is taken as 2. Here, saving is higher for the cases with lower BSP. So, there is larger saving in power for the power-gated design taking BD 1.

Next, in Table 3 the comparative study of our power gated result with the reported result is presented.

Table 3 (a, b). Comparison of % savings of our technique with [12]

(a)

CIRCUIT	%savings of [12]	% savings our approach
bbara	24.88	21.48
cse	-	62.45
dk16	18.89	25.79
dk512	52.51	49.53
keyb	-	80.63
modulo12	19.23	48.55
s1	29.40	43.19
s208	37.37	57.89
s386	51.13	71.61

(b)

CIRCUIT	%savings of [12]	% savings of our approach
s510	61.57	67.42
s820	78.34	79.68
sand	55.84	49.81
bbtas	17.31	37.43
dk27	63.86	55.90
planet	-	57.26
s832	77.32	78.83
ex4	10.05	31.39
donfile	30.03	4.31

7.4   Result Comparison with the Literature

Our power gated result is being compared with the result of [12]. In our work we have considered power of both the sub-FSM when there is a state transition from one to other sub-FSM. To account this effect, two extra terms $P_D(F_1,F_2)Power(F_1)$ and $P_D(F_2,F_1)Power(F_2)$ are considered in developing the power model (Eq. 6) described in Section 5, compared to the power model developed in [12]. Due to the presence of these additional terms in the power model (Eq. 6), the results are bit worse than the results in [12] for the same BD.

For BD 2 our solution gives around 36% average saving, where as solution in [12] shows around 42% saving with respect to NOVA. Average saving of our power gated design with BD 1 is around 51% with respect to NOVA. This saving is more than the saving obtained using our power model and [12] taking BD 2. This is because for BD 1, number of BS is less which results reduction in BSP and the corresponding increase in saving. The comparison of power savings with respect to NOVA for techniques like [12] and our approach considering BD 1 are presented in Table 3.

8   Conclusion and Future Scope

We have presented an efficient technique for synthesizing the FSMs using power-gating targeting dynamic power saving. The idea of combined partitioning and state encoding is introduced in the synthesis process in the genetic algorithm formulation. Existing power model has been modified to account the power consumption during cross transition. The technique worked well as verified by the experimentation with a number of benchmark circuits. The benefit of the scheme presented in the work, is best taken by the circuits having lesser number of BSs. Though, in general power-gating results in good leakage power reduction as in [12], in this paper, leakage power result has not been presented. Low power partitioning and encoding of FSM may increase the area of final circuit. Area result has not been reported in this work. Our future works include, doing experiments to find the impact of leakage and area for this power gated design. The FSM partitioning can be extended to multipartitions, effectiveness of this technique may be examined targeting multilevel circuit synthesis and finally other scope may be to extend the combined partitioning and state encoding process of power gated design to thermal aware FSM synthesis.

References

1. Benini, L., De Micheli, G.: State Assignment for Low Power Dissipation. IEEE Journal on Solid State Circuits, 32–40 (March 1994)
2. Noeth, W., Kolla, R.: Spanning Tree-based State Encoding for Low Power Dissipation. In: Proc. of Design Automation and Test in Europe, pp. 168–174 (March 1999)
3. Venkataraman, G., Reddy, S.M., Pomeranz, I.: GALLOP: Genetic Algorithm based Low Power FSM Synthesis by Simultaneous Partitioning and State Assignment. In: Proc. of 16th IEEE Conf. on VLSI Design, pp. 533–538 (2003)
4. Chow, S.H., Ho, Y.C., Hwang, T., Liu, C.L.: Low power realization of finite state machines-a decomposition approach. ACM Trans. Design Automat. Elect. Syst. 1(3), 315–340 (1996)
5. Monteiro, J.C., Oliveira, A.L.: Finite State machine Decomposition for Low Power. In: Proc. of Design Automation Conference, pp. 758–763 (1998)
6. Giacomotto, C., Singh, M., Vratonjic, M., Oklobdzija, V.G.: Energy Efficiency of Power-Gating in Low-Power Clocked Storage Elements. In: Svensson, L., Monteiro, J. (eds.) PATMOS 2008. LNCS, vol. 5349, pp. 268–276. Springer, Heidelberg (2009)
7. Leverich, J., Monchiero, M., Talwar, V., Ranganathan, P., Kozyrakis, C.: Power Management of Datacenter Workloads Using Per-Core Power Gating. Computer Architecture Letter 8(2) (July-December 2009)
8. Pakbaznia, E., Pedram, M.: Design and Application of Multimodal Power Gating Structures. In: Proc. of the 10th International Symposium on Quality of Electronic Design, pp. 120–126 (2009)
9. Kim, S., Kosonocky, S.V., Knebel, D.R., Stawiasz, K., Heidel, D., Immediato, M.: Minimizing Inductive Noise in System-On-a-Chip with Multiple Power Gating Structures. In: Proc. of the 29th European Solid-State Circuits Conference, pp. 635–638 (2003)
10. Liu, B., Cai, Y., Zhou, Q., Bian, J., Hong, X.: FSM decomposition for power gating design automation in sequential circuits. In: Proc. of the ASICON, pp. 862–865 (2005)

11. Fomina, E., Brik, M., Sudnitson, A., Vasilyev, R.: A New Approach To State Encoding of Low Power FSM
12. Pradhan, S.N., Tilak Kumar, M., Chattopadhyay, S.: Low power FSM synthesis using Power-gating. Integration, the VLSI Journal 44(3), 175–184 (2011)
13. Sentovich, E.M., Singh, K.J., Lavagno, L., Moon, C., Murgai, R., Saldanha, A., Savoj, H., Stephan, P.R., Brayton, R.K., Sangiovanni-Vincentelli, A.L.: SIS: A System for Sequential Circuit Synthesis,
    http://www.eecs.berkeley.edu/Pubs/TechRpts/1992/2010.html
14. Villa, T., Vincentell, A.S.: NOVA: State Assignment of Finite State Machines for Optimal Two-Level Logic Implementation. IEEE Transactions on CAD 9(9), 905–924 (1990)

Design and Implementation of a Linear Feedback Shift Register Interleaver for Turbo Decoding

Rahul Shrestha and Roy Paily*

Department of Electrical and Electronics Engineering,
Indian Institute of Technology Guwahati, Guwahati-781039, Assam, India
{r.shrestha,roypaily}@iitg.ernet.in
http://www.iitg.ac.in

Abstract. Recent wireless communication standards such as 3GPP-LTE, WiMax, DVB-SH and HSPA incorporates turbo code for its excellent coding performance. The interleavers involved in these turbo encoder and decoder play vital role in their performance. In this paper, we have proposed a linear feedback shift register (LFSR) based interleaver for turbo code. The proposed interleaver is compared with existing quadratic permutation polynomial (QPP) and almost regular permutation (ARP) interleavers. The investigation on the hardware implementation of these interleavers were carried out in terms of area and power consumption, and maximum frequency of operation. Hardware implementations were performed in Field Programmable Gate Array (FPGA), as well as in Application Specific Integrated Circuit (ASIC) using 130 nm complementary metal oxide semiconductor (CMOS) technology.

Keywords: Turbo code, Interleaver, CMOS IC Design, FPGA and ASIC.

1 Introduction

In 1993, Berrou et al. proposed a new coding technique so called a turbo code having exceptionally good performance [1]. A turbo code can be described as a refinement of the concatenated encoding structure plus an iterative algorithm for decoding the associated code sequence. It is well studied in the literature that the interleaver has a vital influence on the coding performance of turbo code [2]. Parallel architecture of turbo decoder using multiple soft-input soft-output (SISO) units along with a sliding window approach can significantly reduce the memory requirement and enhance the throughput at the cost of area consumption.

Fig. 1 shows the parallel turbo decoder architecture with M SISO units, corresponding memories and interleaver address generation units. Interleaver design for such a parallel architecture becomes more challenging and are well established

* Both the authors would like to acknowledge Special Manpower Development Programme(SMDP)-II under Govt. of India for providing VLSI design EDA tools at the Indian Institute of Technology Guwahati (IITG) to accomplish the work for this paper.

H. Rahaman et al. (Eds.): VDAT 2012, LNCS 7373, pp. 30–39, 2012.

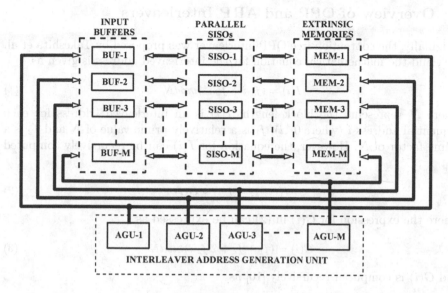

Fig. 1. Parallel turbo decoder architecture

in the literature [3,4]. The most commonly used contention free interleavers are quadratic permutation polynomial (QPP) interleaver for 3GPP-LTE standard [5] and almost regular permutation (ARP) interleaver for WiMax standard [6]. The interleaving patterns can be generated using memory based approach or on-the-fly address generation technique [7]. Memory based approach stores all the interleaving patterns for the entire block length which results in linear dependency of the memory size for interleaving patterns with the block length. This method is impractical for recent wireless standards such as 3GPP-LTE, WiMax, HSPA and DVB-SH because the maximum block lengths for these standards are in the order of several thousand bits. On-the-fly address generation technique generates interleaved address in every clock cycle. However multiple SISO units in the parallel turbo decoder architecture generates soft values simultaneously [8]. Therefore each SISO unit must be associated with an interleaver address generation unit (AGU) to generate multiple interleaved addresses at a time, thus enhancing the throughput of parallel turbo decoder. Requirement of multiple AGUs in parallel turbo decoder arises area and power consumption issues.

In this paper, we have proposed a linear feedback shift register (LFSR) interleaver. We have realized that the contention-free pseudo-random addresses can be produced using LFSR method and the AGU of this interleaver is based on this method. This paper presents the detailed description of the LFSR interleaver architecture. The significant features of LFSR interleaver includes, simplified hardware implementation, reduced on-chip area and limited power consumption. The architectures of QPP and ARP interleavers are also investigated [9,7]. The hardware implementation of LFSR, QPP and ARP interleavers are carried out and the area, power and maximum frequency of operations are compared among them.

2   Overview of QPP and ARP Interleavers

Originally, the contention free QPP interleaver was proposed by Takeshita et al. [10], and the mathematical equation for the interleaved address is given as

$$I(i) = (f_1.i + f_2.i^2)modN \tag{1}$$

where N represents the block length, $I(i)$ is an interleaved address for each sequential address i (where $0<i$), f_1 is a relatively prime value of N and f_2 is a prime factor of N. However, the equation for $I(i)$ can be recursively computed as

$$I(i+1) = I(i) + G(i) \tag{2}$$

where the expression for $G(i)$ in (2) can be expressed as

$$G(i) = (f_1 + f_2 + 2.f_2.i)modN \tag{3}$$

and $G(i)$ is computed recursively [10] as

$$G(i+1) = G(i) + (2.f_2 modN) \tag{4}$$

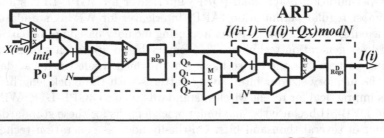

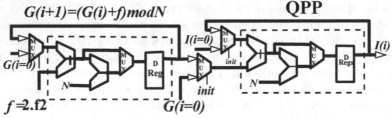

Fig. 2. ARP and QPP interleaver address generation units

Hardware architecture for such a recursive QPP interleaver can be implemented using adders, subtractors, flip-flops and multiplexers [9,7] as shown in Fig. 2. Data width of this architecture depends on the block length of the wireless communication standard. For example, $N=12282$ and $N=6144$ of DVB-SH and

3GPP-LTE requires 14 bits and 13 bits of data width respectively. Similarly the interleaved address of ARP interleaver [9] is given as

$$I(i) = (P_0.i + Q_x)modN \tag{5}$$

This equation can also be recursively computed [9] like QPP interleaver and the hardware architecture for ARP interleaver is also shown in Fig. 2.

3   Proposed LFSR Interleaver

LFSR is basically a shift register whose present state is a linear function of previous state. Feedback polynomial equation of LFSR decides the tapped output of the flip-flops from the shift register. The tapped positions are represented by the power of variables in the feedback polynomial equation. These tapped outputs are XORed and fed back to the input of the shift register. The states of the flip-flops in LFSR represents the pseudo-random pattern, thus tapping all the outputs of flip-flops in LFSR, pseudo-random interleaver addresses can be generated. The operation of LFSR is completely deterministic and its initial value decides the repeating cycle, such an initial value is called seed. Conventional LFSR can never attain the zeroth state, but the interleaver address requires zeroth memory address. We have made the architectural design for LFSR to attain the zeroth state and made it suitable for realizing interleaver AGU for turbo coding.

3.1   Architecture of LFSR Pseudo-random Address Generation Unit

The LFSR AGU can be designed for any block length N, which decides the number of flip-flops and XOR gates in the shift register. In this paper we have proposed an interleaver design for DVB-SH standard of 12282 block length. However, LFSR AGU can also be designed for other standards such as 3GPP-LTE and HSPA standards where the number of flip-flops and XOR gates are proportional to the feedback polynomial equation and the block length. In order to generate the interleaved addresses for 12282 block length, we require 14 flip-flops and the feedback polynomial equation for such LFSR is given as $1+x^3+x^{12}+x^{13}+x^{14}$. The tapped outputs of these 14 flip-flops can generate 1 to 16383 pseudo-random address patterns but we require only 0 to 12281 pseudo-random addresses. Fig. 3 shows the proposed architecture for LFSR interleaver AGU where each flip-flop used in this design is associated with two multiplexers, and there are three XOR gates as per feedback polynomial equation and a comparison unit. The purpose of one bit multiplexers associated with each flip-flop is to make LFSR attain zeroth state. The timing diagram in Fig. 4 shows that, in the 1st clock cycle 'sel1' and 'sel' signals are reset which triggers all the flip-flops to attain 0th state. In the 2nd clock cycle 'sel1' and 'sel' signals are set and reset respectively which supplies seed values to the LFSR flip-flops. From the

3rd clock cycle onwards, 'sel' is set to route the input from preceding flip-flop and 'sel1' is reset. The comparison unit is realized with one 14 bit subtractor and a multiplexer. The interleaved address generated by the flip-flops are subtracted with the block length $N=12282$ and the 'msb' of this subtracted value is used as a select signal for the multiplexer. The comparison unit discards all the interleaved addresses which is greater than $N=12282$.

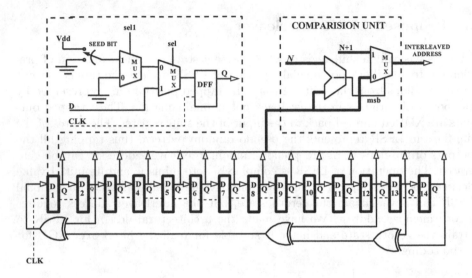

Fig. 3. Proposed architecture of LFSR interleaver address generator unit

3.2   Architecture of LFSR Interleaver

Proposed LFSR pseudo-random AGU is also applicable for parallel turbo decoder as shown in Fig. 1, where each AGU can be replaced with proposed LFSR AGU. In the parallel turbo decoding, entire block length is divided into M smaller sub-blocks and each sub-block is processed by a SISO unit. In order to reduce the latency using on-the-fly address generation units, we need M LFSR AGUs. For example, if the block length $N=12282$ is divided into $M=6$ sub-blocks then each SISO unit needs to process $N/M=2047$ block length. Therefore each LFSR address generation unit can be replicated M times with different seed values, which is possible using those 1-bit multiplexers associated with each flip-flop.

This LFSR AGU can be integrated with Random Access Memory (RAM) and counters to realize a complete interleaver as shown in the Fig. 4. Incoming data stream is sequentially stored in RAM. Based on the address provided by LFSR pseudo random generator, the corresponding data is read from the RAM. Since the addresses generated are random in nature, the output data obtained from RAM are in the interleaved form. There are two mod 12282 counters used in the design, one is an address counter which is used for generating sequential addresses. Sequential addresses generated by this counter is fed to the address line of RAM via multiplexer. This counter is enabled when the incoming data is to be sequentially stored in RAM. The second counter is termed as the reset counter and is used to generate 'select' signal for controlling the multiplexer. During the first 12282 clock cycles the 'rst' signal remains low and the counter output is passed to the RAM as an sequential address. After 12282 clock cycles, 'rst' signal remains high and the pseudo-random address is passed to the RAM. As a result, initially the 12282 soft values are stored sequentially in the RAM and subsequently the 12282 scrambled data are fetched from pseudo-random address locations of the RAM.

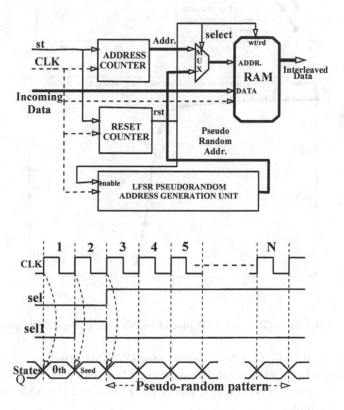

Fig. 4. Proposed architecture of LFSR interleaver and timing diagram of LFSR AGU

4   Experimental Results

In this section, the comparison results of LFSR with QPP and ARP interleaver AGUs are presented from a hardware prospective. These units are implemented

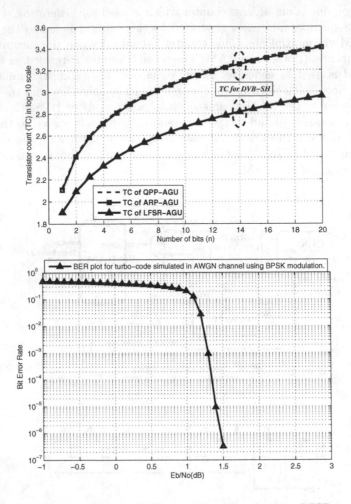

Fig. 5. TC plot for AGUs and BER plot of turbo code using LFSR interleaver

for the block length of (N=12282) suitable for DVB-SH standard and the comparison is carried out in three different ways. These comparisons are initiated with the basic transistor counts, and finally the FPGA and the ASIC implementations of these units.

4.1   Transistor Count

For the block length of N, number of bits required to represent this number is n=$\log_2 N$. As we know, 1-bit transmission-gate-based full-adder requires 24 transistors (Ts), thus n bit adder requires $24n$ Ts [11]. Similarly, 1-bit transmission-gate-based multiplexer requires 4 Ts and n bit multiplexer requires $4n$ Ts.

Table 1. FPGA implementation based comparison of LFSR, QPP and ARP address generation units in target Device(xc5vfx200t-2ff1738)

	LFSR	QPP [9,7]	ARP [9,7]
Number of Slice Registers	44/122880	140/122880	140/122880
Number of Slice LUTs	43/122880	110/122880	110/122880
Critical path delay(nS)	1.781	1.851	1.847
Max. frequency(MHz)	561.498	540.292	541.536

Each D-flip-flop and XOR gate require 8 and 12 Ts respectively. Fig. 2 shows that the QPP address generation unit require two n-bit adders and subtractors, which sums up the transistor count (TC) to $96n$ Ts. There are five n-bit 2:1 multiplexers which is equivalent to $20n$ Ts and two sets of n D-flip-flops which sums up to $16n$ Ts. Therefore the total TC for QPP AGU is $TC_{QPP}=132n$ Ts. The ARP AGU consist of three 2:1 multiplexers and one 4:1 multiplexer where each n-bit 4:1 multiplexer comprises of $12n$ Ts. Number of adders and flip-flops are same as QPP AGU. Therefore the total TC for ARP AGU is $TC_{ARP}=128n$ Ts. LFSR AGU comprises of n D-flip-flops (TC=$8n$ Ts), 3 XOR gates (TC=36 Ts), $2n$ 1-bit 2:1 multiplexers (TC=$8n$ Ts), one n bit subtractor (TC=$24n$ Ts) and one n bit 2:1 multiplexer (TC=$4n$ Ts) which sums up the TC to $TC_{LFSR}=44n+36$. Fig. 5 shows the plot of TC_{QPP}, TC_{ARP} and TC_{LFSR} with respect to n which shows that the transistor count $TC_{LFSR}=10^{2.8}$ and $TC_{QPP} \approx TC_{ARP} \approx 10^{3.2}$ at $n=14$ for the block length of DVB-SH standard. Therefore the analysis clearly shows that LFSR AGU saves approximately 954 transistors in comparison with QPP and ARP AGUs. Fig. 5 also shows the bit error rate (BER) plot of turbo code using LFSR interleaver for $N=12282$ and code-rate (1/3).

4.2 Hardware Implementation Results

Hardware implementation of LFSR, QPP and ARP AGUs were carried out in FPGA for the block length of $N=12282$. Table 1 shows the comparison among these AGUs. It shows that the QPP and ARP AGUs consume more than double the number of LUT slices than LFSR AGU and the frequency of operation of LFSR is approximately 21MHz more than QPP and ARP. ASIC implementation of these AGUs were also carried out in united micro-electronics corporation (UMC) 130nm technology. Logic verification and net-list generations were carried using synthesis tools of SYNOPSYS. Area and power analysis of these AGUs are presented in Table 2. It shows that the area saving of the proposed LFSR AGU is approximately 62% and 59% in comparison with QPP and ARP AGUs respectively. Similarly, the LFSR AGU saves approximately 63% and 60% power consumption in comparison with QPP and ARP AGUs respectively. Investigation on hardware implementations of these AGUs indicates that the proposed LFSR is better than QPP and ARP AGUs in terms of area, power and maximum frequency of operation.

Table 2. ASIC implementation based comparison of LFSR, QPP and ARP address generation units in 130nm Technology

	LFSR	QPP [9,7]	ARP [9,7]
Hierarchical cell count	25	5	4
Combinational area (μm^2)	1137.92	2991.36	2881.28
Non-combinational area (μm^2)	1585.92	4139.52	3763.20
Design area (μm^2)	2723.84	7130.88	6644.48
Total power (mW)	0.495	1.34	1.23

5 Conclusion

In this paper, a detailed analysis of QPP and ARP turbo interleaver architectures for recent wireless communication standards was carried out. A new concept of LFSR interleaver for turbo coding was introduced. Architectures for LFSR AGU and overall LFSR interleaver were proposed. Transistor counts for all these AGUs were estimated. Subsequently, hardware implementation of these AGUs were carried out using FPGA and ASIC. Investigation on these implementation has shown that the proposed LFSR AGU performed better in terms of power, area and frequency of operation in comparison with existing QPP and ARP interleaver AGUs. Thereby, these features of LFSR interleaver makes it highly suitable for parallel turbo decoders, used in recent wireless communication standards, for high throughput, low power and area efficient implementation.

References

1. Berrou, C., Glavieux, A., Thitimajshima, P.: Near Shannon Limit Error-Correcting Coding and Decoding: Turbo-Codes. In: Proc. Int. Conf. Communications, pp. 1064–1070 (May 1993)
2. Woodard, J.P., Hanzo, L.: Comparative Study of Turbo Decoding Techniques: an overview. IEEE Trans. Veh. Technol. 49, 2208–2233 (2000)
3. Hsu, J.-M., Wang, C.-L.: A Parallel Decoding Scheme for Turbo Codes. In: IEEE Int. Symp. Circuit and Systems (ISCAS 1998), vol. 4, pp. 445–448 (1998)
4. Dobkin, R., Peleg, M., Ginosar, P.: Parallel Inerleaver Design and VLSI Architecture for Low-Latency MAP Turbo Decoders. IEEE Trans. VLSI Syst. 13, 427–438 (2005)
5. LTE: Evolved Universal Terrestrial Radio Access (E-UTRA); Multiplexing and channel coding (3GPP TS 36.212 version 10.0.0 Release 10)
6. IEEE Std 802.16m -2011, Part 16: Air Interface for Broadband Wireless Access Systems, Amendment 3: Advance Air Interface
7. Lee, S.-G., Wang, C.-H., Sheen, W.-H.: Architecture Design of QPP Interleaver for Parallel Turbo Decoding. In: IEEE Veh. Technol. Conf. (VTC), pp. 1–5 (2010)

8. Asghar, R., Wu, D., Eilert, J., Liu, D.: Memory Conflict Analysis and Interleaver Design for Parallel Turbo Decoding Supporting HSPA Evolution. In: Euromicro Conf. Digital Syst. Design., Arch., Methods and Tools, pp. 699–706 (2009)
9. Sun, Y., Zhu, Y., Goel, M., Cavallaro, J R.: Configurable and Scalable High Throughput Turbo Decoder Architecture for Multiple 4G Wireless Standards. In: Int Conf on Appl.-Specific Syst., Arch and Processors, pp. 209–214 (2008)
10. Takeshita, O.Y., Costello, D.J.: New Deterministic Interleaver Design for Turbo Codes. IEEE Trans. Inform. Theory 46, 1988–(2006)
11. Weste, N.H.E., Harris, D.: CMOS VLSI Design: A Circuits and Systems Perspective, 3rd edn. Pearson-Addison Welsley, Reading (2005)

Low Complexity Encoder for Crosstalk Reduction in *RLC* Modeled Interconnects

Gunti Nagendra Babu, Brajesh Kumar Kaushik,
Anand Bulusu, and Manoj Kumar Majumder

Department of Electronics and Computer Engineering,
Indian Institute of Technology, Roorkee,
Roorkee, India
{nagendra.babu.iitr,manojbesu}@gmail.com,
{bkk23fec,anandfec}@iitr.ernet.in

Abstract. Most of the encoding methods proposed in recent years have dealt with only *RC* modeled VLSI interconnects. For deep sub-micron (DSM) technologies, the effect of on-chip inductance has increased due to increasing clock frequency, reducing signal rise times and increasing on-chip interconnect length. This issue is a concern for signal integrity and overall chip performance. Therefore, this research work introduces an efficient bus encoder using Bus Inverting (BI) method. This method considerably reduces crosstalk, delay and power dissipation in *RLC* modeled circuits. The proposed encoder dissipates lower power which makes it suitable for current high-speed low power VLSI interconnects. It has been observed that on an average, the proposed encoder reduces power dissipation and propagation delay by 67.86% and 46.78%, respectively.

Keywords: Inductive effects, signal integrity, bus invert method, crosstalk, delay, power dissipation, encoder, and decoder.

1   Introduction

Advancement of VLSI technologies follow the Moore's law for past several decades which states that the number of transistors for an integrated circuit doubles in every two years and the channel length is scaling down at the rate of 0.7/3 years [1]. As the technology scales down to deep sub micron (DSM) regime, wires are placed closer to each other, which increases not only aspect ratio but also coupling capacitance which causes crosstalk noise and excessive signal delay. Propagation delay under the influence of capacitive coupling has become a major determinant of the total power consumption and delay of on-chip busses [2].

The current digital design has to consider inductance of interconnect wires with increasing clock frequency and transistor rise/fall times [3]. Most of the existing noise models and avoidance techniques [4] considered only capacitive coupling. However, at current operating frequencies, inductive-crosstalk effects can be substantial and should be included for complete coupling-noise analysis and reduction. So, this paper primarily focuses on abating power dissipation, crosstalk, propagation delay and chip

H. Rahaman et al. (Eds.): VDAT 2012, LNCS 7373, pp. 40–45, 2012.

size of encoder and decoder of *RLC* modeled interconnects using bus invert (BI) method [5]. However for *RC* modeled interconnects, the worst case crosstalk delay occurs when the adjacent wires have an opposite transition. On the contrary, this worst case pattern is the best case for *RLC* modeled interconnects [3].

In this paper, all possible switching configurations are classified to Type-0, Type-1, Type-2, Type-3 and Type-4 depending on the value of miller coupling factor [6]. Here the proposed method reduces the two undesirable types of crosstalk *i.e.,* Type-0 and Type-1 couplings which are the worst cases in *RLC* type of interconnects. This design reduces the power dissipation by reducing switching activity using BI method. Results show that the power dissipation, crosstalk, propagation delay and encoder size is considerably reduced in comparison previously designed encoders. The paper is framed as follows: Section 2 explains the implementation of CODEC system, section 3 tabulates important results, and finally section 4 draws a brief summary.

2   Implementation of Proposed CODEC

A novel encoder is proposed based on BI method which eliminates worst case crosstalk in *RLC* modeled interconnects. The block diagram of proposed encoder is shown in Fig. 1, which consists of five blocks: Transition detector, Type-A detector, Type-B detector, Latch [6] and XOR stack. The naming conventions used are indicated in the block diagram (Fig. 1).

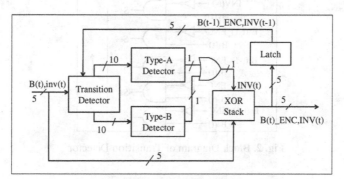

Fig. 1. Block Diagram of Proposed Encoder

A brief description of block diagram is as follows. The first block is the transition detector which detects transition by comparing the present data with the previous data transmitted. The next step after detecting transition is the detection of crosstalk effect of these transitions. The proposed method employs two detectors: Type-A detector used to detect some of the worst case couplings and Type-B detector detects the remaining. The outputs of Type-A and Type-B detectors are used to generate *INV(t)* at the output of OR gate. The *INV(t)* line goes 'high', only if there are one or more worst case couplings. The encoded data is present at the output of XOR stack whose inputs are original data and *INV(t)*. Latch is used to store the encoded data for one clock cycle. After one clock cycle, the stored data (*B(t-1)_ENC, INV(t-1)*) and the data to be transmitted ($B(t)$, $inv(t)$) are fed to the transition detector. Here, the signal $inv(t)$ in the data to be transmitted is assumed to be at logic 'low' initially.

2.1   Transition Detector

There are two types of transitions: 'high' to 'low' transition ($\downarrow$) and 'low' to 'high' transition ($\uparrow$). In order to detect a transition, proposed model compares the present data with the previous. The output of this gate goes 'high', if there is any transition and in the remaining cases it is at logic 'low'. Fig. 2 shows transition detector in which, present data is given to the bubbled input of top five AND gates which detects 'high' to 'low' transition ($\downarrow$) and is fed directly to bottom five AND gates which detects 'low' to 'high' transition ($\uparrow$).

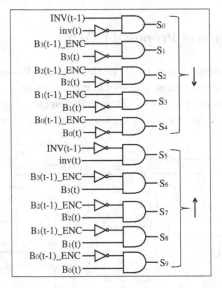

Fig. 2. Block Diagram of Transition Detector

2.2   Type-A and Type-B Detector

Two cases of Type-0 are detected by Type-A detector which is implemented using a three-input NAND gate. The top five signals from transition detector are used and they are logically connected to detect these cases. But coupling occurs between the adjacent lines and it is desirable to divide the five output signals from transition detector into a group of three, which forms three combinations ($S_0S_1S_2$; $S_1S_2S_3$; $S_2S_3S_4$) as shown in Fig. 3(a). Thus, Type-0 coupling due to low to high transition ($\uparrow\uparrow\uparrow\uparrow$) is detected using S_5, S_6, S_7, S_8, S_9 lines. Similarly, another Type-0 coupling, which is of 'high' to 'low' transition ($\downarrow\downarrow\downarrow\downarrow$) is detected using the signal lines S_0, S_1, S_2, S_3 and S_4. The output of OR gate goes 'high' if there is any worst case coupling between the lines (aggressor and victim).

The remaining cases of worst case couplings (Type-1) are detected using Type-B detector which makes use of signal lines from the output of transition detector. In this Type-1 coupling of low to high transition between lines 1, line 2, line 3 are detected using S_0, S_6, S_7 and that of high to low transition is detected using S_5, S_1, S_2 and so on as shown in Fig. 3(b). The model combines all four cases which cause crosstalk and are implemented using one 3-input NAND gate.

When either *N1_out* or *N0_out* becomes 'high', the output of OR gate, *INV(t)* becomes 'high' indicating a worst case coupling. The data bits are fed as one of the input and control line *INV(t)* as other input for XOR stack whose output is encoded data. At the decoder side, this encoded data and control line (*INV(t)*) are given as inputs for decoder which decodes the original data.

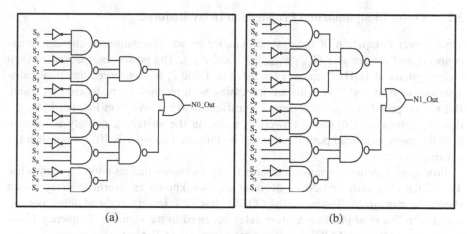

(a)   (b)

Fig. 3. Internal diagram of (a) Type-A detector and (b) Type-B detector

3   Results

HSPICE circuit simulations are performed at 130, 90, 65, 45 and 32nm technology nodes for the proposed encoder. For simulation purpose, the proposed interconnect length is considered as 500μm whereas the other parameters such as width, thickness and spacing are considered as 1μm each. All results of power dissipation and propagation delay are measured for worst case switching (↑↑↑↑↑) where they attain maximum value. The proposed encoder shows a significant reduction in chip area, crosstalk, power dissipation, and propagation delay in comparison with Fan *et al.* [4]. Although internal diagrams of encoder are shown for 4-bit, the model is also extended to 8-bit and 16-bit using shielding method.

3.1   Chip Area Reduction

The total numbers of transistors in 4-bit, 8-bit and 16-bit encoders are compared to Fan *et al.* [4] design in Table 1. The average reduction in number of transistors is almost 57%. As the numbers of transistors are reduced, the chip area is also reduced using this novel encoder.

Table 1. Comparison of components in proposed and Fan *et al.* Encoders

Size of an encoder	Transistors count		Reduction in transistor count (%)
	Fan *et al.*[4]	Proposed method	
4-bit	664	284	57
8-bit	1196	492	59
16-bit	2354	986	58

3.2 Power Dissipation and Propagation Delay Reduced

Total power dissipation of the system includes power dissipation of encoder, interconnects and the decoder (P_{enc}, $P_{interconnects}$ and P_{dec}). The power dissipations of both codec systems at 1GHz frequency are listed in Table 2. It is observed that power dissipations of both codec systems are increasing with technology node and bus width. But the proposed encoder consumes extensively lower power than Fan *et al* [4]. Although, reduction in dynamic power, by reducing the switching activity is same in both the cases, overhead power consumed by proposed encoder is 70% lower than the existing encoders.

Propagation delay at victim line effectively increases due to coupling parasitics. The CODEC system introduces delay of its own known as overhead delay which should be minimized. The proposed CODEC has 47% lesser overhead delay as compared with Fan *et al* [4]. Propagation delay occurred in the signal of frequency 1GHz as it is passed through CODEC systems are compared in Table 3.

Table 2. Comparison of power dissipations of proposed and Fan *et al.* CODECs

Technology node (nm)	Encoders	Power dissipation (µW)			Reduction in power (%)
		4-Bit Encoder	8-Bit Encoder	16-bit Encoder	
130	Proposed	501.90	1348.00	2008.00	64.32
	Fan *et al* [4]	1480.00	3187.00	6516.00	
90	Proposed	275.70	861.40	1103.00	65.15
	Fan *et al* [4]	942.00	1877.00	3754.00	
65	Proposed	166.70	492.10	666.60	70.54
	Fan *et al* [4]	533.90	1440.00	2902.00	
45	Proposed	89.38	256.50	364.50	70.00
	Fan *et al* [4]	341.90	706.30	1323.00	
32	Proposed	38.70	112.00	154.80	73.50
	Fan *et al* [4]	180.50	336.90	624.00	

Table 3. Comparison of propagation delay of proposed and Fan *et al* [4]

Technology node (nm)	Encoders	Propagation delay (ps)			Reduction in delay (%)
		4-Bit Encoder	8-Bit Encoder	16-bit Encoder	
130	Proposed	221.38	221.96	220.47	46.74
	Fan *et al* [4]	415.37	416.51	414.52	
90	Proposed	188.00	188.42	188.02	46.76
	Fan *et al* [4]	350.89	332.35	380.29	
65	Proposed	161.95	160.39	161.96	49.13
	Fan *et al* [4]	315.21	315.67	321.27	
45	Proposed	136.32	136.80	137.49	46.40
	Fan *et al* [4]	254.63	253.12	258.32	
32	Proposed	101.50	104.31	100.36	46.42
	Fan *et al* [4]	190.21	190.43	190.75	

4 Conclusion

This research paper demonstrated reduction in power dissipation and propagation delay using improved circuit design. The proposed design has lesser number of transistors that decreases the chip area. The proposed design reduces the overall size of the circuit by logical simplification; thus there is no trade off parameter for the reduction in power and area. This proposed encoder successfully reduces various design metrics such as circuit area, power dissipation and propagation delay by 55%, 67.86% and 46.78% respectively as compared to existing encoders.

References

1. Elgamel, M.A., Bayoumi, M.A.: Interconnect noise analysis and optimization in deep submicron technology. IEEE Circuits Syst. Mag. 3(4), 6–17 (2003)
2. He, L., Lepak, K.M.: Simultaneous Shield Insertion and Net ordering for Capacitive and Inductive Coupling Minimization. In: Int. Symp. Physical Design, pp. 55–60 (2000)
3. Shang-Wie, T., Yao-Wen, C., Jing-Yang, J.: RLC Coupling-Aware Simulation and On-Chip Bus Encoding for Delay Reduction. IEEE Transaction on Computer-Aided Design of Integrated Circuits and Systems 25(10) (2006)
4. Peng Fan, C., Hao Fang, C.: Efficient RC low-power bus encoding methods for crosstalk reduction. Integration, the VLSI Journal 44(1), 75–86 (2011)
5. Stan, M.R., Burleson, W.P.: Bus-Invert Coding for Low-Power I/O. IEEE Trans. VLSI Syst. 3, 49–58 (2005)
6. Nagendra babu, G., Agarwal, D., Kaushik, B.K., Manhas, S.K.: Power and Crosstalk Reduction using Bus Encoding Technique for RLC Modeled VLSI Interconnect. In: 2nd International Workshop on VLSI, pp. 424–434 (2011)

Analog Performance Analysis
of Dual-k Spacer Based Underlap FinFET

Ashutosh Nandi, Ashok K. Saxena, and Sudeb Dasgupta

Department of Electronics and Computer Engineering,
Indian Institute of Technology Roorkee, Roorkee, Uttarakhand, 247 667, India

Abstract. In this paper we have analysed the analog performance of conventional as well as dual-k spacer based underlap FinFET. Dual-k spacer in underlap FinFET is used to improve the gate electrostatic integrity. The inner high-k spacer helps in better screening out of gate sidewall fringing fields, thereby, increasing transconductance and reducing output conductance with increase in total gate capacitance. We have observed that, as compared to conventional single spacer design, the gain of dual-k spacer based design can be doubled ($\geq$ 6dB) without affecting cutoff frequency. More so, the doping gradient can be relaxed to 9nm/dec in case of dual-k spacer based underlap N/P-FinFET because of excellent control over short channel effects and improved analog performance.

Keywords: Short channel effect (SCE), Dual-k spacer, Figures of Merit (FOM), Electrostatic integrity (EI), Intrinsic gain, Cutoff frequency.

1 Introduction

With tremendous increase in application of battery operated portable devices in the field of cellular phones, wireless receivers, biomedical instruments and others, the demand for low power, high gain with low/moderate frequency of operation emerged as a challenge to VLSI designers. Subthreshold/weak inversion regime of operation achieves this target [1-2]. Short channel effects (SCEs) are of serious concern in nano-scaled devices affecting both digital and analog performance. Among the family of multigate structures, underlap FinFET has potential to suppress SCEs and enhance the performance [3-5]. The effectiveness of gate electrostatic integrity (EI) over channel affect both SCEs and analog figures of merit (FOM) such as transconductance (g_m), output conductance (g_{ds}), early voltage ($V_{EA} = I_{ds}/g_{ds}$), transconductance-to-current ratio (g_m/I_{ds}), intrinsic dc gain ($A_{V0} = g_m/g_{ds}$) and cutoff frequency ($f_T = g_m/2\Pi C_{gg}$). With an increase in the extension length (L_{ext}) of underlap FinFET this FOM are reported to improve further [1]. Dual-k spacer formation is reported recently to be a better alternative in controlling SCEs and improving device performance at nano-scale regime [6-7]. This is due to the barrier modulation capability of inner high-k spacer which shifts the lateral electric field at the gate edge toward drain at low electron concentration, thereby improving performance [1, 6-7].

H. Rahaman et al. (Eds.): VDAT 2012, LNCS 7373, pp. 46–51, 2012.

Present work analyses device analog FOM of dual-k spacer based underlap FinFET with variation of extension length (L_{ext}) and doping gradient. Rest of the manuscript is arranged as follows: Section 2 of the manuscript deals with device structure and simulation method used. Results and discussion is taken up in section 3. Finally, section 4 concludes the paper.

2   Device Structure and Simulation

Fig. 1 Shows a 3-D underlap FinFET structure with following specifications: channel doping (N_a/N_d) = 1×10^{16} cm^{-3}, peak of doping profile (N_{sd}) = 1×10^{20} cm^{-3}, gate work function is 4.5eV for N-FinFET and 4.9eV for P-FinFET, gate length (L_g) = 16nm, gate oxide thickness (T_{OX}) = 1.1nm, fin thickness (T_{fin}) = 8nm, fin height (H_{fin}) = 40nm. SiO$_2$ is used as single low-k spacer ($L_{sp,lk}$) dielectric in conventional FinFET, whereas TiO$_2$ (k=40) as high-k inner spacer ($L_{sp,hk}$) and SiO$_2$ as outer spacer ($L_{sp,lk}$) are used in dual-k spacer based FinFET structures [6]. The spacer extension length L_{ext} = $L_{sp,lk} + L_{sp,hk}$. S/D doping gradient is defined as $|d \log (N_{sd} (x))/dx|^{-1}$.

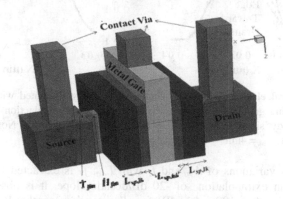

Fig. 1. 3-D Schematic of underlap FinFET

3-D simulations of devices were carried out using TCAD Sentarus device simulator activating lombardi mobility model and drift-diffusion carrier transport model considering quantum corrections at oxide silicon interface [8]. The analog FOM are extracted at I_{ds} = 10 $\mu A/\mu m$ targeting weak/moderate inversion regime of operation of devices. Heavily doped raised source/drain regions are opted for low parasitic resistance [3-4]. However, these parasitic do not affect the device performance at such low drive currents [1].

3   Results and Discussion

Increase in underlap extension length (L_{ext}) from 12nm (0.75 L_g) to 24 nm (1.5 L_g) improves gate controllability with reduced SCEs because of shift in lateral electric field from gate edge toward drain. Therefore, analog FOM is reported to improve by

it [1]. Gate fringe induced barrier lowering (GFIBL) is observed in undoped underlap
FinFETs with operating in strong inversion [9]. At weak/moderate inversion, we have
observed that restricting the high-k dielectric to undoped/low-doped underlap portion
($L_{sp,hk}$) can strengthen the virtually normal gate sidewall fringing fields (E_y and E_z) as
shown in Fig.1. The lateral electric fields (E_x) from drain to source can be shifted
away from gate edge toward drain by strengthening these fringing fields. Fig. 2(a)
shows this shift in lateral electric field with increase in $L_{sp,\ hk}$. This helps in
modulating the energy barrier to drain potential and in fact raises the energy barrier at
weak/moderate inversion regime of operation. The energy band profile is broadened
by depleting the silicon layer beyond the gate edges of FinFET. The electrical length
(L_{elec}), a measure of this energy barrier broadening, increases and the gate electrostatic
integrity ($EI\ \alpha\ 1/L_{elec}$) is improved as shown in Fig. 2 (b) [6].

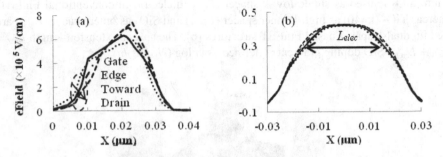

Fig. 2. (a) Lateral electric field at the center of the body simulated with V_{gs} = 0.3V and
V_{ds} = 1.1V, Doping gradient = 5nm/dec. (b) OFF-state lateral conduction band profile at the
center of the body simulated with V_{gs} = V_{ds} = 0V. L_{ext} = 24nm. Notations: $L_{sp,lk}$ ·····,
$L_{sp,\ hk}$ = 2nm ——, $L_{sp,\ hk}$ = 4nm –··–, $L_{sp,\ hk}$ = 6nm ---.

Fig. 3 shows variations of A_{V0} and f_T with L_{ext}. f_T is extracted from current gain
(h21) through an extrapolation of -20 dB/decade slope. It is observed that A_{V0} is
enhanced by more than 100% ($\geq$ 6dB) for all extension lengths. Better screening of
fringing electric fields will increase total gate capacitance (C_{gg}) of dual-k FinFET. As
f_T is dependent upon both g_m and C_{gg}, the increase in C_{gg} is almost compensated by g_m
increase at higher L_{ext}. With increase in L_{ext}, f_T of both low-k and dual-k spacer based
designs are found to be almost equal.

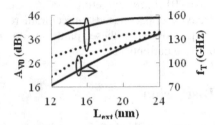

Fig. 3. Variations of intrinsic gain (A_{V0}) and cutoff frequency (f_T) with extension length (L_{ext}).
Doping gradient = 5nm/dec, V_{ds}=1.1V. Notations: Dual-k —— , Low-k ----.

The most crucial aspect of barrier modulation is lowering of g_{ds}. Variation of g_{ds} and g_m is shown in Fig. 4(a). It is observed that g_{ds} of dual-k spacer FinFET is reduced by 56% at L_{ext} = 12nm to 44% at L_{ext} = 24nm. Increase in g_m can be attributed to increase in electron mobility from 20% at L_{ext} = 12nm to 30% at L_{ext} = 24nm. The dual-k spacer increases C_{gg} from 40% at L_{ext} = 12nm to 19% at L_{ext} = 24nm. With increase in g_m the f_T reduction is not significant due to of C_{gg} increase in case of dual-k spacer based design. Therefore, almost same f_T for both low-k and dual-k spacer based FinFET is observed as shown in Fig. 3. The variations of V_{EA} and C_{gg} with L_{ext} are shown in Fig. 4(b).

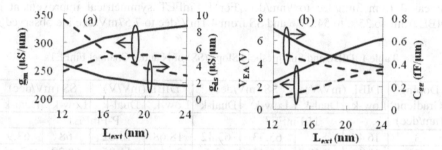

Fig. 4. (a) Variations of trasconductance (g_m) and output conductance (g_{ds}) with extension length (L_{ext}). (b) Variation of Early voltage (V_{EA}) and total gate capacitance (C_{gg}) with extension length (L_{ext}). Doping gradient = 5nm/dec, V_{ds}=1.1V. Notations: Dual-k —— , Low-k ---- .

Transconductance generation efficiency, g_m / I_{ds} is a better criterion than g_m or I_{ds} to assess device performance as it represents the efficiency of the device to convert DC power into AC frequency and gain performance [10]. As $A_{V0} = (g_m / I_{ds}) \times V_{EA}$ therefore increase in both g_m/I_{ds} and V_{EA} increases A_{V0} at different current level. Fig. 5 represents these two factors with normalised drain currents ($I_{ds}/(W/L_g)$).

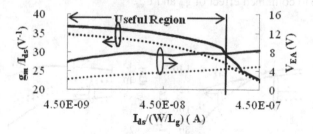

Fig. 5. Variations of g_m/I_{ds} ratio and V_{EA} with normalised drain current $I_{ds}/(W/L_g)$. L_{ext} = 24nm, Doping gradient = 5nm/dec, V_{ds}=1.1V. Notations: Dual-k —— , Low-k ·········· .

Doping profile plays major role in deciding short channel effects (SCEs) and analog performance as the devices are scaled down to nano-scale regime. This is because of intrusion of lateral electric fields into the channel region at higher doping gradients (σ) to reduce the gate electrostatic integrity (*EI*). ITRS 2007 predicts formation of ultra shallow junctions (USJs) targeting σ value of ≤ 2nm/dec to address SCEs and performance issues at nano-scale regime [11]. However, formation of USJ is governed by defect formation and junction leakage, temperature control, equipment maturity, process control, cost effectiveness etc. More so, USJ formation is even more difficult in case of P-FinFET because of annealed limited transient enhanced diffusion (TED) in boron [12]. Therefore, an attempt has been made to address these issues by relaxing doping gradient itself. Drain induced barrier lowering (DIBL) and subthreshold slope (SS) are two main factors of SCE improvement. As shown in Table 1 for N-FinFET the improvement in DIBL is found to be from 50.27% to 54.44% and that in SS is from 2.91mV/dec to 5.48mV/dec when doping gradient is increased from 3nm/dec to 9nm/dec. For P-FinFET symmetrical improvement in DIBL from 46.35% to 54.27% and SS from 4.1mV/dec to 7.57mV/dec are observed.

Table 1. DIBL and Subthreshold Slope (SS) of N and P Channel FinFETs

Doping Gradient (nm/dec)	DIBL (mV/V)		SS (mV/dec)		DIBL (mV/V)		SS (mV/dec)	
	Low-k	Dual-k	Low-k	Dual-k	Low-k	Dual-k	Low-k	Dual-k
	N-FinFET				P-FinFET			
3	16.49	8.2	65.33	62.42	18.68	10.02	68	63.9
5	17.62	8.68	65.45	62.7	21.46	11.05	68.29	63.95
7	22.26	10.06	67.8	63.46	26.7	12.86	69.74	64.58
9	33.34	15.19	70.58	65.1	40.92	18.71	75.39	67.82

Analog FOM are equally affected by use of inner high-k spacer. Fig. 6 plots the variations of A_{V0} and f_T for both N and P-FinFET with doping gradient. For N-FinFET, A_{V0} is observed to be 41.7dB (8.8dB increase) when doping gradient is set as 9nm/dec. For P-FinFET this is found to be 41.08dB (8.12dB increase). Improvement in g_{ds} is accounted for this high increase in A_{V0} at 9nm/dec of doping gradient. It is observed that reduction in f_T is $\leq 16.5\%$ for both N-FinFET and P-FinFET due to combined effect of g_m and C_{gg}.

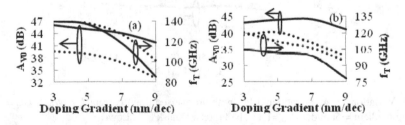

Fig. 6. (a) Variations of A_{V0} sand f_T of N-FinFET and (b) Variations of A_{V0} and f_T of P-FinFET with doping gradient at $I_{ds} = 10 \ \mu A/\mu m$. V_{ds}=1.1V, L_{ext} = 24nm. Notations: Dual-k ——— , Low-k ⋯⋯⋯.

4   Conclusion

Feasible dual-k spacer formation in underlap FinFET is an attractive option in controlling DSDT, SCEs and improving analog FOM. The most crucial aspect of SCE improvement is reduction of output conductance thereby improving the intrinsic dc gain by more than 100% ($\geq$ 6dB) for all extension lengths. Importantly, the doping gradient can be relaxed to 9nm/dec even for dual-k spacer based underlap P-FinFET, where USJ formation is difficult, because of excellent short channel effects and improved analog performance. This will relax the stringent process requirement for USJ formation as predicted by ITRS.

References

1. Kranti, A., Armstrong, G.A.: Source/Drain Extension Region Engineering in FinFETs for Low-Voltage Analog Applications. IEEE Electron Device Lett. 28(2), 139–141 (2007)
2. Interntional Technology Roadmap for Semiconductor, (ITRS) 2005 for Radio Frequency and Analog/Mixed-signal Technologies for Wireless Integration (2005), http://www.itrs.net
3. Kedzierski, J., Ieong, M., Nowak, E., Kanarsky, T.S., Zhang, Y., Roy, R., Boyd, D., Fried, D., Wong, H.-S.P.: Extension and Source/Drain Design for High-Performance FinFET Devices. IEEE Trans. on Electron Devices 50(4), 952–958 (2003)
4. Dixit, A., Kottantharayil, A., Collaert, N., Goodwin, M., Jurczak, M., Meyer, K.D.: Analysis of the Parasitic S/D Resistance in Multiple-Gate FETs. IEEE Trans. on Electron Devices 52(6), 1132–1140 (2005)
5. Trivedi, V., Fossum, J.G., Chodhury, M.M.: Nanoscale FinFETs with Gate-Source/Drain Underlap. IEEE Trans. on Electron Devices 52(1), 56–62 (2005)
6. Vega, R.A., Liu, K., Liu, T.-J.K.: Dopant Segregated Schottky Source/Drain Double Gate MOSFET Design in the Direct Source-to-Drain Tunneling Regime. IEEE Trans. on Electron Devices 56(9), 2016–2026 (2009)
7. Virani, H.G., Gundapaneni, S., Kottantharayil, A.: Double Dielectric Spacer for the Enhancement of Silicon p-Channel Tunnel Field Effect Transistor Performance. Japanese Journal of Applied Physics 50, 04DC04, 1–6 (2011)
8. Sentarus Device User Guide, http://www.synopsys.com
9. Sachid, A.B., Manoj, C.R., Sharma, D.K., Rao, V.R.: Gate Fringe Induced Barrier Lowering in Underlap FinFET Structures and Its Optimization. IEEE Electron Device Lett. 29(1), 128–130 (2008)
10. Kranti, A., Chung, T.M., Raskin, J.-P.: Analysis of Static and Dynamic Performance of Short Channel Double Gate Silicon-on-Insulator Metal Oxide Semiconductor Field Effect Transistor for Improved Cutoff Frequency. Japanese Journal of Applied Physics 44(4B), 2340–2346 (2005)
11. International Technology Roadmap for Semiconductors (2007), http://www.itrs.net
12. Kalra, P.: Advanced Source/drain Technologyy for Nanoscale CMOS, PhD Thesis, University of California, Berkeley (2008)

Implementation of Gating Technique with Modified Scan Flip-Flop for Low Power Testing of VLSI Chips

R. Jayagowri[1] and K.S. Gurumurthy[2]

[1] Department of Electronics and Communication Engg.,
Jawaharlal Nehru Technological University,
Hyderabad, India
rjgowri@rediffmail.com
[2] Department of Electronics and Communication Engg.,
University Visvesvaraya College of Engineering,
Bangalore, India
drksgurumurthy@gmail.com

Abstract. We present a technique to reduce the power of combinational circuits during testing. Power dissipation of IC during test mode is greater than the IC's normal mode of functioning. During testing a significant fraction of test power is dissipated in the combinational circuits. To reduce the test power we proposed a modified structure of scan flip-flop in our previous work. In this paper we present the two possible gating techniques for the modified scan flip-flop to reduce the power dissipation due to unnecessary switching of combinational circuits too. The proposed method is implemented in some of the ISCAS benchmark circuits to observe the percentage of power saving after applying the gating technique. The result of our experiment shows that, about 13%-18.5% more power saving in addition to the proposed scan flip-flop.

Keywords: low power testing, shift cycle, capture cycle, scanflip-flop, gating technique.

1   Introduction

Zorian showed that Power dissipation during test mode of an IC is significantly higher than during normal mode [1]. High power consumption during test affects the yield of the chip. The increased heat due to excess power dissipation can open up reliability issue due to electro-migration. In extreme conditions excess power consumption might even result in chip burn outs also. During testing a significant fraction of total test power is dissipated in the combinational circuits [6]. Testing cycle includes sequence of three different cycles as shift-in, capture and shift-out. During shift-in and shift-out cycle the circuit remains in test mode and during capture cycle the circuit remains in normal mode. The power consumption during shift cycle is directly proportional to the switching activity of the number of components in the circuit due to the serial shifting of test vectors.

H. Rahaman et al. (Eds.): VDAT 2012, LNCS 7373, pp. 52–58, 2012.
© Springer-Verlag Berlin Heidelberg 2012

Different techniques are proposed to reduce the test power during both shift cycle and capture cycle. ATPG dependent method of reducing test power during shift cycle proposed by Dobholkar where test vectors are reordered such that to reduce the number of transition in the circuit by 10% - 14% [2]. Kajihara et al., proposed the software based method to reduce the switching activity in the circuit by filling the don't care value with the value of adjacent bit on the left [3]. This method reduces the switching activity by 36% - 47%. Preferred fill is the software based power reduction method proposed by Santiago in to reduce the switching activity of the circuit during capture cycle. There are few ATPG independent methods of reducing test power [4]. Gerstendorfer proposed a method of adding NOR gate or NAND gate with the scan cell to hold the constant output value in combinational circuit during scanning [5]. Zhang et al., have proposed another gating technique where gating of signal to combinational circuit is through the multiplexer [6]. Swarup Bhunia proposed a technique of inserting extra supply gating transistor in the supply to ground path for the first-level gates at the outputs of the scan flip-flop [7]. This method showed improvement of 62% in area overhead, 101% in power overhead and 94% in delay overhead. Amit Mishra proposed a modified scan flip-flop for low power testing in which the flip-flop disables the slave latch during scan and uses an alternate low cost dynamic latch [8].

In this paper we propose a method of power reduction during the testing. The rest of the paper is organized as follows: Section 2 introduces our proposed modified scan flip-flop called dual mode one latch double edge triggered flip-flop (DMOLDET) scan flip-flop. Section 3 illustrates the proposed technique for saving power during testing by disabling the combinational logic cloud. Section 4 presents experimental results in terms of area, delay, power for a set of specimen circuits by using the proposed scan flip-flop and the amount of power saving by using the gating technique. Section 5 concludes the paper.

2   Proposed Modified Scan Flip-Flop

The double edge triggered flip-flops have been proposed for lower power CMOS digital circuits, for the given data rate they enable halving of the clock frequency and hence they reduce the power dissipation in the clock line [9,10]. The major drawback of the double edge triggered flip-flop is large area requirement. To overcome the drawback of this kind, strollo proposed   the double edge triggered flip-flop using single latch [11]. We propose the new design of scan flip-flop where the one latch double edge triggered flip-flop is used with mux and our proposed design of 'clock driver circuit'[12,13]. The switch level circuit diagram of proposed scan flip-flop is as shown in Fig. 1(A).

With the usage of proposed flip-flop the improvements in terms of area for DFT in the circuit, Speed of testing and test power reduction has been achieved. If the proposed scan flip-flop is used for the sake of testing, then during the normal mode the circuit should function at half frequency of designed (f/2). To overcome this drawback, the new clock driver circuit is proposed in our previous paper as shown in Fig. 1(B).

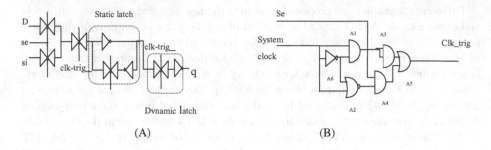

(A)   (B)

Fig. 1. Circuit of the proposed scan flip-flop (A) Switch level circuit excluding the clock driver circuit (B) Logic Diagram of Clock Driver Circuit

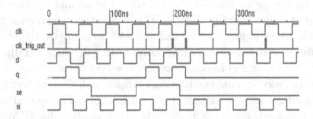

Fig. 2. Simulated output of the single latch scan flip-flop

The gating technique is used between the scan enable and narrow pulse clock generator at falling edge, which helps the circuit to work at half frequency (1/2f) during the test mode and at a designed frequency (f) during normal mode. In the proposed clock driver circuit the AND gate in the circuit diagram is used to sample the data into the latch during a short transparency period in correspondence with clock transition from logic 0 to logic 1 (i.e. positive edge). The NOR gate is responsible for data sampling into the latch during the negative edge of the clock. Production of narrow pulse in the clock driving circuit is shown in Fig. 2. The circuit functions in the testmode when se=1 and the narrow pulses are generated by the clock driver circuit both at the rising edge and falling edge of the system clock. When se=0 the circuit functions in the normal mode, the clock driver circuit generates the narrow pulse only at rising edge of the clock.

In order to apply the test vectors into the circuit the scan flip-flops are stitched as a scan chain. When output of clock driver circuit is high then the data is latched into the scan flip- flops. Since all the latches in the scan flip-flop is positive level triggered it is wide open for the data from first latch to till the output of the last flip-flop in the scan chain. To overcome this problem a simple dynamic latch circuit is connected with the output of every scan flip-flop.

3   Proposed Technique

In this paper we propose two gating methods for our proposed one latch double edge triggered scan flip-flop. They are i) Using the gate at the output of the dynamic latch, ii) Using the gate at the output of the static latch.

The PMOS pass transistor is connected between the output of the dynamic latch and the combinational cloud. The gate of the PMOS pass transistor is connected with the 'se' signal. During the test mode and the PMOS will be in OFF condition it does not allow the data to pass from flip-flop to the combinational circuit. During the functional mode the transistor allows the data to pass from flip-flop to the combinational circuit. Even though PMOS Pass transistor face the threshold drop while passing the logic value of '0' it can be easily compensated by the CMOS circuit in the combo cloud. The circuit arrangement for the gated DMOLDET scan flip-flop is shown in Fig. 3(A). In this gating method, the dynamic latch inverter should be strong enough to drive the fan-out faced by it, due to the combinational circuit connected with it. The strong inverter selection may lead for increase in power dissipation.

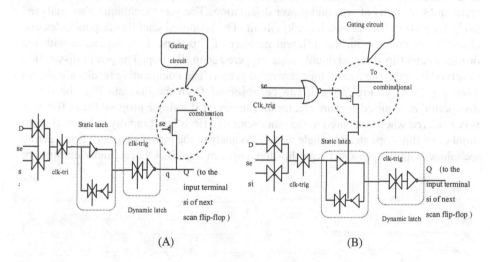

(A)   (B)

Fig. 3. Switch level circuit diagram of the Gating technique (A) PMOS gated DMOLDET scan flip-flop (B) NMOS and NOR gated DMOLDET scan flip-flop

The drawback of the above said technique has been overcome by further optimization in the gating circuit as shown in Fig. 3(B). In this gating method the NMOS can be connected between the output of the static latch and the combinational circuit in the cloud. The gate terminal of NMOS is connected to the output of NOR gate (U1) and the NOR gate's two inputs are clk_trig and se. When both the inputs are at at logic '0' then the value retained in the static latch is passed to the combinational circuit. This helps to select the weak inverter in dynamic latch because it need to drive only the multiplexer of the next scan flip-flop in the scan chain so it reduces the power dissipation. But here the extra silicon area for the amount of NOR gate is need to be sacrificed only once for the entire design. The amount of extra silicon area required for this technique is less when compared to the other gating techniques.

4   Experimental Results

The circuit functionality is verified using NCSIM of cadence tool is shown in Fig 2. The switch level circuit using both the gating techniques is implemented and simulated using cadence spectre with 180nm technology. The simulated output of first proposed gating technique and second proposed technique are shown in Fig. 4(A) and Fig. 4(B) respectively. Fig. 4 clearly shows that there is no switching takes place in the combinational circuit during the signal se = '1' shown in the waveform as 'from_combo' signal. The proposed scan flip-flop is integrated into the different specimen circuits and synthesized using cadence RTL compiler for 180nm technology at a frequency of 100 MHz. The synthesis results are compared with the other techniques in terms of area and power dissipation. The same technique also analyzed using for s1488 (ISCAS bench mark) circuit. The proposed scan flip-flop includes one clock driver circuit with the different number of flip-flops. It is compared with the ordinary scan flip-flop and double edge triggered scan flip-flop. The power dissipation observed by applying a randomly generated vector. The comparative results are shown from Fig. 5(A) to Fig. 5(C). It can be observed from the diagram that the power dissipation & required area are greater for the circuit if a single proposed scan flip-flop is considered when compared to the other scan flip-flops but it rapidly reduces, if more number of flip-flops share a single driver. To analyze the power saving of using gating technique with the proposed scan flip-flop, some of the ISCAS benchmark circuits are

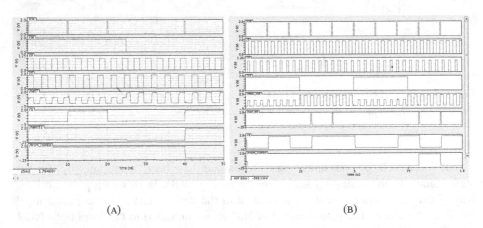

(A)   (B)

Fig. 4. Simulated output of the proposed DMOLDET scan flip-flop with dynamic latch and gating technique for combo at 100 MHz (A) at the output of dynamic latch (B) at the output of static latch

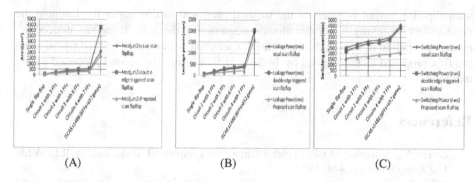

(A)   (B)   (C)

Fig. 5. Comparison of different scan flip-flops (A) Area analysis (B) Leakage power analysis (C) Switching power analysis

taken as specimen circuits. The switching power dissipation before and after gating technique is observed and listed in Table1.

Table 1. Analysis of power dissipation using proposed scan flip-flop with and without gating technique

Specimen circuits	Number of flip-flops	Number of logic gates	Power dissipation(nws)			Percentage of power saving after gating	
			Before gating technique	After first proposed gating technique	After second proposed gating technique	After first proposed gating technique	After second proposed gating technique
s27	3	10	1741.1	1500.61	1487.2	13.81	14.58
s832	5	287	1990.02	1691.517	1630.62	15	18.06
s1488	6	652	2365.77	1924.62	1846.01	18.647	21.97
s344	15	160	3203.22	2754.77	2671.81	13.99	16.59
s526	21	193	4050.16	3462.89	3349.88	14.49	17.29

5   Conclusion

The proposed dual mode one latch double edge triggered scan flip-flop reduces the power dissipation during shift cycle of the scan. This technique is suitable for any scan based testing circuit. This technique can be easily incorporated with other power reducing techniques during testing. From our experimental results of proposed scan flip-flop shows that usage of the proposed scan flip-flop reduces the silicon area by 30% - 45% and the power dissipation by 25% - 35%. The testing speed is improved by 50%. When compared to the scan flip-flop in [8], the proposed scan flip-flop shows 45% reduction in terms of required silicon area and 50% in terms of testing time. Our scan flip-flop output is gated as the method proposed in this paper to eliminate the unnecessary switching in combinational circuit during the scan. It further reduced the power dissipation in the ISCAS benchmark specimen circuits by 13.81-18.647% using the first proposed technique and by 14.58 – 21.97% using the second proposed gating method.

References

1. Zorian, Y.: A distributed BIST control scheme for complex VLSI devices. In: IEEE VLSI Test Symposium, pp. 4–9 (1993)
2. Dobholkar, V., et al.: Techniques to minimize power dissipation in scan and combinational circuits during test application. IEEE Transactions on Computer Aided Design, 1325–1333 (December 1998)
3. Kajihara, S., et al.: Test vector modification for power reduction during scan testing. In: Proceedings VLSI Test Symposium (2002)
4. Ramersaro, et al.: Preferred Fill: A Scalable Method to Reduce Capture Power for Scan Based Designs. In: International Test Conference, pp. 1–10 (2006)
5. Gerstendorfer, S., Wunderlich, H.J.: Minimized power consumption for scan based BIST. In: Proceeding International Test Conference (1999)
6. Zhang, et al.: Power reduction in test-per-scan BIST. In: Proc. Int. OnLine Testing Workshop, pp. 133–138 (2000)
7. Bhunia, S., Mahmoodi, H., Ghosh, D., Mukhopadhyay, S., Roy, K.: Low power scan design using first level supply gating. IEEE Transactions on VLSI System 13(3), 384–395 (2005)
8. Mishra, A., Sinha, N., Satdev, Singh, V., Chakravarthy, S., Singh, A.D.: Modified scan flip flop for low power testing. In: Proceedings 19th IEEE Asian Test Symposium, pp. 367–370 (2010)
9. Hossain, R., Wronski, L.D., Albicki, A.: Low power design using double edge triggered flip flops. IEEE Transaction on VLSI System 2(2), 261–265 (1994)
10. Blair, G.M.: Low power double edge triggered flipflop. Electronics Letters 33(10), 1581–1582 (1997)
11. Strollo, G.M., Napoli, E., Cimino, C.: Low power double edge triggered flip flop using one latch. Electronics Letters 35(3), 187–188 (1999)
12. Jayagowri, R., Gurumurthy, K.S.: Design and Implementation of Area and Power Optimised Novel ScanFlop. International Journal of VLSI design & Communication (VLSICS) 2(1), 37–43 (2011)
13. Jayagowri, R., Gurumurthy, K.S.: A Technique for Low Power Testing of VLSI Chips. In: Proceedings of IEEE International Conference on Devices, Circuits and Systems, pp. 662–665 (2012), doi:10.1109/ICDCSyst.2012.6188654

Post-bond Stack Testing for 3D Stacked IC

Surajit Kumar Roy, Dona Roy, Chandan Giri, and Hafizur Rahaman

Department of Information Technology
Bengal Engineering and Science University, Shibpur
{suraroy,mehulicalcutta,chandangiri}@gmail.com,
rahaman_h@yahoo.co.in

Abstract. In the embedded system design Through-silicon-via (TSV) based 3D stacked ICs (SICs) play an important role in semiconductor industry. But testing of these SICs are required during 3D assembly because different die stacking steps may introduce defects. In this paper, we address test architecture optimization for 3D stacked ICs implemented with hard die means where die-level test architecture is fixed. We consider two different SIC configurations and derive optimal solution to minimize overall test time when complete stack and multiple partial stacks, need to be tested. Results are performed for two handcrafted 3D SICs comprising of various SoCs from ITC'02 SoC test benchmarks. In this work we consider the test architecture optimization for 3D SIC where each die consists of one SoC. We present test schedules and corresponding test lengths for every multiple insertions and also show that total test lengths are decreased with the increasing number of test pins.

Keywords: SIC, DFT, Post-bond testing.

1 Introduction

System-on-chip technology is the packaging of all necessary electronic circuits for a "system" on a single integrated circuit. It comprises with number of cores or modules. In SoC, cores are deeply embedded. So, testing of SoC is required by introducing test access mechanism. Conceptual test access architecture enables modular testing for SoC. Each module under test consists of-a) ATE/BIST: test pattern source and sink that is either off chip or on chip. b) TAM: stimuli and responses travel through the chip to and from the embedded module using TAM. c) Wrapper: provides an interface between the core and its environment. It contains its own instruction register (WIR) for selecting three modes of operations like- bypass (normal operation), INTEST (core internal test), EXTEST (core external test). With advanced semiconductor manufacturing technology complete system is created by attaching multiple device layers to each other through direct wafer or die stacking and bonding of die-on-die. These system chips are commonly referred to as 3D stacked ICs (SICs) [4] as shown in Fig 1 3D SICs are implemented using Through-Silicon-Via.

H. Rahaman et al. (Eds.): VDAT 2012, LNCS 7373, pp. 59–68, 2012.

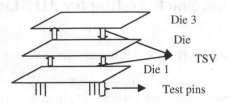

Die 3

Die

TSV

Die 1

Test pins

Fig. 1. Simple example of 3D SIC

3D SoCs provide greater design flexibility, higher on-chip data bandwidth, reduction in average interconnect length [1], [3]. In 3D SIC die stacking steps of thinning, alignment and bonding can introduce defects [1], [2] and during design phase, TSV insertion has an impact on performance. Considering above facts in 3D SIC, test architecture must be able to support testing of individual dies as well as testing of partial and complete stacks. Test architecture optimization must not only minimize the test length, but also needs to minimize the number of TSVs used to route the 3D TAM. Test architecture for 3D SIC is based on modular test approach which allows a) Pre-bond testing: these tests are wafer test and b) Post-bond stack testing: these tests can be carried out on both unpackaged and packaged stacks. Fig 2 shows test flow with multiple test insertions. First, wafer test (pre-bond test) can be used to test die prior to stacking. Next, Die1 and Die2 are stacked and then tested again (post-bond test). Now TSVs are also tested. Similar post bond testing procedure occurs after insertion of Die3. Finally, after assembly and packaging, complete stack test is performed.

Test architecture optimization of 3D SICs can be considered as test architectures for die-level wrapper are either fixed or can be changed. With respect to these two aspects three different test architecture problems can be addressed. **a) Hard dies:** in which test architecture of each SoCs in the stack is already exists. For a hard die 2-D test architecture on the die is fixed. Only 3-D TAM can be controlled by the designer. These dies are less flexible. **b) Soft dies:** test architecture for each die is not predefined; it may be structured during architecture design. In this case, scan chains for each test module are given, but test wrappers for each module and TAM are designed during 3-D TAM design [6]. So, these dies are most flexible. **c) Firm dies:** test architecture of each SoCs in the stack is already exists like hard dies, but serial or parallel conversion hardware may be added to the die to allow fewer test elevators to be used than fixed 2-D TAM width in order to reduce test pin and used TSV.

Some works [4], [5] and [6], have been presented on testing of different type 3D SICs. In [4], problems had introduced with test architecture optimization for both hard and soft dies. Results of stack configurations made up of five SoCs taken from the ITC'02 Test Benchmarks. It focuses only on test length optimization for post-bonded complete stacked ICs. DfT test access architecture [8] for 3D SICs allow for both pre-bond die testing and post-bond stack testing. Different opportunities for optimization on test access architectures are explained in [5]. Minimization of test time for die-internal and die-external tests is explained in [6]. In [4], [6], and [7], the authors give the solution by using integer linear programming. In [7], the authors show a comparison for results between ILP and Greedy algorithm. Firm and soft die [7] are also shown to provide lower test times with an increase in test resources. Since both scenarios result

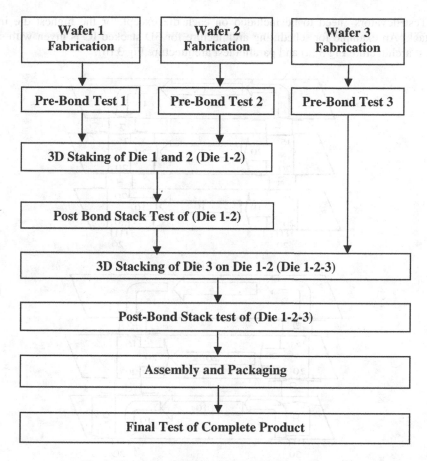

Fig. 2. Test flow with multiple test insertions [6]

in lower test times than the case of hard dies, designers can consider 2-D and 3-D TAM designs as related to optimization problems. Results using these models designer can explore many test solutions for the hard and firm die scenarios in order to prevent sub-optimal allocation of the test resources. In this work we mainly focused on test architecture optimization for 3D SICs where die level test architecture already exist. Our objective is to generate multiple options for testing SIC. Solutions produce optimal TAM designs for multiple schedules, corresponding test lengths and total test lengths.

The rest of this paper is organized as follows. Section 2 uses example to motivate works and outlines the problem definition. Section 3 presents proposed algorithm. Section 4 presents experimental results. Section 5 concludes the paper.

2   Problem Definition

The lowest die is connected to chip I/O pins. To test the non-bottom dies in the stack, test data must enter through test pins. To test other dies in the stack, the TAM must be extended to all dies in the stack. To transport test data up and down the stack,

"TestElevators" need to be included on each die except for the highest die in the stack. An example for scheduling architecture for 3D stacked IC is given with serial test architecture Fig 3 (a) and parallel test architecture Fig 3 (b).

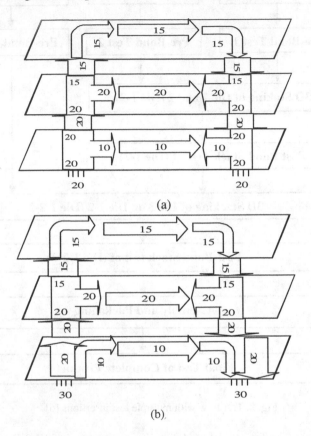

(a)

(b)

Fig. 3. Serial architecture and parallel test architecture of 3D SIC

In the given example, test times for Die 1, 2, and 3 are 200, 300, and 100 cycles respectively. Die 1 requires 20 test pins, and dies 2 and 3 require 40 Test Elevators and 30 Test Elevators, respectively. Fig 3(a) shows if all dies are tested serially. Total of 90 TSVs are used and 40 test pins are necessary. The total test time is the sum of the test times of the individual dies, i.e., 600 cycles. In Fig 3 (b), the number of TSVs used is the same as in Fig 3(a). 60 test pins are required to test Die 1 and 2 in parallel. So, total test time for stack is $100 + \max \{300, 200\} = 400$ cycles.

The problem that has been considered in this paper is as follows: *Given a stack with a set M of dies, total number of test pins W_{max}. For each die $m \in M$, die's number corresponds to its tier. We are given the number of test pins on each die W_m ($W_m \leq W_{max}$), the associated test time (t_m) and a maximum number of TSVs (TSV_{max}) that can be used for TAM design between die $m-1$ and m ($m>1$). The goal is to determine an optimal TAM design and test schedule for each stage of stacking such that the total test time is minimized and number of TSVs used per die does not exceed TSV_{max}.*

3   Proposed Algorithm

```
Input: No. of dies (M), associated test pins
       (W_m), associated test length(t_m), max no.
       of test pins (W_max), set of dies K,
       Max_TSV=TSV_max.
Output: Optimal TAM schedule to minimize test
        length and max no. of TSVs.
  1. begin
  2.    Test length T= 0;
  3.    for (insertion P ← 2 to M ) do
  4.       t=0; K={1, 2,…, P};
  5.       While (K! = Ø) begin
  6.         assign= FALSE;
  7.         if (∑W_m for K dies < = W_max) then
  8.         begin
  9.            assign = TSV_check (K);
 10.            if (assign = = TRUE) then begin
 11.              schedule  as parallel of K dies;
 12.              t_1 = max (t_m) among all dies in K;
 13.            end
 14.         K= Ø;
 15.         end
 16.         else begin
 17.            Find all combinations of dies
                  from K so that ∑W_m≤W_max;
 18.            Let S ← Choose a combination
                  dies such that ∑W_m is maximum;
 19.            assign = TSV_check (S);
 20.            if (assign = = TRUE) then begin
 21.            assign dies as parallel sche
                  dule;
 22.              t_1 = max(t_m) among all dies in S;
 23.            end
 24.         K= K - S;
 25.         end
 26.         Test next combination as serial;
 27.         t = t + t_1;  /* t is the test time
                            for partial stack*/
 28.      end
 28.      Total test length (T) = T + t;/* Fi
                            nal stack time after
                            multiple insertions*/
 30.   end
 31.end
```

Fig. 4. The proposed test scheduling algorithm

```
TSV_check(set of K dies )
 1. begin
 2.          Boolean var, TSV = 0;
 3.          if ({1} ∈ K) then K= K - {1};
 4.          while (K ! = Ø)
 5.          begin
 6.               Choose a die i from K;
 7.               TSV = TSV + Wᵢ;
 8.               K = K - {i};
 9.          end
10.          if (TSVmax< TSV) then
11.               Var = FALSE;
12.          else
13.               Var = TRUE;
14.          return (var);
15. end
```

Fig. 5. The algorithm for TSV check: *TSV_check ( )*

In our work we have assumed that all the SoCs are hard. The principal idea of the proposed algorithm Fig 4 is to enable the parallel testing of SOCs as much as possible. For a given test insertion, K is the set of dies to be tested. First we have tried to test all dies of K in parallel fashion. It is possible when $\sum_1^K W_m$ for K dies is less than or equal to W_{max} and the inter layer TSV constraint is satisfied, which is checked by the *TSV_check ( )* function Fig 5. Then we can assign a schedule of K dies as parallel and test length of this insertion is the maximum test length among K dies. If it is not possible to test all the K dies in parallel, we then find all possible subset of dies from K dies such that $\sum W_m \leq W_{max}$. Among these subsets we have chosen a combination having S number of dies such that $\sum_1^S W_m$ of those dies is maximum and inter layer TSV constraint is satisfied by *TSV_check( )* function. Then assign corresponding dies as parallel schedule and the test length for this schedule is the maximum test length of S dies. The remaining dies of K are scheduled in similar fashion. So, test length of the test insertion is found by adding the test length of all the combination. Final stack test time is found by adding the test length of all the insertions.

The subroutine *TSV_check ( )* is used to calculate total number of TSVs between layer1 and layer2. It is the sum of test pins of all the dies at or above layer2, which are tested in parallel. The maximum number of TSVs between any two consecutive layers is TSV_{max}. If total number of TSVs between layer1 and layer2 is less than or equal to TSV_{max}, then TSV_{max} definitely greater than or equal to total number of TSVs of other consecutive layers and *TSV_check ( )* returns a *true* value.

3.1   Illustrative Example

Now we explain the proposed algorithm with an example. Consider a SIC with five dies, each die has test pins from bottom to top 40, 30, 25, 20, 10 and associated test length for individual dies are 500, 400, 300, 200 and 100 cycles. So, tier numbers are placed 1 to 5 of the stack. Let W_{max} is considered as 70 and maximum TSVs between any two consecutive layers TSV_{max} is 60. When second die is inserted on first die then schedule is 1∥2 because $\sum W_m$ for dies 1 and 2 are 70 and TSVs requirement between layer1and layer2 is less than TSV_{max}. So the test length is 500 cycles. Then third die is inserted on die 1-2 and total number of test pins of die 1, die2 and die 3 is greater than W_{max}. There are a number of combination of dies like (die 1, die 2); (die1, die3); (die1) etc whose total number of test pins is less than or equal to W_{max}. The combination including die1 die 2 has maximum number of test pins among these combinations and requirement between layer1and layer2 is less than TSV_{max}. So they are tested in parallel. Left die 3 has W_m of 30 which is also less than 70. So, die 3 is tested serially after parallel testing of die 1 and die 2. The test length is (500+300) =800 cycles and test schedule is 1||2, 3.Similarly after the insertion of fourth die on die 1-2-3, the test schedule is 1||2, 3||4 and test length is (500+300) = 800 cycles. Finally fifth die is placed on die 1-2-3-4 and test schedule for is 1||2, 3||4||5and the corresponding test length is (500+300) =800 cycles. Hence the total test length including the partial stacks is 2900 (500 + 800 + 800 + 800 = 2900) cycles.

4   Experimental Result

Experimental results are simulated for two handcrafted 3D SICs as in Fig 6 using several SoCs from the ITC'02 SoC test Benchmarks as dies inside SICs. The SoC used are d695, f2126, p22810, p34292 and p93791. For simulation, the algorithm is implemented in C language and run on an Intel Core 2 Duo processor having 1GB RAM in Linux operating system. Number of layers for the SIC are five.

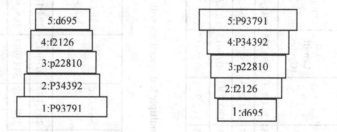

Fig. 6. Two SIC benchmarks SIC1 and SIC2 respectively

In SIC1, the most complex die (p93791) is placed at the bottom, with die complexity decreasing as one move up the stack. The order is reversed in SIC2.

4.1   Results

For problem instances with hard dies, test lengths and TAM widths of different dies are listed in Table 1.

Table 1. Test lengths and number of test pins for hard dies used [6]

Die	p93791	p34392	p22810	f2126	d695
Test length	2608870	2743317	1333098	700665	106391
Test pins	30	25	25	20	15

For a fixed value of TSV_{max} and range of values of W_{max}, Table 2 and Table 3 present results for the two benchmarks SIC1 and SIC2 respectively.

In tables 2 and 3, column1 shows maximum number of TSVs allowed for each die TSV_{max}. Column 2 lists the number of available test pins W_{max}. Column 3 shows test schedule sh.1 after insertion of second die and column 4 represents corresponding test lengths of sh.1. After insertion of third die column 5 and 6 indicates test schedules sh.2 and corresponding test lengths for sh.2. Next, forth die is inserted. Column 7 represents test schedule sh.3 and column 8 gives test lengths of sh.3. Lastly, after inserting fifth die, test schedule sh.4 is given by column 9 and corresponding test length is also given by column 10. Symbol "||" indicates parallel testing and "," represents serial testing. Column 11 represents total test length. Table 4 is a comparison table which compare with respect to total test length and W_{max} for SIC2 and shows same optimum result.

Table 2. Experimental results for multiple test insertions with SIC1

TSV_{max}	W_{max}	Sh1 Die1-2	Test Length (Cycles)	Sh2 Die 1-2-3	Test Length (Cycles)	Sh3 Die 1-2-3-4	Test Length (Cycles)	Sh4 Die 1-2-3-4-5	Test Length (Cycles)	Total Test Length (Cycles)
140	49	1,2	5352187	1,2,3	6685285	2||4,1,3	6685285	2||4,1||5,3	6685285	25408042
140	50	1,2	5352187	1,2||3	5352187	1||4,2||3	5352187	1||4,2||3,5	5458578	21515139
140	69	1||2	2743317	1||2,3	4076415	1||2,3||4	4076415	1||2,3||4||5	4076415	14972562
140	70	1||2	2743317	1||2,3	4076415	1||2,3||4	4076415	1||2,3||4||5	4076415	14972562

Table 3. Experimental results for multiple test insertions with SIC2

TSV_{max}	W_{max}	Sh1 Die1-2	Test Length (Cycles)	Sh2 Die 1-2-3	Test Length (Cycles)	Sh3 Die 1-2-3-4	Test Length (Cycles)	Sh4 Die 1-2-3-4-5	Test Length (Cycles)	Total Test Length (Cycles)
140	49	1||2	700665	1,2||3	1439489	2||3,1||4	4076415	2||4,1||5,3	6685285	12901854
140	50	1||2	700665	1,2||3	1439489	3||4,1||2	3443982	2||5,3||4,1	5458578	11042714
140	69	1||2	700665	1||2||3	1333098	1||3||4,2	3443982	1||2||3,4||5	4076415	9554160
140	70	1||2	700665	1||2||3	1333098	2||3||4,1	2849708	1||4||5,2||3	4076415	8959886

Table 4. Comparision results for SIC2 with [6]

TSVmax	Wmax	Total test length (cycles) for SIC2	Total test length (cycles) [6]
140	49	12901854	12901800
140	50	11042714	11042700
140	69	9554160	9554160
140	70	8959886	8959880

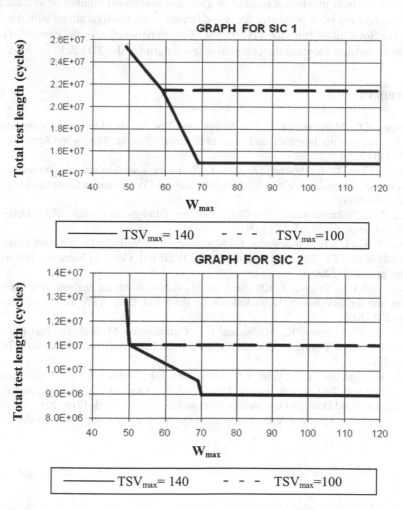

Fig. 7. The total test time with respect to TSV_{max} and W_{max} with hard dies and multiple test insertions according to Table 2 (for SIC1) and Table 3 (for SIC2)

Fig 7 shows the variation in total test time with an increase in the number of test pins W_{max} for SIC1 and SIC2. From figures, it can be observed that both TSV_{max} and W_{max} determine which dies should be tested in parallel and thus total test time for the stack. For a given value of TSV_{max}, increasing W_{max} does not always decreases the test time for multiple test insertion, though test time never increases.

5   Conclusion

In this paper, we have presented an optimization method that provide test schedules for each test insertion and also minimize test time for 3D SIC, either for the final stack test or for any number of multiple test insertions. This method incorporates constraints on both maximum number of TSV and maximum number of available test pins. Results have been presented for two different stack configurations with die made up of five SoCs taken from the ITC'02 SoC Test Benchmarks. In the case of 3D SIC, every test insertion increase the cumulative test length for the 3D stack.

References

1. Iyengar, K.C., Marinissen, E.J.: Test Wrapper and Test Access Mechanism Co-optimization for System-on-chip. International Journal of Electronic Testing, Theory and Appilicatios 18, 213–230 (2002)
2. Wu, X., Chen, Y., Chakrabarty, K., Xie, Y.: Test-access mechanism optimization for core-based three-dimensional SOCs. In: IEEE International Conference on Computer Design, pp. 212–218 (2008)
3. Lee, H.S., Chakrabarty, K.: Test Challenges for 3DIntegrated Circuits. IEEE Design and Test of Computers 26, 26–35 (2009)
4. Noia, B., Goel, S.K., Chakrabarty, K., Marinissen, E.J., Verbree, J.: Test Architecture Optimization for TSV-Based 3D Stacked ICs. In: IEEE Intl. Conf. on European Test Symposium, pp. 24–29 (2009)
5. Marinissen, E.J., Verbree, J., Konijnenburg, M.: A Structured and Scalable Test Access Architecture for TSV-Based 3D Stacked ICs. In: IEEE Intl. Conf. VLSI Test Symposium, pp. 269–274 (2010)
6. Noia, B., Chakrabarty, K., Marinissen, E.J.: Optimization Methods for Post-Bond Die-Internal/External Testing in 3D stacked ICs. In: IEEE Intl. Conf. Test Conference (ITC), pp. 1–9 (2010)
7. Noia, B., Chakraborty, K., Goel, S.K., Marinissen, E.J., Verbree, J.: Test-Architecture Optimization and Test Scheduling for TSV-Based 3-D Stacked ICs. IEEE Transaction on Computer Aided Design of Integrated Circuit and System 30, 1705–1718 (2011)
8. Bushnell, M.L., Agarawal, V.D.: Essentials of electronic testing. Springer Publishers

Translation Validation for PRES+ Models of Parallel Behaviours via an FSMD Equivalence Checker

Soumyadip Bandyopadhyay, Kunal Banerjee,
Dipankar Sarkar, and Chittaranjan R. Mandal

Dept. of Computer Science and Engineering
Indian Institute of Technology Kharagpur, India
{soumyadip,kunal,ds,chitta}@cse.iitkgp.ernet.in

Abstract. Behavioural equivalence checking of the refinements of the input behaviours taking place at various phases of synthesis of embedded systems or VLSI circuits is a well pursued field. Although extensive literature on equivalence checking of sequential behaviours exists, similar treatments for parallel behaviours are rare mainly because of all the possible execution scenarios inherent in them. Here, we propose a translation algorithm from a parallel behaviour, represented by an untimed PRES+ model, to a sequential behaviour, represented by an FSMD model. Several equivalence checkers for FSMD models already exist for various code based transformation techniques. We have satisfactorily performed equivalence checking of some high level synthesis benchmarks represented by untimed PRES+ models by first translating them into FSMD models using our algorithm and subsequently feeding them to one such FSMD equivalence checker.

Keywords: Formal verification, Equivalence checker, PRES+ (Petri Net based Representation of Embedded Systems), FSMD (Finite State Machine with Datapath).

1   Introduction

Embedded systems are becoming pervasive in diverse application domains such as, vehicle control, consumer electronics, communication systems, remote sensing, and various household appliances. They are reactive in nature, with real-time constraints, each being dedicated towards a certain application and must be dependable and efficient. To deal with a broader range of problems and conditions for operation, the algorithms and decision procedures implemented in software have become much sophisticated. In concurrent real-time systems, modular designs have led to complex multitasking systems resulting in intricacies that are difficult to analyze. Finally, designing and deploying of these complex systems are not simple. All of these issues have contributed to a growing concern that current methods for designing and analyzing complex embedded systems are inadequate.

H. Rahaman et al. (Eds.): VDAT 2012, LNCS 7373, pp. 69–78, 2012.

Here, we focus on some aspects related to modeling and formal verification of embedded systems. Many models have been proposed to represent embedded systems [1] such as finite state machines, data flow graphs, communication processes and Petri nets. In this paper, we have used PRES+ models (Petri net based Representation for Embedded Systems) as an extension of classical Petri net models that capture computation, concurrency and timing behaviour of embedded systems [2]. This modeling formalism has a well defined semantics for precise representation of systems.

A typical synthesis flow of complex systems like VLSI circuits or embedded systems comprises of several phases. Each phase transforms/refines the input behavioural specification (of the systems to be designed) with a view to optimizing time and physical resources. Behavioural verification involves demonstrating the equivalence between the input behaviour and the final design which is the output of the last phase. In computational terms, it is required to show that all the computations represented by the input behavioural description, and exactly those, are captured by the output description. The input behaviour undergoes several transformation steps before being mapped to an architecture. Our objective is to verify these transformation steps.

Several code transformation techniques such as, code motions, common subexpression elimination, dead code elimination, etc. may be applied at the preprocessing stage of embedded system synthesis. Recent works [3], [4], [5] have demonstrated the effectiveness of speculation in improving schedule lengths for designs with control flow. List scheduling based on condition vectors (CVLS) [6] improves resource sharing among mutually exclusive operations. Recent work [4], [7] support generalized code motions during scheduling of designs with control flow. The effects of several global code motion techniques in the design are shown in [8]. Literature [9], [10], [11] have shown the effect of code transformation on system performance in terms of energy, power, etc.

Application of code motion techniques during the preprocessing phase of embedded system design increases verification challenges significantly. Some transformation techniques [12], [13], within the basic-blocks [14] describe, where a code never moves beyond the basic block boundary. Verification techniques [15] for such transformations obviously do not work for code motions where code can be moved beyond basic block boundaries. Some recent works [16], [17] target verification of such code motions. For example, a path recomposition based finite state machines with data path (FSMD) equivalence checking method has been proposed in [16] to verify speculative code motions. The equivalence checking method for scheduling verification was reported in [18] works well even when the control structure of the input behaviour is modified by the scheduler. The method can also verify uniform code motion techniques (whereupon code preceding a conditional block are moved to both the branches emanating from the block).

While sequential behaviours can be captured by FSMDs, parallel behaviours can be captured more succinctly using PRES+. Equivalence checkers for FSMD models already exist [19] [20] for code motion technique. It is to be noted that timing constraints are inconsequential for demonstrating data transformation equivalence between the behaviours; this fact allows us to perform equivalence checking using FSMDs. Hence, we may formulate an algorithm to translate a untimed PRES+ model into an FSMD model use an existing FSMD equivalence checker [19].

The paper is organized as follows. Section 2 formally introduces the FSMD and the untimed PRES$^+$ models along with the operational semantics of the latter. Section 3 focuses on the translation mechanism to convert an untimed PRES$^+$ model into an FSMD model. The results obtained when the mechanism was tested on some benchmarks can be found in section 4 and section 5 finally concludes the paper.

2   Preliminaries

2.1   FSMD Models

A finite state machine with data path (FSMD) model is defined as an ordered tuple $F = \langle Q, q_0, I, V, O, f, h \rangle$, where

1. $Q = \{q_0, q_1, ..., q_n\}$ is a finite set of control states.
2. $q_0 \in Q$ is the reset state.
3. I is the set of primary input signals.
4. V is the set of storage variables.
5. O is the set of primary output signals, $O \subseteq V$.
6. $f: Q \times 2^S \to Q$ is the state transition function.
7. $h: Q \times 2^S \to U$ is the update function of the output and the storage variables, where S and U are as defined below
   (a) $S = \{L \cup E_R \mid L$ is the set of Boolean literals of the form b or $\neg b$, $b \in B \subseteq V$ is a Boolean variable$\}$. The set E_R represents the set of status expressions over $I \cup V$ such that $E_R = \{eR0 \mid e \in E_A\}$, where E_A represents a set of arithmetic expressions over $I \cup V$ of input and storage variables and R is any arithmetic relation, $R \in \{=, \neq, >, \geq, <, \leq\}$.
   (b) $U = \{x \Leftarrow e \mid x \in O \cup V$ and $e \in E_A \cup E_R\}$ represents set of storage or output assignments.

2.2   Untimed PRES+ Models

An untimed PRES+ model is a seven tuple $N = \langle P, K, T, I, O, inP, outP \rangle$, where the members are defined as follows. The set $P = \{p_1, p_2, ..., p_m\}$ is a finite non-empty set of places. A place p is capable of holding a token having a value v_p from a domain D_p. A token value may be of type Boolean, integer, etc., or a user-defined type of any complexity (for instance, a structure or a set). The set K denotes the set of all possible token types, i.e., $K = \bigcup_{p \in P} D_p$. The set $T = \{t_1, t_2, \cdots, t_n\}$ is a finite non-empty set of transitions; the relation $I \subseteq P \times T$ is a finite non-empty set of input arcs which define the flow relation from places to transitions − the designation "input" is with respect to transitions; a place p

is said to be an input place of a transition t if $(p,t) \in I$. The relation $O \subseteq T \times P$ is a finite non-empty set of output arcs which define the flow relation from transitions to places; a place p is said to be an output place of a transition t if $(t,p) \in O$. A place $p \in P$ is said to be an in-port iff there is no transition t for which p is an output place, that is, $(t,p) \notin O$, for all $t \in T$. Likewise, a place $p \in P$ is said to be an out-port iff there is no transition t for which p is an input place, that is, $(p,t) \notin I$, for all $t \in T$. The set inP is the set of *in-ports* and the set $outP$ is the set of *out-ports*.

The pre-set $°t$ of a transition $t \in T$ is the set of *input places* of t. Thus, $°t = \{p \in P \mid (p,t) \in I\}$. Similarly, the post-set $t°$ of a transition $t \in T$ is the set of *output places* of t. So, $t° = \{p \in P \mid (t,p) \in O\}$. The pre-set (transitions) $°p$ and the post-set $p°$ of a place $p \in P$ are given by $°p = \{t \in T \mid (t,p) \in O\}$ and $p° = \{t \in T \mid (p,t) \in I\}$, respectively. If the post-set $t°$ of any transition contains n places, then all the places are associated with identical token type, token value and token arrival time; this mechanism is in keeping with the firing rules of Petri net transitions. Thus, $\forall t \in T, \forall p_1, p_2 \in t°, D_{p_1} = D_{p_2}$, also denoted as $D_{t°}$.

For every transition $t \in T$, there exists a transition function f_t associated with t; that is, for all $t \in T$, $f_t \colon D_{p_1} \times D_{p_2} \times \cdots \times D_{p_n} \to D_q$, where $°t = \{p_1, p_2, \ldots, p_n\}$ and $q \in t°$. The function f_t associated with the transition t is used to capture the functional transformation that takes place on the token values associated with the input places of the transition t to produce the token value at its output places. A transition $t \in T$ may have a guard g_t associated with it. The guard of a transition t is a predicate over the token values associated with the input places of transition t; thus, $g_t \colon D_{p_1} \times D_{p_2} \times \cdots \times D_{p_n} \to \{T, F\}$, where $°t = \{p_1, p_2, \ldots, p_n\}$.

2.3   Operational Semantics of an Untimed PRES+ Model

A marking M is an ordered 2-tuple of a subset of places P_M of the net designating presence/absence of token in each place, a mapping val_M of places to token values and a mapping a_M of places to token arrival times; hence, $M = \langle P_M, val_M \rangle$, where, $P_M \subseteq P$ and $val_M \colon P \to D_P$, where $D_P = \bigcup_{p \in P} D_p$. The value $val_M(p)$ of the token in the place p for the marking M is also denoted as v_p^M, where $p \in P_M$; otherwise it is undefined, denoted as ω.

A marking M_0 is an initial marking of the net depicting the places having tokens initially, i.e., at the beginning of a computation. For an initial marking M_0, $P_{M_0} \supseteq I$, the set of input places of the model.

In a PRES+ model, a transition $t \in T$ is *bound* for a given marking $M : \langle P_M, val_M \rangle$ iff all its input places are marked, i.e., $°t \subseteq P_M$.

A bound transition $t \in T$ for a given marking M is *enabled* iff its guard condition g_t is satisfied by the values of the variables associated with its input places, i.e., $g_t(v_{p_1}^M, v_{p_2}^M, \cdots, v_{p_n}^M)$ holds, where $°t = \{p_1, \cdots, p_n\}$. The set of enabled transitions for a marking M is denoted as T_M.

A marking M^+ is said to be a successor of the marking M if $P_{M^+} = \{p \mid p \in t°$ and $t \in T_M\}$; for any marking M and its successor marking M^+, for any place

$p \in t^\circ$, where $t \in T_M$ having $^\circ t = \{p_1, \cdots, p_n\}$ and associated with function f_t, $v_p^{M+} \Leftarrow f_t(v_{p_1}^M, v_{p_2}^M, \cdots, v_{p_n}^M)$.

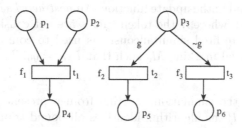

Fig. 1. Places and transitions in a PRES+ model

For illustration of the role of guard conditions of transitions, let us consider the example given in Figure 1. Let M be such that $P_M = \{p_1, p_2, p_3\}$; $v_{p_3}^M$ denotes the value of the token at p_3. The set of bound transitions are $\{t_1, t_2, t_3\}$. Depending upon the guard conditions associated with bound transitions t_2 and t_3, either $\{t_1, t_2\}$ or $\{t_1, t_3\}$ will be enabled. If $g(v_{p_3}^M)$ is true, then $\{t_1, t_2\}$ fires and leads to the marking M_1^+ such that $P_{M_1^+} = \{p_4, p_5, p_6\}$, otherwise $\{t_1, t_3\}$ fires and leads to the marking M_2^+ such that $P_{M_2^+} = \{p_4, p_7\}$.

3   Functional Equivalence Checking Method Using FSMD Equivalence Checking

Karfa et al.[19] have built an equivalence checker for FSMD models. With a view to using this equivalence checker for checking of functional equivalence between the PRES+ models of the original and transformed behaviours, we have devised the following translation algorithm [21] from an untimed PRES+ model to an FSMD model.

3.1   A Translation Algorithm from an Untimed PRES+ Model to an FSMD Model

Unlike FSMD models, the concept of variables is not present in PRES+ models. During translation from an untimed.PRES+ model to an FSMD model, variables must be incorporated in the PRES+ model. Hence, we associate every place with a variable such that all the output places of a transition is associated with a single variable. This association does not violate the operational semantics of the PRES+ model. Note that all the out-places of a transition assume identical token parameters on firing of the transition. Let the input untimed PRES+ model be N and the generated FSMD model be F. For simplicity, we assume that all tokens are of integer type, i.e., $D_p = \mathbb{Z}$ for all $p \in P$.

Let the input untimed PRES+ model be $N = \langle P, K, T, I, O, inP, outP \rangle$ and the translated FSMD model be $F = \langle Q, q_0, I_F, V_F, O_F, f, h \rangle$. The first step of our algorithm computes the following entities in the FSMD model: q_0, I_F, V_F, O_F, U and S. The algorithm then goes on to compute Q: the set of states, f: the state transition function and h: the update function. An *abstracted symbolic simulation* of the PRES+ model, whereby the token values are not considered and all the enabled transitions are fired simultaneously, is used to compute these entities starting from the initial marking M_0 such that $P_{M_0} = q_0$. The major steps are as follows.

1. At each step of the simulation, starting from a present marking M such that $P_M (= q) \subseteq P$ the algorithm identifies all bound transitions of N from P_M. It then identifies the possible subsets of enabled transitions from the bound transitions. For example, let the set of bound transitions be $\{t_1, t_2, t_3\}$, where $°t_2 = °t_3 = \{p\}$, i.e., both t_2 and t_3 emanate from the same place p. Obviously, $g_{t_2} = \neg g_{t_3}$ and only one of them will be satisfied at any instant. Hence the possible subsets of enabled transitions of the above set of bound transitions are $\{t_1, t_2\}$ and $\{t_1, t_3\}$. For each of these subsets of enabled transitions, it constructs the next state (q^+) of F and the successor marking P_{M^+} of the marking M of the PRES+ model N.

2. The parameters of the transition from q to q^+ in F comprising its guard condition and data transformation are then obtained.

Translation Algorithm

1. Given PRES+ model N and initially marked places, i.e., P_{M_0}
   -- $q_0 \Leftarrow P_{M_0}$
   -- $I_F \Leftarrow \{$ Variables associated with $p \mid p \in inP\}$
   -- $V_F \Leftarrow \{$Variables associated with $p \mid p \notin inP \cup outP\}$
   -- $O_F \Leftarrow \{$Variable associated with $p \mid p \in outP\}$
   -- Let $t \in T$ have $°t = \{p_1, p_2, \cdots, p_n\}$ and $t° = \{p'_1, p'_2, \cdots, p'_k\}$. Let the variables associated with p_i, $1 \leq i \leq n$, be v_i and that associated with $p'_i, 1 \leq i \leq k$, be v. Let the transformation function of the transition be $f_t^{(n)}$ and its guard condition be $g_t^{(n)}$. Hence, $v \Leftarrow f_t^{(n)}(v_1, v_2, ..., v_n)$ is put in U and $g_t^{(n)}(v_1, v_2, ..., v_n)$ is put in S.

2. $Q \Leftarrow \{q_0\}$; $Q_{new} \Leftarrow Q$; $Q_{new}^+ \Leftarrow \emptyset$;

3. $\forall q \in Q_{new}$
   (a) $Q_{new} \Leftarrow Q_{new} - \{q\}$; $T_q \Leftarrow \{t \mid °t \in q\}$;
   (b) /* T_q may contain sets of mutually exclusive transitions. All possible subsets of T_q will have to be composed s.t. in a subset exactly one member from each set of mutually exclusive transitions is taken. Each subset will be associated with a set (conjunction) of the guard conditions*/
   -- $\mathcal{T}_q \Leftarrow$ constructSetOfTransitions (T_q)
   -- /* $\mathcal{T}_q \in 2^{T_q}$, the subsets of possible parallel transitions in T_q.*/
   -- $Q_{new}^q = \emptyset$, empty set
   -- /* Q_{new}^q: the set of next states generated for each of the subsets in $\mathcal{T}_q$.*/
   (c) $\forall \mathcal{T} \in \mathcal{T}_q$
      i. $q_{\mathcal{T}}^+ \Leftarrow \bigcup_{t \in \mathcal{T}} t°$; $Q_{new} \Leftarrow Q_{new}^q \cup \{q_{\mathcal{T}}^+\}$
      ii. Let $G_{\mathcal{T}}$ be the set of guards associated with $t \in \mathcal{T}$. In the table of the state transition function f, insert entry
         -- $f(q, G_{\mathcal{T}}) = q^+$
      iii. Let $A_{\mathcal{T}}$ be the set of assignments of the form $\{v \Leftarrow f_t(v_1, v_2, ..., v_n) \mid t \in \mathcal{T}, \{v\} = t°, \{v_1, v_2, ..., v_n\} = °t$ and f_t is the function associated with $t \}$; In the table of the update function h, insert the entry $h(q, G_{\mathcal{T}}) = A_{\mathcal{T}}$; /* members of $A_{\mathcal{T}}$ are carried out in parallel */
      iv. $Q_{new}^+ \Leftarrow Q_{new}^+ \cup Q_{new}^q$;

4. /* Any new state generated */
   – if $Q_{new}^+ = \emptyset$ Exit;
   – else $Q \Leftarrow Q \cup Q_{new}^+$;
   – $Q_{new} \Leftarrow Q_{new}^+$; $Q_{new}^+ \Leftarrow \emptyset$;
   – go to **Step 3**

Figure 2 (b) depicts the FSMD obtained from the PRES+ model of Figure 2 (a), where $I_F = \{a, b\}, O_F = \{f, g\}, V_F = \{c, d, e\}, S = \{e \geq 1, e < 1\}$ and $U = \{c \leftarrow a, d \leftarrow b - 1, e \leftarrow c + d, f \leftarrow 3 * e, g \leftarrow e\}$.

The complexity of the algorithm is determined by that of *Step 3* which is exponential in the number of parallel transitions; the complexity of other steps are linear in number of places and transitions of the model.

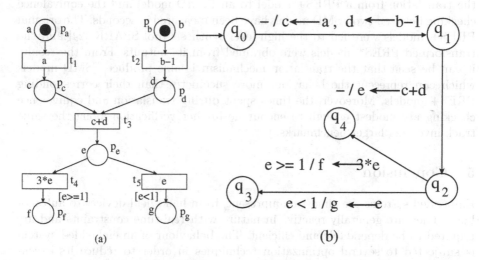

(a)   (b)

Fig. 2. PRES+ model to be converted into FSMD model

3.2 Background of an FSMD Equivalence Checking Method

Karfa et al.[19] have proposed an equivalence checking method of two sequential behaviours. The method consists in introducing cut points in one FSMD, visualizing its computations as concatenation of paths from cutpoints to cutpoints and finally, identifying equivalent finite path segments in the other FSMD; the process is then repeated with the FSMDs interchanged. This method is strong enough to handle most of the code motion techniques.

4 Experimental Results

The algorithm has been implemented and integrated with that of [19]. The tool has been satisfactorily tested on some benchmarks [22] [23] as shown in table 1. The table depicts the sizes of the original (orig) and the transformed (trnsf) PRES+ models in terms of their places and transitions (trans) and that of their

Table 1. Equivalence checking between two PRES$^+$ models via FSMD

Benchmark	Orig PRES+ places	trans	Trnsf PRES+ places	trans	Translated FSMD orig states	trnsf states	Translation time (sec) orig	trans	Equivalence Chk Time (sec)
DIFFEQ	38	18	22	12	15	8	0.0523	0.0278	0.45680
GCD	15	16	12	13	7	6	0.0252	0.0231	0.12867
MODN	18	17	15	14	11	8	0.0258	0.0251	0.23131
PERFECT	17	12	12	9	7	6	0.0257	0.0227	0.75420
TLC	36	39	26	28	20	12	0.0625	0.0321	0.75980

corresponding translated FSMD models in states. The time spent to carry out the translation from a PRES+ model to an FSMD model and the equivalence checking between two FSMD models have been measured in seconds. The original PRES+ models were fed to the high-level synthesis tool SPARK [24] and the transformed PRES$^+$ models were obtained from its outputs. From the results it can be seen that the translation mechanism is able produce FSMD models which can represent the behaviour more succinctly than their corresponding PRES+ models. Moreover, the times spent during translation and equivalence checking are modest enough to encourage further verification along the same track involving larger benchmarks.

5   Conclusion

Embedded systems are almost omnipresent, from hand-held devices to automobiles. They are generally reactive in nature with real-time constraints and are required to be dependable and efficient. The behaviour of an embedded system is subjected to several optimization techniques in order to reduce its execution time, power and area, while preserving its functionality. Several equivalence checkers involving FSMD models [19], [20], [25] have been proposed that can guarantee the correctness of several code motion techniques. However, FSMD models are not suitable to depict parallel behaviours. Hence such specifications can be modeled better using some distributed model of computation such as Petri nets. PRES+ model is equipped to represent a behaviour in embedded systems more efficiently than a normal Petri net. Therefore, it will be helpful if some translation scheme can be deviced that will produce an FSMD model from a PRES+ model such as the one presented in this paper. The main challenge during this translation lies in merging several places in a PRES+ model into a single state of an FSMD, thereby capturing a parallel behaviour in a sequential model. This step is extremely tricky and susceptible to errors if tried by humans. This advocates for developing a mechanized tool for carrying out such translations. Our implementation integrated with that of [19] has been tested satisfactorily on some benchmarks. The times spent translation and then subsequent equivalence checking are modest enough to encourage further experiments on larger benchmarks. Some future work that can be undertaken is to amalgamate our translation tool with those of [20] and [25] as well and perform a comparative study. The presented work should also inspire translation mechanisms between various models of computation to benefit from each of their unique abilities.

References

1. Edwards, S., Lavagno, L., Lee, E.A., Sangiovanni-Vincentelli, A.: Design of embedded systems: Formal models, validation, and synthesis. Proceedings of the IEEE, pp. 366–390 (1997)
2. Cortés, L.A., Eles, P., Peng, Z.: Verification of embedded systems using a petri net based representation. In: ISSS 2000: Proceedings of the 13th International Symposium on System Synthesis, pp. 149–155. IEEE Computer Society, Washington, DC (2000)
3. Gupta, S., Gupta, R., Dutt, N., Nicolau, A.: Coordinated parallelizing compiler optimizations and high-level synthesis. ACM Transactions on Design Automation of Electronic Systems (TODAES) 9(4), 1–31 (2004)
4. Dos Santos, L.C.V., Jress, J.A.G.: A reordering technique for efficient code motion. In: Procs. of the 36th ACM/IEEE Design Automation Conference, DAC 1999, pp. 296–299. ACM, New York (1999)
5. Lakshminarayana, G., Raghunathan, A., Jha, N.K.: Incorporating speculative execution into scheduling of control-flow-intensive design. IEEE Transactions on CAD of ICS 19(3), 308–324 (2000)
6. Wakabayashi, K., Tanaka, H.: Global scheduling independent of control dependencies based on condition vectors. In: DAC 1992: Proceedings of the 29th ACM/IEEE Conference on Design Automation, pp. 112–115 (1992)
7. Rim, M., Fann, Y., Jain, R.: Global scheduling with code motions for high-level synthesis applications. IEEE Transactions on VLSI Systems 3(3), 379–392 (1995)
8. Gupta, S., Dutt, N., Gupta, R., Nicolau, A.: Using global code motions to improve the quality of results for high-level synthesis. IEEE Transactions on CAD of ICS 23(2), 302–312 (2004)
9. Kandemir, M., Vijaykrishnan, N., Irwin, M.J., Ye, W.: Influence of compiler optimizations on system power. IEEE Trans. Very Large Scale Integr. Syst. 9, 801–804 (2001)
10. Kandemir, M., Son, S.W., Chen, G.: An evaluation of code and data optimizations in the context of disk power reduction. In: ISLPED 2005: Proceedings of the 2005 International Symposium on Low Power Electronics and Design, pp. 209–214 (2005)
11. Kandemir, M.T.: Reducing energy consumption of multiprocessor soc architectures by exploiting memory bank locality. ACM Trans. Des. Autom. Electron. Syst. 11(2), 410–441 (2006)
12. Radhakrishnan, R., Teica, E., Vemuri, R.: Verification of Basic Block Schedules Using RTL Transformations. In: Margaria, T., Melham, T.F. (eds.) CHARME 2001. LNCS, vol. 2144, pp. 173–178. Springer, Heidelberg (2001)
13. Eveking, H., Hinrichsen, H., Ritter, G.: Automatic verification of scheduling results in high-level synthesis. In: Proceedings of the Conference on Design, Automation and Test in Europe, DATE 1999, pp. 260–265. ACM, New York (1999)
14. Kim, Y., Kopuri, S., Mansouri, N.: Automated formal verification of scheduling process using finite state machines with datapath (fsmd). In: Proceedings of the 5th International Symposium on Quality Electronic Design, ISQED 2004, pp. 110–115. IEEE Computer Society, Washington, DC (2004)

15. Tristan, J.-B., Leroy, X.: Verified validation of lazy code motion. In: Proceedings of the 2009 ACM SIGPLAN Conference on Programming Language Design and Implementation, PLDI 2009, pp. 316–326. ACM, New York (2009)
16. Kim, Y., Mansouri, N.: Automated formal verification of scheduling with speculative code motions. In: Proceedings of the 18th ACM Great Lakes Symposium on VLSI, GLSVLSI 2008, pp. 95–100. ACM, New York (2008)
17. Kundu, S., Lerner, S., Gupta, R.: Validating High-Level Synthesis. In: Gupta, A., Malik, S. (eds.) CAV 2008. LNCS, vol. 5123, pp. 459–472. Springer, Heidelberg (2008)
18. Karfa, C., Sarkar, D., Mandal, C., Reade, C.: Hand-in-hand verification of high-level synthesis. In: GLSVLSI 2007: Proceedings of the 17th ACM Great Lakes Symposium on VLSI, pp. 429–434. ACM, New York (2007)
19. Karfa, C., Sarkar, D., Mandal, C., Kumar, P.: An equivalence-checking method for scheduling verification in high-level synthesis. IEEE Trans. on CAD of Integrated Circuits and Systems 27(3), 556–569 (2008)
20. Kim, Y., Kopuri, S., Mansouri, N.: Automated formal verification of scheduling process using finite state machines with datapath (fsmd). In: Proceedings of the 5th International Symposium on Quality Electronic Design, ISQED 2004, pp. 110–115. IEEE Computer Society, Washington, DC (2004)
21. Bandyopadhyay, S.: Equivalence checking in embedded systems design verification using pres+ model. CoRR, abs/1010.4953 (2010)
22. Panda, P.R., Dutt, N.D.: 1995 high level synthesis design repository. In: Proceedings of the 8th International Symposium on System Synthesis, ISSS 1995, pp. 170–174 (1995)
23. Gajski, D.D., Dutt, N.D., Wu, A.C.-H., Lin, S.Y.-L.: High-level synthesis: introduction to chip and system design. Kluwer Academic Publishers, Norwell (1992)
24. Gupta, S., Dutt, N., Gupta, R., Nicolau, A.: Spark: a high-level synthesis framework for applying parallelizing compiler transformations. In: Proc. of Int. Conf. on VLSI Design, pp. 461–466. IEEE Computer Society, Washington, DC (2003)
25. Alizadeh, B., Fujita, M.: Automatic Merge-Point Detection for Sequential Equivalence Checking of System-Level and RTL Descriptions. In: Namjoshi, K.S., Yoneda, T., Higashino, T., Okamura, Y. (eds.) ATVA 2007. LNCS, vol. 4762, pp. 129–144. Springer, Heidelberg (2007)

Design of High Speed Vedic Multiplier
for Decimal Number System

Prabir Saha[1], Arindam Banerjee[2], Anup Dandapat[3], and Partha Bhattacharyya[4]

[1] School of Electronics Engineering, Kiit University, Bhubaneswar
sahaprabir1@gmail.com
[2] Dept. of ECE, JIS College of Engineering, Kalyani
banerjee.arindam1@gmail.com
[3] Camelia Institute of Technology and Management, Hoogly
anup.dandapat@gmail.com
[4] Dept. of ETCE, BESU, Shibpur, Howrah-711103
pb_etc_besu@yahoo.com

Abstract. Vedic mathematics is the ancient techniques of mathematics, based on 16 simple sutras (formulae). Decimal number system multiplication technique based on such ancient mathematics is reported in this paper. Improvement in speed was achieved through stage reduction by "Nikhilam Navatascaramam Dasatah (NND)" (all from 9 and last from 10) which was adopted from Vedas, during multiplication. Binary coded decimal (BCD) methodology was incorporated with Vedic mathematics, to implement such multiplier for practical VLSI applications. The functionality of these circuits was checked and performance parameters such as propagation delay, dynamic switching power consumptions were calculated by spice spectre using 90nm CMOS technology. BCD implementation of Vedic multiplier ensures the stage reduction for decimal number, hence substantial reduction in propagation delay compared with earlier reported one, has been investigated. Implementation result offered propagation delay of the resulting (5×5) digit decimal multiplier was only ~5.798ns while the power consumption of the same was ~23.487µW. Almost ~26% improvement in speed from earlier reported decimal multiplier, e.g. parallel implementation methodology, the best architecture reported so far, has been achieved.

Keywords: BCD, Urdhva-tiryakbyham (UT), NND, Vedic Mathematics, High Speed.

1   Introduction

The hardware implementation of decimal arithmetic is becoming a topic of interest to the researchers, for wide application of such arithmetic in the field of human-centric applications [1-3], where exact results are required. Generally, computer algorithms and architectures are based on binary number systems, because, of their simplicity from its counterpart i.e. decimal number systems [4]. However, many decimal numbers cannot be represented exactly in binary format due to finite word-length effect

H. Rahaman et al. (Eds.): VDAT 2012, LNCS 7373, pp. 79–88, 2012.

[4], hence exact implementation is impractical. Recently, decimal arithmetic is becoming commercialized for general purpose computer [5], through Binary Coded Decimal (BCD) encoding techniques.

Substantial amount of research have so far been reported regarding speed improvement and efficient hardware implementation of decimal multiplier [1-11], like RPS algorithm [6], embedded binary multipliers [7], binary multipliers [4], binary counters [8], partial product accumulation and carry save addition [9,10] etc. Among the above mentioned techniques, sequential & parallel implementations are popular to the researches, which also serve the limitations. The sequential implementation of decimal multipliers is based on the iterative process where the partial products are generated once at a time and added to the previously accumulated result [7], thereby; increases propagation delay from its counterpart [10]. To achieve the high speed through sequential approach, several recording scheme like 4221 [9, 11], 5211 [7], was investigated; though, principles behind the multiplication was same for all cases. On the other hand, the digit multiplication was implemented in parallel [4, 10] fashion, resulted better speed and power with the penalty of hardware than earlier reported sequential implementations [2, 3, 6].

Vedic Mathematics is the ancient methodology based on 16 Sutras (Formulae), indicate the potentiality of straightaway calculations. UT and NND both are Sanskrit word means "vertically and crosswise" and "all from 9 and last from 10" respectively are used for multiplication. Numerous works [12-14] have so far been reported on multiplication using Vedic mathematics, but, all the approaches [12-14] have been reported for binary number system, and not extended their work for decimal multiplication.

In this paper we report on a transistor level implementation of decimal multiplier using the formulae of UT and NND from Vedic mathematics. Moreover, to carry-out the transistor level implementation of such multiplier optimized 8421 BCD recording techniques [15] have been adopted in this literature. By employing Vedic mathematics, an N×N digit decimal number multiplication was transformed into one small multiplication and a subtraction. NND sutra is used for the multiplication purpose, with less number of partial products, compared with earlier reports [7,10], to achieve high speed of such multiplication. Transistor level implementation for measuring the performance parameters such as propagation delay, dynamic switching power consumption was calculated by spice spectre using 90nm CMOS technology and compared with previous reported architectures like sequential [7], parallel [10] implementation. The calculated results revealed (5×5) digit multiplier have propagation delay only ~5.798ns with ~23.487μW dynamic switching power.

2   Mathematical Formulation of Vedic Sutras (Formulae)

The potentiality of 'Vedic Mathematics', especially for calculations regarding multiplications, was reported by 'Sri Bharati Krsna Thirthaji Maharaja', in the form of Vedic Sutras (formulae) [16]. In this paper we have concentrated on NND and UT formulae for the reported multiplier.

2.1   "Nikhilam Navatascaramam Dasatah (NND)" Sutra

"Nikhilam Navatascaramam Dasatah (NND)" means "all from 9 and last from 10", have been used to implement the decimal multiplication. Through the multiplication methodology (N×N) digit multiplier is transformed into addition/subtraction and a small (<< N) multiplication, thereby reduces carry propagation leading towards high speed operation. A simple example will suffice to clarify the operations has been shown in Fig. 1, and multiplication procedure has been described in [16,17]. Mathematical description of this sutra can be described hereunder, considering, two operands X and Y.

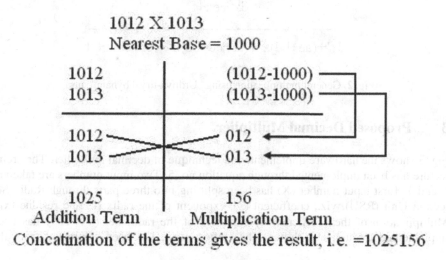

Fig. 1. Illustration of decimal multiplication

$$X = x \times 10^k \pm x_1, \text{ and } Y = x \times 10^k \pm x_2 \qquad (1)$$

Where 'x' is the coefficient, 'k' is the exponent of the radix and x_i ($i \in (1,2)$)   is the residue. Considering that, the two numbers X and Y have the same radix and same coefficient.   Assuming that, P is the product of X and Y, can be formulated as,

$$P = X \times Y = (x \times 10^k \pm x_1) \times (x \times 10^k \pm x_2) \qquad (2)$$

$$= x \times x \times 10^{2k} \pm x \times x_2 \times 10^k \pm x \times x_1 \times 10^k \pm x_1 \times x_2 \qquad (3)$$

$$= x \times 10^k (x \times 10^k \pm x_1 \pm x_2) \pm x_1 \times x_2 \qquad (4)$$

$$= x \times 10^k (X \pm x_2) \pm x_1 \times x_2 \qquad (5)$$

2.2   "Urdhva-Tiryakbyham (UT) " Sutra

The meaning of this sutra is "Vertically and crosswise" and it is applicable to all the multiplication operations. Fig. 2 represents the general multiplication procedure using "Urdhva-tiryakbyham". From Fig. 2, it can be observed that, we have to multiply

(ax^2+bx+c) and (dx^2+ex+f). Where x=10, a,b,c,d,e and f are the digits, i.e., values lies between (0 to 9). This procedure is simply known as array multiplication (sequential) technique. It is an efficient multiplication technique when the multiplier and multiplicand lengths are small, but for the larger length multiplication, this technique is not suitable due to large amount of carry propagation involved here.

$$ax^2+bx+c$$
$$\times$$
$$dx^2+ex+f$$

$$adx^4+(ae+bd)x^3+(af+cd+be)x^2+(bf+ce)x+cf$$

Fig. 2. General multiplication using "Urdhva-tiryakbyham" sutra

3   Proposed Decimal Multiplier

Fig. 3 shows the hardware implementation technique of decimal multiplier. The architecture has been implemented through equation no. 5. Two input numbers are taken as X and Y. First input number (X) has been splitting into three parts through Radix Selection Unit (RSU), viz., coefficient (x), exponent of the radix (k) and residue (x_1). Multiplication of the coefficient by exponent of the radix i.e. $(x \times 10^k)$ has been implemented through left shifter. The shifted result has been subtracted from the

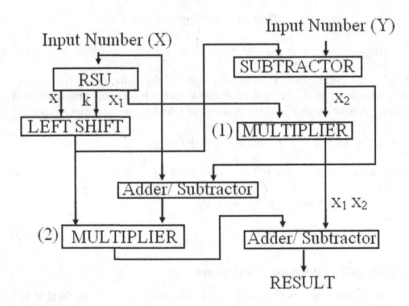

Fig. 3. Hardware implementation technique of decimal multiplier

second input number (Y), to determine the second residue (x_2). The residue (x_1 and x_2) has been multiplied through multiplier (1) and producing result $x_1 \times x_2$. First input number (X) is again added/ subtracted by second residue (x_2) and producing the result ($X \pm x_2$) through adder/subtractor block. This result is multiplied with ($x \times 10^k$) through multiplier (2). Multiplied result is finally promoted towards adder/ sub-tractor; another input of the adder/sub-tractor is taken from (1) multiplier output i.e. ($x_1 x_2$), to generate the final results.

4   Circuit Modules

The advantages of CMOS transmission gate (TG) logic over conventional CMOS and CPL [17] logic are well established. As the CMOS transmission gate consists of one PMOS and one NMOS, connected in parallel, the ON resistance is smaller than even a single NMOS. The circuit modules required for computation decimal multiplication of two numbers are described in the following subsections, have been implemented using TG.

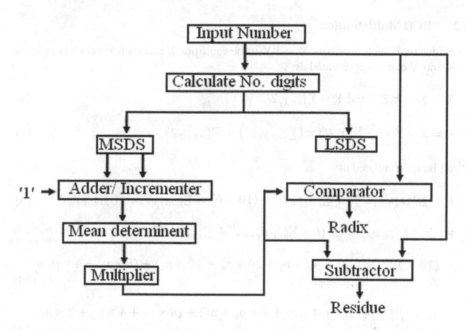

Fig. 4. Hardware implementation technique of Radix Selection Unit (RSU)

4.1   Radix Selection Unit (RSU)

The RSU [17] takes the integer input and calculates the corresponding Coefficient (x) and Exponent of the Radix (k) and Residue (x_i). The implementation methodology is described here. Calculate the digits of input number, i.e. even digit or odd digit number. Odd digit number can be made an even digit number through a concatenation of a '0' before the input number. (Assume that input number is N digit number). Separate the input numbers into two equal halves, i.e., (N/2) in each side. Increment the most significant digit set (MSDS) by '1' and calculate the average of the incremented MSDS and original MSDS. Multiply the average value with $10^{\frac{N}{2}}$, and compare the multiplied result with the input number. If input number is greater than the multiplication result then radix is the incremented MSDS, otherwise original MSDS. Coefficient can be computed as MSDS, and exponent of radix is equal to $k = \frac{N}{2}$. Residue can be computed as, subtracting the input number from radix or vice versa.

Circuit level implementation for RSU has been carried out and shown in Fig. 4. The reported circuit has been shown for 2 digit number for simplicity, for higher digit-set number can be implemented in similar manner. Mean determinant of the given block has been implemented through a single bit right shift and multiplier has been implemented through left shifter. For shifting towards left or right a bidirectional combinational shifter [17] has been used, to achieve the high speed operation.

4.2   BCD Multiplication

Consider two single numbers X and Y to be multiplied, and their product is equal to P. X and Y can be represented as:

$$X = \sum_{i=0}^{3} x_i 2^i \text{ , and } Y = \sum_{j=0}^{3} y_j 2^j \tag{6}$$

$$P = X \times Y = \left(\sum_{i=0}^{3} x_i 2^i\right) \times \left(\sum_{j=0}^{3} y_j 2^j\right) = \sum_{k=0}^{7} p_k 2^k \tag{7}$$

P can be reformulated as:

$$P = \sum_{k=0}^{3} p_{k+4} 2^{k+4} + \sum_{k=0}^{3} p_k 2^k = (10+6) \times \sum_{k=0}^{3} p_{k+4} 2^k + \sum_{k=0}^{3} p_k 2^k \tag{8}$$

$$= 10 \times \sum_{k=0}^{3} p_{k+4} 2^k + \left(6 \times \sum_{k=0}^{3} p_{k+4} 2^k + \sum_{k=0}^{3} p_k 2^k\right) \tag{9}$$

$$= \left(10 \times \sum_{k=0}^{3} p_{k+4} 2^k + 40 \times p_7 + 20 \times p_6 + 10 \times p_5\right) + (8 \times p_7 + 4 \times p_6 + 2 \times p_5 + p_4 + \sum_{k=0}^{3} p_k 2^k) \tag{10}$$

$$= 10 \times \left(\sum_{k=0}^{3} p_{k+4} 2^k + 4 \times p_7 + 2 \times p_6 + p_5\right) + (8 \times p_7 + 4 \times p_6 + 2 \times p_5 + p_4 + \sum_{k=0}^{3} p_k 2^k) \tag{11}$$

Fig. 5 represents the architecture for BCD multiplier. BCD multiplier consists of three main subsections-(i) Binary Multiplier, which has been implemented through array multiplier [18] (ii) First stage BCD converter and (iii) Second stage BCD converter. The inputs to the first stage BCD converter are the higher order and the lower order byte of the multiplier output and the output is the Least Significant Digit (LSD). The two bits carry from the first stage converter is fed to the second stage converter. The other input to the second stage is the higher order byte of the multiplier output. The output of the second stage converter is the Most Significant Digit (MSD).

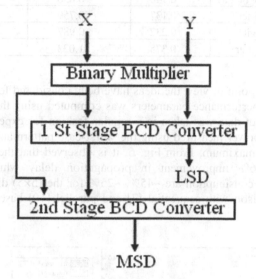

Fig. 5. Hardware implementation of BCD multiplier

4.3   Adder/Sub-tractor

The conventional adder/sub-tractor block has been implemented [18] to perform addition as well as subtraction in a single block, and their performance parameters have been checked using standard 90nmCMOStechnology.

5   Results and Discussions

Transistor level simulation for decimal multiplier circuit was performed through Spice Spectre simulator using 90nm CMOS technology with 1V power supply, operated at 10MHz. Dual threshold voltage(VT) operating mode was considered for simulation to determine the performance parameters. In designing calculation of decimal multiplier like (2×2), (3×3), (4×4) and (5×5) digits, all the individual modules such as BCD multiplier, RSU, Adder/ Subtractor, Logical Shifter was implemented using TG to make the circuit faster. The individual performance parameters such as propagation delay, dynamic switching power consumption and Energy Delay Product (EDP) for different circuit modules, i.e. BCD multiplier, RSU, Adder/Sub-tractor, Logical Shifter is shown in Table1. We focused our main concentration for reducing the propagation delay and dynamic switching power consumption.

Table 1. Performance parameters like propagation delay(ns), dynamic switching power consumption(μW), energy delay product (10^{-24} J-s) analysis of different circuit modules such as Adder/Subtractor, Logical shifter, RSU and BCD Multiplier

Circuit Module	Delay (ns)	Power (μW)	EDP (10^{-24}) J-S
Adder/Subtractor (4-Bit)	0.140	0.856	0.0167
Logical Shifter	0.137	0.759	0.0142
RSU (2-Digit)	0.232	0.987	0.0531
BCD Multiplier	0.375	1.023	0.1438

For the comparison point of view the ideas have been considered form the references and simulated and performance parameters was computed using the same MOSFET technology file. Input data was taken in a regular fashion for experimental purpose. The delay and the power measured using the worst-case pattern and from the output where the delay is maximum. From Fig. 6, it is observed that the proposed design offered ~45%, ~26% improvement in propagation delay while corresponding reduction of power consumption are ~45%, ~25% for the (5×5) digit multiplication circuitry in comparison with sequential [7] and parallel [10] based implementation respectively.

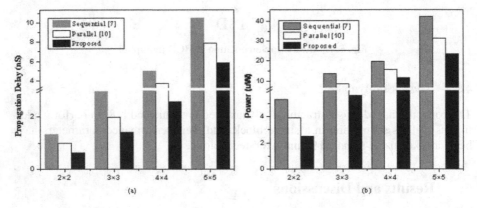

Fig. 6. Performance parameters such as (a) propagation delay (ns), (b) dynamic switching power (μW) consumption of the different architectures, as a function of input number of digits, which have been implemented by Spice Spectre using 90nm CMOS technology file

6   Conclusions

In this paper, we report on a decimal digit multiplication circuitry for practical VLSI implementation, based on ancient Vedic mathematics. Improvement in speed was achieved through significant number of stage reduction through Vedic formulae, resulted in high speed and low power digit multiplication techniques. In multiplication circuitry, an (N×N) bit multiplier implementation was transformed into just one small multiplication (bit length << N) and one adder/sub-tractor implementation, executing the objectives for decimal multiplication. The propagation delay for (5×5) digit decimal multiplication was only 5.798ns while the power consumption of the same was 23.487µW. Improvement in speed were found to be ~45%, ~26% for (5×5) digit decimal multiplication circuitry while corresponding reduction of power consumption were ~45% , ~25%, compared with sequential and parallel implementation respectively.

References

1. James, R.K., Shahana, T.K., Jacob, K.P., Sasi, S.: Decimal Multiplication using compact BCD Multiplier. In: Proc. IEEE Int. Conf. on Electronics Design (ICED 2008), Penang, pp. 1–6 (2008)
2. James, R.K., Jacob, K.P., Sasi, S.: Performance analysis of double digit decimal multiplier on various FPGA logic families. In: Proc. IEEE Int. Conf. on Programmable Logic, Sao Carlos, pp. 165–170 (2009)
3. Sutter, G., Todorovich, E., Bioul, G., Vazquez, M., Deschamps, J.P.: FPGA Implementations of BCD Multipliers. In: Proc. IEEE Int. Conf. on Reconfigurable Computing and FPGAs (ReConFig 2009), Quintana Roo, pp. 36–41 (2009)
4. Véstias, M.P., Neto, H.C.: Parallel decimal multipliers using binary multipliers. In: Proc. IEEE VI Southern Programmable Logic Conference (SPL), Ipojuca, pp. 73–78 (2010)
5. Jaberipur, G., Kaivani, A.: Binary-coded decimal digit multipliers. IET Journal on Computer & Digital Techniques, 377–381 (2007)
6. James, R.K., Shahana, T.K., Jacob, K.P., Sasi, S.: Fixed Point Decimal Multiplication Using RPS Algorithm. In: Proc. IEEE Int. Symp. on Parallel and Distributed Processing with Applications (ISPA 2008), Sydney, pp. 343–350 (2008)
7. Neto, H.C., Vestias, M.P.: Decimal multiplier on FPGA using embedded binary multipliers. In: Proc. IEEE Int. Conf. on Field Programmable Logic and Applications (FPL 2008), Heidelberg, pp. 197–202 (2008)
8. Veeramachaneni, S., Srinivas, M.B.: Novel High-Speed Architecture for 32-Bit Binary Coded Decimal (BCD) Multiplier. In: Proc. IEEE Int. Symp. on Communications and Information Technologies (ISCIT 2008), Lao, pp. 543–546 (2008)
9. Erle, M.A., Hickmann, B.J., Schulte, M.J.: Decimal Floating-Point Multiplication. IEEE Transactions on Computers 58(7), 902–916 (2009)
10. Vazquez, A., Antelo, E., Montuschi, P.: Improved Design of High-Performance Parallel Decimal Multipliers. IEEE Transactions on Computers 59(5), 679–693 (2010)
11. Vazquez, A., Antelo, E., Montuschi, P.: A New Family of High-Performance Parallel Decimal Multipliers. In: Proc. 18th IEEE Symposium on Computer Arithmetic (ARITH 2007), Montepellier, pp. 194–204 (2007)
12. Mehta, P., Gawali, D.: Conventional versus Vedic mathematical method for Hardware implementation of a multiplier. In: Proc. of the IEEE International Conference on Advances in Computing, Control, and Telecommunication Technologies, Trivandrum, pp. 640–642 (2009)
13. Tiwari, H.D., Gankhuyag, G., Kim, C.M., Cho, Y.B.: Multiplier design based on ancient Indian Vedic Mathematics. In: Proc. of the IEEE International SoC Design Conference, Busan, pp. 65–68 (2008)
14. Saha, P., Banerjee, A., Bhattacharyya, P., Dandapat, A.: High Speed ASIC Design of Complex Multiplier Using Vedic Mathematics. In: Proc. of the IEEE, Student Technology Symposium, Kharagpur, pp. 237–241 (January 2011)

15. Bhattacharya, J., Gupta, A., Singh, A.: A high performance binary to BCD converter for decimal multiplication. In: Proc. of the IEEE International Symp. on VLSI Design Automation and Test (VLSI-DAT), Hsin Chu, pp. 315–318 (2010)
16. Maharaja, J.S.S.B.K.T.: Vedic mathematics. Motilal Banarsidass Publishers Pvt. Ltd., Delhi (2001)
17. Saha, P., Banerjee, A., Dandapat, A., Bhattacharyya, P.: ASIC Design of a High Speed Low Power Circuit for Calculation of Factorial of 4-Bit Numbers Based on Ancient Vedic Mathematics. Microelectronics Journal 42(12), 1343–1352 (2011)
18. Saha, P.K., Banerjee, A., Dandapat, A.: High Speed Low Power Complex Multiplier Design Using Parallel Adders and Subtractors. International Journal on Electronic and Electrical Engineering (IJEEE) 07(11), 38–46 (2009)

An Efficient Test Design for CMPs Cache Coherence Realizing MESI Protocol

Mamata Dalui[1] and Biplab K. Sikdar[2]

[1] Department of Computer Science and Engineering, NIT Durgapur, India-713209
[2] Department of Computer Science and Technology, BESU, Shibpur, India-711103
mamata.06@gmail.com, biplab@cs.becs.ac.in

Abstract. This work proposes an efficient test design for verification of cache coherence in CMPs (Chip Multiprocessors). It ensures data coherence more accurate and reliable in a system with thousands of on-chip processors realizing MESI protocol. The design is based on the modular structure of Cellular Automata (CA), a modeling tool invented by von Neumann. A special class of CA referred to as SACA has been introduced to identify the inconsistencies in cache line states of processors' L1 caches. Introduction of segmented CA ensures better efficiency in the design, in terms of number of computations, to detect an inconsistency.

Keywords: Cache coherence, CMP, Fault detection, Coherence controller.

1 Introduction

The major issue in CMPs (Chip Multiprocessors) with thousands of on-chip cores, is the noncompliance of schemes targeted for small systems [1]. The conventional solutions for verification of cache coherence are also not so effective in CMPs. An insignificant defect in the CC (cache coherence controller), responsible for ensuring consistency in L1 caches [2], can lead to a major data inconsistency.

A number of works address the reliability issues in CMPs [3], [4]. The schemes ensuring coherency in CMPs, through frequent communication, are reported in [1], [2], [3], [4]. This communication among L1 caches seriously affects the system performance. The design proposed in [2], is the only effective solution so far been proposed. However, it involves computation intensive steps to detect inconsistencies in different cache data.

The above scenario motivates us to develop a scheme to determine the accuracy in data consistency of the CMPs cache system without a commitment of significant cost. In [7], a CA-based design realizing MSI protocol is reported. The current work targets the design of a test logic entrusted with the verification of data inconsistency in CMPs realizing MESI protocol. It is based on the theory of a special class of cellular automata (CA) referred to as the SACA [5], [6].

The hardware implementation of the proposed test logic can quickly determine the denial of cache coherence in CMPs. The segmentation of CA exploits the

H. Rahaman et al. (Eds.): VDAT 2012, LNCS 7373, pp. 89–98, 2012.
© Springer-Verlag Berlin Heidelberg 2012

inherent parallelism within the solution and thereby reduces the time to get a decision. This SACA based unconventional scheme demands minimum wire communication as well as interconnect access that can lead to reduction in power dissipation. Further, the modular as well as highly scalable structure of cellular automata [5] makes the solution suitable for a system with billions of cores.

2 CA Preliminaries

A Cellular Automaton (CA) can be viewed as an autonomous finite state machine (FSM). A CA cell is having two states - 0 or 1 and the next state (NS) of ith CA cell is $S_i^{t+1} = f_i(S_{i-1}^t, S_i^t, S_{i+1}^t)$, where S_{i-1}^t, S_i^t and S_{i+1}^t are the present states (PS) of the left neighbor, self and right neighbor of the ith cell at time t. f_i is the next state function. On the other hand, the states of cells $S^t = (S_1^t, S_2^t, \cdots, S_n^t)$ at t is the present state of CA.

The f_i can be expressed in the form of a truth table $(Table\ 1)$. The decimal equivalent of the 8 outputs is called Rule R_i. In a 2-state 3-neighborhood CA, there can be 2^8 (256) rules. Five such rules 15, 14, 192, 207, and 240 are illustrated in $Table\ 1$. The first row lists the possible 2^3 (8) combinations of present states of $(i-1)^{th}$, i^{th} and $(i+1)^{th}$ cells at t.

A combination of the present states (1st row of $Table\ 1$) can be considered as Min Term of a 3-variable $S_{i-1}^t, S_i^t, S_{i+1}^t$ switching function and called RMT (rule min term). Column 011 of $Table\ 1$ is the 3rd RMT. The next states corresponding to this RMT are 1 for Rule 15, 14 & 207, and 0 for Rule 192 & 240.

The set R $=< R_1, R_2, \cdots, R_i, \cdots, R_n >$ configures the cells of a CA. If all the R_is are same, the CA is a uniform CA; otherwise it is a non-uniform/hybrid CA. For the current work, we consider null boundary CA as in $Fig.1(a)$.

Table 1. RMTs of the $CA < 15, 14, 192, 207, 240 >$

PS	111	110	101	100	011	010	001	000	Rule
RMT	(7)	(6)	(5)	(4)	(3)	(2)	(1)	(0)	
NS	0	0	0	0	1	1	1	1	15
NS	0	0	0	0	1	1	1	0	14
NS	1	1	0	0	0	0	0	0	192
NS	1	1	0	0	1	1	1	1	207
NS	1	1	1	1	0	0	0	0	240

A CA is reversible if its states form only cycles in the state transition diagram; otherwise, the CA is irreversible $(Fig.1(b))$. The set of states that forms cycle ($7{\rightarrow}7$ and $9{\rightarrow}1{\rightarrow}9$ of $Fig.1(b)$) is referred to as the $attractor$. The attractors of single length cycle, that is, $7{\rightarrow}7$ of $Fig.1(b)$ is of our current interest.

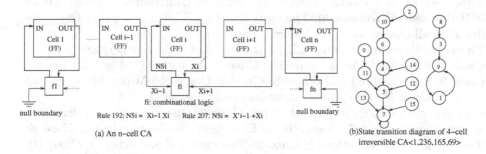

(a) An n–cell CA

Rule 192: NSi = Xi−1 Xi   Rule 207: NSi = X'i−1 +Xi

(b)State transition diagram of 4–cell
irreversible CA<1,236,165,69>

Fig. 1. Null boundary CA

3 Overview of the Proposed Test Design

In CMPs, the second level cache (L2) is shared among all the cores and the first
level caches (L1s) are kept coherent with the help of coherence protocols. In the
current presentation, we have considered the 4-state, Modified (M), Exclusive
(E), Shared (S) and Invalid (I), MESI protocol (Fig.2).

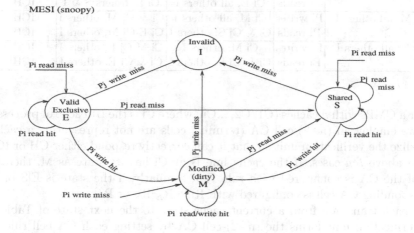

Fig. 2. 4-state MESI protocol

In column 1 of Table 2, we describe the different possible current states in
cache system. All these are coherent states -i.e. when the system is in such states,
the proposed verification unit should respond as CH (coherent). The event shown
in column 2 causes transition of a cache line's (say, B) states at different Cs (L1s)
from a current state to the desired next state (column 3). During this transition a
faulty system may record incorrect states of B at different L1s (noted in column
4). The faulty recording can be due to communication failure or some design

defect in coherence controller (CC). The effect of fault results in either CH or ICH (incoherent) (column 5). The entry 'All Cs I[S]' represents that the cache line B at all the caches are in Invalid [Shared] state.

The verification unit responds CH for the states of cache line B when-

Case 1: All caches (Cs) as I (invalid); **Case 2**: All caches (Cs) as S (shared); **Case 3**: Some caches I and others S; **Case 4**: One cache M (modified) and all others I; **Case 5**: One cache E (exclusive) and all others I.

On the other hand, for incoherent states, **Case 6**: One cache as M, at least one S and others I; **Case 7**: One cache as E, at least one S and others I; **Case 8**: Two caches as M and others I; **Case 9**: Two caches E and others I; **Case 10**: One cache M, one E and others I; - the verification unit should respond ICH.

Table 2. State transitions (MESI protocol) in the event of fault

Current cache states	Event	Desired next states	Faulty next states	Fault effect
All Cs I	Pi writes	Ci M, all others I	Ci M, all others I	CH
	Pi reads	Ci E, all others I	Ci E, all others I	CH
All Cs S	Pi writes	Ci M, all others I	Ci M, all others I	CH
			Ci M, others S & I	ICH
	Pi reads	Ci E, all others I	Ci E, others S & I	ICH
Cs are I & S	Pi writes	Ci M, all others I	Ci M, others S & I	ICH
	Pi reads	Ci E, all others I	Ci E, others S & I	ICH
Cj M, all others I	Pi writes	Ci M, all others I	Ci & Cj M, others I	ICH
	Pi reads	Ci & Cj S, others I	Ci E Cj M, others I	ICH
Cj E, all others I	Pi writes	Ci M, others I	Ci M Cj E, others I	ICH
	Pi reads	Ci & Cj S, others I	Cj & Ci E, others I	ICH

For a CMPs with n caches (C1, C2, ...Cn, where Ci is the L1 cache of processor Pi), we employ an (n+2)-cell CA (terminal cells are not representing a cache) to realize the verification unit so that it can correctly respond either CH or ICH in the above *ten* cases. If the cache line B at Ci has its state as M, then i^{th} cell of the CA is configured with rule R_M. Similarly, if the state is E[S or I], corresponding CA cell is configured with Rule $R_E[R_S$ or $R_I]$.

At each transition from a current cache state to the next state of Table 2, the verification unit forms the (n+2)-cell CA by setting each CA cell rule R_i corresponding to the cache C_i. Then the CA is run for t time steps with all 1s seed. The CA settles to either in an attractor 'CH' for coherent state or in 'ICH' for the incoherent state satisfying all the *ten* cases.

Segmented CA Based Design: The design described above requires $t=n$ (Section 4) time steps to take a decision on coherency. To realize a quick decision, an $(n+2^{p+1})$-cell CA, segmented into 2^p components (terminal cells of a segment are not representing cache) is considered.

For $p=1$, an $(n+4)$-cell CA is partitioned into two segments CA1 & CA2 each of $m = \frac{n}{2}+2$ cells. At each state transition of a cache line, the status information from C_1, C_2 ...$C_{n/2}$ forms CA1 and that of $C_{n/2+1}$...C_n forms CA2 (terminal cells of CA1/CA2 are configured with base rule as described in the next section). The CA1 & CA2 are then run in parallel for $m \approx \frac{n}{2}$ steps. The LSBs of both CA1 & CA2 dictate an inconsistency if exists (Fig. 3(a)).

4   CA Based Test Design

The scheme described in the earlier section demands that the CA constructed from R_M, R_E, R_S & R_I should form single length cycle attractors, preferably single attractor. Further, such a CA (called SACA) should correctly distinguish Case 1-5 and Case 6-10 of Section 3.

Property 1: [6] A rule $\mathcal{R}_i$ can contribute to the formation of single length cycle attractor(s) if at least one of the *RMT*s 0, 1, 4 or 5 is 0, and/or at least one of the *RMT*s 2, 3, 6 or 7 is 1.

Based on *Property1*, the 256 rules are classified [6] in 9 groups (group 0-8). The rule 207 (11001111) is in group 6 as it follows *Property1* for 6 RMTs (Fig.4). *Property 2:* [6] To form a uniform SACA with rule 'r', the 'r' must deny Property 1 for some RMTs.

Rule 48 of group 2 denies Property 1 for 6 RMTs (group 2 in *Table 3*). On the other hand, rule 192 of group 6 denies Property 1 only for 2 RMTs. Both 48 and 192 form SACA for all lengths.

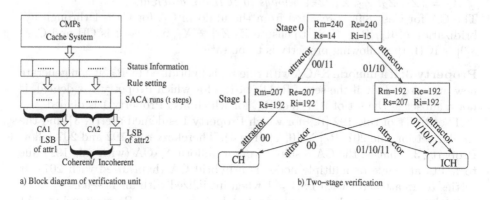

a) Block diagram of verification unit   b) Two-stage verification

Fig. 3. CA based design of verification unit

Selection of R_M, R_E, R_S, & R_I

The rules R_M, R_E, R_S & R_I required for the design should primarily form uniform SACA. That is, these should follow Property 1 and 2. Such SACA rules are shown in Table 3.

In Case 1 & 2 of Section 3, it forms uniform SACA (with attractors X_1 & X_2). For Case 3, 4 & 5, it results in hybrid CA (attractors Y_1, Y_2 & Y_3). Similarly,

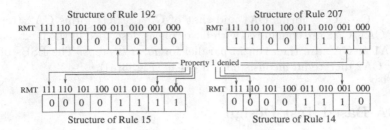

Fig. 4. Structures of rules

Table 3. CA rules for uniform SACA

group	Rule for SACA
2	34, 48
3	2, 16, 32, 42, 56, 98, 112, 162, 176
4	0, 10, 15, 24, 40, 66, 80, 85, 96
	130, 144, 160, 170, 184, 226, 240, 255
5	8, 64, 128, 138, 143, 152, 168, 194, 208, 213, 224
6	136, 192

the CA formed in Case 6 to 10 are also hybrid (attractors Z_1, Z_2, Z_3, Z_4 & Z_5 respectively). The best selection of R_M, R_E, R_S & R_I, therefore, should satisfy

   Cond 1: $A_1 = \{X_1, X_2, Y_1, Y_2, Y_3\}$ *belongs to CH and*

   $A_2 = \{Z_1, Z_2, Z_3, Z_4, Z_5\}$ *belongs to ICH are different.*

The CA for Case 8[9] is resulted from the uniform CA for Case 1 through hybridization of $R_M[R_E]$. Now, to ensure $Z_3[Z_4] \neq X_1$, as Case 1 is CH and Case 8[9] is ICH, the following property is to be satisfied.

Property 3: If a uniform SACA with rule R_o is hybridized by R_h, it can generate new attractors only if the set of RMTs of R_o, for which Property 1 is denied, is not a subset of the set of RMTs of R_h, for which also Property 1 is denied.

   The RMTs of rule 192 [R_o] for which Property 1 is denied are $\{2, 3\}$ and the similar set for rule 207 [R_h] is $\{0, 1\}$ (Fig.4). Therefore, rule 192 and 207 follow Property 3. That is, the CA resulted from a uniform SACA (with rule 192) due to faults at single or multiple nodes is a hybrid CA (hybridized with 207). It settles to an attractor with LSB = 1 when initialized with all 1s seed.

   In the design for $p=1$, we need to select R_M, R_E, R_S & R_I configuring CA1 and CA2 such that CA1 & CA2 as a whole satisfy *cond 1*. Here, both the CA formed for Case 4[5] and Case 8[9] are resulted from hybridization of SACA of Case 1.

   It can be shown that the scheme to select one set of R_M, R_E, R_S & R_I, satisfying *Cond 1*, is hard. Therefore, we propose a 2-stage (Stage 0 & Stage 1) solution to satisfy *Cond 1* assuming even number of L1 caches in the system.

Stage 0: In stage 0, we choose R_M=240, R_I=15, R_E=240 and R_S=14. This combination of rules forms two different classes of CA1 & CA2 with attractors'

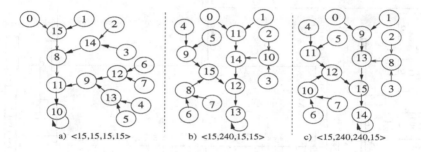

Fig. 5. State transition diagrams of uniform and hybrid CA

LSB pair '00'/'11' & '01'/'10' for all 1s initial seed. LSBs '00'/'11' signify Case 1 (Fig.5(a)), Case 2, Case 3 (not shown), & Case 8, 9, 10 (Fig.5(c)). On the other hand, '01'/'10' signify Case 4, 5 (Fig.5(b)), and Case 6 & 7 (not shown). This classification violates *cond 1* and is corrected in stage 1.

For example, in Case 4, CA1 with rule 15 is hybridized with one 240 and CA2 is uniform with rule 15. These two settle to attractors *attr1* with LSB 1 (Fig.5(b)) and *attr2* with LSB 0 (Fig.5(a)). The LSB pair is '10'. On the other hand, if CA2 is hybridized with rule $240(R_M)$ and CA1 is uniform with rule 15, the attractors' LSB pair is '01'.

Theorem 1. *The null boundary n-cell CA, configured with rule 15 and 240 in any sequence, forms SACA and depth of the CA is n.*

Theorem 2. *If a null-boundary CA, configured with rule 15, is hybridized with rule 14, its state transition behavior remains as that of the uniform CA configured with rule 15 -that is, rule 14 is absorbed into rule 15.*

Stage 1: For differentiating Case 8, 9 & 10 from Case 1, 2 & 3 at the end of stage 0, we select $R_M=207$, $R_E=207$, $R_S=192$ & $R_I=192$. LSBs of the attractors of CA1 & CA2 are then '00' (CH) for Case 1, 2, & 3 and '01'/'10'/'11' (ICH) for Case 8, 9, & 10. Here the terminal cells are set to 192 (base rule).

To distinguish Case 4 & Case 5 from Case 6 & Case 7, we select $R_M=192$, $R_E=192$, $R_S=207$ & $R_I=192$. The presence of 'S' state (Case 6 & Case 7) outputs the LSB pair of the attractors of CA1 & CA2 '01'/'10'/'11' and LSB pair '00' indicates Case 4 & 5. The two stage process is described in Fig.3(b).

Hardware realization

The hardware realization of the design (with $p=1$ i.e. the CA is segmented into CA1 & CA2) is shown in Fig.6. The states M, E, S and I of a cache line are represented as the 00, 01, 11 and 10 respectively. The 32 to 1 multiplexer (MUX) and other combinational logic generate the next state of a CA cell. For example, if the cache line B's state at i^{th} cache (Ci) is 'modified' (R_M) -that is, $P_{i1}P_{i0}=00$ and *attr1* & *attr2* at Stage 0 is 11, then the rule selected for i^{th} CA cell at Stage 1 is 207. In Fig.6, this sets the select lines of MUX as 00111. It implies, output

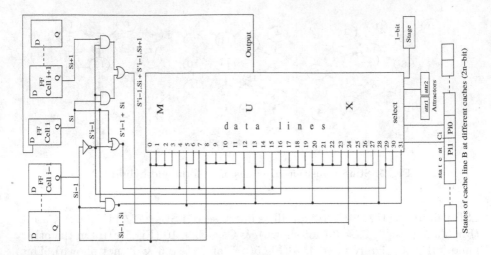

Fig. 6. Hardware realization of the CA based design of verification unit

of the MUX is $S'_{i-1}+S_i$ -that is, rule 207. The part of next state logic (shown in Fig.6), is also shared in realizing the next state logic of cell (i-1) & (i+1).

5   Experimental Results

This section reports experimental results establishing the effectiveness of proposed CA-based test design. In experimentation, we consider CMPs with 16 to 1024 processors (column 1 of Table 4). The possible sequence of states of a cache line B at different C_is is noted in Column 2. The combinations of states for CA1 and CA2 are shown in Column 3 and 4. The *attr1* & *attr2* at stage 0 & stage 1 are noted in the columns 5, 6, 7 and 8 (LSBs indicated by boldfaces). It can be observed that the LSB pair of *attr1* & *attr2* at stage 1 correctly indicates whether the cache states are in coherent state ('00' for coherent(CH), '01'/'10'/'11' for incoherent(ICH), shown in last column).

6   Conclusion

This work proposes an efficient solution for quick determination of data inconsistencies in caches. The solution targets the Chip Multiprocessors with thousands of processor cores. It avoids rigorous computational and communication overhead assuring robust and scalable design. The proposed design is developed around the regular structure of Cellular Automata. This enables simple hardware realization of the design leading to quick identification of cache incoherency.

Table 4. Experimental results

# of P	Cache states	Configuration of		Attractors				Decision
		CA1	CA2	Stage0		Stage1		
				Attr1	Attr2	Attr1	Attr2	
16	I I...I	I I...I	I I...I	1010...10	1010...10	0...0	0...0	CH
	S S...S	S S...S	S S...S	1...0	1...0	0...0	0...0	CH
	I S...I	I S...I	I S...I	1010...10	1010...10	0...0	0...0	CH
		S S...S	I S...I	1...0	1010...10	0...0	0...0	CH
		I I...I	I S...I	1010...10	1010...10	0...0	0...0	CH
		I I...I	S S...S	1010...10	1010...10	0...0	0...0	CH
	I M I...I	I M I...I	I I...I	10...1	10...0	0...0	0...0	CH
	I E I...I	I E I...I	I I...I	10...1	10...0	0...0	0...0	CH
	I M S I...I	I M S...I	I S...I	10...1	10...0	0...1	0...0	ICH
	I E S I...I	I E S...I	I S...I	10...1	10...0	0...1	0...0	ICH
		I M M I...I	I...I	10...0	10...0	0...1	0...0	ICH
	I M M I...I	I M I...I	I M I...I	1...1	1...1	0...1	0...1	ICH
		I E E I...I	I...I	10...0	10...0	0...1	0...0	ICH
	I E E I...I	I E I...I	I E I...I	1...1	1...1	0...1	0...1	ICH
		I M E I...I	I...I	10...0	10...0	0...1	0...0	ICH
	I M E I...I	I M I...I	I E I...I	1...1	1...1	0...1	0...1	ICH
128	I I...I	I I...I	I I...I	1010...10	1010...10	0...0	0...0	CH
	S S...S	S S...S	S S...S	1...0	1...0	0...0	0...0	CH
	I S...I	I S...I	I S...I	1010...10	1010...10	0...0	0...0	CH
		S S...S	I S...I	1...0	1010...10	0...0	0...0	CH
		I I...I	I S...I	1010...10	1010...10	0...0	0...0	CH
		I I...I	S S...S	1010...10	1010...10	0...0	0...0	CH
	I M I...I	I M I...I	I I...I	10...1	10...0	0...0	0...0	CH
	I E I...I	I E I...I	I I...I	10...1	10...0	0...0	0...0	CH
	I M S I...I	I M S...I	I S...I	10...1	10...0	0...1	0...0	ICH
	I E S I...I	I E S...I	I S...I	10...1	10...0	0...1	0...0	ICH
		I M M I...I	I...I	10...0	10...0	0...1	0...0	ICH
	I M M I...I	I M I...I	I M I...I	1...1	1...1	0...1	0...1	ICH
		I E E I...I	I...I	10...0	10...0	0...1	0...0	ICH
	I E E I...I	I E I...I	I E I...I	1...1	1...1	0...1	0...1	ICH
		I M E I...I	I...I	10...0	10...0	0...1	0...0	ICH
	I M E I...I	I M I...I	I E I...I	1...1	1...1	0...1	0...1	ICH

Table 4. (*Continued*)

# of P	Cache states	Configuration of CA1	Configuration of CA2	Attractors Stage0 Attr1	Attractors Stage0 Attr2	Attractors Stage1 Attr1	Attractors Stage1 Attr2	Decision
1024	I I...I	I I...I	I I...I	1010...10	1010...10	0...0	0...0	CH
	S S...S	S S...S	S S...S	1...0	1...0	0...0	0...0	CH
	I S...I	I S...I	I S...I	1010...10	1010...10	0...0	0...0	CH
		S S...S	I S...I	1...0	1010...10	0...0	0...0	CH
		I I...I	I S...I	1010...10	1010...10	0...0	0...0	CH
		I I...I	S S...S	1010...10	1010...10	0...0	0...0	CH
	I M I...I	I M I...I	I I...I	10...1	10...0	0...0	0...0	CH
	I E I...I	I E I...I	I I...I	10...1	10...0	0...0	0...0	CH
	I M S I...I	I M S...I	I S...I	10...1	10...0	0...1	0...0	ICH
	I E S I...I	I E S...I	I S...I	10...1	10...0	0...1	0...0	ICH
		I M M I...I	I...I	10...0	10...0	0...1	0...0	ICH
	I M M I...I	I M I...I	I M I...I	1...1	1...1	0...1	0...1	ICH
		I E E I...I	I...I	10...0	10...0	0...1	0...0	ICH
	I E E I...I	I E I...I	I E I...I	1...1	1...1	0...1	0...1	ICH
		I M E I...I	I...I	10...0	10...0	0...1	0...0	ICH
	I M E I...I	I M I...I	I E I...I	1...1	1...1	0...1	0...1	ICH

References

1. Shivakumar, P., Kistler, M., Keckler, S.W., Burger, D., Alvisi, L.: Modeling the effect of technology trends on the soft error rate of combinational logic. In: International Conference on Dependable Systems and Networks, pp. 389–398 (June 2002)
2. Wang, H., Baldawa, S., Sangireddy, R.: Dynamic Error Detection for Dependable Cache Coherency in Multicore Architecture. VLSI Design (January 2008)
3. Cheng, L., Muralimanohar, N., Ramani, K., Balasubrsmonian, R., Carter, J.B.: Interconnect-Aware Coherence Protocols for Chip Multiprocessors. In: The 33rd IEEE International Symposium on Computer Architecture, ISCA 2006 (2006)
4. Subramanyan, P., Singh, V., Saluja, K.K., Larsson, E.: Energy-Efficient Fault Tolerance in Chip Multiprocessors Using Critical Value Forwarding. In: 2010 IEEE/IIFIP International Conference on Dependable Systems & Networks, DSN (2010)
5. Pal Chaudhuri, P., Roy Chowdhury, D., Nandi, S., Chatterjee, S.: Additive Cellular Automata – Theory and Applications, vol. 1. IEEE Computer Society Press, California (1997) ISBN 0-8186-7717-1
6. Das, S., Naskar, N.N., Mukherjee, S., Dalui, M., Sikdar, B.K.: Characterization of CA Rules for SACA Targeting Detection of Faulty Nodes in WSN. In: Bandini, S., Manzoni, S., Umeo, H., Vizzari, G. (eds.) ACRI 2010. LNCS, vol. 6350, pp. 300–311. Springer, Heidelberg (2010)
7. Dalui, M., Sikdar, B.K.: An Efficient Test Design for Verification of Cache Coherence in CMPs. In: EmbeddedCom 2011 (2011)

An Efficient High Speed Implementation
of Flexible Characteristic-2 Multipliers
on FPGAs

Debapriya Basu Roy and Debdeep Mukhopadhyay

Dept. of Computer Science and Engineering
Indian Institute of Technology Kharagpur, India
{dbroy,debdeep}@cse.iitkgp.ernet.in

Abstract. Multipliers which can support flexible input size are a crucial component of finite field processors. The present paper targets efficient VLSI design of such variable size multipliers, operating on characteristic 2 field polynomials with degree varying to 512 bits. In order to optimize the area, and speed the design employs a sequential architecture, utilizing the Karatsuba-Ofman decomposition. The architecture reduces the critical path by designing an *overlap free* variant of the original Karatsuba algorithm. Apart from exploring wrt. the design parameters, namely levels and thresholding for Karatsuba multipliers, the paper also observes the effect of combinations of overlap free and naive Karatsuba multipliers on the overall area and speed. The results show that on a standard Virtex-4 platform, two levels of overlap free Karatsuba multipliers provides better area-time product and lesser computation delay.

Keywords: Flexible Multiplier, Karatsuba Algorithm, Characteristic-2 Finite Field.

1 Introduction

Extended binary fields ($GF(2^n)$) have significant importance in several mathematical and engineering applications like communication, error correcting codes and cryptography. Multiplication is a key operations, as the more complex algorithm use repeated multiplications, and their performance in turn relies on that of the underlying field multiplier. Unlike application specific circuits, which lacks programmability, an important field of research is to develop cryptographic processors, which are capable of performing finite field operations. For such applications, programmability is imperative, and hence the underlying data-path units should be flexible. However designs of such flexible hardwares can be challenging, as unlike softwares in hardware architectures we do not have the privilege of dynamic memory allocations. Thus the architecture needs to be developed with suitable techniques to optimize area, and yet have a less computational delay. In this paper, we describe the FPGA design of a flexible polynomial multiplier in characteristic-2 field. However it may be noted that we focus on the multiplication steps alone, and not the final modular reduction.

H. Rahaman et al. (Eds.): VDAT 2012, LNCS 7373, pp. 99–110, 2012.
© Springer-Verlag Berlin Heidelberg 2012

Surprisingly, in the literature although there are several works on multiplier designs, but there are very few reported results on flexible multiplier designs. Clearly, the performance of the multiplier design depends on the complexity of the algorithm employed for the multiplication. There are a large number of known multiplication techniques, of quadratic complexity. Multiplication using Fast Fourier Transform (FFT) has lowest algorithmic complexity, $(nlogn)$; however, conversion to the frequency domain has significant overhead for multiplication. Karatsuba algorithm has sub-quadratic complexity $(n^{log_2 3})$ [8] without requiring any conversion. Karatsuba algorithm relies on a decomposition, where we express a multiplication step by few addition operations. However designing a Karatsuba multiplier requires to set the threshold in a proper fashion, thresholding implying the level when we stop the Karatsuba decomposition. Karatsuba algorithm was generalized so that it can support multiplication of polynomials of arbitrary degree [8]. It was shown that in most of the cases simple recursive Karatsuba algorithm works better than the general recursive Karatsuba algorithm.

Overlap free Karatsuba algorithm is introduced in [3]. In this case the input polynomials are divided into odd and even coefficients. The advantage in this algorithm is that it eliminates the overlap in normal Karatsuba algorithm. This property may be exploited while designing a multiplier for flexible dimensions, as it may help to reduce the critical path of each stage of multiplication.

Having fixed the multiplication algorithm, the next important step is to investigate the architecture of the multiplier and their choices. While for fixed length multipliers combinational circuits work, sequential circuits may be preferred for flexible multipliers. The reason for this choice is two fold: a combinational circuit for a flexible length multiplier will imply that the resource required is that of the largest operand size, which means there is huge area wastage. However designing the circuit for a properly chosen underlying dimension, and then iterating the hardware gives an opportunity for proper trade-off between the resource requirement and the computation time needed. The second reason, being in a processor one would expect that a small size multiplication will require less instruction cycles compared to a larger multiplication. Hence keeping uniformity, a flexible multiplier which is often used as an important data-path unit for a processor, would also manifest such a variation when designed with a sequential circuit. However we stress that a proper mixing of sequential and combinational architecture is needed for a better design.

There has been several works in the field of designing multipliers in $GF(2^n)$, where n is fixed. In [1], finite field processor for $GF(2^{163})$ is implemented based on bit parallel word serial multiplier. However the design is suited for ASIC designs. In [7], both parallel and sequential multipliers are proposed. In the core of their architecture, a 64 bit recursive Karatsuba multiplier is employed. The 64 bit recursive Karatsuba multiplier is designed by 16 bit and 32 bit multipliers and this approach is followed in the subsequent higher bit multiplications. As they have showed in the result, the parallel architecture though faster than the sequential one, consumes large area. In [4], a hybrid approach of designing multipliers have been introduced. A 240 bit multiplier is designed by 120 bit, 60 bit and 30 bit multipliers. They have shown that this hybrid approach improves the result wrt. time and area trade-offs. In [5], a hybrid 233 bit combinational Karatsuba multiplier is designed and implemented suited for FPGA platforms. Simple recursive Karatsuba algorithm is followed up to a threshold level, below which generalized algorithm is employed. The design though fully combinational and fast, consumes significant area. Recently in [9] an extensive complexity and implementation analysis of bit parallel Karatsuba-Ofman multiplier is discussed. They have provided methodology for optimum design of Karatsuba multipliers on both ASIC and FPGAs. However to the best of our knowledge, there are no reported works on efficient designs when the arguments are variable; this scenario is the focus of the present paper. In [2], authors have proposed a Karatsuba based Montgomery multiplier. The author have presented their result on 128 bits, 256 bits and 512 bits multipliers.

In this paper, we present the architecture for multiplication of variable sized inputs using overlap free Karatsuba multiplications. The design is capable of multiplying inputs of size upto 512 bits.

The proposed architecture in its core uses 128 bit overlap free Karatsuba combinational multiplier. This combinational multiplier is iterated, depending upon the input size, by the control unit to compute the product. The input multiplicands are split in to odd and even terms according to the overlap free Karatsuba decomposition.

We also investigate performance variation for algorithmic level combination of normal and overlap free Karatsuba algorithm. This multiplier is designed with the goal of using it in a processor.

2 Preliminaries

In this section we will discuss some multiplication algorithms which are required to understand the present paper. Each element of $GF(2^n)$ can be represented as a polynomial of degree n-1. Hence multiplication in $GF(2^n)$ is polynomial multiplication of two elements.

2.1 Schoolbook Multiplication

This is the common method to multiply two polynomials. Let A(x) and B(x) be the element of $GF(2^n)$. Then

$$C(x) = \sum_{i=0}^{n-1} \sum_{j=0}^{n-1} a_i . b_j . x^{i+j}. \tag{1}$$

where

$$A(x) = \sum_{i=0}^{n-1} a_i . x^i, B(x) = \sum_{j=0}^{n-1} b_j . x^j \tag{2}$$

It can be clearly seen that the above algorithm has quadratic complexity. Hence this algorithm is inefficient if no. of bit increases.

2.2   Karatsuba Multiplication

In Karatsuba Multiplication, the operands are divided into two parts. If A(x) and B(x) are the two polynomials, they can be divided into two parts in the following way,

$$A(x) = A_h.x^{n/2} + A_l, B(x) = B_h.x^{n/2} + B_l$$

Their product C(x) can be obtained in the following way. In finite field addition and subtraction is equivalent to xor operation

$$
\begin{aligned}
C(x) &= A(x).B(x) \\
&= (A_h.x^{n/2} + A_l).(B_h.x^{n/2} + B_l) \\
&= (A_h.B_h)x^n + (A_h.B_l + A_l.B_h)x^n/2 + A_l.B_l \\
&= A_h.B_h.x^n + ((A_h + A_l)(B_h + B_l) + A_h.B_h + A_L.B_l)x^{n/2} + A_l.B_l
\end{aligned}
\tag{3}
$$

In the third line of the equation, number of addition required is three and multiplication required is four. Where as in the fourth line, number of addition required is four and multiplication required is three. The speed up in Karatsuba algorithm is obtained by decreasing the number of multiplication and increasing the number of addition, which is less costly operation than multiplication. However Karatsuba decomposition generates over-lapped operands, which involve extra delay.

2.3   Overlap-Free Karatsuba Algorithm

In [3], authors have given a modified algorithm to eliminate those extra xor gate delays due to overlap. This variant of Karatsuba algorithm, known as Overlap-free Karatsuba algorithm. In this section we will illustrate this algorithm.

If A(x) and B(x) are two elements of $GF(2^n)$ and $n = 2m$ then

$$A(x) = \sum_{i=0}^{n-1} a_i.x^i = \sum_{i=0}^{m-1} a_{2i}.x^{2i} + x.\sum_{i=0}^{m-1} a_{2i+1}.x^{2i} \tag{4}$$

$$B(x) = \sum_{i=0}^{n-1} b_i.x^i = \sum_{i=0}^{m-1} b_{2i}.x^{2i} + x.\sum_{i=0}^{m-1} b_{2i+1}.x^{2i} \tag{5}$$

Now if we consider $y = x^2$, then we can write $A(x) = A_e(y) + x.A_o(y)$ and $B(x) = B_e(y) + x.B_o(y)$. Their product C(x) will be

$$
\begin{aligned}
C(x) &= (A_e(y) + xA_o(y))(B_e(y) + xB_o(y)) \\
&= (A_e(y).B_e(y) + y^2 A_o(y).B_o(y)) \\
&\quad + x((A_e(y) + A_o(y))(B_e(y) + B_o(y)) + A_e(y)B_e(y) + A_o(y)B_o(y))
\end{aligned}
\tag{6}
$$

In this case there is no overlap as we have separated the product in even and odd terms.

3   Design of Sequential Overlap Free Karatsuba Multiplier

In this section, we will propose a sequential flexible overlap free Karatsuba multiplier. The full architecture is shown in figure 2. Input to the multiplier is given through a buffer. Input to the buffer are provided as 64 bit block. As in a processor, the operands are stored in registers, it is assumed here that the multiplicands are stored in 64 bit registers. Input buffer stores contents of those registers and pass them to the multiplier. Another input r, denoting the number of 64 bit blocks given as input, is given to the buffer. A signal *load* is made high to indicate the completion of input loading.

The full architecture of the multiplier can be divided into three parts:

- **Splitting:**
  The first step in the algorithm is the splitting of the multiplicands. The architecture has two modules to do this: *break odd-even 256* and the *break odd-even 512*. These blocks are used only if the multiplicands are larger than 128 bits. For multiplicand sizes between 129 to 256, the *break odd-even 256* block is utilized while both blocks are used for multiplicands larger than 256 bits.
- **Combinational Multiplier:** The architecture uses 128 bit combinational overlap free Karatsuba multiplier. The size of combinational multiplier is an important design criteria of the multiplier architecture. If n is the number of iteration required to compute m bit multiplication (m is power of 2) using x bit combinational multiplier (x is power of 2), n is given by following formula

$$n = 3^{log_2(m/x)} \qquad (7)$$

  It is shown in figure 1 that a 512 bit multiplication is same as nine, 128 bit multiplications. Now, each 128 bit multiplication is equivalent to three 64 bit multiplications and nine 32 bit multiplication.
  Thus, 512 bit multiplication can be further split into 27, 64 bit multiplications and 81, 32 bit multiplication. If 128 bit combinational multiplier is used, 512 bit multiplication can be computed by nine iterations of the combinational multiplier. For a 64 bit and 32 bit combinational multiplier, 27 and 81 iterations will be required to compute 512 bit multiplication. As number of iterations increases number of clock cycles required, size of the combinational multiplier is chosen as 128. In [6], the author have shown that below a threshold level, classical multiplication is more efficient than Karatsuba algorithm. In our design, the combinational multiplier uses school book multiplication below a threshold level. Threshold operand size in this combinational multiplier is chosen to be 16.
- **Combining:** Xor block present in the architecture combines the input according to the overlap free Karatsuba algorithm. Output of the combinational multiplier is stored in the 256 bit registers. Contents of those registers are xored and the result is stored in the 512 bit registers. If the operand size

lies between 1-128 the output is obtained at the output of the combinational multiplier. If the operand size lies between 129-256, product is obtained by xoring the contents of 256 bit registers. For the operand size lying between 257-512, product is obtained by xoring the contents of 512 bit registers. A signal *done* is made high to indicate that the product computation is over.

Product is stored in a 1024 bit register. From it, output bits are produced in block of 128 bits. After transferring output, a signal *complete* is made high to indicate that the multiplier is ready to accept another input.

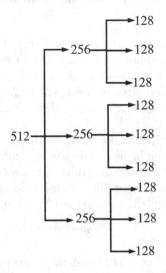

Fig. 1. Breaking of 512 bit multiplication into 9, 128 bit multiplications

3.1   Algorithm Combinations for Multiplier

Multiplication operation can be divided into three stages shown in figure 3. Different stages can be designed by either normal Karatsuba or overlapfree Karatsuba. In the proposed multiplier, splitting of the multiplicands, combinational multiplication and combining the output of combinational multiplier is done according to the overlap free Karatsuba algorithm. The algorithm for these three steps can be changed into normal Karatsuba algorithm and a new architecture can be designed. It is possible to design four different architecture by combining the normal Karatsuba and overlap free Karatsuba. The all possible design configurations are displayed in table 1. We have given a design name to each entry of table 1 and implementation result of them are displayed in section 5.

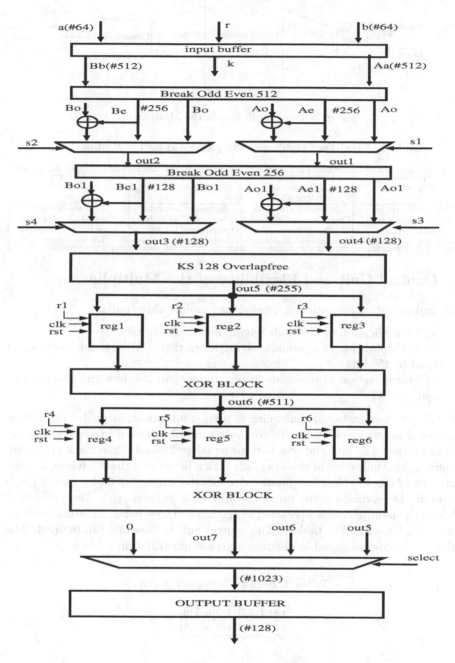

Fig. 2. Design Architecture of the Sequential Overlap Free Karatsuba Multiplier

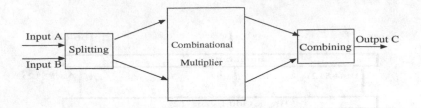

Fig. 3. Different Stages in the Multiplier

Table 1. Algorithm Combinations Implemented for the Multiplication

Splitting Algorithm	Combinational Multiplier Algorithm	Combining Algorithm	Design Name
Normal Karatsuba	Normal Karatsuba	Normal Karatsuba	Normal-Normal
Normal Karatsuba	Overlap free Karatsuba	Normal Karatsuba	Normal-Overlap free
Overlap free Karatsuba	Normal Karatsuba	Overlap free Karatsuba	Overlap free-Normal
Overlap free Karatsuba	Overlap free Karatsuba	Overlap free Karatsuba	Overlap free-Overlap free

4   Control Unit and Flexibility of the Multiplier

The multiplication operation is divided into mainly three parts:

- (a) Multiplication of operands having less than 128 bits
- (b) Multiplication of operands having more than 128 bits and less than or equal to 256 bits
- (c) Multiplication of operands having more than 256 bits and less than or equal to 512

As 128 bit combinational multiplier is used, multiplication up to 128 bits is computed in two clock cycles. To compute multiplication of two operands having more than 128 bits and less than or equal to 256 bits, five clock cycles are required. Multiplication of two operands which have more than 256 bits, is computed in 12 clock cycles. The input r denotes the number of 64 bit blocks given as input. Depending on the input r, value of k is computed. The value of k divides the multiplication operation in the above three parts. Relation between r and k is illustrated in table 2. The control unit is illustrated in figure 4. The value of the control signal in different states is illustrated in table 3.

Table 2. Relation between r and k

r	0	1	2	3	4	5	6	7	8
k	0	1	1	4	4	8	8	8	8

If no. of clock cycle required is c, then the value of c is given by following formula

$$c = 3^{log_2(k/2)} + \lfloor k/4 \rfloor + 1 \qquad (8)$$

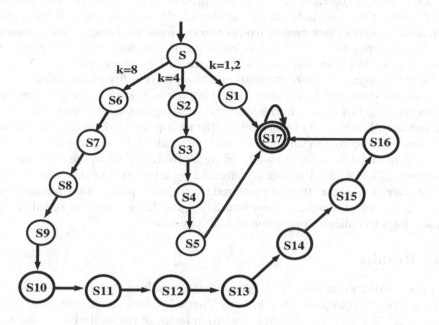

Fig. 4. FSM of Control Unit

Table 3. Control Signals

states	done	s1	s2	s3	s4	r1	r2	r3	r4	r5	r6	select	outputwrite
S	0	1	1	1	1	0	0	0	0	0	0	0	0
S1	0	1	1	1	1	0	0	0	0	0	0	1	1
S2	0	1	1	0	0	1	0	0	0	0	0	0	0
S3	0	1	1	1	1	0	1	0	0	0	0	0	0
S4	0	1	1	2	2	0	0	1	0	0	0	0	0
S5	0	1	1	2	2	0	0	0	0	0	0	2	1
S6	0	0	0	0	0	1	0	0	0	0	0	0	0
S7	0	0	0	1	1	0	1	0	0	0	0	0	0
S8	0	0	0	2	2	0	0	1	0	0	0	0	0
S9	0	1	1	0	0	1	0	0	1	0	0	0	0
S10	0	1	1	1	1	0	1	0	0	0	0	0	0
S11	0	1	1	2	2	0	0	1	0	0	0	0	0
S12	0	2	2	0	0	1	0	0	0	1	0	0	0
S13	0	2	2	1	1	0	1	0	0	0	0	0	0
S14	0	2	2	2	2	0	0	1	0	0	0	0	0
S15	0	2	2	2	2	0	0	0	0	0	1	0	0
S16	0	0	0	1	1	0	0	0	0	0	0	3	1
S17	1	1	1	2	2	0	0	0	0	0	1	2	0

First part of the right hand side indicate the iteration of the combinational multiplier. Next part indicate the number of clock cycles required for register update. An extra clock cycle is required to store the final output into a register.

For example, for a 233 bit multiplication, the multiplicands will come in 4 blocks of 64 bits each(last block will require 23 bits of zero padding). Value of 'r' is set to four and the multiplication is computed in five clock cycles.

Control states can be classified into three parts. State S1 relates to any multiplication up to 128 bits. In this state, no splitting is done. Product is produced in one iteration. State S2 to S5 relate to the multiplication between 129-256 bits. Product is computed in three iteration of the combinational multiplier. An extra state is required for register update. State S6 to S16 relate to the multiplication between 257-512 bits. Product is computed by 9 iteration of the combinational multiplier. Two extra states are required for register update. After product computation, control unit fsm moves into S17 state. In this state, a signal *done* is made high to indicate completion of multiplication.

5 Results

In this section we present the implementation result of the proposed multiplier. the multiplier is implemented on both Virtex-5(xc5vlx330-2fft760) and Virtex-4(xc4vfx140-11ff1517). The implementation result of the multiplier according to the design configuration is presented in table 4. and table 5. 512 bits combinational multiplier when implemented on Virtex-5, slice requirement is found to be 14646 which is much greater than the proposed multiplier. In case of Virtex-4, the slice requirement of 512 bit combinational multiplier is 32,219 which is very high.

Table 4. Implementation Result on Virtex-5(xc5vlx330-2fft760)

Design type	Slices	LUTs	Flip-flops	Time-period (ns)	No. of Bits	Clock Cycles	Computation Time(ns)	AT Product(μs)
Normal-Normal	3035	8485	4396	12.9	1-128	2	25.7	78.1
					129-256	5	64.4	195.3
					257-512	12	154.5	468.8
Normal-Overlap free	3148	8454	4399	12.8	1-128	2	25.7	80.7
					129-256	5	64.1	201.6
					257-512	12	153.8	483.9
Overlap free-Normal	3128	9750	4395	12.9	1-128	2	25.9	80.9
					129-256	5	64.7	202.2
					257-512	12	155.2	485.3
Overlap free-Overlap free	3711	9558	4393	12.1	1-128	2	24.1	89.6
					129-256	5	60.3	223.9
					257-512	12	144.9	537.6

Table 5. Implementation Result on Virtex-4(xc4vfx140-11ff1517)

Design type	Slices	LUTs	Flip-flops	Time-period (ns)	No. of Bits	Clock Cycles	Computation Time(ns)	AT Product(μs)
Normal-Normal	7198	10845	4473	16.1	1-128	2	32.1	230.9
					129-256	5	80.2	577.5
					257-512	12	192.6	1385.9
Normal-Overlap free	6978	10472	4407	16.9	1-128	2	33.9	235.9
					129-256	5	84.6	589.9
					257-512	12	202.9	1415.8
Overlap free-Normal	10052	12974	7850	13.6	1-128	2	27.2	273.5
					129-256	5	68.1	683.7
					257-512	12	163.2	1640.9
Overlap free-Overlap free	7801	12250	4146	13.9	1-128	2	27.8	216.7
					129-256	5	69.4	541.6
					257-512	12	166.6	1299.9

6 Conclusion

In this paper, we have presented a sequential variable size multiplication architecture in $GF(2^n)$. The proposed architecture can support up to 512 bits multiplication. Sequential architecture of the multiplier enable us to optimize area and speed. We have analyzed and implemented all possible combination of *normal* and *overlapfree* Karatsuba. Experimental validation of the multipliers has been performed on Virtex-4 and Virtex-5 platforms. Result shows that $Overlapfree - Overlapfree$ gives better AT product value in Virtex-4 platform. However in Virtex-5 $Normal - Normal$ gives better value of AT product.

References

1. Fourth International Conference on Information Technology: New Generations (ITNG 2007), April 2-4, Las Vegas, Nevada, USA. IEEE Computer Society (2007)
2. Chow, G.C.T., Eguro, K., Luk, W., Leong, P.: A karatsuba-based montgomery multiplier. In: Proceedings of the 2010 International Conference on Field Programmable Logic and Applications, FPL 2010, pp. 434–437. IEEE Computer Society, Washington, DC (2010)
3. Fan, H., Sun, J., Gu, M., Lam, K.-Y.: Overlap-free karatsuba-ofman polynomial multiplication algorithms. IACR Cryptology ePrint Archive 2007:393 (2007)
4. Preneel, B., Tavares, S. (eds.): SAC 2005. LNCS, vol. 3897. Springer, Heidelberg (2006)
5. Rebeiro, C.: Architecture Explorations For Elliptic Curve Cryptography On FPGAs (February 2009)
6. Rebeiro, C., Mukhpodhyay, D.: Power attack resistant efficient fpga architecture for karatsuba multiplier. In: Proceedings of the 21st International Conference on VLSI Design, VLSID 2008, pp. 706–711. IEEE Computer Society, Washington, DC (2008)

7. Wajih, E.-H., Mohsen, M., Medien, Z., Belgacem, B.: Efficient hardware architecture of recursive karatsuba-ofman multiplier. In: 3rd International Conference on Design and Technology of Integrated Systems in Nanoscale Era, DTIS 2008, pp. 1–6 (March 2008)
8. Weimerskirch, A., Paar, C.: Generalizations of the Karatsuba Algorithm for Efficient Implementations. Cryptology ePrint Archive, Report 2006/224 (2006)
9. Zhou, G., Michalik, H., Hinsenkamp, L.: Complexity analysis and efficient implementations of bit parallel finite field multipliers based on karatsuba-ofman algorithm on fpgas. IEEE Transactions on Very Large Scale Integration (VLSI) Systems 18(7), 1057–1066 (2010)

Arithmetic Algorithms
for Ternary Number System

Subrata Das[1], Partha Sarathi Dasgupta[2], and Samar Sensarma[1]

[1] Department of Computer Science & Engineering
University of Calcutta
{dsubrata.mt,sssarma2010}@gmail.com
[2] Management Information Systems Group
Indian Institute of Management Calcutta
partha@iimcal.ac.in

Abstract. The use of multi-valued logic in VLSI circuits can reduce the chip area significantly. Moreover, there are several additional advantages of using multi-valued logic in VLSI over the conventional Binary logic, such as energy efficiency, cost-effectiveness and so on. It has been shown that Base-3 number system is nearly optimal for computation. In this paper we have studied some existing logical operation on ternary number system. We have also discussed some of the existing arithmetic operations using ternary number system. Some new algorithms for arithmetic operations have also been proposed, and shown to be quite efficient in time complexity.

Keywords: Ternary number, trit, arithmetic algorithms, 3-valued logic, VLSI.

1 Introduction

Numbers are counted in tens by human beings simply because we use our ten fingers for counting. Digital computations are based on binary logic because of digital devices having two states: ON and OFF. There are countably infinite number of ways to represent numbers. The number of digits used to represent numbers and the size of the base are two parameters to select a number system. For a unary number system only one symbol is required to represent a number but the number of digits required is high. On the other hand if the value of base is high, then less number of digits is required to represent a number, and the number of different symbols required is large. In order to have an optimal number system the product of base(b) and width (w) (i.e. number of symbols used to represent a number) should be minimized [1] where b^w is a constant. It is found that for optimal result the base should be chosen as e. As 3 is the integer nearest to e, base 3 i.e. ternary number system is a good choice for representing a number. Ternary logic has some advantages over traditional binary logic. The information content can be increased by using ternary logic instead of using conventional binary logic. It is expected that the use of ternary logic in

H. Rahaman et al. (Eds.): VDAT 2012, LNCS 7373, pp. 111–120, 2012.

VLSI implementations should be energy efficient and cost effective[7]. Moreover, arithmetic operations can be performed at higher speed compared to binary logic.

2   Preliminaries

In this section we discuss about some basic concepts of ternary number system, ternary logic and ternary gates.

2.1   Ternary Number

Three different symbols 0,1,2 are used to represent ternary number system.In ternary system the term trit is used to represent ternary digit One of the major issue is how we can represent a negative number in ternary number system. One easy solution is to use signed $3's$ complement representation to represent negative ternary numbers.

$3's$ complement of any ternary number can be obtained as $3^n - N$ where N is the ternary number and n is the number of trits. If the value of sign digit of a ternary number is 0 or 1 then the number can be taken as a positive number and if sign digit is 2 then the number is negative.

For example $A = 02101$, $B = 11210$ are two positive numbers and $C = 21020$ is a negative number since it's sign trit is 2.

2.2   Balanced Ternary Number System

Now instead of using 0, 1 and 2, an alternative representation of the symbols may be as -1, 0 and 1 [2]. For simplicity, the symbol used for -1 is $\bar{1}$. Hereafter, we shall use the notations -1 and $\bar{1}$ to refer to the same value. The ternary number system with this set of symbols is known as a balanced ternary system [2]. Some of the interesting properties of a balanced ternary number system include [2]:

1. The negative number is obtained by interchanging 1 and $\bar{1}$.
2. The sign of a number is given by its most significant nonzero *trit*.
3. The operation of rounding off to the nearest integer is identical to truncation.

3   Application of Ternary Logic in VLSI System

There are several advantages of using ternary logic in VLSI circuits over the conventional Binary logic. For a fixed number of lines for transmitting information it is obvious that more information can be transmitted using ternary logic [7]. With the improvement of fabrication process the devices are scaled down but the scaling rate of interconnect is not same as that of the devices. As a result almost 60% of path delay is due to interconnects [3]. In a VLSI chip almost 60% to 70% area is covered with active devices and rest of the area has interconnects.

This area leads to performance degradation [3]. Using ternary logic the number of interconnections can be reduced to $\frac{1}{log_2^3}$[11]. An energy efficient digital system can be designed using ternary logic as the complexity of interconnects and chip area can be reduced using this logic [7][8]. In electrical circuits power dissipation is mainly due to dynamic switching and current, and sub-threshold leakage current. About 80% of the total power is dissipated due to switching activity [9]. Average Power dissipation due to switching activity is given by P_{avg} $=\frac{1}{2}V_{dd}^2Cf$,where V_{dd} is the supply voltage, C is the load capacitance and f is the frequency of operation. For aperiodic signals the frequency of operation can be estimated by the average number of signal transitions per unit time[9]. Using asynchronous ternary logic signal system the dynamic power is reduced to P_{dyn} $=(\frac{V_{dd}}{2})^2Cf$ [10]. In this system, for the communication line at voltage level $\frac{V_{dd}}{2}$, it is in idle state. Thus in order to transmit one trit of information the voltage level is either high at V_{dd} or low at 0[10].The methods of defining,analyzing and implementing the basic combinatorial circuit with minimum number of ternary multiplexers were discussed in [5].The design and implementation of ternary full adder is described in [4].The design of 2 bit ternary ALU is described in [6].

4   Arithmetic Operation on Ternary Number

In this section we discuss arithmetic operations of ternary number systems such as shift operation, addition, subtraction, multiplication and division.

4.1   Shift Operation Using Balanced Ternary Number System

Arithmetic Right Shift Operation. Arithmetic left shift and right shift operation of balanced ternary numbers were discussed in [12].

4.2   Shift Operation Using Conventional Ternary Number System

Arithmetic Right Shift Operation. With this system after arithmetic right shift operation($Ashr$), the *least significant trit (LST)* is lost. If the *most significant trit (MST)* is 2 before shift operation then after $Ashr$ it will be 2 otherwise after $Ashr$ MST will be 0. If the LST is 1 or 2 then the $Ashr$ of a number A yields $\lfloor \frac{A}{3} \rfloor$.If the LST is 0 then $Ashr$ yields $\frac{A}{3}$.

If A=2120(i.e. $(-12)_{10}$) then $Ashr$ yields 2212 (i.e. $(-4)_{10}$).If A=2121(i.e. $(-11)_{10}$) then $Ashr$ yields 2212 (i.e. $(-4)_{10}$).

If A=1120(i.e. $(42)_{10}$) then $Ashr$ yields 0112 (i.e. $(14)_{10}$).If A=1121(i.e. $(43)_{10}$) then $Ashr$ yields 0112 (i.e. $(14)_{10}$).

Arithmetic Left Shift Operation. With this system after arithmetic left shift operation($Ashl$) the LST become zero. If $R_{n-1}R_{n-2}$ are 00, 01 or 22 then after $Ashl$ MST is lost otherwise a one *trit flip − flap − flop* is needed to store the initial MST.Arithmetic left shift operation yields $A \times 3$.

If $A=121$ (i.e. $(16)_{10}$) then *Ashl* yields 1210 ($(48)_{10}$). If $A=2121$ (i.e. $(-11)_{10}$) then *Ashl* yields 221210 ($(-33)_{10}$).

If $A=2221$ (i.e. $(-2)_{10}$) then *Ashl* yields 2210 ($(-6)_{10}$).

4.3 Addition and Subtraction of Balanced Ternary Numbers

Addition and subtraction of any balanced ternary number can be easily performed using the addition table as in [2]. The following Table 1 shows few example of addition and subtraction of two 4 trits numbers.

Table 1. Examples of Addition and Subtraction of two 4 trits numbers

A	$111\bar{1}(38)$	$11\bar{1}\bar{1}(32)$	$1111(40)$	$1010(30)$	A	$111\bar{1}(38)$	$11\bar{1}\bar{1}(32)$	$1111(40)$	$1010(30)$
B	$1111(40)$	$\bar{1}10\bar{1}(-37)$	$1111(40)$	$\bar{1}1\bar{1}\bar{1}(-40)$	$-B$	$\bar{1}\bar{1}\bar{1}\bar{1}(-40)$	$110\bar{1}(37)$	$\bar{1}\bar{1}\bar{1}\bar{1}(-40)$	$1111(40)$
$A+B$	$100\bar{1}0(78)$	$0\bar{1}11(-5)$	$10001(80)$	$0\bar{1}0\bar{1}(-10)$	$A-B$	$00\bar{1}\bar{1}(-2)$	$10\bar{1}10(69)$	$0000(0)$	$10\bar{1}11(70)$

4.4 Addition and Subtraction of Two Conventional Ternary Numbers

For addition of conventional ternary numbers can be done easily.For substation(A-B) we have to take 3's complement of B and add it to A.3's complement of a number can be easily obtained by interchanging 0 and 2 followed by add 1 to it. Figure 1 shows few examples of addition and subtraction of two conventional ternary numbers.

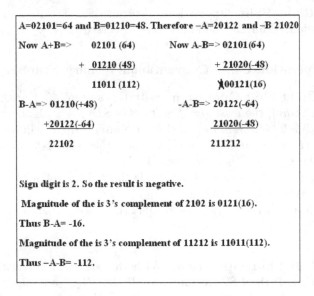

Fig. 1. Addition and subtraction of conventional ternary numbers

5 Algorithm for Multiplication and Division of Two Base-3 Numbers

In this Section we describe multiplication and division of two ternary numbers.

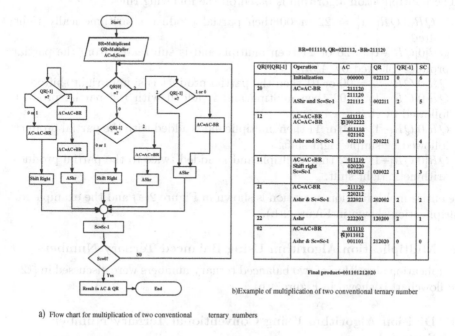

a) Flow chart for multiplication of two conventional ternary numbers

b) Example of multiplication of two conventional ternary number

Fig. 2. Flowcharts for multiplication Algorithm for two conventional ternary numbers

5.1 Multiplication Algorithm Using Conventional Ternary Numbers

A ternary number with a stream of 2 can be expressed as $3^{m+1} - 3^k$ where k is the starting position of 2 and m is the ending position of 2 and counting is start from number 0.As for example $2220 = 3^4 - 3^1$.and $2221 = 3^4 - 3^1 + 1$.

$$2022 = 3^4 - 3^3 + 3^2 - 3^0 . 2122 = 3^4 - 3^3 + 3^2 \times 1 + 3^2 - 3^0.$$

If the number contain only 0 *and* 1 as symbols then we take the usual expression $\sum_{i=0}^{n-1} a_i 3^i$ where $a_i = 0, 1$;

Arithmetic left shift of a number is three times the number.So at the time of multiplication if the multiplier contains stream of 2s we simply Arithmetically left shift the multiplicand.

For multiplication we store multiplicand in a register BR, say, and Multiplier in register QR, say. Initially, we assume that product is zero. This is known as the *partial product*, where a *partial product* is obtained by multiplying the multiplicand with one trit of the multiplier. Now, if the trit of the multiplier is 1 then multiplicand is added with the partial product to generate a new partial product. Now the next trit of the multiplier is multiplied with multiplicand and the product is shifted by one trit to the left and added with the partial product to generate a new partial product. In case of hardware multiplication (using registers), instead of shifting the *multiplicand* × *c* (where *c* is a trit of the multiplier to the left we shift the partial product one trit to the right.

The multiplication algorithm is based on the following rules

1. if $QR[0]QR[-1] = 22$ or 00 then partial product is arithmetically right shifted.
2. $QR[0]QR[-1] = 20$ or 21 then multiplicand is subtracted from the partial product followed by *AShr*.
3. $QR[0]QR[-1] = 00$ or 01 then the partial product is simply right shifted.
4. $QR[0]QR[-1] = 02$ then multiplicand is added with the partial product followed by *AShr*.
5. $QR[0]QR[-1] = 10$ or 11 then multiplicand is added with the partial product followed by simple right shift.
6. $QR[0]QR[-1] = 12$ then multiplicand is added twice to the partial product arithmetic right shift.

The entire multiplication operation is shown in Figure 2(a) and the example for multiplication shown in Figure 2(b).

5.2   Multiplication Algorithm Using Balanced Ternary Numbers

Multiplication algorithm of two balanced ternary numbers were discussed in [12]. The flowchart is shown in Figure 3(b).

5.3   Division Algorithm Using Conventional Ternary Number System

In order to divide a number by another, we store the dividend in register Q and divisor in register M. During division we take a set of trits of dividend and if it has a value less than that of the divisor, then we have to take another trit of dividend and insert 0(zero) in the quotient. On the other hand, if the value of a set of trits of dividend is greater than or equal to the value of the divisor, then either 1 or 2 is inserted in the quotient. For this we have to subtract the divisor from the trits of the dividend; if the result is negative we put 1 in the quotient and add divisor to the result to restore those trits of dividend. This is known as *restoration of the dividend*. If the result of subtraction is positive then quotient is 2.The entire division operation is illustrated in the flowchart of Figure 3(a). The example for division using conventional ternary number system is shown in Figure 5(b).

5.4   Division Algorithm Using Balanced Ternary Number System

The division of two non-negative ternary numbers is discussed in[12] and the flowchart for that algorithm is shown in Figure 4(a). Here we describe the algorithm when the dividend is negative.In this case instead of subtracting the divisor

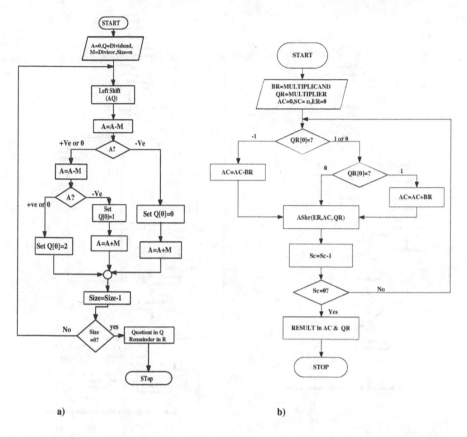

a)   b)

Fig. 3. Flowcharts for (*a*) Division Algorithm for two non negative conventional ternary numbers and (b) Multiplication of two balanced ternary numbers

from the set of trits of dividend is added with the set of trits of dividend.If the result is positive 0 is inserted in the quotient and divisor is subtracted from the result to get back the previous value. This is known as restoration of dividend. If the result of addition between divisor and set of trits of dividend is negative the either $\bar{1}$ (*i.e.* -1 *in decimal*) or $\bar{1}1$ (*i.e.is* -2 *in decimal*) is inserted in the quotient.For this if the result of addition is negative then first $\bar{1}$ is inserted in the quotient then again the divisor is added with the partial result and if the result of this addition is negative or 0 then 1 is inserted in the quotient other wise divisor is subtracted from the last result to restore back the previous result.When all the trits are encountered then if the value of register A is negative then divisor is added with A and the result store in register Q is decremented by 1.The division operation is illustrated in the flowchart of Figure 4(b) and the corresponding example is shown in Figure 5(a). Now using these two algorithms division operation can be easily performed for both negative and non-negative dividends.

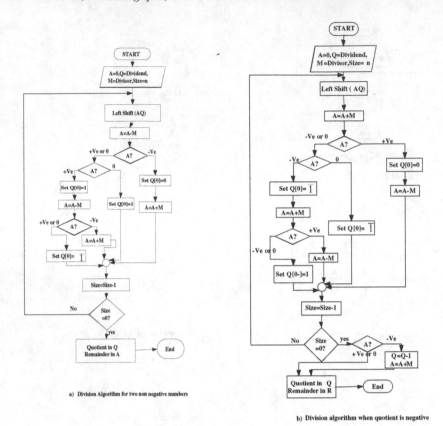

a) Division Algorithm for two non negative numbers

b) Division algorithm when quotient is negative

Fig. 4. Flowcharts for Division Algorithm of two balanced ternary numbers

6   Performance Analysis

6.1   Multiplication Algorithm

In case of multiplication algorithm using conventional ternary number system the complexity of the algorithm will be as follows

1. If the multiplier is 222...2 then number of addition/subtraction operation is only one and number of shit operation is n.So Complexity in this case is $O(n)$.
2. If the multiplier is 000...0 then number of addition/subtraction operation is zero and number of shit operation is n.So Complexity in this case is $O(n)$.
3. For any other multiplier the number of addition/subtraction operation is $O(n)$ and number of shit operation is $O(n)$.So Complexity in this case is $O(n^2)$.

However, for multiplication using balanced ternary number system the complexity is $O(n^2)$. Moreover, using conventional number system maximum range of

Here we divide Ī10ĪĪ by 00111 i.e. -58 by 13. M=00111

Operation	A	Q	Sc
Initialization	00000	-1Ī0-1-1	5
Left Shift AQ	0 00 0-1	10-1-1[]	
A=A+M	00 1 1 1		
A is +Ve Set Q[0]=0	00 1 1 0	10-1-1[0]	
A=A-M	00-1-1-1		
Size=Size-1	000 0-1		4
Left Shift AQ	000-1 1	0-1-1[0][]	
A=A+M	00 1 1 1		
A is +Ve Set Q[0]=0	00 1 1-1	0-1-1[0][0]	
A=A-M	00-1-1-1		3
Size=Size-1	000-1 1		
Left Shift AQ	00-1 1 0	-1-1[0][0][]	
A=A+M	00 1 1 1		
A is +Ve Set Q[0]=0	00 Ī-1Ī	-1-1[0][0][0]	
A=A-M	00-1-1-1		2
Size=Size-1	00-1 1 0		
Left Shift AQ	0-1 1 0-1	-1[0][0][0][]	
A=A+M	0 0 1 1 1		
A is -Ve Set Q[0]=-1	0 0-1 1 0	-1[0][0][0][-1]	
A=A+M	0 0 1 1 1		
A is +ve	0 0 1-1 1		
A=A-M	0 0-1-1-1		
Size=Size-1	0 0-1 1 0		1
Left Shift AQ	0-1 Ī0-1	[0][0][0][-1][]	
A=A+M	0 0 1 1 1		
A is -Ve Set Q[0]=-1	0 0-1 1 0	[0][0][0][-1][-1]	
A=A+M	0 0 1 1 1		
A is +ve	0 0 1-1 1		0
A=A-M	0 0-1-1-1		
Size=Size-1	0 0-1 1 0		
A is negative	0 0-1 1 0	000 -1-1	
A=A+M	0 0 1 1 1	000 0 -1	
Q=Q-1	0 0 1-1 1	00-111	

Remainder= A=(1-11)₃=(7)₁₀   Quotient Q=(00-111)₃=(-5)₁₀

Here we divide (101211)₃ by (201)₃ i.e. 292 by 192 in decimal. M=222022

Operation	A	Q	Sc
Initialization	000000	101211	6
Left Shift AQ	000001	01211[]	
A=A-M	222022		
A is -Ve Set Q[0]=0	222100	011211[0]	
A=A+M	000201		
Size=Size-1	[0]000001		5
Left Shift AQ	000010	1211[0][]	
A=A-M	222022		
A is -Ve Set Q[0]=0	222102	1211[0][0]	
A=A+M	000201		
Size=Size-1	[0]000010		4
Left Shift AQ	000101	211[0][0][]	
A=A-M	222022		
A is -Ve Set Q[0]=0	222200	211[0][0][0]	
A=A+M	000201		
Size=Size-1	[0]000101		3
Left Shift AQ	001012	11[0][0][0][]	
A=A-M	222022		
A is +Ve	[0]000111		
A=A-M	222022		
A is -ve Set Q[0]=1	222210		
A=A+M	000201		2
Size=Size-1	[0]000111		
Left Shift AQ	001111	1[0][0][0][1][]	
A=A-M	222022		
A is +Ve	[0]000210		
A=A-M	222022		
A is +ve Set Q[0]=2	[0]000002	1[0][0][0][1][2]	
Size=Size-1			1
Left Shift AQ	000021	[0][0][0][1][2][]	
A=A-M	222022		
A is -Ve Set Q[0]=0	222120		
A=A+M	000201	[0][0][0][1][2][0]	0
Size=Size-1	[0]00002 1		

Remainder A=00021 and Quotient Q=000120.

b) Quotient is negative and balanced ternary number system

a) Two non negative conventional ternary numbers

Fig. 5. Example for Division Algorithm

n-trit numbers is $3^n - 1$ but in case of balanced ternary number system maximum is $3^{n-1} - 1$. The advantage of using balanced ternary number system subtraction operation can be easily performed.

6.2 Division Algorithm

The complexity of the division algorithm for both conventional and balanced ternary number system is $O(n^2)$. However, in case of balanced ternary number system some extra trits in QR (flip-flap-flop) may be required when $2(1\bar{1})$ is inserted into quotient.

7 Conclusion

In this paper we discuss few algorithms for arithmetic (addition, multiplication, division and arithmetic shift) operations in the conventional and balanced ternary number systems. Some new algorithms have been proposed and their time-complexity analysis have been discussed. There are ample scopes of further work in this number system such as using them in cryptographic systems, exploring their opportunities in efficient power management in VLSI circuits, and so on.

References

1. Hayes, B.: Third Base. American scientist 89(6), 490–494 (2001)
2. Knuth, D.E.: The Art of Computer programming, 3rd edn., vol. 2. Pearson Education
3. Sherwani, N.A.: Algorithms for VLSI Physical Design Automation
4. Srivastava, A., Venkatapathy, K.: Design and implementation of a low power ternary full adder. VLSI Design 4(1), 75–81 (1996)
5. Sathish Kumar, A., Swetha Priya, A.: The Minimization of Ternary Combinational Circuits-A Survey. International Journal of Engineering and Technology 2(8), 3576–3589 (2010)
6. Dhande, A.P., Ingole, V.T.: Design and Implementation of 2-Bit ternary ALU Slice. In: 3rd International Conference SETIT, Tunisia (2005)
7. Balla, P.C., Antoniou, A.: Low Power dissipation of MOS Ternary logic Family. IEEE Journal of Solid State Circuits Sc-19(5) (1994)
8. Lin, S., Kim, Y.-B., Lombardi, F.: CNTFET Based Design of Ternary Logic Gates and Arithmetic Circuits. IEEE Transactions of Nanotechnology 2(11) (2011)
9. Roy, K., Prasad, S.C.: Low Power CMOS VLSI Circuit Design. Wiley, India (2011)
10. Felicijan, T., Furber, S.B.: An Asynchronous Ternary Logic System. IEEE Transaction on Very Large Scale Intregration System 11(6) (2003)
11. Vasundara Patel, K.S., Gurumurthy, K.S.: Multi-valued Logic Addition and Multiplication in Galois Field. In: IEEE International Conference on Advances in Computing, Control and Telecommunication Technologies (2009)
12. Das, S., Sain, J.P., Dasgupta, P., Sensarma, S.: Algorithms for Ternary Number System. In: 2nd International Conference on Computer, Communication, Control and Information Technology, February 25-26. Elsevier Pub., India (2012)

SOI MEMS Based Over-Sampling Accelerometer Design with $\Delta\Sigma$ Output

Dushyant Juneja, Sougata Kar, Procheta Chatterjee, and Siddhartha Sen

Department of Electrical Engineering,
Indian Institute of Technology, Kharagpur, West Bengal, India
juneja.dushyant@gmail.com, sougatakar@ee.iitkgp.ernet.in

Abstract. SOI MEMS provides a class of high dynamic range sensors with superior properties at the cost of lower bandwidth. The present work discusses the development and signal conditioning for one such acceleration sensor along with its back-end signal conditioning and a robust $\Delta\Sigma$ front-end output. Design stages and trade-offs are decided specific to applications and device capabilities. Co-simulation results for the device signal conditioning are found, and good linearity is observed in the same. The sensor hence designed aims specific to low bandwidth, low range, high precision applications in acceleration sensing.

Keywords: MEMS, Accelerometers, Signal Conditioning.

1 Introduction

Advances in modern CMOS technology and chip fabrications have urged instrumentation devices to turn towards fully on-chip solutions for sensing applications. Several such implementations have been done, beginning from simple cantilever based structures for biomedical applications [7] to much more complex surface micro-machined and SOI based comb and gyro structures for pressure and acceleration sensing [1, 2, 8]. Optimal performance of such sensors further requires them to be application specific, and hence special fabrication processes, signal conditioning and packaging technologies may be adopted. Capacitive sensors form a major class of such precision sensors and are suited for wide range of applications. The main principle is to sense the change in capacitance, often differential, due to the effect of sensing parameter. Various methods for the same have also been developed, beginning with square wave excited open loop comb devices [10] to neutral positioned charge amplifier based sensors, both open [1] and closed loop [2, 11, 12] configurations. ADC further serves as the signal conditioning front-end towards producing a more robust output as well as facilitating feedback mechanisms, inherently disturbed owing to non-linear voltage-force square law [11].

Present work discusses one such implementation for acceleration sensing based on comb type SOI MEMS devices. The integrated sensor utilizes static signal conditioning mechanisms in dynamic sensors based on the principle of oversampling, wherein the sampling is kept much higher than the bandwidth. This solves

H. Rahaman et al. (Eds.): VDAT 2012, LNCS 7373, pp. 121–128, 2012.

the constraints posed by chip area and power consumption due to additional supportive circuits such as square wave generators and accompanying demodulators [10, 13]. The saved chip area is instead utilized towards increasing the robustness of the device output using a $\Delta\Sigma$ ADC facilitating single bit digital output at a reduced pin count compared to a conventional ADC. The entire design for the topology and choice for all the above components is done based upon the aim of producing a high precision SOI MEMS device, typically low bandwidth system.

Section 2 discusses the enhancements and the constraints posed by the device, and gives a brief working principle for the sensing action. Section 3 discusses the immediate signal conditioning designed with reference to the device, recognized as the chip back-end in the rest of the work and the final conditioner stage implemented with a high oversampling optimized $\Delta\Sigma$ front-end. Section 4 gives the final simulations for a variety of dc input variations, emulated by capacitance variations. Wide range of static input capacitance variations are observed and the back-end as well as front-end outputs are recorded. Observations hence found confirm well to desired applications.

2   SOI MEMS Accelerometer: Device Description

Conventional MEMS devices are implemented using surface or bulk micro-machining of silicon wafers, as to utilize the excellent mechanical properties offered by silicon for sensing applications. However, due to the requirement of moving parts in applications such as mass sensing [7] and acceleration sensing, the structures so made by above technologies need to be precisely released from the base substrate. Though difficult, it is achieved to some yield using perforated proof mass and lesser feature sizes [9, 10]. Typical comb type accelerometer fabricated with such considerations was needed to have a lower finger dimensions, frequently perforated proof mass and low overall size [9]. This further poses several implications on the performance of the sensor, typically an increased bandwidth, noisy performance and increased range. Stiction, or the unsuccessful release of the MEMS devices, however, still remains a problem only partially addressed by the above solutions, at a considerable cost. Such sensors further find lesser scope in applications requiring higher performance and more precise sensing.

SOI MEMS forms a solution device compared to its more stiction prone surface and bulk micro-machined MEMS counterparts. The solution is essentially in pursuing back side etching instead of conventional surface release steps, better ensuring a successful release of proof mass. Further constraint posed here is increased proof mass owing to finite etching rates, resulting in lower bandwidth systems with more precise sensing. Furthermore due to the back-side etching steps, the device can have larger dimensions and hence more audible variations resulting from changes in the sensing domains. The present implementation discusses the case of a capacitive sensor fabricated with the above process, to attain the goal of an improved performance micro-accelerometer. Section 2.1 discusses the underlying sensing principle. Section 3 thereafter discusses the proposed plan for signal conditioning, on action with the device advantages posed by the SOI MEMS. More elaborate study is presented later in Sections 3.1 and 3.2.

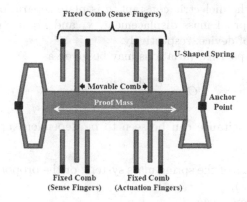

Fig. 1. Simplified device structure in principle

2.1   Device Sensing Principle

Capacitive sensors act with giving an output variation of capacitance with an input variation taken from the sensing environment changes. This output capacitance variation may be due to variation in inter-plate separation as in accelerometers, overlap area as in angular displacement sensors, or dielectric properties as in case of humidity sensors [15]. The present MEMS structure under discussion typically utilizes the first case of changes in gap separation owing to external acceleration change input. Seen from the non-inertial frame of the MEMS device under acceleration, the device may be assumed to be under the action of a pseudo-force proportional to the acceleration input to the device as given by (1), but in opposite direction. This being an equivalent spring mass under external force, tends to displace the proof mass as in attempt to balance the acting forces, by a distance x given by (2), which can be seen to be linear with acceleration. With both the plates energized, the separation forms a differentially balanced capacitor when at rest, the balance of which is disturbed by the input acceleration (or pseudo-force in the non-inertial frame). Resultant capacitance changes may be given as per a general displacement sensor. Since the separation variations are kept tolerably small in MEMS design, the changes in differential capacitance may be approximated to first order in relation to the distance x as given by (3).

$$F = m_p \cdot a_{ext}; \quad m_p \cdot a_{ext} = k_s \cdot x_p \tag{1}$$

$$x_p = \frac{m_p \cdot a_{ext}}{k_s} \tag{2}$$

$$C_1 = C_0 - \Delta C_x \quad \text{and} \quad C_2 = C_0 + \Delta C_x$$

$$\text{where} \quad C_0 = \frac{\epsilon \cdot A_{ov}}{d} \quad \text{and} \quad C_x = \frac{\epsilon \cdot A_{ov} \cdot x_p}{d^2} \tag{3}$$

Here, $\epsilon = \epsilon_r \cdot \epsilon_0$ is the dielectric constant, d is plate separation, A_{ov} is overlap area and x_p is the proof mass displacement. k_s and m_p are equivalent spring constant and mass of device, respectively.

In essence, the capacitive variations may be given as

$$C_x = \frac{\epsilon \cdot A_{ov} \cdot m_p}{d^2 \cdot k_s} \cdot a_{ext} \tag{4}$$

The changes in capacitance can be seen to be dependent upon the following parameters

1. Stiffness and mass of the spring mass system, or the proportionality between x_p and a_{ext} in (2),
2. Input acceleration range,
3. Capacitor base properties, viz dimensions of capacitor and its dielectric properties.
4. Plate separation, or d.

All of these above properties can be varied to get an optimized solution set suiting particular applications. With input acceleration kept within a specified range, the dynamic range for the device can be optimized by variation of the stiffness, device dimensions and plate separation. Utilization of device dimensions in such a optimization necessitates a better, stiction-less fabrication process for the proof mass, such as the SOI MUMPS process from MEMSCAP. The concept here is to pursue the device etching from the wafer backside to the depth desired, instead of front-side etching. This hence also eliminates the need of release step due to inherent release mechanism. This yields higher proof mass, though stiction in fingers may not be completely resolved. Further, the device dimensions can also be varied and can be larger. This gives higher dynamic range owing to better capacitance variations, as also stated by (2) and (4).

3   Signal Conditioning

From the above discussions it could be seen that the SOI devices offer much better properties at the cost of lower bandwidths. A suitable signal conditioning hence would be that which can suitably serve the near-dc variations at a lower cost to give high resolution outputs. Switched capacitor implementations with $\Delta\Sigma$ modulators were hence ideally suited and utilized, with oversampling frequency or switching frequency kept up to 2048 times the input bandwidth. The basic circuit diagram is shown in Fig. 2.

3.1   Back-End Signal Conditioning

The signal conditioning back-end consisted of a charge amplifier along with buffers and anti-aliasing filters. The former served to pick up the low bandwidth variations at the SOI MEMS device output, and convert the same into

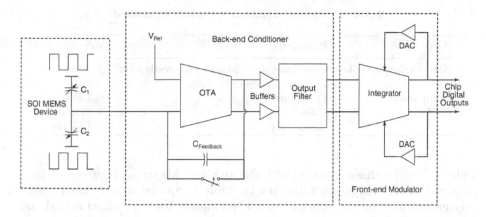

Fig. 2. Elaborate circuit diagram for the signal conditioning scheme, shown integrated with the MEMS device. The same is emulated by differential capacitances. Back-end utilizes an additional switch across amplifier for offset nulling and low frequency noise suppression.

equivalent voltage signals. Oversampling of the same ensured higher resolution from the sensor to the amplifier. A switched capacitor implementation was used due to the reasons explained in Section 3, and also due to their inherent multiple advantages to mid frequency applications [14].

The principle for the back-end is to 'copy' the input capacitance charge to the feedback capacitor, hence to produce an equivalent voltage output necessary to sustain the charge produced. The same is then followed by anti-aliasing processing to filter out the images produced by sampling, and then by a sample and hold circuit and buffer to support the direct chip outputs and the input capacitance from the accompanying ADC. The elaborate circuit is presented in Fig. 2.

3.2 Front End Modulator

The modulator at the chip front end was fabricated to serve multiple functions. The first was to provide a low cost digital interface to the analog signal with a high enough resolution. Secondly, it being an oversampling converter, it heeded excellently to the conditions of the chip with just the need of an extra filter and sampling circuit. It further provided single bit digital output without increasing the cost of the overall chip significantly. Another aim behind the converter was also to obtain a robust enough signal outside the chip to sustain the noises faced by the sensor in application. Being a single bit bit-stream, its transmission to the distant decoding modules like the decimation filter did not pose difficulties. Elaborate design procedures for the modulator have been widely discussed [3–5]. Being an high oversampling device, a low power first order modulator served excellently to the above needs. The modulator was designed in the standard

Table 1. Custom modulator specifications desired

Part	Parameter	Values
Non-overlapping Clock	Complementary phases non-overlap time	≥ 2 ns
	Delayed phases delay time	≥ 2 ns
Comparator	Dead zone	≤ 1 mV
OTA	Gain	≥ 57.8 dB
	Bandwidth	≥ 10 MHz

180 nm CMOS technology along with the back-end. Major modulator guidelines observed in the design are tabulated in Table 1. Special mixed signal design precautions were implemented in layout, prominent being localized digital and analog domains and guard ring separations between the two.

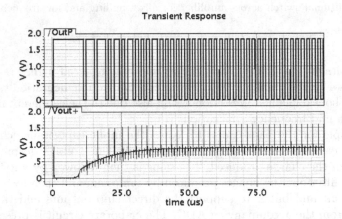

Fig. 3. Transient simulation outputs for sensor at rest, emulated by similar capacitance. OutP is the modulator output, while Vout+ is the back-end output.

4 Integrated Co-simulation Results

Simulations were done by combining the oversampled back-end and the front-end modulator, while the capacitance variations emulated the input acceleration. The transient, resting condition output for the sensor is shown in Fig. 3, while the sensor under acceleration is shown in Fig. 4.

To further show the accuracy of the approach, results were obtained for a large range of capacitive variations to observe the output changes. Since only DC capacitive variations were done, only the output DC value of the modulator was observed. The same are recorded in Fig. 5. The change in output voltage is $500mV$ approximately for $300fF$ change in capacitance which corresponds to the sensitivity of around $1.6mV/fF$. It can be observed that the output showed highly linear variations with the input for the complete range of capacitance

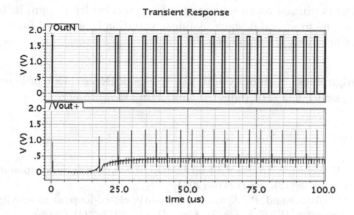

Fig. 4. Transient simulation outputs for sensor under acceleration. Since Vout+ was connected to the negative input node of the modulator, output was taken from OutN instead of OutP.

variation. Similar variations have been found towards the opposite direction, as expected. Variations in modulator output are observed owing to errors in period timings for FFT analysis for a wide output variations. The dynamic range could be tuned using programmable on-chip capacitors.

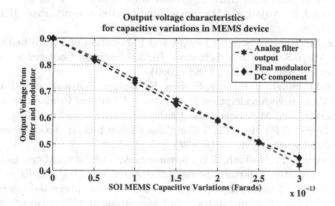

Fig. 5. Filter output and Modulator output DC component plotted against SOI MEMS capacitive variations. The modulator DC component was complemented from positive output OutP, since Vout+ was tied to the negative input of the modulator.

5   Conclusions

SOI MEMS forms an important class of high dynamic range, low input range sensors for precision applications. A contemporary design is presented in this work, with discussions on sensor as well as the signal conditioning approaches.

Oversampling is utilized as an advantage of low bandwidth design, in both the back-end and the front-end designs. A linear variation is observed for a range of input values justifying the approach.

Acknowledgments. Authors would like to thank Department of Science and Technology (DST), Govt. of India for supporting this project.

References

1. Amini, B.V., Ayazi, F.: A 2.5-V 14-bit CMOS SOI capacitive accelerometer. IEEE J. Sol. St. Circ. 39(12), 2467–2476 (2004)
2. Amini, B.V., Abdolvand, R., Ayazi, F.: A 4.5-mW closed-loop micro-gravity CMOS SOI accelerometer. IEEE J. Sol. St. Circ. 41(12), 2983–2991 (2006)
3. Schreier, R., Temes, G.C.: Understanding Delta Sigma Data Converters. Wiley-IEEE Press, New Jersey (2005)
4. Yao, L., Steyaert, M., Sansen, W.: Low-Power Low-Voltage Sigma-Delta Modulators in Nanometer CMOS. Springer (2006)
5. Juneja, D., Kar, S., Chatterjee, P., Sen, S.: Design of Delta Sigma Modulators for Integrated Sensor Applications. In: National Conference on Emerging Trends in Electrical, Instrumentation and Communication Engineering (2012)
6. Franco, S.: Design with Operational Amplifiers and Analog Integrated Circuits, 3rd edn. McGraw-Hill (2002)
7. Kale, N.S., Ramgopal Rao, V.: Design and Fabrication Issues in Affinity Cantilevers for bioMEMS Applications. IEEE J. MEMS 15(6), 1789–1794 (2006)
8. Yazdi, N., Ayazi, F., Najafi, K.: Micromachined Inertial Sensors. Proc. IEEE 86(8), 1640–1659 (1998)
9. Swamy, K.B.M., Kar, S., Sen, S.: Design and Fabrication of PolySi beams for application in Micro-Sensors and Actuators. In: 3rd National Conference on MEMS, Smart Structures and Materials, ISSS (2009)
10. Swamy, K.B.M., Singh, T.P., Kar, S., Sen, S.: Design, Fabrication and Testing of Comb-type Capacitive Acceleration Sensor. In: 3rd National Conference on MEMS, Smart Structures and Materials, ISSS (2009)
11. Kraft, M., Lewis, C.P., Hesketh, T.G.: Closed Loop Silicon Accelerometers. IEE Proc. Circuits, Devices Syst. 145(5), 325–331 (1998)
12. Kraft, M., Lewis, C.P., Hesketh, T.G., Szymkowiak, S.: A Novel Micromachined Accelerometer Capacitive Interface. Sensors and Actuators A68/1-3, 466–473 (1998)
13. Kar, S.K., Sen, S.: Tunable Square-Wave Generator for Integrated Sensor Applications. IEEE Trans. Instrumentation and Measurement (2011) (in press)
14. Brodersen, R.W., Gray, P.R., Hodges, D.A.: MOS Switched-capacitor Filters. Proc. IEEE 67(1), 61–75 (1979)
15. Bentley, J.P.: Principles of Measurement Systems. Pearson Prentice Hall (2005)

Design Optimization of a Wide Band MEMS Resonator for Efficient Energy Harvesting

Goutam Rana[*], Samir Kumar Lahiri, and Chirasree Roy Chaudhuri

Department of Electronics and Telecommunication Engineering,
Bengal Engineering and Science University, Shibpur, West Bengal -711103, India
rana.goutam7@gmail.com

Abstract. Wide band MEMS resonators banking on the principle of amplitude dependent stiffness nonlinearity as reported in few recent publications can stretch the frequency response. A recent report by our group on four internal proof mass based membrane resonator has been observed to vibrate below 350 Hz with more than three closely placed peaks within 2kHz in the frequency response without introducing non-linearity. However, improvements in the design of such wide band MEMS resonators operating in the linear regime are required, so that the lower frequency range can be reduced further. In this paper we have optimized the lateral dimensions and displacements of the internal proof-masses by introducing a figure of merit to estimate the performance of these resonators. The figure of merit incorporates three parameters viz. power output per unit area, lower cut off frequency and no peaks in the operating frequency range within 2 KHz (most of the practical vibration sources lie within it). It has been observed that the resonator with four internal proof-masses each of dimensions $3 \times 2mm^2$ placed 0.5mm apart from each other shows highest figure of merit.

Keywords: low frequency vibration sources, internal proof-mass configuration, MEMS Energy harvester, low impedance.

1 Introduction

The research activities in the fields of different non-conventional energy sources have been intensified over last few decades due to limited resources of conventional energy sources against increasing consumption. The increasing use of different low power devices and wireless sensors has incurred an urgency of making them self-powered. Among many possible ways of making these devices self-powered, mechanical vibration is a potential option due to its almost uninterrupted presence in all places. The well-established method for this conversion is the use of piezo-electric materials in bending mode, which develop voltage when stressed.

Initially, the devices were based on free standing cantilever structures using PZT ceramics [1-4]. The development in MEMS field has introduced the micro-machined structures with thin vibrating layer [5-6]. The advantages of these structures are that they

---

[*] Corresponding author.

H. Rahaman et al. (Eds.): VDAT 2012, LNCS 7373, pp. 129–138, 2012.

can vibrate even with very small source of vibration from ambience. The micro-machined structures generally uses sol gel spin coating of PZT solutions instead of PZT ceramics making the structures less brittle. While few other works also reported using PMN-PT and PVDF materials. The first one is not considered due to high cost while the second one has low piezo-electric coefficients.

A recent work by A.Hajati et al. [7] on, amplitude dependent non-linear stiffness in stretching of resonant frequency band of a doubly clamped beam has made the con-version, of low frequency vibration from natural sources, possible for MEMS struc-tures. Improvements in many aspects, viz.1) effective area of energy conversion, 2) lowering of operating frequency range, and 3) uniformity in deformed shape, have also been reported recently employing square membrane with four rectangular proof-masses [9]. However, improvements in the design of the square membranes and inter-nal proof masses are required, so that the lower frequency range can be reduced further. In this paper we have optimized the lateral dimensions and displacements of the internal proof-masses by introducing a figure of merit to estimate the performance of these resonators. The figure of merit incorporates three parameters viz. power out-put per unit area, lower cut off frequency and no peaks in the operating frequency range within 2 KHz (most of the practical vibration sources lie within it). The lower cutoff frequency and the stress generated on the membrane are estimated from COVENTORWARE10 and the output power is estimated analytically.

2   Design Details

The device proposed for energy harvesting is square membrane consisting of two base layers viz. SiO_2 and Si_3N_4 grown over a Si substrate by thermal oxidation and PECVD methods respectively. Then a conducting layer is grown of Al or Pt/Ti alloy on the top of the membrane. A thin sol-gel PZT layer is then deposited over the con-ducting layer. Now finally a top electrode layer is grown over the PZT top surface. The entire membrane is then subjected to an external load, which is proposed to be modeled separately along with the pillars and then boned with the membrane using adhesive or eutectic die-bonding. To avoid the effect of loads' contribution in mass of the membrane the contacts are made as small as possible.

The primary objective of design is to minimize the resonating frequency as well as the thickness of the membrane to make it vibrate from almost every practical vibrat-ing source whatever small the magnitude is. The decreasing thickness of the membrane results in higher resonating frequency. Thus for minimizing resonating frequency, the membranes lateral dimensions has to be increased. But increasing infi-nitely the dimensions would only lead to disturb the stability of the device. As thermal oxidation and PECVD have limitation in growing thick layers we assumed the values from a standard publication for obtaining the simulation results [7]. The thicknesses of the SiO_2 and Si_3N_4 are assumed to be 1.67μm and 1.56μm respectively. The lateral dimensions of the membrane are optimized to 10mm×10mm.

The internal proof mass orientation plays a vital role in determining the deflection contour and resonating frequency. Four different dimensions of the internal proof-mass are analyzed in three different position of the membrane to obtain an optimized the response of the device.

2.1   Basic Proof Mass Configuration

This configuration contains four rectangular internal proof-masses with different lateral dimension are placed in such a manner that any two consecutive proof-mass forms a T shape among them.   Here four such designs different lateral dimensions of internal proof-masses are analyzed viz. $4 \times 1 \text{mm}^2$, $3 \times 1 \text{mm}^2$, $4 \times 2 \text{mm}^2$ and $3 \times 2 \text{mm}^2$ each with 3 different gaps within them.

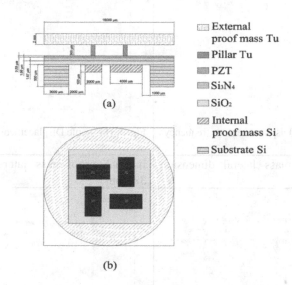

(a)

☐ External
  proof mass Tu

■ Pillar Tu

■ PZT

▨ Si₃N₄

☐ SiO₂

▨ Internal
  proof mass Si

▤ Substrate Si

(b)

Fig. 1. a) Cross-Sectional view of the proposed device with four proof-mass. b) Top view of the lateral dimensions.

3   Design Analysis

3.1   Finite Element Analysis from CoventorWare10

An FEM based commercial tool CoventorWare10 is used to observe the mechanical behavior of the different device structures. The displacement nature of the membrane and the frequency response is observed. All the analysis are performed by clamping the four sides of the membrane for ensuring good clamping an extra 3mm on each side is left for clamping. The displacement contour is achieved by applying a static 0.01μN is applied on the top surface of the external load. The frequency response is observed by applying a harmonic force with amplitude 0.00001μN on the top surface of external proof-mass. The membrane layers and the internal proof-masses are meshed with tetrahedron elements of minimum size 500 and the external proof-mass and the clamped regions of the membrane are also meshed with tetrahedron elements of minimum size 3000.

a.   Internal Proof-Mass Configuration

Internal proof-mass lateral dimension $4\times2\text{mm}^2$	Internal proof-mass lateral dimension $4\times1\text{mm}^2$
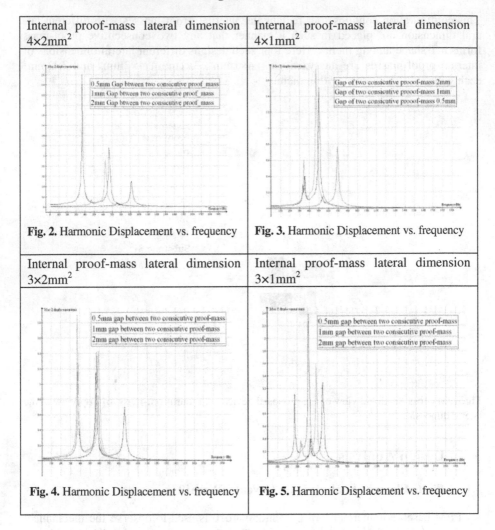	
Fig. 2. Harmonic Displacement vs. frequency	**Fig. 3.** Harmonic Displacement vs. frequency
Internal proof-mass lateral dimension $3\times2\text{mm}^2$	Internal proof-mass lateral dimension $3\times1\text{mm}^2$
Fig. 4. Harmonic Displacement vs. frequency	**Fig. 5.** Harmonic Displacement vs. frequency

b.   External Proof-Mass Design

Among the above designs the lowest frequency is observed in the case with four proof-mass model. The mode shapes are in all the previous analysis with square external proof-mass shows that the 3rd mode affects the membrane most and hence it is dominant over the previous two modes. Also the corners of the external proof-mass are playing a huge role in the first two modes. Therefore, the external should be circular. Next to intensify the loading effect the external proof-mass should be made of a higher density material; this will also ensure negligible shape deformation of the external proof-mass. Also to make this load bearable by the membrane it is applied with help of four pillars, each of $250 \times 250 \mu m^2$ dimension and thickness $300 \mu m$, centered on the four internal proof-mass. The external proof-mass is chosen of 2mm thick Tungsten with 8mm radius.

3.2   Analytical Estimation of Power

Two basic equations for defining the piezo-electricity action of any piezo-electric material [8] are

$$S_1 = s_{11}^E T_1 + d_{13} E_3 \tag{1}$$

$$D_3 = d_{31} T_1 + \varepsilon_{33}^T E_3 \tag{2}$$

Here, S = Mechanical Strain   (dimensionless)
T= Mechanical Stress (Nm^{-2})
E= Electric Field (Vm^{-1})
D= Displacement Current Density (Cm^{-2})
s_{11}^E= Elastic Compliance at constant electric field (m^2N^{-1})
d_{ij}= Piezo-electric Charge Coefficient (CN^{-1})
and,ε_{33}^T= Electric Permittivity at constant Stress (Fm^{-1}).

The first equation depicts the stress-strain relationship but the additional electric-field term describes the effect of piezo-electricity. For feebly piezo-electric materials the second term should be small compared to the first term. The second equation describes the dielectric property of a piezo-electric material. This relation too has piezo-electric effect coupled.

The Ohm's law modified by Maxwell is given by

$$J = \sigma E_3 + \frac{\partial D_3}{\partial t} \tag{3}$$

where, J= Current Density (Am^{-2})
and,σ = conductivity   (mho-m)

Now, for feebly piezo-electric material

$$S_1 = s_{11}^E T_1 \tag{4}$$

In linear elastic region, $s_{11}^E = \frac{1}{Y} \tag{5}$

where, Y= Young's Modules.

For strong dielectric $D_3 = \varepsilon_{33}^T E_3 \tag{6}$

For a situation in between these two extreme conditions, we can assume

$$s_{11}^E T_1 \cong d_{13} E_3 \tag{7}$$

$$and, \varepsilon_{33}^T E_3 \cong d_{31} T_1 \tag{8}$$

For practical situation it is expected that equation (7) & (8) will not be valid. Thus we can assume that

$$d_{13}E_3 = \alpha s_{11}^E T_1 \tag{9}$$

$$\& d_{31}T_1 = \beta \varepsilon_{33}^T E_3 \tag{10}$$

where, $\alpha \ll 1 \& \beta \ll 1$ as under normal circumstances.
From equation (9) & (10) we have

$$E_3 = \alpha \frac{s_{11}^E T_1}{d_{13}} = \frac{1}{\beta} \frac{d_{31}T_1}{\varepsilon_{33}^T} \tag{11}$$

And assuming, $d_{13} = d_{31}$
$$\alpha\beta = \frac{d_{13}^2}{s_{11}^E \varepsilon_{33}^T} \tag{12}$$

Again we know,
$$E_3 = \frac{V}{t} \tag{13}$$

Where, V= voltage (open circuit) developed over PZT surface under no load condition, and t= thickness of the PZT layer.
Equation (11) can be used in equation (13) to obtain voltage expression

$$V = \frac{g_{31}\sigma_1 t}{\beta} \tag{14}.$$

where, $\frac{d_{31}}{\varepsilon_{33}^T} = g_{31} =$ Piezo-electric voltage coefficient   (VNm^{-1}).

Rewriting the equation (2) with help of equation (10) we have

$$D_3 = d_{31}T_1 + \frac{1}{\beta}d_{31}T_1 = \left(1 + \frac{1}{\beta}\right)d_{31}T_1 \tag{15}$$

Clubbing equation (10) & (15) in equation (3) we can write

$$J = \sigma \frac{1}{\beta}\frac{d_{31}T_1}{\varepsilon_{33}^T} + \frac{\partial[(1+1/\beta)d_{31}T_1]}{\partial t} \tag{16}$$

If we assume T_1 to be harmonic, we can write

$$J = d_{31}T_1 \left(\sigma \frac{1}{\beta\varepsilon_{33}^T} + j\omega[1 + 1/\beta]\right) \tag{17}$$

For an effective piezo-material area of 'A' exposed under stress, total short circuit current will be

$$I = JA = d_{31}T_1 \left(\sigma \frac{1}{\beta\varepsilon_{33}^T} + j\omega[1 + 1/\beta]\right) A \tag{18}$$

Therefore, the internal impedance will be

$$Z = \frac{V}{I} = \frac{t}{A} \frac{\sigma - j\omega\varepsilon_{33}^T(1+\beta)}{(\sigma)^2 + (\omega\varepsilon_{33}^T[1+\beta])^2} \tag{19}$$

To estimate the value of β we use the equation (19)

$$Im(Z) = -\frac{t}{A}\frac{\omega\varepsilon_{33}^T(1+\beta)}{(\sigma)^2+(\omega\varepsilon_{33}^T[1+\beta])^2} \tag{20}$$

Assuming that the internal impedance only consist of capacitive and resistive terms

Thus,

$$\frac{1}{\omega C} = \frac{t}{A}\frac{\omega\varepsilon_{33}^T(1+\beta)}{(\sigma)^2+(\omega\varepsilon_{33}^T[1+\beta])^2} \tag{21}$$

Therefore,

$$C = \frac{A}{t}\frac{(\sigma)^2+(\omega\varepsilon_{33}^T[1+\beta])^2}{\omega^2\varepsilon_{33}^T(1+\beta)} \tag{22}$$

From the equation (22) we can have

$$\varepsilon = \frac{(\sigma)^2+(\omega\varepsilon_{33}^T[1+\beta])^2}{\omega^2\varepsilon_{33}^T(1+\beta)} \tag{23}$$

From equation (23) a quadratic equation of βcan be formulated solving which we can estimate the value β.The typical values of different coefficients used in the previous sections are estimated from different available publications for sol-gel spin coated thin-film PZT layers [5, 6, 8, 11]. The different estimated values are ε_r =5000, ε_{33}^T=1.8×10^{-8}, g_{31}= -9.1×10^{-3}Vm/N, $d_{31}=d_{13}=g_{31}e_{33}^T$= -163.8×10^{-12}C/N s_{11}^E=15×10^{-12}m^2/N, σ=5×10^{-5}mho-m, ω=390.8Hz, A=10^{-4}m^2, t=0.53×10^{-6}m. Putting this values in equation (23) and solving for β gives β=0.71.

The maximum power of the device can be estimated from the open circuit voltage and internal impedance expressions.

$$P_{max} = \frac{v^2}{2Re(Z)} \tag{24}$$

Therefore,

$$P_{max} = \frac{(g_{31}T_1t)^2}{2\beta^2\left(\dfrac{t}{A}\dfrac{\sigma}{(\sigma)^2+(\omega\varepsilon_{33}^T[1+\beta])^2}\right)} \tag{25}$$

4   Results and Discussions

Equation (19) shows that to minimize the internal impedance thickness is to be lowered and area has to increase. This clearly signifies the use of thin film piezo-layers instead of thick standalone piezo-ceramics. Also the use of membrane based structures instead of beams is justified. From the various harmonic analysis results, the figure of merit may be determined as:

$$\text{Figure of merit} = \frac{estimated\ power\times no\ of\ peaks\ in\ the\ range\ practical\ vibration\ sources}{lower\ cutoff\ frequency}$$

Table 1. Comparison of the 12designs analyzed

Internal proof-mass dimensions in mm^2	Gap between two consecutive proof-masses in mm	Resonating frequency (in Hz)	No of peaks within 2 KHz	Estimated Power/area (in Watts/cm^2)	Figures of merit
2×4	0.5	370.04	3	0.301	2.44×10^{-3}
	1	463.96	3	0.417	2.7×10^{-3}
	2	720.5	3	0.814	3.25×10^{-3}
1×4	0.5	420.3	4	0.360	2.57×10^{-3}
	1	344.17	4	0.274	3.16×10^{-3}
	2	527.29	3	0.509	2.9×10^{-3}
1×3	0.5	273.59	4	0.209	3.06×10^{-3}
	1	333.35	4	0.263	3.16×10^{-3}
	2	399.35	3	0.334	2.51×10^{-3}
3x2	0.5	378	4	0.598	3.28×10^{-3}
	1	372.8	3	0.304	2.45×10^{-3}
	2	563.24	3	0.567	3.02×10^{-3}

Table 2. Comparison of the frequency response of the different energy harvesters

Model Description	Resonant frequency (in Hz)	Maximum Modal Displacement (µm)	Reference
Doubly clamped beam	500-1000 (non-linear tracking of resonant frequency)	0.1-2.5	Hajati, A., Kim, S.G.: Wide-Bandwidth MEMS-scale piezoelectric energy harvester: Power MEMS, Washington DC,USA, December 1-4 (2009)
Doubly clamped beam	500-1000 (non-linear tracking of resonant frequency)	20-80	Hajati, A., Kim, S.G., Bathurst, S.P., Lee, H.J.: Design and fabrication of nonlinear resonator for ultra wide band energy harvesting application, IEEE 24 conf. on MEMS, Cancun, MEXICO, January 23-27,pp 1301-1304 (2011).
Micro-cantilever beam with proof-mass at tip of free end	13,900	4.5	Jeon, Y.B., Sood, R., Jeong, J.h., Kim S.G.: MEMS power generator with transverse mode thin film PZT. Sensors and Actuators A vol.122 pp16–22. (2005)

Table 2. *(Continued)*

Square membrane With 4 rectangular proof mass (3-2mm^2)	378-2000 (with four closely placed peaks within 2 kHz in the linear regime)	19 (with almost un-iformly spread over the entire membrane)	This paper

The comparison in Table2 shows that the membrane based resonator shows lowered frequency response with multiple peaks in the frequency of interest without entering into non-linear region. Among four proof-mass models, the model with 3x2mm^2 internal proof-mass with 0.5mm separation, is chosen due to its highest figure of merit (3.28×10⁻3) and lower cutoff frequency (378Hz) which is better than the one reported in [9] with 390.8 Hz resonating frequency.

5   Conclusion

This paper optimizes the design of wide band MEMS resonators operating in the linear region through introduction of a figure of merit. The figure of merit incorporates three parameters viz. power output per unit area, lower cut off frequency and no peaks in the operating frequency range within 2 KHz (most of the practical vibration sources lie within it). It has been observed that the resonator with four internal proof-masses each of dimensions 3x2mm2 placed 0.5mm apart from each other shows lower cut off frequency of 378Hz with four closely placed peaks within 2 kHz in the linear region and has the highest figure of merit. The power analysis depicts that a 598mW can be extracted from the optimized device. Using thin layers will enable the device work under very low amplitude vibrations. Tapping the low frequency vibrations will make these devices suitable for use in almost all environments. The device serves the purpose of widening of resonating frequency without entering the device into non-linear region. The low internal impedance of the device also makes it suitable for energy harvesting application.

References

1. Kok, S.-L., White, N.M., Nick, H.N.: Fabrication and characterization of free-standing thick-film piezoelectric cantilevers for energy harvesting. Meas. Sci. Technol. 20(12), 124010, 13 (2009)
2. Roundy, S.J.: Energy Scavenging for Wireless Sensor Nodes with a Focus on Vibration to Electricity Conversion. Thesis submitted in The University of California, Berkeley (2003)
3. Jones, G.P., Beeby, S.P., White, N.M.: Towards a piezoelectric vibration-powered micro generator. IEE Proc. Sci. Meas. Technol. 148, 68R–72R (2001)
4. Roundy, S., Wright, P.K., Rabaey, J.: A study of low level vibrations as a power sources for wireless sensor nodes. Comput. Commun. 26, 1131–1144 (2003)

5. Jeon, Y.B., Sood, R., Jeong, J.H., Kim, S.G.: MEMS power generator with transverse mode thin film PZT. Sensors and Actuators A 122, 16–22 (2005)
6. Choi, W.J., Jeon, Y.B., Sood, R., Jeong, J.-H., Kim, S.G.: Energy harvesting MEMS device based on thin film piezoelectric cantilevers. J. Electroceram. 17(2-4), 543–548 (2006)
7. Hajati, A., Kim, S.G., Bathurst, S.P., Lee, H.J.: Design and fabrication of nonlinear resonator for ultra wide band energy harvesting application. In: IEEE 24th Conf. on MEMS, Cancun, Mexico, January 23-27, pp. 1301–1304 (2011)
8. Eggborn, T.: Analytical Models to Predict Power Harvesting with Piezoelectric Materials. Thesis submitted to the Faculty of the Virginia Polytechnic Institute and State University (2003)
9. Rana, G., Lahiri, S.K., Roychaudhuri, C.: Design and analysis of a membrane based efficient wide band resonator for energy harvesting. In: International Conference on Smart Material Structure & Systems, Bangalore, India (January 2012)
10. Hajati, A., Kim, S.G.: Wide-Bandwidth MEMS-scale piezoelectric energy harvester: Power MEMS, Washington DC, USA, December 1-4 (2009)
11. http://www.noliac.com/Files/Billeder/02%20Standard/Ceramics/ Noliac_CEramics_NCE_datasheet.pdf

Ultra-Low Power Sub-threshold SRAM Cell Design to Improve Read Static Noise Margin

Chandrabhan Kushwah and Santosh K. Vishvakarma

Nanoscale Devices and VLSI/ULSI Circuit & System Design Lab, IIT Indore, India
{chandrabhan,skvishvakarma}@iiti.ac.in

Abstract. Sub-threshold circuit design is a prevalent selection for ultra-low power (ULP) systems. Static random access memory (SRAM) is an important component in these systems therefore ultra-low power SRAM has become popular. Operation of standard 6T SRAM at sub or near-threshold voltages is unfeasible, predominantly due to degraded static noise margin (SNM) and fluctuations in MOSFET currents because of process variations at ultra-low voltages. Hence, many researchers have deliberated divergent configuration SRAMs for sub-threshold operations having 8T, 9T and 10T bit-cells for enhanced stability. Sub-threshold SRAMs have many important design issues such as cell stability, leakage current and area. In this paper, we give a deep insight of sub-threshold SRAM cell design issues and discuss several important circuit techniques. We emphasize on SRAM cell stability during read operation, develop read port circuits to design an ultra-low power sub-threshold SRAM cell. We propose 9T bit-cell that effectively improve read margin, thereby achieving high cell stability at 45nm technology node. The proposed design shows the full functionality of SRAM cell at a voltage down to around 500-200mV. The proposed design employs standard circuit techniques to improve read margins, as well as to allow a large number of bit-cells on single bit-line.

Keywords: SRAM, Sub-threshold, RSNM, ULP.

1 Introduction

This research paper explores the challenges arising from low voltage operation of standard SRAMs and reviews numerous proposed bit-cells by various researchers in past years. Although technology scaling has enabled a dramatic increase in functionality and complexity in integrated circuit (IC) design, one major negative side effect of technology scaling is that leakage power increases significantly from one technology generation to the next and represents one of the main challenges in contemporary system-on-chip (SoC) integration [1, 3]. In addition, the demand for power sensitive designs has grown significantly, mainly due to the fast growth of battery operated portable applications, such as notebook computers, personal digital assistants (PDA), smart phones, etc. To design integrated systems, significant attention has been given to the design of medium performance and low power circuits (tens to hundreds of MHz clock rates). Some popular methods include voltage scaling, switching activity

H. Rahaman et al. (Eds.): VDAT 2012, LNCS 7373, pp. 139–146, 2012.

reduction, architectural techniques, and device sizing and new device structures [2-5]. Voltage scaling is one of the most effective techniques for power reduction in digital VLSI design with some limitations like, loss of static noise margins, current fluctuations due to process variations and limitations on the number of cells connected to a single bit-line. These methods are applicable in medium performance systems which are not suitable for portable battery operated gadgets. Many researchers have suggested operating a circuit in sub-threshold region to reduce power consumption in the range of micro watt [1, 2]. This can be achieved by fix the supply voltage close to the device's threshold voltage which is known as the near-threshold regime. The sub-threshold logic development elevated the need for embedded memories, primarily SRAMs [3, 4]. Researchers have developed several methods for reducing the standby voltage of SRAMs, so the circuit can be run at the optimum speed and then sleep after complete operation to reduce the leakage power consumption. These methods are not suitable for SRAM where data is to be stored for some specific time duration. Therefore reducing the leakage power during active region is necessary. This requirement has led to design SRAM in sub-threshold regime [5].

The 6 transistor (6T) cell which uses cross coupled inverter pair is most commonly used bit-cell in the current SRAM designs shown in Fig. 1 [17]. Different types of SRAM bit-cells have been proposed to improve the memory failure probability at a given supply voltage. This 6T cell is comprised of a cross coupled inverter latch and pair of access transistors that allow differential read and write operations. The positive feedback loop of the cross-coupled inverters makes this structure very robust. The common terminology for the robustness of this cell is achieved with the definition of the Static Noise Margin (SNM), generally calculated as the side of the largest square that fits inside one of the lobes of the butterfly curve [18]. This SRAM cell is working in strong inversion region and therefore the current is linearly depends on device parameters.

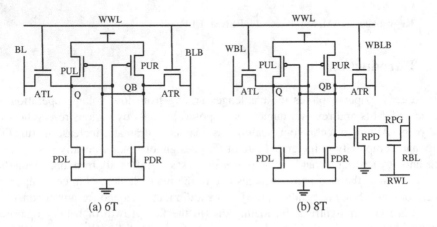

(a) 6T   (b) 8T

Fig. 1. Conventional SRAM cells (a) 6T and (b) 8T

When input voltage at gate of a MOSFET drops below the threshold voltage the device current becomes exponentially dependent on the difference of the gate voltage and threshold voltage. Primarily the sub-threshold memories were presented in 2004 [3, 6, 13, 14]. The group [4] at Purdue showed that operation of a standard 6T SRAM under process variations is problematic. In 2007, Kim's group [6] introduced a standard 8T SRAM cell that functions at voltages as low as 200mV, by utilizing the Reverse short channel effect (RSCE). As a result, increasing the length of a transistor actually lowers V_{TH} in most modern processes until a minimum point. By using access transistors with a channel at this minimum V_{TH} length, the write current is increased, resulting in an equivalent write margin as achieved with a boosted word-line. In addition, the standard 8T topology shown in Fig. 1 decouples the cell node from the bit-line by using additional read path transistors. By doing so, the SNM in read mode becomes equal to that in hold mode. Write SNM at low voltages is achieved by gating the supply voltage to the cell during a write.

In 2008, Chandrakasan's group [8] proposed a standard 8T cell for increased density and achieved low voltage operation through peripheral modifications. Using 8T cell, 30% reduction of area as compared to their 10T cell was achieved. The "zero leakage" readout scheme raises the source of the readout transistor to V_{DD} when the row is deselected, minimizing its DIBL leakage, which almost eliminates the leakage. The reads are further improved by using a differential sensing scheme that eliminates the global variations. The sub-threshold and near-threshold design is fast becoming a popular selection for ultra-low power systems. The operation of standard 6T or 8T SRAMs at sub- or near-threshold voltage is unachievable, primarily due to the degraded static noise margins and extreme fluctuations in the device currents under process variations at low voltages. Therefore we proposed a new design of 9T SRAM cell showing the full functionality at voltages down to 200mV. This design utilizes basic techniques to improve read and write margins, as well as to enable a large number of bit-cells on single bit-line. This cell resembles an 8T cell with a decoupled readout path to solve the read margin problem. Various additional techniques have been used to improve write margins and minimize bit-line leakage.

2   Design of Proposed 9T SRAM Cell

To operate in the sub-threshold/near-threshold and to increase the static noise margin (SNM), structural change of bit-cell has to be considered to enhance the immunity with the process-voltage-temperature (PVT) fluctuations. On the basis of this approach the proposed design gives higher noise immunity than the standard 6T bit cell. Fig. 2 shows the proposed 9T SRAM cell which has one cross-coupled inverter pair. The left side inverter is having one PMOST (PUL) as pull-up device and a combination of a diode connected PMOST (PSL) and NMOST (PDL) as driver. The inverter of right side is made up of one pull up PMOST (PUR) and two NMOST (NSR and PDR) are connected in pull-down path. Since NSR act as a switch between nodes QB and NQB we can control it by SCR. Two access transistors (ATL and ATR) are placed between storage nodes (Q and QB) and write bit lines (WBL and WBLB).

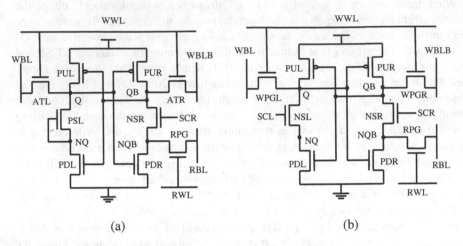

Fig. 2. 9T SRAM cells (a) Proposed and (b) Reference [13]

2.1   Standby Operation

In standby mode, the power supply of SRAM cell is cut off by the NMOS transistor to reduce the leakage power. Also, the supply voltage cannot be reduced randomly as the cell will not be able to hold the true value. Therefore the size of transistors has to be set carefully. As most of the SRAM cells adopt the standard CMOS inverter pair based architecture, therefore their transfer characteristics are similar to the 6T in hold mode. It is for sure not to have any influence on dynamic power and access time of cell. In this mode write word-line (WWL) and read word-line (RWL) are grounded and read bit-line (RBL), SCR and word bit-lines are connected to the power supply.

2.2   Write Operation

It is a challenge to maintain write margin in sub-threshold/near-threshold SRAM design due to small gate overdrive, large load capacitance and severe process variation. We have designed the cell to reduce the pull-down strength so as to achieve better write ability. The value to which node Q can be charged or discharged is closely related to the length of the write period. It is demonstrated that data correctness will not be affected even if the node is charged to a value smaller than a full high signal value or discharged to a value larger than a full low signal value. To write '1' into the cell we will activate NSR switch by applying high logic SCR signal. The read bit-line (RBL) which is used to read the cell is pre-charged to supply voltage and write word-line (RWL) is grounded. The write bit-line (WBL) is connected to supply voltage and WBLB is at ground. We assume that a '0' was written in cell and we can write '1' into the cell by setting WWL to a high logic which will activate access transistors (ATL and ATR) and voltage at storage node Q will be increased. This increased voltage will charge floating node Q and PDR will create low resistance path between QB and ground. To write '0' we will change the polarity of WBL, WBLB and SCR. If we switch-off NSR there will be no path between QB and NQB which makes QB floating and high WBLB charge the QB at high logic while Q is discharged to ground level by PSL and PDL.

2.3   Read Operation

It is known that in SRAM cell design of sub-threshold memories the read failure is the most serious problem as it enforces the smallest margin in contrast with the hold margin and write margin. During the read operation, the values stored in the nodes are transferred to the bit-lines. However, the bit-line capacitance may charge the cell to an increased to a positive value. No matter what the memory structure is, a read failure (RF) event is occurred when the memory stored value "0" is increased to a positive value higher than the trip point (VTRIP). If we increase the threshold voltage while switching from '0' to '1', the read SNM will be increased significantly. To read cell WWL and SCR are grounded and RBL is connected to NQB by applying supply to RWL. If there is '1' stored at Q then PDR will be activated and RBL will be discharged through RPG and PDR. If there is '0' at Q then RBL will remain at its pre-charged value. To increase the read stability, the true value node can be isolated (decoupled) from bit-line so as to allow bit-line discharging. The read current will bypass through the transistor connected between the pseudo and the true storage node. Since NSR is off, the NQB is decoupled from QB during read operation thereby improving read SNM.

3   Simulation and Analysis

Read static noise margin is the figure of merit to evaluate SRAM cells stability. Process parameter severely affects the stability of SRAM and therefore we have simulated the cells on different process corners to see the effect of the threshold voltage variation with other parameters at constant values. Fig. 3 shows the variation in RSNM of proposed cell with power supply at different process corners.

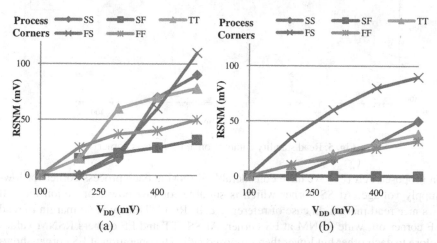

Fig. 3. Read SNM at different process corners for (a) Proposed and (b) Reference cell

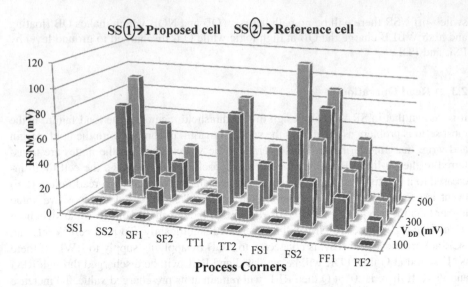

Fig. 4. Read SNM Comparison between proposed and reference cell

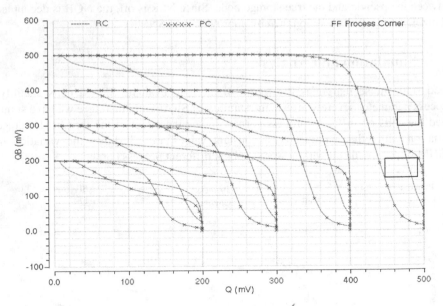

Fig. 5. Read stability comparison at FF process corner

In proposed cell (PC) we have considerable RSNM at each process corner for lower supply voltage. At SS corner which is suitable for low power operation the cell shows nice read margin. In case of reference cell (RC) [11] there is no margin to read at SF corner but wide RSNM at FS corner. At SS, TT and FF corners RSNM values are close to each other but lower then proposed cell. The operation at FS corner shows wide margin to read into the cell. In Fig. 4 it is clear that the proposed cell has larger margin as compared to the reference cell. If we would like to operate the cell for higher performance, we will choose FF corner where the proposed cell shows lesser delay to read and also consumes lower power than the proposed cell. Fig. 5 shows the output waveforms of two cross-coupled inverters to find the RSNM at FF corner. All the values of RSNM are found in the same manner. The RSNM of proposed cell at FF corner is approximately twice than that of the reference cell which is clear from the Fig. 5. If we compare RSNM of both the cells with respect to the threshold voltage variation at minimum and maximum allowable power supply we would get the view as Fig. 6. Since both the cells are having different cell architectures and also the rail-to-rail voltages at 500mV are higher as compared to 200mV power supply so the read currents will be higher which causes different behavior of RSNM variation.

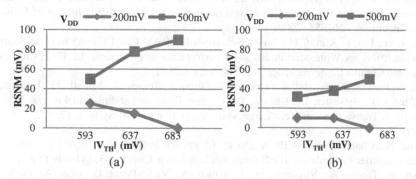

Fig. 6. RSNM variation with transistor V_{TH} (a) Proposed and (b) Reference cell

From Fig. 6 we analyze the effect of threshold voltage (V_{TH}) variation on RSNM of both of the cells. We find that for 500mV power supply the read stability increases with the increase in threshold voltage but for 200mV power supply the read stability decreases. It is clear that RSNM of both the cells vary with threshold voltage but the proposed cell has higher cell stability as compared to the reference cell for different threshold voltages.

4   Conclusion

We designed 9T SRAM cell which can operate in sub-threshold regime with improved read stability at all the process corners. In the range of 200-500mV power supply the proposed cell shows larger RSNM as compared to reference cell. Proposed cell shows same pattern of RSNM variation as reference cell with improved read stability at different power supplies. Proposed cell also provides an effective strategy for total power saving, this approach can be applied to battery operated SoC design.

References

1. Markovic, D., Wang, C.C., Alarcon, L.P., Liu, T.-T., Rabaey, J.M.: Ultralow-Power Design in Near-Threshold Region. Proc. of the IEEE 98, 237–252 (2010)
2. Wang, A., Chandrakasan, A.: A 180-mV subthreshold FFT processor using a minimum energy design methodology. IEEE Journal of Solid-State Circuits 40, 310–319 (2005)
3. Vladimirescu, A., Yu, C., Thomas, O., Huifang, Q., Markovic, D., Valentian, A., Ionita, R., Rabaey, J., Amara, A.: Ultra-low-voltage robust design issues in deep-submicron CMOS. In: The 2nd Annual IEEE Northeast Workshop on Circuits and Systems, pp. 49–52. IEEE (2004)
4. Raychowdhury, A., Mukhopadhyay, S., Roy, K.: A feasibility study of subthreshold SRAM across technology generations. In: Proc. IEEE International Conference on Computer Design: VLSI in Computers and Processors, pp. 417–422. IEEE (2005)
5. Eric, V.: Weak Inversion for Ultimate Low-Power Logic. In: Low-Power CMOS Circuits. CRC Press (2005)
6. Chang, I.J., Kim, J.J., Park, S.P., Roy, K.: A 32 kb 10T Sub-Threshold SRAM Array With Bit-Interleaving and Differential Read Scheme in 90 nm CMOS. IEEE Journal of Solid-State Circuits 44, 650–658 (2009)
7. Kim, T.-H., Liu, J., Kim, C.H.: An 8T Subthreshold SRAM Cell Utilizing Reverse Short Channel Effect for Write Margin and Read Performance Improvement. In: IEEE Custom Integrated Circuits Conference, pp. 241–244. IEEE (2007)
8. Zhai, B., Pant, S., Nazhandali, L., Hanson, S., Olson, J., Reeves, A., Minuth, M., Helfand, R., Austin, T., Sylvester, D., Blaauw, D.: Energy- Efficient Subthreshold Processor Design. IEEE Transactions on Very Large Scale Integration (VLSI) Systems 17, 1127–1137 (2009)
9. Verma, N., Chandrakasan, A.P.: A 256 kb 65 nm 8T Subthreshold SRAM Employing Sense-Amplifier Redundancy. IEEE Journal of Solid-State Circuits 43, 141–149 (2008)
10. Fisher, S., Teman, A., Vaysman, D., Gertsman, A., Yadid-Pecht, O., Fish, A.: Digital subthreshold logic design - motivation and challenges. In: IEEE 25th Convention of Electrical and Electronics Engineers in Israel, pp. 702–706. IEEE (2008)
11. Calhoun, B.H., Chandrakasan, A.P.: A 256-kb 65-nm sub-threshold SRAM design for ultra-low-voltage operation. IEEE Journal of Solid State Circuits 42, 680–688 (2007)
12. Wang, A., Calhoun, B.H., Chandrakasan, A.P.: Sub-threshold design for ultra-low-power systems. Springer (2006)
13. Chang, M.-F., Chang, S.-W., Chou, P.-W., Wu, W.-C.: A 130 mV SRAM with Expanded Write and Read Margins for Subthreshold Applications. IEEE Journal of Solid-State Circuits 46(2) (2011)
14. Itoh, K.: Low-voltage memories for power-aware systems. In: Proc. of the International Symposium on Low Power Electronics and Design, pp. 1–6 (2002)
15. Wang, A., Chandrakasan, A.: A 180mV FFT processor using subthreshold circuit techniques. In: Solid-State Circuits Conference, vol. 1, pp. 292–529 (2004)
16. Calhoun, B.H., Chandrakasan, A.: Analyzing static noise margin for sub-threshold SRAM in 65nm CMOS. In: Proc. of the 31st European Solid-State Circuits Conference, pp. 363–366 (2005)
17. Zhang, K., Hamzaoglu, F., Wang, Y.: Low Power SRAMs in nanoscale CMOS technologies. IEEE Trans. Electron Devices 55(1), 145–151 (2008)
18. Seevinck, E., List, F., Lohstroh, J.: Static-noise margin analysis of MOS transistors. IEEE Journal of Solid-State Circuits SC-22(5), 748–754 (1987)

Workload Driven Power Domain Partitioning

Arun Dobriyal, Rahul Gonnabattula,
Pallab Dasgupta, and Chittaranjan R. Mandal

Department of Computer Science and Engineering,
Indian Institute of Technology Kharagpur, West Bengal, India 721302
pallab@cse.iitkgp.ernet.in, chitta@iitkgp.ac.in,
{grahul.iitkgp,arundobriyaliitkgp}@gmail.com

Abstract. This paper presents a formulation for the problem of partitioning the set of components on a power rail of a low power integrated circuit into power domains based on the usage patterns given by an application specific workload. We present an analysis of the underlying problem, proving that the problem is NP-complete. We propose a greedy algorithm for this problem and compare its solutions with a more exhaustive search based on a genetic algorithm formulation. It is shown through empirical evaluation that the greedy algorithm is in general a well suited algorithm for this problem.

Keywords: low power circuits, partitioning, CAD.

1   Introduction

Large low power digital integrated circuits are typically partitioned into multiple power islands [1, 2]. The on-chip power distribution network places the components on one or more *power rails*, where each power rail supplies a common voltage to all components in the rail. In large system-on-chip (SOC) designs, different circuit components may work at different voltages and different clock frequencies, and therefore components having different voltage / frequency requirements cannot be on the same power rail.

In recent times, designers are advocating the use of fine grained power power gating[3–5] by further partitioning the set of components on a single power rail into subsets (called *power islands*) that are switched ON or OFF together using power gates . There is an ongoing debate on the desired granularity of these power islands[6]. It has been shown[5] that using too many power islands does not necessarily achieve optimal power performance, because the overhead of adding a lot of isolation cells and frequent changes in power states leads to non-trivial wastage of energy. It is also believed that power gating each component individually will create a verification nightmare for the on-chip power management strategy[6]. Therefore clustering individual components into multiple power islands seems to be the more feasible and preferred.

The task of partitioning the set of components having common voltage requirements into multiple power domains is done today mainly by leveraging the

H. Rahaman et al. (Eds.): VDAT 2012, LNCS 7373, pp. 147–155, 2012.
© Springer-Verlag Berlin Heidelberg 2012

domain knowledge of the platform architects regarding possible use cases of the platform. The increasing diversity of applications running on low power platforms and the increasing number of functional components in a SOC are reasons to believe that manual approaches for power domain partitioning will not be possible in near future.

It should be noted that the power domain partitioning problem has been studied from several angles. For example, power domain partitioning in memory units using activity/patterns was studied in [7]. Extending the above work, a polynomial time algorithm for activity based power domain partitioning was presented in [8]. A modification of the sleep time maximization approach was proposed by [9] which added minimization of cut nets to decrease and minimize the power consumption. Though the power domain partitioning problem for SOC components is quite different from the power domain partitioning problem for memories we believe that the role of activity patterns will become increasingly significant in both problem domains. Therefore it is an important requirement to study the power domain partitioning problem for SOC components based on activity patterns. This paper reports the first automated approach towards solving this problem.

The power domain partitioning problem is formally defined as follows.

Given: A set $C = c_1, \ldots, c_N$ of N components with idle state power dissipation, p_i for each $c_i \in C$. A set $Z = z_1, \ldots, z_M$ of M workload patterns, where each $z_j \subseteq C$ is the subset of components that are active in that pattern and frequency f_j for $z_j \in Z$, representing the number of times the pattern z_j was observed in a workload trace.

Optimization Problem: Partition C into k disjoint subsets, $d_1, \ldots, d_k$, such that the total power wasted is minimized. Total power wastage is given by:

$$\text{Power Wastage} = \sum_{z_j \in Z} \left(f_j * \sum_{c_i \in d_u \setminus z_j : d_u \cap z_j \neq \phi} p_i \right). \tag{1}$$

If, $d_u \cap z_j \neq \phi$, is false(no components in power domain d_u is active) in a pattern, z_j then there is no power wastage because the domain can be switched OFF else each component incurs an idle power loss equal to its power rating.

Decision Problem: Given Δ and k, Can we partition C into k disjoint subsets, $d_1, \ldots, d_k$, such that the total power wastage is less than equal to Δ?

Our goal is to solve this optimization problem. Our contributions are as follows:

1. We establish the intractability of the optimization problem in Sec 2.
2. We propose a Greedy Algorithm in Sec 3 which greedily selects and merges two domains based on an intuitive heuristic. This is repeated until the desired k number of domains are obtained.

3. We design a genetic algorithm in Sec 4 and compare the quality of solutions produced by the genetic algorithm with the solutions produced by the Greedy Algorithm in Sec 5 empirically. The results show that there is no significant improvement in the quality of solutions even after many evolutions.

2 Power Domain Partitioning Is NP-Complete

Since we can design a deterministic polynomial time verifier which can check if the given solution admits a power wastage less than Δ, the problem is in NP. To prove that this problem is NP-hard, we show a reduction from the *Minimum sum of Squares* (MSS) problem which is known to be NP-complete[10].

MSS: Given a finite set A containing N elements $a_1, \ldots, a_N$, a size $s(a_i) \in Z^+$ for each $a \in A$, positive integers $k \leq N$ and J, is it possible to partition A into k disjoint sets $A_1, \ldots, A_k$, such that:

$$\sum_{i=1}^{k} \left[\sum_{a \in A_i} s(a) \right]^2 \leq J . \tag{2}$$

Theorem 1. *Power Domain Partitioning is NP-Hard.*

Proof. Given the set A of N elements, $a_1, \ldots, a_N$ and $s(a_i) \in Z^+$, we design an instance of the power domain partitioning. We define a component c_i for each integer a_i (refer Fig 1) with idle state power dissipation, $p_i = s(a_i)$. We introduce N patterns and assign a frequency of $s(a_i)$ for the ith pattern. For the ith pattern, only the component, c_i, is active and the rest are idle.

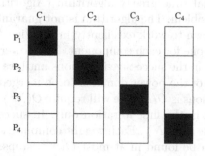

Fig. 1. The construction of the reduction for A={ $a_1, \ldots, a_4$ } elements. Black indicates that the component is active, while White denotes the component is idle.

Consider an arbitrary k partition, B={ $A_1, \ldots, A_k$} for the N components. For the ith pattern, only c_i is active, hence power is wasted for all the other components in its partition A_j. Power wastage in i^{th} pattern is $S_j - s(a_i)$, where $S_j = \sum_{a:a \in A_j} s(a)$.

Considering that the frequency of the ith pattern is also given by $s(a_i)$, the total power wastage due to partition A_i is $\sum_{a:a\in A_i} S_i \times s(a) - \sum_{a:a\in A_i} s(a)^2$.

Therefore, the total power wastage due to the workload is:

$$\text{Power Wastage} = \sum_{i=1}^{k} \sum_{a:a\in A_i} s(a) \times (S_i - s(a))) .$$

$$= (\sum_{i=1}^{k} S_i \sum_{a:a\in A_i} s(a)) - \sum_{i=1}^{k} \sum_{a:a\in A_i} s(a)^2 .$$

$$= \sum_{i=1}^{k} S_i^2 - \sum_{j=1}^{n} s(a_j)^2 . \tag{3}$$

The second term, namely $\sum_{j=1}^{n} s(a_j)^2$ is independent of the partitioning and can be computed a priori. Therefore given a constant J, deciding the satisfiability of:

$$\sum_{i=1}^{k} \left[\sum_{a\in A_i} s(a) \right]^2 \leq J . \tag{4}$$

reduces to deciding whether the power wastage is less than $\Delta = J - \sum_{j=1}^{n} s(a_j)^2$. This completes the reduction and hence the proof of NP completeness.

3   A Greedy Solution

We discuss a polynomial time greedy algorithm (Algorithm 1) for the Power Domain Partitioning problem. The algorithm is not guaranteed to produce optimal solutions but is shown to work excellently in practice. The algorithm starts with N power domains, one for each component. The power domains are merged greedily (two at a time) in the successive iterations until we are left with k power domains. The selection of the power domains to be merged is done greedily.

The number of iterations is $O(N)$. We will require $O(N^2)$ weight computations for the complete graph in the first iteration only. In successive iterations, this step(Line 4) can be done in $O(N)$. Each weight computation needs $O(M)$ time. The minimum edge can be found in at most $O(N^2)$ steps. Line 6 needs $O(M)$ time. Therefore the time complexity of the algorithm is $O(N^3M)$.

4   A Genetic Algorithm Formulation

Genetic Alogorithms are widely employed to solve various optimization problems, in VLSI. They are quite useful in carrying out a restrictive and heuristic based exploration of the design space. The results are reported to be quite promising [11, 12] We designed a Genetic Algorithm for the problem also considering its past success in graph partitioning problems[13, 14]. Our intention

---

Algorithm 1. Greedy k-way Power Domain Partitioning

Input: N components, a number k, M patterns
Output: k power domains

1 $n = N$;
2 Form power domain for each component.
3 **for** $i \leftarrow 1$ **to** $N - k$ **do**
4 | Construct a complete graph of n power domains. For each edge, (j, r),
   | assign weight: w_{jr} = Increase in power wastage if power domain j is merged
   | with power domain r
5 | Choose an edge with minimum edge weight, breaking ties randomly;
6 | Merge the power domains connected by the chosen edge;
7 | $n = n - 1$;
8 **end**
9 *Report k partitions found;*

---

of creating this formulation was to compare the performance of this algorithm with the greedy algorithm.

The Genetic Algorithm for the power domain partitioning problem, runs for a maximum of the user-specified number of evolutions, E, or till a solution having power wastage less than a user-specified upper bound is found, whichever is earlier. It outputs the best partition of the components across all evolutions.

4.1 Problem Encoding

A power domain partitioning instance (N components and k power domains), is encoded in the genetic algorithm framework as follows. Each individual in the population is defined by a chromosome of length N, and represents a partitioning of the N components into k domains. Each chromosome is a sequence of genes where the ith gene has a value j if component C_i belongs to the jth power domain, d_j. The fitness function and the genetic operators are defined as follows:

Fitness Function: The *fitness* of a chromosome is computed as the total power wastage for the partition it represents on the given workload. The fitness function is:

$$\text{Fitness Function} = \sum_{z_j \in Z} \left(f_j * \sum_{c_i \in d_u \setminus z_j : d_u \cap z_j \neq \phi} p_i \right). \tag{5}$$

Lower the Fitness Function value, more is the *Fitness* of the individual.

Cross Over Operator: The crossover operation generates offspring chromosomes by selecting two chromosomes from the current population (parents) by randomly picking a crossover point and then swapping all subsequent genes. The parents are selected randomly to ensure diversity in the population.

Mutation: Genetic algorithms tend to converge upon a local optima. This behavior is avoided by applying mutation operator on the offsprings. The mutation operation selects a random gene in a chromosome with a specified *mutation rate* (μ) and randomizes the value of the gene.

4.2   Runtime Optimizations

The computation of the fitness value of a chromosome greatly affects the running time of the algorithm since the entire workload has to be processed to compute the power wastage. This leads to two types of computation issues, namely:

1. *Repeated Computation.* The Fitness Function is invoked every time the fitness of an individual needs to be computed. Hence repeated computation of the fitness of an individual becomes a bottleneck.
2. *Isomorphic Chromosomes.* In a large population, isomorphic chromosomes representing the same partitioning may come up.

To handle these issues, the fitness function makes an unique encoding of the isomorphic chromosomes, stores it in a global Hash Table along with its fitness value. To calculate the fitness value, the fitness function checks the hash Table, if the particular encoding is not found then it computes the fitness by processing the entire workload trace and then adds a new entry to the hash Table.

The population size is initialized to a user defined value I_p, and this size is maintained across the generations. The initial population I_p is generated randomly and in each generation, offsprings are generated by applying the crossover operation. A mixture of best and random individuals of the resulting population are forwarded to the next generation.

5   Experimental Results

The Genetic Algorithm was implemented using the Java Genetic Algorithm Package (JGAP) on a 2.8 GHz AMD Phenom 2 processor with 4 GB RAM. For generating the test cases, we used a workload trace obtained from a third party evaluation of a cell phone workload on a commercial low power platform architecture. We also developed several randomized workload traces over varying sets of components to test the scalability of our proposed algorithms. The number of patterns were fixed at 7450 for all the experiments.

Table 1. Results on Commercial Workloads

	Optimal	Greedy Algorithm		Genetic Algorithm	
k	$P_{Opt}(\%)$	$P_{Gr}(\%)$	$T_{Gr}(ms)$	Ev	$T_{Ge}(ms)$
2	44.49	44.49	22.51	3.3	18.33
3	29.68	29.68	22.29	3.5	89.72
4	10.20	10.20	20.49	5.7	177.77

Table 2. Results on Random Workloads

Testcase			Greedy		Genetic Algorithm			
N	k	S(%)	$P_{Gr}(\%)$	$T_{Gr}(sec)$	Ev	$T_{Ge}(sec)$	$P_{best}(\%)$	$T_{Ge\_best}(sec)$
45	7	25	64.93	3.76	70.53	29.37	64.72	938.14
45	7	35	55.80	3.92	75.86	30.34	55.68	945.03
45	9	25	62.48	3.72	43.10	33.90	62.06	560.61
45	11	25	58.68	3.68	40.23	65.18	58.26	1551.72
45	11	35	51.63	3.89	51.43	79.24	51.51	1552.24
60	8	35	58.20	9.77	75.12	141.25	75.17	1814.55
60	8	45	48.34	10.06	158.83	190.12	48.31	2442.35
60	11	25	64.43	9.32	56.25	76.01	63.95	2539.98
60	11	35	54.86	9.76	59.00	154.60	54.71	2430.89
60	15	25	58.54	9.21	66.00	212.00	58.06	3678.40
60	15	35	49.42	9.62	78.00	254.76	49.22	3727.93
70	6	35	60.89	16.37	88.89	192.20	60.83	1664.61
70	11	25	66.63	15.16	54.15	190.60	66.06	3301.60
70	13	25	63.29	15.13	61.00	201.41	62.78	4363.98
70	13	35	54.38	15.13	114.40	360.91	54.26	3915.40
70	16	25	61.16	15.19	74.80	281.46	60.70	5479.87
100	15	25	66.01	46.68	111.50	686.54	67.28	30878.87
100	25	15	65.41	41.82	66.30	576.97	65.15	25849.80

Table 3. Effect of Mutation rate on performance of Genetic algorithm

Testcase			Ev			T_{Ge} (sec)		
N	k	S(%)	$\mu = 1/10$	$\mu = 1/30$	$\mu = 1/60$	$\mu = 1/10$	$\mu = 1/30$	$\mu = 1/60$
45	9	25	34.28	28.84	26.27	43.42	41.36	41.43
60	11	25	66.10	64.34	64.52	40.31	39.24	39.35
70	13	25	200.77	201.26	203.75	61.20	61.35	62.11

The trace data for the commercial workbench was collected on a commercial cell phone platform by monitoring the activities of the components under following workloads, a) 720p video playback b) 3D-graphics appl. c) 1080p HD video rec. d) Still Image capture. Since the exact power dissipation values of the components were not given, we used uniform power density across all components.

The parameters used in the experimentations are: a) *N-* the number of components. b) *k-* the desired number of power domains. c) *Sparsity S-* fraction of components that are ON in an usage pattern. d) *Idle Power Dissipation of Components-* the normalized power ratings for the components generated in the range of $[1, 100]$ randomly (motivation for this range is because of the approximate range of power density of each block taken from [15]).

Table 1 compares the proposed algorithms against the optimal power performance values over the commercial work trace, where as Table 2 compares their performance on random work traces. In both the tables, *k* represents the required number of power domains. For all the cases, the results were obtained by averaging over 50 runs of Genetic Algorithm, each time with an initial population of 35 and a mutation rate (μ) of $\frac{1}{10}$ (the probability that a gene mutates). The value of mutation rate and the initial population are to be fixed in general by the users to achieve optimal performance of the genetic algorithm for their problem formulation. The results in Table 3 compare the performance of the genetic algorithm with different mutation rates (μ).

For a given partitioning, the *percentage of power wastage* is computed as (α/β) × 100, where α and β are respectively, the *power wastage* and *the total power consumed* for that partitioning on the entire work trace. In Table 1, Column 2 reports the optimal percentage of power wastage, which was obtained by exhaustively examining all possible ways of partitioning the set of 9 components in that platform. For example, the value $P_{Opt}\% = 44.49$ for $k = 2$ tells us that the best partition of the components into two power domains incurs 44.49% power wastage. We observe that for $k = 4$ the wastage goes down to 10.2%.

The Table 1 reports the percentage power wastage P_{Gr} and the runtime of the algorithm T_{Gr} for the partition obtained greedily. For these test cases, the Greedy Algorithm found the optimal partitioning each time, and hence the P_{Opt} and P_{Gr} values are identical. We also report average number of evolutions, Ev, and the average runtime, T_{Ge}, taken by genetic algorithm to catch up with the Greedy Algorithm in terms of the quality of solution. The average is computed over the 50 different runs of the Genetic Algorithm (with different initial populations). The results presented in Table 1 suggest that the Greedy Algorithm is a better option than the Genetic Algorithm, since it found the optimal solution in all the cases and found it in significantly less time for $k = 3$ and $k = 4$. However, since this test case was gleaned from a platform power management perspective, it does not accurately represent the scale of the problem in a modern SOC with a much larger number of components.

Table 2, on the other hand, reports the results of these algorithms on much larger test cases that were created randomly. In Table 2, T_{Ge_best} reports the time to run the Genetic Algorithm for 2000 evolutions, and P_{best} reports the percentage power wastage for the best solution found after these many evolutions. The remaining columns have the same meaning as in Table 1. From Table 2, it may be observed the genetic algorithm finds a solution which is as good as the one reported by the greedy algorithm, which is not surprising. The significant observation is that the *improvement in solution quality thereafter is only marginal* (less than 1% reduction in percentage power wastage), even though the Genetic Algorithm is run for many more evolutions. This shows that the Greedy Algorithm typically reports a solution which is very close to optimal, if not optimal. As N, k and S are increased the genetic algorithm takes more time to reach a solution comparable to greedy.

The results in Table 3 indicate that there is only a marginal difference in the number of evolutions and the execution time of the genetic algorithm to catch up with the greedy under different mutation rates.

From the results, it can be concluded that in most cases the Greedy algorithm produces the partition which is very close to the optimal partition, and both the algorithms are efficient even for large test benches. These two algorithms have future prospects in workload driven power domain partitioning. Whereas the faster Greedy Algorithm may be useful for rapid design space exploration, the comparatively slower Genetic Algorithm is better suited to identify the near optimal solution in a one-time design scenario.

References

1. Kursun, V., Friedman, E.G.: Multi-voltage CMOS Circuit Design. Wiley (2006)
2. Roy, K., Prasad, S.C.: Low-power CMOS VLSI Circuit Design. Wiley-Inter Science (2000)
3. Lin, T., Chong, K.S., Gwee, B.H., Chang, J.S.: Fine-grained power gating for leakage and short-circuit power reduction by using asynchronous-logic. In: Proc. of ISCAS 2009, pp. 3162–3165 (2009)
4. Kanno, Y., et al.: Hierarchical Power Distribution with Power Tree in Dozens of Power Domains for 90-nm Low-Power Multi-CPU SoCs. IEEE Jour. of Solid State Circuits 42(1), 74–83 (2007)
5. Niedermeier, A., et al.: The challenges of implementing fine-grained power gating. In: Proc. of GLSVLSI (2010)
6. Sperling, E.: How many power islands is too many? (2009), http://chipdesignmag.com/lpd/blog/2009/05/13/how-many-power-islands-is-too-many/
7. Farrahi, A.H., Sarrafzadeh, M.: System partitioning to maximize sleep time. In: Proc. of ICCAD 1995, pp. 452–455 (1995)
8. Farrahi, A.H., et al.: Exploiting Sleep Mode for Memory Partitioning and Other Applications. VLSI Design 7(3), 271–287 (1998)
9. Ghafari, P., et al.: A Low-Power Partitioning Methodology by Maximizing Sleep Time and Minimizing Cut Nets. In: Proc. of the 5th Int. Workshop on SOC for Real-Time Appl. (IWSOC 2005), pp. 368–371 (2005)
10. Garey, M.R., Johnson, D.S.: Computers and Intractability - A guide to the theory of NP-completeness. W.H. Freeman and Company (1979)
11. Mandal, C.A., Chakrabarti, P.P., Ghose, S.: Design space exploration for data path synthesis. In: Proceedings of the Tenth International Conference on VLSI Design, pp. 166–171 (January 1997)
12. Mandal, C., Zimmer, R.M.: A genetic algorithm for the synthesis of structured data paths. In: Thirteenth International Conference on VLSI Design, pp. 206–211 (2000)
13. Maini, H., et al.: Genetic algorithms for graph partitioning and incremental graph partitioning. In: Proc. of Supercomputing 1994, pp. 449–457 (1994)
14. Shazely, S., Baraka, H.A., Wahab, A.H.A., Kamal, H.: Genetic Algorithms in Solving Graph Partitioning Problem. In: Imam, I., Kodratoff, Y., El-Dessouki, A., Ali, M. (eds.) IEA/AIE 1999. LNCS (LNAI), vol. 1611, pp. 155–164. Springer, Heidelberg (1999)
15. Xiao, L., et al.: Fixed-outline thermal-aware 3D floorplanning. In: Proc. of ASP-DAC 2010, pp. 561–567 (2010)

Implementation of a New Offset Generator Block for the Low-Voltage, Low-Power Self Biased Threshold Voltage Extractor Circuit

Rituparna Dasgupta[1], Dipankar Saha[2], Jagannath Samanta[1],
Sayan Chatterjee[2], and Chandan Kumar Sarkar[2]

[1] Department of Electronics & Communication Engineering
Haldia Institute of Technology, Haldia, West Bengal, India
{mithuritu22,jagannath19060}@gmail.com
[2] Department of Electronics & Telecommunication Engineering
Jadavpur University, Kolkata, West Bengal, India
dipsah_etc@yahoo.co.in, {sayan1234,phyhod}@gmail.com

Abstract. In this paper, we have modified a low-voltage, low- power V_T (Threshold Voltage) extractor circuit, and by doing this we have obtained results with greater accuracy. At the same time, the output generated from this circuit is found to be robust enough against supply voltage variations. This scheme is based on the most popular extraction algorithm which essentially starts with I_d versus V_{GS} characteristics of any MOS transistor operating in saturation. Here the V_T extractor block is followed by an offset generator and a feedback block. Now, for the purpose of modification, we have mainly changed the architecture of the offset generator block, keeping rest of the basic blocks unaltered. While doing this we have achieved more accurate results at low supply voltage ranging from 1.2 to 1.8V. In this range, for almost all the cases we found results with excellent accuracy. Whereas, considering the worst case scenario, the maximum deviation from the SPICE-V_T value is found to be only 2.9%. Low power consumption, self-compensation for any second-order effect etc. are the key features for this modified architecture. The paper describes the V_T extraction scheme, as well as, illustrates the techniques and circuit architecture required for the purpose. The results are supported by SPICE simulations.

Keywords: Threshold voltage, second-order effects,square law equation, current mirror, offset generator, channel-length modulation, mobility reduction, body-effect, differential amplifier, transconductance parameter.

1 Introduction

Threshold voltage is an important parameter for MOSFET device. Generally, as the name suggests, a V_T extractor is the circuit that automatically extracts, the threshold voltage of any MOS transistor and delivers the output in form of voltage. There exists a wide range of applications like MOS transistor characterization, level-shifting, temperature compensation; temperature measurement etc. [1].It can also be used as

H. Rahaman et al. (Eds.): VDAT 2012, LNCS 7373, pp. 156–165, 2012.
© Springer-Verlag Berlin Heidelberg 2012

voltage reference which is independent of supply voltage. In modern analog and mixed signal circuit design, the power consumption is one of the most vital issues; because today's portable device applications require low power-dissipation. The limited battery lifetime imposes strict demand on the overall power consumptions of the portable system. New rechargeable battery types such as Nickel-Metal Hydride (NiMH) are being developed with higher energy capacity than that of the conventional Nickel-Cadmium (NiCd) batteries but the energy density of NiMH batteries are still low in view of expanding applications of portable system [2]. Therefore, the major challenge in designing an integrated system is to reduce power dissipation.

Several numerical techniques are already reported for extracting V_T of a MOS transistor. But the numerical techniques available in literature are computationally intense and cannot be suitably used for the real-time on-chip applications [3]. Various real-time V_T extraction schemes and the corresponding circuits which can be utilized to overcome the above said problem are already described in [1], [3-6]. The implementations reported in [3-6] require high supply voltage and long channel MOSFET for their operations.But, while we go for low-voltage, low-power implementation then several second-order effects such as channel-length modulation (λ), mobility reduction (θ), body-effect etc. have to be considered. For low power applications Fikos and Siskos reported, a low voltage accurate CMOS threshold voltage extractor circuit in [7]. This input free circuit includes an offset generator and a feedback loop to achieve low power consumption, compensation of the second order effects and independence of output from the wide variations of the supply voltage range. In our modified low-voltage V_T extractor circuit, the off-set generator block of [7] has been replaced with an all PMOS structure (acting as a differential amplifier) to achieve higher accuracy at low supply voltages. As well as, the replacement of offset generator block makes the circuit output robust enough against supply voltage variations.

2   Conventional V_T Extractor Circuit

The idea of conventional V_T extractor circuit is shown in Fig.1 [8], where M1 is the device under test (DUT). Neglecting channel-length modulation effect and driving the two transistors M1 and M2 directly into saturation, we get

$$I_1 = K_1(V_{GS1} - V_{T1})^2 \tag{1}$$

$$I_2 = K_2(V_{GS2} - V_{T2})^2 . \tag{2}$$

Where the current flowing through the transistor M1 is denoted as I_1 and current through the transistor M2 is denoted as I_2. K_1 and K_2 are the transconductance parameters for M1 and M2 respectively.

Now, choosing $K_1 = 4K_2$, and assuming $V_T = V_{T1} = V_{T2}$, the threshold voltage of the transistor M1 (DUT) becomes,

$$V_T = 2V_{GS1} - V_{GS2} . \tag{3}$$

If we use a current mirror configuration for the current sources I_1 and I_2, and fix the gate voltage V_{GS2}, then V_{GS1} is adjusted automatically.

Table 1 shows the simulation results for the conventional V_T extractor circuit shown in Fig. 1.

The gain-of-two amplifier is mostly implemented by stacking two diode connected transistors. A twin-well process is required for the configuration of stacking transistors, and that is a major disadvantage of this process [9]. Moreover, for the difference operation, we need a differential amplifier (or a subtractor) which makes the circuit more complex and expensive. Stacking of transistors also requires higher supply voltage. Hence, the circuit is not suitable for the low-power operations [8].

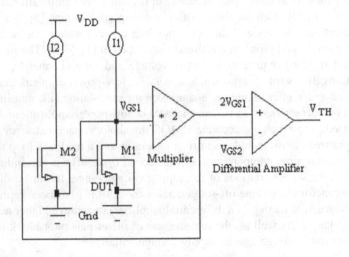

Fig. 1. Conventional V_T extractor circuit

3   Low-Voltage, Low-Power V_T Extractor Circuit

3.1   Operation of the Low-Voltage, Low-Power V_T Extractor Block

The basic V_T extractor block is shown in Fig. 2. It has been assumed that all the transistors in this block are in saturation and the drain current for each MOSFET follows the simple square law equation which is

$$I_{Di} = K_i (V_{GSi} - V_T)^2 . \tag{4}$$

Where, K_i is the transconductance parameter of MOSFET and in Fig.2, $K_1=K_2=K_3=K_4/4 =k$. For the basic V_T extracting block (shown in Fig. 2), if we neglect the body-effect and equate the drain current for M1 (I_{D1}) and drain current for M2 (I_{D2}), we have

$$k(V - V_S - V_T)^2 = k(V_S - V_T)^2 \tag{5}$$

or,
$$V_S = V / 2 . \tag{6}$$

Again, if we equate the drain current for transistor M3 (I_{D3}) and the drain current for transistor M4 (I_{D4}), we get

$$k(V - V_O - V_T)^2 = 4k(V_S - V_T)^2 . \tag{7}$$

Now substituting the value of V_S from (6) into the equation given in (7), we have [7],

$$V_O = V_T . \tag{8}$$

Where, V_O is the output of the circuit shown in Fig. 2.

Table 1. Simulation results of the conventional V_T extractor circuit

V_{DD} (Volt)	Extracted V_T Vo (Volt)	SPICE V_T (Volt)
2.1	1.04	
2.2	1.1	
3.0	1.4	1.0
4.0	1.5	
5.0	2.0	

Consideration of Second-Order Effects. When we consider different second-order effects such as, channel-length modulation (λ), mobility reduction (θ), body-effect etc., then the drain current equation becomes a more realistic one.

Considering λ and θ, we can modify the drain current expression as [7],

$$I_{Di} = K_i (V_{GSi} - V_T)^2 (1 + \theta V_{GSi})^{-1} (1 + \lambda V_{DSi}) . \tag{9}$$

If we substitute the drain current expression of (9) on $I_{D1} = I_{D2}$, it gives the same solution (6) for V_S, that is $V_S = V_{DD} / 2$. Similarly, substituting drain current expression of (9) on $I_{D3} = I_{D4}$, we have [7],

$$K(V - V_O - V_T)^2 [1 + \theta(V - V_O)]^{-1} [1 + \lambda(V - V_O)]$$
$$= 4K(V_S - V_T)^2 [1 + \theta V_O]^{-1} [1 + \lambda V_O] \tag{10}$$

From (10), it can be concluded that V_O will become independent of λ and θ by forcing

$$V = 2V_O .$$

(11)

with proper feedback [7].

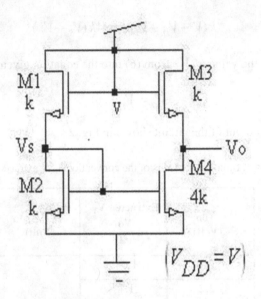

Fig. 2. Basic V_T extractor block

Body-effect has to be considered for the transistors M1 and M3. Therefore their threshold voltages can be modified as,

$$V_T = V_{T0} + \gamma(\sqrt{2\phi_b + |V_{BS}|} - \sqrt{2\phi_b}) .$$

(12)

Where, V_{T0} = Threshold voltage of MOS transistor at zero substrate bias, γ = Body-effect co-efficient, ϕ_b = Substrate fermi potential, V_{BS} = Substrate bias voltage.

Hence, (6) and (8) respectively can be written as follows [7]:

$$V_S = (V - \gamma(\sqrt{2\phi_b + V_S} - \sqrt{2\phi_b}))/2 ,$$

(13)

and

$$V_O = V_{T0} + \gamma(\sqrt{2\phi_b + V_S} - \sqrt{2\phi_b + V_O}) .$$

(14)

Therefore, we can see that the body-effect can be compensated by forcing,

$$V_S = V_O .$$

(15)

3.2   Implementation of the Proposed Offset Generator Block

The undesired output due to the second-order effects can be compensated through voltage V (Fig. 4) by feed backing the current generated through voltage V_{ogen}, which is actually the output of the offset generator block.

In our proposed circuit for the offset generator block, the transistors M5, M6, M7, M8 (Fig. 3) are forming a differential amplifier, where the driving MOSFETs are PMOS transistors. The aspect ratios for the transistors used in this block are all same. As we know, in an n-well process source and substrate terminals of the PMOS devices can be tied together, here transistors M5, M6, M7 and M8 are all bulk source connected. Now for same V_{GS}, M5 and M7 will be conducting the same current. So, equating the drain currents flowing through transistors M5 (I_{D5}) and transistor M7 (I_{D7}), we have,

$$V_{out1} = V_{DD} - V_O + V_{ogen} . \tag{16}$$

Similarly, equating the drain currents flowing through transistors M6 (I_{D6}) and transistor M8 (I_{D8}), we have

$$V_{ogen} = V_{DD} - V_{out1} \tag{17}$$

or,

$$V_{ogen} = V_O - V_{ogen} . \tag{18}$$

Hence, we can see that the block performs the difference operation between the two nodes V_O and V_{ogen}.

3.3   Analysis of the Current Feedback Loop

The feedback loop includes transistors M9, M10 and M11. As these transistors are forming a current mirror structure, therefore drain current flowing through transistor M9 should be equal to the drain current flowing through transistor M11.

Again, from Fig. 4, M9 and M4 are respectively 5 and 4 times wider than the transistor M2. Thus,

$$I_{D9} = I_{D2} + I_{D4} . \tag{19}$$

Substituting the expression of drain current from (4), in (18), we get,

$$V_S = V_{ogen} . \tag{20}$$

Hence, considering (6), (18) and (19) together, we have

$$V = V_O . \tag{21}$$

Thus, V_O is fed back to V by the current mirror formed by transistors M10 and M11, to result an accurate threshold voltage extractor circuit [7]. Fig. 4 shows the low-voltage, low-power V_T extractor circuit, where the implementations of the offset generator block is done with an all PMOS structure.

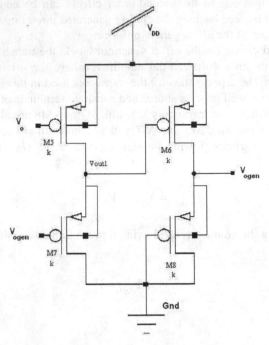

Fig. 3. Proposed circuit for generating the offset voltage

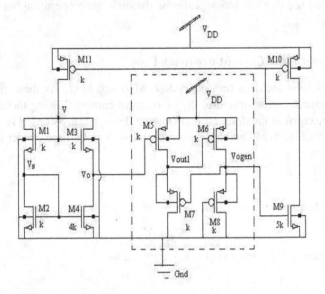

Fig. 4. Low-voltage, low-power V_T extractor circuit, along with the proposed offset generator block

Table 2. Simulation results

	Device dimension	V_{DD} (Volt)	Extracted V_T (Vo) (Volt)	SPICE V_T (Volt)
This Architecture			**0.237**	
[7]	L=160n	1.2	0.335	
Basic Block (Fig. 2)			0.300	0.237
This Architecture			**0.240**	
[7]	L=160n	1.3	0.340	
Basic Block (Fig. 2)			0.250	0.237
This Architecture			**0.230**	
[7]	L=0.5u	1.6	0.230	
Basic Block (Fig. 2)			0.240	0.237
This Architecture			**0.236**	
[7]	L=0.5u	1.7	0.232	
Basic Block (Fig. 2)			0.248	0.237
This Architecture			**0.237**	
[7]	L=0.5u	1.8	0.232	
Basic Block (Fig. 2)			0.250	0.237
This Architecture			**0.940**	
[7]	L=2u	2.1	0.410	
Basic Block (Fig. 2)			0.940	1.0
This Architecture			**1.0**	
[7]	L=2u	2.2	1.0	
Basic Block (Fig. 2)			1.0	1.0
This Architecture			**1.0**	
[7]	L=2u	3.0	1.0	
Basic Block (Fig. 2)			1.04	1.0
This Architecture			**1.0**	
[7]	L=2u	4.0	1.0	
Basic Block (Fig. 2)			1.12	1.0
This Architecture			**1.0**	
[7]	L=2u	5.0	1.0	1.0
Basic Block (Fig. 2)			1.2	

4   Results and Discussions

Table 2 shows the simulation results of the modified architecture, along with the comparison of this scheme with other V_T extraction techniques. The set of results are actually compared with the nominal threshold voltages given by SPICE models, to obtain the accuracy of output for this V_T extractor circuit with proposed offset generator block.It has been observed from the simulation results that the basic V_T extraction block shown in Fig. 2, operates at low supply voltage but its output has been affected by different second-order effects. In the implementation of [7], these second-order effects are compensated by introducing an offset generator block and a current feedback loop to the basic block. Now, considering our modified architecture the V_T extractor circuit works at even lower supply voltages with better accuracy, compared to the other two circuits shown in Table 2. Different device dimensions (L=160n, L=.5u, L=2u) are used while doing the simulation runs. The V_T extractor circuit with the proposed offset generator block gives almost accurate result at a minimum supply voltage of 1.2V; whereas the outputs of other two circuits are not that accurate for this low supply voltage.For the higher supply voltage range (V_{DD}=2.2V to 5V) the outputs of both the circuits (Fig 2. and Fig. 4), with long channel devices (L=2u) show great accuracy. Whereas, at 2.1V the modified circuit gives better result than that is obtained in case of [7].If we consider the average power consumption for the modified V_T extractor circuit then from the graph shown in Fig. 5 , it can be inferred that the circuit consumes much less power for low supply voltages ranging from 1.2 Volt to 1.8 Volt. For a supply voltage of 1.2 Volt, it consumes 0.109 mW of average power; whereas, for a 1.8 Volt supply voltage, the average power consumption is only 0.436 mW. Moreover, the power consumptions for higher supply voltages are also found to be low enough. For a supply voltage of 5 Volt, the modified V_T extractor circuit consumes 5.09 mW of average power.

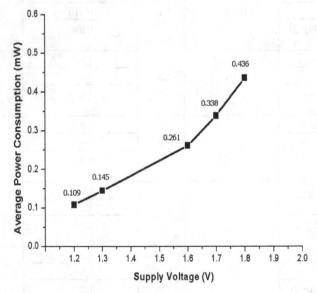

Fig. 5. Average power consumption at different supply voltages

5   Conclusions

The circuit has relatively simple hardware architecture and operates on a supply voltage that can be as low as 1.2 volt. Therefore, looking at the requirement of low-voltage, low-power operations, this modified self-biased V_T extractor circuit emerges as a suitable candidate. Furthermore, the simulation results show that this circuit works with excellent accuracy for a wide range of supply voltage variations (1.2 Volt to 5.0 Volt). Ability to operate at a low supply voltage, extreme accuracy and robustness of the output are the main features of this V_T extractor circuit with the proposed offset generator block. But, one possible drawback of using an all PMOS structure for the offset generator block, is that the cell area tends to be slightly larger, in order to accommodate the n-well for the PMOS transistors.

Acknowledgements. Authors would like to thank SMDP-II project lab., IC Design & Fabrication Centre, Jadavpur University for getting the opportunity to carry out this work using SPICE Tools.

References

1. Wang, Z.: Automatic V_T Extractors Based on An nxn2 MOS Transistor Array and Their Application. IEEE J. Solid-State Circuits, 1277–1285 (1992)
2. Kang, S.M., Leblebici, Y.: CMOS Digital Integrated Circuits. Tata McGraw Hill Education Private Limited, New Delhi (2010)
3. Yu, C.G., Geiger, R.L.: An Accurate and Matching-free Threshold Voltage Extraction Scheme for MOS Transistors. In: Proc. IEEE International Symposium on Circuits and Systems, vol. 4, pp. 115–118 (1994)
4. Johnson, M.G.: An Input-Free V_T Extractor Circuit Using a Two Transistor Differential Amplifier. IEEE J. Solid-State Circuits 28(6), 704–705 (1993)
5. Filanovsky, I.M.: An Input-Free V_T Extractor Circuit Using a Series Connection of Three Transistors. Int. J. Electron. 82(5), 527–532 (1997)
6. Cilingiroglu, U., Hoon, S.K.: An Optimally Self-Biased Threshold-Voltage Extractor. IEEE Transactions on Instrumentation and Measurement 52(5) (2003)
7. Fikos, G., Siskos, S.: Low-Voltage, Low-Power, Accurate CMOS V_T Extractor. IEEE Transactions on Circuits Systems II 48(6), 626–628 (2001)
8. Cilingiroglu, U., Hoon, S.K.: An Accurate Self-Bias Threshold Voltage Extractor Using Differential Difference Feedback Amplifier. In: Proc. IEEE International Symposium on Circuits and Systems, vol. 5, pp. 209–212 (2000)
9. Hoon, S.K., Chen, J.: Threshold Voltage Extraction Circuit. Texas Instruments incorporated, United States patent, patent no. US 6844772B2 (2005)

A High Speed, Low Jitter and Fast Acquisition CMOS Phase Frequency Detector for Charge Pump PLL

Manas Kumar Hati* and Tarun Kanti Bhattacharyya**

Indian Institute of Technology, Kharagpur, India

Abstract. This paper presents the different design schemes of the phase frequency detector (PFD) and compares with the output simulation results. The circuits that have been considered are the tristate linear D-FF type PFD, conventional Phase frequency Detector (conPFD), precharge type phase frequency detector (ptPFD), ncPFD in zero degree phase offset version, modified ncPFD with π rad phase offset, and TSPC-PFD. Although, PFDs are suffered from non ideal effects, therefore, to eliminate these effects a proposed PFD has been designed. The simulation results are focused on exploring the jitter, power dissipation, phase noise, and output noise of the different PFDs. The different PFD circuits are designed using $0.18\mu m$ CMOS process technology with 1.8 V supply voltage.

Keywords: CMOS integrated circuits, phase frequency detector, dead zone, timing jitter, and phase noise.

1 Introduction

Phase locked loops (PLL) are widely used for communication, clock phase synchronization, frequency synthesis, wireless system, digital circuits, high performance microprocessor system, disk drive electronics, and data recovery circuits. Charge pump based PLLs draw most attention due to their simple structure, CMOS compatibility and low phase noise properties. However, there is increasing demand for high frequency operation, low power, and low jitter PLL. A part of a phase locked loop (PLL) based frequency synthesizer as in Fig. 1, is the phase detector (PD) [1]. The phase detectors detect the phase difference (PD) between the reference clk (f_{ref}) and the feedback clk (f_b) from the divider output. Some phase detectors also detect the frequency errors; they are then called phase frequency detectors (PFDs). A PFD is usually built with a state machine with memory elements such as flip-flops [1], is shown in Fig. 2. The most desirable feature of a PFD is to have zero dead zones, which responsible for improving the phase noise performance and to reduce the spurious tones. Dead zone is defined as the undetectable small phase range of a PFD in phase characteristics, which generates a large jitter in the steady state in PLL.

---

* Advanced Technology Development Centre, mkhati@ece.iitkgp.ernet.in
** Dept. of E & ECE, tkb@ece.iitkgp.ernet.in

H. Rahaman et al. (Eds.): VDAT 2012, LNCS 7373, pp. 166–171, 2012.

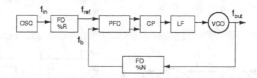

Fig. 1. The block diagram of a frequency synthesizer

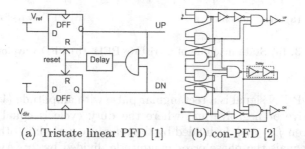

(a) Tristate linear PFD [1]   (b) con-PFD [2]

Fig. 2. (a) Tristate linear phase frequency detector(PFD), (b) Conventional PFD

The maximum operating frequency of a conventional PFD (con-PFD Fig. 2(b)) is limited by about six-gate delays in the reset path. A nc-PFD [4] and a TSPC-PFD [5] are another two high speed PFDs. The ncPFD almost has no dead zone and can operate in high frequency, but it has a four state output [4]. TSPC-PFD has small dead zone and low power also high frequency compare to conventional PFD due to only three gate delays.

Section 2 describes on PFD circuits. Section 3 deals with the non-ideals effects, section 4 describes the proposed PFD. Simulation results are depicted in section 5. The conclusion is given in the last section.

2   PFD Circuit Description

Fig. 2(a) illustrates a common linear tristate PFD architecture using re-settable DFFs, one AND gate and its state diagram is shown in Fig. 3(a). FF1 and FF2 respond to the rising edges of the input clock signals: reference applied to port v_{ref}, and divided output signal at port V_{div}. The duty cycle is not important because FF1 and FF2 respond only to rising edges [1]. PFD waveforms are shown in Fig. 3(b). In Fig. 3(a), three possible conditions are as follows:

(a) Zero: f_{ref} is synchronous with f_b; see the edges marked with ϕ_{e0}. Both UP and DN are very short pulses.
(b) Negative: f_b leads f_{ref}; see the rising edges marked with ϕ_{e1} and ϕ_{e2}.
(c) Positive: f_{ref} leads f_b; see the f_{ref} and f_b rising edges marked with ϕ_{e3}.

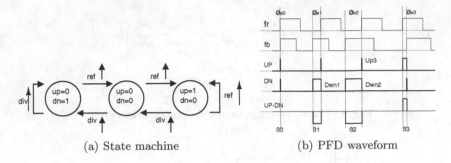

(a) State machine   (b) PFD waveform

Fig. 3. (a) State machine of a tristate PFD, (b) PFD waveform

In Fig. 3(b), UP-DN signal is a rectangular pulse with amplitude $(V_{high} - V_{low})$, which is positive or negative and where the duty cycle is equal to the time distance between f_{ref} and f_b divided by the reference period; in other words the duty cycle is equals the phase error magnitude divided by 2π. Averaging that voltage, like a PLL normally does, we have

$$\overline{(UP - DN)} = (V_{high} - V_{low})\frac{\theta_e}{2\pi} \tag{1}$$

Therefore, PFD gain is $K_{d,PFD} = \frac{(V_{high}-V_{low})}{2\pi}$. In many conventional PFDs, nonideal effects slow down the acquisition, such as missing edge and phase ambiguity. A proposed PFD topology is shown in Fig. 5 that completely eliminates the non-ideal effects is described in section 3.

3   Non Ideal Effects

3.1   Missing Edge

The PFD's characteristic is ideally linear for the entire range of input phase difference from -2π to 2π (upper left of Fig. 4(a)). When the inputs differ in frequency, the phase difference changes each cycle by $2\pi \cdot \frac{(T_{Vref} - T_{Vdiv})}{max(T_{Vdiv}, T_{Vref})}$. However, due to gate delays and parasitic lengthen the ON state of the reset signal, which can cause missing edges, and this effect is never negligible. The effect is shown in Fig. 4(a), when the phase difference goes near 2π, the leading edge of the reference triggers the UP signal until the lagging edge of divider output comes, which resets both the UP and DN signal to low. Due to presence of finite delay of the reset signal, the reset overwrites the next coming edge of the reference clk (V_{ref}), which is supposed to cause the UP to go high. As a result of the missing edge, a discrepancy occurs. The effect appears as a negative output phase differences higher than $2\pi - \Delta$ where $\Delta = 2\pi \frac{t_{reset}}{T_{Vref}}$. Which depends on the reset path delay (t_{reset}) and the reference period (T_{Vref}). Note that t_{reset} is determined by the delay of logic gates in the reset path and which is not a

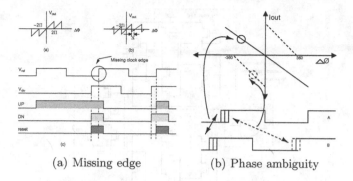

(a) Missing edge   (b) Phase ambiguity

Fig. 4. (a) Finite reset delay cause missing edge, (b) Illustration of phase ambiguity problem in PFD design

function of input frequency. The acquisition slows by how often the wrong information occurs which depends on Δ. At an input frequency ($T_{Vref} = 2.t_{reset}$) where Δ equals π, the PFD outputs the wrong information half the time fails to acquire frequency lock unconditionally. This in turn lead PLL to "Pull out" instead of "Pull in". So, the maximum operating frequency can be expressed as $f_{ref} \leq \frac{1}{2.t_{reset}}$.

3.2 Phase Ambiguity

Another problem is that the two rising edges to be compared are not unique. At any initial state, the circuit can pick, based upon the previous state, any two rising edges shown in Fig. 4(b) (solid and dashed). In other words output current can be in either of the two valid state (solid or dashed). The effect appears as a negative output for phase differences higher than, $2\pi - \Delta$ where, $\Delta = 2\pi \frac{t_{reset}}{T_{Vref}}$ which depends on the reset path delay t_{reset} and the reference clock period T_{Vref}. Note that t_{reset} is determined by the delay of logic gates in the reset path and is not a function of input frequency. Thus, picking the correct edge to start with can shorten the acquisition time.

4   Proposed PFD

A proposed PFD design is shown in Fig. 5. This PFD only compared the two rising edges with smaller phase error. Therefore we eliminate the case when reset signal can overwrite the next coming edge (missing edge) because the reset signal has at least half of the period to go low. Also, it will eliminate the phase ambiguity by always picking the smaller phase error. So, these conditions will be satisfied only when the V_{ref}, V_{div}, UP, and DN are all in high and generates a "reset" high signal at that instant. This could be done with replacing the 2 input AND gate in Fig. 2(a) with 4 input AND gate and out put of the 4-input AND gate should be connected to the reset terminnal. Now with this proposed

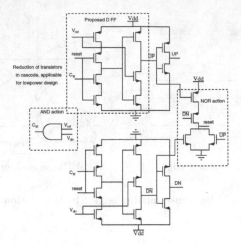

Fig. 5. Proposed PFD, eliminates the non-ideal effects in PFD

architecture the power and area could be saved, which is shown in Fig. 5. Also with this topology, each phase error is mapped uniquely to one possible data point from $-\pi$ to π. Details design of the proposed PFD is not considered here due to brevity.

5   Simulation Results

The performance summary of different PFDs have been reported in Table 1. This proposed PFD can eliminate non-ideal effects found in many PFDs. On the basis of operating frequency the reset delay of the many PFDs could be adjusted. Due to simplicity of the proposed architecture not like con-PFD or linear type PFD, the operating frequency could be very high. From Table 1 it is clear that the proposed PFD jitter, phase noise and o/p noise performance are superior than the other PFDs found in literature. In addition the power consumption of the proposed PFD is lower than the linPFD and conPFD. Although ncPFD is better than the proposed PFD on the basis of power dissipation and phase noise, but it has four output state and could not eliminate the non-ideal effects. The proposed PFD is still a rising edge trigger PFD, the characteristic does not depend on the duty cycle of the inputs. The jitter performance of the proposed PFD is shown in Fig. 6(a) (frequency range 10Hz-10GHz). The deadzone of the proposed PFD is almost zero in simulation and which is measured using a 100fF capacitor at the CP output knowing the current or voltage variation for different clk delays between V_{ref} and V_{div}. Finally, it is clear that the proposed PFD presented in this paper decreases acquisition time (no missing edge and phase ambiguity) and removes the potential of metastability. VCO control signal has been checked using a CP (Charge Pump) and Loop Filter for the two conditions as follows: (i)V_{ref} leads the V_{div} by 800 ps, (ii) V_{ref} lags the V_{div} by 800 ps (Fig. 6(b)).

Table 1. Performance comparisons with different PFD topologies

Different type of PFDs	Jitter$_{ee}$ (fs) (10Hz- 10GHz)	Power diss. (mW)	Phase noise (dBc/Hz)@ 1MHz	o/p-noise (v/sqrtHz)@ 100 kHz	non- ideal effects
linear PFD [1]	422.58	1.650	-139.0	-168.10	yes
con-PFD [2]	550.39	2.940	-133.20	-169.20	yes
ptPFD [3]	843.42	0.100	-126.10	-158.90	yes
nc-PFD [4]*	215.16	0.110	-166.90	-168.70	yes
nc-π rad-PFD [4]*	165.41	0.320	-167.10	-168.80	yes
TSPC-PFD [5]	452.16	0.736	-135.30	-168.00	yes
proposed PFD#	**164.71**	**1.440**	**-132.10**	**-172.90**	**no**

* four ... output... state, # This ...work

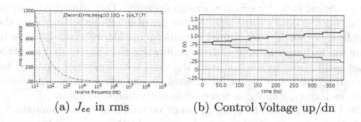

(a) J_{ee} in rms   (b) Control Voltage up/dn

Fig. 6. (a) Jitter response of the proposed PFD in rms, (b) UP/DN control voltage from loop filter output

6   Conclusion

In this paper a high speed, low jitter, and fast acquisition phase frequency detector (proposed PFD) has been designed for CP-PLL operating at 25 MHz. This PFD completely eliminates the missing edge and phase ambiguity problems found in many PFDs. So, this proposed PFD can be broadly used in CP-PLL for high speed, low jitter and fast acquisition purpose.

References

1. Razavi, B.: Design of Analog CMOS Integrated Circuits. McGraw-Hill (2001)
2. West, N.H.E., Eshragrian, K.: Principles of CMOS VLSI Design, 2nd edn. Addison Wesley, Reading (1993)
3. Johansson, H.O.: A Simple Precharge CMOS Phase Frequency Detector. IEEE Journal of Solid State Circuits 33(2) (February 1998)
4. Larsson, P., Svensson, C.: Skew safety and logic flexibility in a true single phase clocked system. In: Proc. IEEE Int. Symp. Circuits and Syst., pp. 941–944 (1995)
5. Kim, S., Lee, K., Moon, Y., et al.: A 960 Mbps/pin interface for skew tolerant bus using low jitter PLL. IEEE Journal of Solid-State Circuits, 691–700 (May 1997)

ILP Based Approach for Input Vector Controlled (IVC) Toggle Maximization in Combinational Circuits

Jaynarayan T. Tudu[1], Deepak Malani[2], and Virendra Singh[2]

[1] Computer Science and Automation, Indian Institute of Science, Bangalore
jayttudu@csa.iisc.ernet.in
[2] Electrical Engineering, Indian Institute Technology, Bombay
malani@ieee.org, viren@ee.iitb.ac.in

Abstract. Dynamic power estimation is a critical requirement in the design of digital logic for effective design decision. The brute-force way of estimating the power is to apply all the possible input vectors. Since the complexity of modern integrated circuits follow Moore's trend this technique can no longer be applied for computationally efficient and accurate power estimation. In the literature different techniques are reported for estimating the power either by generating the worst power consuming input vector or by applying some probability based technique.

We have attempted to generate input vectors that result in maximum possible toggling for combinational circuits. In this work, we have modeled combinational circuits using binary integer linear program(BILP) and solved it using the mixed integer linear programming solver CPLEX. Experimental results on ISCAS-85 benchmarks show that the input vectors generated by our methodology result into maximally possible toggling in the circuit for most of the benchmark circuits[1].

Keywords: Peak power estimation, Combinational circuits, Integer Linear Programming, Input Vector Control (IVC).

1 Introduction

With the shrinking size of transistors, a large number of gates are packed in design of any digital logic circuits today. In other words the transistor density per chip area are gradually increasing with the shrink in transistor size. Coupled with higher operating frequencies, the dynamic power dissipation in these circuits have increased over time. This has developed concerns towards a set of issues manifested due to excessive power consumption like formation of local hotspots, burn-out of chip due to excessive thermal stress and long term reliability issues in modern day integrated circuits. Hence to deal with all these issue there is a need of effective power management in circuit. The effective power management depends upon power distribution network and supply voltage. Hence

---

[1] This research is partly supported under research grant by LSI India Research and Development Pvt. Ltd.

H. Rahaman et al. (Eds.): VDAT 2012, LNCS 7373, pp. 172–179, 2012.
© Springer-Verlag Berlin Heidelberg 2012

for designing of optimized power distribution network and to make decision on supply voltage it is necessary to have a prior knowledge on maximum power that the circuit can consume. The power estimation also helps in evaluating circuit reliability; and in decision-making for packaging and cooling requirement[1] [2].

The power estimation techniques can primarily be categorized into a) Vector less power estimation b) Vector based power estimation. In vector less power estimation generally the estimation is performed based on the analysis of physical properties of circuit parameter. This kind of technique generally uses probability to model the expected switching activity. Though such techniques are very prompt in computing the power number, their accuracies are sometimes far from the reality. The second type of technique tries to bring the accuracy more closer to reality. Therefore it uses a pair of two consequent input vectors or a set of vectors for accurate estimation of power. These techniques although more realistic in estimating power they suffer from longer computation time. This challenge motivate researchers to find out efficient techniques to generate input vectors that can maximally stress the circuit.

The power estimation are generally carried out at different level of abstraction. The power estimation at RTL or high level is computationally easy compared to gate level estimation, gate level estimation is computationally easy compared to device level estimation. As the abstraction level goes down toward towards fine granularity the accuracy increases whereas the computational time increases[1].

In this work we have set forth the objective of worst case power estimation by generating pair of consecutive input vectors. For finding the pair of vectors that will maximally stress the circuit, the computation is modeled with *Binary Integer Linear Programming Model (BILP)*. The BILP formulation is based on the functional behavior of a circuit at gate level, as developed in [3]. The power dissipation can directly be approximated by the amount of toggle that takes place in the circuit nodes. In this work we correlate the worst case dynamic power dissipation with the maximally possible number of toggling nets while the circuit is in active mode. The power that is considered as the model for generating worst case input pattern can be precisely referred as *instantaneous power*. In this work we do not consider the power dissipation over longer duration of time as our focus is centered around the combinational circuits.

The rest of the paper is organized as follows. Section 2 gives an overview of previous approaches in power estimation. Section 3 presents the ILP formulation for worst case dynamic power estimation and generation of corresponding input vectors. In Section 4 the experimental data on ISCAS benchmark circuits and analysis of results are explained. The paper is concluded with future road-map in our approach in Section 5.

2 Previous Work

The power estimation problem is a challenging problem especially when we consider a large circuit having millions of gates with hundreds of primary inputs. The focus in power estimation problem is to efficiently generate consecutive primary input vector pair or a set of vectors and increase the accuracy of prediction i.e. the estimation should be in the close proximity of worst case functional power[2].

A wide variety of directions have been explored in search for accuracy and efficiency in power estimation. Some of the early attempts were made in [4][5] [6][7][8][9]. Devadas et al.[4] have proposed a methodology based on *weighted max-satisfiability* problem. The circuit was represented as *max-satisfiability(max-SAT)* problem and then was solved using exact and approximation algorithm SAT solver. To consider the different load capacitance the formulation of SAT is extended as weighted SAT problem. Some what different idea brought from ATPG(Automatic Test Pattern Generation) technique is proposed by Chuan- Yu Wang et al. [5] [6]. Two methodologies were proposed in [5] for determining lower and upper bounds on maximum power dissipation. To calculate the lower bound, the authors have proposed an ATPG based technique; while for upper bound they have proposed a *monte-carlo* based simulation technique. An improved version, based on D-Algorithm, of this technique is proposed in [6].

Pedram has explored a different technique based on a statistical approach[7]. In similar direction Wu et al.[8] have proposed a technique which uses limiting distribution of extreme order statistics. The challenge in this approach is to show with higher confidence level that the estimated power is indeed the real power. The advantage of this kind of technique is that it does not consume lot of time for computation. More detailed study of the earlier techniques are carried out by Najm[1] and Pedram[2]. Some of the interesting ideas like *cluster-based ATPG Algorithm*[10] and *Genetic Algorithm*[11] based approach on power-up current estimation are also potential in estimating the worst case power.

Recently some of the research has been conducted to formulate the problem as *Boolean Satisfiability(SAT)* or *Pseudo-Boolean SAT* problem. Mangassarian et al.[12] have proposed a technique based on Pseudo-Boolean SAT problem. Sagahyroon et al. have formulated the problem as SAT problem to estimate worst case power and worst case power-up current[13]. The SAT based technique is also shown to be efficient in test pattern generation[14] and low power state assignment[15]. The author have shown that the SAT-based technique is efficient when the problem is solved using commercial SAT solver like CPLEX[16].

In the proposed work we have explored the *Integer Linear Programming(ILP)* based technique to formulate the problem as an optimization problem. This formulated problem is then solved using the commercial tool CPLEX[16]. The experimental data show that our proposed technique can compute the optimal value in reasonably fast CPU time for some of the benchmark circuits. These results show a promising direction to explore increase in computational efficiency for finding maximally stressing test vectors.

3   Formulation of ILP

As expressed earlier, in this paper we have proposed a Binary Integer Linear Programming(BILP) based technique to identify a pair of input vectors to estimate worst case dynamic power dissipation.

For any combinational circuit, we can define two consecutive primary input vectors that will result into maximum toggling among its nets. A combinational circuit can be expressed as an zero-one Integer Linear Program(also known as Binary Integer Linear Programming), with *input-output constraints* and *linearization constraints* as described in the subsections, Sec 3.1 and Sec 3.2, below. One set of constraints express the input-output relation between the gates. Another set of constraints convert a nonlinear integer relation to an ILP formulation. The third set of constraints called as *toggle constraints* defined in Sec 3.3 are modeled to constrain the toggling on a respective net.

3.1 I/O Constraints

The relation between gate inputs and outputs is encoded using a set of constraints. We have used Binary Integer Linear Programming (BIP) to model NOT, NAND, and NOR gates. Let the inputs of a n-input gate be x_1, x_2.., x_n and its output be y. For NOT, NAND and NOR gates, the input-output relations can be expressed as:

NOT: $y = 1 - x_1$
$NAND$: $y = 1 - \prod_i x_i$
NOR: $y = 1 - \sum_i x_i + \sum_{i,j} x_i \cdot x_j + ... + (-1)^n \prod_i x_i$
where $y, x_i \varepsilon [0, 1]$. Similar expression can be derived for other type of gates.

For simplicity we have synthesized the RTL with two input NAND, two input NOR, and Inverter gate only. The constraint for two input gates can be expressed as follows

NOT: $y = 1 - x_1$
$NAND$: $y = 1 - x_1 \cdot x_2$
NOR: $y = 1 - (x_1 + x_2) + x_1 \cdot x_2$

3.2 Linearization Constraints

The constraints used for expressing a logic gate, as described above, consist of non-linear functions where an output variable is a product of input variables. Since an ILP solver requires linear relation between the variables, we need to linearize these equations. We rewrite the product constraints as linear functions by introducing a product variable and three additional constraints for each such variable; as expressed below:

$y = 1 - x_1 \cdot x_2$
$p = x_1 \cdot x_2$
$y = 1 - p$
$such\ that(s.t.)\ \ p \leq x_1$
$s.t.\ \ p \leq x_2$

$s.t.\quad x_1 + x_2 - p \leq 1$
where $x_1, x_2 \varepsilon [0, 1]$.

The above three constraints will ensure the product relation $p = x_1 \cdot x_2$.

3.3 Toggle Constraints

Toggle constraints are defined for each net to measure the toggling event. A two input XOR function is used to detect toggling of a net. The two inputs in this case are values of the net triggered by two consecutive input vectors. Let x_n and x_{n+1} represent values of net x corresponding to two consecutive input vectors. We then define the following five variables to detect the toggle activity.

$$x_n$$
$$x_{n+1}$$
$$\overline{x}_n = 1 - x_n$$
$$\overline{x}_{n+1} = 1 - x_{n+1}$$
$$x_{toggle}^k = x_n \cdot \overline{x}_{n+1} + \overline{x}_n \cdot x_{n+1}$$

The above equation can be rewritten in following way by using linearization constraints:

$$x_{toggle}^k = p_1 + p_2$$
$$p_1 = x_n \cdot \overline{x}_{n+1}$$
$$s.t.\quad p_1 \leq x_n$$
$$s.t.\quad p_1 \leq \overline{x}_{n+1}$$
$$s.t.\quad x_n + \overline{x}_{n+1} - p_1 \leq 1$$
$$p_2 = \overline{x}_n \cdot x_{n+1}$$
$$s.t.\quad p_2 \leq \overline{x}_n$$
$$s.t.\quad p_2 \leq x_{n+1}$$
$$s.t.\quad \overline{x}_n + x_{n+1} - p_2 \leq 1$$

where the variable x_{toggle}^k is toggle variable for k^{th} net, the variables $\overline{x}_n$ and $\overline{x}_{n=1}$ are complement of x_n and x_{n+1} respectively, the variables p_1 and p_2 are intermediate variable introduced to replace the product terms.

The toggle constraints are defined for each of the internal nets which also include the out put nets.

3.4 Objective Function

We have modeled our optimization function to maximize the number of toggling among the nets for a given circuit. This function can be mathematically represented as:

$$Maximize \quad \sum_{i=0}^{N} x_{toggle}^i$$

where N is the total number of internal nets(including the output nets) and x^i_{toggle} is the toggle variable for i_{th} net in the circuit. Note that we have not taken primary input nets in to consideration for toggle maximization because the toggle in primary input does not contribute to power consumption.

Solving for this function generates a pair of consecutive primary input vectors that maximizes number of toggling in the circuit. The solution also guarantee that on the completion of execution of the integer linear program will give rise to optimal primary input vectors which can trigger the maximal toggling in the circuit. However, it is theoretically proved that ILP is NP-Complete problem and hence for some of the circuits it the execution may not terminate in suitably acceptable time. Therefore in such cases the near optimal solution is considered. In this work we have used CPLEX Solver[16] to solve the formulated problem. From experiment it is observed that the CPLEX could able to terminate for most of the circuits in acceptable time limit. The results are analyzed in the following section.

4 Evaluation on ISCAS-85 Circuits

For examining our proposition, we have used benchmark circuits from ISCAS-85. These circuits are simplified into a combination of two input gates as could be used in standard library. We have used CPLEX solver[16] for finding optimal input vector patterns. The Table I summarizes the percentage of nets that toggle with the resulting input vector pairs. In this table, the second column lists the number of primary inputs of the circuit. The third column lists the number of nets in the circuit, equivalent to the total number of internal nets including output nets. The estimated toggles resulting from the CPLEX solver are tabulated in the fourth column. The fifth column show the percentage of nets toggle with respect to the total number of nets in the circuit. In this work we have not considered the number of toggle on fan-out nets.

We observe that for small circuits the solutions result into around 100% down to 80% toggles. However for larger circuits the said toggle percentage varies from 80% down to about 50% depending on the circuit topology and complexity. This is quite expected because as the circuit complexity increases the dependency among the nets also increase.

The computations were done on Intel Xeon CPU operating at 2.0GHz. In this table the solver run time is reported in Time(seconds) column. It can be observed that some of the circuits have executed faster where as other have taken huge amount of time. The longer time is due to the nature of ILP problem being a NP-Complete type.

The experimental results show that the proposed method was able to solve large circuits in reasonably lesser time. For benchmark circuit like c432, the proposed method is performing better compared to SAT-based technique[13].

Table 1. Toggling nets as computed by CPLEX solver

Circuits	No. Primary Input	No. of Nets	Toggle Count	%Toggle	Time(Sec.)
c04	1	4	4	100	0.09
c05	3	8	7	87.5	0.05
c11	3	6	5	83.3	0.02
c14	2	4	3	75	0.03
c17	5	6	6	100	0.02
c432	36	296	243	82	8.86
c499	41	626	360	57.50	3406.00
c880	60	592	491	82.93	21.55
c1355	41	690	415	60.14	3616.48
c1908	33	1291	832	64.44	2371.53
c2670	233	1925	1362	70.75	559.65
c5315	178	4897	2635	53.80	3399.05

5   Conclusion and Future Work

The dynamic power estimation is important for several reasons like power grind design and early design decision. A methodology for formulating the power estimation problem as Binary Integer Linear Programming is proposed. To the best of our knowledge this is for the first time the BILP has been explored for power estimation. An ILP solver, CPLEX, is demonstrated to be useful in generating input vector pairs for toggle maximization. The experimental result motivates further to explore BILP for power estimation.

For more realistic consideration of practical circuits, we plan to incorporate glitches due to contamination delay and propagation delay. Also the estimation can improve when the fan-out are given proper weight. The model can be extended to consider the sequential circuits as well.

Acknowledgements. The authors would like to thank Pramod Subramanyan, Princeton University for his support in BILP formulation of logic circuits.

References

1. Najm, F.: A survey of power estimation techniques in VLSI circuits. IEEE Transactions on Very Large Scale Integration (VLSI) Systems 2, 446–455 (1994)
2. Pedram, M.: Power minimization in IC Design: Principles and Applications. ACM Transactions on Desing Automation of Electronics System 1, 3–56 (1996)
3. Subramanyan, P., Jangir, R.R., Tudu, J., Larsson, E., Singh, V.: Generation of minimal leakage input vectors with contrained nbti degradation. In: East West Design and Test Symposium, EWDTS 2010 (April 2010)
4. Devadas, S., Keutzer, K., White, J.: Estimation of power dissipation in CMOS combinational circuits. In: Proceedings of the IEEE Custom Integrated Circuits Conference, pp. 19.7/1–19.7/6 (May 1990)

5. Wang, C.-Y., Roy, K.: Maximum power estimation for CMOS circuits using deterministic and statistic approaches. In: Proceedings of the Ninth International Conference on VLSI Design, pp. 364–369 (January 1996)
6. Wang, C.-Y., Roy, K., Chou, T.-L.: Maximum power estimation for sequential circuits using a test generation based technique. In: Proceedings of the IEEE Custom Integrated Circuits Conference, pp. 229–232 (May 1996)
7. Pedram, M.: Advanced power estimation technique. In: Mermet, J., Nebel, W. (eds.) Low Power Design in Deep Submicron Technology. Kluwer Academic Publishers (2007)
8. Wu, Q., Qiu, Q., Pedram, M.: Estimation of peak power dissipation in VLSI circuits using the limiting distributions of extreme order statistics. IEEE Transactions on Computer-Aided Design of Integrated Circuits and Systems 20, 942–956 (2001)
9. Polian, I., Czutro, A., Kundu, S., Becker, B.: Power droop testing. In: International Conference on Computer Design, ICCD 2006, pp. 243–250 (October 2006)
10. Li, F., Hi, L., Saluja, K.K.: Estimation of maximum power-up current. In: Proceedings of the 15th International Conference on VLSID (2002)
11. Luo, Z., Xu, Y., Han, Y., Li, X.: Maximum power-up current estimation of power-gated circuits. In: Proceedings of the 5th International Conference on ASIC, vol. 2, pp. 1243–1246 (October 2003)
12. Mangassarian, H., Veneris, A., Safarpour, S., Najm, F., Abadir, M.: Maximum circuit activity estimation using pseudo-boolean satisfiability. In: Design, Automation Test in Europe Conference Exhibition, DATE 2007, pp. 1–6 (April 2007)
13. Sagahyroon, A., Aloul, F.A.: Using SAT-based techniques in power estimation. Microelectronics Journal 38, 706–715 (2007)
14. Aloul, F.A., Sagahyroon, A.: Using SAT based technique in test vector generation. Journal of Advances in Information Technology 1(4), 153–162 (2010)
15. Sagahyroon, A., Aloul, F.A.: Using SAT based technique in low power state assignment. Journal of Circuits, Systems, and Computers 20(8), 1605–1618 (2011)
16. Corporation, IBM ILOG CPLEX optimization studio. IBM Coporation (2010), http://www-01.ibm.com/software/integration/optimization/cplex-optimization-studio/

Comparison of OpAmp Based and Comparator Based Switched Capacitor Filter

Manodipan Sahoo[1] and Bharadwaj Amrutur[2]

[1] School of VLSI Technology, Bengal Engineering and Science University, Shibpur
[2] Department of Electrical Communication Engineering, IISc, Bangalore
manodipansahoo@gmail.com, amrutur@ece.iisc.ernet.in

Abstract. Comparator based switched capacitor circuits provide an excellent opportunity to design sampled data systems where the virtual ground condition is detected rather than being continuously forced with negative feedback in Opamp based circuits. This work is an application of this concept to design a 1st order 330 KHz cutoff frequency Lowpass filter operating at 10 MHz sampling frequency in 0.13μm technology and 1.2 V supply voltage. The Comparator Based Switched Capacitor (CBSC) filter is compared with conventional Two stage Miller compensated Operational amplifier based switched capacitor filter. It is shown that CBSC filter relaxes the constraints like speed ,linearity, gain, stability which would otherwise be hard to satisfy in scaled technologies in Opamp based circuits. The designed CBSC based lowpass filter provides significant power savings compared to traditional Opamp based switched capacitor filter.

Keywords: switched capacitor circuits, sampled data systems, virtual ground, Comparator Based Switched Capacitor(CBSC) filter, Miller compensation.

1 Introduction

As inspired by Moore's law, Technology scaling has been advantageous in terms of packing more transistors in the same die area with improved performance and cost [1]. The higher f_T's (i.e. Transition frequency) of scaled devices can be used effectively for analog design but the low power supply voltage and lower channel length degrade the output signal swing and output resistance of MOS transistors. It is found that due to lower voltage swing in scaled technologies,more power is consumed in $\frac{KT}{C}$ noise limited design for the same Signal to Noise Ratio (SNR) [2].

The design of OpAmp for high open loop DC gain is very challenging, which however is essential to provide an accurate and robust negative feedback. Opamp intrinsic gain (i.e.$g_m r_o$ product) is reduced due to output resistance degradation in scaled technologies. Moreover the output resistance can't be improved a lot by increasing gate length sacrificing the f_T, because in modern devices pocket implants are used to maintain a tight control on the gate [3]. Also at reduced

H. Rahaman et al. (Eds.): VDAT 2012, LNCS 7373, pp. 180–189, 2012.

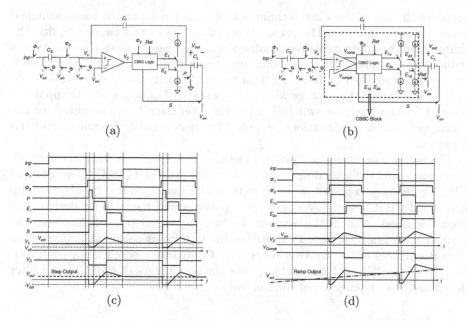

Fig. 1. CBSC Gain stage and Integrator (a) CBSC Gain stage. (b) CBSC Integrator stage. (c) Gain stage timing diagram. (d) Integrator timing diagram.

supply the lower output signal swing prevents the design of cascoded amplifier directing the design of multistage amplifier design at low voltage.

Multistage amplifier design essentially uses some compensation scheme to stabilize the closed loop amplifier in the presence of multiple poles. The compensation capacitor actually increases the power consumption to maintain the same speed of the amplifier.

Different techniques have been developed to compensate for the effects of low OpAmp gain. Dynamic amplifiers have been used to avoid use of dedicated opamps, but they have settling problem when they are switched off [4]. Recently low gain, open loop amplifiers have been used with digital calibration techniques to compensate for the errors in the low gain design [5].

The technique used here is comparator based and was first proposed in a pipelined ADC design [6]. This technique doesn't use high gain operational amplifiers where negative feedback is to be continuously enforced to maintain virtual ground, rather it uses comparator to detect virtual ground and triggers the sampling. Constant current sources are used to charge and discharge the load to compensate for the charge required to maintain virtual ground. Output is sampled only at the sampling instant defined by the detection of virtual ground. Later the same technique was applied to design a 2nd order Sigma-Delta modulator in [7]. In [7] a sampled data integrator is designed, which is the integral part of a Sigma-Delta modulator.Here the integrator charge transfer phase is unidirectional and consists of three sub phases namely Preset,Coarse charge transfer phase and Fine charge transfer phase similar to [6]. This work proposes the use of the same technique to design a comparator based switched capacitor low pass filter. The principal contributions of this paper are, first,the charge transfer phase is bidirectional;second,comparator power consumption is reduced by switching off in the sampling phase;third,an analytical methodology has been adopted to design for a particular linearity-speed specification and lastly a conventional two stage Miller compensated OpAmp and a Comparator based 1st order low pass switched capacitor filter have been compared for the same performance specifications i.e. cutoff frequency, passband gain, stop-band rejection.

The paper is organized as follows. In section II, CBSC gain stage architecture is explained and the main differences between the proposed CBSC Integrator and CBSC gain stage reported in [6] have been elucidated. In section III, OpAmp based and CBSC based low pass filter topologies and their circuit design have been described. Also in this section the linearity-speed tradeoff has been explained analytically. Section IV describes the important results and comparison of performances of the OpAmp based and Comparator based low pass filters. Finally section V concludes and explains the advantages of CBSC based filter design over its OpAmp based counterpart.

2   Comparator Based Switched Capacitor Circuits

2.1   Single Ended CBSC Gain Stage

The comparator based gain stage shown in Fig.1(a) operates on similar two phase cycle as that of Opamp based one. The signals P, E_1, E_2 and S are generated by an asynchronous state machine after the threshold detection comparator. The sampling phase ϕ_1 is the same in both cases. The charge transfer phase consists of three sub phases namely preset (P), coarse charge transfer phase (E_1) and fine charge transfer phase (E_2) to achieve high accuracy and linearity. The charge transfer timing diagram is shown in Fig.1(c). A short preset phase ensures that V_x starts below V_{cm}. The sampling switch S is also closed during the preset phase to preset the load capacitance. The coarse charge transfer phase (E_1) is used to get a rapid rough estimate of the output voltage and virtual ground condition. Due to the high ramp rate used and finite comparator delay this phase generally produces a large overshoot.Once the comparator decides, the charging current source is turned off. The fine charge transfer phase is used to get a far more accurate measurement of virtual ground condition and also the output voltage. The fine phase current is determined by the final offset voltage requirement of the circuit which is limited by the linearity of the system. As the offset requirement is usually very small, the fine phase current is also very small. Now as the comparator detects the second threshold, the sampling switch S is opened and it deposits the sample charge on load capacitor C_L. The discharging current source is turned off a little after the sampling switch opens. Finite comparator delay makes a signal independent constant undershoot each cycle as long as the comparator delay, ramp rate and load capacitance are constant.

2.2   Single Ended CBSC Integrator

The CBSC based integrator architecture is similar to OpAmp based one and is shown in Fig.1(b). The sampling phase is same for both the approaches. Here The charge transfer phase does not have any preset phase because the sampled data based integrator requires memory of the previous output voltage. The preset phase in CBSC gain stage places the virtual ground node to some voltage below V_{cm}(common mode voltage) thus enforcing a unidirectional charge transfer namely charging or coarse charge transfer phase followed by discharging or fine charge transfer phase. In CBSC based integrator we have two current source paths. Those two paths correspond to charging phase(coarse phase) followed by discharging phase(fine phase) and discharging phase(coarse phase) followed by charging phase(fine phase). The control signals $E_{1u},E_{2u},E_{1d},E_{2d}$ are generated by an asynchronous state machine namely the CBSC Control logic shown in Fig.1(b). The timing diagram is shown in Fig.1(d). In ϕ_2 phase V_x goes down, if the input level sampled is above V_{cm} and vice versa. Now if V_x goes down this node alongwith V_{out} is charged first followed by discharging phase. The other current source path is activated if V_x goes up at the onset of charge transfer phase. From the timing diagrams in Fig.1(b) and Fig.1(d) we observe that the CBSC gain stage output is a step for step input whereas CBSC integrator produces ramp output to an input step.

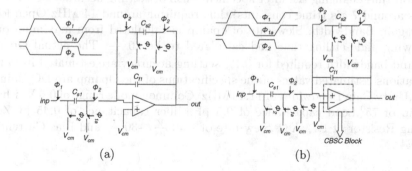

Fig. 2. Low Pass Filter topology (a) 1st order OpAmp-based Low pass filter topology. (b) 1st order CBSC-based Low pass filter topology.

3   Filter Design

3.1   Filter Topology

Filter topology chosen here to compare OpAmp based and CBSC based techniques is a 1st order low pass Switched capacitor filter [8]. The capacitor values are chosen from the filter specifications like Cutoff frequency, Sampling frequency. Sampling frequency is chosen 20 times higher compared to highest input signal frequency of interest to match the continuous time filter response. The OpAmp based and

CBSC based filters are shown in Fig.2(a) and Fig.2(b) respectively. For this particular low pass filter the sampling frequency is 10 MHz,Cutoff frequency is 330 KHz,both C_{s1} and C_{s2} is 0.1 pF and C_{f1} is 0.5 pF.

3.2   Circuit Design

On the first phase ϕ_1, input is sampled onto the sampling capacitor C_{s1} and feedback capacitor C_{s2} is discharged. Bottom plate sampling is used to mitigate charge injection error as ϕ_1 goes low. In the phase ϕ_2, namely the charge transfer phase, the charge on sampling capacitor C_{s1} is dumped onto feedback capacitors C_{f1} and C_{s2}. Two stage Miller compensated opamps are used for integrator design. The finite gain and Bandwidth of opamps shift the poles of the filter transfer function, thus changing the cutoff frequency and stop-band rejection of filter.

Miller Amplifier. Conventional two stage Folded Cascode Miller compensated amplifier [10] is used as the operational amplifier architecture. This architecture has differential input stage cascaded to Class A output stage. Miller compensation is used to stabilize the amplifier ensuring a phase margin of $\phi_M > 60^0$.For 0.1 % settling error,the DC gain requirement is approximately 66dB [10]. Lower gain will not only produce output error but also shifts the poles of filter transfer function thus changing the filter specifications.For settling accuracy of 0.1% requires around 7 τ's (time constants),thus requiring around 14 MHz Open loop Unity gain Bandwidth. Slew rate of opamp is calculated from maximum output swing and settling time and calculated to be 40 $\frac{V}{\mu s}$. The actual Opamp gain and bandwidth required for 0.1% settling accuracy are estimated from the simulations.Estimated values of the specifications of the Opamp are DC Gain of 73dB,Unity Gain Bandwidth of 11.33 MHz ,Common mode range of 0.6 V ,Phase margin of 75^0,Load capacitance of 0.5 pF,Miller capacitance of 0.45 pF,Zero Nulling Resistor of 1.72 $K\Omega$,Slew rate of +40 $\frac{V}{\mu s}$/ -30 $\frac{V}{\mu s}$ and Bias Current of 114 μA .

CBSC Comparator. The threshold detection type CBSC comparator architecture is shown in Fig.3(a) [7]. The threshold detection comparator along with CBSC control logic makes the basic CBSC block shown in Fig.2(b). The comparator consists of three low gain differential amplifiers in cascade with level converters and digital buffers. This comparator consists of multiple open loop stages without any stability problem whereas multistage opamp has stability problem and requires some pole compensation strategy, thus increasing the power consumption. The design constraint in the comparator design is maximum final offset requirement. The offset varies linearly with comparator delay, fine phase current and inversely with load capacitance. Thus to minimize the offset the comparator delay is to be minimized or speed is to be maximized. Further the final signal independent offset can be cancelled only if it is within limits. The comparator speed is maximized using lower dimension input transistors and higher

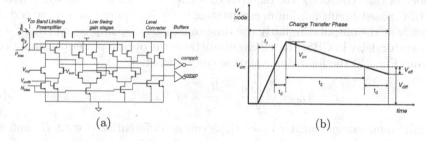

(a)   (b)

Fig. 3. (a)Threshold detection comparator architecture.(b)V_x (positive input node of CBSC stage) during charge transfer phase.

overdrive voltage. Final digital buffers produce rail to rail logic outputs. So in low voltage design the high DC gain and bandwidth requirement of opamp poses a serious challenge and in fact increases the power consumption of amplifier.In comparator design multistage open loop amplifiers can be cascaded without worrying about stability contrary to Opamp design. Very high gain comparators can be designed which increases the resolution voltage of comparator. The only serious challenge being the tradeoff between final offset voltage and comparator speed. This tradeoff is explained in the Speed-Linearity tradeoff in Fig.3(b). Moreover in conventional opamp based circuits the settling accuracy determines the slew rate and bandwidth. In CBSC technique the settling nature is unimportant rather the output voltage accuracy is of concern at the sampling instant. Now V_{res} is defined as [9]:

$$V_{res} = \frac{V_{sup}}{A^N} \tag{1}$$

and τ_{total} is defined as:

$$\tau_{total} = \frac{K \times 2 \times N \times A \times C_{load}}{g_m} = \frac{K \times 4 \times N \times A \times L^2}{3 \times \mu_n \times V_{\text{eff}}} \tag{2}$$

Here V_{sup} is Supply Voltage,A is Stage gain,N is No. of stages,C_{load} is Load Capacitance,g_m is Trans-conductance of input devices ,L is Transistor length ,μ_n is Mobility of NMOS transistor,V_{eff} is Overdrive voltage,V_{res} is Resolution voltage,τ_{total} is Comparator time constant and K is scaling constant .So values of A, N, L and V_{eff} can be suitably chosen for a resolution and speed specification. Comparator average power consumption has been minimized by switching off the comparator during the sampling or ϕ_1 phase. The Threshold detection comparator specifications are Stage Gain(A) of 9.66,No.of stages(N) of 3,stage 3 dB bandwidth of 1.13 GHz,Transistor length of 160 nm,Load capacitance of 10 fF,Overdrive voltage(V_{eff}) of 125 mV,Rising delay for compp and comppb output of 0.95 ns and 0.92 ns,Falling delay for compp and comppb output of 0.72 ns and 0.76 ns and Bias Current of 35 μA.

Linearity-Speed Tradeoff. A tradeoff exists between linearity and speed in both OpAmp and CBSC based circuit. In Opamp based circuit a minimum number of time constants are required to settle to sufficient accuracy. Whereas in CBSC based circuit minimum comparator delay is required to achieve certain accuracy at the output. Similarly the time constant in Opamp based circuit and comparator delay in CBSC based circuit dictates the overall power consumption.

From Fig.3(b) the following equation can be written:

$$T_{total} = \frac{V_{\text{diff}}}{R_1} + \frac{R_1}{R_2} \times t_d + 2 \times t_d \tag{3}$$

For minimum charge transfer time, T_{total} can be differentiated w.r.t R_1 and we arrive at the following equations:

$$R_1 = \sqrt{\frac{R_2 \times V_{\text{diff}}}{t_d}} \tag{4}$$

and

$$T_{total} = 2 \times t_d \times (1 + \sqrt{\frac{V_{\text{diff}}}{t_d \times R_2}}) = 2 \times t_d \times (1 + \sqrt{\frac{V_{\text{diff}}}{V_{\text{off}}}}) \tag{5}$$

Here,V_x is Positive input node of Comparator,V_{cm} is Common mode voltage,t_1 is Coarse charge transfer time,t_d is Comparator + CBSC logic delay,t_2 is Fine charge transfer time,V_{diff} is Maximum input signal amplitude,V_{off} is Final offset at V_x node,V_{ov} is Coarse phase overshoot,R_1 is Coarse phase ramp rate,R_2 is Fine phase ramp rate,T_{total} is Total charge transfer time and C_s is sampling capacitance.These equations are valid as long as it is assumed that comparator delay is signal independent and constant. So as observed from the equations that charge transfer time is minimized for $t_1=t_2$. For a given linearity(V_{off}) and speed(T_{total}) specification there are multiple solutions for R_1,R_2 and t_d. Now the solution should correspond to minimum power consumption as well as realizable current sources. The current sources are implemented as Cascode devices and Output resistance is maintained high enough throughout the output range such that it satisfies the linearity constraint. Floating switches are implemented as Transmission gates and switches connected to either Ground or Supply are NMOS and PMOS transistors respectively. The switches are sized to attain On Resistance(R_{on})of approximately 1 KΩ and Off Resistance(R_{off}) of approximately 100 MΩ.

4   Results and Discussion

Both the OpAmp and CBSC based filters are designed with sampling frequency of 10 MHz. The filter frequency response is extracted by performing DFT of output transient response at different input signal frequencies. The frequency responses are shown in Fig.4(a). The cutoff frequencies are the same for both filters, but there is lesser pass-band gain in CBSC filter than OpAmp based filter because of output offset. The stop-band rejection is approximately 7 dB smaller in CBSC filter than Opamp based one because of higher level of nonlinearity in CBSC-based filter. Two-tone test is used to simulate the performance degradation due to nonlinearity in both filters. The intermodulation distortions in both

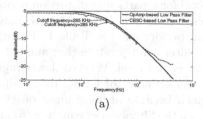
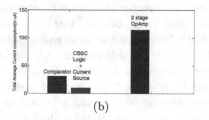

(a)   (b)

Fig. 4. (a)OpAmp and Comparator based Low pass filter frequency response.(b)Average Current consumption comparison of CBSC and OpAmp based Low pass filter.

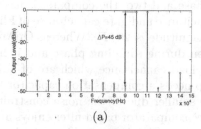
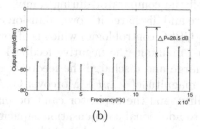

(a)   (b)

Fig. 5. (a)In-band IM3 performance of OpAmp based Low pass filter. (b)In-band IM3 performance of CBSC based Low pass filter.

filters are simulated with tones at 100 KHz and 110 KHz for in-band distortion performance. The 3rd order Intermodulation distortion results are shown in Fig.5(a) and Fig.5(b) for OpAmp and Comparator based low pass filter respectively. If we define the power level(in dBm) difference between signal and 3rd order intermodulation component in-band as ΔP, the in-band IIP3(Input referred third order intercept point) can be roughly approximated as [11]:

$$IIP3(dBm) = \frac{\Delta P}{2}(dB) + P_{in}(dBm) \qquad (6)$$

1st order filters(i.e. both Opamp and CBSC based) are designed at 0.13 μm CMOS technology,1.2V supply voltage , 285 KHz cutoff frequency and Total input referred noise of 203 μV rms.Performances of the filters are summarized in Table 1. So we observe from the Table 1 that the CBSC based filter suffers from significant nonlinearity compared to it's OpAmp based counterpart. This can be attributed to the nonlinearity of the fine current source,which directly degrades the output offset and linearity of the system [6]. Here total in-band noise is assumed to be mainly due to thermal $\frac{KT}{C}$ noise and calculated to be 203 μV rms for sampling capacitor of 0.1 pF. The Dynamic Range(DR) is defined as:

$$DR(dB) = \frac{V_{sig}}{V_{noise}} \qquad (7)$$

where, V_{sig} denotes maximum input signal level for a particular distortion performance and V_{noise} denotes total in-band noise voltage. So DR can be calculated for both filters for the mentioned distortion performance in Table 1. The distortion levels are different as OpAmp based filter can't produce that amount of distortion even at it's highest possible input signal level. Whereas,lower input signal level is used to get good distortion performance of CBSC based filter, further the input level can't be reduced much because of finite input offset of comparator. In-band IIP3 is calculated for both the filters as per equation (6),and it is observed that OpAmp based filter has better IIP3 than CBSC based filter because of it's better distortion performance over the other one. We observe from Fig.4(b) that average current consumption is approximately 2.5 times lower in CBSC based filter than OpAmp based one because of two reasons, one, switching off the comparator during sampling phase and two, the comparator has to charge and discharge it's own diffusion capacitance and gate capacitance of Flip-flops(CBSC control logic) which is of low magnitude($\sim 20fF$). Whereas,OpAmp has to maintain the negative feedback even during sampling phase and it has to charge and discharge the feedback and load capacitance which are of quite high magnitude($\sim 1pF$). Moreover,OpAmp needs a compensation capacitor for stability, and the capacitor can't be made smaller due to the noise constraint. Due to additional compensation capacitance comparator based filter enjoys area advantage over OpAmp based filter. In 0.13 μm technology capacitor area is approximately 1 $\frac{fF}{\mu m^2}$, thus comparator based filter saves approximately 40% area for the same performance specifications. Lastly both the filters are quite insensitive to capacitor mismatch and for a $\pm 5\%$ capacitance mismatch,maximum cutoff frequency variation of CBSC based filter is 0.5%, whereas OpAmp based filter has a maximum of 0.7% cutoff frequency variation.

Table 1. Filter Performance Summary

Parameters	OpAmp based Low pass filter	CBSC based Low pass filter
DC Gain	0 dB	-0.7 dB
In-band IIP3	+21.5 dBm	-3.25 dBm
Total Harmonic Distortion)	2.5%(for 300mV input signal at 100 KHz)	10%(for 50mV input signal at 100 KHz)
Dynamic Range	60 dB	45 dB
Total Average current consumption(without bias and clock generation)	114 μA	41 μA
Total estimated Capacitor Area	1150 μm^2	700 μm^2
Cutoff frequency variation due to $\pm 5\%$ capacitance mismatch	0.68%/0.72%	0.38%/-0.48%

5 Conclusion

In this paper we have applied the CBSC technique to design a 1st order switched capacitor low pass filter. CBSC technique enjoys several advantages like high gain, no stability concern and no settling constraint over opamp based technique whose performance is essentially dictated by gain, stability and settling. CBSC technique relaxes the constraints imposed by conventional closed loop negative feedback opamp based design. The tradeoff for CBSC technique being the final output offset voltage which poses constraint on comparator speed. The nonlinearity of output resistance of current source, signal dependent comparator delay and capacitance variation can potentially produce nonlinearity at the output. But highly linear current source design is easier than designing a high gain OpAmp in scaled technologies which clearly makes CBSC based design a potential candidate for scaled technologies in future. The noise analysis for Switched capacitor integrators are not straightforward because conventional steady state noise analysis can't be applied due to the transient nature of the CBSC circuit and this is to be investigated in future. Further the differential CBSC integrator stage can be investigated to reap the benefits of a differential design like inherent extraneous noise immunity, higher signal swing, high linearity.

References

1. Moore, G.: Cramming more components on integrated circuits. Electronics 38(8) (April 1965)
2. Sansen, W., et al.: Towards Sub 1V Analog Integrated circuits in submicron standard CMOS technologies. In: IEEE Int. Solid State Circuits Conference, Dig. Tech. Papers, pp. 186–187 (February 1998)
3. Buss, D.: Device issues in the integration of analog/RF functions in deep submicron digital CMOS. IEEE IEDM Technical Digest, 423–426 (December 1999)
4. Copeland, M.A., Rabaey, J.M.: Dynamic amplifiers for M.O.S Technology. Electronics Letters 15(10), 301–302 (1979)
5. Murmann, B., Boser, B.: A 12-bit 75-MSamples/s pipelined ADC using open loop residue amplification. IEEE JSSC 38(12), 2040–2050 (2003)
6. Sepke, T., Fiorenza, J.K., Sodini, C.G., Holloway, P., Lee, H.-S.: Comparator-based switched-capacitor circuits for scaled CMOS technologies. IEEE JSSC 41(12) (December 2006)
7. Momeni, M., Basinschi, P.B., Glesner, M.: Comparison of Opamp based and Comparator based Delta-Sigma modulation. Design, Automation and Test in Europe (2008)
8. Schaumann, R., Valkenberg, M.E.: Design of Analog Filters. Oxford University Press (2006)
9. Johns, D., Martin, K.: Analog Integrated Circuit Design. John Wiley and sons, Inc. (1997)
10. Baker, R.J.: CMOS Circuit Design, Layout, and Simulation. John Wiley and sons, Inc. (2005)
11. Behzad Razavi, R.F.: Microelectronics. Prentice-Hall (1998)

Effect of Malicious Hardware Logic on Circuit Reliability

Sanjay Burman[1], Ayan Palchaudhuri[2], Rajat Subhra Chakraborty[2],
Debdeep Mukhopadhyay[2], and Pranav Singh[1]

[1] Centre for Artificial Intelligence and Robotics
C.V. Raman Nagar, Bangalore, India – 560093
[2] Department of Computer Science and Engineering
Indian Institute of Technology Kharagpur
Kharagpur, India – 721302
rschakraborty@cse.iitkgp.ernet.in

Abstract. Malicious modifications of integrated circuits have emerged as a potent threat to circuit and system security and reliability. In this paper, we present theoretical models of different types of commonly investigated malicious hardware logic to estimate their effect on circuit reliability, specifically those malicious circuit modifications that cause functional failure of circuits ("hardware Trojans"). Simulation results show close match to the theoretically predicted trends.

Keywords: Logic simulation, Hardware Trojan, Malicious logic, Reliability, Theoretical Modeling.

1 Introduction

The ever-increasing complexity of modern ICs imply that not only IC manufacturing being outsourced, external parties (e.g. CAD software and hardware IP suppliers) are increasingly getting involved in all aspects of the design process. With so much loss of control over every stage of the IC design and manufacturing process for economic motivations, it has become difficult to ensure their trustworthiness. It has been shown that an intelligently designed and inserted malicious hardware logic (MHL) can evade most traditional testing and verification techniques, since such analysis is equivalent to the *Halting Problem*, according to *Rice's Theorem* [2]. Such security breaches can prove to be disastrous in critical situations.

The main feature of MHLs which makes them difficult to detect and prevent against in general is their "stealthiness". They activate and manifest their activity (commonly through circuit malfunctions, in which case they are termed "hardware Trojans") very rarely, under internal circuit logic conditions that might be impossible to emulate during the finite duration of post–manufacturing testing, using a relatively small number of test vectors [1]. Ingenious MHL designs are reported in the technical literature frequently, with effects as varied as *functional failures*, *performance degradation*, *information leakage* and *denial-of-service* [1].

H. Rahaman et al. (Eds.): VDAT 2012, LNCS 7373, pp. 190–197, 2012.
© Springer-Verlag Berlin Heidelberg 2012

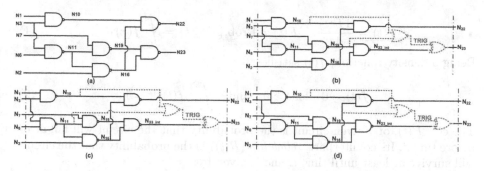

Fig. 1. The *c17 ISCAS–85* circuit and three different inserted combinational Trojans. Trojan–1 and Trojan–3 are triggered and cause malfunction for 2 out of 32 possible input vectors. Trojan–2 is triggered relatively more often and cause malfunction for 4 out of the 32 possible input vectors.

Highly sensitive testing techniques have been proposed in recent years that have been shown to be capable of detecting extremely small circuit modifications in industry–standard circuits [3–7]. However, as of now, the competing problems of MHL design and MHL detection is a "cat-and-mouse game", with no definite clear winner. Undetected MHLs can potentially affect the functional lifetime of an IC by decreasing the mean time between failures. Therefore, it is essential that we study the impact of undetected MHLs on mean time between failures in real–world deployments. *This is the topic that we concentrate on in this paper, and try to develop mathematical models of reliability for widely-studied hardware Trojans.* We validate our models using circuit simulations

The rest of the paper is organized as follows. In Section 2, we discuss mathematical modeling to estimate circuit reliability in general. In Section 3, we mathematically analyze the effect of inserted and undetected MHLs on circuit reliability for several types of MHLs, with supporting simulation and experimental results. We conclude in Section 4.

2   Background: Mathematical Modeling of Circuit Reliability

In this section, we would treat circuit reliability and associated metrics from a relatively abstract mathematical viewpoint, without concentrating on the actual cause of circuit failure. Our definitions and notation would follow those given in [8], and would use relatively simple analytical models of circuit failure.

Suppose a circuit starts operating at time $t = 0$ and remains operational until it is hit by a failure for the first time at time $t = T$. Then, T is the *lifetime* of the component, and let T be a random variable distributed according to the *probability density function* (pdf) $f(t)$. If $F(t)$ is the cumulative distribution function (cdf) for T, then, $f(t)$ and $F(t)$ are related by:

$$f(t) = \frac{\mathrm{d}\,F(t)}{\mathrm{d}\,t}, \quad F(t) = \mathrm{Prob.}\{T \le t\} = \int_0^t f(\tau)\,\mathrm{d}\tau \tag{1}$$

Being a density function, $f(t)$ satisfies:

$$f(t) \ge 0 \quad \text{for}\, t \ge 0 \quad \text{and} \quad \int_0^\infty f(t)\,\mathrm{d}t = 1 \tag{2}$$

The cdf, $F(t)$, of a given circuit is the probability that the circuit will fail at or before time t. Its counterpart, *reliability* $(R(t))$ is the probability that the circuit will survive at least until time t, and is given by:

$$R(t) = \mathrm{Prob.}\{T > t\} = 1 - F(t) \tag{3}$$

Perhaps the most important quantitative metric used to estimate reliability is the *failure rate* or *hazard rate*, denoted by $\lambda(t)$, and defined as:

$$\lambda(t) = \frac{f(t)}{1 - F(t)} = \frac{f(t)}{R(t)} \tag{4}$$

$\lambda(t)$ denotes the conditional instantaneous probability of a circuit failing, given it is yet to fail at time t. Since $\frac{\mathrm{d}\,R(t)}{\mathrm{d}\,t} = -f(t)$, we have $\lambda(t) = -\frac{1}{R(t)}\frac{\mathrm{d}\,R(t)}{\mathrm{d}\,t}$. For circuits which have a failure rate that is constant over time (which is the most commonly considered model for ICs), i.e. $\lambda(t) = \lambda$, we have:

$$\frac{\mathrm{d}\,R(t)}{\mathrm{d}\,t} = -\lambda R(t) \tag{5}$$

Solving eqn. (5) with the initial condition $R(t) = 0$ leads to:

$$R(t) = e^{-\lambda t} \quad \text{for}\, t \ge 0 \tag{6}$$

Eqn. (6) leads to the following expressions:

$$f(t) = \lambda e^{-\lambda t} \quad \text{and} \quad F(t) = 1 - e^{-\lambda t} \quad \text{for}\, t \ge 0 \tag{7}$$

Besides λ, another important parameter that characterizes circuit reliability is the *mean time to failure* (MTTF), which is the expected lifetime of the circuit, and is given (assuming a constant failure rate) by:

$$\mathrm{MTTF} = \mathrm{E}[T] = \int_0^\infty t f(t)\,\mathrm{d}t = \int_0^\infty \lambda t e^{-\lambda t}\,\mathrm{d}t = \frac{1}{\lambda} \tag{8}$$

A major part of our analysis for different types of MHLs would be devoted to modeling how the presence of a undetected MHL modifies the values of the failure rate and MTTF of a circuit. Depending on the nature of the inserted MHL, the circuit may or may not recover its original functionality. However, in the analyses that follow, we would assume the interval between the start of functioning of a circuit and its first functional failure due to the activation of a MHL as defining the lifetime of the circuit.

Table 1. Combinational Trojans: Trigger Condition and Trojan Activation Probability

Trojan	Trigger Condition	Troj. Activation Probability
Trojan–1	$N10 = 0, N19 = 0$	2/32
Trojan–2	$N10 = 0, N11 = 0$	4/32
Trojan–3	$N10 = 0, N16 = 0$	2/32

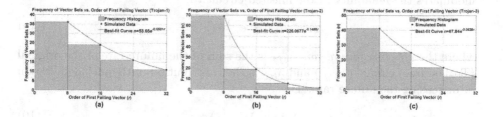

Fig. 2. Failure trends of the $c17$ circuit with three types of inserted combinational Trojans (shown in Figs. 1(b)–(d))

3 Malicious Hardware Logic and Reliability: Analysis and Results

In this section, we give examples of different common and widely studied MHLs, and analyze their effect on circuit reliability.

3.1 Combinational Trojans

As a running example, we would use the $c17$ circuit from the *ISCAS–85* combinational circuit suite. The $c17$ circuit was chosen because of its inherent simplicity (the entire circuit consists of six two–input NAND gates), and this choice does not take into consideration the fact that the Trojan concerned is easily detectable. However, as would be evident from the analysis, the technique of estimating the reliability and the quantitative metrics derived are applicable for circuits of arbitrary complexity. Fig. 1(a) shows the $c17$ circuit. It has five primary inputs ($N1$, $N2$, $N3$, $N6$ and $N7$); two primary outputs ($N22$ and $N23$), and four internal nodes ($N10$, $N11$, $N16$ and $N19$).

Figs. 1(b)–(d) show the $c17$ circuit with three different inserted simple combinational Trojans. Each of these three Trojans consists of one NOR gate and one

Table 2. Combinational Trojans and Associated Mean Time to Failure[†]

Trojan	b_{est}	$\text{MTTF}_{\text{trojan,est}} = \frac{1}{b}$	$\text{MTTF}_{\text{trojan,est}}$ (95% Conf. Int.)	$\text{MTTF}_{\text{trojan,av}}$
Trojan–1	0.0501	19.96	[19.09,20.94]	19.15
Trojan–2	0.1489	6.72	[5.79,6.93]	6.81
Trojan–3	0.0628	15.92	[15.47,16.41]	16.35

†The MTTF is in terms of the number of input vectors applied before the first circuit failure.

XOR gate, and each of them are triggered and cause circuit malfunction by the simultaneous occurrence of logic–0 at two selected internal nodes of the circuit. Table 1 shows the trigger conditions and the activation probabilities of the three inserted Trojans obtained by exhaustive simulation of the possible input values.

Assuming that the only effect of combinational Trojans is functional failure of the circuit, and does not include *ageing*, the presence of a combinational Trojan modulates the reliability of the infected circuit to:

$$R(t) = e^{-\lambda_{eff}t} \tag{9}$$

where the *effective failure rate* λ_{eff} is the sum of the failure rate of the original (Trojan–free) circuit (λ_{org}) and λ_{tro} is the contribution of the included Trojan in increasing the failure rate. Thus,

$$\lambda_{eff} = \lambda_{org} + \lambda_{tro} \tag{10}$$

If $MTTF_{org}$ is the original $MTTF$ and $MTTF_{eff}$ is the effective $MTTF$ due to the presence of the Trojan, the change in $MTTF$ value is given by:

$$\Delta MTTF = MTTF_{eff} - MTTF_{org} = \frac{MTTF_{org}}{1 + \frac{\lambda_{org}}{\lambda_{tro}}} \tag{11}$$

To observe the actual failure trend of the $c17$ circuit, we simulated the three circuits shown in Figs. 1(b)–(d) with 100 sets of random vectors, each set consisting of 32 vectors. However, each set of 32 vectors did not consist of all possible vectors 00000 to 11111, and hence, the set of test vectors were truely random. Figs. 2(a)–(c) show frequency histogram of the number of failures (n) that occur in the intervals 0–8, 9–16, etc., in a set of 32 vectors, considering the average over 100 vector sets. The upper range of the intervals are denoted by r. Thus, the time is discretized in terms of the number of vectors applied. This curve is representative of the failure probability density function of the Trojan-infected circuit. The best–fitted curves of the form $n = ae^{-br}$ were obtained using $MATLAB$. The parameter b, which is interpreted as representative of the $MTTF$ of the circuit, can also be estimated by averaging the time to failure for the different vector sets, following the *Method of Moments* [8]. Table 2 shows the estimated and average value (as obtained by averaging the first instance of failure of the vector sets) of the $MTTF$ (considering only the presence of Trojan), along with the 95% confidence interval for the estimated value. From the plots and the table, it is evident that the data and the data trends fitted very well to the theoretically predicted trend.

3.2   Synchronous Counter Based Sequential Trojan

A synchronous counter-based Trojan acts as a "silicon time–bomb" and causes malfunction after an inserted free-running counter driven by the system clock reaches a terminal count value. The synchronous counter-based Trojan modulates the circuit failure probability density function differently compared to the conditional triggered Trojans, because the Trojan is guaranteed to be activated after the count has reached its terminal value. Let T_{tro} be the time required for the counter to reach its terminal count. Then, for $0 \leq t < T_{tro}$, the circuit failure probability function $(F(t))$ is identical to that of the original Trojan, whereas for $t \geq T_{tro}$, $F(t) = 1$. This implies the following form of the failure probability density function:

$$f(t) = \lambda e^{-\lambda t} \left[u(t) - u(t - T_{tro}) \right] + e^{-\lambda T_{tro}} \delta(t - T_{tro}) \tag{12}$$

where $u(t)$ is the *unit step function* defined by:

$$u(t) = \begin{cases} 1 & \text{for } t \geq 0 \\ 0 & \text{otherwise} \end{cases} \tag{13}$$

and $\delta(t)$ is the *Unit Impulse Function* defined by:

$$\delta(t) = \begin{cases} 1 & \text{for } t = 0 \\ 0 & \text{otherwise} \end{cases} \tag{14}$$

Clearly, $f(t) \geq 0$ for non–negative value of t as defined above, and it can be easily verified that the above definition of $f(t)$ satisfies $\int_0^\infty f(t)\, dt = 1$ as follows:

$$\int_0^\infty f(t)\, dt = \int_0^{T_{tro}} \lambda e^{-\lambda t}\, dt + e^{-\lambda T_{tro}} \int_0^\infty \delta(t - T_{tro})\, dt = 1 \tag{15}$$

using the *Sampling property* of $\delta(t)$, i.e. $\int_{-\infty}^\infty f(t)\delta(t - t_0)\, dt = f(t_0)$. The *failure probability* $F(t)$ is the given by:

$$F(t) = \int_0^t f(\tau)\, d\tau = \begin{cases} 1 - e^{-\lambda t} & \text{for } t < T_{tro} \\ 1 & \text{for } t \geq T_{tro} \end{cases} \tag{16}$$

To determine the $MTTF$, we consider two different cases: (a) $\frac{1}{\lambda} \geq T_{tro}$ and (b) $\frac{1}{\lambda} < T_{tro}$. When $\frac{1}{\lambda} \geq T_{tro}$, the circuit is expected to fail due the activation of the Trojan before it fails due to other reasons. However, there is still a finite probability of the circuit failing in the time interval $0 \leq t < T_{tro}$. Hence, if $\frac{1}{\lambda} \geq T_{tro}$,

$$MTTF_{eff} = T_{tro} - T_{tro} \int_0^{T_{tro}} f(t)\, dt = T_{tro} \left[1 - (1 - e^{-\lambda T_{tro}}) \right] = e^{-\lambda T_{tro}} T_{tro} \tag{17}$$

and the corresponding $\Delta MTTF$ is:

$$\Delta MTTF = -\left(\frac{1}{\lambda} - e^{-\lambda T_{tro}} T_{tro} \right) = -T_{tro} \left(\frac{1}{k} - e^{-k} \right) \tag{18}$$

where $k = \lambda T_{tro}$ is a dimensionless parameter and $0 < k < 1$.

When $\frac{1}{\lambda} < T_{tro}$, the circuit is expected to fail due to other reasons before it fails due to the activation of the Trojan. Hence, if $\frac{1}{\lambda} < T_{tro}$,

$$MTTF_{eff} = MTTF_{org} = \frac{1}{\lambda} \tag{19}$$

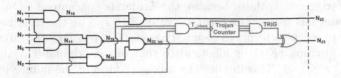

Fig. 3. $c17$ with an asynchronous binary counter–type Trojan. The reset signal for the Trojan counter has not been shown for simplicity.

Table 3. Asynchronous Sequential Trojan: Trigger Condition and Trigger Probability[†]

Trojan	States	Troj. Cnt. Inc. Cond.	Trigg. Cond.	Troj. Act. Prob. (est.)
Trojan–4	$2^3 = 8$	↑ for $T_{clock} = N11\&N16\&N19$	$T_{count} = 3'b111$	0.0406
Trojan–5	$2^4 = 16$	↑ for $T_{clock} = N11\&N16\&N19$	$T_{count} = 4'b1111$	0.0191

[†]The Trojan activation probability was estimated by simulations with a set of 3200 random vectors.

and the corresponding change in $MTTF$ is:

$$\Delta MTTF = 0 \tag{20}$$

3.3   Asynchronous Counter Based Sequential Trojan

The asynchronous counter–based sequential Trojan is triggered by successive occurrence of rare events at chosen internal circuit nodes (instead of the system clock). Eqns. (10) and (11) are still valid. In addition, if the number of state transitions required before the Trojan causes a circuit malfunction is larger, the value of $MTTF$ can be also be expected to be greater.

Fig. 3 shows the $c17$ circuit with an inserted sequential Trojan. The Trojan is an asynchronous binary counter which increases its count whenever a positive edge occurs on the net T_{trojan}, which in turn is derived by AND–ing nodes $N11$, $N16$ and $N19$. The Trojan flips the logic–value at the primary output node $N23$ whenever the count reaches $(2^n - 1)$. Two different such Trojans were

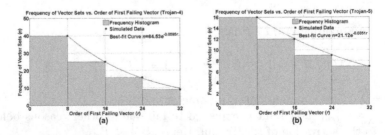

Fig. 4. Failure trends of the $c17$ circuit with two types of inserted sequential Trojans (described in Sec. 3.3)

Table 4. Asynchronous Sequential Trojans and Associated Mean Time to Failure [†]

Trojan	b_{est}	$\text{MTTF}_{\text{trojan,est}} = \frac{1}{b}$	$\text{MTTF}_{\text{trojan,est}}$95% Conf. Int.	$\text{MTTF}_{\text{trojan,av}}$
Trojan–4	0.0595	16.81	[14.91,19.28]	19.10
Trojan–5	0.0351	28.52	[26.32,31.12]	30.22

[†]The MTTF is in terms of the number of clock cycles passed before the first circuit failure.

considered: Table 3 shows the Trojan clocking and activation conditions, along with the activation probability estimated through simulations using 3200 test vectors. Fig. 4 shows the simulated failure trends of the $c17$ circuit infected with two types of Trojans: 3–bit asynchronous counter (Trojan–4) and 4–bit asynchronous counter (Trojan–5). Table 4 shows the $MTTF$ extracted from the best–fitted curve and by averaging the simulation data. Again, the $MTTF$ derived from the best–fit curve and from the simulation data agree very well, and as expected, the circuit with the more difficult to activate Trojan (Trojan–5) has a smaller $MTTF$.

4   Conclusion

In spite of recent advances in malicious hardware logic (MHL) detection and prevention techniques, undetected MHLs remain a great threat. We have theoretically investigated the effect of several types of undetected MHLs on circuit reliability and expected lifetime, with supporting simulation and experimental results.

References

1. Karri, R., Rajendran, J., Rosenfeld, K., Tehranipoor, M.: Trustworthy hardware: identifying and classifying hardware Trojans. IEEE Computer 43(10), 39–46 (2010)
2. Huffmire, T., Irvine, C., Nguyen, T.D., Levin, T., Kastner, R., Sherwood, T.: Handbook of FPGA Design Security. Springer, Dordrecht (2010)
3. Aarestad, J., Acharyya, D., Rad, R., Plusquellic, J.: Detecting Trojans through leakage current analysis using multiple supply pad $IDDQ$. IEEE Trans. Inf. Forensics Security 5(4), 893–904 (2010)
4. Rad, R., Plusquellic, J., Tehranipoor, M.: A sensitivity analysis of power signal methods for detecting hardware Trojans under real process and environmental conditions. IEEE Trans. VLSI Syst. 18(12), 1735–1744 (2010)
5. Koushanfar, F., Mirhoseini, A.: A unified framework for multimodal submodular integrated circuits Trojan detection. IEEE Trans. Inf. Forensics Security 6(1), 162–174 (2011)
6. Potkonjak, M., Nahapetian, A., Nelson, M., Massey, T.: Hardware Trojan horse detection using gate-level characterization. In: Proc. Design Automation Conference (DAC 2009), pp. 688–693 (2009)
7. Banga, M., Hsiao, M.S.: A region based approach for the identification of hardware Trojans. In: Proc. IEEE International Workshop on Hardware-Oriented Security and Trust (HOST 2008), pp. 40–47 (2008)
8. Koren, I., Krishna, C.M.: Fault–tolerant Systems. Morgan Kaufmann Publishers, Francisco (2007)

A Modified Scheme for Simultaneous Reduction of Test Data Volume and Testing Power

Sruthi P.R. and M. Nirmala Devi

Amrita Vishwa Vidyapeetham, Coimbatore, India
sruthirk@gmail.com, m_nirmala@cb.amrita.edu

Abstract. Today's electronic systems, with ever-growing demand for mobile computing devices, are more complex, fast and energy efficient. Cost and quality are the major issues in testing these circuits. The test data storage requirements, along with the operating frequency and channel capacity, have a significant impact on the test cost. This paper presents a new compression scheme based on Alternating Variable Run-length (AVR) codes for reducing the test data. Weighted transition based reordering scheme is adopted prior to the compression scheme to improve the compression ratio (CR). By applying an appropriate mapping scheme, sufficient reduction in power has been achieved. The scheme is also found to have a maximum of 10% increase in compression ratio when compared to the conventional frequency directed run-length codes (FDR) codes and extended FDR (EFDR) codes without any significant on-chip area overhead. The experiments are performed on ISCAS'89 benchmark circuits.

Keywords: Difference vector, Modified AVR codes, Test data compression, Test power reduction, Weighted transition based reordering.

1   Introduction

With the recent advancements in process technology, the integration density has evolved as a new paradigm, resulting in larger designs with more number of scan cells and more number of faults. The test cost is directly related to test data volume and hence the test data transfer time [1]. Another major problem faced in system-on-chip (SOC) test integration is test power. The power consumption in test mode is considerably higher than in normal mode. Though numerous methods are presented in literature so far, there are only few methods that handle both the issues of increased data volume and power dissipation simultaneously during testing. The testing problem is further aggravated by the use of intellectual property (IP) cores, which remains hidden from the system integrator.

Structural methods require design modifications for reducing test volume and testing time [2]. Though the compaction techniques can reduce the test data without introducing additional hardware overhead, it affects the fault coverage of non-modeled faults [3]. Built-in self-test (BIST), [4-6] methodology reduces the need for expensive automatic test equipment (ATE). The memory requirements of ATE and the limitations in channel capacity would invite test data compression schemes. In test

H. Rahaman et al. (Eds.): VDAT 2012, LNCS 7373, pp. 198–208, 2012.
© Springer-Verlag Berlin Heidelberg 2012

data compression technique, additional on-chip hardware is added before and after the scan chains. This hardware decompresses the test stimulus coming from the tester [7].

Existing test-data compression techniques can be classified into three types [8]: code-based [9-17] compression techniques, linear-decompression based [18, 19], and broadcast-based schemes [20]. In cases, where no modifications can be applied to the cores of the scan chain, or neither automatic test pattern generation nor fault simulation tools can be used, code based compression schemes are found to give better results. Many compression techniques, such as statistical coding [10] based on frequency of occurrence, run-length codes like Golomb codes [11], Frequency Directed Run-length (FDR) codes [14], Extended Frequency Directed Run-length (EFDR) codes [16], and Variable Input Huffman Coding (VIHC) [15], dictionary coding [9], constructive codes [7] have been proposed to reduce the test data volume. These techniques partition the original test set into symbols and then replace each symbol with a code word to form the compressed data.

Power dissipation during test application must also be addressed. State transitions that are not possible in normal mode are often possible during test mode [21]. It was shown that test data volume and test power can be reduced simultaneously using Golomb coding [6]. The main idea was to map the don't cares in the test vectors to zero. This results in long runs of zeros that can be efficiently compressed using Golomb codes. However, the test power can be reduced further if don't cares were mapped suitably to derive test sets that minimize switching activity. This was proposed in [6] using alternating run-length (AR) codes.

This paper presents a new algorithm which aims at achieving the two major goals of test vector compression and reduced test power simultaneously using a reordering scheme. It was shown in [5] that the use of appropriate reordering scheme combined with FDR code resulted in a considerable increase in compression ratio. But, by using a compression scheme which considers both 0s as well as 1s for compression the compression ratio can be further improved. This is considered in the proposed design by incorporating modified AVR coding [22] with some modifications. The results show that the use of this coding results in better compression and have significant reduction in switching activity due to proper filling mechanism followed in the reordering algorithm adopted. The reduction in switching activity in turn reduces the peak power as well as average power.

The paper is organized as follows: Section 2 gives a brief introduction into the various schemes adopted in this paper including AVR codes, the power estimation technique used and the existing ordering techniques. Section 3 introduces the modified AVR codes along with its decompressor architecture. Section 4 presents the experimental results of the proposed test data compression on its compression ratio and test power. Section 5 summarizes the paper.

2   Background

In this section, we provide a theoretical background of AVR codes and modified AVR codes, a brief description of the power estimation method, which is used throughout this paper. The characteristics of low-power test sequences to correlate test data compression and scan-in power are also briefly described here.

2.1   Alternating Variable Run-Length (AVR) Codes

A run is a consecutive sequence of equal symbols that can be encoded using two elements: the repeating symbol and the number of times it appears. It was shown in [14], that an FDR code is very efficient for compressing data that has few 1s and long runs of 0s. However, for data streams that are composed of both runs of 0s and 1s, the FDR code is rather inefficient. So, it is important to have a code that can efficiently compress both runs of 0s and runs of 1s. A detailed description about this coding scheme and the decoder architecture is described in [22]. The compression achieved can be improved further by considering the relationship between two consecutive runs. This relationship has been exploited here and hence a slight modification has been made on the AVR code explained earlier.

If two consecutive runs have the same run-length, then the second run can be encoded using a small code word. If the second run is runs of 0 then it is encoded as 000 else encoded as 111, accordingly called Type 1 coding or Type II coding respectively. The significance of these two code is that they do not appear as the code word in any of the groups and hence during decoding it would be simpler to get back the original data. Fig.1 shows an encoded data that was obtained using FDR (T_{FDR}), AVR (T_{AVR}) and modified AVR code (T_{MAVR}). The input data (T_D) has both runs of 0s and runs of 1s. For the same input data stream, FDR coding results in 58 bits while only this is reduced to 22 bits using modified AVR coding.

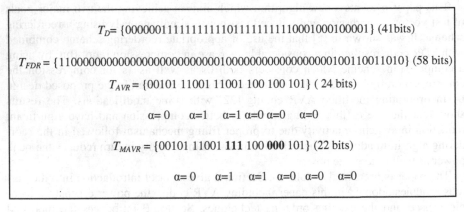

Fig. 1. Example of FDR coding, AVR coding and Modified AVR coding

2.2   Power Estimation Analysis

The main goal of any compression scheme is to reduce the volume of test data. Each compression scheme fills don't cares in the test set differently which might affect the power consumption of the components that finally receive the uncompressed data from the decoder unit [13]. Compression techniques that lower the power encode vectors to have fewer transitions while decoding. Reducing the number of transitions in test vectors reduces the switching activity and power during scan-in operation [13]. A minimum transition fill [21], replicates the value of the most recent care bit for all unspecified positions until the next care bit whose value will be used for the following bits. A genetic algorithm based heuristic to fill the don't cares is proposed in [23]. A significant improvement in dynamic power and leakage power over various existing don't care filling algorithms were obtained.

Though the scan power reduction is not the main focus of this paper, the compression technique also reduces the scan-in power. Scan-in power refers to the power consumption of elements in the scan chain during scan-in operation. To analyze the scan-in power, the weighted transition metric (WTM) is used to estimate the power dissipation during scan testing. The WTM model [24] shown to be correlated with the power dissipation in the circuit. The WTM models the fact that the scan in power for a given vector depends not only on the number of transitions in it, but also on their relative positions. Let l and $t_j=\{t_{j,1},\ t_{j,2},...,\ .t_{j,l}\}$ be the scan chain length and a scan vector respectively, with $t_{j,1}$ scanned in before $t_{j,2}$ and so on. The weighted transition metric for t_j, denoted WTM_j, [24] is given by:

$$WTM_j = \sum_{i=1}^{l-1}(l-i)\times(t_{j,i}\oplus t_{j,i+1}) \tag{1}$$

If the T_D contains n vectors $\{t_1,\ t_2....,t_n\}$ then the average scan in power P_{avg} and peak scan-in power P_{peak} are estimated using (2) and (3) respectively.

$$P_{avg} = \frac{\sum_{j=1}^{n}\sum_{i=1}^{l-1}(l-i)\times(t_{j,i}\oplus t_{j,i+1})}{n} \tag{2}$$

$$P_{peak} = \max_{j\in\{1,2,3,...n\}}\{\sum_{i=1}^{l-1}(l-i)\times(t_{j,i}\oplus t_{j,i+1})\} \tag{3}$$

2.3   Ordering Algorithms

In scan circuits, power dissipation during test is a function of two parameters; the order in which the tests are applied and the order in which the scan flip flops are chained to form the shift register. The switching activity can be reduced by modifying the former and apply it to the CUT. These techniques can be applied during external testing or deterministic BIST. Test vector reordering can be used to solve the low correlation between consecutive test vectors. One such scheme [25] reorders the scan cells such that the test sequence shifted in has the minimum switching activity during test application. The greedy algorithm based reordering process uses the minimum hamming distance between them to reduce the scan power [26]. In case of IP cores, an artificial intelligence based reordering of scan vector, for capture power reduction was presented in [27]. Weighted transition based reordering was proposed in [5]. This is an extension of the hamming distance based reordering [28] where the first vector was kept unfilled until all vectors are reordered. The run-based reordering approach [29] is based on reordering test frames to give bigger run lengths of 0s. As this approach uses scan frame reordering, this scheme is not suitable for IP cores. The weighted transition based reordering is used as the basic scheme of the proposed algorithm in this paper.

3   Problem Formulation

In [5], weighted transition based reordering, column wise bit filling, and difference vector (WTR-CBF-DV) mechanism was adopted to improve the compression. It was noticed in that the amount of compression in those schemes could be further improved. This is due to the fact that using FDR coding compression on the reordered vectors, need not provide much compression if the test sequence had more number of 1s than 0s. Even after taking the difference vectors, the number of 1s resulting in some circuits was found to be considerable by using this scheme. From our previous work [25], it was noticed that the modified AVR code which takes both runs into consideration was found to have better compression results. The relationship between consecutive runs was also considered there. The WTR-CBF-DV mechanism was found to give better results for the scan-in power reduction. Both the average as well as the peak power was shown to have reduced by incorporating appropriate reordering and don't care filling mechanisms. A combination of the above described reordering scheme and the modified AVR code is presented in this paper. This scheme aims at achieving both higher compression ratios as well as reduced test power.

3.1   Major Contributions

1. It was noticed that the test sequences had repeating consecutive runs and in the existing schemes both these runs were coded using the same code word. To avoid this, modified AVR code is introduced where the relationship between two consecutive runs is also considered. The AVR codes are found to have smaller code word length compared to many other codes and hence the replacement with smaller code word would yield better compression.
2. In order to achieve a simultaneous reduction in test power as well as test volume reduction, a reordering of test vectors were done prior to compression. The WTR-CBF-DV algorithm adopted here, fills the don't cares keeping in mind test power reduction. Also, the CB fill adopted helps to reduce the capture power to a large extend.

3.2   Modified Algorithm

The test vectors required for executing the algorithm is obtained from an ATPG. The algorithm uses the WTR-CBF-DV algorithm [5] with a difference in the compression scheme adopted.

1. Find the test vector with minimum number of don't care bits in the given test set. If more than one vector have this then MT fill those vectors and calculate WTM for

each vector. The vector with minimum WTM among them would be placed as the first vector of the reordered set.

2. To find the next vector of the reordered set, find the hamming distance of each vector from the first vector of the reordered set. If more than one vector with minimum hamming distance then:

   — Columwise bit (CB) fill each vector and calculate WTM of each of these vectors.
   — Select the vector with minimum WTM as the next vector of the reordered set.

3. Repeat steps 1 and 2 until all the vectors are reordered.
4. Apply difference vector mechanism.
5. Perform modified AVR coding;

   — Count the run-length.
   — If it differs from the previous run-length (initially its set to 0), then perform the conventional AVR coding else perform either type I or type II coding checking if its runs of 0 or runs of 1.

6. Compute the compression ratio.

3.3   Decompressor Architecture

The compressed data has to be decompressed on-chip and fed to the CUT. The decompressor, decompresses the encoded test set T_E and produces the primary set T_D. The complete decompressor architecture is shown in Fig 2. The decoder is simple and it is independent of the pre-computed test set and the CUT.

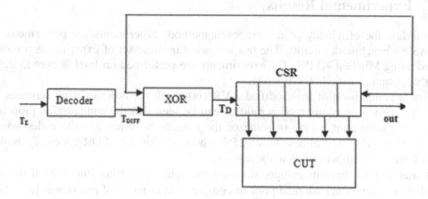

Fig. 2. The complete decompressor architecture [14]

This decoder architecture is slightly modified from conventional AVR coding after considering the relationship between two consecutive runs. For this, an extra register in included in the architecture to keep an account of the previous run-length. To account for the difference vectors, an XOR gate followed by a cyclical scan register has been included. The extra register keeps the value of the previous run. First the incoming prefix is compared with the two values *000* and *111*. If it is found to be same then the value stored in the register is chosen and fed to the *(k+1)* bit counter else the decoder behaves as a conventional AVR decoder. The decoder operation is very much similar to that in [22] except for the extra register. The decoder for the modified AVR code and the state diagram [25] for the finite state machine (FSM) are shown in Fig. 3 (a) and Fig 3 (b) respectively.

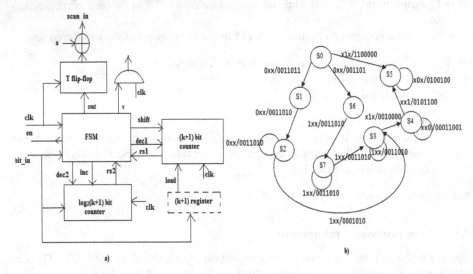

Fig. 3. a) The decoder architecture of modified AVR code [25] b) State diagram for FSM [25]

4   Experimental Results

To validate the efficiency of the proposed method, experiments are performed on ISCAS'89 benchmark circuits. The test sets used in these set of experiments are obtained using MinTest ATPG. The experiments are performed on Intel ® core i5 2.30 GHz workstation with 4.00 GB RAM.

First a comparison of the modified AVR code with the other existing schemes is done in terms of the compression ratio. It can be seen that the compression ratio increases by maximum 1.49% in some of the circuits by using MAVR codes when compared to AVR and almost by 25.25% when compared to FDR codes. T_D is the size of original number of bits in the test set.

It was noticed that this compression scheme could be further improved if proper reordering schemes are adopted prior to compression in terms of test power [22]. For this different reordering scheme were combined with the MAVR codes. The results of this are shown in Table 2. Here, initially HDR-CBF-DV mechanism is adopted and this was combined with the existing FDR codes and then the reordering scheme was slightly modified to WTR-CBF-DV combined with FDR codes. It was observed that the compression ratio improved slightly. This was then combined with the proposed MAVR codes. It can be seen clearly that this further improved the compression ratio on an average 4.66%.

Table 1. Comparison between FDR[14], EFDR[16] , AVR[22], and MAVR

Circuit	Size of T_D (bits)	Percentage of compression (%)			
		FDR [14]	EFDR [16]	AVR [22]	Modified AVR (Proposed)
s5378	23754	47.991	57.986	61.943	62.310
s9234	35479	41.79	49.351	59.366	59.937
s13207	165200	81.306	82.531	85.614	86.440
s15850	76986	66.205	70.993	**75.946**	**77.438**
s38417	164739	**43.259**	58.978	69.064	**69.151**
s38584	199106	60.922	66.121	71.770	71.905

Table 2. Comparison of compression ratios using different compression schemes

Circuit	Percentage of compression (%)		
	HDR-CBF-DV+FDR	WTR-CBF-DV+FDR [5]	WTR-CBF-DV+MAVR (Proposed)
s5378	58.34	57.28	61.31
s9234	52.89	54.72	**63.71**
s13207	82.23	84.03	86.25
s15850	67.63	68.87	74.10
s38417	52.79	60.46	64.32
s38584	57.46	59.79	**63.46**

Table 3. Comparison of average power

Circuit	MT FILL [16]	HDR-CBF-DV [28]	WTR-CBF-DV [5]
s5378	11522	14236	11009
s9234	14106	16756	18476
s13207	94885	121637	125386
s15850	70894	89486	96458
s38417	437935	677843	658957
s38584	481173	527092	633478

The scan-in power calculation for all the circuits using this WTR-CBF-DV is then analyzed. The results are projected in Table 3 and Table 4. Table 3 shows the average power consumed in the circuits by adopting different filling mechanisms. It is known the amount of power dissipated largely depends on the filling mechanism adopted. The power calculations are done using WTM described in section 2.2. It can be seen that the WTR-CBF-DV mechanism when used resulted in minimum average as well as peak power.

Table 4. Comparison of peak power

Circuit	MT FILL [16]	HDR-CBF-DV [28]	WTR-CBF-DV [5]
s5378	3465	12142	11254
s9234	4022	14563	13492
s13207	7879	129317	102745
s15850	13659	87685	64573
s38417	118078	543472	437854
s38584	86305	412274	332789

5   Conclusion

An efficient code based compression scheme is presented which is found to have a higher compression ratio than other existing schemes. An appropriate reordering scheme is adopted prior to the compression scheme to achieve better compression result. The proposed design demands no extra on-chip area overhead. Experiments are performed on ISCAS'89 benchmark circuits and are found to have an increase in compression ratio. The peak power and average power is found to have reduced by using proper reordering scheme.

Acknowledgement. We sincerely thank Prof. Nur. A. Touba for providing us with the MinTest ATPG vectors.

References

1. Hirech, M.: Test cost and test power conflicts: EDA perspective. In: Proceedings of the 28th IEEE VLSI Test Symposium (VTS 2010), Santa Cruz, Calif., USA, p. 126 (2010)
2. Hamzaoglu, I., Patel, J.H.: Reducing test application time for full scan embedded cores. In: Proc. Int. Symp. Fault-Tolerant Comput., pp. 260–267 (1999)
3. Jau-Shien, C., Chen-Shang, L.: Test set compaction for combinational circuits. In: Proceedings of Test Symposium, pp. 20–25 (1992)
4. Denq, L.-M., Hsing, Y.-T., Wu, C.-W.: Hybrid BIST scheme for multiple hetero-geneous embedded memories. IEEE Des. Test Comput. 26(2), 64–72 (2009)
5. Mehta, U.S., Dasgupta, K.S., Devashrayee, N.M.: Research Article: Weighted Transition Based Reordering, Columnwise Bit Filling, and Difference Vector: A Power-Aware Test Data Compression Method. VLSI Design, Article ID 756561, 8 pages (2011)
6. Chandra, A., Chakrabarty, K.: Reduction of SOC test data volume, scan power and testing time using alternating run length codes. In: Proceedings of the 39th Design Automation Conference (DAC 2002), New Orleans, La, USA, pp. 673–678 (2002)

7. Touba, N.A.: Survey of test vector compression techniques. IEEE Design and Test of Computers 23(4), 294–303 (2006)
8. Wang, L.-T., Wu, C.-W., Wen, X.: VLSI Test Principles and Architectures. Morgan Kaufmann, San Mateo (2006)
9. Li, L., Chakrabarty, K., Touba, N.: Test data compression using dictionaries with selective entries and fixed-length indices. ACM Trans. Des. Autom. Electron. Syst. 8(4), 470–490 (2003)
10. Jas, M.-E.N.A., Ghosh-Dastidar, J., Touba, N.: An efficient test vector compression scheme using selective Huffman coding. IEEE Trans. Comput.-Aided Des. Integr. Circuits Syst. 22(6), 797–806 (2003)
11. Chandra, A., Chakrabarty, K.: System on a chip test data compression and decompression architectures based on Golomb codes. IEEE Trans. Comput.-Aided Des. Integr. Circuits Syst. 20(3), 355–368 (2001)
12. Kavousianos, X., Kalligeros, E., Nikolos, D.: Optimal selective Huffman coding for test-data compression. IEEE Trans. Computers 56(8), 1146–1152 (2007)
13. Nourani, M., Tehranipour, M.: RL-Huffman encoding for test compression and power reduction in scan applications. ACM Trans. Des. Autom. Electron. Syst. 10(1), 91–115 (2005)
14. Chandra, A., Chakrabarty, K.: Test data compression and test resource partitioning for system-on-a-chip using frequency-directed run-length (FDR) codes. IEEE Trans. Computers 52(8), 1076–1088 (2003)
15. Kavousianos, X., Kalligeros, E., Nikolos, D.: Test data compression based on variable-to-variable Huffman encoding with codeword reusability. IEEE Trans. Comput.-Aided Des. Integr. Circuits Syst. 27(7), 1333–1338 (2008)
16. El-Maleh, A.H.: Test data compression for system-on-a chip using extended frequency-directed run-length code. IET Comput. Digital Tech. 2(3), 155–163 (2008)
17. Jas, A., Touba, N.: Test vector decompression using cyclical scan chains and its application to testing core based design. In: Proc. Int. Test Conf., pp. 458–464 (1998)
18. Koenemann, B.: LFSR-Coded Test Patterns for Scan Designs. In: Proc. European Test Conf. (ETC 1991), pp. 237–242. VDE Verlag (1991)
19. Czysz, D., Kassab, M., Lin, X., Mrugalski, G., Rajski, J., Tyszer, J.: Low-power scan operation in test compression environment. IEEE Trans. Comput.-Aided Design Integr. Circuits Syst. 28(11), 1742–1754 (2009)
20. Shah, M.A., Patel, J.H.: Enhancement of the IllinoisScan Architecture for Use with Multiple Scan Inputs. In: IEEE Computer Soc. Ann. Symp. VLSI (ISVLSI 2004), pp. 167–172. IEEE CS Press (2004)
21. Butler, K.M., Saxena, J., Fryars, T., Hertherington, G., Jain, A., Lewis, J.: Minimizimg Power Consumption in Scan Testing: Pattern Generation and DFT techniques. In: Proc. ITC, pp. 355–364 (2004)
22. Ye, B., Zhao, Q., Zhou, D., Wang, X., Luo, M.: Test data compression using alternating variable run-length code. Integration, the VLSI Journal, 167–175 (2010)
23. Kundu, S., Chattopadhyay, S.: Efficient don't care filling for power reduction during testing. In: Proceedings of the International Conference on Advances in Recent Technologies in Communication and Computing (ARTCom 2009), pp. 319–323 (2009)
24. Sankaralingam, R., Oruganti, R., Touba, N.: Static Compaction Techniques to Control Scan Vector Power Dissipation. In: Proc. of IEEE VLSI Test Symposium, pp. 35–42 (2000)

25. Sruthi, P.R., Nirmala Devi, M.: Modified AVR coding for test data compression. In: Proceedings of Seventh International Workshop on Unique Chips and Systems UCAS-7, New Orleans, La, USA, pp. 40–46 (2012)
26. Girard, P., Landrault, C., Pravossoudovitch, S., Severac, D.: Reducing power consumption during test application by test vector ordering. In: Proceedings of the IEEE International Symposium on Circuits and Systems (ISCAS 1998), pp. 296–299 (1998)
27. Mehta, U.S., Dasgupta, K.S., Devashrayee, N.M.: Artificial intelligence based scan vector reordering for capture power minimization. In: Proceedings of the IEEE International Symposium on VLSI, ISVLSI 2011 (2011)
28. Mehta, U.S., Dasgupta, K.S., Devashrayee, N.M.: Hamming distance based reordering and column wise bit stuffing with difference vector: a better scheme for test data compression with run length based codes. In: Proceedings of the 23rd International Conference on VLSI Design (VLSID 2010), Bangalore, India, pp. 33–38 (2010)
29. Fang, H., Chenguang, T., Xu, C.: RunBasedReordering: a novel approach for test data ompression and scan power. In: Proceedings of the IEEE International Conference on Asia and South Pacific Design Automation (ASP-DAC 2007), Yokohama, Japan, pp. 732–737 (2007)

Reusable and Scalable Verification Environment for Memory Controllers

Kiran Kumar Abburi[1], Siva Subrahmanya Evani[1],
Sajeev Thomas[1], and Anup Aprem[2],*

[1] Analog Devices India Pvt. Ltd., Bangalore
[2] India Institute of Science, Bangalore

Abstract. With the increase in design complexity, verification times are growing significantly. Reuse of verification environment is an important means of reducing the verification effort. This paper address the problem of developing a reusable and a scalable verification environment for memory controllers. Though the architecture of different memory controllers varies significantly, they share a common transactional property. This property is exploited to develop a reusable verification environment. The proposed transactional verification environment coupled with the assertion based latency checkers achieve near cycle-accurate efficiency. The proposed verification environment is also scalable to verify memory controllers with multiple ports. We applied the above approach for the verification of three memory controllers, and results showed significant improvement in productivity and effectiveness.

1 Introduction

Advances in circuit technology and new trends in computer architecture are leading to tremendous increase in computational capability of processors. However, memory speeds are increasing at a much lower rate compared to computational capability. Many innovative architectures are evolving to bridge this performance gap between logic and memory. While memory hierarchy schemes are targeting to reduce the average memory access latency [1], techniques such as out-of-order and speculative execution are aiming to hide the memory access latency [2]. These techniques are increasing the design complexity of processors, especially memory controllers, making its verification difficult and time consuming.

Memory controllers manage the flow of data going to and from the memory devices. Architecture of memory controllers varies significantly depending on its performance expectations and memory access protocol. However, they share a common transactional property. We used this property to develop a transactional verification framework, which is independent of the memory controller's architecture, for functional verification. Furthermore, we developed assertion based latency checkers for performance verification.

---

* Anup Aprem's contribution to this work is during his association with Analog Devices.

H. Rahaman et al. (Eds.): VDAT 2012, LNCS 7373, pp. 209–216, 2012.

A transaction based verification environment for memory controller has been already proposed in [3]. However, physical read back based data checking method used in this environment limits the randomization of read/write sequences and fail in detecting corner case bugs. Furthermore, the verification environment proposed in [3] does not scale well for verification of memory controllers with multiple ports. Our paper, presents solutions to these problems.

Network calculus based performance verification model that computes the worst-case bounds on latencies of memory accesses has been proposed in [4] . Deriving tight bounds for latency using this model is very complex. To overcome this problem, we split the memory transaction into three components and modeled latency of each component using assertions. The proposed assertion based latency checkers are simple and efficient.

This paper is organized as follows. Section 2 presents brief description of memory controllers. Section 3 explains the verification environment and its components. Section 4 describes the assertion based latency checkers developed for performance verification. Section 5 explains the procedure to reuse and scale the verification environment for memory controller with multiple ports. Section 6 reports the verification results. Finally, Section 7 concludes the paper.

2   Memory Controller Description

Memory controller is a digital logic circuit which manages the flow of data between System-on-Chip (SoC) and memory devices. Fig. 1. depicts the block diagram of the memory controller. Memory controller is connected to SoC buses like Advanced eXtensible Interface (AXI), Advanced High-performance Bus (AHB), Advanced Peripheral Bus (APB), etc. to issue memory requests and configure registers. Register slave interface logic enables the access to memory mapped registers. Memory slave interface converts the high-level bus requests into low-level memory requests, and it have FIFOs to improve performance by handling multiple outstanding transactions. Control logic converts the requests from memory slave interface logic to memory accesses suitable to memory protocol. Memory controllers that interface with on-chip memories often have multiple memory slave interfaces and memory ports to support huge bandwidth requirements of processor. Memory controllers that interface with off-chip memories share its memory port to multiple memory devices due to pin-count limitation.

3   Generic Verification Environment

The generic verification environment is developed by extending the base classes of Verification Methodology Manual (VMM)[5]. The architecture of transaction based verification environment for memory controller is shown in Fig. 2. Register framework of the verification environment configures the registers of the memory controller with randomly generated configuration commands. VMM Register Abstraction Layer (RAL) package [6] is used to develop this framework, which makes it reusable for all peripherals using the same register bus protocol.

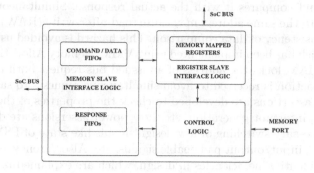

Fig. 1. Block diagram of memory controller

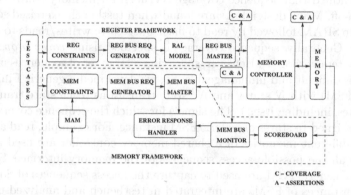

Fig. 2. Verification environment for a memory controller

Memory framework of the verification environment verifies the memory controller in the configured mode by issuing randomly generated read/write bus requests. Memory bus protocols have transactional property i.e they have handshaking signals for receiving a request and sending a response after execution of a request. Memory framework compares data of each bus transaction after receiving a response to that transaction, and any data mismatch can be traced to find the design bug. This makes the verification environment independent of memory controller's architecture and reusable.

Memory bus master issues randomly generated bus requests to the memory controller. Memory bus monitor monitors the bus and passes each transaction data as a packet to the scoreboard after receiving the response from design. Scoreboard gets the data corresponding to address of bus transaction through back-door PLI access from memory and compares with the bus transaction data. Unlike the physical read back method (immediate read after a write) of [3], our back-door access based data checking method allows the randomization of read/write sequences and improve the functional verification efficiency.

Memory controller gives an error response if it cannot successfully process the bus request. Error response handler computes the expected error response of each bus request and compares it with the actual response. Simultaneous read and write request to the same address may cause read-after-write (RAW) hazard and result in inconsistency of data comparison. This hazard is avoided using memory scheduler, which has been implemented using VMM Memory Allocation Manager (MAM) [6]. MAM locks the address of an issued bus request until the response for that transaction is received to avoid simultaneous requests to same address.

Functional assertions are developed to check the properties of the design like bus protocols, interrupt generation, etc. Low power assersions are developed to identify unnecessary switching of few design signals like state of FSMs, memory control signals, input/output pad enable signals, etc. Also, latency assertions are developed to identify inefficiencies in design, which are explained in more detail in section 4.

In addition to the traditional coverage metrics like code and functional coverage, we identified that sequence coverage is crucial for memory controller verification sign-off. Many design bugs are found when testbench exercised sequences like write to SRAM followed by read to flash, successive writes/reads to different banks, etc. Generally, sequence coverage is specified using *cover property* construct of system verilog [7]. However, specifying a large set of sequences using this construct is difficult and unmanageable. So, we developed a generic Finite State Machine (FSM) with N states and N^2 state transitions (each state transition to all the states, including itself). The signals for which the sequence coverage is required is assigned to states of generic FSM instance. For example, read and write signals to different memories of a shared memory controller are used as states to capture all the possible access sequences of the memory interface. Similarly, instances of generic FSM are used to capture the access sequences of SoC buses. All these instances of FSMs are integrated in testbench and analyzed using the code coverage tool.

4   Assertion Based Latency Checkers

Latency of a bus transaction is the number of cycles taken by a memory controller to return the response to SOC after receiving a bus request. It varies due to many factors like number of pending requests in the command FIFOs of same memory slave interface, number of high-priority pending requests from other memory slave interfaces, etc. Network calculus based approach, presented in [4], to modeling a single equation for computing *bus request to bus repsonse* latency is difficult due to these dependencies. So we split the bus transaction into three components, as shown in Fig. 3, to isolate the dependencies and efficiency of each component is verified. Each bus transaction latency is the sum of latency of these three components.

Efficiency of *bus request to memory request* latency and *memory grant to bus response* latency depend on efficient utilization of command and response FIFOs. This is verified by checking the following conditions using assertions.

− If the *command / response* FIFO is not full, *bus request / memory grant* should be accepted immediately.

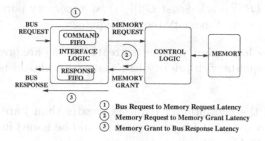

① Bus Request to Memory Request Latency
② Memory Request to Memory Grant Latency
③ Memory Grant to Bus Response Latency

Fig. 3. Execution flow of an bus transaction in a memory controller

– If the *command / response* FIFO is not empty, *memory request / bus response* should be generated immediately.

These assertions are instantiated on all memory slave interfaces of the memory controller.

Control logic of the memory controller processes memory requests from memory slave interfaces, and returns grants after its completion. For a memory controller with M memory slave interfaces and N memory ports, control logic can receive a maximum of 2M (M reads, and M writes) simultaneous requests to a memory port. As each memory port support only one access (either read or write) at a time, priority scheme is implemented in control logic to process multiple requests to a memory port in sequence. Control logic processes simultaneous requests to different memory ports in parallel.

```
generate
    for(i = 0; i < N; i++) begin : loop_I
        for(j = 2M – 1;  j >= 0;  j––) begin : loop_J
            property LATENCY_CHK;
                @(posedge CLK)
                    ($rose(R[i][j]) || (R[i][j] && $past(G[i][j]))) |-> ((G[i][j:0] == 0) && R[i][j]
        && (R[i][2M−1 :j+1] != 0))[*0 : $] ##1 ((G[i][j] == 0) && R[i][j])[*n] ##1 G[i][j];
            endproperty
        end
    end
endgenerate
```

Fig. 4. Assetions for checking latency and priority of memory requests

LATENCY_CHK in Fig. 4 is an assertion property and *generate* construct with two *for* loops make $N * 2M$ instances of this property to check $N * 2M$ memory request signals. R and G are two-dimensional arrays that store the request and grant signals tapped from the design. j^{th} request and grant signal to the ith memory port can be accessed by $R[i][j]$ and $G[i][j]$ respectively, where $i \in \{0, 1, \ldots, N-1\}$ and $j \in \{0, 1, \ldots, 2M-1\}$. The assertion is triggered whenever there is a new request ($rose(R[i][j])$) or after receiving a grant if there is a pending request $(R[i][j] \&\& \$past(G[i][j]))$ to a memory port. It checks both the priority and latency of memory request signals.

Priority: As long as high-priority requests greater than j are present $(R[i][2M - 1 : j + 1]! = 0)$, requests with priority less than $j + 1$ should not be processed $(G[i][j : 0] == 0)$.

Latency: After all the high-priority requests greater than j are processed $(R[i][2M - 1 : j + 1] == 0)$, grant for j^{th} request should be issued in n cycles, where n is latency of control logic to process a request.

5   Reusability and Scalability

Verification environment is reused to verify different memory controllers with minor setup changes in few components as shown in Fig. 5 Constraints are changed according to specification of the memory controller, back-door access functions in the scoreboard are changed according to memory models and error response handler is updated with the types of transactions for which error response is expected. Similarly, coverage and assertions corresponding to memory and register buses are reused directly, while coverage and assertions of memory port are changed according to the memory protocol. The latency check assertions presented in the section 4 are also tailored according to the memory controller's architecture.

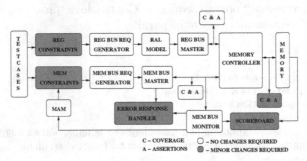

Fig. 5. Re-use of verification environment for different memory controller

A memory controller with M memory slave interfaces executes M bus requests simultaneously. Verification environment for such a memory controller is built by instantiating all the components of memory framework M times as shown in Fig. 6. Each memory framework injects bus requests independently and verifies the corresponding data/response of these transactions. Bus requests to the same address from different SoC buses may cause read-after-write (RAW) and write-after-write (WAW) hazards and result in false test failures. These hazards are avoided by using a common MAM to all the memory frameworks. MAM locks the address issued by a memory framework until its response is received to avoid simultaneous requests to the same address.

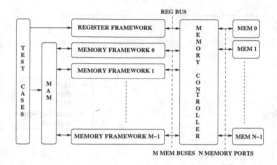

Fig. 6. Verification environment for a memory controller with multiple ports

6 Results

The verification environment presented in this paper is used for three different memory controllers : L2 controller, Static Memory Controller (SMC), Double Data Rate (DDR) Controller. Verification environment was first developed for L2 controller, and it was reused to verify SMC and DDR controllers. Table. 1 presents the verification effort of these memory controllers. This reuse of verification environment saved about 8 person weeks each for DDR and SMC. Total verification time is the sum of verification environment development time, and simulation and debug time. Percentage of verification time saved (S) is computed as.

$$S = T_s/(T_s + T_v) * 100$$

where T_s is the time saved by reuse of verification environment and T_v is the total verification time. 25% and 16% of verification time is saved for SMC and DDR respectively. This verification effort reduction will continue in the forthcoming projects also.

Table 1. Verification effort of three different memory controllers

Block	Verification Environment Development time (in Person Weeks)	Simulation & Debug Time (in Person Weeks)	Total Verification Time (T_v) (in Person Weeks)	% of Verification Time Saving (S)
L2	12	25	37	-
SMC	4	20	24	25
DDR	4	38	42	16

Fig. 7. shows the percentage of design bugs found with verification time. We can observe that bugs are found in SMC and DDR from 2nd week itself due to the reuse of verification environment. Randomly generated tests are simulated continuously until the design is stable i.e no test failures are reported for a long time (atleast 2 weeks). Verification is signed off after achieving 100% coverage on stable design.

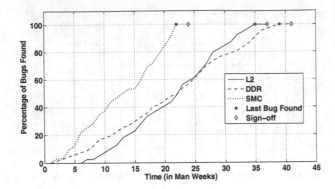

Fig. 7. Percentage of bugs found vs Person weeks spent

7 Conclusion

The proposed transactional verification framework coupled with the assertion based latency checkers proved to be robust for verification of memory controllers. The reduction in the verification effort by reusing and scaling the verification environment for different memory controllers is significant. Other challenges that need to be addressed to further reduce the verification effort are simulation and debug time reduction.

References

1. Wu, D., Zou, X., Dai, K., Deng, C., Lin, S.: Memory system design and implementation for a multiprocessor. In: ICCET (April 2010)
2. Wang, P.H., Wang, H., Collins, J.D., Grochowski, E., Kling, R.M., Shen, J.P.: Memory latency-tolerance approaches for Itanium processors: out-of-order execution vs. speculative precomputation. In: Eighth International Symposium on High-Performance Computer Architecture (February 2008)
3. Wu, Y., Yu, L., Lan, L., Zhou, H.: A Coverage-driven Constraint Random-based Functional Verification Method of Memory Controller. In: The 19th IEEE/IFIP International Symposium on Rapid System Prototyping (June 2008)
4. Henriksson, T., van der Wolf, P., Jantsch, A., Bruce, A.: Network Calculus Applied to Verification of Memory Access Performance in Socs. In: IEEE/ACM/IFIP Workshop on Embedded Systems for Real-Time Multimedia (October 2007)
5. Synopsys, VMM Standard Library User Guide
6. Synopsys, VMM Register Abstraction Layer User Guide
7. Spear, C.: System Verilog for Verification: A guide to Learning the Testbench Language Features

Design of a Fault-Tolerant Conditional Sum Adder

Atin Mukherjee and Anindya Sundar Dhar

Electronics and Electrical Communication Engg. Dept., IIT Kharagpur
mukherjeeatin@gmail.com,
asd@ece.iitkgp.ernet.in

Abstract. Fault tolerance is the ability of a system to retain its normal operation without failure when some part of the system fails to operate properly. It increases the wear-out time for any system at a cost of increased hardware. Fault tolerant approaches must be incorporated in any safety-critical system for continuing its job without failure even if an error occurs in the system. Adder is the most essential block in any digital architecture. In this Paper we present the design of a fault tolerant conditional sum adder with an efficient testing methodology and self-reconfiguring approach.

Keywords: fault tolerant, self-reconfigurable, dynamic recovery, conditional sum adder.

1   Introduction

Adder is an absolutely essential block in any digital system. Ripple carry adder is most popular in different types of computing machines because of its simple architecture. But in the era of speed, ripple carry adder is losing its priority because of its larger operational time due to delay in carry propagation. Different types of fast adders (e.g. carry look-ahead, carry select, conditional sum) have been proposed [1]. The addition is much faster in case of conditional sum adder (CSA) as here the higher bit addition operations do not rely on conventional carry propagation mechanism.

By making any system self-reconfigurable, we increase the system's reliability and durability. In general, fault tolerant architectures are mainly used in various critical applications like satellites, defense systems, safety measures, operational equipments, railway signaling etc., where the systems failing to operate properly may cost severe damage or affect human life. Design of fault tolerant architectures are getting priorities in recent trends to decrease the probability of failure of a system.

There are mainly two approaches of hardware fault recovery. We have opted for the dynamic recovery method for its less hardware requirement over the fault masking method. In dynamic recovery method, spare components are activated upon the failure of any currently active components. In this Paper, we have presented the design philosophy of a reconfigurable CSA that can be utilized to make a VLSI architecture fault tolerant. We assume only single fault can affect one CSA block at a time. We can use our self-reconfigurable CSA can replace any ordinary adder in any digital system replacing an ordinary adder in the system to decrease the probability of error and increase the reliability of the system.

H. Rahaman et al. (Eds.): VDAT 2012, LNCS 7373, pp. 217–222, 2012.

2   Conditional Sum Adders

Conditional sum adder is a modified version of carry select adder using 1-bit blocks. In carry select adder duplicated hardware are used to pre-compute multiple outcomes and the correct outcome is selected. In CSA, the incoming n-bits are divided into smaller k-bit groups. For each k-bit group, two sets of sum and carry_out are computed assuming both carry_in=0 and carry_in=1. Once the real value of the incoming carry is known, correct set of outputs are chosen without waiting for the carry to further propagate [2].

The main computational block in a CSA is known as conditional cell (CC). Logic design of a CC block is shown in figure 1. Table 1 represents the truth table for the CC block.

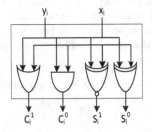

Fig. 1. Logic design of CC

Table 1. Truth table of CC

x_i	y_i	C_i^1	C_i^0	S_i^1	S_i^0
0	0	0	0	1	0
0	1	1	0	0	1
1	0	1	0	0	1
1	1	1	1	1	0

As a representative example, a simple 7-bit CSA module with all its data inputs and outputs is shown in figure 2.

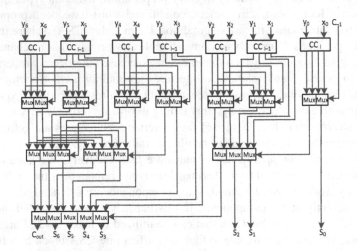

Fig. 2. A 7-bit CSA

3   Design of a 7-bit Fault Tolerant CSA

Many works are available in literature, where attempts have been made to have the complete system fault tolerant at a time. Those approaches are system dependent and difficult to apply to any other system. But it will be more hardware efficient and cost effective to make a system module wise fault tolerant. For efficient testing purpose, an iterative logic array (ILA) should be designed as C-testable [3], where required test patterns are independent of the size of the ILA. To decrease the number of test vectors and making the overall procedure easy, we make our CSA system C-testable.

3.1   Fault Modeling

To make the CSA C-testable, we group 2-bit operands along with two CCs and first level of MUXes as shown in figure 3, which we call conditional selection cell (CSC). We use four such CSCs along with some more MUXes for second and third level MUXing to design the full 7-bit CSA. Next to make the full CSA structure fault tolerant, we shall run each CSC with required input patterns for testing and compare the results with the desired outputs. If any mismatch is there, the CSC block must be faulty! Now, instead of replacing the faulty CSA completely, we will use one spare CSC and if any of the working CSC is found to be faulty, the spare one will start working bypassing the faulty one so that the system works properly.

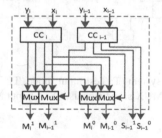

Fig. 3. Block diagram of CSC

In test mode, the required test patterns are applied to the system to check its functionality by comparing the coming outputs with the desired ones stored in a lookup table of size 4x6 only. If any CSC is identified as faulty then the inputs to that faulty and subsequent CSCs will be bypassed to next CSCs and the corrected outputs from error free CSCs will be fed to the next level of MUXes.

3.2   Making the Architecture Fault Tolerant

To make the system symmetric and cascadable, the first CC included in one CSC with the input patterns as shown in figure 4. We need extra two level of selection MUXes for input and output selections in the CSA system to select correct inputs and outputs bypassing the faulty CSA, if any.

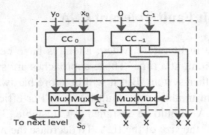

Fig. 4. Inputs and outputs of CSC0 (X=ignored)

To make the CSA self-reconfigurable, we use five CSC blocks as shown in figure 5. MUX select signals will select which CSCs are active and corresponding outputs are taken and fed to the next level of MUXes to complete the full CSA operation.

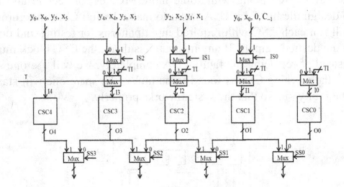

Fig. 5. Self-reconfigurable CSC system (T: Test input mode, TI: Test Inputs, I: Inputs to CSC, O: Outputs from CSC, IS: Input MUX select signals, SS: Output MUX select signals)

3.3   Testing of CSA

The testing of CSC serves two purposes; one is testing of conventional CC and the other is testing of MUXes in CSC. CSC has four inputs and hence normally 16 test patterns should exhaustively test a CSC. The output function of a 2-input MUX with inputs A and B and select line SEL is expressed as: Z=SEL?A:B; i.e., Z=A, if SEL =1 and Z=B, if SEL=0. The minimal test set [4] for detecting functional faults of a 2-input MUX is: {(Z | SEL, A, B) = (1 | 0, 0, 1), (0 | 0, 1, 0), (1 | 1, 1, 0), (0 | 1, 0, 1)}.

For testing of the CC, the cell has been modified in [5] with one more extra input test (T) as shown in figure 6. When T=1, the system runs in test mode and T=0 indicates normal mode of operation. The truth table of modified CC remains same with T=0, but changes with T=1 as shown in Table 2. Four test patterns (with T=1) suffice to test a normal CC with two inputs exhaustively. It is observed that MUX input lines of a CSC should get only (0, 1) or (1, 0) inputs for exhaustive testing. By properly adjusting the inputs to CSC we design the test patterns for the CSC (Table 3), where only four test patterns suffice to test the two CCs and four MUXes exhaustively.

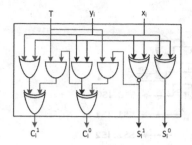

Fig. 6. Modified CC

Table 2. truth table of modified CC with T=1

x_i	y_i	C_i^1	C_i^0	S_i^1	S_i^0
0	0	0	1	1	0
0	1	1	0	0	1
1	0	1	0	0	1
1	1	0	1	1	0

Table 3. Complete Test Pattern for CSC with modified CC (T=1)

Test Patterns	y_i	x_i	y_{i-1}	x_{i-1}	M_i^1	M_{i-1}^1	M_i^0	M_{i-1}^0	S_{i-1}^1	S_{i-1}^0
0	0	1	0	0	1	0	1	1	0	1
1	0	1	0	1	0	1	1	0	0	1
2	0	1	1	0	0	1	0	1	0	1
3	1	0	1	1	0	1	0	0	1	0

The desired test patterns can easily be generated using one simple 2-bit counter and one Ex-OR gate as shown in figure 6. The same counter and circuitry can also be used to generate the desired outputs for given test patterns (illustrated in fig 6).

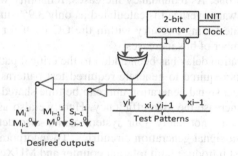

Fig. 7. Test Pattern Generation Circuit (INIT= Initialization signal)

3.4   Mux Select Signal Generation

Each generated output for the given input pattern is compared with desired output stored in the lookup table (of size 4x6) and depending on their mismatch, the corresponding Mux Select lines are asserted by the simple circuitry as shown in figure 7. If any of the output is erroneous for at least one of the test patterns, the complete CSC is assumed to be faulty and MUX select signals are changed to bypass that CSC. It takes only four clock pulses to check the outputs as generated in every clock pulse with the given test patterns. The Clr (clear) and the Clk (clock) signals are identical to that of INIT and Clock signal of the test pattern generator circuit.

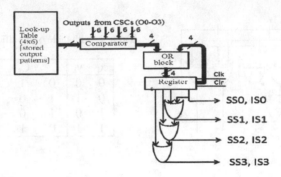

Fig. 8. Mux Select Signals Generation Unit

4   Discussions and Conclusions

In quadded logic or TMR/TIR processes, area overhead is very high to make an architecture self-reconfigurable. In TMR, the full system is triplicated and in case of quadded logic, area requirement is about four times of the original design. But in our design, we divide the 7-bit CSA into four identical submodule CSCs with second and third level of MUXing and use one CSC as spare and increase in area is about 25% only for the extra CSC along with some extra MUXes for choosing inputs to and outputs from the error free CSCs. Our design is cascadable in the sense that, we can cascade two designed self-reconfigurable CSAs by feeding one's final Carry_out to the Carry_in of the other one. As redundancy increases, reliability will also be higher in this case. In [5], hardware overhead is calculated as only 3.9% due to the use of modified CC to incorporate testing circuitry within the CC itself for 16-bit adder. Overhead decreases as number of bits increases.

Three mux propagation delay has been added to the critical path. Only one test pattern generation unit is required to generate required test patterns for all CSCs in the system. One mux select signal generation unit can be time shared among several fault tolerant modules to increase the area efficiency. Here we also assume that MUXing circuitry and registers are not faulty. Our system cannot also detect any fault in test pattern or MUX select signal generation circuitries. To incorporate fault tolerant features in them, we must introduce fault tolerant counter and MUXes in the system.

References

1. Biernat, J.: Fast fault-tolerant adders. International Journal Critical Computer-Based Systems 1(1/2/3), 117–127 (2010)
2. Koren, I.: Computer Arithmetic Algorithms. A K Peters (2011)
3. Lu, S.K., Wang, J.C., Wu, C.W.: C-testable design techniques for iterative logic arrays. IEEE Trans. VLSI Systems 3, 146–152 (1995)
4. Miczo, A.: Digital logic testing and simulation. John Wiley & Sons, New Jersey (2003)
5. Li, J.F., Hsu, C.C.: Efficient testing methodologies for conditional sum adders. In: Proc. Asian Test Symp., pp. 319–324 (2004)

SEU Tolerant Robust Latch Design

Mohammed Shayan[1], Virendra Singh[2], Adit D. Singh[3], and Masahiro Fujita[4]

[1] Indian Institute of Science Bangalore
shayan@cedt.iisc.ernet.in
[2] Indian Institute of Technology Bombay
viren@ee.iitb.ac.in
[3] Auburn University, USA
adsingh@auburn.edu
[4] University of Tokyo, Japan
fujita@ee.t.u-tokyo.ac.jp

Abstract. With the scaling of technology node and voltage levels, VLSI circuits are facing the challenge of tolerance to soft errors normally caused by alpha particle or neutron hits. These radiation strikes, resulting into bit upsets referred to as single-event upsets (SEUs), may be catastrophic in few sensitive applications and severely undermine the quality and reliability in other applications. In this paper we propose two novel SEU tolerant latch designs RHL-A and RHL-B. Our latch designs are area efficient in comparison with the earlier proposals. Simulation results show that the proposed latch designs is extremely robust as it does not flip even for a transient pulse with 58 times the $Qcrit$ of a standard latch cell. Compared to standard latch, RHL-A uses 40 percent more transistors and is 65 percent slower, whereas RHL-B uses 60 percent more transistors but is 65 percent faster.

Keywords: Soft Error Upsets, Radiation hardening, Critical charge, Collection time constant, Ion track establishment constant.

1 Introduction

Semiconductor market driven by consumers insatiable desire for higher density, more functionality and low power is moving towards smaller devices and lower operating voltages. As the device dimension, frequency and voltage scale, there are new challenges which come up with each technology node. Increased sensitivity to radiation is one such challenge.

With the relentless reducing of the minimum feature size of VLSI integrated circuits there is a corresponding reduction in the dimensions of diffusion nodes. This results in a reduced diffusion capacitance. It has implication in terms of increased susceptibility to radiation. The reduction in supply voltage reduces the noise margin of the circuit. The increased clock frequency further increases the probability of soft errors. This problem particularly severe in electronic circuits designed for space applications and is also becoming cause of concern for territorial applications.

H. Rahaman et al. (Eds.): VDAT 2012, LNCS 7373, pp. 223–232, 2012.
© Springer-Verlag Berlin Heidelberg 2012

There are two ways of dealing with this challenge. One is to prevent soft errors from occurring i.e, preventive mechanism. The other way is to detect the occurrence of such errors and then take corrective measures i.e, reactive mechanism. Device and circuit level solutions fall under the former approach. Architectural or system level solutions falls under the later approach. Device level modifications involve improving the transistor itself.

At the circuit level, many designs have been proposed to avoid soft errors [1], [2], [3]. Some of them are discussed in next section. System level solution presented in [4], [6] exploits the fact that not all soft errors may affect the functionality of a system and keeps off the corrective action until it becomes essential. Traditionally memory elements have been protected at the system level by error correcting codes [1]. It may be more expensive to protect latches and flip flops using parity or error correcting codes.

When particles like neutron, protons and heavy cosmic ions strike the diffusion regions in a transistor, they deposit charge; the flow of charge causes a voltage fluctuation on that node. The minimum amount of charge needed to change the voltage level from V_{ss} to V_{dd} and vice-versa, is called the critical charge, Q_{crit}. A neutron or alpha particle strike manifests itself as a transient charge disturbance that would usually last for around 60ps [5]. The current pulse that results from a particle strike is traditionally described as a double exponential function [17] as follows,

$$I(t) = \frac{Q}{\alpha - \beta}(e^{\frac{-t}{\alpha}} - e^{\frac{-t}{\beta}}) \tag{1}$$

Here Q is the amount of charge deposited as a result of the ion strike, while α is the collection time constant for the junction and β is the ion track establishment constant. When a circuit has been modified in such a manner so that its tolerance towards soft error has increased, it is said to be hardened against soft errors.

2   Previous Work

Kumar et.al. proposed [7] a technique to reduce the magnitude of a transient pulse by filtering action of multiple pass transistors. The pass transistors are always on, these pass transistors work as low pass filters as shown in Fig. 1. The input glitches that are of lesser width than that of the delay of the pass gate are filtered. However this only decreases the probability of upset and does not eliminate it. This also adds to path delay.

Hungse and Patel [8] explored inserting a resistor in the most effective place in the circuit to obtain information redundancy in time thus achieving radiation hardened latch. Ochoa [9] proposed the use of poly resistors to divide voltage amplitudes of transients and to delay the transients such that it dies before the upset as shown in Fig.4. Polysilicon resistive hardening is an unattractive proposal as pointed out by Rockett [10] et.al. because it would require polysilicon with high resistivity which leads to process control problems of laying a large resistance. Moreover polysilicon is very sensitive to the doping concentration, polysilicon structure and grain sizes. These techniques are in turn sensitive to

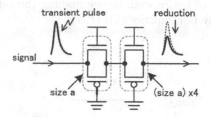

Fig. 1. Filtering of transient pulse [7]

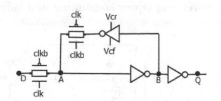

Fig. 2. Tunable SEU tlerant latch [16]

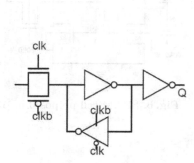

Fig. 3. Unhardened latch

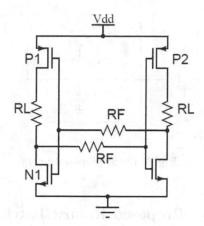

Fig. 4. Resistively decoupled SRAM [9]

thermal processing steps. Tunable latch proposed in [16] tunes the loop delay. However the flaw here is it tunes delay in one direction. As shown in our results, it makes node A in Fig. 4 even more susceptible than the unhardened latch in Fig. 3.

In [11] feedback loop is blocked to prevent the transient pulse from propagating along the loop. However this design has serious limitations as pointed out in [12] and [13]. The node voltages recover slowly and not fully. The cell also requires periodic refresh pulses.

Another hardened latch was proposed by Omana et al. [18] as shown in Fig.5. The circuit relies on redundant path and addition of special output stage (C element) to recover from the strike. However, the cost in area is more. The combinatorial circuit driver will see double capacitance increasing the area and power in combinational circuitry.

A 10T SRAM cell was proposed by Sudipta et al. [13]. For providing SEU immunity 4 extra transistors are introduced to the standard SRAM cell as shown in Fig.6. In the design a PMOS with its source connected to body is used. This necessitates separate wells for the two transistors increasing area. It also ties the huge n-well to substrate capacitance to the source i.e. changing the source voltage would mean to change the voltage of entire well. Hence making the cell slower and power consuming and spice may not capture this effect.

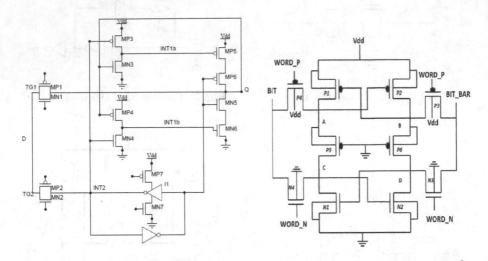

Fig. 5. Latch proposed in [18]   **Fig. 6.** SRAM cell proposed in [13]

3 Proposed Robust Latch

This section describes our proposed soft error resilient latch design. Our approach does not use polysilicon hardening and at the same time brings in the benefit of filtering than just mere voltage division. It overcomes the need of a separate well for PMOS. It does not need periodic refresh signals as well.

When the drain voltage of a PMOS is at V_{dd} volts and NMOS is at 0 Volt, they are not susceptible to SEU (provided body voltages of PMOS and NMOS are V_{dd} and 0 Volt respectively) because the charge deposited does not observe potential difference to travel and cannot give rise to current. The charges may get recombined in the substrate. Thus depending upon the data value at the drain one of the transistors in an inverter is immune and other is susceptible to strike. Thus in an inverter when the drain is at logic '1' NMOS is susceptible to strike and PMOS is immune and vice versa. Our approach aims to isolate the two drains. We use four transistors P5, P6, N5, N6 that are always 'ON' to isolate the PMOS drain from NMOS drain as shown in Fig.7.

3.1 Sensitivity Analysis

Case 1: First we consider the case when V1a=V1=V1b=0 and V2a=V2=V2b=1. We can straightaway see that P6, P2, N1, N4 and N5 are SEU immune, because their drain, body and source terminals are at the same potential. However transistors P1, P4, P5, N2 and N6 are susceptible to SEUs because their drain voltages are different from their body terminals. In the left stack N1, N4, N5, P4 and P5 are ON and P1 is OFF. Let us consider that a particle strikes at P4 (P5 or P1) making node V1A (V1) momentarily go to logic 1 (V_{dd}). It is worth to mention here that the drain voltage cannot go beyond V_{dd} because the moment it reaches V_{dd}, there is no further voltage difference between the body and drain, thus any further charge separation is prevented. However V1b will see lesser fluctuation due to the voltage division and filtering action of P5, N4 and N5; hence drive of N2 is lesser than that of N1. N2 and series of N1 and N4 are cross coupled. If series of N1 and N4 are sized so as to have equal strength of N2 then series of N1 and N4 will win over N2 and sink the charge at V1a. When V1a goes high due to SEU, it turns P2 off and hence does not change the state of node V2a. Thus we see that a momentary full scale voltage fluctuation at V1a or V1 cant change the state of any of the other 4 nodes, hence V1a (V1) eventually gets restored by P5, N5, N4 and N1.

Now take a case when an SEU occurs at N2 and causes V2b to go to 0 or radiation strike at N6 causes V2 to go to 0. However V2a will see lesser glitch due the voltage division and filtering action of P6 and N6 hence drive strength of P1 is lesser than that of P2. Series of P4 and P1 are sized so as to have equal strength of P2, since the drive of P2 is max it will prevail over series of P4 and P1 and charge V2b (V2) to its previous value. Furthermore, when V2b goes to zero, it only switches off N1; therefore it does not cause any state change at V1a.

Case 2: When V1a=V1=V1b=1 and V2a=V2=V2b=0, the situation is simply the opposite to the previous case. Therefore it can be explained similarly.

Case 3: We now consider the effect of radiation strike at pass transistors P3 and N3. We do not consider SEU strike at the *Din* lines assuming that it is being strongly driven to recover from a radiation strike. Let us take the case of N3. It will be susceptible to SEU when V1b=1and this case is similar to an SEU strike at N4 when V1b=1 provided N3 is OFF. The *Din* line can be at 1 or 0, it hardly makes any difference because only the magnitude of subthreshold current changes. Similarly, P3 is susceptible when node V1a=0 and this case is same as when SEU strikes P4. Therefore pass transistors are also SEU immune in our design. Radiation strike at P7 or N7 causes output to glitch. However, as the

Table 1. Transistor Sizes(W/L) in μm

P1	0.64/0.12	N1	0.32/0.12	P5	0.16/0.12	N5	0.16/0.24
P2	0.32/0.12	N2	0.16/0.12	P6	0.16/0.12	N6	0.16/0.24
P3	0.64/0.12	N3	0.16/0.12	P7	0.32/0.12	N7	0.16/0.12
P4	0.64/0.12	N4	0.32/0.12				

inverter is being driven by V2a and V2b, the output will recover eventually. This glitch can be treated as a combinatorial glitch if the latch is driving combinatorial part. The time of recovery is dependent on the sizing of transistors driving V2. P6, P5 can be made of minimum size. A unit NMOS is of resistance R, unit PMOS is of resistance 2R assuming the mobility of NMOS is twice that of

PMOS. In order to have balance in NMOS stack and PMOS stack N5, N6 are of minimum width and twice the length of the other transistors. The sizing of transistors is as shown in Table 1.

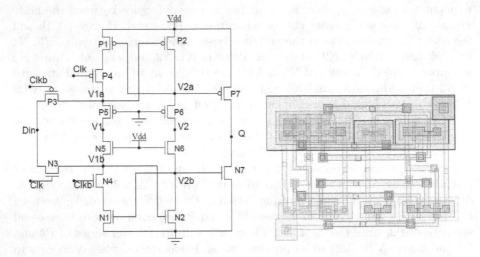

Fig. 7. Proposed Latch RHL-A   **Fig. 8.** Layout of the Latch RHL-A

4   Simulation Results

We have simulated the proposed designs using SPICE in 130 nm technology. We used 0.13 μm logic process model files of UMC and considered $V_{dd} = 1.2$V for all the simulations. Table 2 shows pre-layout comparisons with other proposals normalized to the unhardened latch in Fig 3. For calculating Q_{crit}, we have used the exponential current model mentioned in equation 1 to model an SEU. The constants $\alpha = 0.2$ns, $\beta = 0.05$ns were taken as used in [14]. SEU at the drain of an NMOS is modeled as an outgoing exponential current pulse and incoming current pulse in case of PMOS. To simulate SEU strike on a transistor we connected the current source to the drain of the transistor. We calculated Q_{crit} by increasing the amplitude of current in equation.1 till the value in cell is flipped. Power was calculated from ELDO tool chain. It shows that our proposal with 4 extra transistors is highly robust than any other except for [18] which has double the number of transistor count and consumes more power. Latch [18] flips its value only when there is strike at more than two nodes. Hence Q_{crit} of this latch is not given, in the corresponding column of Table 2 it is mentioned as MBU. For latch [16] Q_{crit} was calculated for all possible values of V_{cr} and V_{cf}.

Post layout simulation with double exponential current source with α 0.2 nS and β 0.05 nS as used in [14] are shown in Table 4. The proposed design RHL-A incurs an area penalty of 50 percent (Fig. 8) and RHL-B incurs 66.6 percent (Fig. 12) compared to more than 100 percent in the dice cell as well as the design

Table 2. Comparison table (pre-layout)

latch	Q_{crit}	delay	power	transistor count
[18]	MBU	0.5	1.464	2
[15]	5	1.34	0.79	1
[16]	0.79	0.83	1.04	1.2
[13]	1.93	1.92	1.46	1.2
RHL-A	29	1.97	1.25	1.4
RHL-B	29	0.392	1.259	1.6

Table 3. Post-layout Simulation results

	Q_{crit}	Q_{crit} increase	Delay	Delay increase
Normal latch	0.0225 pC	x 1	164.32 pS	x 1
RHL-A	1.32 pC	x 58.7	271.7 pS	x 1.65
RHL-B	1.32 pC	x 58.7	57.5 pS	x 0.35

proposed in [18] and 82 percent in [13]. Area overhead is calculated by counting the number of metal tracks [22].

The voltage waveforms at various internal nodes, when SEU strikes transistor N5 of RHL-A are shown in Fig. 9. We observed only a small bump at the point at V1a. We have verified that the proposed cell does not flip due to strike at other nodes also as in Fig.10. Simulations show similar results for RHL-B.

4.1 Delay Penalty

The increased delay of RHL-A shown in Table 3 is because the ON transistors are not driven to full as the nodes V1a (V2a) and V2b (V1b) do not swing to perfect 0 and V_{dd} respectively. The nodes V1a and V2a can only go down to

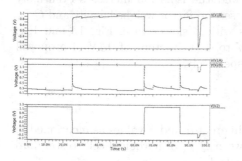

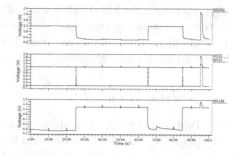

Fig. 9. Effect of SEU strike at N5   **Fig. 10.** Effect of SEU strike at P6

approximately V_{pT}, the nodes V1b and V2b can only go to approximately (V_{dd} - V_{nT}). The delay penalty is high, we make further modifications to get high performance. In RHL-B a parallel path is added from D to Q in Fig. 11 through a transmission gate. It takes 6 more transistors which results in 66.6 percent area overhead. However, it gives better performance than unhardened latch. It is also SEU tolerant as shown in table 3.

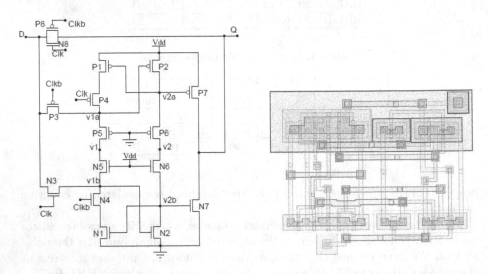

Fig. 11. Proposed latch RHL-B   -   **Fig. 12.** Layout of latch RHL-B

4.2   Varying Supply Voltage

With decrease in supply voltages, charge at nodes decreases resulting in low Q_{crit}. This is shown by the almost linear Q_{crit} vs V_{dd} graph in Fig. 14. For the hardened latch there is a second factor that affects Q_{crit}, with decrease in V_{dd} drive of P5, P6, N5, N6 decreases and the isolation increases eventually Q_{crit} increases. As Fig. 13 shows initially second factor weighs heavily and Q_{crit} increases, reaches a peak and decreases with a slower rate. Fig. 13 and Fig. 14 show Q_{crit} for V_{dd} varying from 1.2V to 0.8V in steps of 0.1V of proposed hardened latch and unhardened latch respectively.

4.3   Varying α and β

The Table 4 gives Q_{crit} calculations for different α and β values as mentioned in [14], [20], [19], [21]. Worst case ratio between Q_{crit} of hardened cell to standard cell is 28 as shown in column 4 of the Table 4.

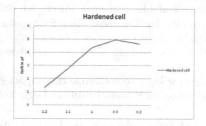

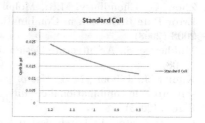

Fig. 13. Q_{crit}vs V_{dd} **Fig. 14.** Q_{crit} vs V_{dd}

Table 4. Q_{crit} for different α and β

Q_{crit} in pC	α=0.2ns β=0.05ns	α=0.164ns β=0.05ns	α=0.25ns β=0.063ns	α=0.15ns β=0.038ns
RHL-A	1.32	2.28	0.748	2.69
Standard Latch	0.0225	0.021	0.027	0.013
Increase X	58	108	28	206

5 Conclusion

In this paper, we proposed improved designs of SEU tolerant latch RHL-A and RHL-B. The designs have been extensively simulated in SPICE and their effectiveness has been thoroughly verified against the widely used exponential current model. Moreover, we do not rely on subthreshold current or periodic refresh signals. In terms of area overhead, our designs are more economical compared to previous proposals. The cell does not flip even for a Q_{crit} of 1.32pC i.e. 58 times of normal latch. RHL-A incurs 50 percent area penalty and is slower by 65 percent. RHL-B incurs 66.6 percent area penalty and is faster by 65 percent compared to standard latch.

References

1. Naeimi, H., DeHon, A.: Fault Secure Encoder and Decoder for NanoMemory Applications. IEEE Transactions on Very Large Scale Integration (VLSI) Systems 17(4) (April 2009)
2. Sasaki, Y., Namba, K., Ito, H.: Soft Error Masking Circuit and Latch Using Schmitt Trigger Circuit. In: Proceedings of 21st IEEE International Symposium on Defect and Fault Tolerance in VLSI Systems, pp. 327–335 (October 2006)
3. Lin, S., Yang, H., Luo, R.: A New Family of Sequential Elements With Built-in Soft Error Tolerance for Dual-VDD Systems. IEEE Trans. On VLSI Systems 16(10) (October 2008)
4. Sootkaneung, W., Saluja, K.K.: Sizing Techniques for Improving Soft Error Immunity in Digital Circuits. In: Proceedings of ISCAS 2010 (2010)

5. Zhou, Q., Choudhury, M.R., Mohanram, K.: Tunable Transient Filters for Soft Error Rate Reduction in Combinational Circuits. In: European Test Symposium 2008 (2008)
6. Mukherjee, S.: Architecture Design for Soft Errors. Morgan Kaufmann publishers (2008)
7. Kumar, J., Tahoori, M.B.: Use of pass transistor logic to minimize the impact of soft errors in combinational circuits. In: Workshop on System Effects of Logic Soft Errors (2005)
8. Cha, H., Patel, J.: Latch design for transient pulse tolerance. In: International Conference in Computer Design, pp. 385–388 (October 1994)
9. Ochoa, Axness, Weaver, H.: A proposed new structure for SEU immunity in SRAM employing drain resistance. IEEE Electron Device Letters EDL-8(11) (November 1987)
10. Rockett, L.R.: A SEU hardened CMOS latch design. IEEE Transactions on Nuclear Science 35(6) (December 1988)
11. Nicolaidis, M., Perez, R., Alexandrescu, D.: Low-cost Highly-robust Hardened Cells Using Blocking Feedback Transistors. In: 26th IEEE VLSI Test Symposium (2008)
12. Lin, S., Kim, Y.-B., Lombardi, F.: A Novel Design Technique for Soft Error Hardening of Nanoscale CMOS Memory. In: IEEE International Midwest Symposium on Circuits and Systems (2009)
13. Sudipta, Anubhav, Singh, V., Saluja, K., Fujita, M.: SEU tolerant SRAM cell ISQED (2011)
14. Garg, R., Jayakumar, N., Khatri, S.P., Choi, G.S.: Circuit-Level Design Approaches for Radiation-Hard Digital Electronics. IEEE Trans. on Vary Large Scale Integration (VLSI) Systems 17(6) (June 2009)
15. Liang, W., Suge, Y., Yuanfu, Z.: Low-Overhead SEU-Tolerant Latches. In: Proc. International Conference on Microwave and Millimeter Wave Technology, pp. 1–4 (2007)
16. Xiaoxuan, S., Li, N., Farwell, W.D.: Tunable SEU-Tolerant Latch. IEEE Trans. on Nuclear Science 57, 3787–3794 (2010)
17. Messenger, G.C.: Collection of charge on junction nodes from ion tracks. IEEE Trans. Nucl. Sci. NS-29(6), 2024–2031 (1982)
18. Omana, M., Rossi, Metra: Novel High Speed Robust Latch. In: IEEE International Symposium on Defect and Fault Tolerance in VLSI Systems (2009)
19. Nagpal, C., Garg, R., Khatri, S.P.: A delay-efficient radiation-hard digital design approach using CWSP elements. In: Proc. Des. Autom. Test Eur., pp. 354–359 (March 2008)
20. Namba, K., Ikeda, T., Ito, H.: Construction of SEU tolerant flipflops allowing enhanced scan delay fault testing. IEEE Trans. Very Large Scale Integr (VLSI) Syst. 18(9), 1265–1276 (2010)
21. Zhou, Q., Mohanram, K.: Gate sizing to radiation harden combinational logic. IEEE Trans. Comput.-Aided Design Integr. Circuits Syst. 25(1), 155–166 (2006)
22. Weste, N., Harris, D.: CMOS Vlsi Design, 4th edn. Pearson Education

Design of Content Addressable Memory Architecture Using Carbon Nanotube Field Effect Transistors

Debaprasad Das, Avisek Sinha Roy, and Hafizur Rahaman

School of VLSI Technology, Bengal Enginnering and Science University, Shibpur, Howrah
dasdebaprasad@yahoo.co.in, avishek2by@gmail.com,
rahaman_h@it.becs.ac.in

Abstract. The work in this paper designs a 4-bit content addressable memory (CAM) architecture using carbon nanotube field effect transistors (CNTFETs). CAM is a special class of memory that is used to search a given data inside the memory. CAMs are used in high speed serach operations such as network routers. The proposed design is very efficient in terms speed and power as compared to its CMOS counterpart.

Keywords: Content Addressable Memory (CAM), Carbon Nanotube Field Effect Transistor (CNTFET), Delay, Power.

1 Introduction

With the advancement of CMOS technology the devices are scaled down aggressively. This has resulted in several small geometry issues in the nanometer regime such as short channel effects, reduced control over the gate, increased leakage current, increased process variation, etc. Therefore, there is a drive towards developing an alternate to the traditional CMOS technology. Among several alternatives that have been proposed, carbon nanotube field effect transistor (CNTFET) has been the most promising candidate in replacing traditional CMOS devices due to its similar I-V characteristics as that of CMOS devices [1].

The work in this paper designs a complete 4-bit CAM architecture using MOSFET-like CNTFET. The design is implemented using the Verilog-AMS CNTFET model obtained from [3]. The simulation is performed in Cadence Analog Design environment (Virtuoso). The design is simulated for both match and mismatch conditions. The performance of the CNTFET based design is investigated by calculating the delay and power dissipation of the circuit.

The rest of the paper is organized as follows. Section 2 describes the basics of CNTFET. The architecture and design of CAM is discussed in Section 3. Section 4 presents the simulation results followed by the conclusions in Section 5.

2 Carbon Nanotube Field Effect Transistor

Carbon nanotube (CNT) is a rolled graphene sheet in the form of a cylinder. Depending on the direction of rolling (chirality) it exhibits metallic or semiconducting properties. While the metallic CNTs are being explored for VLSI interconnect,

H. Rahaman et al. (Eds.): VDAT 2012, LNCS 7373, pp. 233–242, 2012.
© Springer-Verlag Berlin Heidelberg 2012

semiconducting CNTs are considered for the channel region of high speed transistors due to their near ballistic electron transport. There are three different types of proposed carbon nanotube field effect transistor (CNTFET) structures: Schottky barrier – carbon nanotube field effect transistor (SB-CNTFET), MOSFET-like CNTFET, and band-to-band tunneling – carbon nanotube field effect transistor (BTBT-CNTFET). In this section we have described the basics of above three types of CNTFET.

CNTFET has a very similar structure to that of MOSFET where semiconducting single-wall carbon nanotubes (SWCNTs) are used in the channel region. The structures of different types of CNTFET are shown in Fig. 1.

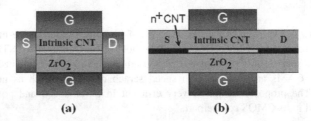

(a)   (b)

Fig. 1. Different types of CNTFETs: (a) Schottky barrier (SB) CNTFET (b) MOSFET-like CNTFET

In SB-CNTFET the channel is made of intrinsic semiconducting CNT and direct contacts of the metal with the semiconducting nanotubes are made for source and drain regions. The device works on the principle of direct tunneling through the Schottky barrier (SB) at the source-channel junction. The barrier-width is modulated by the application of gate voltage, and thus, the transconductance of the device is controlled by the gate voltage.

In MOSFET-like CNTFET doped CNTs are used for the source and drain regions and channel is made of intrinsic semiconducting CNT. A tunable CNTFET with electrical doping is also proposed. It works on the principle of barrier-height modulation by the application of gate potential. In [6] it has been shown that MOSFET-like CNTFET is superior as compared to SB-CNTFET. Therefore in this paper we have used the MOSFET-like CNTFETs to design CAM cell.

The band-to-band tunneling (BTBT) CNTFET is suitable for ultra low power applications due to its extremely small ON currents [6]. SWCNT is used between the source and drain regions. There are two gates: one is called (silicon) Si back gate which controls the electrical characteristics of the CNT near the drain and source regions, and the other one is called aluminium (Al) gate which controls the electrical characteristics of the nanotube in the middle portion giving rise to ideal switching behaviour [7].

The electrical characteristics of SWCNT are determined by chirality of the nanotube. The chiral vector of SWCNT is given by

$$C = na_1 + ma_2 \qquad (1)$$

where n and m are integer pair. A CNT is metallic if $n = m$ or $(n - m) = 3i$, where i is an integer. Otherwise the CNT is semiconducting. The diameter of the CNT is given by

$$D = \frac{a\sqrt{n^2 + nm + m^2}}{\pi}$$

(2)

where $a = \sqrt{3}b$ and $b = 0.142$ nm is the C-C bond length. The bandgap is inversely proportional to the CNT diameter (D) as given by

$$E_g = \frac{0.84}{D} \text{eV}.$$

(3)

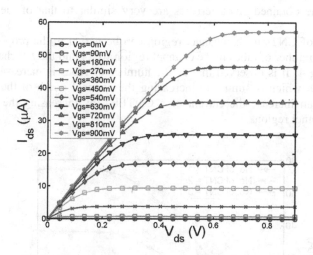

Fig. 2. Drain current of NCNTFET as a function of drain-to-source and gate-to-source voltage

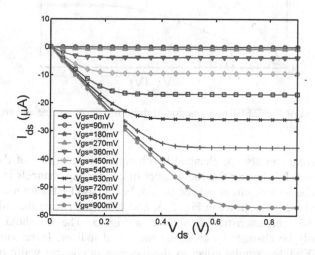

Fig. 3. Drain current of PCNTFET as a function of drain-to-source and gate-to-source voltage

The threshold voltage of the CNTFET is also a function of CNT diameter given by

$$V_{th} = \frac{E_g}{2e}$$

(4)

The SPICE compatible equivalent circuit of MOSFET-like CNTFET is proposed by Deng and Wong in [4, 5]. The proposed model in Verilog-AMS is simulated in Cadence virtuoso environment to obtain the *I-V* characteristics of CNTFET.

Fig. 2 and 3 show the *I-V* characteristics of CNTFET of n-type and p-type conducting channel. The obtained characteristics are very similar to that of the traditional MOSFET.

The number of CNTs in the channel region can be varied in the proposed model. By varying the number of tubes in the channel region we obtain the *I-V* characteristics as shown in Fig 4. It is observed that as the number of tubes is increased the drain current increases which is similar to increasing the channel width of the MOSFET. Therefore we can increase the current of a CNTFET by increasing the number of tubes in the channel region.

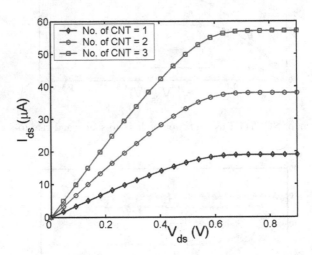

Fig. 4. Drain current of NCNTFET as a function of drain-to-source voltage and no. of CNTs in the channel

The drain current can also be changed by changing the chirality of the nanotube used in the channel. It is known that the number of conducting channels in a CNT is a function of the diameter or chiral indices (n, m). For a CNTFET with $n=19$ and $m=0$ we have obtained the plots shown in Fig. 2, 3, and 4. By increasing the chiral index n we obtain the *I-V* characteristics as shown in Fig. 5. The threshold voltage of CNTFET can only be changed by changing the chiral indices. Increasing the chiral index n of CNTFET has similar effect as the increase in channel width of the MOS transistors.

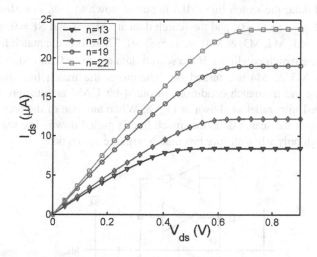

Fig. 5. Drain current of NCNTFET as a function of drain-to-source voltage and chiral index n. No. of CNTs = 1 in this case.

3   Design of CAM Architecture

The architecture of a 4-bit CAM is illustrated in the schematic diagram shown in Fig. 6. A 4-bit serach data is the input to the CAM. There are four memory locations at which four data are stored. Each stored word has a match line. The match lines are connected to the encoder through match-line-sense amplifiers (MLSA). The match lines indictate whether the stored word matches with the serach data or do not match. When the stored data matches with serach data, the corresponding match line becomes high. The encoder generates the address of the stored data that is matched.

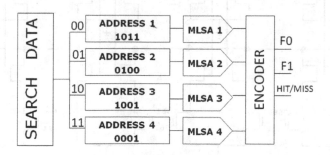

Fig. 6. Architecture of 4-bit CAM

The architecture of the CAM cell is shown in Fig. 7. The search data and its complement are applied to the search lines (SL) and ($\overline{\text{SL}}$), respectively. Before, the search operation the match line (ML) is precharged to high. When the search data does not match the stored data, the match line (ML) is pulled down to low. For example if the stored data are D = 1 and $\overline{D} = 0$, and the search data are SL = 1 and $\overline{SL} = 0$, all the pull-down transistors (M1, M2, M3, & M4) are turned off. Therefore, the match line remains high, indicating the match condition. If the search data are SL = 0 and $\overline{SL} = 1$, the pull-down transistors M3 & M4 are turned on. Therefore, the match line discharges to ground, indicating the mismatch condition. In our 4-bit CAM architecture four CAM cells are connected in parallel as shown in Fig. 8. When any one of the four stored bits does not match with the search data, the match line is pulled down. The match line remains at logic high only when all four bits match with the stored data.

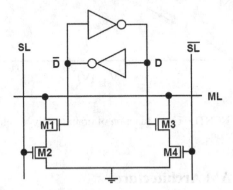

Fig. 7. A NOR type CAM cell

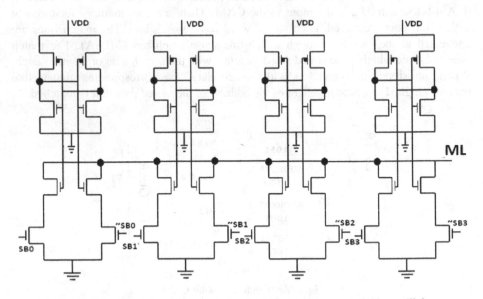

Fig. 8. Schematic of an address block with 4 CAM cells connected in parallel

In this design we have used current race match line sense amplifier (MLSA) as shown in Fig. 9. In this scheme the match line (ML) is precharged to low by setting signals mlpre and $\overline{en}$ to high. During this phase the search data are also placed in the search lines SL and $\overline{SL}$. In the next phase (evaluation phase), the signals mlpre and $\overline{en}$ are both set to low. If the match line is in the match state, then the match line is charged up to logic high through the pMOS and current source. In this phase the match line is charged up to a very small voltage in case of data mismatch. Therefore, the match line sensing transistor (M_{SENSE}) is turned off and the output becomes low. In the data match condition the match line remains at logic high making the transistor M_{SENSE} turned on and the output becomes high.

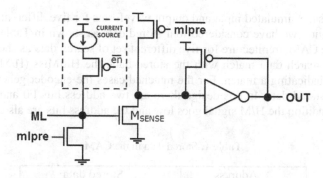

Fig. 9. Schematic of match line sense amplifier (current race MLSA) [2]

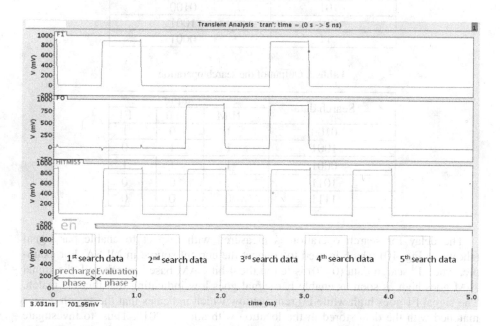

Fig. 10. Simulated input and output waveforms of the 4-bit CAM for five different search data

The design is implemented using MOSFET-like CNTFET. The model of MOSFET-like CNTFET is obtained from [3]. The chirality taken for all PCNTFETs used in the CAM cell is (19, 0). Similarly for all NCNTFETs, the chirality is chosen same as (19, 0). The number of tubes used in each PCNTFET and NCNTFET is 3. The chirality and number of tubes used in the match line sense amplifier and encoder are same as used in the CAM cell.

4   Simulation Results

Fig. 10 shows the simulated input and output waveforms for five different search data. In the simulation we have considered four stored data as shown in Table 1. We have simulated the CAM architecture for five different set of search data as shown in Table 2. When the search data match with the stored data, the Hit/Miss (H/M) output becomes high, indicating a match. For the matched cases the encoder generates the address of the stored data. In this design there are two address bits F0 and F1. For the mismatch condition the H/M signal goes low and the address bits are also set to low.

Table 1. Stored data in the CAM

Address	Stored data
00	1011
01	0100
10	1001
11	0001

Table 2. Output of the search operation

Search data	Output		
	H/M	F0	F1
0100	1	0	1
1001	1	1	0
0001	1	1	1
1011	1	0	0
1111	0	0	0

The delay for search operation is measured with respect to enable bar signal (shown in Fig. 10) which is used to connect the current source in MLSA. For example, when 1st search data (0100) is fed to the 4-bit CAM based search cell, the signal H/M goes high as soon as enable bar signal goes low indicating that there is match. The signal F1 goes high while F0 remains low which indicates that the search data is matched with the data stored in the location with address "01". Thus, to investigate the speed of the search operation, the rise and fall delay times of the signals F0, F1, and H/M are measured with respect to the enable bar signal. After the 1st search data is fed, it is then followed by a precharge phase where the match line (ML) is set to logic zero. The precharge phase is immediately followed by the evaluation phase where the enable bar signal goes low and thus depending on the second search data the match line indicates whether there is a match or mismatch. Similarly, for all other search data the corresponding rise time and fall time are calculated for both MOSFET and CNTFET based operation. Fig. 10 shows the output waveforms for different search data.

Table 3 shows the delay results. It is observed that CNTFET based design shows significantly less delay as compared to that of MOSFET based design. It is also observed that the rise and fall delays are symmetrical in the proposed design.

Table 3. Delay of the design

PARAMETER			MOSFET		CNTFET	
			Rise	Fall	Rise	Fall
Delay (ps)	1st search data	F1	63.17	37.99	16.07	15.98
		H/M	88.49	63.63	21.96	21.38
	2nd search data	F0	59.83	35.29	15.71	16.09
		H/M	81.78	58.24	21.21	21.33
	3rd search data	F0	66.72	40.82	16.6	16.2
		F1	63.01	38.41	16.22	16.15
		H/M	84.41	64.88	21.17	21.7
	4th search data	H/M	57.98	33.05	15.42	15.85

Table 4 shows power dissipation of the design. It is observed that CNTFET based design has 17.4% less power dissipation as compared to that of MOSFET based design.

Table 4. Power dissipation of the design

PARAMETER	MOSFET	CNTFET
POWER(μW)	53.45	44.15

5   Conclusions

In this work we have designed a 4-bit content addressable memory array using carbon nanotube field effect transistors. The speed-power performance of the design is compared with that of the CMOS based design. It has been found that the proposed design has 2–4x speed improvement over the CMOS counterpart. The power dissipation is also significantly less in the proposed design as compared to that of CMOS based design.

References

1. International Technology Roadmap for Semiconductors (ITRS) reports,
   http://www.itrs.net/reports.html
2. Pagiamtzis, K., Sheikholeslami, A.: Content-addressable memory (CAM) circuits and architectures: a tutorial and survey. IEEE Journal of Solid-state Circuits 41(3), 712–727 (2006)
3. Stanford University CNFET Model Web site,
   http://nano.stanford.edu/model.php?id=23
4. Deng, J., Wong, H.-S.P.: A compact SPICE model for carbon-nanotube field-effect transistors including nonidealities and its application—Part I: Model of the intrinsic channel region. IEEE Trans. Electron Devices 54(12), 3186–3194 (2007)
5. Deng, J., Wong, H.-S.P.: A compact SPICE model for carbon-nanotube field-effect transistors including nonidealities and its application—Part II: Full device model and circuit performance benchmarking. IEEE Trans. Electron Devices 54(12), 3195–3205 (2007)
6. Raychowdhury, A., Keshavarzi, A., Kurtin, J., De Kaushik Roy, V.: Carbon Nanotube Field-Effect Transistors for High-Performance Digital Circuits—DC Analysis and Modeling Toward Optimum Transistor Structure. IEEE Trans. Electron Devices 53(11), 2711–2717 (2006)
7. Appenzeller, J., Lin, Y.-M., Knoch, J., Avouris, P.: Band-to-band tunneling in carbon nanotube field-effect transistors. Phys. Rev. Lett. 93(19), 196805 (2004)

High-Speed Unified Elliptic Curve Cryptosystem on FPGAs Using Binary Huff Curves

Ayantika Chatterjee and Indranil Sengupta

School of Information Technology
Indian Institute of Technology Kharagpur, India
cayantika@gmail.com, isg@iitkgp.ac.in

Abstract. Conventional Elliptic Curve (EC) cryptosystems are subjected to side channel attacks because of their lack of unifiedness. On the other hand, unified cryptosystems based on Edwards curves have been found to be slow. The present paper proposes the first VLSI design of binary Huff curves, which also lead to unified scalar multiplication. Several optimized architectural features have been developed to utilize the FPGA resources better, and yet lead to a faster circuit. Experimental results have been presented on the standard NIST curves, and on state-of-the-art $GF(2^{233})$ to show that the design is significantly faster than other unified EC cryptosystems.

Keywords: Binary Huff Curve (BHC), Elliptic Curve Cryptography (ECC), FPGA.

1 Introduction

Elliptic curve cryptography (ECC) is favored in the world of Public Key Cryptography (PKC) due to its smaller key size requirement over RSA. Hence ECC started a new era in the field of public key cryptosystems, once it was introduced by Miller and Koblitz in the year 1985 [9,10]. Considering a point on the curve $(x, y) \in GF(2^n) \times GF(2^n)$, and the curve constants $a_1, a_2, a_3, a_4, a_6 \in GF(2^n)$, the Weierstrass form of Elliptic curve is defined as:

$$y^2 + a_1 xy + a_3 y = x^3 + a_2 x^2 + a_4 x + a_6$$

The security of ECC is mainly the hardness of its ECDLP property. To implement this scalar multiplication, point addition and doubling are necessary operations. But, the addition laws on ECC are not unified, hence the difference of the doubling and addition laws make the system vulnerable against SCA [7].

Due to these reasons, different forms of ECC have been investigated which are capable of having unified addition and doubling laws. Binary Huff Curve [5] is a solution of such problems which is the binary extension of Huff's model [8]. The main advantage of this curve is the presence of unified addition and doubling law and hence processor based on this curve is expected to be simple side channel

H. Rahaman et al. (Eds.): VDAT 2012, LNCS 7373, pp. 243–251, 2012.

attack preventive. We show in this paper, that the unified addition for BHC can be efficiently implemented on FPGA resources to lead to a processor which is faster than other unified curve namely binary Edwards curves.

The remaining part of this paper is organized as follows. In section 2, properties and algorithms related to BHC are discussed. Our contribution about the detailed design of the processor are described in detail in section 3. At the end, the time and area requirement of this design are explained and the results are compared with some previous implementations in section 4.

2   Binary Huff Curves

A binary Huff curve [5] is defined as the set of projective points $(X : Y : Z)$ F_{2^m} satisfying the equation, considering $a, b \in F^*_{2m}$ and $a \neq b$:

$$E : aX(Y^2 + YZ + Z^2) = bY(X^2 + XZ + Z^2); \qquad (1)$$

- There are three points at infinity satisfying the curve equation, namely $(a : b : 0)$, $(1 : 0 : 0)$, and $(0 : 1 : 0)$.
- This curve is birationally equivalent [5] to the Weierstrass elliptic curve $v(v + (a + b)u) = u(u + a^2)(u + b^2)$.
- This curve deals with unified addition laws, but the laws are complete in certain proper subgroups, which can be used for most cryptographic applications.

Let, sum of two points (X_1, Y_1) and (X_2, Y_2) be (X_3, Y_3). The resultant point on the projective curve is defined according to the following addition formulas. In this paper, we shall concentrate on the design of a ECC processor based on projective unified addition laws of BHC. This can be evaluated as:

Table 1. Addition Law

$$m_1 = X_1 X_2; m_2 = Y_1 Y_2; m_3 = Z_1 Z_2;$$
$$m_4 = (X_1 + Z_1)(X_2 + Z_2) + m_1 + m_3;$$
$$m_5 = (Y_1 + Z_1)(Y_2 + Z_2) + m_2 + m_3;$$
$$m_6 = m_1 m_3; m_7 = m_2 m_3; m_8 = m_1 m_2 + m_3^2;$$
$$m_9 = m_6(m_2 + m_3)^2; m_{10} = m_7(m_1 + m_3)^2;$$
$$m_{11} = m_8(m_2 + m_3); m_{12} = m_8(m_1 + m_3);$$
$$X_3 = m_4 m_{11} + \alpha.m_9;$$
$$Y_3 = m_5 m_{12} + \beta.m_10;$$
$$Z_3 = m_{11}(m_1 + m_3);$$

Here, $\alpha = \frac{a+b}{b}$ and $\beta = \frac{a+b}{a}$ are two constants and the total cost of this projective addition is $15M + 2D$ (M implies multiplication and D implies multiplication with constants).

3   Design of the BHC Based Processor

The design modules of an ECC processor based on BHC are described here. In spite of providing security against simple side channel attacks, unified addition laws of BHC are expected to be slower compared to other traditional ECC processors. Hence, we have mostly concentrated on enhancing the speed of this design. Different techniques are adapted to minimize the number of clock-pulses like precomputation and storage of multiplication values (The above projective addition law shows that multiplications with constants α and β are required, hence we have precomputed and stored the values in order to save the clock-cycles), enhancement of keymodification module and parallelized scheduling of operations. Apart from these modifications, the arithmetic logic unit(ALU) has been suitably designed with techniques ideal for FPGA platforms. The architecture has three main modules:

- **Register module** stores the data intermediate data.
- **Keymodification module** convert the key from its binary to ternary form.
- **Arithmetic Logic Unit(ALU)** deals with addition, multiplication and final inversion operations.

3.1   Register File Architecture Details

Figure 1 describes the register details of the implemented architecture. Two constant values are precomputed and total 9 register files are used for storing intermediate data. Two input multiplexers are used for fetching initial inputs and precomputed values from ROM. Three output multiplexers MuxOUT1, Mux-OUT2 and MuxOUT3 are used for selecting register values as input to the ALU module. In this design, 25-bit control word is used for data control in register module. $CW_0 - CW_8$ are used for writing output of the operation C_0 in any of the 9 registers namely $RA_1, RA_2, RB_1, RB_2, RC_1, RC_2, RD_1, RD_2$ and $RE1$. For example, if CW_0 is high, output is written in $RA1$, CW_1 is for $RA2$ and so on. Similarly, $CW_8 - CW_{17}$ are used to decide the destination register for the output of operation C_1. CW_{24} and CW_{25} control the output of $MC0$ and $MC1$. If CW_{24} is low, then ALU output of operation C_0 gets stored in registers, else value from ROM is selected for storing in the registers. CW_{25} similarly controls the choice between the output of operation C_1 and ROM. $RD2, RA1, RB2, RC2$ are fed as input to the multiplexer $M01$ and output $A1$ serves as one of the input to ALU. Similarly, $M02$ and $M03$ works with the input set of $(RA_2, RB_1, RC_1 and RF_2)$ and (RD_1, RE_1, RC_1, RD_2). $CW_{18} - CW_{23}$ controls these three multiplexers, each with 2 selection lines and inputs to the ALU are determined.

Table 2. Projective Addition

Clock	State	Operation1(C_1)	Operation1(C_0)
1	Initial	$RA_1 \leftarrow X_1$	$RB_1 \leftarrow X_2$
2	Initial	$RB_1 \leftarrow Z_1$	$RB_2 \leftarrow Y_2$
3	Initial	$RD_1 \leftarrow Z_1$	$RD_2 \leftarrow Z_2$
4	S_1		$RC_1 \leftarrow RA_1.RA_2$
5	S_2		$RC_2 \leftarrow RB_1.RB_2$
6	S_3		$RB_1 \leftarrow RD_1.RD_2$
7	S_4		$RA_1 \leftarrow (RA_1 + RA_2).$ $(RA_2 + RD_2)$
8	S_5		$RD_1 \leftarrow RC_1.RC_2$
9	S_6		$RB_2 \leftarrow RC_2.RB_1$
10	S_7		$RA_2 \leftarrow RB_1.RB_2$
11	S_8		$RD_2 \leftarrow (RD_1 + RB_2)$ $(RA_2 + RD_1)$
12	S_9		$RB_2 \leftarrow (RC_1 + RB_1).RD_2$
13	S_{10}	$RE_1 \leftarrow \beta$	$RC_2 \leftarrow (RB_1 + RC_2).$ $(RB_1 + RC_2)$
14	S_{11}		$RC_2 \leftarrow (RC_2 + RB_1)$ $(RC_2 + RB_1)$
15	S_{12}		$RE_1 \leftarrow RC_1.RE_1$
16	S_{13}	$RD_2 \leftarrow (RC_2 + RB_1)$	$RC_2 \leftarrow RE_1.RC_2$
17	S_{14}	$RE_1 \leftarrow \alpha$	$RE_2 \leftarrow (RA_1 + RD_2).$ $(RA_2 + RD_1)$
18	S_{15}	$RA_2 \leftarrow 1$	$RC_1 \leftarrow RC_1.(RA_2 + RB_2)$
19	S_{16}	$RB_2 \leftarrow (RC_2 + RA_2)$	$RC_1 \leftarrow (RE_1 + RC_1)$
20	S_{17}	$RA_2 \leftarrow (RD_2 + RA_2)$	$RD_2 \leftarrow (RC_1 + RA_1).$ $(RD_1 + RB_1)$

3.2 Proposed Architecture for Keymodification Module

The key-modification unit uses ternary logic to reduce the number of point operations. Ternary representation [6] is a special technique to reduce the time required to compute kP. Here, k is represented as the sums and differences of power of 2. In this representation, large sequences of 1 get replaced by $(1, 0, -1)$. The keymodification module explained in [3] is enhanced in this design and keymodification is performed in parallel with the point addition operation to make the design faster. Initially, a few clock pulses are used solely for key-bit shifting. Then the same clock pulses are used for both key-bit modification and addition operation. Number of initial clock pulses for shifting (say, n) are determined based on the required clock-pulses for point addition or point doubling.

Considering k-bit key, n can be determined from the following relation $3 + 17 * n \geq k$ for BHC. 17 clock pulses are required for each addition or doubling states of BHC with 3 initial clock pulses for data loading from ROM as shown in table 2. For our implementation, 233-bit key is considered. Hence, 14 clock pulses are required solely for initial key-shifting compared to the previous design explained in [3], where 233 clock pulses are used for modification of 233-bit key. This initial key-bit shifting is mainly important to avoid any overlap between any key-bit modification operation and point addition/doubling operation based on the same key-bit.

In actual implementation, $1, 0, -1$ is represented as $00, 01, 11$ respectively. If $P = (x_1, y_1)$ be a point on the curve, negation of point P is $-P(x_r, y_r)$ and it is evaluated as [5]:

$$x_r = \frac{y_1(b + ax_1y_1)}{a + bx_1y_1} \tag{2}$$

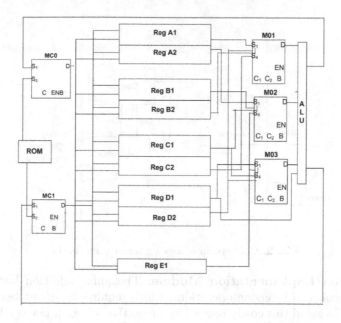

Fig. 1. Register module of the processor

$$and \quad y_r = \frac{x_1(a + bx_1y_1)}{b + ax_1y_1} \tag{3}$$

Every 0 is handled by doubling and 1 is handled by one addition along with a doubling. However, -1, which is represented as 11 requires one addition and doubling as it is required for 01 and another negation as explained in Equation. 2 and 3.

3.3 Arithmetic Logic Unit

Arithmetic logic unit(ALU) performs the computation of field addition, field multiplication and the final inverse calculation for projective to affine conversion. The ALU consists of two main submodules:

- **Hybrid Karatsuba Multiplier Block:** The field multiplication is performed by Hybrid Karatsuba multiplier. Simple and general Karatsuba are clubbed together in Hybrid Karatsuba multiplier. The General Karatsuba is better for maximum utilization of LUT for smaller bits, while Simple Karatsuba is beneficial for minimizing gate counts for higher bits. As mentioned in [12], we have the threshold of the multiplier at $m \leq 29$, to improve the LUT utilization of the circuit.

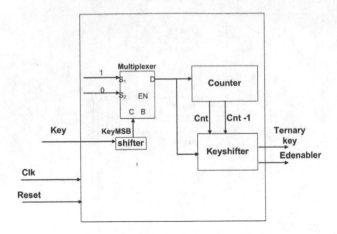

Fig. 2. Conversion of key by ternary method

- **Inversion Implementation Module:** The affine addition laws require large number of inversion operations, which requires large number of clock-cycles. To avoid this costly operation, projective addition law is adapted. In this case, a single inversion is required to convert the projective result to affine one. Quad Itoh-Tsujii algorithm is effective for saving the clock cycles in inversion implementation [3]. In each step, the input is raised to the power of four with the quadblock rather than raising to the power of 2 as it is done in conventional Itoh-Tsujii algorithm.

Table 3. Comparison of the Proposed $GF(2^m)$ ECCP with FPGA based Published Results

Work	Platform	Field m	Slices	LUTs	Gate Count	Freq (MHz)	Latency (ms)	Latency /bit (ns)
Saqib [14]	XCV3200	191	18314	-	-	10	0.056	293
Pu [11]	XC2V1000	193	-	3601	-	115	0.167	865
Ansari [1]	XC2V2000	163	-	8300	-	100	0.042	257
Chelton [4]	XCV2600E	163	15368	26390	238145	91	0.033	202
	XC4V200	163	16209	26364	264197	153.9	0.019	116
Chester *et.al* [12]	XCV3200E	233	20325	40686	333063	25.31	0.074	317
	XC4V140	233	20917	39303	334709	64.46	0.029	124
BEC [3]	XC4V140	233	21816	35003	240064	50	0.170	729
BHC	XC4V140	233	20,437	39,034	273,221	81	0.073	313

The overall ALU consists of multiplier unit and a few multiplexers. The inputs A_0, A_1, A_2, A_3 are typically fetched from register module. M_1 and M_2 are two 8 : 1 multiplexers, which are used for the selection of inputs to the multiplier.

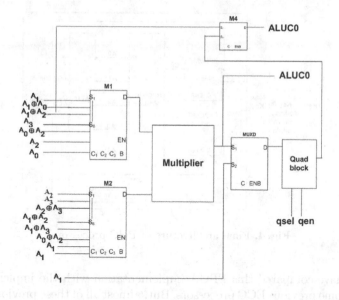

Fig. 3. ALU of BHC Processor

M_3 is used for controlling input to the quad block and the M_4 is used for selection of the final output. Figure 3 depicts the final ALU architecture and figure 4 shows the overall BHC processor in $GF(2^{233})$.

4   Analysis and Verification of the Result

The proposed architecture is implemented in Virtex4 FPGA device. The design is verified with its software equivalent coded using Rosing's library [13].

   The efficiency of the design is measured depending on the total time required for computing the scalar multiplication kP. If the total length of the key(k) is l and the Hamming weight is h and 22 clock pulses are required for inversion, then the total number of clock pulses required are (excluding 14 clock pulses required solely for initial key-shifting of the key-modification module):

$$\text{Number of clock pulses} = 3 + 17(l - 1) + 17(h - 1) + 22 \qquad (4)$$

During the calculation of number of clock-cycle requirement as mentioned in table 3, half of the bits of the 233-bit key are considered to be one and no consecutive ones are considered. Hence, this is the worst case scenario, where effectively there is no gain for the presence of keymodification module [3]. In actual scenario, the probability of existing consecutive blocks of 1 are almost one and that will in turn increase the speed of the design. Some of the mathematical computations also show, number of blocks of 1 will increase with the number of bits. To the best of our knowledge, there is no previous implementation on BHC,

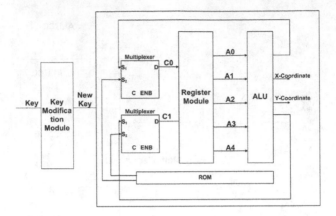

Fig. 4. Final architecture of BHC processor

hence we have compared this FPGA implementation with the implementation results of some previous ECC processors. But, almost all of these previous designs are non-unified except BEC. Since, BEC [2] also has the side channel attack preventive unified property, comparisons between these two curves are of great importance in practical cryptographic applications. Comparison result shows that BHC being complete for some specific subgroups, is much faster compared to BEC.

Table 3 shows comparisons with several other existing ECC processors also. For better comparisons among different fields, a scaling factor is multiplied with the slice and required time [12], The number of slices hold a quadratic relationship due to presence of multiplier block, hence the factor is considered as $(233/m)^2$ and the scaling factor for time is $233/m$. In all the comparisons, *latency/bit* is considered rather than *latency* only since the previous ECC implementations are in different fields.

Finally, BHC based design is unified as well as complete and this BHC based processor can be considered as the first FPGA implementation of the **fastest, unified** processor in the ECC domain.

5   Conclusion

To the best of our knowledge, this is the first FPGA implementation based on BHC processor. The main feature of any hardware ECC implementation is the trade-off between security and efficiency. Being defined in certain proper subgroups, BHC can maintain both security as well as speed of computation. Hence, this BHC based design can be considered as first reported state-of-the-art FPGA processor having the capability of simple side channel attack prevention with unified laws along with faster computation ability compared to other unified processors.

References

1. Ansari, B., Hasan, M.A.: High Performance Architecture of Elliptic Curve Scalar Multiplication. Tech. rep., Department of Electrical and Computer Engineering, University of Waterloo (2006)
2. Bernstein, D.J., Lange, T., Farashahi, R.R.: Binary edwards curves. Cryptology ePrint Archive, Report 2008/171 (2008), http://eprint.iacr.org/
3. Chatterjee, A., Sengupta, I.: Fpga implementation of binary edwards curve using ternary representation. In: GLSVLSI 2011: Proceedings of the 21st ACM Great Lakes Symposium on VLSI. ACM, Lausanne (2011)
4. Chelton, W.N., Benaissa, M.: Fast Elliptic Curve Cryptography on FPGA. IEEE Transactions on Very Large Scale Integration (VLSI) Systems 16(2), 198–205 (2008)
5. Devigne, J., Joye, M.: Binary Huff Curves. In: Kiayias, A. (ed.) CT-RSA 2011. LNCS, vol. 6558, pp. 340–355. Springer, Heidelberg (2011)
6. Hoffstein, J.: An introduction to mathematical cryptography. Springer (2009)
7. Izu, T., Takagi, T.: Exceptional Procedure Attack on Elliptic Curve Cryptosystems. In: Desmedt, Y.G. (ed.) PKC 2003. LNCS, vol. 2567, pp. 224–239. Springer, Heidelberg (2002)
8. Joye, M., Tibouchi, M., Vergnaud, D.: Huff's Model for Elliptic Curves. In: Hanrot, G., Morain, F., Thomé, E. (eds.) ANTS-IX. LNCS, vol. 6197, pp. 234–250. Springer, Heidelberg (2010)
9. Koblitz, N.: Elliptic curve cryptosystems. Mathematics of Computation 48, 203–209 (1987)
10. Miller, V.S.: Use of Elliptic Curves in Cryptography. In: Williams, H.C. (ed.) CRYPTO 1985. LNCS, vol. 218, pp. 417–426. Springer, Heidelberg (1986)
11. Pu, Q., Huang, J.: A Microcoded Elliptic Curve Processor for $GF(2^m)$ Using FPGA Technology. In: 2006 International Conference on Communications, Circuits and Systems Proceedings, vol. 4, pp. 2771–2775 (June 2006)
12. Rebeiro, C., Mukhopadhyay, D.: High Speed Compact Elliptic Curve Cryptoprocessor for FPGA Platforms. In: Chowdhury, D.R., Rijmen, V., Das, A. (eds.) INDOCRYPT 2008. LNCS, vol. 5365, pp. 376–388. Springer, Heidelberg (2008)
13. Rosing, M.: Implementing Elliptic Curve Cryptography. Manning Publications Co., Sound View Ct. 3B Greenwich (1998)
14. Saqib, N.A., Rodríiguez-Henríquez, F., Diaz-Perez, A.: A Parallel Architecture for Fast Computation of Elliptic Curve Scalar Multiplication Over $GF(2^m)$. In: Proceedings of the 18th International Parallel and Distributed Processing Symposium (2004)

A 4 × 20 Gb/s 2^9-1 PRBS Generator for Testing a High-Speed DAC in 90nm CMOS Technology

Mahendra Sakare, Mohit Singh, and Shalabh Gupta

Department of Electrical Engineering,
Indian Institute of Technology(IIT)-Bombay, Mumbai, India
mahendras@iitb.ac.in

Abstract. This paper presents a 4 × 20 Gb/s 2^9-1 pseudo-random binary sequence (PRBS) generator in 90nm CMOS technology to test a 4-bit 20 GS/s digital to analog converter (DAC). The architecture results in generation of four de-correlated sequences from a single 9-bit LFSR (linear feedback shift register) with minimal circuitry. Improved CML (current mode logic) multiplexer design ensures peak-to-peak jitter of 1.7 psec, and negligible amplitude variation. The data latches are clocked at half-rate in order to reduce power dissipation, and are followed by 2:1 multiplexers to achieve the desired data-rate, consuming 51mW per output lane (total 204 mW) of power from a 1 V supply. The PRBS and DAC can together be used for generating pseudo-random multi-level test symbol sequences for high-speed communication links.

1 Introduction

To increase the capacity by improving spectral efficiency, multi-level modulation formats are explored in modern broad-band data communications. PRBS generators are desirable to provide high speed test data patterns and high speed DACs are needed to generate the multi-level signal. Minimum requirement for covering all transitions is satisfied by using a 2^m-1 PRBS generator to test an m-bit input of DUT [1]. For 4 de-correlated sequence generation, 2^7-1 PRBS generator are used in [2]−[3], which doesn't cover all transitions until power consuming, shifting of initial condition circuit is not incorporated, and 2^{31}-1 bit PRBS generator is used in [4], which takes longer time to cover maximum length sequence (MLS) and have increased circuitry because of number of DFF is proportional to size of PRBS generator. This increases power, area and cost. In [2], comparison between various multi-lane series and parallel PRBS generators are dissucssed and have chosen one minimal circuitry PRBS generator topology.

In this paper, selection of correct PRBS generator topology is discussed for multi channel output and a multi-channel multiplexing technique depending on tapping of PRBS generator is proposed which covers all transitions with minimal circuitry. In general, low voltage swing (approx. 200mV) for clock signal is used to reduce power in CML. Incomplete switching of differential pairs causes problem of residual currents in transistors that are supposed to be off. This problem is more prominent in MUX. In this paper, solution of this residual current is proposed which results a balanced output voltage, low jitter CML MUX.

H. Rahaman et al. (Eds.): VDAT 2012, LNCS 7373, pp. 252–257, 2012.

2 Multi-channel Multiplexing Technique

The aim of this multi-channel multiplexing technique is to generate 4 de-correlated sequences that cover all transitions to test high speed DACs using PRBS in efficient manner. Fig 1 shows the need of all transition coverage for assessment of true dynamic behavior of DAC. Multi-channel multiplexing technique states that for exhaustive testing of an m-bit DAC, (a) each channel should be more than one clock cycle apart and (b) multiplexing is applied on ≤2m-bit linear feedback shift register (LFSR) which has minimum number of XORs ensuring maximum DFF output is used to generate testing sequence for minimal circuitry.

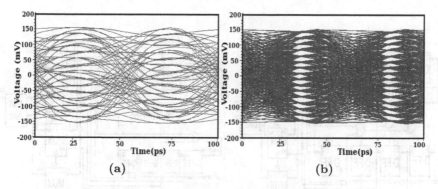

Fig. 1. Eye diagram of (a)2^6-1 (25% transition coverage)and (b)2^9-1 (100% transition coverage) PRBS generator testing 4 bit DAC

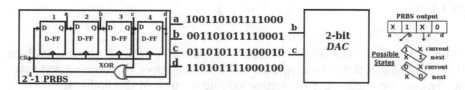

Fig. 2. Block diagram showing DAC testing with one clock cycle delayed PRBS output covers half of total transitions because of two bits are fixed

For example, Fig. 2 shows 4 bit PRBS generator output is applied to the one clock cycle delayed inputs to DAC then it covers only half of the total transitions because of two bits are fixed. Fig 3 shows each MUX output is 2 clock period apart to each other and $2^n \times 2^n = 2^{2n}$ PRBS generator is requried for covering all transitions for n-bit DAC(Fig 3). Therefore, 2^8-1 PRBS generator is required to cover all transitions for 4 output channels. Characteristic equation of 2^8-1 LFSR is

$$x^8 + x^6 + x^5 + x^4 + 1 = 0 \tag{1}$$

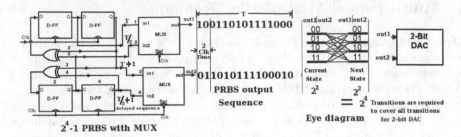

Fig. 3. Block diagram showing DAC testing with two clock cycle delayed PRBS output covers all transitions

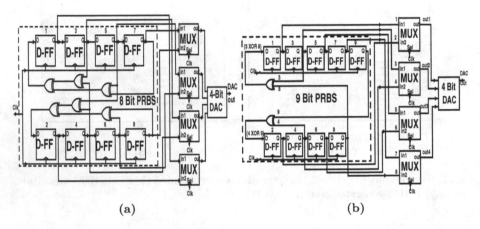

Fig. 4. Block diagram of (a) 2^8-1 PRBS generator (b)$2^9 - 1$ PRBS generator testing 4 bit DAC

These 4 tappings make circuit complex as shown in Fig. 4a. Critical path in this case includes 2 XOR gates. This is further improved by choosing one extra bit, circuit complexity and capacitive loading at most of the nodes are reduced because of less number of required XOR gates. Characteristic equation of 2^9-1 LFSR is

$$x^9 + x^5 + 1 = 0 \tag{2}$$

Less number of tappings reduce circuit complexity as shown in Fig. 4b.

2^9-1 PRBS generator completes exhaustive testing in 511 clock cycles including the 0-0 transition which is missing in the test done using 2^8-1 PRBS generator. Area required is also approximately 10% less in 2^9-1 PRBS generator as compare to 2^8-1 PRBS generator. This technique removes the logic depth and reduces power consumption by minimum one gate and increases the maximum operating frequency. To the best of our knowledge, this $2^9 - 1$ PRBS generator is most efficient topology for testing 4-bit DAC.

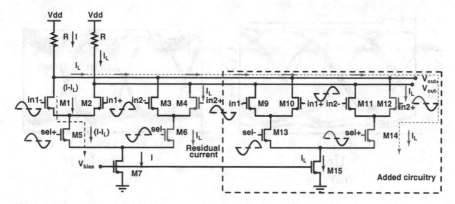

Fig. 5. Circuit diagram of the proposed 2:1 MUX showing added circuitry for solving residual current problem

3   PRBS Generator Circuit Design Techniques

A single LFSR core is used to generate 4 de-correlated sequences results in low power per channel. CML latches, D flip-flops, XORs, buffers and MUXes are needed to combine the parallel sequences into the final high speed PRBS. The main problem in the conventional 2:1 MUX is imperfect switching of Differential pairs due to low swing signals. Significant current flows through the transistors even in the off state, causing two output voltage levels for 'high' and two output levels for 'low' state and variation in rise and fall time at the output. This current varies depending on circuit configurations, specifications and technology. As technology is scaling down, this residual current is increasing. In 90nm technology, it can be one fourth of total bias current. To avoid this in the proposed MUX, extra current is added through extra differential amplifiers with current capacity of this residual current, as shown in Fig. 5. Other cases work in similar fashion. It draws 5mA current including amount of extra current i.e. 1mA which is flowing from extra circuitry. It draws extra 1mA current but it improves MUX output response significantly so this extra power loss in manageable.

The latch and CML XOR merged with latch to reduce delay are working with 10 Gb/s data-rate with 10 GHz clock frequency by drawing 3 mA current individually [5]. 10Gb/s CML buffer draws 5mA current [6]. For the 20Gb/s buffer, the active feedback technique is used because it can extend the gain-bandwidth product by a factor of the ratio of f_T and bandwidth of the amplifier [7]. This buffer is working with 20-Gb/s data-rate with single ended output voltage swing of 280mV. This also helps MUX output to improve further. It draws 8mA current.

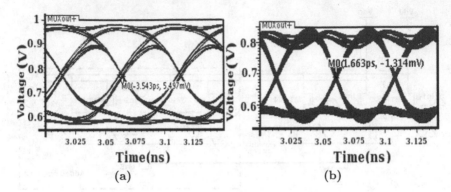

Fig. 6. Eye diagram of 2:1 MUX (a) conventional 2:1 MUX (b) proposed 2:1 MUX

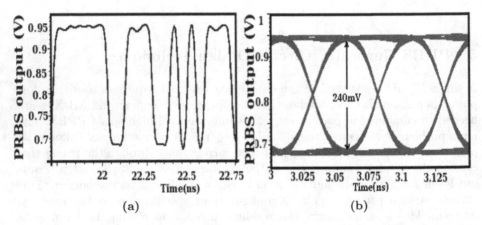

Fig. 7. Eye-diagram of CMOS PRBS generator showing 20Gb/s output data with 240mV eye opening and <1ps jitter$_{pp}$

4   Simulation Results

Eye diagram of 2^9-1 PRBS generator output is shown in Fig. 7b. Simulation is performed in typical-typical process at 100°C temperature. PRBS output is 240 mV single ended voltage swing with common mode of 0.8 V. This simulation is carried out with sinusoidal wave of 10GHz clock frequency including interconnect capacitance. This is working fine with process, temperature and voltage variations. Eye-diagram (Fig. 1b) clearly shows all transition levels are covered in equal proportion after DAC.

Table 1. Comparison with other published work

Ref.	Technology	f_T (GHz)	Data-rate	MLS	Power per lane	FOM* ($\frac{pJ}{bit}$)
[3]	CMOS 0.13 um	80	1×20Gb/s	2^7-1	0.84 W@1.5V	6
[5]	CMOS 0.13 um	NA	1×24Gb/s	2^7-1	274 mW@1.5V	1.63
[2]	0.13 um SiGe BiCMOS	150	4×23Gb/s	2^7-1	60 mW@2.5V	0.37
[4]	CMOS 0.18 um	NA	3×12Gb/s	2^{31}-1	262 mW@1.8V	0.7
[8]	0.25 um SiGe BiCMOS	75	1×25Gb/s	2^9-1	151 mW@2.85V	0.67
This work	CMOS 90 nm	120	4×20Gb/s	2^9-1	51 mW@1V	0.57

$$FOM^* = Power/(log_2(MLS) \times DataRate)$$

5 Conclusion

The 4×2^9-1 PRBS generator, which is designed in 90nm CMOS technology, generates data at 10-Gb/s and produces 20-Gb/s data rate after multiplexing. This module offers low jitter$_{pp}$ (<1 ps) and eye opening of 240 mV. It is suitable for high speed transmitters and testing high speed DAC to comply stringent input requirement. The PRBS core draws 115 mA and multiplexer draws 88 mA from a 1 V supply.

Acknowledgments. The authors would like to thank TCS funding at IIT Bombay.

References

1. Singh, M., Sakare, M., Gupta, S.: Testing of high-speed dacs using prbs generation with "alternate-bit-tapping". In: DATE, pp. 1–6 (2011)
2. Laskin, E., Voinigescu, S.P.: A 60 mw per lane, 4× 23-gb/s 2^7-1 prbs generator. IEEE Journal of Solid-State Circuits 41, 2198–2208 (2006)
3. Kim, J., Kim, J., Jeong, D.: A 20-gb/s full-rate 2^7-1 prbs generator integrated with 20-ghz pll in 0.13-μm cmos. In: IEEE A-SSCC 2008, pp. 221–224 (2008)
4. Sham, K., Bommalingaiahnapallya, S., Ahmadi, M., Harjani, R.: A 3×5-gb/s multilane low-power 0.18-μm cmos pseudorandom bit sequence generator. IEEE Transactions on Circuits and Systems II: Express Briefs 55, 432–436 (2008)
5. Weiss, F., Wohlmuth, H.D., Kehrer, D., Scholtz, A.: A 24-gb/s 2^7 - 1 pseudo random bit sequence generator ic in 0.13 -μm bulk cmos. In: ESSCIRC, pp. 468–471 (2006)
6. Heydari, P.: Design and analysis of low-voltage current-mode logic buffers. In: Fourth Inter. Symp. on Quality Electronic Design, pp. 293–298 (2003)
7. Galal, S., Razavi, B.: 10-gb/s limiting amplifier and laser/modulator driver in 0.18-μm cmos technology. IEEE Journal of Solid-State Circuits 38, 2138–2146 (2003)
8. Laemmle, B., Sewiolo, B., Weigel, R.: A $2^9 - 1$ up to 25gb/s m-sequence generator ic for uwb radar applications in a low-cost sige bicmos technology. In: German Microwave Conference, pp. 1–4 (2009)

VLSI Architecture for Bit Parallel Systolic Multipliers for Special Class of GF(2^m) Using Dual Bases

Hafizur Rahaman[1], Jimson Mathew[2], A.M. Jabir[3], and Dhiraj K. Pradhan[2]

[1] Department of Information Technology,
Bengal Engineering and Science University, Shibpur, India
[2] Computer Science Dept., University of Bristol, Bristol, UK
[3] Dept. of Computer Science and Electronics, Oxford Brookes University, Oxford, UK
rahaman_h@it.becs.ac.in, ajabir@brookes.ac.uk,
{jimson,pradhan}@cs.bris.ac.uk

Abstract. This paper presents the efficient VLSI architecture for bit parallel systolic multiplication over dual base for trinomial and pentanomial in$GF(2^m)$ for effective use in RS decoders. This architecture supports pipelining. Here irreducible trinomial of form $p(x)=x^m+x^n+1$ and pentanomial of the form $p(x) = x^m+x^{k+2}+ x^{k+1}+x^k+1$ generate the fields in $GF(2^m)$. For ECC algorithms, NIST recommends the five reduction polynomials which are either trinomial or pentanomial. Since the systolic multiplier has the features of regularity, modularity and unidirectional data flow, this structure is well suited to VLSI implementations. For trinomial, the systolic structure of proposed bit parallel dual multipliers requires only m^2 two inputs AND gates and at most (m^2-1) two inputs EXOR gates. For pentanomial, it requires only m^2 two inputs AND gates and (m^2+3m-3) two inputs EXOR gates. The proposed multipliers have clock cycle latency of m. The length of the largest delay path and area of this architecture are less compared to the bit parallel systolic multiplication architectures reported earlier. This architecture can also operate over both the dual-base and polynomial base.

Keywords: Finite Field, RS codes, bit parallel, systolic, error correction.

1   Introduction

Finite field or Galois Field arithmetic operations over $GF(2^m)$ find widespread applications in public-key cryptography [1], the implementation of Reed-Solomon (RS) decoders and encoders[11], error detecting and correcting code[8], VLSI testing[9], digital signal processing[10]. The addition, multiplication, division and inversion over $GF(2^m)$ are the essential operations in design of the RS decoders and encoders [11, 21]. The multiplication is the main operation for implementing RS codecs due to the overall coding algorithms and also hardware complexity of circuits implementing the operation. Two basic operations over $GF(2^m)$ are addition and multiplication. Addition over $GF(2^m)$ is relatively straightforward to implement, requiring m 2-input EXOR gates. Multiplication operation is much more expensive

H. Rahaman et al. (Eds.): VDAT 2012, LNCS 7373, pp. 258–269, 2012.
© Springer-Verlag Berlin Heidelberg 2012

in terms of gate count and clock cycle. Other operations of the $GF(2^m)$ fields like exponentiation, division, and inversion can be performed by repeated multiplications. There are different equivalent representations of the elements of the finite field over $GF(2^m)$ e.g. Polynomial base (PB), normal base, and dual base. The dual basis multipliers are the most hardware efficient multipliers available, both in bit-serial and in bit-parallel forms [17-18]. Again, the problem of a dual basis multiplier operating over two different bases can largely be avoided by choosing the bases appropriately. In this case, the required basis conversion requires little or no extra hardware [17, 22]. It is therefore often convenient to take the operating basis of an RS codec to be the dual basis.

Based on different base representation, a variety of architectures for multiplication have been proposed. For high speed VLSI implementation, the preferred architecture for multiplication is the systolic array architecture. The systolic array multipliers in $GF(2^m)$ can be classified into four categories, namely bit serial, bit-parallel, hybrid and digit-serial. The bit serial architecture has minimum area and minimum throughput among all the categories. The problem with serial architecture is its latency. The most widely used bit serial multiplier is dual basis Berlekamp bit serial multiplier [11]. This multiplier requires less hardwire. PB bit-serial and bit-parallel systolic multipliers were presented in [3-4, 6]. The bit parallel multiplier needs largest area and provides maximum throughput. Mastrovito has proposed an algorithm along with its hardware architecture for PB multiplication [6] known as the Mastrovito multiplier. A formulation for Polynomial basis multiplication and generalized bit-parallel hardware architecture for special reduction polynomials, namely: trinomials, equally spaced polynomials (ESPs), and two classes of pentanomials has been presented in [23]. A testable polynomial basis bit parallel multiplier circuits over $GF(2^m)$ was presented in [20]. Although bit-serial dual basis multipliers have been widely employed in applications such as RS encoders [3], it has been shown in [18] that it is advantageous for employing bit-parallel dual basis multipliers in more complex circuits such as RS decoders and syndrome calculators. Dual basis inversion architecture was presented in [21]. A finite field dual basis bit-serial systolic multiplier architecture suitable for RS codes implementation was proposed in [24].

In this paper, we present the simplified bit parallel and systolic architectures for dual basis finite field multiplication over $GF(2^m)$, where the finite fields are generated by irreducible trinomial and pentanomials.

2   Preliminaries

2.1   Polynomial Multiplication

Let $GF(N)$ denote a set of N elements, where N is a power of a prime number, with two special elements 0 and 1 representing the additive and multiplicative identities respectively and two operator addition '+' and multiplication '.'. The GF(N) defines a finite field, if it forms a commutative ring with identity over these two operators in which every element has a multiplicative inverse. Finite fields can be generated with primitive polynomials of the form $P(x) = x^{m-1} + \sum_{i=0}^{m} p_i x^i$, where $p_i \in GF(2)$ [9]. It is conventional to represent the elements of $GF(2^m)$ as a power of the primitive element α where α is the root of $P(x)$, i.e. $P(\alpha) = 0$. The set $\{1, \alpha, \ldots, \alpha^{m-1}\}$ is referred to as polynomial basis or standard basis. Each element $A \in GF(2^m)$ can be expressed with respect to the PB as a polynomial of degree m over $GF(2)$, i.e. $A(x) = \sum_{i=0}^{m-1} a_i x^i$ where $a_i \in GF(2)$. Given A, $B \in GF(2^m)$, PB multiplication over $GF(2^m)$ can be defined as $C(x) = A(x).B(x) \mod P(x)$. In practice $C(x)$ is obtained in two steps: polynomial multiplication and modulo reduction.

2.2 Dual Basis Multiplication

Let F_p^m denote the set of all linear function $f: GF(p^m) \rightarrow GF(p)$. A well known linear function is the trace function which is frequently used to produce the finite field multipliers. We follow the definition of the duality of two bases [14, 17] as given below.

Definition 1: Let $\{\lambda_i\}$ and $\{\mu_i\}$ be bases for $GF(2^m)$, let f be the linear function $f: GF(2^m) \rightarrow GF(2)$ and let $\beta \in GF(2^m)$, $\beta \neq 0$. Then the bases are said to be dual with respect to f and β if

$$f(\beta \lambda_i \mu_j) = \begin{cases} 1 & \text{If } i=j \\ 0 & \text{if } i \neq j \end{cases}$$

Here $\{\lambda_i\}$ is the standard basis and $\{\mu_i\}$ is the dual basis. The following theorem represents a generalized representation of Berlekamp bit-serial multiplier.

Theorem 1 [14]: Let a, b, $c \in GF(p^m)$ such that $c = ab$. Further, let α be a root of the defining irreducible polynomial for the field, let $\beta \in GF(2^m)$, $f \in F_2^m$ and represent a over the polynomial basis by $a = \sum_{i=0}^{m-1} a_i \alpha^i$, *Then the following relation holds.*

$$\begin{bmatrix} f(b\beta) & f(b\beta\alpha) & \cdots & f(b\beta\alpha^{m-1}) \\ f(b\beta\alpha) & f(b\beta\alpha^2) & \cdots & f(b\beta\alpha^m) \\ \cdots & \cdots & \cdots & \cdots \\ f(b\beta\alpha^{m-1}) & f(b\beta\alpha^m) & \cdots & f(b\beta\alpha^{2m-2}) \end{bmatrix} \begin{bmatrix} a_0 \\ a_1 \\ \cdots \\ a_{m-1} \end{bmatrix} = \begin{bmatrix} f(c\beta) \\ f(c\beta\alpha) \\ \cdots \\ f(c\beta\alpha^{m-1}) \end{bmatrix} \tag{1}$$

We have modified eqn. (1) as follows.

$$\begin{bmatrix} c_0 \\ c_1 \\ \cdots \\ c_{m-2} \\ c_{m-1} \end{bmatrix} = \begin{bmatrix} b_0 & b_1 & b_2 & \cdots & b_{m-1} \\ b_1 & b_2 & \cdots & \ddots & b_m \\ \cdots & \cdots & \cdots & \cdots & \cdots \\ b_{m-2} & \ddots & \ddots & \cdots & b_{2m-3} \\ b_{m-1} & b_m & b_{m+1} & \cdots & b_{2m-2} \end{bmatrix} \times \begin{bmatrix} a_0 \\ a_1 \\ \cdots \\ a_{m-2} \\ a_{m-1} \end{bmatrix} \tag{2}$$

Where $b_k = f(b\beta\alpha^k)$ $(k = 0, 1, \ldots 2m - 2)$ and $c_k = f(c\beta\alpha^k)$ $(k = 0, 1, \ldots m - 1)$. If f and β are taken as in the preceding definition, c_k and b_k $(k = 0, 1, \ldots m - 1)$ in eqn.(1) are the dual-basis coefficients of c and b, respectively. Thus to make use of eqn. 1 in a systolic multiplier one must first generate the values of b_k ($k= m, m+1, …2m-2$).

If $p(x) = \sum\limits_{i=0}^{m-1} p_i x^i + x^m$ is the defining irreducible polynomial for the field, then

$$b_m = f(b\beta\alpha^m) = f(b(\beta\sum\limits_{j=0}^{m-1} p_j\alpha^j)) = \sum\limits_{j=0}^{m-1} p_j f(b\beta\alpha^j) = \sum\limits_{j=0}^{m-1} p_j b_j$$

and then $b_{m+k} = f(b\beta\alpha^{m+k}) = f(b(\beta\sum\limits_{j=0}^{m-1} p_j\alpha^{j+k})) = \sum\limits_{j=0}^{m-1} p_j f(b\beta\alpha^{j+k}) = \sum\limits_{j=0}^{m-1} p_j b_{j+k}$

Then in general, $b_{m+k} = \sum\limits_{j=0}^{m-1} p_j b_{j+k}$ (3)

Where b_{m+k} ($k= 0, 1, …, m-2$) are the dual basis coefficients of b and α is root of $p(x)$.

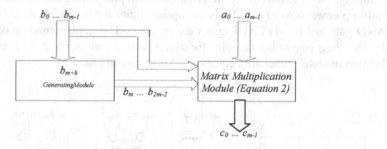

Fig. 1. Bit Parallel Dual Basis Multiplier Architecture

3   Proposed Multiplier Architecture

3.1   Bit Parallel Dual Basis Multiplier Architecture

For implementation of the multiplier architecture, first we will have to generate the values of b_{m+k} from eqn. (3) and then carry out the matrix multiplication given in eqn. (1). Now, we consider the implementation of this multiplication algorithm in the design of a bit-parallel systolic multiplier. The general structure of bit parallel dual basis architecture over $GF(2^m)$ is shown in the Fig. 1. In this work, first we develop simplified structure for Bit Parallel Dual Basis Multiplier Architecture for Trinomial and pentanomial over $GF(2^m)$. Then we present the dual basis bit parallel systolic architecture for Trinomial and pentanomial over $GF(2^m)$.

3.1.1   Bit Parallel Dual Basis Multiplier Architecture for Trinomial over $GF(2^m)$

In this section, we present a Bit Parallel Dual Basis Multiplier Architecture over $GF(2^m)$ in which an irreducible Trinomial of degree m generates the finite field over $GF(2^m)$. Let us consider the irreducible trinomial of the form $p(x) = x^m + x^n + 1$

generating the fields over $GF(2^m)$. If $b= \sum_{i=0}^{m-1} b_i\mu_i$ is the dual basis representation of b and $a= \sum_{i=0}^{m-1} a_i\alpha^i$, is the polynomial basis representation of a. The product bits $c_i (i = 0, 1, ...m-1)$ become available on the output lines. The following equation will generate the terms b_{m+k}.

$$b_{m+k}=b_k+b_{n+k} \text{ for } k = 0 \text{ to } (m-2) \tag{4}$$

Using equation (4), equation (2) is modified for the trinomial as given below.

$$\begin{bmatrix} b_0 & b_1 & b_2 & \cdots & b_{m-1} \\ b_1 & b_2 & \cdots & \ddots & b_0 + b_n \\ \cdots & & \cdots & \cdots & \cdots \\ b_{m-2} & \ddots & \ddots & \cdots & b_{(m-3)} + b_{n+(m-3)} \\ b_{m-1} & b_0 + b_n & b_1 + b_{n+1} & \cdots & b_{(m-2)} + b_{n+(m-2)} \end{bmatrix}$$

To implement equation (2), we require m^2 AND gate and (m^2-m) EXOR gates and, similarly, $(m-1)$ EXOR gates are required for implementing the equation (3), i. e. for full implementation of dual basis multiplier circuit for trinomials over $GF(2^m)$, the m^2 AND gate and (m^2-1) EXOR gates are required. The implementation of equation (3) for the "b_{m+k} generating module" for trinomial is shown in Fig.2. The "matrix multiplication module" generating equation (2) is shown in Fig. 3.

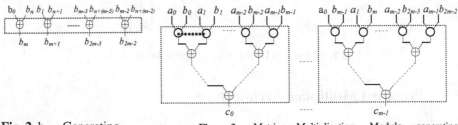

Fig. 2. b_{m+k} Generating Module for trinomial

Fig. 3. Matrix Multiplication Module generating equation (2)

Example 1: Consider the irreducible trinomial $p(x) = x^4+ x^3+1$. The above derivation for the formulation of a bit-parallel dual basis multiplier over $GF(2^4)$ defined by the primitive polynomial $p(x)=x^4+x^3+1$ can also be formulated as follows.

The two inputs of the multiplier are $B=(b_0,b_1,b_2,b_3)$ and $A=(a_0,a_1,a_2,a_3)$. The polynomial representation of $GF(2^4)$ elements is as follows: $B(x)= b_0+b_1x+b_2x^2+b_3x^3$ and $a(x) = a_0+a_1x+a_2x^2+a_3x^3$, where $a,b \in GF(2^4)$. But in this implementation, one operand will be in dual basis. If $(1,\alpha, \alpha^2,\alpha^3,)$ is in the polynomial basis, then $(\alpha^2,\alpha,1,\alpha^3)$ will be in the dual basis of B[23]. In the dual basis, $B(x)=b_0x^2+ b_1 x+ b_2+ b_3x^3$.

$$\text{The product } C(x)= B(x) \times A(x) \tag{6}$$

If B is in the dual basis then, the multiplication result C will be in the dual basis also. From the coefficients of the equation (6), the expressions for b_{m+k}, and $0 \geq k \geq 2$ are derived below.

$$b_4 = b_0 + b_3; \ b_5 = b_1 + b_4; b_6 = b_2 + b_5.$$

The multiplication matrix for the above generating polynomials is given below.

$$\begin{bmatrix} b_0 & b_1 & b_2 & b_3 \\ b_1 & b_2 & b_3 & b_4 \\ b_2 & b_3 & b_4 & b_5 \\ b_3 & b_4 & b_5 & b_6 \end{bmatrix} \begin{bmatrix} a_0 \\ a_1 \\ a_2 \\ a_3 \end{bmatrix} = \begin{bmatrix} c_0 \\ c_1 \\ c_2 \\ c_3 \end{bmatrix}$$

Table 1. Comparison with Polynomial Basis on Trinomial

Multiplier	#AND2	#EXOR2	Time Delay
$p(x) = x^m + x + 1$			
Mastrovito[6]	m^2	$m^2 - 1$	$T_A + T_X\{1 + \lceil log_2{}^m \rceil\}.$
Arch. [23]	m^2	$m^2 - 1$	$T_A + T_X\{2 + \lceil log_2{}^{m-1} \rceil\}.$
Propoposed	m^2	$m^2 - 1$	$T_A + T_X\{1 + \lceil log_2{}^m \rceil\}.$
$p(x) = x^m + x^n + 1, 1 < n > m/2$			
Mastrovito[6]	m^2	$m^2 - 1$	$T_A + T_X\{2 + \lceil log_2{}^m \rceil\}.$
Arch. [23]	m^2	$m^2 - 1$	$T_A + T_X\{2 + \lceil log_2{}^{m-1} \rceil\}.$
Propoposed	m^2	$m^2 - 1$	$T_A + T_X [\{1 + \lfloor (m-2)/(m-n) \rfloor\} + \lceil log_2{}^m \rceil].$
$p(x) = x^m + x^{m/2} + 1$			
Mastrovito [6]	m^2	$m^2 - m/2$	$T_A + T_X\{1 + \lceil log_2{}^m \rceil\}.$
Arch. [23]	m^2	$m^2 - 1$	$T_A + T_X\{1 + \lceil log_2{}^m \rceil\}.$
Propoposed	m^2	$m^2 - 1$	$T_A + T_X [\{1 + \lfloor (m-2)/(m-n) \rfloor\} + \lceil log_2{}^m \rceil].$
$p(x) = x^m + x^n + 1, m/2 < n > m$			
Mastrovito [6]	m^2	$m^2 - 1$	$T_A + T_X [\{1 + \lfloor (m-2)/(m-n) \rfloor\} + \lceil log_2{}^m \rceil].$
Arch. [23]	m^2	$m^2 - 1$	$T_A + T_X [\{1 + \lfloor (m-2)/(m-n) \rfloor\} + \lceil log_2{}^{m-1} \rceil].$
Propoposed	m^2	$m^2 - 1$	$T_A + T_X [\{1 + \lfloor (m-2)/(m-n) \rfloor\} + \lceil log_2{}^m \rceil].$
$p(x) = x^m + x^{m-1} + 1$			
Mastrovito [6]	m^2	$m^2 - 1$	$T_A + T_X\{m-1 + \lceil log_2{}^m \rceil\}.$
Arch. [23]	m^2	$m^2 - 1$	$T_A + m T_X.$
Propoposed	m^2	$m^2 - 1$	$T_A + T_X [\{1 + \lfloor (m-2)/(m-n) \rfloor\} + \lceil log_2{}^m \rceil].$

Time Delay: Assume, T_A is the delay through a two input AND gate and T_X is the delay through a two input EXOR gate. The delay through the matrix multiplication module may be calculated as $\{T_A + T_X \lceil log_2{}^m \rceil\}$. For trinomial, the Hamming weight (hw) of the polynomial is 3. The delay through "b_{m+k} Generating Module" is $[T_X\{(1 + \lfloor (m-2)/(m-n) \rfloor\} \lceil log_2{}^{(hw-1)} \rceil] = [T_X\{(1 + \lfloor (m-2)/(m-n) \rfloor\} \lceil log_2{}^{(3-1)} \rceil] = [T_X\{1 + \lfloor (m-2)/(m-n) \rfloor\}]$. Overall delay through the multiplier $= T_A + T_X [\{1 + \lfloor (m-2)/(m-n) \rfloor\} + \lceil log_2{}^m \rceil]$. Table 1 shows that the time–space complexity of our proposed dual basis architecture is the same as or lower than the polynomial basis architecture reported earlier.

3.1.2 Bit Parallel Dual Basis Multiplier Architecture for Pentanomial over GF(2^m)

Let us consider the irreducible pentanomial of the form $p(x) = x^m + x^{n+2} + x^{n+1} + x^n + 1$ generating the fields over GF(2^m). From the following expression, we can derive the expression for b_{m+k} for $k = 0$ to $(m-2)$.

$$b_{m+k} = b_k + b_{n+k} + b_{(n+1)+k} + b_{(n+2)+k} \text{ for } k = 0 \text{ to } (m-2) \tag{7}$$

The expressions for b_{m+k} for the pntanomials are given below.

$$b_m = b_0 + b_n + b_{n+1} + b_{n+2} \; ; b_{m+1} = b_1 + b_{n+1} + b_{n+2} + b_{n+3}; \; b_{m+2} = b_2 + b_{n+2} + b_{n+3} + b_{n+4}$$
$$..., b_{2m-2} = b_{m-2} + b_{n+m-2} + b_{n+m-1} + b_{n+m}$$

To implement equation (2) for the pentamonials, we require m^2 AND gate and (m^2-m) EXOR gates and, similarly, $\{(m-1) \times 3\}$ EXOR gates are required for implementing equation (3), i.e. for full implementation of the dual basis multiplier circuits for pentamonials over GF(2^m), the m^2 AND gate and (m^2+2m-3) EXOR gates are required.

Example 2: Consider the irreducible pentanomial $p(x) = x^8 + x^4 + x^3 + x^2 + 1$. The expressions for b_{m+k}, and $0 \geq k \geq 6$ are derived below.

$$b_8 = b_0 + b_2 + b_3 + b_4 \; ; b_9 = b_1 + b_3 + b_4 + b_5 \; ; b_{10} = b_2 + b_4 + b_5 + b_6 \; ; b_{11} = b_3 + b_5 + b_6 + b_7;$$
$$b_{12} = b_4 + b_6 + b_7 + b_8 \; ; b_{13} = b_5 + b_7 + b_8 + b_9 \; ; b_{14} = b_6 + b_8 + b_9 + b_{10}$$

Calculation of Time Delay: The delay through the "matrix multiplication module" may be calculated as $T_A + T_X \lceil \log_2{}^m \rceil$. The Hamming weight (*hw*) of the polynomial is 5. The delay through "b_{m+k} *Generating Module*" is $[T_X\{(1+\lfloor (m-2)/(m-n) \rfloor \} \lceil \log_2{}^{(hw-1)} \rceil] = [T_X\{(1+\lfloor (m-2)/(m-n) \rfloor \} \lceil \log_2{}^{(5-1)} \rceil] = [T_X\{1+\lfloor (m-2)/(m-n) \rfloor \}2]$

Total through the multiplier $= T_A + [T_X\{2(1+\lfloor (m-2)/(m-n) \rfloor)\} + \lceil \log_2{}^m \rceil]$.

Table 2 shows that the time–space complexity of our proposed dual basis architecture for the pentanomials is of the same order or lower than the polynomial basis architecture reported earlier.

Table 2. Comparison with Polynomial Basis on Pentanomial

Multiplier	#AND2	#EXOR2	Time Delay
Arch.	m^2	m^2+2m-3	$T_A + T_X\{6 + \lceil \log_2{}^m \rceil\}$.
Arch. [ ]	m^2	m^2+2m-3	$T_A + T_X\{4 + \lceil \log_2{}^{m-1} \rceil\}$.
Propoposed	m^2	m^2+2m-3	$T_A + [T_X\{2(1 + \lfloor (m-2)/(m-n) \rfloor)\} + \lceil \log_2{}^m \rceil]$.

3.2 Systolic Dual Basis Multiplier

3.2.1 Systolic Architecture for Trinomial over GF(2^m)

If b over the dual basis is represented by $b = \sum_{i=0}^{m-1} b_i \mu_i$ and a over the polynomial basis is represented by $a = \sum_{i=0}^{m-1} a_i \alpha^j$, and a, b, $c \in$ GF(2^m), we can derive the following expressions for the product c over dual basis from equation (2).

$$c_0 = b_0 a_0 + b_1 a_1 + \ldots + b_{m-1} a_{m-1}$$
$$c_1 = b_1 a_0 + b_2 a_1 + \ldots + b_m a_{m-1}$$
$$\ldots$$
$$c_{m-1} = b_{m-1} a_0 + b_m a_1 + \ldots + b_{2m-2} a_{m-1}, \text{ where } b_{m+k} (k \geq 0) \text{ are given by eqn. (3).}$$

The following algorithm can be used to generate the "matrix multiplication" component of equation (2).

Algorithm (Product)

Input: *A(x), B(x),* and *m.*

Output: *C(x) = A(x).B(x) mod g(x).*

Initialize: *for (j = 0; j<= m-1; j=j+1), c(0, j)=0};*
A = [a₀,a₁, ...,aₘ₋₂, aₘ₋₁], B = [b₀,b₁ ,..., b₂ₘ₋₃, b₂ₘ₋₂]

1. *for i in 1 to m do*
2. *for j in 0 to (m-1) do*
3. *c(i, j) = c (i-1, j) + a(i-1). b(i-1+j)*
4. *end for*
5. *left shift one bit position of B.*
6. *end for*

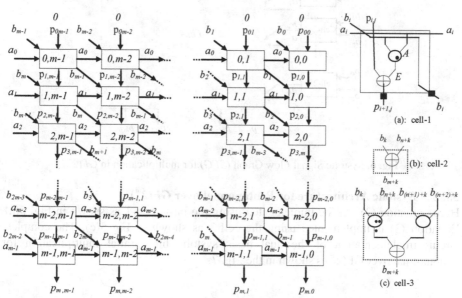

Fig. 4. Systolic Signal Flow Graph *(SFG)* for multiplication in *GF(2ₘ)*

Fig. 5. Basic Cell Implementing Architecture

A systolic signal flow graph (SFG) and corresponding basic cell over $GF(2^m)$ based on the above algorithm are presented in the Fig. 4 and Fig 5(a) respectively. The i's and j's represent the rows and a columns of the SFG, respectively. In general the SFG consists of $\{m{\times}m\}$ basic cells for multiplication over $GF(2^m)$. The basic cell in the ith row and j^{th} column computes $p_{(i+1,\ j)}^{\text{th}}$ internal product of algorithm-1. The final product $P(x)$ in vector form is given by array of $p(m, j)$'s. To implement the SFG as a bit parallel multiplier, the outputs of the basic cells can be latched using D-flip-flops. This implementation consumes m^2 2-input EXOR gates, m^2 2-input AND gates and $2m^2$ D-flip flops. The primary inputs of the SFG are assumed to be unlatched. This requires m clock cycles to calculate one product.

3.2.2   Systolic Architecture for Trinomial over $GF(2^m)$

The general structure for bit parallel dual basis systolic architecture for the trinomial over $GF(2^m)$ of form $p(x)= x^m+ x^n+1$ is shown in the Fig. 6. This structure is constructed using two cells. We introduce cell-1 as shown in Fig. 5(a) to generate eqn. (2) and also introduce cell-2 as shown in Fig. 5(b) for generating eqn. (3).

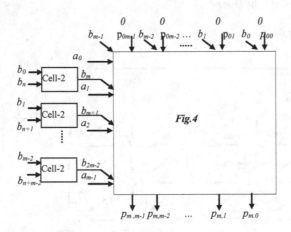

Fig. 6. Systolic Signal Flow Graph *(SFG)* for multiplication in $GF(2^m)$

3.2.3   Systolic Architecture for Pentanomial over $GF(2^m)$

Here, equation (2) will be implemented using the basic cell-1 as shown in Fig. 5(a). Equation (3) is implemented using the cell-3 as shown in Fig 5(c). The complete circuit implementation of the dual basis systolic bit parallel multiplication for pentanomial over $GF(2^m)$ is shown in the Fig. 7.

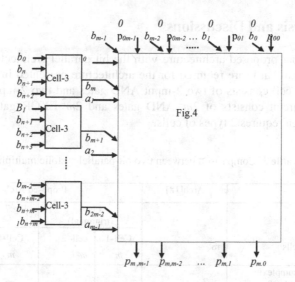

Fig. 7. Systolic SFG for multiplication in $GF(2^m)$ with the generator polynomial of $g(x) = x^m + x^{n+2} + x^{n+1} + x^n + 1$

3.3   Circuit Complexity and Time Delay

To implement equation (2), we require m^2 cell-1 as shown in Fig 5(a). Each cell-1 consists of one 2-input AND gate, one 2-input EXOR gate and two D-flip-flops. For systolic implementation of multiplier for trinomial with the generator polynomial $g(x) = x^m + x^n + 1$, the cell-2 as shown in Fig.5(b) implements equation(3). It requires $(m-1)$ cell-2. Each cell-2 consists of one 2-input EXOR gate and one D-flip-flop. The overall implementation for the dual basis multiplication over $GF(2^m)$ for trinomial requires m^2 2-input AND gates, $m^2 + (m-1)$ 2-input EXOR gates and $2m^2 + (m-1)$ D-flip-flops.

Similarly, for systolic implementation of the multipliers for the pentanomials with the generator polynomial $g(x) = x^m + x^{n+2} + x^{n+1} + x^n + 1$, the cell-1s implement equation(2) and the cell-3s as shown in Fig.(3) implements equation (3).Each cell-3 consists of three 2-input EXOR gate and one D-flip-flop. Hence, the total hardware requirement for dual basis multiplication over $GF(2^m)$ for the pentanomials requires m^2 2-input AND gates, $m^2 + 3m - 3$ 2-input EXOR gates and $2m^2 + (m-1)$ D-flip-flops.

The delay in each cell-1 of the "matrix multiplication module" is $T_A + T_X$. For the trinomial implementation, as shown in the 6, the time delay may be calculated as $m(T_A + T_X)$. For the pentanomial based implementations as shown in Fig. 8, the time delay may be calculated as $(m-1)T_A + (m+1)T_X$. The proposed multipliers have clock cycle latency of m. After the initial delay, the results can be produced continuously as one per each clock cycle.

4   Analysis and Discussions

We compare our proposed architecture with the bit parallel architecture described in [18]. The overall hardware required for the architecture presented in [18] consists of m^2 cells. Each cell consists of two 2-input AND gates and two 2-input EXOR gates. The overall circuit consists of $2m^2$ AND gates and $2m^2$ EXOR gates in total. Our proposed design requires 2 types of cells.

Table 3. Comparison between two bit-parallel systolic multipliers

Properties	Arch[18]	Proposed Arch.			
		Fig.6 (trinomial)		Fig.7 (pentanomial)	
		Cell-1	cell- 2	Cell-1	cell- 3
Number of cells	m^2	m^2	$m-1$	m^2	$m-1$
Circuit complexity # of AND2	$2m^2$	m^2	-	m^2	-
# of EXOR2	$2\,m^2$	m^2	$m-1$	m^2	$3(m-1)$
# of D-flip-flops	$3\,m^2$	$2m^2$	$m-1$	$2m^2$	$m-1$
Critical Path	$(2m-1)\,[T_A + T_X]$	$m(T_A+T_X)$		$(m-1)T_A+(m+1)T_X$	
latency	M	m		M	

The cell-1 consists of one 2-input AND gate and one 2-input EXOR gate. The cell-2 consists of one 2-inputEXOR gate only and cell-3 consists of three 2-input EXOR gates. The architecture based on the trinomial implementation uses cell-1 and cell-2, and that based on pentanomial uses cell-1 and cell-3. The number of D-flip-flops has been reduced significantly compared to the earlier designs [18]. Table 3 shows that the circuit complexity is much lower than the architecture of [18]. The critical path delay is much lower compared to the earlier architecture [18]. From table 3, it is observed that the proposed dual basis multiplier is hardware efficient and faster.

5   Conclusions

The paper presented a simplified dual-basis bit-parallel systolic multiplier architecture over GF(2^m), which can be pipelined and which requires less hardware compared to that required in the conventional BP systolic multiplier architecture reported earlier. Based on the trinomials and pentanomials, we have given an exact complexity analysis of the dual basis multipliers. Our proposed multiplier can also operate over both the dual base and polynomial base. The proposed multiplier provides shorter longest path delay compared to the existing architectures.

References

1. Kumar, S., Wollinger, T., Paar, C.: Optimum Digit Serial $GF(2^m)$ Multipliers for Curve-based Cryptography. IEEE TC 55(10), 1306–1311 (2006)
2. Fenn, S.T.J., Benaissa, M., Taylor, D.: Bit-Serial Dual Basis Systolic Multipliers for GF(2m). In: ISCAS 1995, vol. 3, pp. 2000–2003 (1995)
3. Koc, C.K., Sunar, B.: Mastrovito Multiplier for all Trinomial. IEEE TC 48(5), 522–527
4. Hasan, M.K., Bhargava, V.K.: Division and bit-serial multiplication over $GF(q^m)$. IEE Proc. E 139(3), 230–236
5. Furness, R., Benaissa, M., Fenn, S.T.J.: Generalized Triangular Basis Multipliers for the Design of Reed-solomon Codes. In: IEEE Workshop on Signal Processing Systems, pp. 202–211 (1997)
6. Mastrovito, E.D.: VLSI Architectures for Computation in Galois Fields. PhD thesis, Linkoping Univ, Sweden (1991)
7. Wang, C.L., Lin, J.L.: Systolic Array Implementation of Multipliers for $GF(2^m)$. IEEE TCAS 38(7), 796–800 (1991)
8. Reed, L.S., Chen, X.: Error-Control Coding for Data Networks. Kluwer Academic (1999)
9. Gulliver, T.A., Serra, M., Bhargava, V.K.: The Generation of Primitive Polynomials in $GF(2^m)$ with Independent Roots and Their Application for Power Residue Codes, VLSI Testing and Finite Field Multipliers Using Normal Bases. Int'l J. Electronics 71(4), 559–576 (1991)
10. Blahut, R.E.: Fast Algorithms for Digital Signal Processing. Addison Wesley (1985)
11. Berlekamp, E.R.: Bit-serial Reed-Solomon encoders. IEEE Trans. Inform. Theory 28(6), 869–874 (1982)
12. Yeh, C.S., Reed, I.S., Truong, T.K.: Systolic multi-pliers for finite fields GF (2^m). IEEE TC 33(4), 357–360 (1984)
13. Fenn, S.T.J., Benaissa, M., Taylor, D.: Dual basis systolic multipliers for $GF(2^m)$. IEE Computers & Digital. Tech. 144(1) (January 1997)
14. Fenn, S.T.J., Benaissa, M., Taylor, D.: GF (2^m) multiplication and division over the dual basis. IEEE TC 45(3), 319–327 (1996)
15. Fenn, S.T.J., Benaissa, M., Taylor, D.: Division in GF (2^m). Electron. Letter 28, 2259–2261 (1993)
16. Wang, C.L., Lin, J.L.: Systolic array implementation of multiplier for finite fields GF (2^m). IEEE TCAS 38(7), 796–800 (1991)
17. Hsu, I.S., Truong, T.K., Deutsch, L.J., Reed, I.S.: A comparison of VLSI architectures of finite field multipliers using dual, normal or standard bases. IEEE TC 37(6), 735–737 (1988)
18. Kim, C.H., Hong, C.P., Kwon, S.: A Digit-Serial Multiplier for Finite Field $GF(2^m)$. IEEE TVLSI 13(4), 467–483 (2005)
19. Kim, K.W., Lee, K.J., Yoo, K.Y.: A new digit-serial systolic multiplier for finite fields $GF(2^m)$. In: ICII 2001, Beijing, vol. 5, pp. 128–133 (November 2001)
20. Rahaman, H., Mathew, J., Pradhan, D.K.: C-testable bit Parallel Multipliers over $GF(2^m)$. In: VLSI 2007, India (2007)
21. Fenn, S.T.J., Benaissa, M., Taylor, D.: Finite Field Inversion over the Dual Basis. IEEE TVLSI 4(1), 134–137 (1996)
22. Fenn, S.T.J.: Optimised algorithms and circuit architectures for performing finite field arithmetic in Reed-Solomon codecs. Ph.D. dissertation, The Univ. Huddersfield (1993)
23. Reyhani-Masoleh, A., Hasan, M.A.: Low Complexity Bit Parallel Architectures for Polynomial Basis Multiplication over $GF(2^m)$. IEEE Transactions on Computers 53(8), 945–959 (2004)
24. Fenn, S.T.J., Taylor, D., Benaissa, M.: A dual basis systolic multiplier for $GF(2^m)$. INTEGRATION, the VLSI Journal 18, 139–149 (1995)

A Synthesis Method
for Quaternary Quantum Logic Circuits

Sudhindu Bikash Mandal[1], Amlan Chakrabarti[1], and Susmita Sur-Kolay[2]

[1] A.K. Choudhury School of Information Technology, University of Calcutta, India
[2] Advanced Computing and Microelectronics Unit, Indian Statistical Institute, India

Abstract. Synthesis of quaternary quantum circuits involves basic quaternary gates and logic operations in the quaternary quantum domain. In this paper, we propose new projection operations and quaternary logic gates for synthesizing quaternary logic functions. We also demonstrate the realization of the proposed gates using basic quantum quaternary operations. We then employ our synthesis method to design of quaternary adder and some benchmark circuits. Our results in terms of circuit cost, are better than the existing works.

Keywords: Quaternary algebra, Quaternary quantum logic gates, Quaternary logic synthesis, Quaternary adder.

1 Introduction

Quaternary quantum computing is gaining importance in the field of quantum information theory and quantum cryptography as it can represent a Galois Field(4) quantum system by the basis states $|0\rangle$, $|1\rangle$, $|2\rangle$ and $|3\rangle$. The unit of information is called a *qudit* which is characterized by a wave function $|\psi\rangle$ [1,2] expressed as a linear superposition of basis states. Multi-valued quantum algebra comprises the rules for a set of basic logic operations that can be performed on qudits. While in [3] the structure of a multi-valued logic gate is proposed which is experimentally feasible with a linear ion trap scheme for quantum computing; this approach can produce large dimensional circuits. A universal architecture for multi-valued reversible logic is given in [4], but quantum realization of the circuits thus obtained is not apparent. The universality of n-qudit gates is presented in [5], but no algorithms for synthesis were given. Al-Rabedi et al. proposed in [6] the minimization technique for multi-valued quantum Galois field sum of products (QGFSOP). Quaternary logic is one of the promising multi-valued quantum logic systems. The binary logic functions can be expressed by grouping 2-bits together into equivalent quaternary value [7]. This theoretically reduces the total volume of the physical devices needed to approximately $1/log_2^4$, i.e. $1/2$ the volume needed for binary system [7].

The realization of a given quaternary quantum function as a quantum circuit requires a set of gates for the quaternary logic operations. In [8], the realization of quaternary Feynman and Toffoli gates using 1-qudit and 2-qudit quaternary

H. Rahaman et al. (Eds.): VDAT 2012, LNCS 7373, pp. 270–280, 2012.

Muthukrishnan-Stroud gates (M-S Gate)[3] are illustrated. The QGFSOP expressions can be realized by using these Feynman and Toffoli gates [8]. The method of synthesizing incompletely specified multi-output quaternary function using quaternary 1-qudit gates and multi-qudit controlled gates has been proposed in [9]. But this synthesis method is not applicable for any arbitrary quaternary functions. In [10], a heuristic alogorithm is proposed for minimization of a QGFSOP expression for multi-output quaternary logic functions using a Quaternary Galois Field Decission Diagram (QGFDD). But no quantum gate level implementation was provided. In this paper, our specific contributions are as follows:

- new projection operation for synthesizing quaternary logic functions;
- new quaternary logic gates, namely Generalized Quaternary Gate (GQG), permutative quaternary Controlled Cyclic Shift gate (C^2CS) and Modulo4 addition gate;
- new simplification rules for reduction in gate count and circuit levels for multivalued quantum circuits.

The rest of the paper is organized as follows. We provide the preliminary concepts of multivalued quantum computing in section 1. We propose the qua- ternary algebra with a new projection operation in section 2. In section 3, we introduce some new quaternary logic gates. The proposed synthesis methodology along with its simplification rules are presented in section 4. The synthesis results for some example circuits and their comparison with related work are given in section 5. Concluding remarks appear in section 6.

2   Quaternary Algebra

A brief summary of the quaternary addition, multiplication and NOT operations as well as the quaternary projection operations L, J and (the new one) P are presented next.

2.1   GF(4) Arithmetic

Quaternary Galois field GF(4) is an algebraic structure consisting the set of elements Q={0, 1, 2, 3}. The addition (+) and multiplication (.) operations over GF(4) are shown in the Table 1.

Table 1. GF(4) Addition and Multiplication

+	0	1	2	3		.	0	1	2	3
0	0	1	2	3		0	0	0	0	0
1	1	0	3	2		1	0	1	2	3
2	2	3	0	1		2	0	2	3	1
3	3	2	1	0		3	0	3	1	2

2.2   Quaternary Logical NOT

The logical NOT in quaternary quantum system is defined as $NOT(a) = a + 1$, where $'+'$ denotes the modulo 4 addition, and $a = \{0, 1, 2, 3\}$.

2.3   Quaternary Projection Operations L, J and P

We present nine projection operations, grouped into three types L_i, J_i, and P_i, where $i = \{0, 1, 2, 3\}$. While L_i and J_i types were defined earlier [11,12] as

$L_i(a) = 1$ if $a = i$ and 0 otherwise, and $J_i(a) = 2$ if $a = i$ and 0 otherwise.

We introduce the new P_i type operations, which are defined as

$P_i(a) = 3$ if $a = i$ and $a = 0$ otherwise.

Table 2 presents the truth tables for L_i, J_i, and P_i types of operators as well as for the derived operators L'_i, J'_i and P'_i. The L_i, J_i and P_i operations are commutative, associative and distributive over AND and OR logic.

Table 2. Truth table of projection operations L_i, L'_i, J_i, J'_i, P_i, P'_i

a	0	1	2	3	a	0	1	2	3	a	0	1	2	3	a	0	1	2	3
$L_0(a)$	1	0	0	0	$J_2(a)$	0	0	2	0	$L'_0(a)$	0	1	1	1	$J'_2(a)$	2	2	0	2
$L_1(a)$	0	1	0	0	$J_3(a)$	0	0	0	2	$L'_1(a)$	1	0	1	1	$J'_3(a)$	2	2	2	0
$L_2(a)$	0	0	1	0	$P_0(a)$	3	0	0	0	$L'_2(a)$	1	1	0	1	$P'_0(a)$	0	3	3	3
$L_3(a)$	0	0	0	1	$P_1(a)$	0	3	0	0	$L'_3(a)$	1	1	1	0	$P'_1(a)$	3	0	3	3
$J_0(a)$	2	0	0	0	$P_2(a)$	0	0	3	0	$J'_0(a)$	0	2	2	2	$P'_2(a)$	3	3	0	3
$J_1(a)$	0	2	0	0	$P_3(a)$	0	0	0	3	$J'_1(a)$	2	0	2	2	$P'_3(a)$	3	3	3	0

3   Quaternary Logic Gates

The definitions of the existing quaternary logic gates as well as a few newly introduced quaternary logic gates are provided below. We also show the implementation of the newly proposed gates using basic quantum ternary operations.

3.1   Quaternary Feynman, Quaternary Toffoli, MAX and MIN Gates

The 2-qudit Quaternary Feynman gate [8] is defined as:

Feynman(A, B) = $A + B$, where $'+'$ operator is addition over GF(4)(Figure 1.a).

The quaternary 3-qudit Toffoli gate [8], shown in Figure 1.b is defined as:

Toffoli(A, B, C) = $A.B + C$, where A and B are the control inputs and C the target input, $'+'$ and $'.'$ operators are addition and multiplication over GF(4).

We use the quaternary MAX and MIN gates [13] respectively to replace the OR and the AND gates. These two gates are defined as

$$\text{MAX}(A_1, A_2, .., A_n, B) = \begin{cases} A_i \text{ if } A_i \geq A_j,\ i \neq j \text{ and } A_i \geq B; \\ B \text{ if } \forall i, B \geq A_i; \end{cases}$$

$$\text{MIN}(A_1, A_2, ...A_n, B) = \begin{cases} A_i \text{ if } A_i \leq A_j,\ i \neq j \text{ and } A_i \leq B; \\ B \text{ if } \forall i, B \leq A_i; \end{cases}$$

where $i = \{1, 2, 3...n\}$ (Figures 2.a, 2.b). The quaternary Feynman and Toffoli gates can be realized using quaternary M-S gates [7,8], defined as (Figure 2.c)

M-S$(A, B) = Z$ operation on B if $A = 3$, otherwise B, where Z is one of the 24 shift operations [10] shown in Table 3.

Table 3. Shift Operations over GF(4) [10]

Symbol	Operation	Symbol	Operation	Symbol	Operation	Symbol	Operation
x^{+0}	$x = x$	x^{021}	$x = 2x + 2$	x^{23}	$x = x^2$	x^{0231}	$x = 2x^2 + 2$
x^{+1}	$x = x + 1$	x^{032}	$x = 2x + 3$	x^{01}	$x = x^2 + 1$	x^{03}	$x = 2x^2 + 3$
x^{+2}	$x = x + 2$	x^{132}	$x = 3x$	x^{0213}	$x = x^2 + 2$	x^{13}	$x = 3x^2$
x^{+3}	$x = x + 3$	x^{012}	$x = 3x + 1$	x^{0312}	$x = x^2 + 3$	x^{0123}	$x = 3x^2 + 1$
x^{123}	$x = 2x$	x^{023}	$x = 3x + 2$	x^{12}	$x = 2x^2$	x^{02}	$x = 3x^2 + 2$
x^{013}	$x = 2x + 1$	x^{031}	$x = 3x + 3$	x^{0132}	$x = 2x^2 + 1$	x^{0321}	$x = 3x^2 + 3$

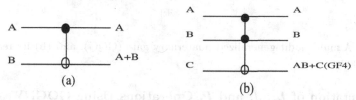

Fig. 1. (a) 2-qudit Quaternary Feynman gate (b) 3-qudit quaternary Toffoli gate

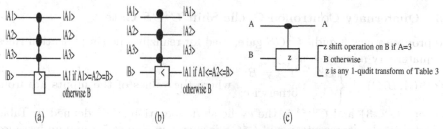

Fig. 2. (a) Quaternary MAX gate, (b) Quaternary MIN gate, (c) Quaternary M-S gate

3.2   Generalized Quaternary Gate

A new generalized quaternary gate (GQG) is required to realize the 24 shift operations [10] given in the Table 3. It is a multi-qudit gate shown in Figure 3.a. The controlling input of GQG can be used to select the 1-qudit shift operation on the target input. The GQG is formally defined as

$$GQG(A_1, A_2, .., A_n, B) = \begin{cases} B \text{ shift } X & \text{if } A_1, A_2, .., A_n = 0; \\ B \text{ shift } Y & \text{if } A_1, A_2, .., A_n = 1; \\ B \text{ shift } Z & \text{if } A_1, A_2, .., A_n = 2; \\ B \text{ shift } W & \text{if } A_1, A_2, .., A_n = 3; \\ B & \text{otherwise;} \end{cases}$$

The realization of a GQG gate using quaternary M-S gates, is shown in Figure 3.b.

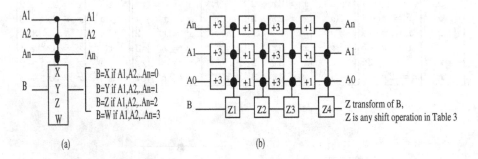

(a)   (b)

Fig. 3. (a) A multi-qudit generalized quaternary gate (GQG), and (b) its realization using M-S gates

Implementation of L_i, J_i and P_i Operations Using GQG. We can implement the L_i, J_i and P_i operations by using a GQG, as shown in Figures 4.a, 4.b and 4.c respectively. For L_i, J_i and P_i type operations, we set GQG(a,1), GQG(a,2) and GQG(a,3) respectively.

3.3   Quaternary Controlled Cyclic Shift C^2CS Gate

We propose a new 3-qudit C^2CS gate, used for realizing the simplification rules for quaternary minterms, as

$$C^2CS(A, B, C) = \begin{cases} C^{0123} & \text{if } A \neq B; \\ C & \text{otherwise;} \end{cases}$$ where the values of the inputs are from

the set $\{1, 2, 3\}$ and C^{0123} is the cyclic shift operation x^{0123} defined in Table 3. The symbolic representation of C^2CS is shown in Figure 5.a and an instance of this gate is shown in Figure 5.b, where x^{0123} shift operation is applied on C if $A = 1$, $B = 3$ or $A = 3$, $B = 1$. The realization of the C^2CS gate using M-S gates is shown in Figure 6.

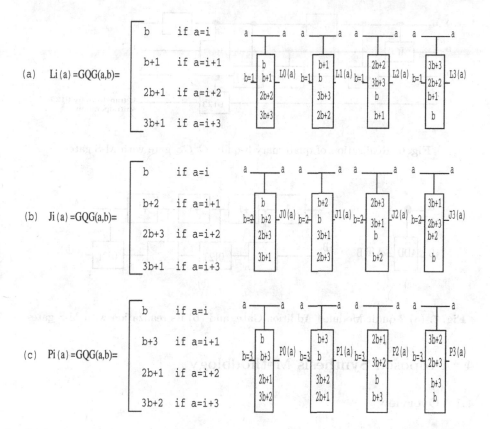

Fig. 4. GQG based realization of quaternary projection operations: (a)L_i, (b)J_i and (c)P_i

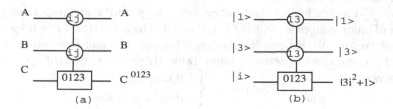

Fig. 5. (a) Quaternary 3-qudit C^2CS gate, and (b) an instance of it

3.4   A New Modulo4 Addition Gate

We introduce the new 2-qudit quaternary Modulo4 Addition gate as: ADD(A, B)= $A \oplus B$, where $\oplus$ represent the modulo 4 addition. This gate can be used as a template for simplification of adder circuits. The symbolic representation of ADD gate is shown in Figure 7.a and the realization using quaternary M-S gate is shown in Figure 7.b

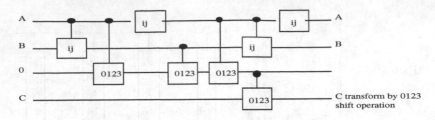

Fig. 6. Realization of quaternary 3-qudit C^2CS gate with M-S gates

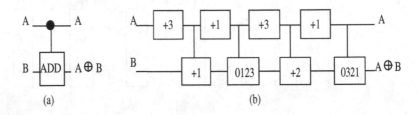

Fig. 7. (a) 2-qudit Modulo4 Addition Gate, and (b) its realization with M-S gates

4   Proposed Synthesis Methodology

4.1   Overview

Consider an m-variable quaternary quantum logic function

$f(a_1, a_2, \ldots, a_m) = \sum_{i=0}^{n}(\text{minterms for } one\,)_i + \sum_{j=0}^{p}(\text{minterms for } two)_j + \sum_{k=0}^{s}(\text{minterms for } three)_k,$

where $\sum$ implies logical quaternary OR, n, p and s are respectively the number of input vectors for which f is 1, 2 and 3. Thus, f is 0 for $(4^m - n - p - s)$ of the input vectors. We express the minterms for *one*, *two* and *three* using the L_i, J_i and P_i operations respectively. From Table II, we can state that $\prod_{i=1}^{m} L_0(a_i)$

$= \begin{cases} 1 \ if \ \forall i \ a_i = 0; \\ 0 \ if \ \exists \ i \ a_i = 1, \ 2 \ or \ 3; \end{cases} \quad \prod_{i=1}^{m} L_1(a_i) = \begin{cases} 1 \ if \ \forall i \ a_i = 1; \\ 0 \ if \ \exists \ i \ a_i = 0, \ 2 \ or \ 3; \end{cases}$

$\prod_{i=1}^{m} L_2(a_i) = \begin{cases} 1 \ if \ \forall i \ a_i = 2; \\ 0 \ if \ \exists \ i \ a_i = 0, \ 1 \ or \ 3; \end{cases} \quad \prod_{i=1}^{m} L_3(a_i) = \begin{cases} 1 \ if \ \forall i \ a_i = 3; \\ 0 \ if \ \exists \ i \ a_i = 0, \ 1 \ or \ 2; \end{cases}$

$\prod_{i,p,k,s=1}^{m} L_0(a_i).L_1(a_p).L_2(a_k).L_3(a_s) = \begin{cases} 1 \ if \ \forall i, p, k, s \ a_i = 0, \ a_p = 1, \ a_k = 2, \ a_s = 3; \\ 0 \ if \ \exists \ i, \ p, \ k, \ s \ a_i = 1, \ 2 \ or \ 3, \ a_p = 0, \ 2 \ or \ 3, ; \\ a_k = 0, \ 1 \ or \ 2, \ a_s = 0, \ 1 \ or \ 2; \end{cases}$

where $i + p + k + s = m$.

Hence, the minterms for which $f = 1$ are

1. $\prod_{i=1}^{m} L_0(a_i = 0)$, 2. $\prod_{i=1}^{m} L_1(a_i = 1)$, 3. $\prod_{i=1}^{m} L_2(a_i = 2)$,
4. $\prod_{i=1}^{m} L_3(a_i = 3)$, 5. $\prod_{i,p,k,s=1}^{m} L_0(a_i = 0).L_1(a_p = 1).L_2(a_k = 2).L_3(a_s = 3)$.

Similarly from Table 2, the minterms for which $f = 2$ are

1. $\prod_{i=1}^{m} J_0(a_i = 0)$, 2. $\prod_{i=1}^{m} J_1(a_i = 1)$, 3. $\prod_{i=1}^{m} J_2(a_i = 2)$,
4. $\prod_{i=1}^{m} J_3(a_i = 3)$, 5. $\prod_{i,p,k,s=1}^{m} J_0(a_i = 0).J_1(a_p = 1).J_2(a_k = 2).J_3(a_s = 3)$.

The minterms for which $f = 3$ are

1. $\prod_{i=1}^{m} P_0(a_i = 0)$, 2. $\prod_{i=1}^{m} P_1(a_i = 1)$, 3. $\prod_{i=1}^{m} P_2(a_i = 2)$,
4. $\prod_{i=1}^{m} P_3(a_i = 3)$, 5. $\prod_{i,p,k,s=1}^{m} P_0(a_i = 0).P_1(a_p = 1).P_2(a_k = 2).P_3(a_s = 3)$.

4.2 Simplification Rules

Next, we define six simplification rules derived from Table 2

1. $L_i(a).0 = 0$, $J_i(a).0 = 0$ and $P_i(a).0 = 0$
2. $L_i(a).1 = L_i(a)$, $J_i(a).2 = J_i(a)$ and $P_i(a).3 = P_i(a)$
3. $L_i(a) + 0 = L_i(a)$, $J_i(a) + 0 = J_i(a)$ and $P_i(a) + 0 = P_i(a)$
4. $L_i(a) + 1 = 1$, $J_i(a) + 2 = 2$ and $P_i(a) + 3 = 3$
5. $L_i(a).L_i'(a) = 0$, $J_i(a).J_i'(a) = 0$ and $P_i(a).P_i'(a) = 0$
6. $L_i(a) + L_i'(a) = 1$, $J_i(a) + J_i'(a) = 2$ and $P_i(a) + P_i'(a) = 3$

Simplification Rules for Reducing Ancilla Qudits. For gate level realization of L_i, J_i, and P_i we need an ancilla qudit for each of them. Further, to synthesize an m-variable quaternary function with n minterms specified in our proposed methodology, we have maximum of $n * m$ ancilla qudits. However, we can reduce the number of ancilla qudits by the following three simplification rules based on the new quaternary C^2CS gate and Table 2:

7. $L_i(a)L_j(b) + L_j(a)L_i(b) = C^2CS(a_{ij}, b_{ij}, 0)$, $J_i(a)J_j(b) + J_j(a)J_i(b) = C^2CS$
$(a_{ij}, b_{ij}, 1)$ and $P_i(a)P_j(b) + P_j(a)P_i(b) = C^2CS(a_{ij}, b_{ij}, 2)$ Where $i, j = \{1, 2, 3\}$

8. $L_i(a).L_i(a) = L_i(a)$, $J_i(a).J_i(a) = J_i(a)$ and $P_i(a).P_i(a) = P_i(a)$

9. $L_i(a_1)L_i(a_2)..L_i(a_n) = L_i(a_1, a_2, .., a_n)$, $J_i(a_1)J_i(a_2)..J_i(a_n) = J_i(a_1, a_2, .., a_n)$, and $P_i(a_1)P_i(a_2)..P_i(a_n) = P_i(a_1, a_2, .., a_n)$, $i = \{0, 1, 2, 3\}$.

5 Synthesis of Quaternary Functions

5.1 2-qudit Quaternary Arbitrary Function

The truth table for the 2-qudit arbitrary function $f(a, b)$ is given in Table 4.

Table 4. Truth table of 2-qudit $f(a, b)$

a , b	00	01	02	03	10	11	12	13	20	21	22	23	30	31	32	33
$f(a,b)$	0	3	1	2	3	3	2	0	1	2	1	3	2	1	3	2

We re-write the function $f(a, b)$ using our proposed methodology as

$f(a, b) = L_0(a)L_2(b) + L_2(a)L_0(b) + L_2(a)L_2(b) + L_3(a)L_1(b) + J_0(a)J_3(b) + J_1(a)J_2(b) + J_2(a)J_1(b) + J_3(a)J_0(b) + +J_3(a)J_3(b)P_0(a)P_1(b) + P_1(a)P_0(b) + P_1(a)P_1(b) + P_2(a)P_3(b)+P_3(a)P_2(b)$

By using simplification rules 7 and 9, we get

$f(a,b)=C^2CS(a_{02}, b_{02}, 0) + L_2(a, b) + L_3(a)L_1(b) + C^2CS(a_{03}, b_{03}, 1) + C^2CS(a_{12}, b_{12}, 1) + J_3(a, b) + C^2CS(a_{10}, b_{10}, 2) + C^2CS(a_{23}, b_{23}, 0) + P_1(a, b)$

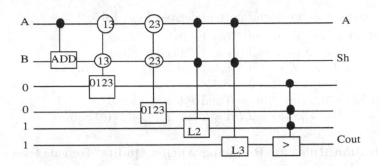

Fig. 8. Quaternary 2-qudit Half Adder by our synthesis method

5.2 Quaternary Adder

We synthesize the 2-qudit half and full adder circuits using our proposed methodology and these circuits are simplified with the use of Modulo4 Addition gate. But the details are not provided due to limitation of space. The gate level implementation of 2-qudit half and full adder are shown in Figure 8 and 9 respectively.

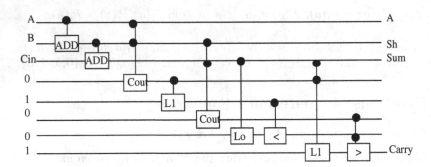

Fig. 9. Quaternary 2-qudit Full Adder by our synthesis method

5.3 Comparison of Results

The quantum cost of the half and the full adder circuits, as shown in Figures 10 and 11, and of the benchmark circuits such as *sum2*, *rd53*, *rd73*, *xor5* are evaluated in terms of the number of M-S gates used. The number of M-S gates required to realize a 2-qudit Feynman gate, a 3-qudit Toffoli, MAX and MIN gates are 5, 17, 6, 6 respectively [7,13]. To realize the new GQG, C^2CS, ADD gates we need 8 M-S gates for each of them. The M-S gate count cost comparison of our circuits with that in [14] are given in Table 6. While the second column of the table indicates the maximum number of ancilla qudits required to synthesize the above mentioned circuits, the third column shows the number of ancilla qudits required after using our simplification rules in Section 4.2. The columns 4, 5 and 6 establish that although our design has a small increase in cost for the circuits $rd53$, $rd73$, $xor5$, the results for the 2-qudit quaternary half and full adder shows that there is more than 50% reduction in the M-S gate count cost compared to [14].

Table 5. Comparison of Quantum cost by our method vs. [14]

Circuit	maximum ancilla qudits	Reduced ancilla qudits	# Levels Ours	# Levels [14]	Total Cost Ours	Total Cost [14]
Half Adder	36	6	6	23	46	114
Full Adder	120	17	17	40	128	304
Sum2	24	0	4	-	8	-
mul2	16	5	5	-	40	-
ham3	135	95	25	-	135	-
rd53	275	245	15	-	120	-
rd73	475	435	35	-	280	-
xor5	150	120	7	-	56	-

6 Conclusion

In this paper, we have proposed a methodology for logic synthesis of quaternary quantum circuits. We have defined a minterm based approach of expressing a quaternary logic function using L_i, J_i and P_i operations. We have also stated the simplification rules for the method. Quaternary half adder, full adder and some benchmark circuits synthesized by our method, use fewer ternary quantum gates and hence reduce quantum realization cost compared to earlier method in [14]. While the number of levels is fewer in our synthesis, the number of ancilla bits is higher. A synthesis methodology for reduction of the number of ancilla qudits is being investigated.

References

1. Nielsen, M.A., Chuang, I.L.: Quantum Computation and Quantum Information. Cambridge University Press (2002)
2. Ekert, A., Zeilinger, A.: The physics of quantum information, pp. 1–14. Springer, Berlin (2002)
3. Muthukrishnan, A., Stroud Jr., C.R.: Multi-Valued Logic Gates for Quantum Computation. Phys. Rev. A62, 0523091-8 (2000)
4. Picton, P.: A Universal Architecture for Multiple-Valued Reversible Logic. Multiple-Valued Logic - An International Journal 5, 27–37 (2000)

5. Brylinski, J.L., Brylinski, R.: Universal Quantum Gates. To appear in Mathematics of Quantum Computation. CRC Press (2002), LANL e-print quant-ph/010862
6. Perkowski, M., Al-Rabadi, A., Kerntopf, P., Mishchenko, A., Chrzanowska-Jeske, M.: Three-Dimensional Realization of Multivalued Functions Using Reversible Logic. In: Booklet of 10th Int. Workshop on Post-Binary Ultra-Large-Scale Integration Systems (ULSI), Warsaw, Poland, pp. 47–53 (May 2001)
7. Khan, M.M.M., Biswas, A.K., Chowdhury, S., Tanzid, M., Mohsin, K.M., Hasan, M., Khan, A.I.: Quantum realization of some quaternary circuits. In: TENCON 2008 - 2008 IEEE Region 10 Conference, November 19-21, pp. 1–5 (2008)
8. Khan, M.H.A.: Quantum Realization of Quaternary Feynman and Toffoli Gates. In: International Conference on Electrical and Computer Engineering, ICECE 2006, December 19-21, pp. 157–160 (2006)
9. Khan, M.H.A.: Synthesis of incompletely specified multi-output quaternary function using quaternary quantum gates. In: 10th International Conference on Computer and Information Technology, ICCIT 2007, December 27-29, pp. 1–6 (2007)
10. Khan, M.H.A., Siddika, N.K., Perkowski, M.A.: Minimization of Quaternary Galois Field Sum of Products Expression for Multi-Output Quaternary Logic Function Using Quaternary Galois Field Decision Diagram. In: 38th International Symposium on Multiple Valued Logic, ISMVL 2008, May 22-24, pp. 125–130 (2008)
11. Mandal, S.B., Chakrabarti, A., Sur-Kolay, S.: Synthesis Technique for Ternary Quantum Logic. In: 41th International Symposium on Multiple-Valued Logic, Tuusula, pp. 218–223 (2011)
12. Herrmann, R.L.: Selection and implementation of a ternary switching algebra. In: Spring Joint Computer Conference, Atlantic City, pp. 283–290 (1968)
13. Giesecke, N., Kim, D.H., Hossain, S., Perkowski, M.: Search for Universal Ternary Quantum Gate Sets with Exact Minimum Costs. In: Proceedings of RM Symposium, Oslo, May 16 (2007)
14. Khan, M.H.A.: A recursive method for synthesizing quantum/reversible quaternary parallel adder/subtractor with look-ahead carry. Journal of Systems Architecture 54, 1113–1121 (2008)

On the Compact Designs of Low Power Reversible Decoders and Sequential Circuits

Lafifa Jamal[1], Md. Masbaul Alam Polash[1],
M.A. Mottalib[2], and Hafiz Md. Hasan Babu[1,*]

[1] Dept. of Computer Science and Engineering, University of Dhaka, Dhaka-1000, Bangladesh
{lafifa,polash_csedu}@yahoo.com, hafizbabu@hotmail.com
[2] Dept. of CIT, Islamic University of Technology, Gazipur, Bangladesh
mottalib@iut-dhaka.edu

Abstract. Conventional logic dissipates more power by losing bits of information whereas reversibility recovers bit loss from the unique input-output mapping. Reversible Computation has high promise of low power consumption. In this paper, we have proposed a new 4x4 reversible gate (namely BJ gate) which is used to design reversible J-K flip-flop. We have also proposed the design of low power reversible decoders, reversible sequence counter and reversible instruction register. These circuits are analyzed with the existing ones. The comparative results show that the proposed designs of reversible decoders and sequential circuits outperform the existing designs in terms of numbers of gates, garbage outputs and quantum cost. Some lower bounds on the number of gates and garbage outputs of the proposed decoder circuits have also been proposed.

Keywords: Reversible Logic, Reversible Decoder, Reversible Sequence Counter, Reversible Instruction Register, Quantum Cost, Low Power Circuit.

1 Introduction

Energy loss is a very important issue in modern VLSI designs. Though the improvement in higher-level integration and the advancement of new fabrication processes have significantly reduced the heat loss over the last decades, physical limit exists in the reduction of heat. According to Landauer [1], in logic computation, every bit of information loss generates $kT\ln2$ joules of heat energy, where k is Boltzmann's constant of 1.38×10^{-23} J/K and T is the absolute temperature of the environment in which the operation has been performed. Reversible circuits are fundamentally different from traditional irreversible ones. In reversible logic, no information is lost, i.e., the circuit that does not lose information is reversible. Bennett [2] showed that zero energy dissipation would be possible if the network consists of reversible gates only. Thus reversibility will be an essential property for the future circuit design.

Synthesis of reversible logic is more complicated than irreversible one as it imposes many design constraints [3]. A reversible circuit therefore should have the

---

* Corresponding author.

H. Rahaman et al. (Eds.): VDAT 2012, LNCS 7373, pp. 281–288, 2012.
© Springer-Verlag Berlin Heidelberg 2012

following attributes [4]: garbage output and number of reversible gates should be as minimal as possible, input lines that are either 0 or 1, known as constant input, should be as minimal as possible.

In this paper, we have proposed a new 4×4 reversible gate (namely BJ gate) and different reversible circuits with improvement in terms of cost comparing with the existing designs. The different circuits are reversible 2-to-4 decoder, 3-to-8 decoder, J-K flip-flop, sequence counter and instruction register.

2   Basic Definitions and Literature Overview

This section describes basic definitions and ideas related to reversible logic.

2.1   Reversible Gate

A Reversible Gate is a k-input, k-output (denoted by $k×k$) circuit that produces a unique output pattern [5, 6] for each possible input pattern. Reversible Gate is a circuit in which the number of inputs and outputs is equal and there is a one-to-one correspondence between the vector of inputs and outputs [6].

Let the input vector be I_v, output vector be O_v and they are defined as follows, $I_v = (I_i, I_{i+1}, I_{i+2}, \ldots, I_{k-1}, I_k)$ and $O_v = (O_i, O_{i+1}, O_{i+2}, \ldots, O_{k-1}, O_k)$. For each particular i, there exists the relationship $I_v \leftrightarrow O_v$.

2.2   Garbage Output

Garbage is the number of outputs added to make an n-input k-output Boolean function $((n, k)$ function) reversible. In other sense, a reversible logic gate has an equal number of inputs and outputs $(k×k)$ and all the outputs are not expected. Some of the outputs should be considered to make the circuit reversible and those unwanted outputs are known as garbage outputs [7].

To perform Ex-OR between two inputs, we can use the Feynman gate [8], but in that case, one extra output will be generated as well, which is the garbage output in this regard (shown in Fig. 1).

2.3   Feynman Gate, Fredkin Gate and HNF Gate

The input vector, I_v and output vector, O_v for 2×2 Feynman Gate (FG) [8] is defined as follows: $I_v = (A, B)$ and $O_v = (P = A, Q = A \oplus B)$. The block diagram for 2×2 Feynman gate is shown in Fig. 1.

The input vector, I_v and output vector, O_v for 3×3 Fredkin Gate (FRG) [9] is defined as follows: $I_v = (A, B, C)$ and $O_v = (P = A, Q = A'B \oplus AC, R = AB \oplus A'C)$. The block diagram for 3×3 Fredkin gate is shown in Fig. 2.

The input vector, I_v and output vector, O_v for 4×4 HNF Gate [10] is defined as follows: $I_v = (A, B, C, D)$ and $O_v = (P = A, Q = A \oplus C, R = B, S = B \oplus D)$. The block diagram for 4×4 HNF gate is shown in Fig. 3.

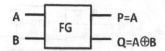

Fig. 1. Block Diagram of a 2×2 Feynman Gate

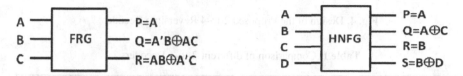

Fig. 2. Block Diagram of a 3×3 Fredkin Gate   **Fig. 3.** Block Diagram of a 4×4 HNF Gate

2.4 Quantum Cost

The quantum cost of a circuit is the minimum number of 2×2 unitary gates to represent the circuit keeping the output unchanged. The quantum cost of a 1×1 gate is zero and that of any 2×2 gate is the same, which is one [11, 12]. The quantum costs of FG and FRG are one and five respectively [11, 12].

2.5 Delay

According to [13], delay is defined as follows:

The delay of a logic circuit is the maximum number of gates in a path from any input line to any output line. This definition is based on the following assumptions:

- Each gate performs computation in one unit time.
- All inputs to the circuit are available before the computation begins.

The delay of the circuit of Fig. 1 is obviously one, as it is the only gate in any path from input to output.

3   Proposed Design of Different Reversible Circuits

In this section, we have proposed the designs of reversible 2-to-4 decoder, 3-to-8 decoder, 4×4 BJ gate, J-K flip-flop, sequence counter and instruction register. We have also compared the circuits with the existing designs.

3.1   Reversible 2-to-4 Decoder

A reversible 2-to-4 Decoder has been designed using one Feynman gate and two Fredkin gates, shown in Fig. 4. This optimized design produces one garbage bit. The performance comparison of different decoders has been shown in Table 1.

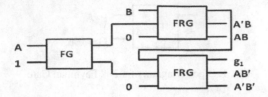

Fig. 4. Design of the Proposed 2-to-4 Reversible Decoder

Table 1. Comparison of different 2-to-4 Decoders

2-to-4 Decoder	No. of Gates	Garbage Output	Delay	Quantum Cost
Proposed Method	3	1	3	11
Existing design[14]	4	2	4	14

3.2   Reversible 3-to-8 Decoder

A reversible 3-to-8 Decoder has been designed using one 2-to-4 reversible decoder and four Fredkin gates as shown in Fig.5. This proposed design produces two garbage bits. The performance comparison of different 3-to-8 decoders has been shown in Table 2.

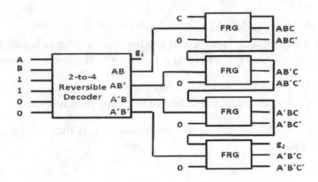

Fig. 5. Design of the Proposed 3-to-8 Reversible Decoder

Table 2. Comparison of different 3-to-8 Decoders

3-to-8 Decoder	No. of Gates	Garbage Output	Delay	Quantum Cost
Proposed Method	7	2	7	31
Existing design[14]	11	6	11	38

Lemma 1: An n-to-2^n reversible decoder can be realized by at least 2^n-1 gates.

Proof: According to Fig. 4, a 2-to-4 ($n=2$) decoder can be realized by $3(=2^2-1)$ reversible gates (1 FG and 2 FRGs). Similarly, a 3-to-8 ($n=3$) decoder requires one 2-to-4

decoder and 2^2 Fredkin gates (shown in Fig. 5). So, the total number of reversible gates required for 3-to-8 decoder is $(2^2-1)+2^2=7(=2^3-1)$. Hence an n-to-2^n decoder can be realized by at least 2^n-1 reversible gates.

Lemma 2: An n-to-2^n reversible decoder generates at least n-1 garbage outputs.

Proof: According to Fig. 4, a 2-to-4 (n=2) decoder generates 1 garbage outputs. Similarly, a 3-to-8 (n=3) decoder generates 2 garbage outputs and so on. Hence an n-to-2^n decoder generates at least n-1 garbage outputs.

3.3   Proposed BJ Gate

In this section, a new 4×4 reversible gate, namely BJ gate, is proposed (shown in Fig. 6). The truth table of the proposed gate is shown in Table 3. From the truth table, it can be established that there is a one-to-one correspondence between input and output vector.

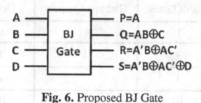

Fig. 6. Proposed BJ Gate

Table 3. Truth table of the proposed gate

Input				Output			
A	B	C	D	A	$AB \oplus C$	$A'B \oplus AC'$	$A'B \oplus AC' \oplus D$
0	0	0	0	0	0	0	0
0	0	0	1	0	0	0	1
0	0	1	0	0	1	0	0
0	0	1	1	0	1	0	1
0	1	0	0	0	0	1	1
0	1	0	1	0	0	1	0
0	1	1	0	0	1	1	1
0	1	1	1	0	1	1	0
1	0	0	0	1	0	1	1
1	0	0	1	1	0	1	0
1	0	1	0	1	1	0	0
1	0	1	1	1	1	0	1
1	1	0	0	1	1	1	1
1	1	0	1	1	1	1	0
1	1	1	0	1	0	0	0
1	1	1	1	1	0	0	1

The proposed BJ gate can be used as universal gate, which is shown in Fig. 7. In this paper, this gate is used to design a reversible J-K FF (shown in Fig. 8) to minimize the number of gates and garbage outputs. The improvement of the J-K FFs is highlighted in Table 4.

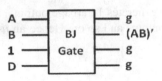
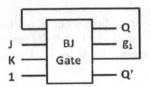

Fig. 7. Proposed BJ Gate as Universal Gate   **Fig. 8.** Reversible J-K FF

Table 4. Comparison of different J-K FFs

J-K FF	No. of Gates	Garbage Outputs	Delay	Quantum Cost
Proposed Method	1	1	1	12
Existing design[15]	3	3	3	14
Existing design[16]	4	3	4	18
Existing design[17]	10	12	10	30

3.4   Reversible Sequence Counter

A reversible sequence counter can be designed using four J-K FFs, which produces four garbage bits (shown in Fig. 9). Table 5 shows the performance of the proposed reversible sequence counter using the proposed J-K FF and existing JK-FFs [15, 16, 17].

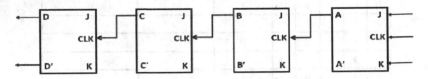

Fig. 9. Proposed Design of Reversible Sequence Counter

Table 5. Comparison of different counters

Sequence Counter	No. of gates	Garbage Outputs	Delay	Quantum Cost
This work	4	4	4	48
Existing design[15]	12	12	12	56
Existing design[16]	16	12	16	72
Existing design[17]	40	48	40	120

3.5   Reversible Instruction Register

A reversible Instruction Register has been designed using four HNF gates and four J-K FFs, which produces five garbage bits (shown in Fig. 10). Table 6 shows the performance of different IRs using the proposed J-K FF and existing JK-FFs [15, 16, 17].

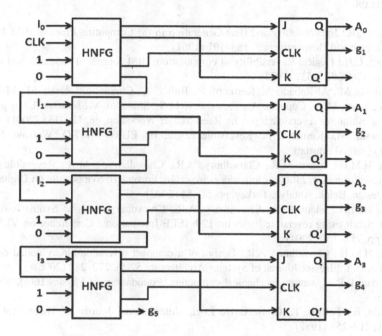

Fig. 10. Proposed Reversible Design of Instruction Register

Table 6. Comparison of different instruction registers

Instruction Register	No. of gates	Garbage Outputs	Delay	Quantum Cost
Proposed Method	8	5	8	64
Existing design[15]	16	13	16	64
Existing design[16]	20	13	20	80
Existing design[17]	44	49	44	128

4   Conclusions

This paper is mainly focused on the design of reversible decoders and sequential circuits. A new reversible BJ gate has been proposed here. This gate is used to design the sequential circuits. It is demonstrated that the proposed designs of reversible decoders and sequential circuits are highly optimized in terms of numbers of reversible gates, garbage outputs and quantum cost than the existing designs. Moreover, the lower bounds on the number of gates and number of garbage outputs have been established for the proposed decoder circuits. The proposed circuits will be useful for implementing the reversible control unit, quantum computers, reconfigurable computer [8, 9] etc.

References

1. Landauer, R.: Irreversibility and Heat Generation in the Computing Process. IBM Journal of Research and Development 5, 183–191 (1961)
2. Bennett, C.H.: Logical Reversibility of computation. IBM Journal of Research and Development 17(6), 525–532 (1973)
3. Perkowski, M., Al-Rabadi, A., Kerntopf, P., Buller, A., Chrzanowskajeske, M., Mischenko, A., Khan, M.A., Coppola, A., Yanushkevich, S., Shmerko, V., Jozwiak, L.: A general decomposition for reversible logic. In: Reed-Muller Workshop, pp. 119–138 (2001)
4. Perkowski, M., Kerntopf, P.: Reversible Logic. In: EURO-MICRO, Warsaw, Poland (2001) (invited tutorial)
5. Babu, H.M.H., Islam, M.R., Chowdhury, A.R., Chowdhury, S.M.A.: Reversible Logic Synthesis for minimization of full-adder circuit. In: Euromicro Symposium on Digital System Design, Belek, Antalya, Turkey, pp. 50–54 (2003)
6. Babu, H.M.H., Islam, M.R., Chowdhury, A.R., Chowdhury, S.M.A.: Synthesis of full-adder circuit using reversible logic. In: 17th IEEE International Conference on VLSI Design, pp. 757–760 (2004)
7. Babu, H.M.H., Chowdhury, A.R.: Design of a compact reversible binary coded decimal adder circuit. Elsevier Journal of Systems Architecture 52(5), 272–282 (2006)
8. Feynman, R.P.: Quantum mechanical computers. Foundations of Physics 16(6), 507–531 (1986)
9. Fredkin, E., Toffoli, T.: Conservative Logic. International Journal of Theoretical Physics 21, 219–253 (1982)
10. Haghparast, M., Navi, K.: A Novel Reversible BCD Adder for Nanotechnology Based Systems. American Journal of Applied Sciences 5, 282–288 (2008)
11. Perkowski, M.: A hierarchical approach to computer-aided design of quantum circuits. In: 6th International Symposium on Representations and Methodology of Future Computing Technology, pp. 201–209 (2003)
12. Smolin, J., Divivcenzo, D.P.: Five two-qubit gates are sufficient to implement the quantum fredkin gate. Physical Review 53(4), 2855–2856 (1996)
13. Biswas, A.K., Hasan, M.M., Chowdhury, A.R., Babu, H.M.H.: Efficient Algorithms for Implementing Reversible Binary Coded Decimal Adders. Elsevier Journal of Microelectronics 39(12), 1693–1703 (2008)
14. Huda, N., Anwar, S., Jamal, L., Babu, H.M.H.: Design of a Reversible Random Access Memory. Dhaka University Journal of Applied Science and Engineering 2, 31–38 (2011)
15. Sayem, A.S.M., Ueda, M.: Optimization of reversible sequential circuits. Journal of Computing 2(6) (2010)
16. Thapliyal, H., Ranganathan, N.: Design of Reversible Latches Optimized for Quantum Cost, Delay and Garbage Outputs. In: 23rd International Conference on VLSI Design, pp. 235–240 (2010)
17. Thapliyal, H., Srinivas, M.B., Zwolinski, M.: A beginning in the reversible logic synthesis of sequential circuits. In: Proc. the Military and Aerospace Programmable Logic Devices Intl. Conf., Washington (2005)

Delay Uncertainty in Single- and Multi-Wall Carbon Nanotube Interconnects

Debaprasad Das and Hafizur Rahaman

School of VLSI Technology, Bengal Engineering and Science University, Shibpur, India
dasdebaprasad@yahoo.co.in, rahaman_h@it.becs.ac.in

Abstract. Carbon nanotube (CNT) has become the promising candidate for replacing the traditional copper based interconnect systems in future VLSI technology nodes. This paper analyzes delay uncertainty due to crosstalk in the Single- and Multi-wall CNT bundle based interconnect systems. Results are compared with traditional copper based interconnect systems. It is shown that the average crosstalk induced delay is within 60.5% over normal interconnect delay for double MWCNT as compared to 76.6% for copper and 72-75.2% for SWCNT and MWCNT bundle based interconnects. The average delay uncertainty with respect to Cu interconnects for SWCNT bundle based interconnect is found to be 75.3% and 84.6% for densely and sparsely packed SWCNT bundles, respectively, whereas it is 84.3% for MWCNT bundle and 61.6% for double MWCNT based interconnects.

Keywords: Carbon Nanotube (CNT), Single-wall Carbon Nanotube (SWCNT), Double-wall Carbon Nanotube (DWCNT), Multi-wall Carbon Nanotube (MWCNT), Crosstalk delay, Very Large Scale Integration (VLSI).

1   Introduction

In the recent past there has been a tremendous amount of research in finding out an alternative to the traditional copper (Cu) based interconnect due to its susceptibility to electromigration, increased resistivity and crosstalk noise with the technology scaling. Carbon nanotubes (CNTs) have been regarded as possible replacement for the traditional Cu based interconnects in future technology nodes [1]. In this work we have investigated the delay uncertainty due to crosstalk in different form of CNT based interconnect systems. As the signal switching speed increases and the density of interconnect grows, the crosstalk phenomena due to the coupling capacitances between interconnects have become a major challenge to the physical designers. The crosstalk delay problem arises when both aggressor and victim nets switch simultaneously either in same or opposite directions.

Carbon nanotubes are cylinders made off rolled graphene sheets whose diameter is of the order of nanometer. CNTs exhibit excellent electrical, mechanical, and thermal properties. CNTs can be either metallic or semiconducting depending on their chirality [1]. While the semiconducting CNTs are being considered for nanoelectronic devices, the metallic CNTs are being considered for on-chip interconnects. CNTs are classified into single-wall (SWCNT) and multi-wall (MWCNT). For on-chip

H. Rahaman et al. (Eds.): VDAT 2012, LNCS 7373, pp. 289–299, 2012.
© Springer-Verlag Berlin Heidelberg 2012

interconnects, a bundle of SWCNTs, mixed SWCNT/MWCNT or only MWCNTs are of special interest due to their excellent electrical conductivity.

The equivalent circuit model of SWCNT is proposed by Burke in 2002 [2]. Since then a number of investigations have been carried out to explore the performance of the CNT based interconnect systems. It has been found that CNTs are better suited for long interconnects as compared to Cu wires [3-9]. The crosstalk effects in SWCNT and MWCNT bus architecture is analyzed in [10] by Rossi *et al.* Lei and Yin in [11] have investigated the temperature effects on crosstalk delay and noise in SWCNT and DWCNT interconnect. The work in [12] has investigated the crosstalk effects in both SWCNT and DWCNT bundles of dimension corresponding to the ITRS technology nodes by Shao-Ning Pu *et al.* A time and frequency domain model is proposed for crosstalk analysis in SWCNT bundle and MWCNT interconnects in [13–15] by D'Amore *et al.* Sun and Luo in [16] have proposed a statistical model for analyzing crosstalk noise in SWCNT based interconnect systems. Two SWCNTs are considered and crosstalk noise induced by the statistical variation of interconnect parameters due to process variation has been modeled in [16]. Chiariello *et al.* in [17] analyzes frequency dependent crosstalk noise in CNT bundle based interconnects considering CNT inductance and resistance. W. C. Chen *et al.* in [18] have investigated the crosstalk delay for SWCNT based interconnect systems considering three-line interconnect array. In [19] crosstalk overshoot/undershoot analysis is presented for SWCNT bundle based interconnects. Though a number of works have analyzed crosstalk in CNT based interconnect systems, none of the previous works analyzes delay uncertainty due to crosstalk in SWCNT bundle and MWCNT bundle based interconnect systems. Previous works have shown that delay through SWCNT bundle and MWCNT based interconnect is less as compared to traditional Cu based interconnects for intermediate and global wires. However, crosstalk may speedup or slowdown a net depending on the relative switching of aggressor and victim nets, which in turn introduces delay uncertainty. The motivation behind this study is to explore the impact of crosstalk on the delay uncertainty in SWCNT and MWCNT bundle based interconnects of dimension corresponding to a future (Year 2019, 16 nm) ITRS technology node.

The rest of the paper is organized as follows. Section 2 describes the CNT equivalent model. Section 3 presents the results of crosstalk delay analysis in different interconnects systems. The conclusions are drawn in Section 4.

2   Equivalent Circuit Model for CNT

This section presents the equivalent circuit modeling of SWCNT, SWCNT bundle, MWCNT, and MWCNT bundle based interconnect systems.

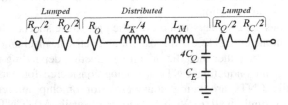

Fig. 1. Equivalent circuit of Single-Wall Carbon Nanotube (SWCNT)

2.1   Models for SWCNT

The electrical equivalent circuit model of an individual CNT as shown in Fig. 1 is proposed by Burke [2]. The resistance of a CNT is modeled by three parts (i) contact resistance (R_C), (ii) quantum (R_Q) resistance, and (iii) ohmic resistance (R_O). L_K and L_M are the kinetic and magnetic inductances and C_Q and C_E are quantum and electrostatic capacitances, respectively.

2.2   Models for SWCNT Bundle

Due to the large resistance of single SWCNT, a bundle of SWCNT is proposed for the interconnect. However, due to the lack of control on chirality a bundle consists of both metallic and semiconducting nanotubes (Fig. 2). Statistically, it has been found that 1/3 (P_m) [9] of the nanotubes are metallic and the rests are semiconducting. In this paper, a bundle with all metallic CNTs is termed as densely packed bundle, and a bundle with both metallic and semiconducting CNTs is termed as sparsely packed bundle. As the sparsely packed bundle may have metallic CNTs surrounded by semiconducting CNTs, we have modeled sparsely packed bundle considering larger inter-CNT spacing i.e., $x > d + \delta$.

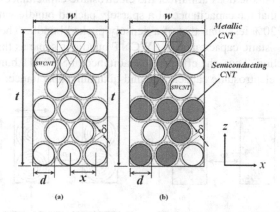

(a)   (b)

Fig. 2. Schematic of SWCNT bundle (a) all metallic (b) mixture of metallic and semiconducting

Resistance of CNT Bundle

The resistance of a CNT bundle of length l consisting of n_{CNT} SWCNTs is expressed as [12]

$$R_b = R_{CNT} / (P_m \cdot n_{CNT}) \tag{1}$$

where P_m is the metallic fraction of CNTs in the bundle and R_{CNT} is total resistance of an isolated SWCNT.

Inductance of CNT Bundle

The CNTs have both kinetic and magnetic inductances. The kinetic inductance of the bundle is expressed as [12]

$$L_b^K = l \cdot L_K / (P_m \cdot 4n_{CNT}) \tag{2}$$

The work in [3] has calculated the magnetic inductance of the CNT bundle by dividing the magnetic inductance of an isolated CNT by the number of CNTs which underestimates the magnetic inductance. The works [5, 6] have neglected magnetic inductance of CNTs. To accurately model the magnetic inductance we follow the modeling technique in [28] based on the partial element equivalent circuit (PEEC) method.

Capacitance of CNT Bundle

The quantum capacitance of CNT bundle is given by

$$C_b^Q = l \cdot 4C_Q \cdot (P_m \cdot n_{CNT}) \tag{3}$$

The electrostatic capacitance of a SWCNT bundle is almost equal to that of Cu wire of same cross-sectional dimensions [23]. It has also been found that metallic fraction (P_m) of CNTs in a bundle does not affect the electrostatic capacitance significantly. In [23] it is reported that the capacitance of a sparsely packed bundle with four CNTs at the corners is just 20% less than that of a densely packed bundle. Therefore, we have assumed the electrostatic capacitance of SWCNT bundle is same as that of Cu wire of identical cross-section. Thus, the effective capacitance of SWCNT bundle is the series combination of its electrostatic capacitance and quantum capacitance.

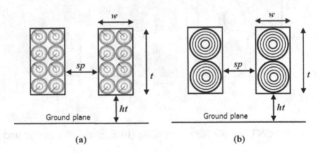

(a)   (b)

Fig. 3. MWCNT bundle based interconnect (a) bundle with four MWCNTs in vertical direction (b) bundle with two MWCNTs in vertical direction

2.3   Models of MWCNT

MWCNT is a carbon nanotube structure with a number of concentric shells. The outer diameter of MWCNT varies from a few to hundreds of nanometer and the spacing between the walls, δ is 0.34 nm [1]. An MWCNT is modeled by N number of conducting channels where N is determined by sum of conducting channels ($N=\Sigma N_i$) in individual shells [4]. We have neglected contact resistance as MWCNT with low contact resistance is demonstrated in [22].

2.4 Models for MWCNT Bundle

We have considered two different structure of interconnect using MWCNT bundle as shown in Fig. 3. This structure is suitable only when aspect ratio is two. Otherwise, smaller diameter MWCNTs must be used to fit the MWCNTs within the specified interconnect cross-section. In [23], [25], and [27] it reported that the electrostatic coupling and ground capacitances of CNT bundle of smaller diameter CNTs, are same as that of Cu wire of equal dimension. Hence, we have assumed electrostatic and coupling capacitance for the smaller diameter MWCNT bundle based interconnect (Fig. 3a), same as that of Cu wire. For MWCNT bundle with large diameter MWCNTs (Fig. 3b), the capacitance is calculated using the model described in [25].

3 Crosstalk Delay Analysis in CNT and Cu Interconnects

Crosstalk is a phenomenon which arises due to the coupling capacitance between the parallel interconnects. We have considered a coupled interconnect system with three identical interconnects in the same layer. Fig. 4 shows the circuit model with one victim and two aggressor nets, used for crosstalk analysis. When victim and aggressor nets switch in the same direction the signal transition becomes faster and the delay through interconnect is decreased (speed-up). Alternately, when aggressor nets switch in the opposite direction to victim, the signal transition becomes slower and the delay through interconnect is increased (slow-down). The accuracy of the crosstalk delay analysis depends on interconnect parasitic (RLC) circuit elements and relative switching of the neighboring nets. Crosstalk delay introduces delay uncertainty in the signal transition times which adversely affects the timing of the VLSI circuits.

3.1 Simulation Results and Discussions

Inverting buffers are designed for the driver and load in the circuit schematic shown in Fig. 4. The SPICE models are used from predictive technology model (PTM)

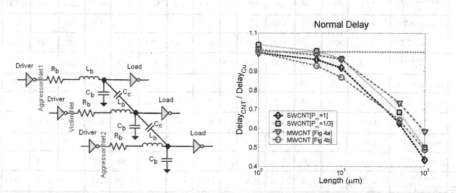

Fig. 4. Schematic diagram of a coupled interconnect system

Fig. 5. Normal delay ratio of CNT and Cu based interconnect as a function of length

source [24]. The simulations are performed for 16 nm technology node using Cadence spectre simulator and delay values are calculated. It has been assumed that all three nets switch at the same time. For worst case delay two aggressor nets are switched in opposite direction of victim whereas for best case all are switched in the same direction. Aggressor nets are kept quiet for normal delay calculation. The results are shown in Table 1. We have considered two SWCNT configurations: (i) 100% metallic ($P_m=1$) SWCNT bundle with perfect contact ($R_C = 0\ \Omega$) and (ii) 33.3% metallic ($P_m=1/3$) SWCNT bundle with imperfect contact ($R_C = 100\ k\Omega$). The MWCNT based interconnect configurations (Fig. 3) are considered with perfect contact.

Table 1. Crosstalk Induced Interconnect Delay for Different Interconnect Length

Length (μm)	Transition	Total delay = Driver delay + Normal interconnect delay + Crosstalk induced delay (ps)					Percentage change in delay due to crosstalk over normal interconnect delay $= \dfrac{Delay_{xtalk} - Delay_{normal}}{Delay_{normal}} \times 100$					Percentage increase in delay with respect Cu interconnect $= \dfrac{Delay_{CNT} - Delay_{Cu}}{Delay_{Cu}} \times 100$			
		Cu	SWCNT [$P_m=1$]	SWCNT [$P_m=1/3$]	MWCNT Bundle1	MWCNT Bundle2	Cu	SWCNT [$P_m=1$]	SWCNT [$P_m=1/3$]	MWCNT Bundle1	MWCNT Bundle2	SWCNT [$P_m=1$]	SWCNT [$P_m=1/3$]	MWCNT Bundle1	MWCNT Bundle2
1	Worst case [↑↓↑]	4.51	4.49	4.67	4.56	4.35	13.8	13.6	14.6	14.0	10.4	-0.45	3.60	1.15	-3.55
	Normal [0↓0]	3.96	3.95	4.08	4.00	3.94						-0.36	2.85	0.91	-0.60
	Best case [↓↓↓]	3.55	3.54	3.64	3.58	3.62	-10.4	-10.4	-10.8	-10.5	-8.1	-0.32	2.44	0.84	2.00
	Worst case [↓↑↓]	3.49	3.47	3.67	3.55	3.43	10.0	9.9	10.6	10.2	7.7	-0.66	5.22	1.63	-1.74
	Normal [0↑0]	3.17	3.15	3.32	3.22	3.18						-0.60	4.65	1.49	0.32
	Best case [↑↑↑]	2.87	2.85	2.99	2.90	2.91	-9.5	-9.5	-10.0	-9.9	-8.4	-0.53	4.16	1.07	1.60
5	Worst case [↑↓↑]	9.91	9.55	9.98	9.85	8.37	63.9	63.5	64.6	64.9	50.4	-3.56	0.69	-0.61	-15.49
	Normal [0↓0]	6.04	5.84	6.06	5.97	5.57						-3.32	0.26	-1.18	-7.87
	Best case [↓↓↓]	3.97	3.85	3.96	3.93	4.05	-34.4	-34.0	-34.7	-34.2	-27.3	-2.81	-0.14	-0.95	2.01
	Worst case [↓↑↓]	7.20	6.60	7.35	7.00	5.95	53.9	48.3	56.0	53.1	36.1	-8.33	2.04	-2.78	-17.37
	Normal [0↑0]	4.68	4.45	4.71	4.57	4.37						-4.84	0.66	-2.23	-6.54
	Best case [↑↑↑]	3.45	3.31	3.47	3.41	3.47	-26.2	-25.6	-26.4	-25.4	-20.6	-4.10	0.32	-1.18	0.49
10	Worst case [↑↓↑]	17.12	15.94	16.66	16.60	13.90	97.8	96.3	98.3	95.2	84.2	-6.89	-2.66	-3.03	-18.81
	Normal [0↓0]	8.65	8.12	8.40	8.50	7.55						-6.16	-2.88	-1.72	-12.79
	Best case [↓↓↓]	4.52	4.24	4.35	4.35	4.61	-47.8	-47.8	-48.2	-48.8	-38.9	-6.21	-3.69	-3.67	1.95
	Worst case [↓↑↓]	13.52	11.32	12.76	12.39	10.06	97.8	86.1	95.6	93.8	70.8	-16.28	-5.61	-8.39	-25.62
	Normal [0↑0]	6.84	6.08	6.53	6.39	5.89						-11.00	-4.54	-6.49	-13.87
	Best case [↑↑↑]	4.11	3.70	3.92	3.92	4.13	-39.9	-39.1	-40.0	-38.7	-29.9	-9.91	-4.75	-4.68	0.41
50	Worst case [↑↓↑]	98.61	65.29	70.86	74.48	59.03	170.4	149.5	161.2	160.9	134.0	-33.79	-28.14	-24.47	-40.13
	Normal [0↓0]	36.46	26.17	27.13	28.54	25.23						-28.23	-25.58	-21.72	-30.80

Table 1. (*Continued*)

Best case [↓↓↓]	11.46	7.77	8.15	8.70	10.02	-68.6	-70.3	-70.0	-69.5	-60.3	-32.24	-28.93	-24.08	-12.60
Worst case [↓↑↓]	97.11	51.41	60.83	65.75	50.48	176.2	172.1	177.5	173.5	140.4	-47.06	-37.36	-32.29	-48.02
Normal [0↑0]	35.16	18.89	21.92	24.04	20.99						-46.26	-37.64	-31.61	-40.29
Best case [↑↑↑]	11.07	6.53	7.21	8.11	9.41	-68.5	-65.4	-67.1	-66.3	-55.2	-40.99	-34.84	-26.71	-14.99
Worst case [↑↓↑]	286.91	128.66	147.35	167.03	125.60	228.8	162.8	180.9	182.8	149.6	-55.16	-48.64	-41.78	-56.22
Normal [0↓0]	87.26	48.96	52.46	59.06	50.32						-43.89	-39.87	-32.32	-42.33
100 Best case [↓↓↓]	25.55	12.45	13.67	16.43	18.66	-70.7	-74.6	-73.9	-72.2	-62.9	-51.29	-46.50	-35.69	-26.97
Worst case [↓↑↓]	291.11	104.75	133.73	159.35	116.12	167.4	189.0	191.9	186.3	154.5	-64.02	-54.06	-45.26	-60.11
Normal [0↑0]	108.87	36.25	45.81	55.65	45.63						-66.71	-57.92	-48.88	-58.09
Best case [↑↑↑]	25.80	10.41	12.44	15.68	17.87	-76.3	-71.3	-72.9	-71.8	-60.8	-59.66	-51.80	-39.23	-30.73
Average value of percentage change in delay due to crosstalk over normal interconnect delay =						76.6	72.0	75.2	74.1	60.5				

It is observed from the results [5th column in Table 1] that the Cu based interconnects are better (note that some numbers are positive indicating less Cu delay than CNT) for short interconnects. But for longer interconnects (>10 μm) SWCNT and MWCNT bundle show better performance. For instance sparsely packed SWCNT bundle of length 50 μm shows 32.7% reduction in delay as compared to Cu and double MWCNT shows 44% reduction. The 4th column in Table 1 shows the percentage change in delay due to crosstalk for different interconnect systems. It is observed that as the interconnect length increases the percentage change in delay due to crosstalk increases for all types of interconnects. The average change in delay due to crosstalk is 76.6%, 72%, 75.2%, 74.1%, and 60.5% for Cu, densely packed SWCNT bundle, sparsely SWCNT bundle, MWCNT bundle, and double MWCNT, respectively. Figures 5, 6, and 7 show the relative comparison of delay in Cu and CNT based interconnects.

In Figures 5, 6, and 7, the delay ratio of 1.0 is the line that decides the relative performance of CNT over Cu based interconnects. When the ratio is greater than unity Cu is better and if the ratio is less than unity CNT is better. From Figures 5, 6, and 7 it is evident that the CNT is better for longer interconnects of length greater than 10 μm. The double MWCNT configuration shows superior performance over Cu and SWCNT bundle based interconnects (Fig. 5). The crosstalk has also less impact on delay for double MWCNT based interconnects, which indicates double MWCNT configuration is less susceptible to crosstalk delay than SWCNT/MWCNT bundles.

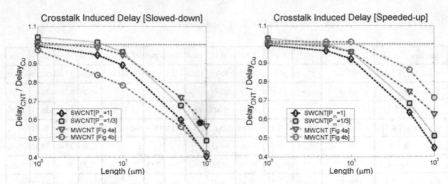

Fig. 6. Delayed crosstalk induced delay ratio of CNT and Cu based interconnect as a function of length. Rise and fall delays are averaged.

Fig. 7. Speeded crosstalk induced delay ratio of CNT and Cu based interconnect as a function of length. Rise and fall delays are averaged.

Table 2 shows the delay uncertainty values for different interconnect systems of different length (1 μm ≤ l ≤100 μm). It is found that as the interconnect length increases, the delay uncertainty of CNT based interconnects reduces in comparison to that of Cu based interconnects. The 100 μm long interconnect shows 40%, 48.4%, 55.9% and 39% delay uncertainty (average value corresponding to rise and fall transition) w.r.t. Cu for densely packed, sparsely packed, and MWCNT bundle (Fig. 3a &b) based interconnects, respectively. This result indicates that double MWCNT configuration has least delay uncertainty due to crosstalk amongst other types of interconnect considered in this work. Fig. 8 shows the delay uncertainty for different interconnect systems of length 1 μm ≤ l ≤100 μm.

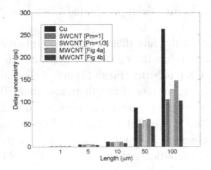

Fig. 8. Delay uncertainty vs. interconnect length.

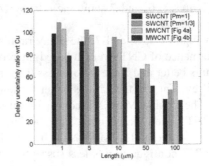

Fig. 9. Delay uncertainty w.r.t. Cu vs. interconnect length.

Table 2. Delay Uncertainty for Different Interconnect Length

Length (μm)	Victim Transition	Delay uncertainty (Δτ) = Worst Delay – Best Delay (ps)					Delay uncertainty w.r.t. Cu $=100\times\dfrac{\Delta\tau_{CNT}}{\Delta\tau_{Cu}}$			
		Cu	SWCNT [Pm=1]	SWCNT [Pm=1/3]	MWCNT Bundle 1	MWCNT Bundle 2	SWCNT [Pm=1]	SWCNT [Pm=1/3]	MWCNT Bundle 1	MWCNT Bundle 2
1	↓	0.96	0.95	1.03	0.98	0.73	99.0	107.9	102.3	75.8
	↑	0.62	0.61	0.68	0.65	0.51	98.8	110.1	104.2	82.8
5	↓	5.94	5.70	6.02	5.92	4.33	95.9	101.2	99.6	72.8
	↑	3.75	3.29	3.88	3.59	2.48	87.8	103.6	95.8	66.2
10	↓	12.60	11.70	12.31	12.25	9.29	92.9	97.7	97.2	73.7
	↑	9.41	7.62	8.85	8.47	5.93	80.9	94.0	90.0	63.0
50	↓	87.14	57.52	62.71	65.77	49.01	66.0	72.0	75.5	56.2
	↑	86.04	44.87	53.62	57.64	41.06	52.2	62.3	67.0	47.7
100	↓	261.36	116.21	133.68	150.60	106.94	44.5	51.1	57.6	40.9
	↑	265.31	94.34	121.30	143.67	98.25	35.6	45.7	54.2	37.0
Average delay uncertainty w.r.t. Cu							75.3	84.6	84.3	61.6

3.2   Comparison with Other Works

In [10] crosstalk delay has been analyzed in interconnect considering three parallel SWCNTs and MWCNT with three concentric SWCNTs. For SWCNTs and MWCNTs of length 10 μm, the work in [10] reports 82% and 94% delay uncertainty without using shielding. In this work the delay uncertainty for 10 μm long interconnect shows: a) 86.9% for densely packed SWCNT bundle, b) 95.8% for sparsely packed bundle, c) 93.6% for MWCNT bundle (Fig. 3a), d) and 68.4% for double MWCNT (Fig. 3b). The work in [9] doesn't provide the delay uncertainties due to crosstalk. It only considers DWCNT bundle but not MWCNT. It has been found in our analysis that the delay uncertainty for MWCNT bundle of Fig. 4b shows better results than MWCNT bundle of Fig. 3a. The densely packed SWCNT bundle show much better delay uncertainty than sparsely packed SWCNT bundle. The relative merit of CNT based interconnects w.r.t. Cu is illustrated in Fig. 9. As the length increases delay uncertainty decreases indicating longer CNT based interconnects are less susceptible to crosstalk induced delay. Among four different CNT based interconnects considered in this work, double MWCNT shows the least delay uncertainty. Therefore we may conclude that MWCNT bundle of large diameter is least impacted due to crosstalk delay.

4   Conclusions

In this paper the crosstalk delay is analyzed in SWCNT bundle, MWCNT bundle, and Cu based interconnect systems for 16 nm technology node. It is shown that the average crosstalk induced delay is within 60.5% over normal interconnect delay for double MWCNT as compared to 76.6% for copper and 72-75.2% for SWCNT/MWCNT bundle based interconnects. The average delay uncertainty w.r.t. Cu interconnects for SWCNT bundle based interconnect is found to be 75.3% and 84.6% for densely and sparsely packed SWCNT bundles, respectively, whereas it is 84.3% for MWCNT bundle and 61.6% for double MWCNT based interconnects. The MWCNT bundle with large diameter MWCNTs is better for crosstalk delay avoidance. The densely packed SWCNT bundle with perfect contact is also suitable for longer interconnects.

References

1. ITRS reports, http://www.itrs.net/reports.html
2. Burke, P.J.: Luttinger Liquid Theory as a Model of the Gigahertz Electrical Properties of Carbon Nanotubes. IEEE TNANO 1(3), 119–144 (2002)
3. Srivastava, N., Li, H., Kreupl, F., Banerjee, K.: On the Applicability of Single-Walled Carbon Nanotubes as VLSI Interconnects. IEEE TNANO 8(4) (2009)
4. Naeemi, A., Meindl, J.D.: Compact Physical Models for Multiwall Carbon-Nanotube Interconnects. IEEE EDL 27(5), 338–340 (2006)
5. Naeemi, A., Sarvari, R., Meindl, J.D.: Performance Comparison Between Carbon Nanotube and Copper Interconnects for Gigascale Integration (GSI). IEEE EDL 26(2) (2005)
6. Raychowdhury, A., Roy, K.: Modeling of Metallic Carbon-Nanotube Interconnects for Circuit Simulations and a Comparison with Cu Interconnects for Scaled Technologies. IEEE TCAD 25(1), 58–65 (2006)
7. Nieuwoudt, A., Mondal, M., Massoud, Y.: Predicting the Performance and Reliability of Carbon Nanotube Bundles for On-Chip Interconnect. In: ASPDAC, pp. 708–713 (2007)
8. Maffucci, A., Miano, G., Villone, F.: Performance Comparison Between Metallic Carbon Nanotube and Copper Nano-Interconnects. IEEE Trans. Advanced Packaging 31(4) (2008)
9. Pasricha, S., Kurdahi, F.J., Dutt, N.: Evaluating Carbon Nanotube Global Interconnects for Chip Multiprocessor Applications. IEEE TVLSI 18(9), 1376–1380 (2010)
10. Rossi, D., Cazeaux, J.M., Metra, C., Lombardi, F.: Modeling crosstalk effects in CNT bus architectures. IEEE TNANO 6(2), 133–145 (2007)
11. Jia, L., Yin, W.-Y.: Temperature Effects on Crosstalk in Carbon Nanotube Interconnects. In: Proc. Asia-Pacific Microwave Conference, pp. 1–4 (2008)
12. Pu, S.-N., Yin, W.-Y., Mao, J.-F., Liu, Q.H.: Crosstalk Prediction of Single- and Double-Walled Carbon-Nanotube (SWCNT/DWCNT) Bundle Interconnects. IEEE TED 56(4) (2009)
13. D'Amore, M., Sarto, M.S., Tamburrano, A.: Signal Integrity of Carbon Nanotube Bundles. In: Proc. IEEE Int. Symposium on Electromagnetic Compatibility, pp. 1–6 (2007)
14. D'Amore, M., Sarto, M.S., Tamburrano, A.: Transient analysis of crosstalk coupling between high-speed carbon nanotube interconnects. In: Proc. IEEE Int. Symposium on Electromagnetic Compatibility, pp. 1–6 (2008)
15. D'Amore, M., Sarto, M.S., Tamburrano, A.: Fast Transient Analysis of Next-Generation Interconnects Based on Carbon Nanotubes. IEEE TEMC 52(2), 496–503 (2010)
16. Sun, P., Luo, R.: Analytical Modeling for Crosstalk Noise Induced by Process Variations among CNT-based Interconnects. In: Proc. IEEE Int. Symposium on Electromagnetic Compatibility, pp. 103–107 (2009)
17. Chiariello, A.G., Maffucci, A., Miano, G., Villone, F.: High Frequency and Crosstalk Analysis of VLSI Carbon Nanotube Nanointerconnects. In: Proc. EMC Europe, Int. Symposium on Electromagnetic Compatibility, pp. 1–4 (2009)
18. Chen, W.C., Yin, W.-Y., Jia, L., Liu, Q.H.: Electrothermal Characterization of Single-Walled Carbon Nanotube (SWCNT) Interconnect Arrays. IEEE TNANO 8(6), 718–728 (2009)

19. Das, D., Rahaman, H.: Crosstalk analysis in Carbon Nanotube interconnects and its impact on gate oxide reliability. In: Proc. ASQED, pp. 272–279 (2010)
20. Kim, W., Javey, A., Tu, R., Cao, J., Wang, Q., Dai, H.: Electrical contacts to carbon nanotubes down to 1 nm in diameter. Appl. Phys. Lett. 87, 173101-1–173101-3 (2005)
21. Sarto, M.S., Tamburrano, A.: Single-Conductor Transmission-Line Model of Multiwall Carbon Nanotubes. IEEE TNANO 9(1), 82–92 (2010)
22. Sato, S., et al.: Novel approach to fabricate carbon nanotube via interconnects using size-controlled catalyst nanoparticles. In: Proc. Int. Interconnect Technol. Conf., pp. 230–232 (2006)
23. Naeemi, A., Meindl, J.D.: Design and Performance Modeling for Single-Walled Carbon Nanotubes as Local, Semiglobal, and Global Interconnects in Gigascale Integrated Systems. IEEE TED 54(1), 26–37 (2007)
24. Predictive Technology Model, http://ptm.asu.edu/
25. Nieuwoudt, A., Massoud, Y.: On the Optimal Design, Performance, and Reliability of Future Carbon Nanotube-Based Interconnect Solutions. IEEE TED 55(8), 2097–2110 (2008)
26. Naeemi, A., Meindl, J.D.: Performance Modeling for Single- and Multiwall Carbon Nanotubes as Signal and Power Interconnects in Gigascale Systems. IEEE TED 55(10), 2574–2582 (2008)
27. Li, H., Yin, W.-Y., Banerjee, K., Mao, J.-F.: Circuit Modeling and Performance Analysis of Multi-Walled Carbon Nanotube Interconnects. IEEE TED 55(6), 1328–1337 (2008)
28. Nieuwoudt, A., Massoud, Y.: Understanding the Impact of Inductance in Carbon Nanotube Bundles for VLSI Interconnect Using Scalable Modeling Techniques. IEEE TED 5(6), 758–765 (2006)

A Fast FPGA Based Architecture
for Sobel Edge Detection

Santanu Halder[1], Debotosh Bhattacharjee[2],
Mita Nasipuri[2], and Dipak Kumar Basu[2]

[1] Department of CSE, GCETTB, Berhampore, Murshidabad-742101, India
[2] Department of CSE, Jadavpur University, Kolkata, 700032, India

Abstract. This paper presents an efficient FPGA based architecture for Sobel edge detection algorithm in respect of both time and space complexity. Various edge detection algorithms are typically used in image processing, artificial intelligence etc. In this paper the Sobel edge detection algorithm using hardware description language and its implementation in Field Programmable Gate Array (FPGA) device is presented in an efficient way. Sobel edge detection algorithm is chosen due to its property of less deterioration in high levels of noise. The result shows a significant improvement of time and space complexity over an existing architecture.

Keywords: Sobel edge detection, hardware implementation, VHDL, FPGA.

1   Introduction

Edge detection algorithms are widely used in various research fields like Image Processing, Video Processing, Artificial Intelligence etc. Edges are most important attribute of image information and a lot of edge detection algorithms are defined in literature [2-5]. Sobel edge detection algorithm is chosen among of them due to its property of less deterioration in high level of noise. FPGA is becoming the most dominant form of programmable logic [4-6] over past few years and it has advantages of low investment cost and desktop testing with moderate processing speed and thereby offering itself as suitable one for real time application. This paper describes an efficient architecture for Sobel edge detector which is faster and takes less space than the architecture proposed by Tanvir A. Abbasi and Mohd. Usaid Abbasi [1] in 2007. The current work not only saves time but also takes less space than the architecture of Tanvir A. Abbasi et al. [1] and hence is more suitable for a real time system.

This paper is organized as follows: The Section 2 presents the brief description of the Sobel edge detection algorithm. Section 3 presents the top level design of Sobel edge detection hardware. Section 4 depicts the proposed system architecture for Sobel edge detection. Section 5 shows the experimental results and finally Section 6 concludes and remarks about some of the aspects analyzed in this paper.

H. Rahaman et al. (Eds.): VDAT 2012, LNCS 7373, pp. 300–306, 2012.

2   Algorithm for Sobel Edge Detection

The Sobel Edge Detection Operator is 3×3 spatial mask. It is based on first derivative based operation. The Sobel masks are defined as:

$$H1 = \begin{matrix} -1 & -2 & -1 \\ 0 & 0 & 0 \\ 1 & 2 & 1 \end{matrix} \qquad (1)$$

$$H2 = \begin{matrix} -1 & 0 & 1 \\ -2 & 0 & 2 \\ -1 & 0 & 1 \end{matrix} \qquad (2)$$

Suppose the pixel value of a 3×3 sub-window of an image is as shown as in Fig. 1.

D0	D1	D2
D3	D4	D5
D6	D7	D8

Fig. 1. The pixel intensity values of a 3×3 sub-window of an image

Applying the Sobel mask on the sub-window of Fig. 1 yields

$$G_x = (D6 + 2 \times D7 + D8) - (D0 + 2 \times D1 + D2)$$

$$= f1 - f2 \text{ Where, } \quad f1 = (D6 + 2 \times D7 + D8) \text{ and } f2 = (D0 + 2 \times D1 + D2) \qquad (3)$$

$$G_y = (D2 + 2 \times D5 + D8) - (D0 + 2 \times D3 + D6)$$

$$= f3 - f4 \text{ Where, } f3 = (D2 + 2 \times D5 + D8) \text{ and } f4 = (D0 + 2 \times D3 + D6) \qquad (4)$$

Now the maximum value of f1, f2, f3 and f4 is 4×255. As here we are designing an 8-bit Sobel Edge Detection Architecture, so to limit the value of f1, f2, f3 and f4 to a maximum of 255, we divide the each term by a factor of 4. Therefore Eq-3 and Eq-4 can be rewritten as:

$$G_x = \frac{1}{4} f1 - \frac{1}{4} f2 \qquad (5) \qquad\qquad G_y = \frac{1}{4} f3 - \frac{1}{4} f4 \qquad (6)$$

The Sobel output for one group of pixel (3×3 sub-window) is calculated as per the method given in Eq-7.

$$G = |G_x| + |G_y| \qquad (7)$$

To limit the value of G to a maximum of 255, the value of G is divided by a factor of 2. So, the Eq-7 can be rewritten as:

$$G = \frac{1}{2} \times (|G_x| + |G_y|) \qquad (8)$$

To reduce the number of division operations, we can rewrite Eq-5 and Eq-6 as:

$$G_x = \frac{1}{8} \times f1 - \frac{1}{8} \times f2 \qquad (9) \qquad\qquad G_y = \frac{1}{8} \times f3 - \frac{1}{8} \times f4 \qquad (10)$$

Now the value of G can be calculated using Eq-7. Suppose the Threshold value given by the user is T. Then the output $D_{O/P}$ will be 0 if T is greater than G or 1 if T is less than G as shown in Eq-11.

$$D_{O/P} = 0 \qquad \text{if } T > G$$
$$= 1 \qquad \text{if } T < G \tag{11}$$

Now consider the following four cases depending on the values of Gx and Gy:

Case 1: if Gx ≥ 0 and Gy ≥ 0 then

$$G1 = \tfrac{1}{8} \times ((f1 - f2) + (f3 - f4)) \qquad \text{[Using Eq-9, Eq-10 and Eq-7]}$$

$$= \tfrac{1}{8} \times \begin{pmatrix} D6 + 2 \times D7 + D8 - D0 - 2 \times D1 \\ + D2 + D2 + 2 \times D5 + D8 - D0 \\ - 2 \times D3 - D6 \end{pmatrix}$$

$$= \tfrac{1}{4} \times ((D5 + D7 + D8) - (D0 + D1 + D3))$$

$$= \tfrac{1}{4} \times (f5 - f6) \qquad \text{Where, } f5 = (D5 + D7 + D8) \text{ and } f6 = (D0 + D1 + D3) \tag{12}$$

Case 2: if Gx ≥ 0 and Gy ≤ 0 then

$$G2 = \tfrac{1}{8} \times ((f1 - f2) + (f4 - f3)) \qquad \text{[Using Eq-9, Eq-10 and Eq-7]}$$

$$= \tfrac{1}{8} \times \begin{pmatrix} D6 + 2 \times D7 + D8 - D0 - 2 \times D1 \\ - D2 + D0 + 2 \times D3 + D6 - D2 \\ - 2 \times D5 - D8 \end{pmatrix} = \tfrac{1}{4} \times ((D3 + D6 + D7) - (D1 + D2 + D5))$$

$$= \tfrac{1}{4} \times (f7 - f8) \qquad \text{Where, } f7 = (D3 + D6 + D7) \text{ and } f8 = (D1 + D2 + D5) \tag{13}$$

Case 3: if Gx ≤ 0 and Gy ≥ 0 then

$$G3 = \tfrac{1}{8} \times ((f2 - f1) + (f3 - f4)) \qquad \text{[Using Eq-9, Eq-10 and Eq-7]}$$

$$= \tfrac{1}{8} \times \begin{pmatrix} D0 + 2 \times D1 + D2 - D6 - 2 \times D7 \\ - D8 + D2 - 2 \times D5 + D8 - D0 \\ - 2 \times D3 - D6 \end{pmatrix} = \tfrac{1}{4} \times ((D1 + D2 + D5) - (D3 + D6 + D7))$$

$$= \tfrac{1}{4} \times (f8 - f7) \tag{14}$$

Case 4: if Gx ≤ 0 and Gy ≤ 0 then

$$G4 = \tfrac{1}{8} \times ((f2 - f1) + (f4 - f3)) \qquad \text{[Using Eq-9, Eq-10 and Eq-7]}$$

$$= \tfrac{1}{8} \times \begin{pmatrix} D0 + 2 \times D1 + D2 - D6 - 2 \times D7 \\ - D8 + D0 + 2 \times D3 + D6 - D2 \\ - 2 \times D5 - D8 \end{pmatrix} = \tfrac{1}{4} \times ((D0 + D1 + D3) - (D5 + D7 + D8))$$

$$= \tfrac{1}{4} \times (f6 - f5) \tag{15}$$

Therefore, based on the value of Gx and Gy, four values of Gi (G1, G2, G3 and G4) are produced according to Eq-12 to Eq-15. So, the confusion arises around the four values of Gi (i=1 to 4) to determine the final value of G from them. Now, if Case 1 is true, then Gx $\geq$ 0 and Gy $\geq$ 0. Now, as Gx $\geq$ 0, then f1 $\geq$ f2 and as Gy $\geq$ 0 then f3 $\geq$ f4. Therefore we can write:

$$G2 = \tfrac{1}{8} \times ((f1 - f2) + (f4 - f3)) \leq \tfrac{1}{8} \times ((f1 - f2) + (f3 - f4)) \leq G1$$

$$G3 = \tfrac{1}{8} \times ((f2 - f1) + (f3 - f4)) \leq \tfrac{1}{8} \times ((f1 - f2) + (f3 - f4)) \leq G1$$

$$G4 = \tfrac{1}{8} \times ((f2 - f1) + (f4 - f3)) \leq \tfrac{1}{8} \times ((f1 - f2) + (f3 - f4)) \leq G1$$

Hence we can conclude that if Case 1 is true, then G1 is greatest among Gi (i=1 to 4) values. Similarly, it can be shown that if Case 2 or Case 3 or Case 4 is true then G2 or G3 or G4 is largest between the Gi (i=1 to 4) values respectively. Therefore we can write:

$$G = \max (G1, G2, G3, G4) \tag{16}$$

Alternatively,
$$G = \max \left(\left| \tfrac{f5}{4} - \tfrac{f6}{4} \right|, \left| \tfrac{f7}{4} - \tfrac{f8}{4} \right| \right) \tag{17}$$

Or, $G = \max \left(|f9 - f10|, |f11 - f12| \right)$ Where $f9 = \tfrac{f5}{4}, f10 = \tfrac{f6}{4}, f11 = \tfrac{f7}{4}, f12 = \tfrac{f8}{4}$ (18)

Or, $G = \max (f13, f14)$ Where $f13 = |f9 - f10|$ and $f14 = |f11 - f12|$ (19)

Now, from Eq-11 and Eq-19, we can write:

$$
\begin{aligned}
D_{O/P} &= 0 &&\text{If } T > f13 \text{ and } T > f14 \\
&= 1 &&\text{Otherwise}
\end{aligned}
\tag{20}
$$

The present work uses the equations from Eq-12 to Eq-20 to find the edges in an image using Sobel Operator. In traditional method, the equations from Eq-3 to Eq-11 are used for Sobel Edge detection. To calculate the values of f1, f2, f3 and f4, 8 Addition and 4 Multiplication operations are needed. To find the values of Gx and Gy from Eq-9 and Eq-10, four division and two subtraction operations are required. Again Eq-7 claims one more addition operation to compute the value of G. But using the equations of our method (Eq.-12 to Eq-20), some addition and multiplication operations can be reduced which improves both the space and time complexity of the architecture. Table-1 shows the comparison study between the traditional method and the method proposed in this paper in terms of number of operations needed to find the edges from an image with size m × n.

3   Top Level Design

The top level design of Sobel edge detection architecture is shown in Fig. 2. The proposed architecture takes eight 8-bit pixel values and one 8-bit threshold value as input. Finally the system generates one 1-bit pixel value which is either 0 or 1 based on the threshold value supplied by the user.

Fig. 2. The Top Level Design of Sobel Edge Detection Algorithm

4   System Architecture

The proposed architecture for the generation of Sobel edge detection algorithm is shown in Fig 3. The modeling of the internal architecture of each block is designed using Very high-speed integrated circuit Hardware Description Language (VHDL) and each block is controlled by a global clock. The various blocks for this architecture are next described:

Adder/Divider Block: Each of these blocks take three 8-bit pixel values and divide by 4 after adding them.

Subtractor Block: This block subtracts two 8-bit pixel values, takes the absolute value of the result and produces the result in 8-bit pixel value.

Comparator Block: The comparison of the resultant values from a given threshold value is performed by this block. The output of this block is edge detected binary image having only two pixel values i.e. 0 or 1. This block produces a 0 value if both f13 and f14 are less than the threshold value T and produces a 1 value otherwise.

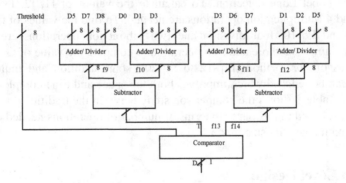

Fig. 3. Proposed architecture for Sobel edge detection algorithm

5   Experimental Results

The Sobel edge detection architecture was implemented using VHDL, synthesized for a Xilinx Spartan 3 XC3S50-5PQ208 FPGA with simulation on the Modelsim 6.2c from Mentor Graphics Corporation. Tanvir A. Abbasi et al also used the same Spartan kit for their experimental result. In this paper, the test images with size 512×512 pixels with 256 gray levels are used. In the proposed method, number of additions and multiplications are reduced to 2097152 from 2359296 and to 262144 from 1048576 respectively over the traditional method for a 512×512 image. The comparison study of device utilization summary is given in Table 2 and Table 3 shows the comparison study of timing summary.

Table 1. Comparison study of device utilization summary

		No. Of Slices	No. of Slice Flip Flops	No. of 4 input LUTs	No. of Bonded IOBs
Total		768	1536	1536	124
T. A. Abbasi et al [1]	Usage	204	280	202	81
Our Method	Usage	76	47	107	57

Table 2. Comparison study of timing summary

	Max. Frequency	Min. Period	Time needed for 512×512 image	Time needed for 1024×768 image
T. A. Abbasi et al [1]	134.756 MHz	7.420 ns	1.95 ms	5.84 ms
Our Method	204.750 MHz	4.884 ns	1.28 ms	3.84 ms

Fig. 4 shows the edge detected images using the proposed method with the given threshold values.

Threshold=12   Threshold=13   Threshold = 36   Threshold = 30

Fig. 4. Original Images and corresponding Sobel Images

6   Conclusion

The proposed FPGA based architecture for Sobel edge detection algorithm is capable of operating at a speed of 190.840 MHz. which is much better than the architecture proposed by Tanvir A. Abbasi et al. in 2007. This frequency ensures the high speed computation of Sobel edge detector in real time processing system. This architecture uses only 16% slices on Xilinx Spartan 3 XC3S50-5PQ 208 FPGA which allows implementing some more parallel processes with this architecture on the same FPGA.

References

1. Abbasi, T.A., Abbasi, M.U.: A proposed FPGA Based Architecture for Sobel Edge Detection Operator. Journal of Active and Passive Electronic Devices 2, 271–277 (2007)
2. Chanda, B., Dutta Majumder, D.: Digital Image Processing and Analysis. Prentice-Hall of India (2001)
3. Gonzalez Rafael, C., Woods Richard, E.: Digital Image Processing. Pearson Education (2002)
4. Jenkins, J.H.: Designing with FPGA and CPLDs. Prentice-Hall Publication (1994)
5. Weste, N.H.E., Eshraghian, K.: Principles of CMOS VLSI Design: A Systems Perspective. Pearson Education, Asia (2000)
6. Wakerly, J.F.: Digital Design: Principles and Practices. Pearson Education, Asia (2002)

Speech Processor Design for Cochlear Implants

Arun Kumarappan and P.V. Ramakrishna

nura_k@ymail.com, pvramakrishna@annauniv.edu

Abstract. In this paper, a DFT based speech processor model is developed for the evaluation of different parameters associated with the design of external processor used in a typical cochlear implant system. The key design parameters chosen for investigation in the present work are the bit precisions required at different stages, the impact of increasing the number of channels or stimulant electrodes, the impact of errors in the frequency and amplitude stimulated by individual electrodes. Detailed simulations are first carried out in MATLAB to identify acceptable values for the various design parameters. The design is then mapped on to an FPGA to identify the gate level complexity involved in realizing the processor. The result shows that electrode misplacement (frequency error) can be easily rectified by varying accordingly the channel center frequencies chosen in the external processor. The results presented show that 12- bit precision for formant frequency channels and 8-bit precision for the other channels are adequate to ensure that the normalized Mean Square Error (MSE) is less than 5%. In case of misplaced electrodes, it is shown that allowing for tunability of center frequency of each channel in steps of 10Hz results in the performance improvement by nearly 70% in terms of MSE.

Keywords: Cochlear Implant (CI), speech processor, Continuous Interleaved Sampling (CIS) algorithm, DFT, Acoustic stimulation.

1   Introduction

Cochlear implants are used to render speech recognition ability in certain types of profoundly deaf persons. A typical multi-channel cochlear implant system [1] [2] has an external speech processor unit, an implantable electrode stimulator unit and a wireless power & data transfer unit. The speech processor unit decomposes the audio signal into sub-bands and then the electrode stimulator unit excites the electrode placed in the inner ear with the amplitude of the respective sub-band. Prior studies have established that the Continuous Interleaved Sampling (CIS) algorithm implemented in the external processor provides the highest speech comprehension rates among patients [1]-[3]. It is well known that the speech processor parameters such as channel count, channel allocation, and amplitude mapping have a strong impact on speech perception. Further, due to variations from individual to individual, it is neither possible to precisely place the electrodes to invoke specific frequency responses, nor it is possible to predict the exact amount of stimulant current needed to invoke a specific intensity of response. After surgery, tuning of the speech processor is needed to achieve the desired speech reception. Although all the aforementioned issues are

H. Rahaman et al. (Eds.): VDAT 2012, LNCS 7373, pp. 307–316, 2012.

known and addressed [1]-[5], quantitative estimates to aid in the design of the external processor are not easily available in the literature. The implementation of a DSP based speech processor for laboratory experiments is discussed in [6]-[8], but the bit precisions required and the post-surgical tunability that needs to be provided in the external processor are not addressed. The present paper aims to address these issues.

The rest of the paper is organized in the following sequence. The methodology adopted in the work is discussed in detail in Section II. The simulation results and realization of the external processor in an FPGA are discussed in Section III and Section IV briefly discusses the conclusions.

2   Speech Processor Methodology

A typical multichannel cochlear implant system is shown in Fig.1. It comprises of an external speech processor, the implantable electrode stimulator unit and power transfer unit.

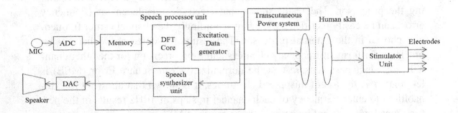

Fig. 1. Cochlear Implant System

The speech processor unit captures the speech signals with the aid of microphone and ADC. Then it stores the digitized samples in memory for processing. The captured sound signal is decomposed in to sub bands using the DFT core. The DFT bins are grouped in accordance with the frequency allocated as per the CIS scheme and the summation of the grouped DFT bins decides the corresponding electrode's excitation amplitude. In order to evaluate the quality of the speech signal stimulated by the electrodes, one can tap the electrode signals to drive a speech synthesizer/DAC unit to reconstruct the speech signal. Using a pair of inductively coupled coils, wireless transfer of power and data needed by the stimulator unit is carried out. One coil is placed behind the ear and other one is implanted inside the human skin. The stimulator unit implanted in the inner ear excites the electrode with the amplitude determined by the speech processor.

Fig.2 shows the flowchart for the computations to be carried out in a speech processor and speech reconstruction process, the latter being included only for the present study. The speech processor is designed with the flexibility of sweeping its various parameters. In the speech processing section, audio signal from the microphone is split into small data packets. In the present design, the audio codec's sampling frequency and data bit resolution used for capturing the speech signal can be varied.

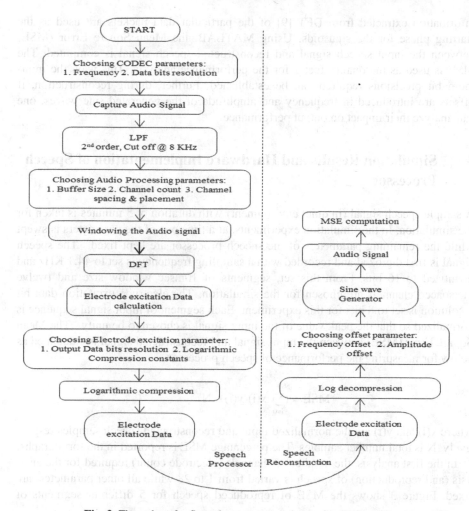

Fig. 2. Flow chart for Speech processor and speech reconstruction

The digitized speech signal from the audio codec is filtered using a second order low pass filter with a cut off frequency of 8 KHz. Depending on the selected buffer size, the captured speech signal is divided into small data packets for DFT processing, after which the various DFT bins are combined to form N number of signal bands (channels). The chosen number of channels, channel spacing and adjacent channel overlap parameters decide the decomposed signal bands. The average power of each band is computed by averaging the grouped DFT bins. After deciding the excitation data bit resolution and logarithmic compression parameters, the electrode excitation data for the various electrodes is calculated. This process is repeated to compute the excitation information for the full length of audio input.

Speech reconstruction [9] is carried out by generating N number of sine waves with amplitudes derived from the electrode excitation data. The frequencies of the sine waves are set equal to the electrode placement frequencies. The phase information extracted from DFT [9] of the particular data packets are used as the starting phase for the sinusoids. Using MATLAB, the Mean Square Error (MSE) between the input speech signal and reconstructed speech signal is computed. The MSE is used as the quality factor for the performance analysis. This way, the minimum bit precisions required can be established. Further, during reconstruction, if offsets are introduced in frequency and amplitude of the generated sine waves, one can analyze their impact on output performance.

3   Simulation Results and Hardware Implementation of Speech Processor

A sample speech signal (in quiet environment) with duration of 5 minutes is taken for the simulation. In the simulation experiments, at a time one of the parameters is swept while the remaining parameters of the speech processor are kept fixed. The speech signal is first digitized and recorded with a sampling frequency is set to 44.1 KHz and quantized to 16 bits. From this set, segments of 10msec window size and twelve melspaced channels are chosen for the simulation. The electrode excitation data bit resolution is set to 8 bits for this experiment. Each segment of input signal sequence is normalized so that the peak value of the input signal is chosen to be unity. The Mean Square Error (MSE) between the input signal and reconstructed signal is calculated as below for measuring the performance of speech processor.

$$MSE = (\sum_{i=0}^{N}(x(i)\text{-}y(i))^2/N)$$

where x(i) and y(i) are the normalized input and reconstructed speech samples respectively. N is total number samples. The percentage MSE is reported in the form graphs.

In the first analysis, the number of channels (electrode count) required for the analysis (and reproduction) of speech is varied from 1 to 28 while all other parameters are fixed. Figure 3 shows the MSE of reproduced speech for 5 different segments of

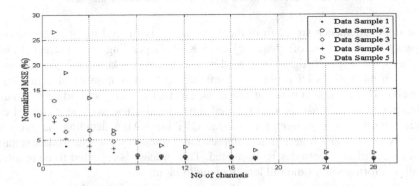

Fig. 3. Percentage of MSE as a function of channels for five different samples of speech signal. Each sample is 40ms duration speech signal

speech signal. It can be seen that the MSE shows a wide variation while using lower number of channels and this is due to variation of the frequency content of the particular speech data samples. If one uses the average of MSE across different speech samples, it is observed that the increasing the number of channels up to 12 is likely to be beneficial for cochlear implant users. The MSE improves by about 90%, from a single channel system to a 12 channel system, while the performance improvement is less significant beyond 12 channels.

Next, the same input speech is added with the White Gaussian Noise (WGN), noise samples generated in MATLAB and the simulation similar to that of Fig.3 is carried out for the noisy environment. Figure 4, shows that for 4db SNR, the performance improves rapidly up to a channel count of 12, but this increase became less prominent for higher number of channels. For the 8 db SNR case, 12 electrodes are sufficient to obtain nearly the same SNR as for the noiseless case. In the noisy environment it is possible to improve the MSE by adopting algorithms such as the one reported [11], but this aspect is not the focus of the present work.

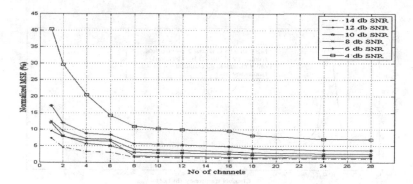

Fig. 4. Percentage of MSE as a function of channel for different SNR values. SNR of speech signal varied from 14 db to 4 db in steps of 2db

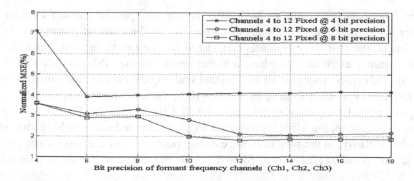

Fig. 5. MSE as a function of three formant frequency channel bit precision. Rest of the channels kept with default channel precision. MSE plot for three default channel precision reported.

The next set of simulations is aimed at evaluating the impact of varying the bit precision. The resolution of excitation amplitudes of the three formant frequency channels (channel 1 2 & 3 of 12 channel system) is varied from 4 to 18 bits. This variation of the bit precision for the formant channels is studied while fixing the bit precision of the remaining channels first at 4 bits, then at 6 bits and then finally at 8 bits. As shown in Fig.5, the MSE converged at 12 bits for the formant frequency channels while keeping the precision of other channels amplitudes at 8 bits.

Placing the electrode in the cochlea to stimulate precisely the specific frequency of the channel is a challenging task, and incorrect placement results in frequency offset while reconstruction. In the next experiment, the sine waves used for the speech reconstruction are generated with +/- 10% frequency offset from the corresponding center frequencies used for the analysis of speech. Offset is introduced in one channel at a time, and MSE performance related to that offset is observed and plotted in Fig.6. It is observed that formant frequency channels are more sensitive to frequency offset and result in a higher MSE. However, this performance degradation can be overcome by changing the center frequency of the channel taken for the analysis

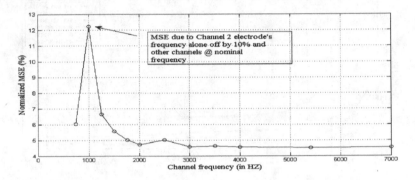

Fig. 6. MSE as a function of channel center frequency for 12 different trials. In each trial one channel's center frequency is offset by 10%.

Fig.7 presents the results of MSE after tuning the specific channel's center frequency (corresponding to the analysis carried out in the external processor). In this experiment, the first three channels considered for the tuning process, since the formant frequency electrodes shift have a higher impact on the MSE (as shown in Fig 6). Initially, the center frequency of the channel under question (electrode or reconstruction frequency) is offset from fc by nearly +10%. Then during the tuning process, the analysis channel frequency shifted from (0.9fc) Hz to (1.1 fc) Hz in the steps of 10Hz. At each step, the MSE is computed. Fig.7 depicts reduction in MSE, where for the sake of clarity, in the plot, only the extreme positions and that too for one particular channel frequency is shown. Similar results are obtained for other channels as well.

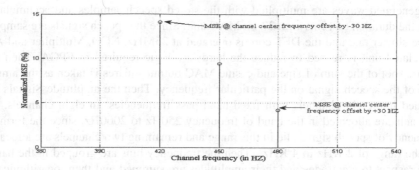

Fig. 7. MSE as a function of channels center frequency. In the experiment one reconstructed speech channel's center frequency is offset by 10% and the channel's center frequency tuned from fc-30 Hz to fc+30 Hz in steps.

Fig.8 shows the performance analysis for the mismatch in the electrode excitation amplitude. It can be seen that the error observed is small for fifteen percent (plus or minus) mismatch in the excitation amplitude in channel frequencies below 1 KHz range. This can be eradicated by changing the amplitude mapping function implemented in speech processor.

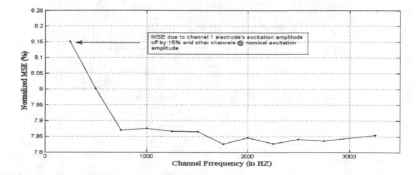

Fig. 8. MSE as a function of channel center frequency for 12 different experiments. In each experiment one channel's amplitude used for the reconstruction is offset by +15%.

Based on the above estimates obtained, the speech processor based on the DFT core is implemented in Altera Cyclone II FPGA (Device: EP2C35F672C8). Fig.9 shows the DFT core implementation, in which the external audio front end ADC is used to capture the speech signal. In the FPGA, audio signal is stored alternately in two RAM blocks of size 8 Kbits each. A second order low pass filter with cut off frequency 8 KHz is used to filter the input signal and then taken as input for the DFT core and the frequency estimation is carried out. In the DFT processor, sine and cosine waves were generated with 7-bit output precision using a single Number Controlled Oscillator (NCO) with 12 bit accumulator. This is used for generating these sine and cosine waves in the region of 0 - 4 KHz with the resolution of 100Hz. Then the generated waves are multiplied with the stored speech samples and accumulated over the duration of 10ms with 27-bit MAC unit. Since the speech signals are sampled at the slower rate and the DFT core is operated at 25MHz, NCO, Multiplier and Accumulated unit is reused to reduce the hardware logic required in FPGA. Then the square root of the sum of sine and cosine MAC output squares is taken as the amplitude of the speech signal on the particular frequency. Then the amplitude Signals are divided into eight channels with fixed band pass frequencies. In eight channels, six channels are allocated in the band of frequency 250Hz to 2000Hz, since the formant frequency of speech signals lie in this range and remaining two channels are allocated for the range of 2 KHz to 4 KHz. Then the frequency bins are grouped in the bands with respect to electrodes and their amplitudes are summed and then logarithmically compressed to obtain the excitation amplitudes of the various electrodes. These 8-bit excitation amplitudes are encoded along with the channel number and sent out to the transmitter coil.

For evaluating the performance, the speech signal is reconstructed form the excitation amplitude information. On the reconstruction side, each channel has a dedicated Look Up Table (LUT) based sine wave which is generated using 12-bit NCO running in accordance with the sampling frequency. All the sine waves are summed and then it sent to the audio CODEC for driving the speaker. Table1 shows the area report for the Speech processor (reported by the Altera Quartus II software).

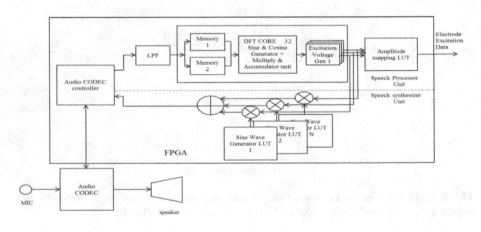

Fig. 9. Hardware implementation of speech processor

Figure 10 and Figure 11 shows the power spectral density of the input speech data samples and power spectral density of reconstructed speech signal for the duration of 10ms. The 8-channel speech processor and reconstruction unit is used for this experiment. Then PSD for the data samples are plotted in MATLAB. The PSD of reconstructed speech signal is same as that of input speech in the region of less than 4 KHz, since electrode excitation channels are allocated in this region only. Moreover in the above 4 KHz region, speech signal strength is less.

Table 1. Area Report For The Speech Processor

Area Report	Usage
Logic Element	2464 (7% of device)
Combinational Function	2343
Dedicated Logic Registers	802
Memory Bits	16384
Estimated Fmax/ Operating Frequency	96.2MHz

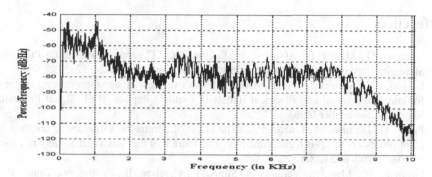

Fig. 10. Power Spectral Density of original speech signal

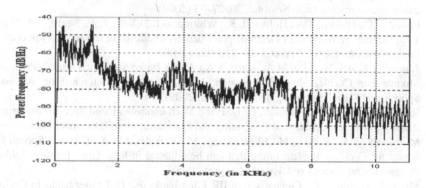

Fig. 11. Power Spectral Density of reconstructed speech signal

4   Conclusion

In this paper a simple procedure has been reported for designing and evaluating the speech processor for use in a typical cochlear implant system. The developed system is flexible in terms varying the speech processor's parameters such as DFT buffer size, excitation amplitude resolution, electrode channel offset and amplitude mismatch correction. Five parameters of speech processor are examined in this paper and based on which the external speech processor hardware is implemented in an FPGA. The simulations show that 12 channels are sufficient for the 8dB SNR. Frequency offset in the channel has the significant impact in the performance degradation while the excitation amplitude offset is not so detrimental. The center frequency of the channel tuned in steps of 10Hz to shows the performance improvement in speech reception by 70%. The result shows that excitation of the formant frequency channels with 12- bit precision and remaining channels with 8-bit precision is sufficient from the speech reconstruction purposes. The hardware reconstructed speech spectrum indicates the implemented speech processor results are comparable to MATLAB simulation results.

References

1. Stickney, G., Mishra, L., Assmann, P., Loizou, P.C.: Comparison of speech Processing Strategies Used in the Clarion Implant Processor. Ear and Hearing 24, 12–19 (2003)
2. Loizou, P.C.: Mimicking the HUMAN EAR An overview of signal-processing strategies for converting sound into Electrical signals in cochlear implant. IEEE Signal Processing Magazine (September 1998)
3. Poroy, O., Dorman, M., Loizou, P.C.: The effect of parametric variations of cochlear implant processors on speech understanding. The Journal of the Acoustical Society of America 108(2), 790–802 (2000)
4. Grolman, W., Maat, A., Verdam, F., Simis, Y., Carelsen, B., Freling, N., Tange, R.A.: Spread of excitation measurements for the detection of electrode array foldovers: A prospective study comparing 3-dimensional rotational x-ray and intraoperative spread of excitation measurements. Otol. Neurotol. 30, 27–33 (2009)
5. Finley, C.C., Holden, T.A., Holden, L.K., Whiting, B.R., Chole, R.A., Neely, G.J., Hullar, T.E., Skinner, M.W.: Role of electrode placement as a contributor to variability in cochlear implant outcomes. Otol. Neurotol. 29, 920–928 (2008)
6. Ahmad, T.J., Ali, H., Ajaz, M.A., Khan, S.A.: A Dsk Based Simplified Speech Processing Module For Cochlear Implant Research. In: International Conference on Acoustics, Speech, and Signal Processing, ICASSP (April 2009)
7. Raja Kumar, K., Seetha Ramaiah, P.: DSP and Microcontroller based Speech Processor for Auditory Prosthesis. Advanced Computing and Communications (December 2006)
8. Morbiwala, T.A., Svirsky, M., El-Sharkway, M., Rizkalla, M.: A PC-Based Speech Processor for Cochlear Implant fitting that can be adjusted in Real-Time. In: 48th Midwest Symposium on Circuits and Systems (August 2005)
9. Mourad, G., Adnen, C.: Comparison of IIR Filter banks and FFT Filter banks in Cochlear Implant Speech Processing Strategies. Journal of Electrical Systems 8(1), 76–84 (2012)
10. Tuo, L., Tian, G., Qin, G.: Study on Mobile Phone-based Speech Processor for Cochlear Implant. Communications and Mobile Computing, 110–113 (April 2011)
11. Kim, G., Loizou, P.C.: Improving Speech Intelligibility in Noise Using Environment-Optimized Algorithms. IEEE Transactions on Audio, Speech, and Language Processing 18(8), 2080–2090 (2010)

An Efficient Technique for Longest Prefix Matching in Network Routers

Rekha Govindaraj[1], Indranil Sengupta[2], and Santanu Chattopadhyay[1]

[1] Department of Electrical and Electronics Communication Engineering
Indian Institute of Technology, Kharagpur, India
[2] IIT Kharagpur
rekha.graj@gmail.com, santanu@ece.iitkgp.ernet.in

Abstract. Network Routers find most defined path for an arriving packet by the destination address in the packet using longest prefix matching (LPM) with Routing table entries. In this paper we propose a new Ternary Content Addressable Memory (TCAM) based system architecture for the LPM problem in routers. The proposed architecture eliminates sorting of table entries during table update [1][2]. It also eliminates the priority encoder needed to find the longest prefix match in conventional techniques .This has advantage in large capacity routing tables as proposed technique uses a priority encoder only of size equal to the number of bits in destination address to find the longest prefix length. To implement the proposed method for LPM, TCAM cell is modified by including two control transistors which control connection of cell either with Bit Match Line (BML) or with Word Match Line (WML). Functionality of modified cell is verified by simulating 32-bit TCAM word in UMC 180 nm technology in Spectre. Difference in search cycle time has been observed to be comparable to the conventional TCAM. The proposed technique completely reduces the LPM problem to only three search cycles in proposed TCAM memory architecture. As in recent times router table update rate has increased along with its capacity, proposed architecture is expected to be advantageous over conventional in large capacity and high update rate routing tables, due to elimination of sorting [2] and storage of any extra information on new entry [3].

Keywords: Longest prefix matching, Hardware solution, Ternary content addressable memory.

1   Introduction

Content Addressable Memory (CAM) has a special feature of addressing memory directly by content rather than by address [1]. The memory finds application in implementing lookup-table functions, such as, Hough transformation [4], Huffman coding/decoding [5], LZ compression [6] and also classifying and forwarding Internet Protocol packets in network routers [7][8][9][2]. In recent days internet services demand very high data transmission rate and high speed network routers. Longest prefix match constitutes one of the major problems in such domains. This work is oriented to address LPM problem in Internet Protocol packet forwarding.

H. Rahaman et al. (Eds.): VDAT 2012, LNCS 7373, pp. 317–326, 2012.

1.1   Background Work

Several software and hardware scheme have been proposed for LPM. Most of the hardware solutions are based on Content Addressable Memory (CAM) to store the table. As Ternary CAMs provide single cycle search operation, it can implement lookup table for IP packet forwarding. Fig. 1 shows the conventional scheme to find forwarding port for an arriving packet arrived from its destination address. Along with search operation we need longest prefix match (LPM) of multiple strings in table to forward packet on most defined and logical shortest path. Hardware solution for LPM using TCAM, with high power consumption, sorting requirements and high speed requirements in internet facilities [1] remain to be another serious problem of concern in research. Internet services demand high speed packet forwarding and high capacity routing tables need high table update rate. Many works have been reported to improve search time but to improve the update rate. These works [3] either need extra data storage with the routing table or simply employ better sorting techniques [2, 3]. In Reconfigurable CAM(RCAM) scheme we need the size of SRAM cell transistors to be adjusted depending on maximum number of possible matches with a given destination address as mask bits are read in wired-AND manner to find the longest prefix length and also proceeds in three phases [10]. RCAM scheme is not suitable for large capacity routing tables though provide a promising solution to small and medium size CAMs.

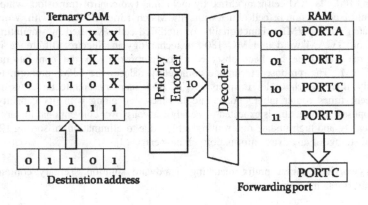

Fig. 1. Conventional Packet forwarding scheme with TCAM entries in sorted order of decreasing prefix length

We propose a similar scheme which can completely eliminate sorting in update of table and updating is made as simple as inserting a new entry into the table. Longest prefix matching problem is reduced to three cycles of search operation. There is a lot of research going on in improving search performance in TCAM, so the scheme can be a promising solution to LPM problem with increasing demand in internet service speed.

Proposed scheme and architecture for realization are explained in coming sections.

1.2   Our Contribution

We propose a high speed technique for longest prefix matching to find most defined path for the given destination address in packet header. Fig. 2 shows a pictorial representation of the proposed scheme for packet forwarding in network routers. To find longest prefix match, the technique proceeds in three search cycles. First and third search cycles are on word match line as in conventional TCAM and the second search cycle is performed on Bit match line which is an extra search line included in the proposed architecture. It aids in finding the length of longest prefix once all the matches with the given destination address are found.

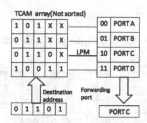

Fig. 2. Proposed scheme for IP packet forwarding

To support second phase of search for longest prefix length two new minimum size transistors are added to conventional TCAM cell in search circuitry of the cell as shown in Fig. 3 inside thick dotted lines. In the figure two SRAM cells are shown inside thin dotted lines, rest of transistors in search circuitry are of minimum size. This method is based on fact that a don't care bit gives match with any bit and its complement but binary 1/0 gives miss with its complement always. The technique eliminates priority encoder used in conventional method replacing it with a smaller sized priority encoder whose size is restricted to number of bits in destination address of IP packet. Also sorting is not required during table update. The complete problem of LPM is reduced to three search cycles in he proposed architecture.

2   Proposed Architecture

Proposed technique for longest prefix matching problem proceeds in three phases of search cycle. A pictorial representation of complete architecture for proposed scheme is as shown in Fig. 4. In the figure the terms TC, SLn,WMLn,BMLn stand for TCAM cell, Search data line n, word match line nth word, Bit match line at nth bit position respectively. Length of longest prefix match is indicated

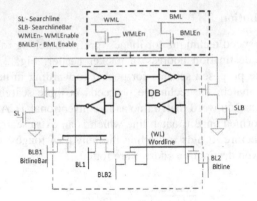

Fig. 3. TCAM cell in the proposed architecture

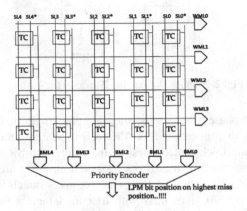

Fig. 4. Architecture for proposed scheme for solution to LPM problem

by highest miss position on BML lines. Size of priority encoder used is limited by number of bits in destination address.

The scheme proceeds in three phases of search cycles as explained below.

TCAM array

0	1	1	1	0	X	X	X	0
1	0	1	0	X	X	X	X	1
1	1	0	1	X	X	X	X	0
0	0	1	X	X	X	X	X	0
1	0	1	0	0	1	X	X	1
0	1	1	1	0	0	X	X	0
1	1	0	1	1	X	X	X	0
1	0	1	X	X	X	X	X	1

LPM position (arrow pointing to row 5)

Search data: 1 0 1 0 0 1 1 0

Word Match vector

Fig. 5. Find all matches in forwarding table for the destination address

In the first phase all the matches corresponding to the destination address in packet are found as similar to conventional TCAM architecture. Fig. 5 depicts the first phase to find all matches of destination address.

Second phase of search is performed on new Bit match search lines included to find longest prefix length only out of the lines matched in first search. We have to find single miss on this line and first miss from right gives the length of longest prefix. Search data is the complement of destination address. Fig. 6 shows a pictorial representation of second phase search cycle. Priority encoder whose size is limited by number of bits in destination address.

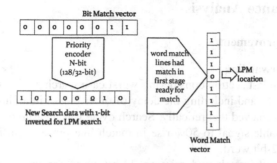

Fig. 6. Complemented destination address in search data and longest prefix length is first miss position from right

In the third phase of search cycle, destination address bit at longest prefix length position (from second phase) is complemented and the search is performed only on lines matched in first phase. Similar to second cycle, corresponding lines are selected by control signal BMLEn in respective TCAM cells. Longest prefix match will give miss with complement bit in longest prefix position of destination address. Fig. 7 shows the change in data vectors in third search cycle and location of LPM among forward table entries is found.

Fig. 7. Find LPM entry at miss on WML lines

Priority encoder used in this architecture is same as the one used in conventional TCAM [1] but of smaller size. So the area overhead is negligible only the bit match line amplifiers for BML are needed.

Updating routing table is as simple as inserting a new entry into the table, does not involve sorting. No further storage of any extra information about the new entry is required.

2.1   Details of Proposed Architecture

2.1.1   TCAM Cell and Difference in Search Cycle Time Compared with Conventional TCAM

Two transistors which connect the TCAM cell to either Bit Match line or Word match line are introduced to support architectural implementation of proposed technique. Newly introduced transistors are of minimum size in technology and SRAM cells in TCAM   realization   are kept same as in conventional TCAM   compared to Reconfigurable CAM architecture, which also eliminates priority encoder and sorting needs SRAM cell sizing to read selected bit lines in wired-AND method [10].

32-bit conventional TCAM word and modified TCAM 32-bit word are simulated to compare difference in search cycle time, 0.25ns of time difference is observed which can be neglected by considering worst case search cycle time as 2ns for high capacity memory. Search cycle time for conventional TCAM and Modified TCAM words were found to be 1.47ns and 1.69ns respectively. For three search cycles 6ns of time is needed. Hence the packet forwarding rate of 160Mhz can be achieved which is comparable to speed achieved.

2.1.2 Match Line Sensing Scheme

To verify functionality of proposed TCAM cell and to compare with the conventional TCAM memory search cycles segmented match line sensing scheme [11]. Same match line sense amplifiers are used for both conventional and modified TCAM architectures to measure difference in search cycle between them.

3   Performance Analysis

3.1   Speed Improvement

3.1.1 Packet Forwarding

As we discussed in last section considering worst case search cycle time to be 2ns for large memory blocks and including the delay of other blocks in architecture ,160Mhz line speed can be achieved theoretically. Search cycle was measured as from 50% rise of Match Line Enable signal to 50% rise in match line sense amplifier output signal during match of 32-bit word.

Search cycle with match and miss in 32-bit word for the proposed and conventional TCAM words are as shown in fig. 8, Fig. 9 and Fig. 10, 11 respectively.

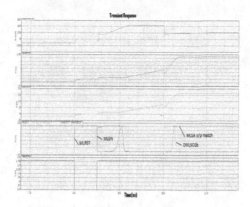

Fig. 8. Match in 32-bit proposed TCAM word

3.1.2 Update Time

Updating the routing table is just as inserting new entry into the table as technique does not need the entries to be in sorted order. This is advantageous when we have larger size routing tables and high frequency update of table as in recent days and IPv6 packets as prefix length can be of various lengths and destination address has 144-bits rather than 32-bits in IPv4 packets.

3.2 Area Overhead

Two extra transistors are included in new TCAM cell but priority encoder of size equal to the table entries is eliminated and the technique does not require any extra memory [12] to improve performance and eliminates sorting for longest prefix matching solution [2]. This includes negligible area overhead in large routing tables compared RCAM architecture and conventional TCAM architectures.

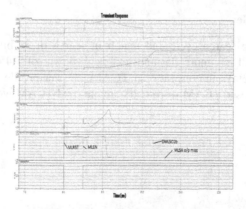

Fig. 9. Miss in 32-bit proposed TCAM word

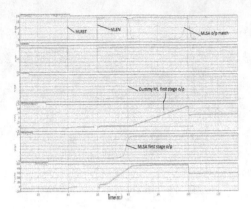

Fig. 10. Match in 32-bit conventional TCAM word

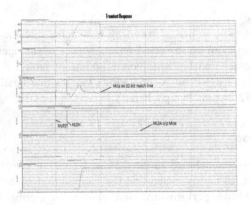

Fig. 11. Miss in 32-bit conventional TCAM word

3.3   Power Profile

Power profile during search cycle and match in search of 32-bit word is observed. Modified TCAM cell has more flat and less peak power of 1.458mW compared to peak power of 6.262mW in conventional TCAM. Power profile is as shown in Fig. 12, Fig. 3.3 for proposed TCAM word and conventional TCAM word respectively.

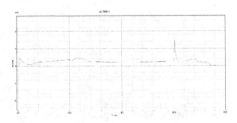

Fig. 12. Power profile for 32-bit proposed TCAM word in match case

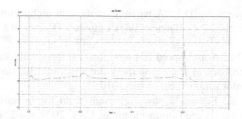

Fig. 13. Power profile for 32-bit conventional TCAM word in match case

4   Conclusion

In this paper a new solution to longest prefix matching problem in network routers for packet forwarding has been proposed. The scheme completely eliminates sorting during update time and priority encoder in conventional architecture. The method is suitable for large capacity routing tables which need frequent update and large priority encoders to find LPM for packet forwarding. Due to introduction of extra bit match lines (BML), inverters and priority encoder of size of number of bits in destination address area overhead will be high for small and medium capacity routing tables but still improves update time so will be advantageous when update rate is very high in small and medium capacity routing tables.

By employing better search techniques and match line sense amplifier circuits performance can be further improved to provide promising solution to next generation high data rate demands.

References

1. Pagiamtzis, K., Sheikholeslami, A.: Content-addressable memory (cam) circuits and architectures: A tutorial and survey. IEEE Journal of Solid State Circuits 41 (2006)
2. Panigrahy, R., Sharma, S.: Sorting and searching using ternary cams. IEEE Micro 23, 44–53 (2003)
3. Kasnavi, S., Vincent, P., Gaudet, C., Amaral, J.N.: A hardware based longest prefix matching scheme for tcams. In: IEEE International Symposium on Circuits and Systems, ISCAS 2005, vol. 4, pp. 3339–3342 (2005)
4. Nakanishi, M., Ogura, T.: Real-time cam-based hough transform and its performance evaluation. Machine Vision Appl. 12, 59–68 (2004)
5. Komoto, T.H.E., Nakamura, T.: A high speed and compact size jpeg huffman decoder using cam. In: VLSI Circuit Design Technology Symposium, pp. 37–38 (1993)
6. Wei, B., Tarver, R., Kim, J., Ng, K.: A single chip lampel-ziv data compressor. In: Proc. IEEE Int. Symp. Circuits Syst. (ISCAS), vol. 3, pp. 1953–1955 (1993)
7. McAuley, A.J., Francis, P.: Fast routing table lookup using cams. In: Proc. IEEE INFOCOM, vol. 3 (1993)
8. Huang, J.L.N.F., Chen, W.E., Chen, J.: Design of multi-field ipv6 packet classifiers using tcams. In: Proc. IEEE GLOBECOM, vol. 3 (2001)
9. Chao, H.: Next generation routers. Proc. IEEE 90 (September 2002)

10. Nourani, M., Vijayasarathi, D.S.: A reconfigurable cam architecture for network search engines. In: International Conference on Computer Design, ICCD 2006, pp. 82–87 (October 2007)
11. Syed Iftekhar Ali, M.: A high speed and low-power ternary cam design using match-line segmentation an feedback in sense amplifiers. In: Proc. of 13th International Conference on Computer and Information Technology (2010)
12. Mishra, T., Sahni, S.: Petcam- a power efficient tcam for forwarding tables. In: IEEE Symposium on Computers and Communications, ISCC 2009, pp. 224–229 (2009)

A Faster Hierarchical Balanced Bipartitioner for VLSI Floorplans Using Monotone Staircase Cuts

Bapi Kar[1], Susmita Sur-Kolay[2],
Sridhar H. Rangarajan[3], Chittaranjan R. Mandal[1]

[1] Indian Institute of Technology, Kharagpur, India
[2] Indian Statistical Institute, Kolkata, India
[3] IBM India Systems & Technology Engineering Lab (ISTEL)

Abstract. This work proposes an improved heuristic algorithm for top-down hierarchical Monotone Staircase Bipartitioning of VLSI floorplans using breadth-first traversal to reduce the runtime to $O(nk)$ at each level of the hierarchy, where n and k denote respectively the number of blocks and nets in the given floorplan. This multi-objective optimization problem calls for a trade off between maximizing the quality of area (number) balanced bipartition, and minimizing the number of cut nets at each level of the hierarchy by a trade-off parameter $\gamma \in [0,1]$. The area balanced bipartition is known to be a NP-hard problem. The proposed approach obtains a bipartition as close to balanced (ideally equal area or number as the case may be) as possible along with a minimal net cut. We obtain convex weighted linear cost as high as 0.998 for $\gamma = 0.4$, and the runtime does not exceed 1 second for any of the circuits in MCNC/GSRC Hard floorplanning benchmarks. This method, without using maxflow algorithm, is much faster and simpler than the earlier maxflow-based approach, without sacrificing the quality of the solution.

Keywords: VLSI floorplan, balanced bipartition, top-down hierarchy, routing region definition, monotone staircase cut.

1 Introduction

In VLSI Design Methodology, global routing(GR) is an important stage that greatly impacts the quality and performance of a circuit being realized in silicon. In case of infeasible routing solution, block placement and hence floorplanning (Chip-planning) must be done repetitively until a feasible routing solution is attained. This is a bottleneck to ascertain a good time-to-market. Moreover, channel routing demands a safe (cycle free) routing order; it is shown [7,8] that non-sliceable floorplans do not cater safe (acyclic) routing order using slicing tree method as it does for a sliceable floorplan (see Figure 1). In [3,8], it is shown that Monotone Staircase Channels provide a *tree like routing order* irrespective of the sliceability of the floorplan and can also tackle the Switch-Box routing problem [7]. Moreover, the flexibility in resizing the area of monotone staircase channels is conducive to efficient channel utilization and avoidance of routing congestion in the channel.

H. Rahaman et al. (Eds.): VDAT 2012, LNCS 7373, pp. 327–336, 2012.

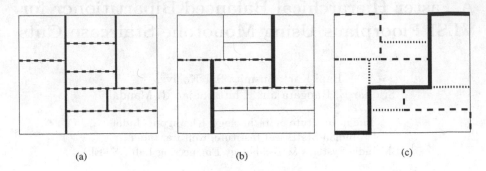

(a)   (b)   (c)

Fig. 1. Hierarchical Floorplan Bipartition: (a) sliceable floorplan and (b) non-sliceable floorplan with cutlines only; (c) non-sliceable floorplan with monotone staircase cuts

Previous work on Monotone Staircase Bipartition of VLSI floorplans [5] proposed an iterative maxflow-based heuristic approach for *Area Balanced Monotone Staircase Bipartition Problem*, P_{ac} with minimum net cut. It was also proved that P_{ac} is NP-hard. In [9], it is shown that a circuit graph can be balanced bipartitioned by a max-flow based iterative node-merging technique. This algorithm using an $O(n^3)$ push-relabel algorithm [1] for computing the max-flow in each iteration leads to $O(n^4)$ time for a maximum of $O(n)$ iterations. An improvement was then suggested in [9] as an iterative flow augmenting method similar to Ford-Fulkerson algorithm [1] with the worst case time complexity $O(nm)$, where n and m denote the number of vertices and edges in the graph respectively. But, this cannot guarantee a monotone staircase cut [4].

Meanwhile, a linear time algorithm for *Number Balanced Monotone Staircase Bipartition* employing depth-first traversal was given in [2]. Their algorithm, namely *Block_Labeling*, gives monotone staircases by labeling the blocks one by one until $\lfloor n/2 \rfloor$ blocks are labeled which form the left partition. However, this is not directly adaptable in the context of Area Balanced Bipartitioning. Moreover, their problem formulation does not consider any net cut. Since a minimum net cut obtained otherwise (as cited in previous works) may not always lead to a monotone staircase, our work proposes a method based on breadth-first traversal of BAG without using maxflow-based algorithm. This work is focused on getting a set of monotone staircase cuts first, and subsequently computing the corresponding net cuts. We pick the best monotone staircase with a specific balance factor and the corresponding net cut for a given trade-off parameter γ (see Section 3). Similar to [5], the present work can obtain Monotone Staircase based Number Balanced Bipartition with minimum net cut by using *Area/Number mode selection*.

The organization of this paper is as follows: Section 2 gives some preliminaries for the Monotone Staircase Bipartition problem, while the details of the proposed method is based on *breadth-first traversal* appear in Section 3. Results and relevant discussion are presented in Section 4, while Section 5 has the concluding remarks.

2   Preliminaries

Previous works on Area Balanced Monotone Staircase Bipartition [4,5] suggested two different heuristic approaches for circuits with only two terminals ($t = 2$) and with multi-terminal nets ($t > 2$) respectively. The present work is an improvement over the aforementioned work and generalized for k-terminal nets ($t \geq 2$). Moreover, it converges on larger circuits consisting of hundreds of blocks. We give a faster *Hierarchical Monotone Staircase Bipartitioning* algorithm such that every cut is a monotone staircase cut and hence the resulting channels are (strictly) monotone increasing (or decreasing) staircase channels at alternate levels of the hierarchy. However, there exist a few trivial cuts, i.e. a cut in a sub-floorplan having two blocks at the leaf level of the hierarchy, are merely vertical or horizontal cuts belonging to both types. These may be termed as *degenerated* monotone staircase cuts.

We revisit the formulation of *block adjacency graph* (BAG) [4] using floorplan information of the blocks and their relative positions. It is defined as an unweighted directed graph, $G(V, E)$ where $V = \{v_i | v_i$ corresponds to block $b_i\}$ and E is the set of directed edges $e_{ij} = (v_i, v_j)$ such that block b_i is to the *left of or above* its adjacent block b_j in the floorplan. This definition caters to a *monotonically increasing staircase* (MIS) cut. The source and sink vertices of the BAG are chosen as the blocks at top-left (indeg=0) and bottom-right (outdeg=0) corners of the floor respectively.

Similarly, in the BAG to obtain a *monotonically decreasing staircase* (MDS) cut, however, the edges are defined as follows: there exists a directed edge e_{ij} $=(v_i, v_j) \in E$ from a block (b_i) which is to the *left of or below* another adjacent block b_j. The source and sink vertices in this case are identified as the bottom-left (indeg=0) and top-right (outdeg=0) cornered blocks in the floor respectively. Both the cases are demonstrated in Figure 2. From now on, we shall use n and m to denote number of vertices and edges of BAG respectively.

We use the following lemma [4] and refer to it as the *Monotone Staircase (MS) Property* of a cut for a given BAG, henceforth.

Lemma 1. *If $e_{ij} \in E$ is an arc in BAG, $G(V,E)$, then there exists at least one monotone staircase in the floorplan such that the blocks b_i and b_j appear in the left and right partitions respectively, and there exists no staircase with b_i in the right partition and b_j in the left partition.*

3   Algorithm for Balanced Monotone Staircase Bipartition

We formulate the top-down hierarchical Monotone Staircase Bipartitioning problem for VLSI floorplans by using BAG formulation for MIS or MDS. Since the problem of area balanced mincut (P_{ac}) is a multi-objective optimization problem, we reiterate the objectives as:

- balance ratio $\delta = \min(A_l, A_r)/\max(A_l, A_r)$ be maximized, and
- number of cut nets(k_c) in the partition be minimized,

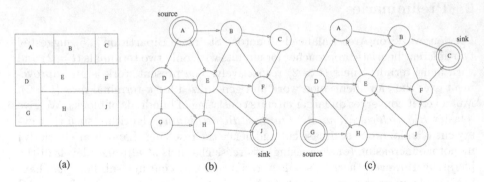

Fig. 2. (a) A floorplan, and its corresponding block adjacency graphs for (b) a MIS, and (c) a MDS

where A_l and A_r are the area of the left and the right partitions respectively. For number balanced bipartition problem (P_{nc}), δ is defined as $\min(n_l, n_r)/\max(n_l, n_r)$, where n_l and n_r are the respective number of blocks in the left and the right partitions.

We take the same convex function as defined in [5] along with the *trade-off parameter* γ as:

$$Cost = \gamma \times \delta + (1 - \gamma) \times (1 - k_c/k) \qquad (1)$$

where k_c is the number of nets cut in a given partition and k is the total number of nets that exist in the (sub) floorplan. Our objective is to maximize the function cost so that δ is maximized and k_c is minimized for a given value of γ. We also need to ensure that the value of cost is maximum for a specific value of γ. In [5], few specific values of $\gamma \in [0,1]$ were suggested from experimental results. Based on the type of BAG (MIS or MDS), at each level of the hierarchy, we obtain multiple monotone staircase cuts starting from the trivial one (Lemma 3 in [4]) i.e. the left partition contains the source vertex only. Subsequent iterations for adding adjacent blocks, take place until a point of convergence is reached (ideally at $W/2$) based on the total weight (area of the floor), W and a predefined user input, ϵ (<1), based weight bounds $[(1-\epsilon)W/2, (1+\epsilon)W/2]$.

In Figures 3(a)-(d), we illustrate the steps of creating the queue-based partition of the (sub) floorplan using BAG (MIS in the current example). Figure 3(a) depicts that this method starts with the source vertex A, at the top left corner for MIS and subsequently its adjacent vertices {D,B,E} are processed. The blocks B and D are eligible to be added (in any order) to the left partition as there is no *back edge* from the right to the left partition. If E is added as an adjacent block of A prior to either B or D, there would be a back edge (B,E) or (D,E) thus violating Lemma 1. In that case, E cannot be added as an adjacent block of A. However, E can be added as an adjacent block of either B or D in a latter pass thus forming a valid staircase comprising A,B,D and E. It is also to be noted that, at each step of adding a block to the left partition, it has to

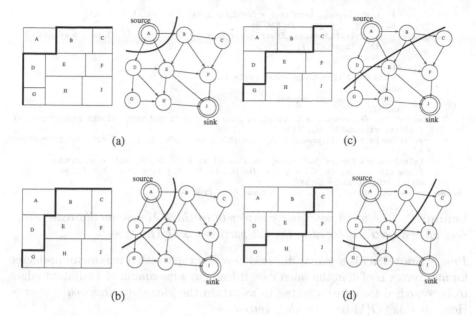

Fig. 3. Four iterations of our method for balanced bipartitioning of a floorplan by a MIS cut

be ensured that the weight of the left partition is either less than $(1-\epsilon)W/2$, or converge when it lies within the aforementioned weight-bound.

This iterative bipartitioning method converges when the weight of the left (and hence the right) partition is within these two bounds. It takes longer time to converge a monotone staircase with a very good value of δ (close to 1) when ϵ is very small [9], e.g. 0.05. Conversely, a larger ϵ (>0.2) leads to a faster convergence but inferior value of δ that results in a sub-optimal solution (an MIS/MDS cut in this case). We choose the best cut with the maximum cost among the set of possible cuts at each level of the hierarchy, to obtain an optimal monotone staircase cut.

The algorithm *GenerateMSCut* is based on iterative breadth-first traversal (without using any maxflow-based algorithm) of the BAG, while strictly obeying the *monotone staircase property*.

GenerateMSCut(G, N, γ, ϵ, Balance)

1. Create a Queue, Q; size(Q) = $2|V|$. /*$G = (V, E)$*/
2. W = $\sum_i Wt(b_i)$ when Balance = 1(Area Balance mode); = $|V|$, otherwise(Number Balance Mode).

   lb_wt = $(1-\epsilon)*W/2$ and ub_wt = $(1+\epsilon)*W/2$.
   /* Let Left partition be L and S be the source vertex in G with indeg = 0.*/
3. Initially, L= $\varnothing$, Wt(L) = 0, $level\_no$ = 0.
   Enqueue(S), S.level = $level\_no$; Enqueue($\varnothing$).
4. while (Wt(L) $\notin$ [lb_wt, ub_wt]) do
   (a) while (Q $\neq \varnothing$) do
       i. v_i = Dequeue(Q).
       ii. if ($v_i \neq \varnothing$) then

```
        A.  L = L ∪{v_i}; Level(v_i) = level_no ; Wt(L) ← Wt(L) + Wt(v_i).
        B.  for v_j ∈ adj(v_i) in BAG do
              if IsValid_Monotone_Staircase = true && (Wt(L) + Wt(v_j)) in [lb_wt,ub_wt]
              then Enqueue(v_j);
              end for.
     iii. else
              if (Q = ∅) then break inner while loop.
              else
              Increase level_no; Enqueue(∅).
              end if.
        end while. /*Inner while loop: gives B_l and B_r; left and right blocks respectively*/
    (b)  findNetPartition(B_l, B_r, N)
        /*findNetPartition() produces N_l, N_r and N_c; the left, right and cut nets respectively
        */
    (c)  Calculate the Convex Cost using Equation(1) with B_l, B_r, N_c and N as inputs.
    (d)  Store the cut object, C_i = {Cost, B_l, B_r, N_l, N_r, N_c} to a list, λ = {C_i}.
    end while. /*Outer while loop*/
 5. Return the cut object, C_max with Maximum Cost from λ.
```

Lemma 2. *The worst case time complexity to check Monotone Staircase Property after a vertex is added to the left partition is O(1).*

Proof. Since BAG is a planar directed acyclic graph with a maximum in-degree for any vertex is of 4, in the worst case it leads to a maximum of 4 adjacent edges to be searched for a given vertex to ascertain the *monotone staircase property.* Hence it takes $O(1)$ time for each vertex.

Lemma 3. *The worst case time complexity for Monotone Staircase Cut Generation at a given level of hierarchy is O(n), where n is the number of blocks.*

Proof. We start from the source vertex of BAG and traverse all the adjacent vertices in a breadth-first search manner and simultaneously check for the validity of the *monotone staircase property* to enqueue them in the queue. Thus it has $O(n)$ enqueue operations in the worst case for all the blocks except the sink vertex, and $O(1)$ operation to check the staircase property for each vertex. It can also be stated that the BAG is a planar graph with the cardinality of the edge set E is $O(n)$ and amortized analysis for each vertex yields total $O(m)$ time for all enqueued vertices. Thus the total time complexity turns out to be $O(n + m)$, which is again $O(n)$.

Lemma 4. *The number of Monotone Staircase Cuts obtained by GenerateMS-Cut algorithm at a given level of hierarchy is O(n).*

Proof. Once a block is added to the left partition, it remains in the same partition and results in a distinct monotone staircase. This holds initially when the left partition contains only the source vertex of the BAG. Addition of one or more blocks continues for at most $n - 1$ iterations until the sink vertex in the BAG is encountered. The right partition must contain at least the sink vertex for a valid staircase. Thus, the number of distinct monotone staircases considered by this algorithm pertains to the number blocks added in each step to the left partition and hence is $O(n)$ in the worst case.

The nets at a given level of hierarchy, are either cut nets whose terminals are present on either side of the staircase cut, or belong entirely within one of the two partitions. The nets with all terminals entirely within the left (right) partition are termed as the left (right) *uncut nets*. Further, the cut nets are assigned to the left (right) partition if they have *at least* two terminals in the left (right) partition. Thus, in the left (right) partition, the uncut nets along with the (modified) cut nets having terminals belonging to the left (right) partition constitute the total nets for that partition and are to be considered for MIS (MDS) cut generation at the next level of the hierarchy.

Lemma 5. *The worst case time complexity for the net bipartition at a given level of hierarchy is $O(k)$, where k is the number of nets in the (sub) floorplan.*

Proof. We need to check all the nets in a given (sub) floorplan to determine whether these are *cut net* or belong entirely to the left or the right partition. Thus, the worst case time complexity is $O(k)$.

Lemma 6. *The worst case time complexity of GenerateMSCut algorithm at a given level of hierarchy is $O(nk)$.*

Proof. From Lemmas 3, 4 and 5, generation of each staircase takes $O(n)$ time. There are $O(n)$ distinct staircases in the worst case, and the net bipartition takes $O(k)$ for each staircase. Thus, the total time complexity is $O(n+nk)$, i.e. $O(nk)$.

3.1   Hierarchical Framework

The top-down hierarchical procedure *GenerateMSCTree* generates a hierarchy tree called *MSC Tree* for a given floorplan and *GenerateMSCut* gives the breadth-first traversal based balanced bipartitioning for min-cost monotone staircase cuts (ms-cuts) at each hierarchical node given in the previous section. The procedure *ConstructBAG* is based on Lemma 1 in Section 2. Here B, F, N, *stype* and *Balance* denote blocks, floorplan topology, nets, staircase type namely MIS (MDS), and area (number) balance mode respectively. The first call to *GenerateMSCTree* is for the entire floor along with *stype* as MIS, and specific values for γ and ϵ (see Section 4 for the experimental details), and the resulting cut gives the *root cut* of the MSC Tree.

GenerateMSCTree (B,N,F,stype,γ,ϵ,Balance)

```
1. G = ConstructBAG(B, F, stype). /* G = (V,E)*/
2. Node.Cut = GenerateMSCut(G, N, γ, ε, Balance).
3. if |Bₗ| ≥ 2 then
     lNode = GenerateMSCTree(Bₗ, Nₗ, Fₗ, stype, γ, ε, Balance).
   end if
4. if |Bᵣ| ≥ 2 then
     rNode = GenerateMSCTree(Bᵣ, Nᵣ, Fᵣ, stype, γ, ε, Balance).
   end if
5. Node.Left = lNode, Node.Right = rNode.
6. return Node.
```

Theorem 1. *Algorithm GenerateMSCTree for Hierarchical Monotone Staircase Cut Generation takes $O(nk\log n)$ time.*

Proof. From Lemma 6, each hierarchy takes $O(nk)$ time in the worst case. The procedure *ConstructBAG* takes $O(n)$ since BAG is a planar graph. The depth of the hierarchy i.e. height of the MSC Tree is $O(\log V)$, as the tree is (nearly) a balanced binary tree. Hence, the total taken time is $O((n + nk) \log n)$, i.e $O(nk \log n)$.

4   Experimental Results

In order to verify the correctness and efficiency, we test our algorithm on MCNC and GSRC Hard floorplanning benchmark circuits given in Table 1. The floorplans are generated using ParquetFP tool [6]. We modified a few nets having connectivity with IO Pads and consider only the modified nets with $t \geq 2$ excluding IO Pads.

Table 1. MCNC and GSRC (Hard) Benchmark Circuits

Suite	Circuit	Blocks	Nets (original)	Nets (modified)
MCNC	apte	9	97	44
	hp	11	83	44
	xerox	10	203	183
	ami33	33	123	84
	ami49	49	408	377
GSRC	n10	10	118	54
	n30	30	349	147
	n50	50	485	320
	n100	100	885	576
	n200	200	1585	1274
	n300	300	1893	1632

Our algorithm was implemented in C programming language and run on a Linux platform (2.8GHz, 4GB). Unlike the previous work on monotone staircase bipartitioning [5] which presented their results for MCNC benchmark circuits only with several values of γ, we assume a specific value of γ to be 0.4. We achieved maximum runtime of less than 1 second for all the circuits in both MCNC and GSRC Hard benchmark suite. Table 2 summarizes the values of the maximum convex cost and the runtimes for all the modified MCNC and GSRC Hard benchmark circuits to produce their respective hierarchical partition tree, *MSC Tree*.

In Table 3, we compare the maximum *Cost* and runtime of the maxflow based work [5] with those obtained by our proposed method. It is to be noted that their work [5] did not report results on GSRC benchmark circuits.

We also verified our algorithm with a tight example created from a floorplan topology in [5] as shown in Figure 4(a) containing 11 blocks and 44 nets (derived from the *hp* benchmark circuit). The dimensions of the individual blocks are computed accordingly. The values obtained are $Cost = 0.976$ for the cut highlighted in Figure 4(b) with $\gamma = 0.4$ and $\epsilon = 0.05$. It took only three iterations to converge for the said cut with a runtime of 4 msecs. The resulting *MIS Channel* is highlighted with thicker lines in Figure 4(a).

Table 2. Maximum *Cost* and runtime for area-balanced and number-balanced mode by our method (γ=0.4)

Benchmark		Area-balanced mode			Number-balanced mode		
Suite	Circuit	ϵ	*Cost* (max)	runtime(s)	ϵ	*Cost* (max)	runtime(s)
MCNC	apte	0.05	0.995	0.005	0.05	0.920	0.003
	hp	0.15	0.936	0.003	0.05	0.933	0.002
	xerox	0.05	0.989	0.009	0.05	0.867	0.007
	ami33	0.05	0.980	0.014	0.05	0.950	0.011
	ami49	0.40	0.997	0.023	0.05	0.954	0.016
GSRC	n10	0.10	0.998	0.008	0.05	0.867	0.004
	n30	0.10	0.998	0.006	0.05	0.950	0.006
	n50	0.15	0.987	0.050	0.015	0.950	0.011
	n100	0.15	0.990	0.062	0.05	0.960	0.061
	n200	0.20	0.989	0.432	0.05	0.962	0.437
	n300	0.35	0.979	0.656	0.05	0.962	0.617

Table 3. Comparison between our method and [5] of maximum convex cost over all levels and runtime (γ=0.4)

Benchmark		Area Balance Mode				Number Balance Mode			
Suite	Circuit	Max-Cost ([5])	Max-Cost (Ours)	Runtime ([5])	Runtime (Ours)	Max-Cost ([5])	Max-Cost (Ours)	Runtime ([5])	Runtime (Ours)
MCNC	apte	0.469	0.995	0.013	0.005	0.641	0.920	0.007	0.003
	hp	0.486	0.936	0.016	0.003	0.775	0.933	0.009	0.002
	xerox	0.767	0.989	0.022	0.009	0.723	0.867	0.015	0.007
	ami33	0.752	0.980	0.029	0.014	0.732	0.950	0.021	0.011
	ami49	0.802	0.997	0.095	0.023	0.960	0.954	0.069	0.016
GSRC	n10	-	0.998	-	0.008	-	0.867	-	0.004
	n30	-	0.998	-	0.006	-	0.950	-	0.006
	n50	-	0.987	-	0.050	-	0.950	-	0.011
	n100	-	0.990	-	0.062	-	0.960	-	0.061
	n200	-	0.989	-	0.432	-	0.962	-	0.437
	n300	-	0.979	-	0.656	-	0.962	-	0.617

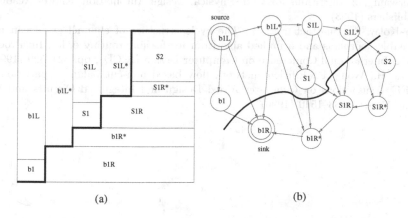

(a)   (b)

Fig. 4. Example of (a) Floorplan[5] with MIS Channel, and (b) BAG with MIS Cut

5   Concluding Remarks

In this paper, we present a novel heuristic algorithm for Monotone Staircase Bipartitioning of a VLSI floorplan with better accuracy and runtime. However, there is scope of improvement in this algorithm such as BAG modeling for non-mosaic floorplans generated by ParquetFP tool [6], by inserting dummy blocks in the white space to make it mosaic and more compact. The insertion of these dummy blocks would give a generic modeling of the routing resources as in the case of ideal mosaic floorplans and will facilitate a robust monotone staircase channel based global routing. The *number of bends* in the staircase at a given level of the hierarchy may also be minimized and therefore considered as the third objective for this optimization problem.

References

1. Cormen, T., et al.: Introduction to Algorithms, 3rd edn. MIT Press (2009)
2. Dasgupta, P., et al.: Monotone Bipartitioning Problem in a Planar Point Set with Applications to VLSI. ACM Transactions on Design Automation of Electronic Systems 7(2), 231–248 (2002)
3. Guruswamy, M., Wong, D.: Channel Routing Order for Building-Block Layout with Rectilinear Modules. In: Proc. of IEEE International Conference on Computer-Aided Design (ICCAD), pp. 184–187 (1988)
4. Majumdar, S., et al.: On Finding a Staircase Channel with Minimum Crossing Nets in a VLSI Floorplan. Journal of Circuits, Systems and Computers 13(5), 1019–1038 (2004)
5. Majumdar, S., et al.: Hierarchical Partitioning of VLSI Floorplans by Staircases. ACM Transactions on Design Automation of Electronic Systems 12(1), Article 7 (2007)
6. Parquet FloorPlanner, Rev-4.5, University of Michigan (2006), http://vlsicad.eecs.umich.edu/BK/parquet
7. Sherwani, N.: Algorithms for VLSI Physical Design Automation. Kluwer Academic Publishers (1993)
8. Sur-Kolay, S., Bhattacharya, B.: The cycle structure of channel graphs in non-sliceable floorplans and a unified algorithm for feasible routing order. In: Proc. of IEEE International Conference on Computer Design (ICCD), pp. 524–529 (1991)
9. Yang, H., Wong, F.: Efficient network flow based min-cut balanced partitioning. IEEE Transactions on Computer Aided Design and Integrated Circuits and Systems 15(12), 1533–1540 (1996)

Test Data Compression for NoC Based SoCs Using Binary Arithmetic Operations

Sanga Chaki and Chandan Giri

Department of Information Technology
Bengal Engineering and Science University, Shibpur
{s.chaki27,chandangiri}@gmail.com

Abstract. Network-on-chip (NoC) is the most effective communication structure for System-on-Chip (SoC) components. Test data compression is essential to reduce test data volume, to decreases test costs. In this paper, a test compression and decompression solution is proposed based on binary arithmetic operations. Experimental results for full scan test data set of ISCAS'89 benchmarks are demonstrated. The major advantages include high compression ratio and a low cost decoder. It is observed that the proposed compression method achieves a compression ratio as high as 93.56% for ISCAS'89 benchmarks.

Keywords: NoC testing, Horizontal test data compression.

1   Introduction

One of the most fundamental issues in Network-on-Chip (NoC) design is that of test related parameters optimization to reduce test costs. The combination of test data compression and NoC based test scheduling allows a drastic reduction of the system test time. As all the cores of the SoC must be adequately tested, the amount of test data required tremendous. Conventional external testing [1] involves storing all test vectors and test response on the Automated Test Equipment (ATE). But these testers have limited speed, data memory, channel capacity on top of being extremely expensive. So, the bandwidth between the tester and chip becomes small, increasing test time. Reducing the test-data volume by compression is a viable option. The original test data is compressed off line, stored in the ATE, and decompressed on-chip to restore the initial data. The test results are compacted before being sent back to the tester. The scheme presented in this paper is based on the horizontal test data compression method [8].

The organization of the paper is as follows. In Section 2, a literature survey is presented. Sections 3 and 4 present the compression procedure and the decompressor architecture. Experimental results are reported in Section 5, and the conclusions are drawn in Section 6.

2   Literature Survey

A wide range of literature on test data compression methods include the Code-based schemes [2-5], which encode test cubes by using data compression codes. The data is

H. Rahaman et al. (Eds.): VDAT 2012, LNCS 7373, pp. 337–342, 2012.

partitioned into symbols; the compressed data is formed by replacing symbols with code words. Run-length-based codes [1] investigate compression of scan vectors by encoding runs of repeated values. In Dictionary codes [1] the original data is partitioned into n-bit symbols and a dictionary to store each unique symbol is used. Statistical coding [10] partitions the original data into n bit symbols and assigns variable-length code words based on each symbol's frequency of occurrence. Constructive codes exploit the fact that each n-bit scan slice typically contains relatively few care bits. The Linear-decompression-based schemes [7] decompress the data using only linear operations like LFSRs and XOR networks. The Broadcast-scan-based schemes [1] rely on broadcasting the same values to multiple scan chains. Vertical compression schemes [2], horizontal compression schemes [8], and schemes that address compression in both directions [9], are also present.

3   Proposed Compression Scheme

3.1   Motivational Example

In the proposed compression scheme, individual test vectors (*TVs*) are compressed and stored in the ATE memory. During test, the ATE sends the compressed slices to an 1 *to n* on chip decompressor that feeds the n scan chains.

The example *TV* to be compressed, shown in Fig. 1(a) is considered. Fig. 1(b) represents the *TV* after it is divided into n-bit sub-vectors. Here, the unit size n is taken as 8 bits, and the length of *TV*, m is 47 bits. The last zero bit is appended so that *TV* can be divided into 6 groups of 8 bits each. All the don't care bits are replaced by zero bits. The binary differences between consecutive groups are computed, using the two's complement binary subtraction rule, and each of them is used to generate each of the parts of the compressed TV_C. These parts are depicted in Fig. 1(c). The details of the method are discussed in the next sub-section. The data actually sent through the ATE to the on chip decompressor, TV_S, is shown in Fig. 1(d). The Fig. 1(e) gives the restored groups, which together forms the single test vector, TV_A that is applied for testing.

3.2   Compression Algorithm

In the proposed compression algorithm represented in Fig. 2, each *TV* is divided into a number of n bit slices. In the next step, a constant *MAX* is defined and assigned an integer value closest to m, such that, $MAX \% n = 0$ and $MAX >= m$.

Next, all the don't-care bits in the *TV* are assigned 0 values and $(MAX - m)$ number of 0 bits are appended to the *TV*, so that the length of the updated *TV* is equal to *MAX* bits. This is the reason of calculating the *MAX* value in the previous step. Each *TV* is now divided into (MAX/n) number of n-bit groups or units. For two consecutive n-bit groups, say $GROUP_{(i/n)}$ and $GROUP_{((i/n)+1)}$, the binary difference is calculated using the two's complement binary subtraction rule. From each such difference value, a part of the whole compressed vector is generated. Here, i is the counter variable which increments by n after each operation.

If a difference is zero, the compressed part consists of a single zero bit, as illustrated in Fig. 3(a). On the other hand, if the difference is non-zero, the sign is checked. If the difference is positive, a pair of bits of values one and zero is added before the difference value to create the compressed part of $(n+2)$ bits. But if the difference is negative, a pair of bits, both of values one is added before the difference value to create the compressed part of $(n+2)$ bits, detailed in Fig. 3(b). In this additional pair of bits, the value of the first bit is always one, signifying that the next $(n+1)$ bits should be treated as a single unit and the second bit signifies the sign of the magnitude contained in the next n bits. Each such part is appended to get each compressed TV.

xxxxxxxxxx0xx0xxxx00xx1xxxxxxxxxxx00xxxx0x0xxxx
(a) Original 47-bit test vector

G1	xxxxxxxx	P 1	-	S1	0	G1	00000000
G2	xx0xx0xx	P2	0	S2	0	G2	00000000
G3	xx00xx1x	P3	1100000010	S3	1100000010	G3	00000010
G4	xxxxxxxx	P 4	1000000010	S4	1000000010	G4	00000000
G5	xx00xxxx	P 5	0	S5	0	G5	00000000
G6	0x0xxxx0	P 6	0	S6	0	G6	0000000
(b) TV		**(c) TVC**		**(d) TVs**		**(e) TVA**	

Fig. 1. Example of compressed test sequence, $n = 8$ bits

Procedure TV_Compression

1.   Inputs : n = unit size, TVs of length m-bits from a test set
2.   Define MAX such that
a.   If m%n = 0 then MAX = m;
b.   Else MAX = m + (n - m%n);
3.   For each input T V of m-bits
a.   Update TV: Assign 0 values to all Don't-Care bits.
Append (MAX - m) number of 0 bits, make length of Updated_TV = MAX;
b. Initialize i = 0, For the (i/n)th and ((i/n)+1)th groups of n-bits in Updated_TV
i. Assign binary difference between two consecutive groups to Bin_diff[n];
ii. From Bin_diff[n] create a   Compressed_TV_part:
If all bits of Bin_diff[n]=0 then Define Part[1] = {0};
Else Define Part[n+2], Part[0]=1
Now, if Bin_diff[n]>0, assign Part[1]=0;
Else assign Part[1]=1;
Then store Bin_diff[n] in last n bits of Part[n+2];
iii.   Append the computed Compressed_TV_part to the Compressed_TV;
iv.   i = i+n;
c. Return Compressed_TV;
4.   Repeat for each T V;

Fig. 2. The Compression Algorithm

The entire procedure is repeated for all the *TV*'s in the set under consideration. It is to be remembered that the compressed *TV* is actually an ordered collection of pre-processed differences between a set of *n* bit groups. So, to recover the original *TV* from its compressed counterpart, the first group of *n* bits is necessary. Thus, the compressed vector and a) if the first *n* bits of the original *TV* contain a specified bit of value *1*, a bit of value *1* and the first *n* bits of the original *TV*, added at the beginning of the compressed *TV* are sent, b) else a *0* bit, added at the beginning of the compressed *TV* is sent.

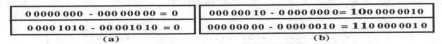

0 0000 000 - 000 000 00 = 0	000 000 10 - 0 000 000 0= 1 00 000 0010
0 000 1010 - 00 001 0 10 = 0	000 000 00 - 0 0000 0010 = 1 1 0 0000 0010
(a)	(b)

Fig. 3. Encoding of difference values for *n*= 8 bits

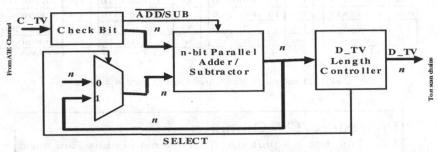

Fig. 4. The Proposed Decompression Architecture

4   Decompression Scheme – Proposed Architecture

In this section, the decompression scheme is detailed. The values of *n*, *m* and *MAX* remain the same as in compression. The proposed decompression architecture, presented in Fig. 4, has three main components – the *Check Bit* component, the *n*-bit parallel *Adder/Subtractor* and a *Length Controller* for the test vector being decompressed. The *C_TV* is applied to the *Check Bit* component first. The operations regarding the checking of bit values occur here, after which, either *n C_TV* bits or *n* zero bits are sent to the *n*-bit parallel *Adder/Subtractor* as the augend (minuend). The *Check Bit* component also provides the *Adder/Subtractor* with the $\overline{ADD/SUB}$ signal, which decides the operation performed by it, addition ($\overline{ADD/SUB}$ is low) or subtraction ($\overline{ADD/SUB}$ is high), depending on the incoming bit values of the *C_TV*. The *n*-bit addend (subtrahend) is provided through a multiplexer. For the first *n C_TV* bits, the addend (subtrahend) is always *n* zero bits. Otherwise, it is the *n*-bits of the *D_TV*, computed in the previous step. The *multiplexer* is controlled by the *SELECT* signal, generated by the *D_TV Length Controller*. This component reduces the number of bits in the regenerated test vector from *MAX* number of bits to *m* number of bits, and restores it to its original length. It can feed *n* number of scan chains at a time. As soon as a complete test vector is regenerated, the *SELECT* signal turns low, indicating the start of the next *C_TV* and an *n* zero bits addend (subtrahend). After the first *n*-bits of the *C_TV* are processed to get the first *n*-bits of the *D_TV*, *SELECT* again turns high and remains so, until the whole *D_TV* is regenerated.

5   Experimental Results

In this section, the results of applying the proposed test data compression scheme on ISCAS'89 benchmarks full scan test data are reported. The compression algorithm was implemented in C programming language and run on an Intel Core 2 Duo processor, having 512 MB RAM, in Linux operating system. The test sequences used are high in don't care percentage. The values of *n* that are considered here for experimental purpose are 8 bits, 16 bits, 24 bits and 64 bits. In table 1 the row %X denote don't – care percentage. The rows C Volume and C Ratio% give the compressed volume and the compression ratio percentage respectively. The best compression percentage achievable for each circuit is reported in the last row. Table 2 presents a comparison of the work with other code-based compression schemes proposed in the literature. Results presented in row "Proposed" give the maximum % compression obtained for any *n* value as given in Table 1. The proposed compression scheme results in much better compression percentage with respect to average compression % of all circuits, as shown in the column "Improvement%".

Table 1. Compression ratio for the proposed scheme for varying unit sizes

Circuits		s5378	s9234	s15850	s13207	s38417	s38584
%X		96.26	90.69	98.70	98.06	98.40	98.80
n (bits)	Compression Parameters	Obtained Compression Results					
8	C Volume (bits)	6632	9549	11809	22785	19953	26742
	C Ratio %	**69.30**	**65.31**	80.24	86.23	86.22	83.98
16	C Volume (bits)	7080	11168	11489	14494	12293	20268
	C Ratio %	68.39	60.70	**81.02**	91.24	91.51	87.92
24	C Volume (bits)	8800	13610	12450	13165	10353	19890
	C Ratio %	59.26	53.56	79.43	**92.22**	92.92	**88.08**
32	C Volume (bits)	7596	15066	15010	13251	10905	21861
	C Ratio %	66.10	46.98	75.82	91.99	92.47	86.97
64	C Volume (bits)	9660	20418	24468	18080	9325	30718
	C Ratio %	62.27	28.15	60.59	89.07	**93.56**	81.69
Best Compression %		**69.30**	**65.31**	**81.02**	**92.22**	**93.56**	**88.08**

Table 2. Comparison of compression values with other schemes

Scheme Name	Circuits						Avg.(%)	Improvement%
	s5378	s9234	s15850	s13207	s38417	s38584		
Proposed	69.30	65.31	81.02	92.22	93.56	88.08	**81.58**	-
Fit.[8]	54.76	45.17	53.21	65.90	66.65	57.07	**57.13**	24.45
GOL.[2]	37.11	45.25	62.83	79.75	28.38	57.17	**51.74**	29.84
R-HF[3]	53.75	47.59	67.34	82.51	64.17	62.40	**62.96**	18.62
SHC[4]	55.10	54.20	66.00	77.00	59.00	64.10	**62.57**	19.01
MDC[6]	56.20	54.70	72.80	86.50	61.80	71.20	**67.20**	14.38
ARITH[5]	54.00	58.00	68.00	84.00	56.00	57.00	**62.83**	18.75

6   Conclusion and Future Work

A simple method for test data compression and decompression has been presented with the aim of reducing required ATE channels. The proposed compression scheme is highly dependent on long stretches of don't cares. Some possible future works include exploring alternatives with respect to don't care assignment. It is observed that the proposed compression method achieves a compression ratio as high as 93.56% for ISCAS'89 benchmarks.

References

1. Touba, N.A.: Survey of Test Vector Compression Techniques. In: Proc. of IEEE Design & Test of Computers, vol. 23(4), pp. 294–303 (2006)
2. Chandra, A., Chakrabarty, K.: SoC Test Data Compression and Decompression Architectures based on Golomb Codes. IEEE Trans. on CAD 20(3), 355–368 (2001)
3. Tehranipoor, M.H., Nourani, M., Arabi, K., Afzali-Kusha, A.: Mixed RL-Huffman Encoding for Power Reduction and Data Compression in Scan Test. In: International Symposium on Circuits and Systems, vol. 2, pp. 681–684 (2004)
4. Jas, A., Ghosh-Dastidar, J., Mom-Eng, N., Touba, N.A.: An Efficient Test Vector Compression Scheme Using Selective Huffman Coding. IEEE Trans. on CAD of Integrated Circuits and Systems 22(6), 797–806 (2003)
5. Hashempur, H., Lombardi, P.: Application of Arithmetic Coding for Compression of VLSI Test Data. IEEE Trans. on Computers 54(9), 1166–1177 (2005)
6. Ping, L.S., Len, L.C., Chen, J.E., Jan, C.J., Lun, L.K., Ching, W.W.: A Multilayer Data Copy Test Data Compression Scheme for Reducing Shifting-in Power for Multiple Scan Design. IEEE Trans. on VLSI Systems 15(7), 767–776 (2007)
7. Wang, L.-T., Wu, C.-W., Wen, X.: VLSI Test Principles and Architectures: Design for Testability. Morgan Kaufmann (2006)
8. Dalmasso, J., Flottes, M.-L., Rouzeyre, B.: Fitting ATE Channels with Scan Chains: A Comparison between a Test Data Compression Technique and Serial Loading of Scan Chains. In: 3rd IEEE International Workshop on Electronic Design, Test and Applications, DELTA 2006 (2006)
9. Liang, H.-G., Hellebrand, S., Wunderlich, H.J.: Two dimensional test data compression for scan-based deterministic BIST. In: European Test Workshop, pp. 291–298 (2001)
10. Yu, Y., Xi, G., Qiao, L.: Multiscan-based Test Data Compression Using UBI Dictionary and Bitmask. In: 20th Asian Test Symposium, pp. 279–284 (2011)

Particle Swarm Optimization Based BIST Design for Memory Cores in Mesh Based Network-on-Chip

Bibhas Ghoshal[1], Subhadip Kundu[1],
Indranil Sengupta[1], and Santanu Chattopadhyay[2]

[1] Department of Computer Science and Engineering
[2] Department of Electronics and Electrical Communication Engineering
Indian Institute of Technology, Kharagpur
Kharagpur-721302, India

Abstract. Network-on-Chip (NoC) based Built-In-Self Test (BIST) architecture is an acceptable solution for testing embedded memory cores in Systems-On-Chip. The reuse of the available on-chip network to act as Test Access Mechnism brings down the area overhead as well as reduces test power. However, reducing the time to test still remains a problem due to latency in transporting the test instruction from BIST circuit to the memory cores. We have proposed a NoC based test architecture where a number of BIST controllers are shared by memory cores. A Particle Swarm Optimization (PSO) based technique is used (i) to place the BIST controllers at fixed locations and (ii) to form clusters of memories sharing the BIST controllers. This reduces the test instruction transport latency which in turn reduces the total test time of memory cores. Experimental results on different sizes of mesh based NoC confirm the effectiveness of our PSO based approach over heuristic techniques reported in literature as well as used in the industry.

1 Introduction and Background

The embedded memory content in Systems-On-Chip (SoCs) have increased from one-tenth to more than three fourth of the chip area today and will continue to increase[1]. With more and more memories embedded in circuits, accessibility becomes an issue in tester based methods making Built-in-Self Test (BIST) the solution of choice. Memory BIST (MBIST) research has developed a class of algorithms, called March algorithms [2], that are the most commonly used tests for detecting faults in memories. The MBIST architecture that can implement the March test algorithm comprises of a BIST controller and a memory with a wrapper[2]. The area cost of BIST circuit is usually small with respect to the area of the memory under test. However, in SoCs with large number of embedded memories, if each memory has a self contained BIST circuit then the area overhead will be very high. Test area overhead reduction while allowing at-speed testing can be achieved if an on-chip network is implemented as test

H. Rahaman et al. (Eds.): VDAT 2012, LNCS 7373, pp. 343–349, 2012.

access mechanism (TAM) for testing memory cores. However, the test instruction transport latency negatively impacts the test time.

In this paper, we propose a two-level test architecture having BISTed memory cores interconnected by a mesh type NoC. The proposed architecture aims at reduced test instruction transport latency at minimum area overhead. A fixed number of BIST controllers are placed at calculated locations and each controller is shared by a group of memory cores. We have formulated the memory grouping problem as a placement problem considering reduction of test instruction transport latency as the only objective. The locations of the BIST controllers are computed using the Particle Swarm Optimization(PSO) algorithm and memory cores are assigned to the controllers based on a greedy approach. Experimental results for transport latency obtained from the PSO based approach is compared with Neighbourhood Allocation (NA) technique. The NA technique is a heuristic allocation technique of assigning cores which are physically close to the controllers for reduced test time and is currently used in the industry[3]. The rest of the paper is organized as follows. Section 2 surveys the work already done in the field of Memory BIST optimization. Section 3 discusses the proposed two level test architecture. Section 4 formulates the memory grouping problem as a placement problem. Section 5 details the PSO technique for solving the optimization problem. Section 6 discusses the experimental results and section 7 provides the conclusions.

2   Related Work

Research suggests that the approaches taken so far have explored two main directions to gain improvement in performance of MBIST by hardware sharing: *Parallel and serial interconnection techniques of BIST wrapper sharing*[4],[5] and *Memory grouping algorithms for optimized area, power and time*[3],[6]. However, if memories are working at high frequencies, and placed physically far apart, then testing memories at-speed with a shared BIST becomes impossible. In such a situation, the preferred solution is to utilize the on-chip network as test access mechanism. However, not much research has been done on exploring the NoC based BIST technique and to the best of our knowledge only Liu etal. [7] have proposed a NoC based MBIST. The proposed BIST scheme applies test operations to multiple memories in a pipeline. The memories are divided into two groups, one group of memories receives the read test operation and the other receives the write test operation. Therefore, the number of memories that can be tested in parallel under a limited test power consumption increases. However, the test instruction transport latency remains same and in worst case is the diameter of the mesh.

3   Proposed Test Architecture

Figure 1 shows a 3x3 mesh based NoC consisting of cores and routers interconnected by bidirectional links. The cores present have been classified as Memory

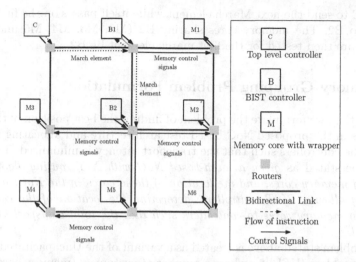

Fig. 1. Test Architecture showing both First level and Second level of transport

cores with wrappers, BIST controllers and Top Level Controller. The Top level contoller (C) is a logic core that receives March test commands from the external test source and delivers them to the network. For brevity, we assume all memory cores are homogeneous.

A MATS+ type March instruction

$$\{\Uparrow (w0); \Uparrow (r0, w1); \Downarrow (r1, w0)\}$$

for testing stuck at faults is used as an example to illustrate the instruction flow. The MATS+ instruction is a sequence of three March elements. A March element is a sequence of operations applied to each cell before proceeding to the next cell. An operation can be reading or writing of 0 or 1.

First Level of Transport: The NoC is first configured to operate in test mode. C receives the MATS+ test instruction from external tester and splits it into constituent March elements. The first March element,

$$\{\Uparrow (w0)\}$$

alongwith the path information is packetized and passed on to the network for delivery to the nearest BIST controller B1 as shown in Figure 1. The routing technique considered is X-Y routing and wormhole switching is used. The flit size considered is 32 bits.

Second Level of Transport: The BIST controller B1 on receiving the test packet from C, decodes the March element and issues memory level control signals (for example Read/Write signal) to each of the memory cores sharing B1 (M1 in Figure 1) following a multi-cast technique. When each memory core sharing B1 completes the test for the first March element, and if no fault is detected, B1 requests C to send the next March element while itself passes on the first March element to B2. The memory cores sharing B2 (M2, M3, M4, M5 and M6 in Figure 1) are then tested for the first march element by B2.

4   Memory Grouping Problem Formulation

In this section, we formulate the problem of finding the best position of the BIST controllers in the proposed NoC based test architecture and allocating memory cores to the controllers such that the transport latency is minimized. The problem can be stated as *given a mesh-based NoC with X-Y routing algorithm; a number of memory cores, and the location of these cores in the NoC; maximum number of allowed BIST controllers; determine the location of the controllers and assign memory cores to controllers such that the total transport latency is minimized.*

The problem stated above is treated as a variant of the Uncapacitated Facility Location problem (UFL)[8], where a number of customers (memory cores) have to be alloted to a number of facilities (BIST controllers) such that the total cost is minimized. The total cost in the UFL problem is the distance travelled by a customer to its nearest serving facility. In the problem stated above the total cost is the sum of setup cost (C_{setup}) and service cost ($C_{service}$).

The set up cost (C_{setup}) of a BIST controller is the total latency in transporting the March instruction to each of the BIST controllers. The service cost ($C_{service}$) of a BIST controller is the maximum of the number of hops from the BIST controller to its alloted memory cores. The mathematical formulation is as follows:

$C_{setup} = (h_{C-B1}) + (h_{B1-B2})$

$C_{service} = Max((h_{B1-M1})) + Max((h_{B2-M2}),(h_{B2-M3}),(h_{B2-M4}),(h_{B2-M5}),(h_{B2-M6}))$

where, (h_{i-j}) is the number of hops from block i to block j.

The objective function $Z = Min (C_{total})$ where, $C_{total} = C_{setup} + C_{service}$ subject to the constraints that the maximum number of controllers to be alloted is fixed and each memory core is alloted to exactly one BIST controller.

5   PSO Based Optimization Algorithm

Research suggests that metaheuristic solutions have been preferred over exact solutions for the UFL problem, as it is an NP-hard problem. Since, the problem stated in the previous section can be treated as a variant of the UFL problem, we have also used a metaheuristic approach like Particle Swarm Optimization (PSO) for the problem. We have chosen PSO over methods like Genetic algorithm and search techniques due to its ease of use and fewer parameters to handle [8]. Particle Swarm Optimization (PSO)[9] is a population based stochastic technique which is initialized with a group of particles with random position and searches for optima by updating their position through generations.

Particle Structure: n-bit binary array, n being the total number of possible controller position. So a 1 in i^{th} position indicates presence of a controller in the ith location, and 0 otherwise.

Fitness Function: Objective function mentioned in the previous section.

Global Best (GB) and Particle Best (PB): Particle best of a particle has the minimum fitness among all particles generated through changes to that particle, across generations. Within a particular generation, the particle resulting in the minimum fitness function is the global best. Both GB and PB (for a particle) are updated after each iteration.

Evolution of Particles: We define Mask operators to find the new position of a particle. Mask operators are calculated separately based on GB and PB positions. Mask operator is calculated by comparing bit by bit with GB and the particles current position. If controller is present/absent at a particular bit position in both GB and particle then bit at the same location of the Mask operator is set to 0 and 1 otherwise. In other words, when a bitwise-XOR is performed between particles current position and mask operator, it will produce GB. However, not all bits are XOR-ed. Based on a random probability, certain bits in particle position are left unaltered. The rest is found by XOR-ing the current position with Mask operator. After applying the mask operators for GB, the particle positions also go through the same process for their respective PB. The position obtained after applying the PB mask operator is considered as the particles new positions.

Termination Condition: We stop running the algorithm, if the particle which has minimum fitness, does not change for the last 20 generations. We also use a maximum iteration condition (200 considered in this problem), to terminate the process.

6   Experimental Results and Evaluation

Since there is no published work for the optimization problem stated in this paper, we have compared our PSO based method with a heuristic method, Neighbourhood Allocation method (NA) similar to the approach taken in [3]. In the PSO based approach, the number of allowed BIST controllers are placed at locations using the Mask operator technique explained in the previous section. After the BIST controlles have been placed, memory cores are alloted to them using a greedy approach. We simulated the NA and PSO based techniques using gcc on a 2.0 GHz dual core Linux workstation with 4 Gb memory. Both the NA and the PSO optimization programs were run for 15 runs and 200 iterations were used for the PSO approach. The experimental results are shown in Table 1. The values in Table 1 represent calculated fitness values. The percentage allotment is the percentage of total number of blocks in the test architecture that are BIST controllers. From Table 1, it is found that the best percentage improvement of PSO based approach over NA technique is obtained with a mesh size of 32x32 and with 25% allotment.

Table 1. Cost values calculated for different mesh sizes wih different percentage allotment of blank spaces for BIST controllers

Mesh size	Technique	Allotment		
		25%	50%	75%
4x4	NA[3]	30.00	21.62	20.73
	PSO	24.67	17.73	17.65
8x8	NA[3]	96.63	52.46	43.00
	PSO	54.66	31.13	31.00
16x16	NA[3]	144.00	76.00	67.00
	PSO	71.00	50.00	54.00
32x32	NA[3]	323.61	132.53	105.46
	PSO	122.13	97.53	91.00

7 Conclusion

In this work, we have proposed a two-level test architecture to reduce the test instruction transport latency for BISTed memory cores. We also proposed a PSO based approach to locate a finite number of BIST contollers in the test architecture such that the transport latency can be further reduced. The results show that as the number of BIST controllers increase, the cost value decreases indicating reduction in transport latency.

References

1. Marinissen, E.J., Prince, B., Keltel-Schulz, D., Zorian, Y.: Challenges in embedded memory design and test. In: Proceedings, Design, Automation and Test in Europe (DATE), vol. 2, pp. 722–727 (March 2005)
2. Bushnell, M.L., Agrawal, V.D.: Essentials of electronic testing for digital, memory, and mixed-signal VLSI circuits. In: Frontiers in Electronic Testing. Kluwer Academic (2000)
3. Chien, T.-F., Chao, W.-C., Li, C.-M., Chang, Y.-W., Liao, K.-Y., Chang, M.-T., Tsai, M.-H., Tseng, C.-M.: Bist design optimization for large-scale embedded memory cores. In: Proceedings of the IEEE/ACM International Conference on Computer-Aided Design (ICCAD), pp. 197–200 (November 2009)
4. Huang, Y.-J., Li, J.-F.: A low-cost pipelined bist scheme for homogeneous rams in multicore chips. In: Proceedings, 17th Asian Test Symposium (ATS), pp. 357–362 (November 2008)
5. Denq, L.-M., Wu, C.-W.: A hybrid bist scheme for multiple heterogeneous embedded memories. In: Proceedings, 16th Asian Test Symposium (ATS), pp. 349–354 (October 2007)
6. Miyazaki, M., Yoneda, T., Fujiwara, H.: A memory grouping method for sharing memory bist logic. In: Proceedings, Asia and South Pacific Conference on Design Automation, p. 6 (January 2006)

7. Liu, H.-N., Huang, Y.-J., Li, J.-F.: Memory built-in self test in multicore chips with mesh-based networks. IEEE Micro 29(5), 46–55 (2009)
8. Guner, A.R., Sevkli, M.: A discrete particle swarm optimization algorithm for uncapacitated facility location problem. J. Artif. Evol. App. 2008, 10:1–10:9 (2008)
9. Kennedy, J., Eberhart, R.: Particle swarm optimization. In: Proceedings, IEEE International Conference on Neural Networks, vol. 4, pp. 1942–1948 (November 1995)

An Efficient Multiplexer
in Quantum-dot Cellular Automata

Bibhash Sen[1], Manojit Dutta[1],
Divyam Saran[1], and Biplab K. Sikdar[2]

[1] CSE Dept., National Institute of Technology Durgapur
[2] CST Dept., Bengal Engineering and Science University, Shibpur,
bibhash.sen@cse.nitagp.ac.in,
{nitdmono,divyamsaran}@gmail.com, biplab@cs.becs.ac.in

Abstract. Quantum-dot Cellular Automata (QCA) technology is considered as the alternative to state-of-the-art CMOS due to its extra low-power, extremely dense and high speed structures at nano-scale. This paper proposes a novel design of 2:1 multiplexer in QCA, targeting better area efficiency and reduced input to output delay.

Keywords: Quantum-dot Cellular Automata (QCA), Multiplexer.

1 Introduction

The fundamental unit of QCA based design is the 3-input *majority gate* [1]. On the other hand, Multiplexer (MUX) is an important part in implementing signal control system and memory circuitry. The existing QCA based MUX designs are of large cell count. It increases the complexity of logic circuit simultaneously increasing the delay in logic realization.

2 The Proposed QCA Multiplexer

A quantum dot is a region where an electron is quantum-mechanically confined. A quantum cell consists of such quantum dots at each corner of a square and contains two free electrons [1]. The electrons can quantum-mechanically tunnel among the dots and settle either in polarization P=-1 (logic 0) or in P=+1 (logic 1). Timing in QCA is accomplished by the cascaded clocking of four distinct and periodic phases [1].

The output expression for a 2:1 multiplexer is $Out = I1.Sel + I0.\overline{Sel}$ (I0 and I1 are data inputs, Sel is the select line). This can also be represented using majority function as $Out = M3(M1(\overline{Sel}, I0, 0), M2(Sel, I1, 0), 1)$. It infers that a 2:1 multiplexer design requires 3 majority gates and 1 inverter. The structure shown in Fig.1(a) is the QCA realization of proposed multiplexer.

The performance of proposed multiplexer is compared with the recent designs in Fig. 1(b) in terms of area, speed and complexity. It significantly reduces the

H. Rahaman et al. (Eds.): VDAT 2012, LNCS 7373, pp. 350–351, 2012.

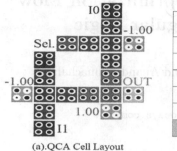

Design	Complexity (in Cell Count)	Area (in μm²)	Latency (in clock-cycle)
K. Kim et. al. '07	88	0.14	1
V. Mardiris et. al.'08	66	0.14	1
T. Teodsio et. al. '07	46	.08	1
S. hashemi et.al. '08	36	0.06	0.75
A. Roohi et. al. '11	27	0.03	0.75
Proposed Mux	19	0.02	0.75

(a).QCA Cell Layout   (b)

Fig. 1. QCA multiplexer (a) Cell layout (b) Comparison

cell count via reduction in wire length, permitting a fast timing (reduced clock zone). The simulation is done with QCADesigner [2].

Design capability of proposed mux is further analysed with existing one in implementing a two input XOR-gate, a D-latch as shown in Table 1.

Table 1. Performance analysis of proposed Mux with previous design [3]

Parameters	XOR Gate			D-Latch		
	in[3]	proposed Mux	Improvement(%)	in[3]	proposed Mux	Improvement(%)
Complexity (# Cell)	29	27	6.89	36	26	27.77
Area(in μm^2)	0.03	0.02	33.33	0.03	0.02	33.33
Latency(in C.Cycle)	1	0.75	25	2	2	equal

3   Conclusion

A 2:1 multiplexer in QCA is presented. It significantly reduces the cell count via reduction in wire length, permitting a fast timing (reduced clock zone).

References

1. Lent, C.S., Taugaw, P.D.: A device architecture for computing with Quantum dots. Proceedings of IEEE 85(4), 541–557 (1997)
2. Walus, K., et al.: Univ. of Calgary, Canada (2002),
   http://www.atips.ca/projects/qcadesigner
3. Roohi, A., Khademolhosseini, H., Sayedsalehi, S.: A Novel Architecture For QCA. IJCSI 8(6(1)) (November 2011)

Integrated Placement and Optimization Flow for Structured and Regular Logic

Vikram Singh Saun, Suman Chatterjee, and Anand Arunachalam

Synopsys
{vikrams,sumanc,anand}@synopsys.com

Abstract. A physical synthesis flow for data path circuits is proposed that integrates bit-slice tiling and gate size selection in traditional P&R tool, which outperforms traditional P&R tool in power and timing. This approach also reduces effort and multiple iterations of manual flow.

1 Introduction

The traditional P&R tools cannot exploit the regular bit-sliced structure of the data path circuits, causing signal and clock skew among different bits, and congested routing. A data path circuit placed in bit-sliced pattern, as shown in Fig. 1, not only minimizes the skew but also creates well planned routing[1][2].

In manual flow, designer has to make sure that the data path circuit is placed in bit-sliced pattern and gate sizes are optimal, and multiple iterations may be needed to meet power and performance, leading to longer design cycles.

In this paper, a flow is proposed that integrates bit slice tiling and optimal gate size selection with the mainstream P&R tool.

2 Structure Aware Placement

The proposed flow as shown in Fig. 2 has been implemented in a mainstream P&R tool. The designer has to provide data path structure information as input in the form of a matrix, called DP group, similar to data path shown in Fig. 1. DP group defines relative locations of gates of data path structure.

With simple modeling of DP group as a single gate, the placement engine of the traditional P&R tool is utilized to decide locations of DP groups. This enables the designer not to consider data path structures as hard macros during floor-planning.

Each gate of DP group is exposed to the optimizer along with non-structured logic, so optimization (i.e. sizing) on these gates are done keeping whole design in view and designer does not have to worry about choosing optimal gate size, reducing multiple iterations of manual flow.

The tiling algorithm aligns gates of rows and columns. The tallest gate of a row defines its height and widest gate of column defines its width, so that alignment can be achieved.

H. Rahaman et al. (Eds.): VDAT 2012, LNCS 7373, pp. 352–353, 2012.

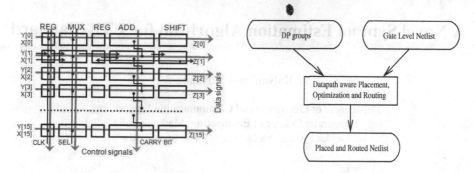

Fig. 1. Bit Slice Placement   **Fig. 2.** Proposed Data-path Design Flow

3   Experimental Results

The proposed flow (Flow-2) is compared with traditional P&R flow (Flow-1) for 5 designs with 90nm and below technology nodes, having number of gates ranging between 11k and 506k, with 12% to 60% data path logic.

Table 1. Critical Path Slack(CPS)

Design	Flow-1	Flow-2
A	-0.175	0.00219
B	-0.44	-0.19
C	-0.28	-0.26
D	-0.265	-0.245
E	-0.11	0

Table 2. Total Power

Design	Flow-1	Flow-2
A	5.1	4.42
B	55.4	52.5
C	2.97	2.75
D	85	77.2
E	124	117

With proposed approach, CPS has been improved in all designs as shown in the table 1. The table 2 shows that power is better too, across all designs.

4   Conclusion

The proposed flow improves power and critical path slack compared to the traditional P&R tool. This seamless automation not only reduces manual effort of custom designers but also eliminates multiple iterations, leading to shorter design cycle and time to market.

References

1. Leveugle, R., Safinia, C., Magarshack, P., Sponga, L.: Data path implementation: bit-slice structure versus standard cells. In: Proc. of Euro ASIC 1992, pp. 83–88 (1992)
2. Ienne, P., Griessing, A.: Practical experiences with standard cell based data path design tools. Do we really need regular layouts? In: Proc. of DAC, pp. 396–401 (1998)

A Novel Symbol Estimation Algorithm for LTE Standard

K. Kalyani and S. Rajaram

Department of Electronics and Communication Engineering
Thiagarajar College of Engineering, Madurai, India
{k_kalyani,rajaram_siva}@tce.edu

Abstract. In this paper, CORDIC based Givens Rotation QR Decomposition (QRD) for a 3GPP Long Term Evolution (LTE) receiver is proposed. The QRD block implemented with the use of CORDIC, eliminate the computation of Norm function. These CORDIC based blocks are compared with conventional blocks and found that the proposed design has an improvement in terms of area. This design has minimal hardware and computational complexity to meet the requirements of LTE standard.

1 Architecture of QR Decomposition Using CORDIC Algorithm

The upcoming 3GPP long term evolution (LTE) standard receiver [1] will support data rate up to 100 Mbps. In this work, the CORDIC based Given's rotation QR Decomposition (QRD) for LTE receiver [1] is proposed.

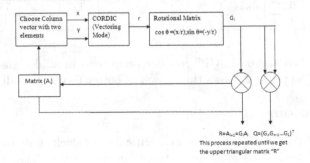

Fig. 1. Proposed Architecture for QRD Using CORDIC

In the LTE receiver [1], the transmitted symbol **s** can be estimated by ML detection by solving $\mathbf{S'} = \mathrm{argmin}\left\| y - Hs \right\|^2$ (1) which gives the optimal result. Instead of solving (1), the symbol estimation can be simplified by using QRD of **H**. In ML detection using QRD, substitute $\mathbf{s'} = \mathrm{argmin}\left\| y' - Rs \right\|^2$ (2) where $y' = Q^H y$ is used. As **R** is in upper triangular form, approximation of **s'** is computationally simpler with the aid of (2). With this practice, the computational complexity is lowered. When this channel matrix **H** is decomposed using Given's rotation algorithm, for every iteration,

H. Rahaman et al. (Eds.): VDAT 2012, LNCS 7373, pp. 354–356, 2012.

the matrix **H** will be multiplied with rotational matrix **G** which consist of sine and cosine angles. In conventional QRD, these angles are calculated by norm of that vector followed by division operation. In this proposed algorithm, the norm operation which consists of multiplication, addition and square root function are replaced simply by CORDIC. Thus reduce the hardware and computational complexity of LTE receiver. The proposed Given's rotation based QRD using CORDIC is given below.

Step 1: Consider a matrix **A** as channel matrix **H**.

Step 2: Identify an element to make as zero, assign that element as 'y' and element which is placed in one row above and also in the same column is assigned as 'x'.

Step 3: Apply 'x' and 'y' into CORDIC [2] which is operated in vectoring mode to compute norm of that vector 'r'. when 'y' become zero, final x=r.

Step 4: Calculate $\cos\theta = (x/r)$; $\sin\theta = (y/r)$; G_1 is a rotational matrix. Substitute the values of $\sin\theta$ and $\cos\theta$ in the rotational matrix G_1.

Step 5: Take matrix multiplication between G_1 and **A**. we got the matrix A_{11} with least lower triangular element equal to zero.

Step 6: To make next lower triangular value equal to zero. Take the matrix A_{11} and repeat the above procedure from Step 2 until the upper triangular matrix **R** for the given matrix will be found.

Step 7: Then orthogonal matrix **Q** is computed by $Q = (G_n....G_3G_2G_1)^T$

2   Simulation and Implementation

The VHDL coding for conventional and CORDIC based QRD for LTE are simulated and downloaded onto Xilinx xc3s1000-4fg456. The simulation and comparison results are given below.

Fig. 2. Simulation result for conventional Given's rotation QRD

Fig. 3. Simulation result for CORDIC based Given's rotation QRD

Table 1. Comparison of Conventional and CORDIC Based Given's rotation QRD

S.No	Resources	Available	conventional QRD	QRD using CORDIC	% of improvement
1.	Slices	7680	729	375	94.4%
2.	4 input LUT	15360	1307	665	96.54%

3   Conclusion

Thus it is evident from the comparison result that the number of slices, lookup tables that are required in FPGA implementation of QR Decomposition using CORDIC is tremendously reduced, thereby making our design cost effective and area efficient. By reduction of hardware and computational complexity of QRD module, the 3GPP LTE receiver will become efficient.

References

1. Salmela, P., Antikainen, J., Pitkänen, T., Sivén, O., Takala, J.: 3G Long Term Evolution Baseband Processing with Application-Specific Processors. International Journal of Digital Multimedia Broadcasting 2009, Article ID 503130, 13 pages (2009)
2. Hu, Y.H.: CORDIC-based VLSI Architectures for Digital Signal Processing. IEEE Signal Processing Magazine (July 1992)

Impact of Dummy Poly on the Process-Induced Mechanical Stress Enhanced Circuit Performance

Naushad Alam, Bulusu Anand, and Sudeb Dasgupta

MEV Group, ECE Department, IIT Roorkee, India
{nalamdec,anandfec,sudebfec}@iitr.ernet.in

Abstract. In this work we studied the impacts of number of fingers in strain engineered MFGSs on the circuit performance designed using multi-finger gate structures (MFGSs) for three different layout scenarios. We studied the stress induced in the channel of MFGSs by decoupling different stress sources and dependence of channel stress on the layout of gate structures. Stress induced by shallow trench isolation (STI) and tensile/compressive etch stop liner (t/c-ESL) decreases with increase in the number of fingers (NF); whereas, eSiGe/eSiC stress increases with increasing number of fingers. Stress from different sources are additive in nature and overall stress profile is the resultant of stress from all the sources. We observed that the use of dummy poly reduces the LDE of variability due to stress, though, at the cost of increased area.

Keywords: ESL, eSiGe, eSiC, Multi-Fingered Gate Structure, Process-induced mechanical Stress, STI.

1 Introduction

In this work we systematically study and develop an understanding of the layout-dependent effects (LDE) variability (we concentrate on regular layouts used in standard cell libraries) of various stress sources (t/c-ESL, eSiGe, eSiC, and STI) by decoupling the stress from individual sources. We study the impact of the use of dummy poly in strain engineered MFGSs and observe that the use of dummy poly help reduce the LDE variability in MFGSs. We use Synopsys Sentaurus TCAD process simulation to generate strain engineered MFGSs and Synopsys HSPICE circuit simulation to evaluate the performance characteristics. A detailed discussion of our TCAD and HSPICE simulation setup has been presented in [1].

2 Results

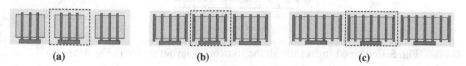

     (a)   (b)   (c)

Fig. 1. Simplified schematic of MFGS layout with number of fingers NF=3, (a) without dummy poly, (b) with dummy poly on STI, and (c) with dummy poly on STI and Active

H. Rahaman et al. (Eds.): VDAT 2012, LNCS 7373, pp. 357–359, 2012.

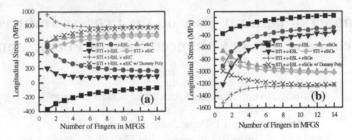

Fig. 2. Stress in MFGSs for different layout contexts, (a) NMOSFET, (b) PMOSFET

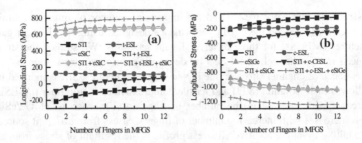

Fig. 3. Stress in (a) NMOSFET and (b) PMOSFET for layout shown in Fig. 1(c)

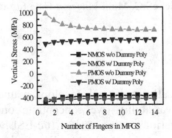

Fig. 4. Combined stress from all the stress sources for layout in Fig. 1(a) and (b)

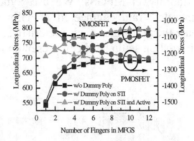

Fig. 5. Combined stress from all the sources for layout shown in Fig. 1(a) - (c)

Table 1. Percentage change in FO4 delay of cells w.r.t. cells Without dummy poly

Cell	With one dummy poly			With two dummy poly		
	Tplh	Tphl	Tpd	Tplh	Tphl	Tpd
Inv_x1	17.60	9.05	13.07	12.28	6.29	9.11
Inv_x2	10.53	4.32	7.24	7.54	2.54	4.89
Inv_x4	4.39	1.12	2.67	1.92	-0.37	0.72
Nand2_x1	14.02	6.30	10.39	10.88	3.76	7.53
Nand2_x2	3.36	2.82	3.11	2.54	-0.65	1.09
Nand2_x4	0.27	0.75	0.48	-0.53	-2.36	-1.37
Nor2_x1	12.91	4.53	8.24	9.22	2.415	5.43
Nor2_x2	5.30	1.00	2.93	2.03	-0.50	0.63
Nor2_x4	1.58	0.5	0.98	1.05	-1.35	-0.27

3   Conclusion

In this work we studied the impact of number of fingers in strain engineered MFGSs on the circuit performance designed using MFGSs for three different layout scenarios. Stress induced by STI and ESL decreases with increase in number of fingers; whereas, eSiGe/eSiC stress increases with increasing number of fingers. Stress from different sources are additive in nature and overall stress profile is the resultant of stress from all the sources. We observed that the use of dummy poly reduces the LDE variability due to stress, though, at the cost of increased area.

Reference

1. Alam, N., Anand, B., Dasgupta, S.: Process induced mechanical stress aware poly-pitch optimization for enhanced circuit performance. In: IEEE ISQED, pp. 717–722 (2012)

A Novel Approach to Voltage-Drop Aware Placement in Large SoCs in Advanced Technology Nodes

Biswajit Patra[1], Santan Chattopadhyay[2], and Amlan Chakrabarti[2]

[1] Qualcomm
bpatra@qualcomm.com
[2] University of Calcutta
{scelc,acakcs}@caluniv.ac.in

Abstract. High supply voltage drops in a circuit may lead to significant performance degradation and even malfunction in lower technology nodes like 45nm and below. Existing placement algorithms do not model voltage drops as an optimization objective and thus causes problems in power-integrity convergence. To remedy this deficiency, we propose a methodology to place the high power consumptions logic in lower IR (voltage) drop regions. We divide the whole floor plan into different buckets after doing an early voltage drop analysis, assuming virtual current sources in every 5u, at the lowest level metal on the PG grid. We propose to plug-in package, PCB parasitic and perform an early static and dynamic IR drop analysis by industry standard tools. The key efforts in this regard were logic clustering and region based placement. The placement regions are planned such that the high frequency logic blocks are placed in low IR drop buckets and low frequency logic blocks are placed in higher voltage drop regions. Our experimental results show 11 % improvement in peak voltage drop and 19% improvement in average voltage drop.

Keywords: Layout, physical design, placement, power, voltage (IR) drop.

1 Introduction

The power delivery network (PDN) design is a challenging task in most of the SOC (system on chip) design houses. A typical PDN consists of a voltage regulator module (VRM), power and ground routing on PCB (printed circuits board) and package, decoupling capacitors located at different locations, and the chip residing on top of the package. Below 45nm design node, we observe increased voltage drop along power supply networks [1] as increasing device density leads to increased supply current, and higher clock frequency leads to more significant inductance effect which brings additional supply voltage drop [2]. On the other hand, decreased supply voltage need for wireless handheld devices forces semiconductor industry to make transistor at threshold voltage for given technology node and leaves a smaller noise margin for signal transition, which makes a transistor more sensitive to supply voltage degradation. Less severe supply voltage degradation still leads to transistor performance degradation, e.g., 10% supply voltage degradation could be responsible for 10% to 16 % performance degradation, and the effect is super-linear.

H. Rahaman et al. (Eds.): VDAT 2012, LNCS 7373, pp. 360–363, 2012.
© Springer-Verlag Berlin Heidelberg 2012

In this paper our specific contributions are as follows: A) A new proposal for supply voltage degradation aware placement. B) Our experimental results evaluated for three industrial designs show an average 11% improvement in worst-case voltage degradation and 19% improvement in average voltage degradation, with only around 1 % wire length increase, which proves to be better than the related research work [3].

2   Methodology

We used Apache's RedHawk tool [4] for voltage drop (static and dynamic) analysis. RedHawk provides an accurate time-domain voltage and current information at every cell and transistor in the design that can be correlated to silicon measurements [4]. Static voltage drop on a power-grid network is obtained by solving Ohm's Law for the PG network, V_{static} (static voltage drop) computed at every node by using matrix inversion simulation. The I_{avg}(average current) is estimated based on frequency and worst case I_{avg} is assigned at every 5u in lowest metal layers to do early analysis. The resistance is estimated for each wire and via based on the technology (extraction) parameters and their layout topology (geometry sizes, placement and densities). The static drop is estimated starting at the voltage sources through all the power/ground routings terminating at the current sinks located inside die. The metal and via electro-migration violations are simultaneously determined with static voltage drop by considering the static current densities as well to make sure no electromigration violations in PG grid. We used the following steps to perform the proposed placement methodology:

Step 1: Extraction of PCB and package parasitics by using an industry standard tool.

Step 2: Designing of the PG (Power and ground) mesh and assigning current sources at every 5u whose values depend upon the current density for a given a chip.

Step 3: Running the static and dynamic voltage drop simulations by using Apache's RedHawk tool.

Step 4: Finding out the regions, which are having higher voltage drop. The higher voltage drop occurs due to the fact that their exist parasitic (RLC) variations from *PCB* power pins to different parts of the floor plan.

Step 5: Creation of bounds (regions of 200 u by 200 u) for high frequency logics where IR drop will be lesser on the floor plan .We can create bounds by any industry standard tools and take the design for placement optimizations, followed by clock tree synthesis and routing.

Step 6: Running the IR drop analysis to evaluate results for validating our methodology.

3   Results

For verifying our methodology we took three industry standard in house designs (varying from 5 to 8 million placeable instances and frequency from 100 MHz to 1 GHz). We have seen in all the three designs, there is a significant improvement in average / worst case static and dynamic voltage drop values. The key takeout points are (i) the voltage drop values mentioned in below tables (Table 1 & 2) for overall system level i.e. from VRM (voltage regulator module) to standard logic cells placed on the digital die, as compared to [3] looking at die level and (ii) we can do this analysis much early in design cycle so this helps for quicker turnaround time (TAT) . Static IR drop ($I_{avg} * R_{eff}$) is the product of average current flowing through the standard cell and resistance (R_{eff}) from VRM to the standard cell. The average IR drop is the sum of IR drop for all standard cells divided by the total number of cells. The worst case IR drop is the worst voltage drop seen over an instance among all instances in the design. The dynamic IR drop ($V_{dynamic}$) over an instance can be represented as: $I(t) * R_{eff} + L_{eff} * di/dt$, where $I(t)$ is the instantaneous current flowing through the standard cell, $Reff$ is effective resistance from VRM to standard cell and L_{eff} is the effective impedance from VRM to standard cells placed inside digital die .

Table 1. Static IR drop results

	V_{static} Average (Before using our approach)	V_{static} Worst case (Before using our approach)	V_{static} Average (After using our approach)	V_{static} Worst case (After using our approach)
Design A	8.05 mV	12.9 mV	6.71 mV	11.65 mV
Design B	9.09 mV	11.92 mV	7.6 mV	9.29 mV
Design C	6.6 mV	10.82 mV	5.01 mV	9.5 mV

Table 2. Dynamic IR drop results

	$V_{dynamic}$ Average (Before using our approach)	$V_{dynamic}$ Worst case (Before using our approach)	$V_{dynamic}$ Average (After using our approach)	$V_{dynamic}$ Worst case (After using our approach)
Design A	81 mV	119 mV	67.5 mV	107.2 mV
Design B	89.1 mV	109 mV	74.25 mV	98.2 mV
Design C	67.5 mV	82 mV	57 mV	74 mV

4   Conclusion

We have proposed placement methodology for supply voltage degradation reduction after doing an early IR drop analysis taking into PCB parasitic, package parasitic and floor plan with PG grid. Our experimental results show an average 11% improvement of worst-case voltage degradation and 19% improvement of average voltage degradation without any significant degradation of quality in terms of timing, congestion, routing with around 1% increase in total wire length at post route stage . This is done at system level so whole system is optimized. We can use this flow during early phase of the SOC design, as this gives enough confidence to design houses to take early product decisions.

References

[1] Bai, G., Bobba, S., Hajj, I.N.: Simulation and Optimization of the Power Distribution Network in VLSI Circuits. In: Proc. of Int. Conf. Computer-Aided Design, pp. 481–486 (2000)

[2] Bobba, S., Hajj, I.N.: Estimation of Maximum Current Envelope for Power Bus Analysis and Design. In: Proc. of ACM/IEEE Int. Symp. Physical Design, pp. 141–146 (1998)

[3] Kahng, A.B., Liu, B., Wang, Q.: Supply Voltage Degradation Aware Analytical Placement. In: Proc. of the 2005 International Conference on Computer Design, ICCD 2005 (2005)

[4] Shen, et al.: Full-chip Vector less Dynamic Power Integrity Analysis and Verification Against 100uV/100ps-Resolution Measurement. In: Proc. of the IEEE Custom Integrated Circuits Conference, pp. 509–512 (2004)

Design and Implementation
of Efficient Vedic Multiplier Using Reversible Logic

P.Saravanan, P. Chandrasekar, Livya Chandran,
Nikilla Sriram, and P. Kalpana

Department of ECE, PSG College of Technology,
Coimbatore, Tamil Nadu, India

Abstract. Reversible logic is considered as the emerging technologies in the field of optical computing, low power design and Nano electronics. It has been proved that reversible logic ideally dissipates zero power. In Digital Signal Processing (DSP) applications, multiplier plays an important role. Hence in this work, we proposed an efficient multiplier design using Nikhilam sutra of Vedic Mathematics and implemented it in reversible logic. The proposed implementation gives minimum number of ancilla inputs, garbage outputs and quantum cost there by reducing the computation time.

Keywords: Vedic Multiplication, Reversible Logic, Quantum Computing.

1   Introduction

Multiplier plays an important role in Digital Signal Processing (DSP) systems. Multiplier design using vedic mathematics reduces complexity and computation time [1]. Researchers have proved that Reversible logic ideally dissipates zero power [2]. In this paper, an efficient multiplier is designed using vedic mathematics and implemented in reversible logic. The proposed multiplier achieves high performance and consumes low power.

2   Basic Reversible Logic Gates

Reversible gate is an n x n gate having 1-1 mapping between inputs and outputs [3,4].

NOT Gate: It is a 1 x 1 gate which complements input and has unit quantum cost.

CNOT Gate(Feynman): It is a 2 x 2 gate with 1st output (Garbage) is same as 1st input and 2nd output is "exclusive or" of two inputs and has unit quantum cost.

Toffoli Gate: It is 3 x 3 gate which is a generalization of CNOT gate with two garbage outputs. It has quantum cost of 5.

Peres Gate: It is a 3 x 3 gate and can perform the operation of a half-adder and two Peres gates are combined to form one full adder. It has quantum cost of 4.

H. Rahaman et al. (Eds.): VDAT 2012, LNCS 7373, pp. 364–366, 2012.

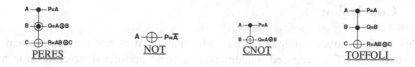

Fig. 1. Basic Reversible Gates

3 Nikhilam Sutra of Vedic Mathematics

Nikhilam sutra performs efficient multiplication of numbers nearer to base 100 [1].

Algorithm.
step1: Subtract inputs X,Y from 100,
   (t1=100-X, t2=100-Y).
step2: Multiply **t1** and **t2**, **(PL=t1*t2)**.
step3: Subtract **t2** from **X**, **(PH =X-t2)**.
step3: Merge **PH** and **PL**,**(Out={PH,PL})**.

Example: $\{xx_{10},yy_{10}\}= (xx00)_{10}+(yy)_{10} =(xxyy)_{10}$

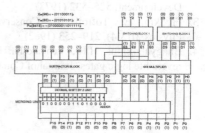

Fig. 2. Nikhilam sutra Multiplier

4 Implementation in Reversible Logic

All the sub-blocks shown in Fig. 2 has been implemented in reversible logic using reversible gates as depicted in Fig. 3. The Switching block gives values equivalent to subtracted inputs as given in step1 of the algorithm. The Merging unit joins PH, PL and gives out the final product (P15-P0).

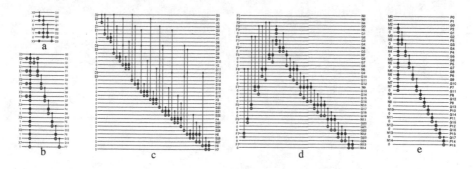

Fig. 3. a. Switching Block. **b.** Subtractor block. **c.** 4x4 multiplier. **d.** Decimal shift by 2 unit. **e.** Adder

5   Conclusion

In this work, a novel multiplier using vedic mathematics has been implemented in reversible logic. The proposed implementation is an optimized structure in terms of less number of garbage outputs, ancilla inputs and quantum cost. The proposed 8-bit multiplier uses 83 ancilla inputs, 94 garbage outputs and has quantum cost of 458.

References

1. Tiwari, H.D., Gankhuyag, G., Kim, C.M., Cho, Y.B.: Multiplier design based on ancient Indian Vedic Mathematics. In: IEEE International Conference on SoC Design. IEEE (2008)
2. Bennett, C.H.: Logical reversibility of computation. IBM Journal of Research and Development, 525–532 (1973)
3. Fredkin, E., Toffoli, T.: Conservative logic. International Journal of Theoretical Physics 21(3-4), 219–253 (1982)
4. Bhagyalakshmi, H.R., Venkatesha, M.K.: Optimized reversible BCD adder using new reversible logic gates. Journal of Computing 2(2) (2010) ISSN 2151-9617

Design of Combinational and Sequential Circuits Using Novel Feedthrough Logic

Sauvagya Ranjan Sahoo and Kamala Kanta Mahapatra

Department of Electronics & Communication Engg.
National Institute of Technology
Rourkela, India
{sauvagya.nitrkl,kmaha2}@gmail.com

Abstract. In this paper a circuit design technique to reduce dynamic power consumption of a new CMOS domino logic family called feedthrogh logic (FTL)is presented. The proposed modified circuit has very low dynamic power consumption compared to recently proposed circuit techniques for FTL logic styles. The proposed circuit is simulated using 0.18 μm, 1.8 V CMOS process technology. We compare an 8-bit ripple carry adder and a D-latch designed by both FTL and proposed FTL structure in terms of power consumption, average propagation delay and clock rate.

Keywords: Dynamic CMOS Logic circuits, Low power, Ripple Carry Adder (RCA).

1 Introduction

The design of low power CMOS integrated circuits, while maintaining its high performance is a challenge for the designers. The various design techniques [1] [2] proposed in the last two decades trade power for performance. Dynamic logic circuits [3] as compared to static CMOS offer more advantage in terms of area and speed. However the major drawback of domino logic, an important dynamic logic family is its excessive power dissipation due to switching activity and requirement of inverters during cascading of logic blocks. To improve the performance of CMOS logic circuits in terms of speed and power further a new logic family called FTL was proposed in [4]. The FTL concept was successfully used for the design of low power and high performance arithmetic circuits.

2 Proposed Modified FTL

The dynamic power consumption of the FTL [4] structure is improved by the modified circuit shown in Fig. 1. This circuit reduces V_{OL} by inserting one additional PMOS transistor T_{P2} in series with T_{P1}. The insertion of additional PMOS reduces the source voltage of T_{P2} below V_{DD}. Due to ratio logic the output node pulled to logic low voltage i.e. V_{OL} which is less than the V_{OL} of existing FTL structure in [4]. This reduction in V_{OL} causes significant reduction in dynamic power consumption.

H. Rahaman et al. (Eds.): VDAT 2012, LNCS 7373, pp. 367–369, 2012.

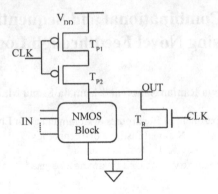

Fig. 1. Modified FTL

3   Performance Analysis

Table 1. Comparison Between FTL and proposed modified FTL

8-bitRCA	Logic Family	Power (μW)	t_p (ns)	PDP (μW * ns)	f_{max} (GHz)
	FTL	552.5	0.457	252.492	1.91
	MODIFIED FTL	356.2	0.612	217.994	1.53
D-Latch	FTL	50.7	0.359	18.201	2.57
	MODIFIED FTL	28.23	0.512	14.453	1.81

4   Conclusions

In this paper, we proposed a modified FTL structure for low power application. The simulation result shows that the RCA designed by proposed scheme consumes 35.5% less power as compared to existing FTL structure. The simulation result for both combinational and sequential circuit confirms that power delay product of the proposed circuit is much better than that of existing FTL structure but the modified FTL suffers from reduction in speed.

References

1. Vangal, S., Hoskote, Y., Somasekhar, D., Erraguntla, V., Howard, J., Ruhl, G., Veerama-chaneni, V., Finan, D., Mathew, S., Borkar, N.: A 5-GHz floating point multiply-accumulator in 90-nm dual V_T CMOS. In: Proc. IEEE Int. Solid-State Circuits Conf., San Francisco, pp. 334–335 (2003)
2. Mathew, S., Anders, M., Bloechel, B., Nguyen, T., Krishnamurthy, R., Borkar, S.: A 4 GHz 300 mW64b integer execution ALU with dual supply voltages in 90nm CMOS. In: IEEE Int. Solid State Cir. Conf., pp. 162–163 (2004)
3. Rabaey, J.M., Chandrakasan, A., Nikolic, B.: Digital Integrated Circuits: A Design perspective, 2nd edn. Prentice-Hall, Upper saddle River (2002)
4. Navarro-Botello, V., Montiel-Nelson, J.A., Nooshabadi, S.: Analysis of high performance fast feed through logic families in CMOS. IEEE Trans. Cir. & Syst. II 54(6), 489–493 (2007)

Efficient FPGA Implementation
of Montgomery Multiplier Using DSP Blocks

Arpan Mondal, Santosh Ghosh,
Abhijit Das, and Dipanwita Roy Chowdhury

Department of Computer Science and Engineering
IIT Kharagpur, WB - 721302, India
arpanmondal@live.com, santosh.ghosh@gmail.com,
{abhij,drc}@cse.iitkgp.ernet.in

Abstract. In this paper, an efficient Montgomery modular multiplier is designed exploiting the efficiency of inbuilt multiplier and adder soft-cores of DSP blocks. 256×256 bit multiplier has been implemented with (i) fully parallel, (ii) pipelined and (iii) semi parallel architectures that consumes upto 16 DSP48E1 64×64 bit soft-cores provided by Xilinx 12.4 ISE Design Suite. Performances with respect to area, operating frequency and design latency have been compared.

Keywords: Montgomery Multiplier, FPGA design, DSP blocks.

1 Introduction

The most critical operation behind all cryptographic operations is the chained modular multiplication. The efficiency of the implementations is measured by the computing power, energy consumption and memory usage. The proposed method of Peter L. Montgomery[2], in 1985, is a very efficient algorithm for modular multiplication in hardware. The input variables are transformed into Residue Number System (RNS) to replace the costly division operation of hardware by simple shift operations. The re-transformation of the output from RNS to integer domain gives the actual result. Montgomery Multiplication[2] is feasible for the algorithms that involves lot of multiplications with respect to the same modulus as the ratio between transformation overhead and actual modular arithmetic becomes much lower.

2 Efficient Design of Montgomery Multiplier

The implementations of the Montgomery multiplier is classified mainly into two categories : bit-wise and block-wise. Implementation of the entire algorithm without using any explicit multiplication tends to a complex design of the algorithm.

H. Rahaman et al. (Eds.): VDAT 2012, LNCS 7373, pp. 370–372, 2012.

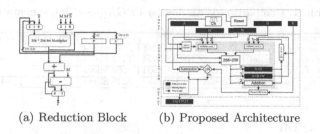

(a) Reduction Block   (b) Proposed Architecture

Fig. 1. 256 × 256 bit Montgomery Multiplication

The architecture shown in Fig.1(a) is the basic block diagram of the Montgomery Reduction Algorithm. Detailed architecture for hardware implementation is given in Fig.1(b). The 256 × 256 bit multiplier is the main multiplication block which affects the overall performance of the architecture. Fully parallel, pipelined and semi-parallel multiplication blocks, shown in Fig. 2(a), 2(b) and 2(c) respectively, built using the efficiency of modern FPGAs have been applied in the design to compare and analyze the performance.

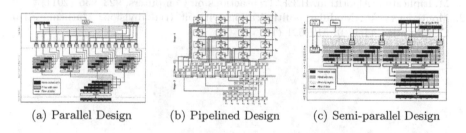

(a) Parallel Design   (b) Pipelined Design   (c) Semi-parallel Design

Fig. 2. 256 × 256 bit Multiplier Architectures

3   Experimental Results and Analysis

Fig. 3(a) and 3(b) respectively shows the macro statistics and the performance graph of the implemented designs. Comparison with similar FPGA based implementation has been done in Table 1 providing the design details.

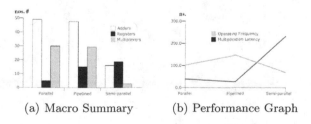

(a) Macro Summary   (b) Performance Graph

Fig. 3. Diagrammatic Representation of Performance

Table 1. Comparison With Similar FPGA-based Implementation

Implementation	Device	Logic blocks	DSP blocks	Freq. (MHz)
Huang et al.[1]	Xilinx 6000FF1517-4	2176 Slices	64	116.4
Proposed (Semi-parallel)	Xilinx XCHVHX250T	1572 Slices	4	69.94
Proposed (Fully-parallel)	Xilinx XCHVHX250T	2106 Slices	16	102.67
Proposed (Pipelined)	Xilinx XCHVHX250T	2346 Slices	16	147.62

4   Conclusion

In this paper, we have presented a block-based area optimized hardware design of Montgomery Multiplication on DSP platform. The power consumption of the design is low because of the usage of DSP48E1 soft-cores. The performance of the design in terms of computational speed and resource balancing proves the overall effectiveness and the general validity of the approach.

References

1. Huang, G., El-Ghazawi: New Hardware Architectures for Montgomery Modular Multiplication Algorithm. IEEE Transactions on Computers, 923–936 (2011)
2. Montgomery, P.: Modular multiplication without trial division. Mathematics of Computation 44(170), 519–521 (1985)

Independent Gate SRAM Based on Asymmetric Gate to Source/Drain Overlap-Underlap Device FinFET

Naveen Kaushik, Brajesh Kumar Kaushik, Davinder Kaur, and Manoj Kumar Majumder

Indian Institute of Technology-Roorkee, Roorkee, India
{navinpph,bkk23fec,dkaurfph,m1985dec}@iitr.ernet.in

Abstract. The read-write ability of SRAM cells is one of the major concern in nanometer regime. This paper analyzes the stability and performance of asymmetric FinFET based different schematic of 6T SRAM cells. The proposed structure exploits asymmetrical behavior of current to improve read-write stability of SRAM. By exploiting the asymmetricity in proposed structure, contradiction between read and write noise margin (RNM and WNM) is relaxed. The overall improvements in static, read and write noise margins for proposed asymmetric FinFET based independent gate SRAM (IGSRAM) are 28%, 71%, and 31% respectively.

Keywords: FinFET, IGSRAM, SNM, RNM, WNM, leakage current.

1 Introduction and Device Design

Multigate FinFET devices have gained enormous importance in area of nanometer regime due to their better performance supported by quasi-planar structure [1]. The device structure is suitable for application in next generation SRAM technology due to their reduced leakage current and short channel effects (SCE). This research work proposes a novel asymmetric 6T independent gate SRAM (IGSRAM) based on asymmetric lateral diffusion (ALD) FinFET.

The proposed ALD device has a structure that is similar to the conventional FinFET except for asymmetric source and drain lateral diffusion (Fig. 1). The device parameters are summarized in Table 1. The drain and source terminals have asymmetrically lower and higher doping lateral diffusions respectively. Although, the lower lateral doping at drain side reduces source to drain current (I_{sd}) but for $V_{ds}>0$, I_{ds} will not be affected, since extra potential barrier (EPB) is neutralized for positive V_{ds}.

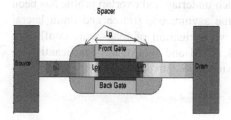

Fig. 1. Novel asymmetric FinFET

Table 1. TCAD Device Parameters

Device Parameters	Values
Gate length	32 nm
Oxide thickness	1.6 nm
Channel Doping	Intrinsic
Metal work function for n	4.55 ev
Metal work function for p	4.75 ev
Drain and source doping	1e+20

H. Rahaman et al. (Eds.): VDAT 2012, LNCS 7373, pp. 373–374, 2012.

2   Performance Analysis for FinFET Based 6T SRAM

The proposed tied and independent gate schematics of SRAM are shown in Fig. 2(a) and 2(b) respectively. Performance is analyzed for SNM, RNM and WNM. Generally, SNM in SRAM depends on V_{TH} of FinFETs. A higher V_{TH} implies lower drive current making write operation more difficult and resulting in higher SNM. Therefore, higher V_{TH} is preferred to obtain higher stability. Proposed ALD FinFET has high V_{TH} due to EPB thus limiting the drive current. Cell flipping is more difficult which leads to increase in SNM as shown in Table 2. RNM can be increased by downsizing the access transistor as shown in Fig. 2(b). On the other hand, WNM improves for a stronger access and weaker pull up FinFET device as compared to conventional MOSFET.

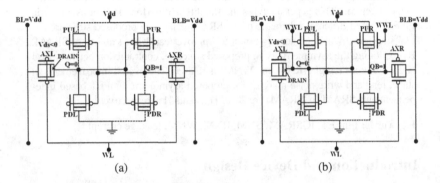

Fig. 2. (a) Tied and (b) independent gate schematic of 6T SRAM

Table 2. Percent Improvement in SNM, RNM and WNM for proposed schematics

Types	SNM	RNM	WNM
AD FinFET	19.2	8.5	8.6
ADSE FinFET	21.1	14.1	9.4
ALD FinFET	23.5	19.3	12.4
Proposed ALD IGSRAM	28	71	31

3   Conclusion

This paper proposed a novel IGSRAM in which underlap and overlap profile has been used at drain and source sides along with the asymmetric source and drain lateral diffusions. Asymmetry is exploited to achieve mitigation of read–write conflict in SRAM. The performances in terms of SNM, RNM and WNM are significantly improved for proposed device structure in comparison to conventional one.

Reference

1. Goel, A., Gupta, S.K., Roy, K.: Asymmetric Drain Spacer Extension (ADSE) FinFETs for Low-Power and Robust SRAMs. IEEE Trans. Electron Devices 58(2), 296–308 (2011)

VLSI Architecture for Spatial Domain Spread Spectrum Image Watermarking Using Gray-Scale Watermark

Sudip Ghosh[1], Somsubhra Talapatra[1], Debasish Mondal[1], Navonil Chatterjee[1], Hafizur Rahaman[1], and Santi P. Maity[2]

[1] School of VLSI Technology, Bengal Engineering and Science University, Shibpur, India
{sudip_etc,rahaman_h}@yahoo.co.in,
{s_talapatra,mondal_debasish86}@rediffmail.com,
navonilchatterjee@yahoo.in
[2] Department of Information Technology,
Bengal Engineering and Science University, Shibpur, India
spmaity@yahoo.com

Abstract. In this paper we propose a spatial domain Spread Spectrum (SS) watermarking scheme which effectively eliminates security problem while increasing robustness and enhancing perceptual quality of watermarked image. VLSI implementation using Field Programmable Gate Array (FPGA) has been developed for the algorithm.

Keywords: VLSI, FPGA, Spread Spectrum, Digital Watermarking.

1 Introduction

The objective of this paper is to design VLSI architecture for the given image watermarking algorithm that caters to the need of media authentication as well as secure transfer of image [2]. In this paper, the architecture that has been created for the given Spread Spectrum watermarking algorithm [1], enables watermarking to be implemented instantaneously at the time of capturing the image rather than using a software procedure that calls for greater execution time.

2 Proposed Method

The following subsection describes different steps in watermark embedding process respectively. Here, grey-scale watermark is embedded directly to the pixel values of each block of the cover image using SS modulation [3].

1. The cover image is taken as F, where $F = \{F_{ij}, 1 \leq i \leq F_{length}, 1 \leq j \leq F_{width}\}$, while $F_{ij} \in \{0, 1,..,255\}$, where F_{length}= image length and F_{width}=image width.
2. The watermark image is taken as W, where $W = \{W_{ij}, 1 \leq i \leq W_{length}, 1 \leq j \leq W_{width}\}$, while $W_{ij} \in \{0,1,..,15\}$, where W_{length}= length and W_{width} = width.
3. The partitioning of the cover and watermark image into NxN non overlapping blocks where N = 2,4,8,16 etc.

H. Rahaman et al. (Eds.): VDAT 2012, LNCS 7373, pp. 375–376, 2012.

4. The PN (Pseudo Noise) sequence generated $S = \{s_1, s_2, ..., s_{LxL}\}$, si $\in \{0, 1\}$.
5. The embedding rule is given as:

$$F^e = F + KS \qquad \text{if } b_j = \text{`0'}$$
$$F^e = F - KS \qquad \text{if } b_j = \text{`1'}$$

The architecture of the proposed watermark algorithm is shown in figure below.

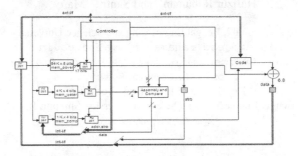

Fig. 1. Datapath of the Embedding Unit

We consider a 4 bits/pixel of size (64 x 64) and 8bits/pixel of size (256 x 256) grayscale images as watermark and the cover image respectively for experiment purpose. The cover image is partitioned in (8 x 8) non-overlapping blocks and the watermark image is partitioned in (2 x 2) non-overlapping blocks.

The synthesis of the watermark embedding have been implemented on Xilinx (ISE version8.1) based FPGA. We have chosen Virtex series of FPGA to fit the complexities of the design. The device used is xc2vp30-7ff896 for the implementation and the language used is VHDL. The behavioral simulation was done with Synopsys VCS-MX to verify the functionality of the design. The power consumption is 650 mw and the maximum frequency is 82.204 MHz.

3   Conclusion

The algorithm is simple with low computation cost and can be easily implemented in hardware. Digital design of the proposed algorithm using FPGA is also developed and thus makes it suitable for real time authentication as well as secured communication.

References

1. Ghosh, S., Ray, P., Maity, S.P., Rahaman, H.: Spread Spectrum Image Watermarking with Digital Design. In: IEEE International Advance Computing Conference (IACC 2009), pp. 868–873 (2009)
2. Mohanty, S.P.: A secure digital camera architecture for integrated real-time digital rights managements. Journal of Systems Architecture: the EUROMICRO Journal Archive 55(10-12) (October 2009)
3. Cox, I.J., Kilian, J., Leighton, F.T., Shamoon, T.: Secure spread spectrum watermarking for multimedia. IEEE Transactions on Image Processing 6(12), 1673–1687

A Photonic Network on Chip with CDMA Links

Soumyajit Poddar, Prasun Ghosal, Priyajit Mukherjee,
Suman Samui, and Hafizur Rahaman

Bengal Engineering and Science University, Shibpur
Howrah 711103, WB, India
{poddar18,priyajit.sp,samuisuman}@gmail.com, prasun@ieee.org,
rahaman_h@yahoo.co.in

Abstract. Currently, photonic network on chips utilize dense wavelength division multiplexing by modulating multiple high bandwidth wavelength channels from an on-chip broadband LASER source. We use adaptive Code Division Multiple Access techniques with the above method to allocate a single wavelength channel to multiple transceivers, each one being allocated a unique PN code.

Keywords: CDMA, On-chip communication, Photonic NoC.

1 Introduction

Photonic interconnect promises to deliver bandwidth in tens of Gigabits per second (10Gbps) with Bit Error Rate (BER) many orders below wired and wireless interconnect. However if Dense Wave-length Division Multiplexing (DWDM) is used, then aggregate bandwidths of several 100s of Gbps can be obtained. The major limitation of photonic interconnects is the large area required and also limited broadcast ability. In this paper we have proposed a solution that needs a fraction of the area required in previous photonic NoCs.

2 Architecture of the Proposed Network on Chip

This work uses Code Division Multiple Access Techniques [1] in addition to photonic interconnect. Such an approach results in a very simple ring topology and hence the number of micro rings is reduced to less than hundred. This directly translates to a fraction of the area requirement of previous approaches.

Our Network on Chip is a 3D chip with two layers (Physical plane) stacked one on top of the other communicating via TSVs. The physical plane contains IP cores and their communication resources. The routing plane consists of both wavelength division multiplexed photonic interconnect and its related electrical backend. Local communication refers to intra-cluster traffic and global communication refers to inter-cluster traffic. Intra cluster traffic takes place by means of the Mesh network in the logical plane while inter cluster traffic takes place with the help of the CDMA photonic interconnect on the routing plane. The proposed

H. Rahaman et al. (Eds.): VDAT 2012, LNCS 7373, pp. 377–378, 2012.

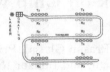

Fig. 1. The proposed Photonic Topology

photonic topology is shown in Figure 1. In the routing plane, the routers in the lower plane send/receive data to the upper plane by means of TSVs. The data of the lower logical plane must be stored in FIFOs before they are dispatched to their destinations. The CDMA Tx sends data simultaneously by all wavelengths. There is a facility to enable or disable each wavelength's driver and send data to corresponding modulator. As A-T protocol is used, so for receiving from cores of 3 different clusters we need to have one micro ring and CDMA receiver pair.

3 Experimental Results

The OMNeT++ open network simulation platform [2] has been used in conjunction with PhoenixSim [3] environment to simulate our work. We have used the methods and formulae provided in PhoenixSim to calculate our optical power budget. A simple C language program has been written with the above methods and formulae to find out the improvement of our proposed scheme over that of the photonic NoC mentioned in [4]. Total area required by our scheme is just 1 sq-mm in the die. The photonic loss is about two orders of magnitude lesser than in [4].

4 Conclusion

Our approach has been mainly to reduce component count while at the same time maintain the high performance of the NoC. Significant improvements in loss reduction has been obtained.

References

1. Wang, X., Ahonen, T., Nurmi, J.: Applying CDMA Technique to Network-on-Chip. IEEE Transactions on Very Large Scale Integration (VLSI) Systems 15(10), 1091–1100 (2007)
2. Chan, J., Hendry, G., Biberman, A., Bergman, K., Carloni, L.P.: PhoenixSim: A simulator for physical-layer analysis of chip-scale photonic interconnection networks. In: Design, Automation & Test in Europe Conference & Exhibition (DATE), March 8-12, pp. 691–696 (2010)
3. http://www.omnetpp.org
4. lightwave.ee.columbia.edu/?s=research&p=phoenixsim

Simulation Study of an Ultra Thin Body Silicon On Insulator Tunnel Field Effect Transistor

Partha Sarathi Gupta[1], Sayan Kanungo[1],
Hafizur Rahaman[1], and Partha Sarathi Dasgupta[2]

[1] Bengal Engineering and Science University, Howrah, West Bengal, India
[2] Indian Institute of Management Calcutta, India

Abstract. This paper presents a modified UTB SOI TFET structure and a thorough simulation study of various device design parameters on this structure.

Keywords: UTB-SOI-TFET, Band-to-Band Tunneling, Sub-threshold Swing.

1   Introduction

In this work ,we have proposed a modification to the conventional UTB SOI TFET structure which shows a significant improvement in the Sub-threshold Swing. A thorough simulation study has been carried out to study the impact of variations in structural parameters on the on-state/off-state current ratio and sub-threshold swing of the proposed structure.

2   Simulation Results

Figure.1 and Figure.2 illustrates the generic UTB SOI TFET structure and modified UTB SOI TFET structure respectively.

Fig. 1. Generic UTB-SOI TFET Structure   **Fig. 2.** Modified UTB-SOI TFET Structure

Table 1. Comparitive Study of the Device performance

TFET Structure	On-state/off-state current ratio	Sub-threshold Swing
UTB-SOI- TFET	6.86×10^7	77.520
Modified TFET	9.90×10^7	53.114

H. Rahaman et al. (Eds.): VDAT 2012, LNCS 7373, pp. 379–380, 2012.

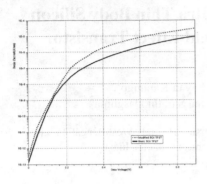

Fig. 3. Transfer Characteristics comparison

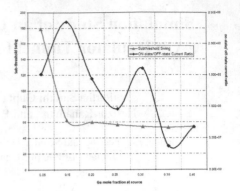

Fig. 4. Study of Ge mole fraction on Ion/ Ioff and SS

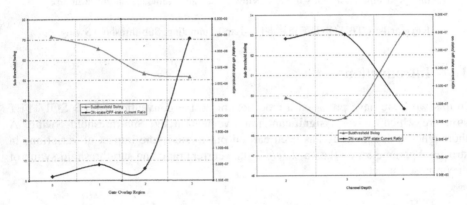

Fig. 5. Study of gate overlap on Ion/ Ioff and SS

Fig. 6. Study of channel thickness on Ion/ Ioff and SS

3   Conclusion

The modified UTB-SOI-TFET structure presented in this work shows a sub-threshold swing of 53.11 mv/decade and an Ion/Ioff ratio of about 10^8, making it a suitable candidate for low power applications.

References

1. Choi, W.Y., Park, B.-G., Lee, J.D., Liu, T.-J.K.: Tunneling Field-Effect Transistors (TFETs) With Subthreshold Swing (SS) Less Than 60 mV/dec. IEEE Electron Device Letters 28(8) (August 2007)
2. Gandhi, R., Chen, Z., Singh, N., Banerjee, K.: Vertical Si-Nanowire n-Type Tunneling FETs With Low Subthreshold Swing ($\leq$ 50 mV/decade) at Room Temperature. IEEE Electron Device Letters 32(4) (April 2011)

Routing in NoC
on Diametrical 2D Mesh Architecture

Prasun Ghosal and Tuhin Subhra Das

Bengal Engineering and Science University, Shibpur
Howrah 711103, WB, India
prasun@ieee.org, tuhinbcrec@gmail.com

Abstract. Network-on-Chip (NoC) has proven itself as a viable alternative for the on-chip communication among processing cores in recent years. In Diametrical 2D Mesh architecture, advantages of routing include smaller network diameter as well as larger bisection width. Again, fast network access requires a well-constructed optimal routing algorithm. Our proposed routing algorithm ensures that the packet will always reach the destination through the shortest path and it is deadlock free.

Keywords: NoC routing, Diametrical 2D mesh, On-chip communication.

1 Introduction

Network-On-Chip(NoC) is a new paradigm used for making inter-connections between IP cores on a system-on-chip(SoC) [3]. It brings notational improvement over conventional Bus and Crossbar interconnection. In NoC [2], system module such as processor, memories and specialized IP exchange data using network as a public transportation sub-system for the information traffic.

1.1 Routing on NOC

Routing on NoC is similar to routing on any network. A routing algorithm determines how the data is routed from sender end to receiver end. In NoC, routing algorithm should be implemented by simple logic and require size of data buffers should be minimal.

2 Proposed Routing

We propose a Modified extended XY routing for Diametrical 2D mesh Topology. This routing algorithm is very similar to Extended XY routing and XY routing, Modified Extended XY is very simple due to simple addressing scheme and structural topology.

H. Rahaman et al. (Eds.): VDAT 2012, LNCS 7373, pp. 381–382, 2012.

3   Experimental Results

The proposed algorithm is implemented in a standard desktop environment running Linux operating system on a chipset with Intel Pentium processor running at 3 GHz using GNU GCC compiler. The important section of a sample run is shown below.

```
[student@localhost26 ~]$ gcc diametric_algo.c
[student@localhost26 ~]$ ./a.out
give size of diametric matrix
5
give value of xdest 4
give value of ydest 4
give value of xcurr 0
give value of ycurr 0
current node is(0 0)
current Xdiff is 4
current Ydiff is 4
After diametr routing current node is (3 3)
current Xdiff is 1
current Ydiff is 1
After xy routing current node is(3 4)
current Xdiff is 1
current Ydiff is 0
After xy routing current node is(4 4)
current Xdiff is 0
current Ydiff is 0
Packet has reached the detination
```

4   Conclusion

Diametrical 2D Mesh was proposed to cope up with the disadvantages of 2D Mesh architecture such as large network diameter and high power consumption. But the algorithm proposed in [1] was not able to fully utilize the benefit of Diametrical 2D Mesh and in some cases the packet is not reaching to its destination node. In our proposed algorithm those issues have been solved and the proposed deterministic algorithm is able to fully exploit the benefit of Diametrical 2D Mesh architecture. Our proposed algorithm is a deterministic one. So, future works may be to make it adaptive in order to address the issues like network congestion and faulty network issues.

References

1. Reshadi, M., Khademzadeh, A., Reza, A., Bahmani, M.: A Novel Mesh Architecture for On-Chip Networks. D & R Industry Articles, http://www.design-reuse.com/articles/23347/on-chip-network.html
2. A survey of Architectural Design and Implementation Tradeoffs in Network on Chip System, http://www.danmarconett.com/downloads/NoCSurveyPaper.pdf/
3. Benini, L., De Micheli, G.: Networks on Chips: A new SoC Paradigm. IEEE Computer, 70–78 (2003)

Reversible Circuits:
Recent Accomplishments and Future Challenges for an Emerging Technology[*]
(Invited Paper)

Rolf Drechsler[1,2] and Robert Wille[1]

[1] Institute of Computer Science, University of Bremen
Group of Computer Architecture, D-28359 Bremen, Germany
{drechsle,rwille}@informatik.uni-bremen.de
[2] Cyber-Physical Systems
DFKI GmbH, D-28359 Bremen, Germany
rolf.drechsler@dfki.de

Abstract. Reversible circuits build the basis for emerging technologies like quantum computation and have promising applications in domains like low power design. Hence, much progress in the development of design solutions for this kind of circuits has been made in the last decade. In this paper, we provide an overview on reversible circuits as well as their applications. We discuss recent accomplishments and, finally, have a look on future challenges in the design of circuits for this emerging technology.

1 Introduction

Reversible circuits represent an emerging technology based on a computation paradigm which significantly differs from conventional circuits. In fact, they allow bijective operations only, i.e. n-input n-output functions that map each possible input vector to a unique output vector. Reversible computation enables several promising applications and, indeed, superiors conventional computation paradigms in many domains including but not limited to quantum computation or low power design (see e.g. [1,2,3]). But since reversible logic is subject to certain characteristics and restrictions, the design methodology of circuits and systems following the reversible computation paradigm significantly differs from the established (conventional) design flow.

However, much progress in the development of design solutions for reversible circuits has been made in the last decade: In particular, methods for synthesis have been developed (see e.g. [4]). These got manifested in first publicly available design tools [5] and enabled the design of initial circuit representations available at benchmark libraries [6]. Encouraged by these work, researchers now are striving for more scalability – a first hardware description language already is available [7]. These promising results build the basis for the development of a design flow which is competitive to the design of conventional circuits.

---

[*] This work was supported by the German Research Foundation (DFG; DR 287/20-1).

H. Rahaman et al. (Eds.): VDAT 2012, LNCS 7373, pp. 383–392, 2012.
© Springer-Verlag Berlin Heidelberg 2012

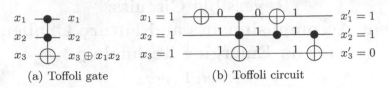

(a) Toffoli gate   (b) Toffoli circuit

Fig. 1. Toffoli gate and Toffoli circuit

In this paper, we provide an overview on reversible circuits as well as their applications. We discuss recent accomplishments and, finally, have a look on future challenges in the design of circuits for this emerging technology. References to the respective original work are provided for further reading.

2   Reversible Circuits

A Boolean function $f : \mathbb{B}^n \to \mathbb{B}^m$ over the variables $X := \{x_1, \ldots, x_n\}$ is *reversible* iff (1) its number of inputs is equal to the number of outputs (i.e. $n = m$) and (2) it maps each input pattern to a unique output pattern. Reversible functions are realized by reversible circuits. A *reversible circuit* G is a cascade of reversible gates, where fanout and feedback are not directly allowed [1]. Each variable of the function f is thereby represented by a *circuit line*, i.e. a signal through the whole cascade structure on which the respective computation is performed. Computations are performed by *reversible gates*. In the literature, reversible circuits composed of *Toffoli gates* are frequently used. A Toffoli gate is composed of a (possibly empty) set of *control lines* $C = \{x_{i_1}, \ldots, x_{i_k}\} \subset X$ and a single *target line* $x_j \in X \setminus C$. The Toffoli gate inverts the value on the target line if all values on the control lines are assigned to 1 or if $C = \emptyset$, respectively. All remaining values are passed through unaltered.

Fig. 1(a) shows a Toffoli gate drawn in standard notation, i.e. control lines are denoted by ●, while the target line is denoted by ⊕. A circuit composed of several Toffoli gates is depicted in Fig. 1(b). This circuit maps e.g. the input 111 to the output 110 and vice versa.

3   Applications of Reversible Circuits

Several promising applications of reversible circuits have been shown – with quantum computation and low power design being the most prominent examples. In this section, we briefly review possible research areas which are advanced by reversible circuits.

3.1   Quantum Computation

In a quantum computer [1], information is represented in terms of *qubits* instead of bits. In contrast to Boolean logic, qubits do not only allow to represent Boolean 0's and Boolean 1's, but also the superposition of both. In other words, using quantum computation and qubits in superposition, functions can be evaluated with different possible input assignments in parallel. Unfortunately, it is not possible to obtain the current state of a qubit. Instead, if a qubit is measured, either 0 or 1 is returned depending on a respective probability.

Nevertheless, using these quantum mechanical phenomena, quantum computation allows for breaching complexity bounds which are valid for computing devices based on conventional mechanics. The Grover search [8] and the factorization algorithm by Shor [9] rank among the most famous examples for quantum algorithms that solve problems in time complexities which cannot be achieved using conventional computing. The first algorithm addresses thereby the search of an item in an unsorted database with k items in time $O(\sqrt{k})$, whereas conventional methods cannot be performed using less than linear time. Shor's algorithm performs prime factorization in polynomial time, i.e. the algorithm is exponentially faster than its best known conventional counterpart. First physical realizations of quantum circuits have been presented e.g. in [10].

Reversible circuits are of interest in this domain since all quantum operations inherently are reversible. Since most of the known quantum algorithms include a large Boolean component (e.g. the database in Grover's search algorithm and the modulo exponentiation in Shor's algorithm), the design of these components is often conducted by a two-stage approach, i.e. (1) realizing the desired functionality as a reversible circuit and (2) map the resulting circuit to a functionally equivalent quantum circuit (using methods introduced e.g. in [11,12]).

3.2 Low Power Design

Pioneering work by Landauer [13] showed that, regardless of the underlying technology, loosing information during computation causes power dissipation. More precisely, for each "lost" bit of information, at least $k \cdot T \cdot \log(2)$ Joules are dissipated (where k is the Boltzmann constant and T is the temperature). Since today's computing devices are usually built of elementary *gates* like AND, OR, NAND, etc., they are subject to this principle and, hence, dissipate this amount of power in each computational step.

Although the theoretical lower bound on power dissipation still does not constitute a significant fraction of the power consumption of current devices, it nonetheless poses an obstacle for the future. Fig. 2 illustrates the development of the power consumption of an elementary computational step in recent and expected future CMOS generations (based on values from [14]). The figure shows that today's technology is still a factor of 1,000 away from the Landauer limit and that the expected CMOS development will reduce this to a factor of 100 within the next 10 years. However, a simple extrapolation also shows that the trend cannot continue with the current family of static CMOS gates as no amount of technological refinement can overcome the Landauer barrier. Moreover, the Landauer limit is only a *lower* bound on the dissipation. Gershenfeld has shown that the actual power dissipation corresponds to the amount of power used to represent a signal [15], i.e. Landauer's barrier is closer than immediately implied by the extrapolation from Fig. 2.

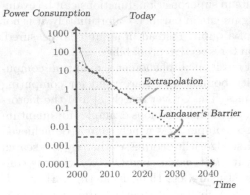

The figure illustrates the development of the power consumption of an elementary computational step in recent CMOS generations (based on values from [14]). The power consumption is thereby determined by CV_t^2, where V_t is the threshold voltage of the transistors and C is the total capacitance of the capacitors in the logic gate. The capacitance C is directly proportional to $\frac{LW}{t}$, i.e. to the length L and the width W of the transistors. Reducing these sizes of transistors enables significant reductions in the power consumption as shown in the extrapolation. However, this development will reach a fundamental limit when power consumption is reduced to $k \cdot T \cdot \log(2)$ Joule.

Fig. 2. Power consumption Q in different CMOS generations

Since reversible circuits bijectively transforms data at each computation step, the above-mentioned information loss and its resulting power dissipation does not occur. Because of this, reversible circuits manifests themselves as the only way to break this fundamental limit. In fact, it has been proven that to enable computations with no power consumption at all, the underlying realization must follow reversible computation principles [16]. These fundamental results motivate researchers in investigating this direction further. First physical realizations have been presented e.g. in [2].

3.3   Further Applications

While quantum computation and low power design represent the most prominent application areas of reversible circuits, promising results have been achieved in other domains as well.

An obvious filed is for example the design of encoding and decoding devices. Since encoders and decoders always realize reversible one-to-one mappings, the application of reversible circuits is a reasonable choice. However, so far, most of such devices are implemented in a conventional, i.e. irreversible, manner and, therefore, miss potential benefits in their design. An exception provides the approach recently presented in [3] where, for the first time, encoders and decoders for the on-chip communication between different components of a system-on-a-chip have been designed by means of reversible circuits.

As another domain, adiabatic circuits [17] utilize signals that, in order to avoid power losses, switch their states very slowly. When the power dissipation from switching transitions has been suppressed to a minimum, the static power dissipation caused by leaking devices in advanced, extremely miniaturized process technologies will become very substantial. Regardless of the computing paradigm, the static energy is present in virtually all transistor circuits. However, reversible circuits have the advantage that they naturally are suited for adiabatic switching without any extra circuitry.

Finally, program inversion provides a proper application for reversible computation. Motivated e.g. through debugging purposes, the question how to automatically derive the inverse of a given program is addressed. As most of the existing programs follow the conventional, i.e. irreversible, computation paradigm, program analysis techniques (e.g. [18]) or interpretive solutions (e.g. [19]) are applied so far. However, programs based on a reversible, i.e. invertible, computation paradigm would allow an inherent and obvious program inversion.

4   Design of Reversible Circuits

Motivated by the promising applications outlined above, design and synthesis of reversible circuits became an active research area where a significant amount of approaches has been presented over the last years. This section provides an overview of the initial contributions and the recent accomplishments in this area. Based on this, future challenges and possible solutions to them are discussed.

4.1   The Beginning

First approaches for synthesis of reversible circuits relied on simple function representations such as permutations or truth tables. Somewhat later, more compact data-structures like decision diagrams, positive-polarity Reed-Muller expansion, or Reed-Muller spectra have been utilized for this purpose. Complementary, also exact synthesis approaches, i.e. methods ensuring minimality of the resulting circuits, have been proposed. An overview of these methods is e.g. provided in [4]. The given functions need thereby to be reversible. Since this is not the case for many practically relevant functions, a pre-processing step often is performed first which embeds the desired non-reversible functionality into a proper reversible function [20,21].

Until today, these approaches build the basis of the design of reversible circuits and can be used e.g. to realize basic building blocks for reversible computations. However, the scalability of all these approaches is limited. That is, the methods are applicable for relatively small functions, i.e. functions with at most 30 variables only. Hence, after the initial development of synthesis methods for this upcoming emerging technology, researchers began to strive for more scalable design solutions.

4.2   Recent Accomplishments

While being an open research problem for many years, how to automatically realize large functions and more complex logic as reversible circuit has been tackled by recently presented solutions. More compact function representations like *Binary Decision Diagrams* (BDDs) [22] have been applied for this purpose. In contrast to the synthesis approaches outlined above, a hierarchical synthesis scheme is thereby applied. That is, the (possibly very large) function to be synthesized, is decomposed into smaller sub-functions. The decomposition is repeatedly applied until a sub-function results for which a building block exists. By

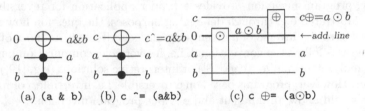

Fig. 3. Circuits obtained by HDL-based synthesis

accordingly composing these building blocks, a circuit representing the desired function results.

The development of this paradigm in the domain of reversible circuit design eventually led to the definition and consideration of a *Hardware Description Language* (HDL) for reversible circuits in [7]. In order to ensure reversibility in the description, this HDL distinguishes thereby between reversible operations (denoted by $\oplus=$) and not necessarily reversible *binary operations* (denoted by $\odot$). The former class of operations assigns values to a signal on the left-hand side. Therefore, the left-hand side signal must not appear in the expression on the right-hand side. Furthermore, only a restricted set of assignment operations exists, namely increase (+=), decrease (-=), and bit-wise XOR (^=). These operations preserve the reversibility (i.e. it is possible to compute these operations in both directions). In contrast, binary operations, e.g. arithmetic, bit-wise, logical, or relational operations, may not be reversible. Thus, they can only be used in right-hand expressions which preserve the values of the respective inputs. In doing so, all computations remain reversible since the input values can be applied to reverse any operation. For example, to describe a multiplication (i.e. a*b), a new free signal c must be introduced which is used to store the product (i.e. c^=a*b is applied). In comparison to common (non-reversible) languages, this forbids statements like a=a*b.

Having an HDL description like this, automatic synthesis of complex reversible circuits became applicable for the first time. Again, a hierarchical synthesis paradigm is thereby applied [7]. That is, existing realizations of the individual operations are combined so that the desired circuit is realized.

While this represents a significant step towards design of complex reversible circuits, the resulting realizations suffer from having a very large number of additional circuit signals. This is caused by the fact that building blocks representing non-reversible operations usually require additional circuit lines with constant inputs 0. For example, the AND operation (a & b) – a typical binary operation – is non-reversible. In order to realize the AND nevertheless, an additional circuit line with a constant input is required as shown in Fig. 3(a). However, since binary operations can only be applied in combination with a reversible assignment operation, these lines principally are not necessary (e.g. the overall statement c ^= (a & b) can be realized without additional lines as shown in Fig. 3(b)). But determining the respective circuits for arbitrary combinations of reversible assignment operations and binary operations is a cumbersome task.

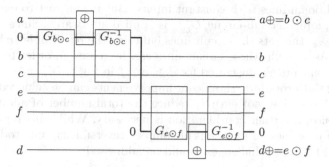

Fig. 4. Improved HDL-based synthesis

Hence, so far HDL synthesizers realize reversible circuits using the hierarchical scheme as illustrated in Fig. 3(c)[1] for a general statement c $\oplus$= (a $\odot$ b). That is, first the respective building block(s) for binary operations are solely applied. This requires additional circuit lines. Afterwards, the intermediate results from the binary operations (buffered in the additional circuit lines) are applied together with the building block(s) of the corresponding reversible assignment operation.

4.3   Future Challenges

With the recent accomplishments, the scalability of synthesis approaches for reversible circuits has significantly been improved. Although further improvements and extensions concerning the available descriptions means are still desired (e.g. more complex data-types, support of sequential behavior, etc.), the specification and realization of complex reversible circuits at a high level became possible. But as outlined above, the resulting circuits still suffer from having too many circuit lines. A first approach addressing this issue is already available [23]. However, as e.g. shown in [24], these promising results are still far away from the optimum. Hence, after progress concerning the scalability has been made, how to reduce the number of additional circuit lines remains an open problem.

A possible direction to solve this issue might be to "undo" the values of intermediate results once they are not needed any longer. Then, no new additional lines might be required to buffer upcoming intermediate results. Instead, the existing (reset) signals can be re-used. The general idea is briefly illustrated in Fig. 4 by means of the following two generic HDL statements:

```
a ⊕= (b ⊙ c);
d ⊕= (e ⊙ f);
```

First, two sub-circuits $G_{b\odot c}$ and $G_{a\oplus=b\odot c}$ are added ensuring that the first statement is realized. This is equal to the established procedure from Fig. 3(c) and

---

[1] Circuit lines drawn through the blocks represent thereby signals whose values are preserved.

leads to additional lines with constant inputs. But in contrast to existing HDL synthesizers, a further sub-circuit $G_{b\odot c}^{-1}$ is applied afterwards. Since $G_{b\odot c}^{-1}$ is the inverse of $G_{b\odot c}$, this sets the circuit lines buffering the result of $b\odot c$ back to the constant 0. As a result, these circuit lines can be reused in order to realize the following statements as illustrated for $d\oplus=e\odot f$ in Fig. 4.

Following this procedure, significant improvements can be achieved. However, even this solution does not entirely reduce the total number of additional lines to none. Hence, a further consideration is necessary. While this represents one of the major obstacles for synthesis of complex reversible circuits today, beyond that also the following challenges should be addressed:

- Quantum costs [11,12] are mainly applied as cost metric to evaluate the synthesized reversible circuits so far. But beyond that, also other, more technology-specific constraints should be considered (e.g. transistor cost [25] or nearest-neighbor requirements [26,27]).
- In order to realize practical reversible circuits, sequential behavior has to be supported. Initial work considering this issue can be found e.g. in [28,29,30] but requires more research to become applicable for complex designs.
- Followed by the increasing power of the synthesis methods, also new verification issues will emerge. Hence, developing appropriate checkers particularly for complex reversible designs is a logical next step. Researchers can thereby build on first results achieved for equivalence checking (see e.g. [31,32]) and even debugging [33].
- Furthermore, questions related to test of reversible circuits more and more becomes of interest. A basis builds the work presented e.g. in [34,35]. However, with ongoing progress in the development of further (and larger) physical realizations, new test models and ATPG approaches are needed.
- Finally, all these methods and approaches have to be combined to an integrated design flow. Although first simple flows are provided e.g. through tools like RevKit [5], this remains the long-term challenge of research in the domain of reversible circuit design.

5   Conclusions

Reversible circuits are an emerging technology with promising applications. In the last decade, synthesis of reversible circuits has intensely been studied and impressive accomplishments have been made. Starting from first synthesis approaches applicable to functions represented by permutations or truth tables, today it is possible to design and synthesize complex circuits using a reversible hardware description language. However, HDL-based synthesis still suffers from the fact that circuits with a large number of lines are generated. In this paper, a brief overview on reversible circuits and their applications, recent accomplishment, as well as future challenges has been provided.

References

1. Nielsen, M., Chuang, I.: Quantum Computation and Quantum Information. Cambridge Univ. Press (2000)
2. Berut, A., Arakelyan, A., Petrosyan, A., Ciliberto, S., Dillenschneider, R., Lutz, E.: Experimental verification of landauer's principle linking information and thermodynamics. Nature 483, 187–189 (2012)
3. Wille, R., Drechsler, R., Oswald, C., Garcia-Ortiz, A.: Automatic design of low-power encoders using reversible circuit synthesis. In: Design, Automation and Test in Europe, pp. 1036–1041 (2012)
4. Drechsler, R., Wille, R.: From truth tables to programming languages: Progress in the design of reversible circuits. In: Int'l Symp. on Multi-Valued Logic, pp. 78–85 (2011)
5. Soeken, M., Frehse, S., Wille, R., Drechsler, R.: RevKit: An Open Source Toolkit for the Design of Reversible Circuits. In: De Vos, A., Wille, R. (eds.) RC 2011. LNCS, vol. 7165, pp. 64–76. Springer, Heidelberg (2012), RevKit http://www.revkit.org
6. Wille, R., Große, D., Teuber, L., Dueck, G.W., Drechsler, R.: RevLib: an online resource for reversible functions and reversible circuits. In: Int'l Symp. on Multi-Valued Logic, pp. 220–225 (2008), RevLib, http://www.revlib.org
7. Wille, R., Offermann, S., Drechsler, R.: SyReC: A programming language for synthesis of reversible circuits. In: Forum on Specification and Design Languages, pp. 184–189 (2010)
8. Grover, L.K.: A fast quantum mechanical algorithm for database search. Theory of Computing, 212–219 (1996)
9. Shor, P.W.: Algorithms for quantum computation: discrete logarithms and factoring. In: Foundations of Computer Science, pp. 124–134 (1994)
10. Vandersypen, L.M.K., Steffen, M., Breyta, G., Yannoni, C.S., Sherwood, M.H., Chuang, I.L.: Experimental realization of Shor's quantum factoring algorithm using nuclear magnetic resonance. Nature 414, 883 (2001)
11. Barenco, A., Bennett, C.H., Cleve, R., DiVinchenzo, D., Margolus, N., Shor, P., Sleator, T., Smolin, J., Weinfurter, H.: Elementary gates for quantum computation. The American Physical Society 52, 3457–3467 (1995)
12. Miller, D.M., Wille, R., Sasanian, Z.: Elementary quantum gate realizations for multiple-control toffolli gates. In: Int'l Symp. on Multi-Valued Logic, pp. 288–293 (2011)
13. Landauer, R.: Irreversibility and heat generation in the computing process. IBM J. Res. Dev. 5, 183 (1961)
14. Zeitzoff, P., Chung, J.: A perspective from the 2003 ITRS. IEEE Circuits & Systems Magazine 21, 4–15 (2005)
15. Gershenfeld, N.: Signal entropy and the thermodynamics of computation. IBM Systems Journal 35(3-4), 577–586 (1996)
16. Bennett, C.H.: Logical reversibility of computation. IBM J. Res. Dev. 17(6), 525–532 (1973)
17. Patra, P., Fussell, D.: On efficient adiabatic design of MOS circuits. In: Workshop on Physics and Computation, Boston, pp. 260–269 (1996)
18. Glück, R., Kawabe, M.: A method for automatic program inversion based on LR(0) parsing. Fundamenta Informaticae 66(4), 367–395 (2005)
19. Abramov, S., Glück, R.: The universal resolving algorithm and its correctness: inverse computation in a functional language. Science of Computer Programming 43(2-3), 193–229 (2002)

20. Maslov, D., Dueck, G.W.: Reversible cascades with minimal garbage. IEEE Trans. on CAD 23(11), 1497–1509 (2004)

21. Miller, D.M., Wille, R., Dueck, G.: Synthesizing reversible circuits for irreversible functions. In: EUROMICRO Symp. on Digital System Design, pp. 749–756 (2009)

22. Wille, R., Drechsler, R.: BDD-based synthesis of reversible logic for large functions. In: Design Automation Conf., pp. 270–275 (2009)

23. Wille, R., Soeken, M., Drechsler, R.: Reducing the number of lines in reversible circuits. In: Design Automation Conf., pp. 647–652 (2010)

24. Wille, R., Keszöcze, O., Drechsler, R.: Determining the minimal number of lines for large reversible circuits. In: Design, Automation and Test in Europe, pp. 1204–1207 (2011)

25. Thomson, M.K., Glück, R.: Optimized reversible binary-coded decimal adders. J. of Systems Architecture 54, 697–706 (2008)

26. Khan, M.H.A.: Cost reduction in nearest neighbour based synthesis of quantum boolean circuits. Engineering Letters 16, 1–5 (2008)

27. Saeedi, M., Wille, R., Drechsler, R.: Synthesis of quantum circuits for linear nearest neighbor architectures. Quantum Information Processing 10(3), 355–377 (2011)

28. Chuang, M., Wang, C.: Synthesis of reversible sequential elements. In: ASP Design Automation Conf., pp. 420–425 (2007)

29. Nayeem, N.M., Hossain, M.A., Jamal, L., Babu, H.: Efficient design of shift registers using reversible logic. In: Int'l Conf. on Signal Processing Systems, pp. 474–478 (2009)

30. Himanshu, H., Ranganathan, N.: Design of reversible sequential circuits optimizing quantum cost, delay, and garbage outputs. J. Emerg. Technol. Comput. Syst. 6, 14:1–14:31 (2010)

31. Viamontes, G.F., Markov, I.L., Hayes, J.P.: Checking equivalence of quantum circuits and states. In: Int'l Conf. on CAD, pp. 69–74 (2007)

32. Wille, R., Große, D., Miller, D.M., Drechsler, R.: Equivalence checking of reversible circuits. In: Int'l Symp. on Multi-Valued Logic, pp. 324–330 (2009)

33. Wille, R., Große, D., Frehse, S., Dueck, G.W., Drechsler, R.: Debugging of Toffoli networks. In: Design, Automation and Test in Europe, pp. 1284–1289 (2009)

34. Polian, I., Fiehn, T., Becker, B., Hayes, J.P.: A family of logical fault models for reversible circuits. In: Asian Test Symp., pp. 422–427 (2005)

35. Wille, R., Zhang, H., Drechsler, R.: ATPG for reversible circuits using simulation, Boolean satisfiability, and pseudo Boolean optimization. In: IEEE Annual Symposium on VLSI, pp. 120–125 (2011)

Power Problems in VLSI Circuit Testing*

Farhana Rashid** and Vishwani D. Agrawal

Auburn University
Department of Electrical and Computer Engineering
200 Broun Hall, Auburn, AL 36849 USA
fzr0001@tigermail.auburn.edu, vagrawal@eng.auburn.edu
http://www.eng.auburn.edu/~vagrawal

Abstract. Controlling or reducing power consumption during test and reducing test time are conflicting goals. Weighted random patterns (WRP) and transition density patterns (TDP) can be effectively deployed to reduce test length with higher fault coverage in scan-BIST circuits. New test pattern generators (TPG) are proposed to generate weighted random patterns and controlled transition density patterns to facilitate efficient scan-BIST implementations. We achieve reduction in test application time without sacrificing fault coverage while maintaining any given test power constrain by dynamically adapting the scan clock, accomplished by a built-in hardware monitor of transition density in the scan register.

Keywords: Test power, test time, transition density, weighted random patterns, built-in self-test, scan testing.

1 Introduction

Controlling power dissipation in large circuits during test is a major concern in the VLSI industry. High power dissipation occurs during test because, unlike the normal mode operation of the system, correlations between consecutive test patterns do not exist in the test mode [6, 7]. To increase the correlation between consecutive vectors during testing, several techniques have been proposed for creating low transition density in pattern sets and thus control the power dissipation. However, this in turn increases the test application time as the test has to run for longer time to reach sufficient fault coverage. Increase in test time is also undesirable.

In this work we show that by properly selecting the characteristics of either weighted random patterns (WRP) or transition density patterns (TDP) for a given circuit we can reduce the test time that is proportional to the number of vectors. In some cases, we may also get higher fault coverage because many

* Research supported in part by the National Science Foundation Grants CNS-0708962 and CCF-1116213.
** Present Address: Intel Corporation, 1501 S. Mo-Pac Expressway, Suite 400, Austin, TX 78746 USA, farhana.rashid@intel.com.

H. Rahaman et al. (Eds.): VDAT 2012, LNCS 7373, pp. 393–405, 2012.

random-pattern resistant faults become detectable by WRP or TDP. Section 3 describes experiments run on the ISCAS89 benchmark circuits and compares the test lengths to reach certain fault coverage for weighted random patterns and transition density patterns against the conventional "purely" random patterns.

New test pattern generators (TPG) proposed in Section 4 produce vectors with desired weights or transition densities. Section 5 shows that the test time can be further reduced while maintaining any given power constrain by using a dynamically adaptive scan clock [15, 16]. Section 6 reports simulation results.

2   Background

Weighted random patterns have been used before to reduce test length for combinational circuits [1–3, 8]. Proper selection of the input probability can increase the efficiency of test vectors in detecting faults, resulting in reduced test time [10]. Therefore, to achieve higher fault coverage with shorter test lengths weighted pseudo random patterns are used [5].

Weighted random patterns (WRP) in which the probability of 1, $p1$, instead of being 0.5, can be set to any value in the range [0, 1] have certain advantages. Recent papers discuss low power test using weighted random and other reduced activity patterns. The power dissipation of scan patterns is related to the transitions they produce in the scan register. It is reported that with reduced activity patterns the fault coverage rises slowly and for the same required coverage a larger number of patterns are needed. Thus, a reduced power test may take longer time.

Much work has been reported on the generation and application of WRP in BIST and random testing since the 70s. We cite only a few references here [8, 10]. The primary purpose of WRP is to increase the rate of fault detection and reduce the test time. They are also known to reduce power consumption [22].

Transition density patterns (TDP) are primarily used for reducing power consumption during test [12, 20]. Their potential for enhancing the fault coverage, the main topic this paper, has not been explored before. Transition density for a signal or a circuit was originally defined for estimating the dynamic power as the number of signal transitions per unit time [11].

We consider built-in self-test of full-scan circuits. A hardware test pattern generator (TPG) feeds bits serially into the scan chain. A test controller switches between test and normal modes to perform test-per-scan of the combinational logic as scan-out response bits are sent serially to a signature analyzer (SA). Typical TPGs use a linear feedback shift register (LFSR) or cellular automata (CA) to generate equiprobable 0s and 1s [19].

In scan BIST when the circuit is clocked in the scan mode, the shifting of pattern in the scan register produces transitions that cause power consumption in flip-flops and the combinational circuit. We can call them source transitions. The number of source transitions per clock is the total number of transitions in the bit-stream held in the scan register. As the scan register is loaded during scan-in, the probability of transitions in the incoming bit-stream determines the average number of transitions that the register will contain. The scanned-in pattern is applied to the combinational logic during normal mode of a test-per-scan process. We do not consider the activity caused by the capture bits on which the scan-in does not have a direct control. Thus, the probability of transitions in the scan-in bits defines the transition density patterns (TDP).

3 Fault Coverage of WRP and TDP

We experimentally examine the fault coverage capabilities of weighted random patterns and transition density patterns.

3.1 Weighted Random Patterns

A Matlab program was written to construct different test vector sets. Each set contained 10,000 vectors but with different weights. Here, the weight is defined as the probability $p1$ of a bit being 1 in a vector. The weights are varied from 0.1 to 0.95 at 0.05 intervals. Thus, 18 sets of vectors are constructed for the weights 0.1, 0.15, 0.2, etc., up to 0.95.

Target fault coverage was set at 95% of the total faults and fault simulation was done using the 18 vector sets mentioned above. The number of vectors needed to reach the target fault coverage by each vector set was recorded. For every circuit that was simulated there exists one specific weight that resulted in the shortest test length. The number of vectors obtained in this experiment for s1269 circuit as a function of the weight (probability of 1 in the scan-in bits) is shown in Figure 1. For this circuit the minimum vectors required for achieving the 95% target fault coverage is 22, obtained for weight $p1 = 0.6$.

3.2 Computing Best Case Transition Density from Best Case Weight

The transition density of the best case weighted random patterns can be estimated. The transition density in an uncorrelated-bit sequence that has a 0 probability of $p0$ and 1 probability of $p1$ is given by $p0p1 + p1p0$ since a transition occurs when a 1 follows a 0 or a 0 follows a 1. However, $p0 = 1 - p1$, thus, the transition density can be calculated as:

$$TD = (1 - p1)p1 + p1(1 - p1) = 2p1(1 - p1) \tag{1}$$

Hence, from Figure 1, for circuit s1269, if best case weighted random pattern has a 1-bit probability of 0.6 then the corresponding transition density will be $2 \times 0.6 \times 0.4 = 0.48$.

This implies that if a test vector set is constructed to have a transition density of 0.48, then that vector set will generate an effective test for the circuit with shortest test length. In other words it can be assumed that a vector set of average transition density of 0.48 will result in detecting more faults with fewer vectors when compared to the numbers of vectors applied with transition densities higher or lower than 0.48.

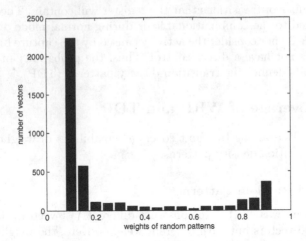

Fig. 1. Number of test-per-scan vectors for 95% coverage in s1269 when 1-probability (p1) of scan-in bits was weighted

3.3   Transition Density Patterns

If bits are generated randomly, the probabilities of generating a 1 or a 0 are equal, i.e., $p0 = p1 = 0.5$. Hence the transition density of the bit stream is $2 \times p0 \times p1 = 0.5$. To generate a transition density higher or lower than 0.5, bits must be generated with negative or positive correlation, respectively. Therefore, the bit stream will contain shorter runs of consecutive 1s or 0s for a transition density higher than 0.5 and longer runs of consecutive 1s or 0s for a transition density lower than 0.5.

A Matlab program was written to generate test vector sets, each containing 10,000 vectors but with different transition densities. Here also the transition density was varied from 0.1 to 0.95, with 0.05 intervals. The vector set generated for 0.1 transition density has longer runs of 1s and 0s in consecutive bit positions. Likewise the vector set having transition density of 0.95 has very short runs of 1s and 0s in consecutive bit positions.

Target fault coverage was set to 95% of the total faults and then fault simulation was done using these 18 vector sets. In each case the number of vectors needed to reach the target fault coverage was recorded. For every circuit we simulated, there existed a best transition density (TD) that resulted in the shortest test length. Figure 2 shows a bar chart of the number of transition density vectors obtained from fault simulation experiments to reach 95% fault coverage in circuit s1269. A vector set generated with 0.5 transition density has the best fault detecting capability with smallest number (only 24) as compared with the other transition density vector sets.

A set of ISCAS89 benchmark circuits was used for fault simulation with the transition density vector sets and weighted random vector sets. Table 1 shows the best case results obtained from fault simulation using AUSIM [18]. The table shows the numbers of vectors that achieved 95% fault coverage. The third column

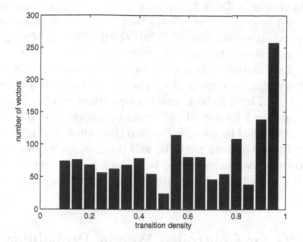

Fig. 2. Number of test-per-scan vectors for 95% coverage in s1269 for various transition densities of scan-in bits

Table 1. Best case weighted random and transition density vectors for 95% fault coverage in ISCAS89 circuits obtained from fault simulation of Matlab-generated patterns. Boldface numbers show the best choice for a circuit

Circuit name	Target FC (%)	Weighted random vectors			Transition density vectors	
		$p1$	No. of vectors	$TD = 2p1(1-p1)$	Best TD	No. of vectors
s298	77.1	**0.6**	**18**	0.48	0.55	423
s382	95	**0.3**	**56**	0.42	0.45	124
s510	95	**0.4**	**136**	0.48	0.5	152
s635	95	**0.9**	**97**	0.18	0.1	1883
s820	95	**0.45**	**2872**	0.495	0.45	5972
s1196	95	**0.55**	**1706**	0.495	0.45	2821
s1269	95	**0.6**	**22**	0.48	0.5	24
s1494	98.8	0.5	4974	0.5	**0.45**	**3158**
s1512	95	0.75	538	0.375	**0.2**	**338**

gives the weighted random bit probability ($p1$) that required minimum number of vectors shown in column 4. In column 5, the probability $p1$ of column 3 is used to compute transition density from equation 1.

The last two columns of Table 1 give the best case transition density (TD) and the corresponding number of vectors obtained from simulation. The differences in the transition densities of columns 5 and 6 can be because the two were obtained from two different statistical test samples. Also, equation 1, used for computing TD in column 5, assumes uncorrelated neighboring bits, an assumption that is yet to be validated for our transition density vectors.

However, unlike highly efficient weighted random patterns the patterns constructed based on transition density were not able to detect 100% of faults for some circuits. As shown in Table 1, the weighted random patterns and the transition density based vectors do not always have the same effectiveness. Which is better, often depends upon the circuit. While the generation of weighted random patterns is well understood, transition density patterns need further study.

Note that weighted random bits have a transition density of their own. But our transition density patterns generated by the toggle flip-flop always have equal number of 0s and 1s. Though the transition density of weighted random bits as obtained from equation 1 for any $p1$ can never be higher than 0.5, our transition density patterns generated by a toggle flip-flop (Section 4) can produce transition densities greater than 0.5. Such patterns will produce high power consumption, which can be lowered by the adaptive test clock procedures [15] as discussed in a Section 5, if the vectors gave accelerated fault coverage. This aspect needs additional study.

4   BIST-TPG for Controlled Weight Probability and Transition Density

We propose a new test pattern generator (TPG) for producing vectors of desired weights or transition densities. The illustration in Figure 3 contains a 28-bit external linear feedback shift register (LFSR) using the polynomial $p(x) = x^{28} + x^3 + 1$. The Scan Bit Generator block consists of AND gates, inverters, an 8-to-1 MUX to select from eight different probabilities of a bit being 1, and a toggle flip-flop. A simple finite state machine (FSM) provides the select inputs to the MUX. The Scan Bit Generator produces eight different weighted random bit sequences. The weights are constructed by ANDing two or more outputs from non-adjacent cells of the LFSR.

As shown in Figure 3, any one among eight weights for the probability $p1$ of a bit being 1, i.e., 0.125, 0.25, 0.375, 0.4375, 0.5, 0.625, 0.75 and 0.875, respectively, is selectable by an 8-to-1 MUX. The probability of a bit being 1 or 0 at the output of any cell of the LFSR is 0.5. These are signals W[0] through W[1]. One of these is directly fed to an input of the MUX. Two outputs from two non-adjacent cells were ANDed to produce a weight 0.25, three outputs from three non-adjacent cells are ANDed to produce a weight 0.125, and inverting these two weights we get weights 0.75 and 0.875, respectively. For generating a weight 0.375, the weight 0.75 is again ANDed with another cell output that is not adjacent to any of those two cells that are used in creating the 0.75 weight. Similarly, for generating a weight 0.4375, the weight 0.875 is ANDed with another non-adjacent cell output. Finally, to construct a weight 0.625, the weight 0.375 is inverted. An FSM controls the three select lines of the 8-to-1 MUX to choose any intended probability $p1$ for WRP_bits.

A toggle flip-flop constructed with a D flip-flop and an XOR gate produces bits with transition density $TD = p1$ from the weighted random bits of weight $p1$ as shown in Figure 3. Through the select lines of the MUX, weight $p1$ is selected as the bit sequence fed to one of the inputs of the XOR gate; the other input line of the XOR gate is the output of the D flip-flop. The selected weight

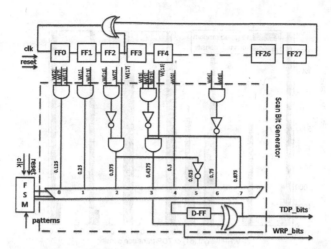

Fig. 3. Test pattern generator (TPG). Equiprobable 0-1 bit outputs, W[0] through W[27], of a 28-bit LFSR are transformed into weighted random pattern (WRP) and transition density pattern (TDP) bits for scan-in.

$p1$ thus controls the transition density at the output of the XOR gate. A 1 in the bit sequence will produce a transition at the output of the XOR gate and a 0 will produce no transition. The resulting TDP_bits at the output of the XOR gate have a probability of a transition to occur, which is same as the weight $p1$ selected from the MUX.

Output WRP_bits or TDP_bits from TPG of Figure 3 feeds the scan chain input of the circuit under test (CUT). For multiple scan chains, the Scan Bit Generator block in TPG is copied multiple times to generate inputs scan_in1, scan_2, etc., for scan chains, as discussed in the next section. The LFSR outputs, {W[i]}, are permuted differently as they are supplied to the duplicated blocks to reduce correlation among the scan chain inputs.

Figure 4 shows that the proposed TPG for WRP and TDP is capable of producing vectors with the desired weight ($p1$) or transition density. The bars in the figure show the numbers of TPG test-per-scan vectors for 95% fault coverage in s1512 as determined by fault simulation. The best cases are 406 TDP vectors for $TD = 0.25$ and 768 WRP vectors for $p1 = 0.75$. These are within statistical variation from the data for s1512 in Table 1, which was obtained by fault simulation of Matlab-generated patterns. The best cases there were 338 TDP vectors for $TD = 0.2$ and 538 WRP vectors for $p1 = 0.75$.

5   Dynamic Control of Scan Clock in BIST Circuit with Modified TPG

Recent work shows that by deploying a dynamic test clock control scheme in scan testing we can reduce test time while maintaining any given peak power limit [14–17]. We extend that technique to multiple scan chains and then use

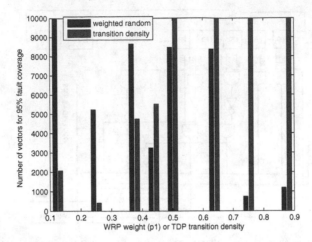

Fig. 4. Performance of transition density and weighted random patterns of s1512

the transition density or weighted random patterns produced by the TPG of the last section. The scheme automatically adjusts the scan clock to keep the test power constrained while reducing the test application time. Our objective is to examine the test time reduction benefits of various types of patterns.

The adaptive scheme of scan clock in scan-BIST consists of a separate inactivity monitor for each scan chain, which keeps track of total inactive bits entering the scan chain as shown in Figure 5. In addition, a frequency divider block provides different frequencies to choose from by a control clock select block. The scanning in of the bits of a test vector starts with the slowest test clock and depending on the number of inactive bits scanned in, the scan clock frequency is gradually increased. We assume that the captured vector produces worst-case activity of 1, that is, the scan chains are filled with alternating 1s and 0s prior to scan-in. We use a TPG with multiple scan bit generator blocks as described in the previous section, along with a finite state machine that selects the weight or transition density from the TPG as shown in Figure 5. The finite state machine (FSM) takes the number of the patterns applied as inputs from the BIST controller and controls the wight or transition density of the test vectors.

The circuit under test (CUT) in Figure 5 has a built-in self-test (BIST) architecture with flip-flops inserted on all primary inputs (PI) and primary outputs (PO). All flip-flops are configured into multiple (e.g., four, as shown in the figure) scan chains of nearly equal lengths [13, 15]. Unlike the Illinois scan [9] where identical bits are broadcast to all chains, this TPG supplies (presumed, though not verified) independent bits, scan_in1 through scan_in4, to CUT, which in the figure has four scan chains. Under the control of a BIST controller once, using the scan mode, all chains are filled with bits from TPG, one normal mode clock cycle captures the circuit response in flip-flops. Then, again using the scan mode

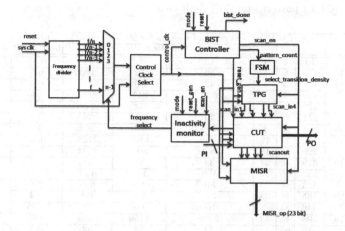

Fig. 5. Adaptive scan clock scheme with modified TPG

as the next pattern is scanned in the captured bits are supplied to a multi-input signature register (MISR) [4, 19]. This completes the application of one test-per-scan vector.

We can pre-determine the best case transition density with the modified TPG and run the whole test session with a pre-selected transition density. Also the circuitry to dynamically adapt the scan clock will help speed up the test clock by monitoring the inactivity and, therefore, keep the whole test session power-constrained. The time reduction in scan-in will be dominated by the largest scan chain and for a transition density TD and the number of frequencies available to adapt from v, the reduction in scan-in time is given by [13, 15],

$$\text{Test time reduction} = \frac{1}{2}(1 - TD) - \frac{1}{2v} \tag{2}$$

6   Experimental Results

Experiments were done on ISCAS89 benchmark circuits. Table 2 shows the comparison between the number of vectors needed to reach 90% fault coverage for each of the circuits. It is to be noted that for each circuit there exists a particular weight or a particular transition density that results in the shortest test length. Consider s13207 circuit with the conventional BIST using a fixed frequency clock. For a 90% target fault coverage, Table 2 gives 4262 random ($p1 = 0.5$) vectors, 2127 WRP ($p1 = 0.35$) and 1490 TDP ($TD = 0.3$). We use the conventional BIST with random vectors as the reference for test time. When the BIST is implemented with TDP, the test time will be reduced by $100 \times (4262 - 1490)/4262 = 65\%$. There will be additional gain with adaptive clock.

So, we examine the reduction in test application time when a dynamic scan clock scheme is used [15]. Results for a selected set of ISCAS89 circuits are given

Table 2. Test lengths for random and best-case weighted random (WRP) and transition density (TDP) patterns for 90% fault coverage in ISCAS89 circuits

Circuit	DFFs	Gates	PIs	POs	Number of vectors for 90% coverage			$p1$ for best WRP	TD for best TDP
					Random, $p1 = 0.5$	Best WRP	Best TDP		
s27	3	10	4	1	15	5	12	0.15	0.6
s298	14	119	3	6	52	52	> 10000	0.5	0.0
s382	21	158	3	6	42	30	16	0.3	0.4
s386	6	159	7	7	621	317	609	0.35	0.4
s344	15	160	9	11	50	34	> 10000	0.45	0.0
s510	6	211	19	7	70	84	76	0.4	0.5
s420	16	218	18	1	> 10000	300	263	0.9	0.1
s832	5	287	18	19	1380	1126	2128	0.45	0.55
s820	5	289	18	19	962	806	1524	0.45	0.45
s641	19	379	35	24	38	31	41	0.7	0.55
s713	19	393	35	23	109	131	139	0.75	0.55
s967	29	394	16	23	746	268	656	0.4	0.45
s953	29	395	16	23	746	312	458	0.4	0.35
s838	32	446	34	1	> 10000	488	491	0.95	0.15
s1238	18	508	14	14	2506	1759	2598	0.55	0.45
s991	19	519	65	17	34	34	23	0.5	0.75
s1196	18	529	14	14	675	537	712	0.65	0.3
s1269	37	569	18	10	14	10	12	0.6	0.85
s1494	6	647	8	19	460	416	266	0.6	0.4
s1488	6	653	8	19	438	410	247	0.6	0.55
s1423	74	657	17	5	12	6	11	0.85	0.2
s1512	57	780	29	21	46	46	78	0.5	0.6
s13207	669	7951	31	121	4262	2127	1490	0.35	0.3
s15850	597	9772	14	87	2463	2463	3293	0.5	0.3

in Table 3. In each case four scan chains of nearly equal length were inserted using the BIST architecture of Figure 5. Test times for all three types of vectors shown in Table 2 were obtained by simulation.

As an example, consider s13207 again. Since flip-flops are added to primary inputs (PIs) and primary outputs (POs), total scanned flip-flops are $669 + 31 + 121 = 821$. Given there are four nearly equal scan chains, the longest chain has $\lceil 821/4 \rceil = 206$ flip-flops. For fixed frequency test a clock period of 40ns is assumed. This is generally specified on the basis of the maximum energy consumption by a vector and the power dissipation capability of the circuit. Test time for 4262 random vectors is calculated as [4],

$$\text{Test time} = (207 \times 4262 + 206) \times 40\text{ns} = 35.3\text{ms} \qquad (3)$$

Similarly, the test time for 2127 WRP vectors is 17.6ms and that for 1490 TDP vectors is 12.3ms. For this circuit, the shortest vector set is for TDP, which reduces the test time to $100 \times (35.3 - 12.3)/35.3 = 0.65\%$ of the random vector test time.

For the adaptive scheme, we use four clocks ($v = 4$) of periods 40ns, 30ns, 20ns and 10ns. Assuming the worst case activity from the captured bits, we begin each scan with the slowest clock of 40ns, which is sped up by the activity monitoring circuitry. Test times for the three types of vectors were obtained by simulation of the BIST circuit as 31.6ms, 16.2ms and 10.2ms, respectively, as shown in Table 3. When we compare the adaptive clock BIST with the best transition

Table 3. Comparing test times for 90% coverage by conventional random (R), weighted random (WRP) and transition density (TDP) patterns when adaptive scan clock is used

Circuit	Types of patterns				
	Random (R), $p1 = 0.5$ test time (ns)	Weighted random (WRP)		Transition density (TDP)	
		Best $p1$	Test time (ns)	Best TD	Test time (ns)
s298	10050	0.5	10050	0.5	1974026
s382	10320	0.3	6661	0.4	8287
s510	18200	0.4	19570	0.4	19852
s820	348392	0.4	268971	0.4	504453
s953	418073	0.4	162371	0.3	231833
s1196	264652	0.6	221416	0.3	262350
s1488	124572	0.6	117901	0.5	72831
s13207	31565011	0.35	16180025	0.3	10149712
s15850	16341260	0.5	16341260	0.3	20109065

density patterns and the conventional fixed clock random pattern BIST, the test time reduction is $100 \times (35.3 - 10.2)/35.3 = 71\%$.

Once again, time reduction is measured as the time required for the vectors to be scanned-in using fixed scan clock minus the time required for the vectors to be scanned-in using the variable scan-clock. We see a significant reductions in test application time in s13207 and s1488 as the best case transition density vectors were applied along with the dynamic adaptive scan clock scheme.

7   Conclusion

For scan-BIST testing it is important to note that both power and test time contribute to the test cost as well as quality of the test. Transition density can be effectively selected for any circuit analogous to weighted random patterns to generate test session with shorter test length. Table 2 shows that for certain circuits, 90% fault coverage can be achieved with a minimal number of vectors if transition density patterns are used. Once the transition density is known the test application time can be further reduced by dynamically controlling the test clock keeping the test power under control as shown in Table 3. Thus, this work contributes towards generating high quality tests with reduced test application time and keeping the test power constrained.

Renewed interest in low power test patterns [12, 20, 21] has shown applications of low toggle rate vectors for reducing test power. Low toggle rate is often associated with slow rise in fault coverage. In this paper, we show that this is not necessarily true when the toggle rate (or transition density) is suitably determined for the circuit under test. Even higher toggle rates can be used when they provide quicker fault coverage because power consumption can be constrained by an adaptive scan clock, thus reducing the overall test time on balance.

References

1. Agrawal, P., Agrawal, V.D.: On Improving the Efficiency of Monte Carlo Test Generation. In: Digest of 5th International Fault Tolerant Computing Symp., Paris, France, pp. 205–209 (June 1975)
2. Agrawal, P., Agrawal, V.D.: Probabilistic Analysis of Random Test Generation Method for Irredundant Combinational Networks. IEEE Trans. Computers C-24, 691–695 (1975)
3. Agrawal, P., Agrawal, V.D.: On Monte Carlo Testing of Logic Tree Networks. IEEE Trans. Computers C-25, 664–667 (1976)
4. Bushnell, M.L., Agrawal, V.D.: Essentials of Electronic Testing for Digital, Memory and Mixed-Signal VLSI Circuits. Springer (2000)
5. Eichelberger, E.B., Lindbloom, E.: Random-Pattern Coverage Enhancement and Diagnosis for LSSD Logic Self-Test. IBM Jour. Research and Development 27(3), 265–272 (1983)
6. Girard, P.: Low Power Testing of VLSI Circuits: Problems and Solutions. In: Proc. First IEEE Symp. Quality Electronic Design (ISQED), pp. 173–179 (March 2000)
7. Girard, P.: Survey of Low-Power Testing of VLSI Circuits. IEEE Design & Test of Computers 19(3), 80–90 (2002)
8. Hartmann, J., Kemnitz, G.: How to Do Weighted Random Testing for BIST. In: Proc. IEEE/ACM International Conf. Computer-Aided Design, pp. 568–571 (November 1993)
9. Hsu, F., Butler, K., Patel, J.H.: A Case Study on the Implementation of Illinois Scan Architecture. In: Proc. International Test Conf., pp. 538–547 (2001)
10. Majumder, A.: On Evaluating and Optimizing Weights for Weighted Random Pattern Testing. IEEE Trans. Computers 45(8), 904–916 (1996)
11. Najm, F.: Transition Density: A New Measure of Activity in Digital Circuits. IEEE Trans. CAD 12, 310–323 (1993)
12. Rajski, J., Tyszer, J., Mrugalski, G., Nadeau-Dostie, B.: Test Generator with Pre-selected Toggling for Low Power Built-In Self-Test. In: Proc. 30th IEEE VLSI Test Symp., pp. 1–6 (April 2012)
13. Rashid, F.: Controlled Transition Density Based Power Constrained Scan-BIST with Reduced Test Time. Master's thesis, Auburn University, Alabama, USA (May 2012); A talk based on this thesis was presented in a student forum at the 21st IEEE North Atlantic Test Workshop, May 10 (2012)
14. Shanmugasundaram, P.: Test Time Optimization in Scan Circuits. Master's thesis, Auburn University, Alabama, USA
15. Shanmugasundaram, P., Agrawal, V.D.: Dynamic Scan Clock Control for Test Time Reduction Maintaining Peak Power Limit. In: Proc. 29th IEEE VLSI Test Symp., pp. 248–253 (May 2011)
16. Shanmugasundaram, P., Agrawal, V.D.: Dynamic Scan Clock Control in BIST Circuits. In: Proc. Joint IEEE Int. Conf. on Industrial Electronics and 43rd Southeastern Symp. on System Theory, pp. 237–242 (March 2011)
17. Shanmugasundaram, P., Agrawal, V.D.: Externally Tested Scan Circuit with Built-In Activity Monitor and Adaptive Test Clock. In: Proc. 25th International Conf. VLSI Design, pp. 448–453 (January 2012)
18. Stroud, C.E.: AUSIM - Auburn University SIMulator, http://www.eng.auburn.edu/users/strouce/ausim.html (accessed on March 6, 2012)
19. Stroud, C.E.: A Designer's Guide to Built-In Self-Test. Springer (2002)

20. Tehranipoor, M., Nourani, M., Ahmed, N.: Low Transition LFSR for BIST-Based Application. In: Proc. 14th IEEE Asian Test Symposium, pp. 138–143 (December 2005)
21. Udavanshi, S.: Design of Low Power and High Fault Coverage Test Pattern Generator for BIST. Master's thesis, Thaper University, Patiala, India (July 2011)
22. Wang, S.: Generation of Low Power Dissipation and High Fault Coverage Patterns for Scan-Based BIST. In: Proc. International Test Conf., pp. 834–843 (2002)

Author Index